miss vickie's
BIG BOOK OF
PRESSURE COOKER RECIPES

miss vickie's
BIG BOOK OF
PRESSURE COOKER RECIPES

* * * * * * *

Vickie Smith

WILEY

John Wiley & Sons, Inc.

This book is printed on acid-free paper. ♾

Published by John Wiley & Sons, Inc., Hoboken, New Jersey
Published simultaneously in Canada

Cover Credits: Thanks to Khun Rikon for the pressure cooker; Joan Platt Pottery for the plate;
La Cafetiore for the linens; and Gallo for the Sonoma Reserve 2003 Cabernet Sauvignon.

Cover Photography by Ben Fink
Cover prop styling by Mary-Ellen Weinrib
Cover food styling by Alison Attenborough
Book design and composition by Ralph Fowler

For general information about our other products and services, please contact our Customer Care Department within the United States at (800) 762-2974, outside the United States at (317) 572-3993 or fax (317) 572-4002.

Wiley also publishes its books in a variety of electronic formats. Some content that appears in print may not be available in electronic books. For more information about Wiley products, visit our web site at www.wiley.com.

Library of Congress Cataloging-in-Publication Data

Smith, Vickie (Vickie L.), 1947–
Miss Vickie's big book of pressure cooker recipes / Vickie Smith.
p.   cm.
ISBN 978-0-7645-9726-8 (paper)
1. Pressure cookery.   I. Title.
TX840.P7S65 2008
641.5'87—dc22
2007006913

Printed in the United States of America
10 9 8 7 6 5

Contents

Acknowledgments

This cookbook is dedicated to my family, for their cheery encouragement of my adventures in pressure cookery. A special acknowledgment goes to the memory of those wonderful cooks, my relatives from bygone days when the pressure cooker was the queen of the kitchen. Their collected recipes and tips were the treasured resource that provided the foundation for *Miss Vickie's Big Book of Pressure Cooker Recipes.*

I am indebted to everyone at John Wiley & Sons, but most especially, I owe a heartfelt thanks to Justin Schwartz, who serendipitously happened across my website one day and envisioned a new cookbook. Your enthusiasm launched this amazing adventure in cookbook writing, and I am deeply grateful that you provided me with this marvelous opportunity.

I would like to express a special thank you to my most proficient editor, Christine DiComo. Your patient understanding, your many invaluable suggestions, and your expertise in guiding me through the editorial process added the final polish to ensure a successful ending to my endeavors.

Introduction

Long before there were cookbooks and master chefs, there were just ordinary cooks. Cooking is a journey of discovery that becomes an enjoyable adventure along the way, and with that in mind, the recipes in this book are designed to take maximum advantage of the full potential of today's modern pressure cookers.

In the heyday of pressure cookery, the years centering around World War II, pressure cookers were a mainstay in kitchens across America. Nowadays, Grandma's trusty old pressure cooker has been replaced with modern engineering marvels featuring the state-of-the-art pressure-valve mechanisms, the best features of professional-quality cookware, and superior safety systems. With the arrival of modern pressure cookers comes a renewed interest in the lost art of pressure cookery, and many American cooks are rediscovering the original fast-food machine.

You'll find plenty of tempting new recipes, some of the most popular recipes from my Web site, and the old-fashioned favorites that will take you back in time to sample the sort of comfort foods you may remember from childhood. Along with my own original recipes, I've collected distinctive and old-fashioned family favorites and revamped them to take advantage of today's modern pressure cookers. Knowing that today's cooks are busy and often pressed for time, I've included lots of quick recipes and one-pot meals, as well as updated versions of some classic heirloom recipes that will remind you of dinners with the whole family gathered around the kitchen table at home. Wherever possible, I've used commonplace ingredients so you won't have to set off on a foraging expedition in search of odd ingredients or obscure spices. Throughout this book, the recipes are planned for four to six servings unless noted otherwise. I've always found that portion sizes are as varied as the people sitting at your table, their appetites, and, of course, their level of self-indulgence, so eat hearty!

If you have questions about pressure cookers, or the recipes and techniques used in this book, you'll find more information, articles, and recipes available on my Web site, http://missvickie.com. You can also post questions by clicking on the Forum link, or just e-mail me at: dearmissvickie@gmail.com.

The History of the Pressure Cooker

THE FIRST VERSION of a pressure cooker was created in 1680 by Denis Papin. He made a large cast-iron vessel with a lid that locked and named it a "steam digester." His invention raised cooking temperatures by 15 percent over boiling, and accordingly reduced cooking time. However, regulating the steam and temperature was difficult, and explosions were common.

The development of pressure canners came long before home-sized pressure cookers were available. The canning process was a by-product of the Napoleonic Wars. Malnutrition was rampant in the 18th century, and preserving food was mostly guesswork that relied on dried or salt-cured meats and fish, grains, dried peas, and beans, as well as root vegetables and apples that could be stored over the winter.

Napoleon, gathering a massive army for his Russian campaign, was desperate for a means to provision his troops. He offered a prize of twelve thousand francs to anyone who could find a reliable means of preserving food. In 1795, Nicholas Appert, a Parisian candy maker, invented a method that would prevent food from spoiling by placing fresh meat and vegetables in wide-mouthed glass jars, which were then heated in a boiling-water bath. Finally, the hot jars were sealed with corks. As the jars cooled, a vacuum was formed that sucked the cork tight into the jar, after which the seal was coated with pitch, a process Appert called "Appertisation."

By 1804, Appert opened the first vacuum-canning plant. His nephew, Raymond Chevallier-Appert, improved upon Papin's pressure retort when he designed and patented a pressure vessel to vacuum seal foods, an invention that would lead to the eventual development of the canning industry. The canning process was a vitally important French military secret, but the process soon leaked out, and, in 1810, Englishman Peter Durance patented the use of metal cans rather than glass jars. In 1813, Bryan Dorkin and John Hall perfected canning and set up the first commercial cannery in England. Not long after, canning companies sprang up all over the country. The new "tinned" foods were first used to feed the British army and navy, and the troops that battled at Waterloo had canned rations. In 1812, Thomas Kensett emigrated to the United States and established the first U.S. canning facility in New York, producing canned oysters, meats, fruits, and vegetables.

Despite the development of pressure canning, no one really understood why it worked to preserve food and keep it from spoiling. Not until some 50 years later would Louis Pasteur explain why canning was so effective, when he demonstrated that microorganisms cause food to spoil and high heat destroys them.

Early Home Canning

In 1902, the first commercial pressure-cooker patents in the United States described huge, industrial-size pressure vessels, or "retorts," used by commercial canneries. Smaller, fifty-gallon-capacity pressure pots were soon developed for use in hotels, restaurants, schools, and institutions. Homemakers had only the hot-water-bath method to can foods at home, and while this worked for some foods, cured meat was still safer than canned versions. In 1905, Northwestern Steel and Iron Works, located in Eau Claire, Wisconsin, began manufacturing canning retorts for canneries. Thirty-gallon canners and then smaller ten-gallon models became available that were more suitable for home canning.

The Development of Pressure Cooking

The term "pressure cooker" first appeared in print in 1915 with the arrival of new, lightweight aluminum canners manufactured for home use. In the days before refrigeration, thrifty housewives everywhere wanted a pressure canner to preserve food. In 1917, the U.S. Department of Agriculture determined that pressure canning at 15 pounds per square inch was the only safe method of preserving low-acid foods and meats.

In 1938, Alfred Vischler introduced his Flex-Seal Speed Cooker at a New York City trade show, and the "pressure saucepan" was an instant success. As people migrated from a farming lifestyle in the country and moved to the cities and suburban living, modern housewives found the smaller size of the new pressure cookers very convenient. At just 4 quarts, this aluminum pressure cooker was big enough to cook a meal, but small enough to be manageable in everyday use by the average housewife. Vischler's idea was so successful that it wasn't long before other manufacturers in America and Europe were retooling their foundries and mass-producing many brands of pressure cookers to keep up with the growing popularity.

The small, cast-aluminum pressure cookers enjoyed widespread popularity in most American homes. Every store carried a wide selection of pressure cookers, and cooking demonstrations were so popular that many early television shows featured well-known chefs preparing meals in pressure cookers. Pressure cookers were also commonplace appliances in busy hotels and upscale restaurants. Even transcontinental airliners used pressure cookers in their onboard galleys to serve hot meals to passengers on long flights.

Wartime Necessity

In 1941, at the start of World War II, there were eleven companies producing pressure cookers, but aluminum was needed for the war effort, and its use became tightly regulated. It wasn't long before the manufacturing of aluminum pressure cookers came to a halt. Many housewives donated their aluminum cookware to be melted down in support of the war effort. With widespread food and fuel shortages, the War Production Board encouraged victory gardens and a return to home canning. Large canners made of steel (not the stainless kind) were made available, but hard to come by and they were manufactured under strict government control. Cooks who held onto their prewar pressure cookers shared them with friends and neighbors, and the humble pressure cooker fast became a necessity rather than merely a convenient piece of cookware.

The Decline and Fall of Pressure Cookery

In 1945, with the war ending, the pent-up demand for pressure cookers was tremendous, and soon there were 85 U.S. manufacturers vying for consumer attention. Young families were in the making, and newly married housewives rushed out to buy a new pressure cooker so that they could cook the same recipes that Mom made. Companies that formerly produced aluminum airplane components were suddenly in the cookware business, but they made better airplane parts than they did pressure cookers and problems quickly developed. Production methods favored quantity rather than quality, and competition was so steep that many manufacturers began cutting costs.

A glut of cheap, poorly designed, shoddily made pressure cookers flooded the market from the late 1940s through the '50s. Those postwar pressure cookers earned a bad reputation—they turned into exploding bombs, often redecorating the kitchen in red beets or green pea soup. These inferior pressure cookers were accidents waiting to happen, and when they failed—as they often did—the boiling contents spewed all over everything and everyone in the vicinity. Catastrophic failures occurred so frequently that the term "pressure cooker" took on a whole new meaning, and became synonymous with imminent disaster, an all-too-familiar association that still persists today.

Pressure Cookery Becomes a Lost Art

As word spread about these flawed postwar pressure cookers, people became increasingly reluctant to use them. Cooks stopped using pressure cookers, sales plummeted, and the upstart cookware manufacturers quickly went out of business until only a handful remained. Diehard pressure-cooker users resurrected their old, but reliable, prewar units and waited for the industry to produce a safer product. Burdened with overstocked warehouses, the few remaining manufacturers were reluctant to invest in research and development or the expense of retooling their factories for a new design that would have to face a skeptical consumer market. Marked with a bad reputation and pushed aside by the arrival of newer, modern cooking methods such as the microwave oven, pressure-cooker usage rapidly declined, and the art of pressure cookery nearly disappeared in the U.S.

A Bad Reputation Still Persists

In the 1970s, there was a brief resurgence in pressure-cooker popularity, as many young people were drawn to a rural, back-to-nature lifestyle. Young folks hauled their mothers', grandmothers', or great aunts' vintage pressure cookers and canners out of attics, basements, and garages. Those same unreliable postwar contraptions were once again being passed on to the next generation as family heirlooms and put back into service, and the old stories of pressure-cooker disasters continued. Unfortunately, some of those antique pressure cookers are *still* being passed around, perpetuating the bad reputation of problematic, poorly manufactured pressure cookers.

Pressure Cookery Returns with Sleek European Styling

As American cooks were shelving their pressure cookers in the 1950s, manufacturers in Europe and Asia were reaping the benefits of postwar reconstruction and investing capital in developing new pressure cookers. In much of the world, cooking fuel—natural gas, propane, and electricity—is very costly or in limited supply, and a pressure cooker is considered *de rigueur*, a daily necessity for millions of cooks. With improved pressure-valve systems and redundant safety features, a new breed of completely safe and reliable pressure cookers found a steady market.

Despite the success overseas, it took a long time before foreign manufacturers penetrated the American market with their advanced models. India, Japan, Spain, Switzerland, France, and Germany now manufacture pressure cookers for sale in the U.S. In contrast to the old-style pressure cookers that predominate in America, the advanced and vastly improved foreign imports are much easier to use. Pressure-cooker aficionados began snapping up the new European pressure cookers, marveling at the advanced safety features, quiet operation, and new features like a scorch-resistant layered base and a quick release.

Although pressure cookers have been marketed for home cooking in the United States for nearly a century, the arrival of these modern, state-of-the-art cookers has revived the enthusiasm for this time-saving kitchen tool. Widespread advertising has brought with it a resurgence of interest in pressure cookery, and this old-fashioned cooking method is suddenly new again. TV infomercials and high-end department stores are marketing pressure cookers with fancy new names, touting the "latest, greatest, new invention" to cooks who would never have considered buying an "old-fashioned" pressure cooker. Still, American manufacturers, perhaps wary that customers will not accept these chic, high-tech marvels, have again been slow to adapt to the new designs and modern improvements, so the original jiggle-top model remains the U.S. standard.

Modern Pressure-Cooker Excellence

All over America, cooks are once again rediscovering the benefits of modern pressure cookery. The new pressure cookers appeal to busy cooks with hectic schedules, demanding jobs, active families, and little spare time for cooking. The modern pressure cooker is the perfect solution for anyone looking for healthier recipes and faster, economical ways to prepare nutritious home-cooked meals. In defining the new, modern pressure cookers, the first thing to look for is an advanced pressure-regulating system with an enclosed spring valve, a quick-release mechanism to release pressure automatically, and multiple built-in safety features. Durable, high-quality stainless steel construction with a heavy, three-ply base is also a must.

The Benefits of Modern Pressure Cookers

FORGET ABOUT YOUR GRANNY'S tales of exploding pressure cookers and those old stories about dinner decorating the kitchen ceiling or family dinners consisting of overcooked foods and mushy vegetables. The old-style, classic, weighted pressure regulators have become a distant memory, nothing more than a vintage relic from Grandma's era. Those noisy, rattling, hissing pressure regulators are now outdated relics of bygone days. Say goodbye to hot ovens and standing in front of a stove, constantly watching and stirring a pot. It's time to take a good look at today's new pressure cooker. More and more people are discovering, or rediscovering, the completely safe and very easy-to-use modern pressure cooker.

Originally invented over 300 years ago, the pressure cooker is simply a large, heavy pot with a special lid that locks over the pot and forms an airtight seal. With the steam trapped inside, the pressure increases, forcing the temperature to rise above the boiling point. Fortunately for contemporary cooks, the pressure cooker has undergone significant changes and improvements over time, making it the perfect cooking method for today's hectic lifestyle.

Lifestyles may have changed from the early days of pressure cooking, but we still want to serve nutritious, homemade meals and spend less time in the kitchen. For many pressed-for-time people, the definition of cooking has gone from scratch cooking to the mechanics of assembling a meal from assorted cans and packages of commercially prepared foods. Modern pressure cookers offer the best solution with fast, easy, home-cooked meals, and even the busiest cooks can serve nutritious and healthy home-cooked meals more quickly and cheaply than going out for fast food.

A Healthier Lifestyle

If you want to eliminate junk food, expensive fast food, and prepackaged "dinners" with a high content of fat, salt, and other unwanted additives, then a pressure cooker is the answer. Serve your family wholesome, nutritious, home-cooked meals in record time.

Cooking methods can have a big impact on the nutrient content of the foods we eat. Not surprisingly, pressure cooking retains more vitamins and minerals than other cooking methods because foods are cooked quickly in little water or air, and that means better nutrition, taste, and value. The pressure cooker is perfect for cooking tender-crisp fresh vegetables that retain their texture and bright colors in low-fat and vegetarian recipes. Pressure cooking is virtually fat free, as fats are drained away from meats while the meats stay moist and juicy. The superheated steam within a pressure cooker actually intensifies natural flavors, so you can use less salt and still get great taste.

Ecologically Friendly

The pressure cooker is not only very efficient, it is a time, energy, and labor saver for your kitchen. It's also easy on the environment because reduced cooking times conserve energy and reduce fuel costs. The pressure cooker cooks 70 percent faster than conventional cooking methods, and because all the heat is trapped inside the pot, the kitchen remains cooler, easing the strain on your wallet with lower fuel bills during the warm months. Over time, that adds up to money saved that you can spend on something else. Also, since very little steam is vented by modern pressure cookers, there is almost no cooking odor or oily residue to pollute your kitchen and home.

Lower Food Costs

Using a pressure cooker means that you can save money at the supermarket. Increase your buying power by purchasing the less expensive, tougher cuts of meat and using a pressure cooker to serve tender, succulent, and delicious roasts. A package of dried beans can be on the table in minutes, and for just the cost of your loose pocket change. An inexpensive, wholesome, and nutritious one-pot meal can be served in less than 15 minutes, just as quickly as, and certainly much less expensively than, any fast food. The pressure cooker intensifies natural flavors, so you can use less additives like salt and sugar, and fewer seasonings or expensive spices, and still achieve excellent taste in a fraction of the time required by other cooking methods. Fans of once-a-week-cooking can buy food in bulk sizes, or take advantage of sales, to cook up large quantities of food in short order using a pressure cooker.

Safe and Reliable

Today's modern pressure cookers are completely re-engineered and totally "goof-proof," which means they are very easy to use and 100 percent safe. With their advanced design and improved valve and vent systems, modern pressure cookers offer as many as six safety systems that prevent the kind of accidents that made the old-style pressure cookers so notorious. A good-quality stainless steel pressure cooker will last a lifetime and can be used on virtually any heat source, including natural gas, propane, electric, and heat induction stoves.

Versatility

A wide variety of foods can be cooked in the pressure cooker, including grain, meat, seafood, vegetables, fruit, rice, and pasta in just minutes. An endless variety of recipes, from main dishes, casseroles, and soups and stews to desserts, snacks, and side dishes can be quickly and easily prepared in a modern pressure cooker. Cook separate meals for fussy eaters, or someone with special dietary needs, at the same time the regular meal is cooking. By using accessory pans and my PIP cooking method (see page 37), it's now possible to cook a wider variety of dishes than ever before. Plan on two- and even three-course meals made all at once in a pressure cooker

Easy to Use

The modern pressure cooker, with spring-loaded valves and reliable pressure indicators, takes the guesswork out of pressure cooking. Gone are the days of overcooked, mushy food and those noisy, jiggling weights and clouds of escaping steam. Using today's modern pressure cooker is easier than ever. Once the lid is locked, there is no more standing in front of a hot stove and constantly stirring a boiling pot. With its heavy three-ply base, today's modern pressure cooker does not require constant attention to maintain a stable pressure throughout the cooking process.

Fast and Saves Time

Your pressure cooker is the original "fast food" machine. The pressure cooker can reduce cooking time to just one third of conventional cooking methods, and that's extra time you can spend on other activities. Imagine, a savory beef stew in just fifteen minutes—that's faster than you can set the table—or a roast chicken in only a half an hour. You can forget about all those trips out for fast food and forget about frozen dinners when it's just as fast to cook a homemade meal in the pressure cooker.

Takes the Place of Other Cookware

Really a multi-purpose pot, the pressure cooker will save space and money rather than buying various types of cookware and that may only be used occasionally. Use your pressure cooker as a:

Dutch oven: Use a regular lid and your pressure cooker becomes a Dutch oven for braising and slow simmering.

Steamer: Either under pressure, or with a regular basket and lid, cook perfect rice or risotto, tender-crisp veggies, and delicate fish and seafood, or steam a fancy holiday pudding.

Saucepan: Use the cooker as a heavy-bottomed pan that will not scorch thick sauces.

Deep fryer: While you cannot fry under pressure, the heavy pot without the pressure lid can be used to fry fish, French fries, tempura, and doughnuts.

Braising pot: Tender braised meats and veggies cooked in a flavorful sauce are standard fare.

Poaching pot: Poach fish, fruit, and even eggs in just minutes.

Baking pan: Yes, breads and cakes can be cooked in a pressure cooker.

Browning pan: The heavy pressure cooker does an excellent job of browning meats; no need to wash an extra skillet.

Sterilizer: Use the pressure cooker to sterilize baby bottles and even medical instruments in an emergency.

Water bath canning kettle: Use a large pressure cooker with a regular lid as a water-bath canner for processing high-acid foods like jelly and jam.

Add a Pressure Cooker to Your Emergency Preparedness Kit

During an emergency or power outage, a pressure cooker can be used with a solar stove, or barbecue grill, and even with wood or charcoal fires to prepare food without a stove. A pressure cooker can be used to provide safe drinking water during an emergency. Because of its large size, the pot can be used for washing clothes, dishes, and even the baby.

A Pressure Cooker Is Indispensable in and out of the Kitchen

RV travelers, hikers, and hunters will find the pressure cooker very convenient for quick meals on the go. Cook several foods at the same time, or enough to feed the entire family or even just a single serving. A pressure cooker takes up less space, and serves as a multi-purpose, all-in-one pot. Campers can use a pressure cooker for high-altitude cooking on many types of heat sources. Boaters will find a pressure cooker indispensable in the galley for quick, hearty meals even in rough weather.

How Does It Do That Thing It Does?

ALL PRESSURE COOKERS OPERATE by the same principle. The pot is an enclosed system. Heat builds steam, which produces the pressure to cook the food faster. Pressure is controlled by adjusting the heat. Safety devices are designed to vent off excess pressure, and the pressure must be released before opening the lid. That's it in a nutshell. To understand how a pressure cooker works, you need to know just a little about physics. The principles behind a pressure cooker have not changed since its earliest invention; it cooks faster because the temperature is hotter than conventional cooking methods. At sea level a pot of water will boil at a temperature of 212°F and no matter how long you continue to boil that pot, it will never get any hotter. By trapping steam inside a tightly closed pot, pressure increases and the heat rises. All pressure cookers use a pressure-valve mechanism to create an internal environment ranging from 3 to 15psi (pounds per square inch). At 15psi, the temperature inside the pressure cooker is 250°F, which is 38°F hotter than boiling, and that means foods cook very quickly.

In addition to using a much higher pressure and temperature, the pressure cooker also creates live steam. A very successful cooking medium, steam is the most efficient cooking method, and the perfect choice for everything from delicate seafood and tender-crisp vegetables to large cuts of meat. Under high pressure, the fiber in food breaks down more rapidly, and even the toughest cut of meat becomes tender.

It Isn't a Pressure Fryer

It's a common misconception of some first-time pressure cooker owners that they can cook fried chicken just like the "Colonel" by substituting a pressure cooker for a pressure fryer. "Broasted" chicken, a popular cooking process, requires the use of a commercial pressure fryer made for the restaurant industry. A pressure cooker *is not* a pressure fryer, and it is extremely dangerous to use more oil than the manufacturer recommends, which is usually only ¼ cup.

A shallow, skillet-like, pressure fry pan *is not* a pressure fryer either; it is intended for braising chops and steaks. Used properly, today's modern pressure cookers are very safe, but they are not intended for boiling hot oil under pressure. The same gasket that performs well at 250°F in normal use may melt away in the 400°F heat of boiling oil, creating a potential for serious damage and injury. Please read the warnings in your owner's manual for the restrictions on using oil, and follow the manufacturer's recommendations.

There are special pressure fryers available specifically for that purpose. They operate at a much lower pressure than the standard pressure cooker, and have several additional safety features, but the two are not interchangeable.

It Isn't a Pressure Canner

In the early years of canning, in the 1940s, small pressure saucepans were introduced as an alternative to large, heavy home canners. Homemakers thought they could use their small pressure cookers for canning by adding a few minutes to the processing time. However, this proved to be unsafe and was never adequately tested or approved.

The USDA has made great advances in the science of home canning. In 1989, canning guidelines were markedly changed to keep abreast of new scientific testing and improved food-safety information. It is no longer recommended to use a pressure cooker for home canning because a fully loaded canner takes a longer time for heating and cooling than the much smaller pressure cooker. The heat-up and cool-down times of a pressure canner loaded with a rack and jars are taken into account when determining the total processing time established by lab testing to ensure the safety of home-canned foods.

Canning is now an exact science requiring updated and lab-tested canning directions, specialized equipment, and accurate timing based on altitude and jar size to properly process foods for safe consumption. It's not safe to can "homemade recipes" because without knowing the pH factors of the ingredients used, it's impossible to determine correct processing times. Can the separate ingredients for your favorite recipes and then combine them as you cook the meal. Alternately, can a tested recipe that is similar to yours, and then incorporate your special seasoning and other ingredients in preparing your family recipes at serving time. You should never make any adjustments to the ingredients in a tested canning recipe because any change in the pH factor will affect the accuracy of the processing time.

USDA guidelines have changed dramatically and food preservation is more precise and much safer than ever, but always use up-to-date and tested canning instructions. The most accurate, up-to-date, and dependable guidelines are in the current bulletins put out by the USDA, and these are available free or cost only a few cents from your local county extension office. They will also have the current processing times that are specific to your altitude.

Pressure-Cooking Techniques

MOST PEOPLE never go beyond learning one or two basic pressure cooker techniques, but there are actually several different ways of using moist heat for poaching, stewing, braising, steaming, and boiling. By using these techniques most foods can be cooked in the pressure cooker.

Boiling

Boiling is cooking by immersing food in boiling water, and, contrary to what you may think, there are very few foods that need to be boiled when using the pressure cooker. In general, boiling under pressure is reserved for the toughest cuts of meats, or those that have been salt cured, brined, pickled, or smoked. Corned beef or hams might be fatty and salty, and boiling may help leach out some of the fat and salt. Smoked or pickled tongue, beef heart, smoked ham hocks, pork neck bones, pigs feet, etc., are examples of meats that do quite well when boiled. If it suits your taste, the broth from cured and smoked meats can be quite rich and flavorful and provides a much-needed hearty flavor in recipes for dried beans, stews, and soups. The broth should be skimmed of fat before using, and can be frozen for later use. Another instance where boiling can produce satisfactory results is with game meats like venison and fowl, which may be tough or have a strong flavor. The broth may be discarded or skimmed of fat and then used or frozen for later use. Boiling is also the preferred method of cooking when the resulting broth is more important than the foods cooked in it. The pressure cooker excels at soup stocks made from root vegetables, beef bones, or poultry carcasses.

Braising

Braising is a good method for cooking cheaper cuts of tough meats in the pressure cooker because it converts the connective tissue, called collagen, into gelatin and makes the meat tender and moist. Use the pressure cooker to first brown the meat in fat, and then add enough plain water or a flavoring liquid such as wine, stock, or broth, separately or in combinations to barely cover the ingredients. This will form the basis of a delicious sauce or gravy to accompany the dish. The popular Italian dish osso buco of braised veal shanks is a good example of braising done in the pressure cooker.

Stewing

This is another method of moist-heat cooking, typically made with enough liquid to cover the ingredients. Stews differ from soups in that the pieces of food are usually cut larger, and the broth is thickened before serving. Just about any food can be stewed in pressure-cooker recipes, including meats, vegetables, grains, fruits, and seafood. Stewing not only tenderizes tougher cuts of meat, but also allows the flavors of the ingredients to blend deliciously. Whether it's a French ragoût, a Hungarian goulash, or an Indian mulligatawny, stews are a universal favorite, and the pressure cooker will make this family favorite in just a few minutes. After browning the meat, pour off excess fat and add the liquid, herbs, and spices. Vegetables with shorter cooking times are usually added after the meat is partially cooked. The gravy is thickened after pressure cooking has finished.

Poaching

This is similar to braising, except there is no added fat and the food is covered by a well-flavored stock or broth. Poaching is fast, and best used with foods that are tender or delicate, such as eggs, fruits and vegetables, chicken, and fish. The modern pressure cooker can be used to cook poached dishes in record time while retaining the vibrant color and texture of delicate foods.

Steaming

Steaming requires no added fat, preserves more nutrients, and retains the taste, texture, and color of foods. Steam rice, grains, meats, poultry, fish and seafood, fruits, vegetables, and even casserole-style dishes in the pressure cooker. Use a rack or trivet to lift a steamer tray or basket, an inserted pan, or a foil packet above the water level and you'll maximize the full potential of your pressure cooker.

Steam Roasting

You won't believe how easy it is to cook a large roast or a whole chicken in the pressure cooker. Steam roasting drains the fat away from the meat and produces flavor-rich broth that can be used for gravy or defatted and used in stews and soups. Meats should be browned first to develop taste, color, and aroma. The pan is deglazed, and enough water is added for the length of the cooking process, plus an additional amount equal to the quantity of broth or gravy desired. Use a foil Helper Handle (see page 42) to place the meat on an elevated rack that is well above the water level. As an alternative to pan browning, meats can be popped in the oven or under the broiler after pressure cooking. Add a glaze if desired, and baste the meat until the skin begins to brown and crisp.

A Buyer's Guide to Modern Pressure Cookers

THE OLD FAMILIAR, NOISY, rattling, jiggling pressure regulators and hissing, spitting pressure cookers of Grandma's day are thankfully long gone. The new, advanced designs of modern pressure cookers are completely reliable and totally safe. While features may vary slightly between brands and models, the new-generation pressure cookers are easy to operate and a joy to use. Today's new, precision spring-valve pressure cookers are very quiet and much easier to use than the older designs with those rocking weights perched on a vent pipe. The new pressure cookers have a closed system with very little escaping steam. Because there is practically no evaporation, only a small amount of water is required, and that preserves the maximum amount of nutrients, flavor, and color of foods during cooking.

Choose Carefully

Purchasing a modern pressure cooker is an investment, and there are specific features to look for when considering which brand suits your needs. Among the best examples of top-of-the-line models are those offered by the Swiss-made Kuhn-Rikon (kuhn-rikon.com) and the Spanish-made Fagor (fagor-america.com). Most manufacturers offer several models to choose from, each with different features and various sizes to suit the needs and budgets of every customer.

There are many brands and styles available from American, European, Indian, and Asian manufacturers, but choose wisely. Some of these companies, while well regarded in their respective countries, are virtually unknown in the U.S., and it may be difficult to find replacement parts for these little known imports. There are only a few companies making pressure cookers in the U.S., and most models are still based on the old classic style used in the original 1940s concept of a "pressure saucepan." Some U.S. manufacturers are now incorporating modern improvements in their products, while others are blending some modern improvements with that same old noisy, jiggling pressure regulator designed nearly a century ago.

In addition to the standard stovetop pressure cookers, there are various electric appliances, microwavable devices, and other low-pressure cookers. These fads may come and go, but the modern stovetop pressure cooker still dominates the market by offering far more safety features, durability, speed, longevity, and versatility than the rest of the field. Whichever brand you select, always buy from a reputable, well-established company.

Choose Stainless Steel Construction

For durability, usefulness, and easy maintenance look for pressure cookers made from good-quality stainless steel. The label should indicate [18/10] (chromium steel/nickel steel), making it very strong. Stainless steel can be used on all types of stoves, including ceramic, and induction or glass-top stoves,

natural gas, propane, and electric. In an emergency, disaster, or power outage, a stainless steel cooker can be used on wood or charcoal fires, camp stoves, and outdoor grills. Its unique surface has no pores or cracks to harbor dirt, grime, or bacteria, making stainless steel one of the most hygienic surfaces for food. It will not react to acidic foods, and it will not rust, pit, stain, or become discolored like other types of cookware. Stainless steel is easy to clean, and the base of most pressure cookers can be easily washed in the dishwasher.

Choose a Three-Ply Base

One of the most important features of good-quality cookware is a thick, encapsulated base that is highly heat conductive and heat diffusing. The heavy base heats faster and more evenly, and retains heat longer, which means less heat is needed to maintain pressure, and that translates into a greater variety of foods and recipes that can be prepared. The heavy base allows cooks to use a high-heat setting to rapidly pressurize the cooker, and then drop to a very low heat to stabilize and maintain pressure without the need of any further adjustments. This feature on modern pressure cookers is essential to prevent hot spots that cause burning and scorching, a notable problem with some pressure cookers.

Choose the Standard Pressure Setting

In pressure cookery, we use pressure settings, or pounds per square inch (psi) rather than temperatures to gauge the heat and determine how fast foods will cook. When pressure cookers were first introduced, they had just one setting of 15psi, and that has remained the accepted standard for nearly a century. Modern pressure cookers should conform to the accepted standard because most recipes, including the ones in this book, use this setting. In fact, the 15psi setting is so common that it is largely taken for granted, and many pressure cooker recipes don't even mention pressure unless it differs from the standard 15psi.

Before purchasing any new pressure cooker, check the specifications carefully to be sure it is capable of meeting the 15psi standard. Nonstandard pressure cookers that use less than 15psi defeat the greatest benefit of pressure cookery—speed. These nonstandard pressure cookers may include a few recipes, but in order to use any other pressure-cooker recipe it must first be adapted. This means the cooking time has to be increased to compensate for the lower pressure. Longer cooking times can diminish the nutritional value of foods, and pose an increased danger of scorching food on the bottom of the cooker. They also can create unexpected and sometimes unpleasant results, not to mention wasting your valuable time.

A Choice of Pressure Settings

Some pressure cookers offer more than one pressure setting. Since the vast majority of pressure-cooker recipes are designed around the universally accepted standard of 15psi, you may never need any other pressure setting. The lower pressure settings are occasionally used for foods that foam, froth, or expand during cooking. Some recipes for delicate foods, cakes or breads that need to rise, or long-cooking foods like English holiday puddings, may call for a lower pressure setting.

Select Accurate Pressure Indicators

Unlike older pressure cookers, the modern pressure cooker now has a device that accurately indicates pressure within the pot. This new feature eliminates the guesswork and uncertainty of knowing when the cooker has reached the desired pressure. Most brands use a colored or marked pop-up indicator (think Butterball turkey) to show that the cooker is pressurized, which makes it much easier to know when to begin timing the recipe.

Look for Enhanced Safety Features

The majority of pressure-cooker accidents are caused by "operator error," but modern pressure cookers have so many new, built-in safety features that they are safe even under the most severe conditions. Top-of-the-line models offer as many as five or six integrated safety features, while there may only be two or three in less expensive models. The new and improved safety mechanisms are designed to prevent the sort of accidental over-pressuring and clogged vent pipes that were once associated with older styles of pressure cookers; even the old-fashioned "overpressure plug" has been eliminated.

An interlocking lid is the first line of defense, making it impossible to open the lid while the cooker is still pressurized. Some models even offer a "lid lock" as an additional safety feature. At the first sign of too much pressure, there is an audible hissing as the excess steam is vented from the valve stem. Should overpressuring continue, or if the valve should become clogged, the gasket will be pushed out through an aperture on the side of the lid, safely venting the pressure.

Select a Quick Pressure Release Method

In addition to the natural and cold water release methods found on early pressure cookers, the modern versions offer a quick-release mechanism that drops the pressure without losing heat. This quick-release feature permits cooks to interrupt the cooking process to add other ingredients or check for doneness without significantly lowering the temperature of the cooker. Cooking can be resumed very quickly again when the lid is closed and the heat turned back up.

What about Size?

Pressure cookers come in sizes from a small 2-quart size intended for pressure braising to enormous 10- and 12-quart units, as well as every size in between. Regardless of the size you choose, remember that a pressure cooker can only be filled two-thirds full for most foods, and only half full for dried beans and other foods that foam, froth, or expand during cooking. The size you choose may depend on your available storage space, the number and size of portions you prepare, your particular cooking style, or your budget. While even the largest pressure cooker is capable of cooking the smallest amounts of food, large amounts cannot be cooked in a small one. For most practical purposes, a pressure cooker of 6 quarts is the minimum size to consider. If your budget allows it, a 7- to 8-quart model will make it easier to accommodate a wider selection of accessory pans and bowls that will extend the usefulness of your investment and permit you to cook an even wider variety of recipes.

Choose carefully, and buy the largest model you can afford. Larger pressure cookers can easily cook whole chickens, large roasts, spareribs, and whole ears of corn. If you like to cook ahead, or make meals in advance, then the larger pressure cookers will let you cook in quantity and freeze portions. The larger size will allow you to use the base when you want to employ the pot for conventional cooking. A tall pressure cooker is preferable to a short one because there is more room for large, bulky foods, and a greater choice of accessory pans. Tall pots also come to pressure slightly quicker. When browning foods, less oil will splatter out of a tall pressure cooker.

Why Handles Are an Important Consideration

A pressure cooker with a long handle on one side and a shorter helper handle on the opposite side is easier to manage than one with just a single handle or only short handles. The longer handles will keep your hands away from the heat, protect your fingers from accidentally touching the side of a hot pot, and will stay cool on the range top. The long handle will make it easier to carry a heavy pot, and provides some advantage when locking or removing the lid. Look for cookware with phenolic or similar heat-resistant handles and knobs that stay cool to the touch while cooking. This type of material also permits the base unit to go into a preheated oven up to 300°F, but check for specific manufacturer recommendations.

The Value of the Warranty

A good-quality stainless steel pressure cooker can be expected to last at least 25 years, and many vintage units have served one family, and then passed on from one generation to the next. As a thrifty shopper, look for long warranties as a good indicator of a quality product, and expect at least a ten-year warranty to protect your investment. The length and warranty coverage varies widely and some companies place unreasonable restrictions on what they cover, making it difficult for the consumer to obtain satisfactory service, so be sure to read carefully. Replaceable parts like gaskets are not covered under warranty.

The Importance of Readily Available Replacement Parts

All pressure cookers will need new replacement seals or gaskets from time to time. Before making a purchasing decision, it's essential to know that the manufacturer supports the product by supplying information on where to purchase replacement gaskets and other parts when needed. Other replaceable parts, such as handles and knobs, may need to be replaced occasionally, and most are attached in such a way that they can be removed easily when necessary. Some of the better pressure cooker manufacturers carry additional accessory items such as regular lids, steaming and baking trays, pasta baskets, and even egg poachers in addition to regular replacement parts.

Pressure Cookers and Nonstick Finishes

Be a wise and informed shopper. As with any expensive piece of cookware, pressure cookers are a long-term investment that will provide decades of reliable service, but a nonstick finish may not fare as well. Many manufacturers of nonstick finishes do not recommend using a dishwasher, and that means more cleanup work for the busy cook. If you already own a pressure cooker with an applied finish, check the warranty before using any accessory pans, as they may damage the interior.

My Supercalifragilisticexpialidocious Pressure Cooker

If you have the misfortune of owning a pressure cooker made by some obscure or unknown manufacturer or a company that has gone out of business, or a vintage model that is no longer in production, your orphan pressure cooker may need to be retired. Be leery of discount stores and online auctions that sell liquidation merchandise. That bargain-priced pressure cooker may not be such a good deal when you discover that you can't read the foreign-language owner's manual and there is no service or any source of replacement parts available in the U.S. Orphaned pressure cookers can sometimes be repurposed and used as ordinary large cooking pots. For safety reasons, never attempt to use any sort of homemade gasket or try to substitute gaskets from other makes and models of pressure cookers.

For Owners of Electronic Pressure Cookers

Check the owner's manual to find the temperature or psi settings for the appliance. As long as they meet the standard 15psi rule, electric pressure cookers can use many of the same recipes as stovetop models. There are many makes and models of electric pressure-cooker appliances, all with different operating instructions, and I do not propose to give detailed mechanical instructions for each and every one. In general, use the brown setting to do the initial browning or sautéing, and then close the lid and select the high pressure setting on the timer as recommended in the recipe. When the time is up, depressurize the appliance according to the manufacturer's directions and open the lid. Recipe instructions remain the same whether it is a stovetop or electric pressure cooker. The exceptions are recipes that call for a cold water release which is not an option for electric appliances. Recipes that use the interrupted cooking method (see page 38) may not be practical for use in some electric pressure cookers because of the limited choices on pressure release methods.

Step-by-Step Pressure-Cooker Instructions

WHETHER YOU'RE A NOVICE or have just purchased a new pressure cooker, thoroughly read the owner's manual to familiarize yourself with the basic principles, new terminology, and techniques associated with pressure cookery. Keep the manual in a safe place for quick reference. If you have lost the original owner's manual that came with your cooker, usually replacements are available at little or no cost by contacting the manufacturer.

Before You Begin

Every time you use a pressure cooker, it should be carefully inspected. Make sure that it is clean inside and out before each and every use. Lift or turn the pressure valve to make sure it moves freely and check the housing assembly or connecting screw to see that it is secure. Examine the vent pipe if your cooker uses the classic jiggle-top pressure regulator, making sure it's clean and open. Check the handles on the pot and the lid to see that they are firmly attached, tightening the screws as necessary. The gasket and other replaceable rubber or silicon seals should be in good condition, with no signs of tears or other deterioration such as gumminess or brittleness. Replace the parts if there are any suspicious areas or other signs of deterioration. The gasket should fit snugly in its place in the lid.

Follow Recipe Directions

Always use a pressure cooker recipe or refer to the Pressure-Cooking Time Charts (see page 83) for the correct time and release methods. Don't rely on guesswork when it comes to pressure cooking. A mistake in choosing the proper cooking method, timing, or release method will yield unsatisfactory results in short order.

Adding Liquid to the Pressure Cooker

Before cooking anything in a pressure cooker, there must be some sort of liquid inside the pot to generate enough steam to pressurize the cooker. The minimum amount of water or liquid required depends on two factors: (1) the length of cooking time, and (2) the cooking method, but *not* the amount of food in the pressure cooker. Modern pressure cookers can use as little as less than ½ cup of water or other cooking liquids, but check the owner's manual for the minimum amount as recommended by the manufacturer. This amount of liquid is usually sufficient for approximately 15 minutes of pressure-cooking time, and longer cooking times will require correspondingly more liquid. I strongly recommend using the test drive (see page 30) to determine what amount of water is best for your brand when cooking for longer periods of time.

Filling the Pressure Cooker

Never exceed the maximum fill level on any pressure cooker. Some units have these maximum fill levels conveniently marked on the inside of the pot. Do not exceed the two-thirds full level for most ingredients. The exceptions are foods that are mostly liquids, and foods that foam, froth, or expand during cooking, in which case the maximum is only half full.

Pressurizing the Cooker

Place the pressure cooker on the correct size burner, one that is no larger, or slightly smaller, than the diameter of the base. Do not use a burner that is larger, or a super-high BTU heating element. Set the heat on high initially, to rapidly pressurize the cooker. Once high pressure (15psi) is reached, as shown by the pressure indicator, immediately lower the heat to the lowest possible setting that will stabilize and still maintain pressure. Now it's time to begin actually timing the recipe according to the directions.

Cooking and Timing

If using a model with the classic pressure regulator, or jiggle top, it should rock three to five times per minute. If it is in constant motion, the heat is too high and it needs to be adjusted to a lower setting. As with any other cooking method that uses high heat, such as frying, broiling, or grilling, the pressure cooker should not be left unattended. Always—let me repeat that—always use a timer. A digital timer is preferred because it can be carried with you on a lanyard, clipped on a belt, or pocketed so you will never forget about the pressure cooker. When the cooking time is up, remove the pressure cooker from the heat source and proceed with the release method recommended in the recipe.

Releasing Pressure

Before the lid can be removed from the pressure cooker, the pot must be depressurized. This is an important final phase of pressure cooking, and the choice of pressure release methods can have a great impact on the food inside. There are three methods (see page 30) for releasing the pressure in a modern stovetop pressure cooker: (1) the natural release method, (2) the quick release method, and (3) the cold water release method. Using the correct pressure release method is the final phase of pressure cooking and affects the successful outcomes of most recipes. Individual recipes and the Pressure-Cooking Time Charts (see page 83) will indicate which release method to use at the end of the cooking process.

Opening the Cooker

As a matter of routine safety, be certain the cooker is completely depressurized before unlocking and removing the lid. The pressure indicator will have dropped, but a simple test of moving or lifting the pressure valve or regulator will verify that the cooker has depressurized if there is no sound of escaping steam. When you have verified that the cooker is completely depressurized, open the lid, tipping it away from you to avoid coming into contact with the escaping hot steam.

Pressure-Cooker Safety

MODERN PRESSURE COOKERS have many more safety features than ever, making them completely safe and reliable. The new pressure cooker has a lid-locking system that prevents the lid from being removed until the pressure inside has returned to normal. Top-quality brands will have a total of five, or even six, safety features. If you are a novice at cooking, especially pressure cooking, read and follow the directions in your owner's manual, and even more importantly, understand how the pressure cooker operates, and become familiar with all the terms and methods used.

Ten Golden Rules of Pressure Cookery

Regardless of the type of pressure cooker you own, these basic safety rules apply to all brands and models.

1. Check to see that the vent or valve systems are clean and in good working order before using the pressure cooker.

2. Never use less than the minimum amount of liquid as recommended by the manufacturer, or as required for the length of cooking time.

3. Do not exceed the two-thirds full level for most recipes. The exception is foods that are mostly liquids, and foods that foam, froth, or expand during

cooking, in which case half full is the maximum fill level.

4. Use high heat to establish the desired pressure, immediately reduce the heat to the lowest possible level to stabilize and maintain that pressure, and then begin timing.

5. For best results, always use a recipe or check the Cooking Time Charts (see pages 84 to 106), carefully following the directions for the proper cooking technique, amount of liquid, cooking time, and pressure release methods.

6. Always set a timer, and, as with any other kitchen appliance that cooks rapidly and uses high temperatures, do not leave the pressure cooker unattended.

7. Never use more than ¼ cup of fats or oils or exceed the maximum as recommended by the manufacturer.

8. Use the natural release method (see page 31) for foods that are mostly liquids or that foam, froth, or expand, or foods with a skin or peel, and most cuts of meat.

9. When using the cold water release method (see page 30), do not allow water to run directly over the vent or valve system.

10. Always be sure the pressure has dropped back to normal before opening the locking lid on a pressure cooker.

Five Formulas for Foods that Foam, Froth, or Expand

When using a pressure cooker for foods that foam, froth, or expand, there are additional safety rules that apply. Examples include dried beans or peas, pasta, rice, and grain, and some varieties of fruit.

1. Always use a pressure cooker that is 5 quarts in size or larger.

2. If necessary, adjust the recipe, but do not exceed the half-full level.

3. To minimize foaming, use 1 or 2 tablespoons of cooking oil.

4. Pay careful attention to adjusting the heat to the lowest possible setting immediately after the cooker comes to pressure to avoid scorching problems.

5. Depressurize the cooker by using either the natural or the cold water release method.

Check Your Pressure Cooker Before and After Each Use

Do a visual inspection before using the pressure cooker. Pay close attention to the lid with its gasket, vents, and valve systems, to be sure everything is clean and in good working order. On pressure cookers that use the old-style, jiggling pressure regulator, hold the lid up to the light and look through the vent pipe to be sure it's clear. Check the overpressure plug on your jiggle-top cookers, looking for cracking in the rubber, and be sure the little metal rod is loose and moves up and down freely. On the newer, modern pressure cookers that use a pop-up-type, spring valve pressure regulator, be sure the pop-up button or rod moves up and down without sticking. On the pressure cookers using a dial or knob setting, be sure that the mechanism rotates easily.

Ten-Point Safety Checklist

Before purchasing, or using any new pressure cooker, or trying to use the one you discovered in granny's attic, make sure can it pass my Ten-Point

Safety Checklist. To protect your investment and for obvious safety reasons, all questions require a "yes" answer.

1. Can you identify the manufacturer, and is the company still in business?

2. Can you identify the model number or name, and is that unit still being manufactured?

3. Are replacement parts and accessory items easily available from more than one source?

4. Is an owner's manual included, or can a replacement copy still be obtained from the manufacturer?

5. If used, is the pressure cooker in good condition and free of pitting or signs of undue wear or misuse?

6. Are the handles well attached, free of cracks or nicks, and does the manufacturer still offer replacements?

7. Are all the necessary parts available, and can they still be obtained from the manufacturer?

8. If the pressure cooker has a gauge, has it been tested for accuracy to make sure it is actually able to maintain pressure as indicated?

9. Are there any stains or discoloration caused by leaks around the lid or valve fittings that may indicate the lid does not seal properly?

10. Does the pressure cooker have at least three safety features, including an interlocking lid, an over-pressure valve or vent, and a gasket release slot in the lid?

Pressure: Getting It, Keeping It, Releasing It

THE MODERN PRESSURE COOKER is easier to operate than the old-time versions that required constant attention to keep the pressure adjusted properly. The heavy encapsulated base and modern spring valves have solved the mystery of pressure cooking. Some novice pressure-cooker users are under the impression that they must only use recipes specially designed just for their particular brand. Not true! As long as a pressure cooker meets the 15psi standard, virtually all recipes designed for pressure cooking can be used.

How to Achieve and Maintain Pressure

All pressure cookers use heat to generate pressure. Center the pressure cooker on a burner that is slightly smaller than the diameter of the base. Do not use any oversized heating element or a super-high BTU setting when pressure cooking. The cooker is brought to high pressure (15psi) over high heat until the pressure indicator shows that it is pressurized. Once pressure is achieved, immediately lower the heat to the lowest possible setting that will stabilize and then maintain that pressure. Begin timing at this point, and set a timer for the length of time indicated in the recipe.

Depending on your pressure cooker, there may be more than one pressure setting available, generally corresponding with 5, 10, and 15psi. At 5 pounds, the internal temperature is 228°F; at 10 pounds, it's 240°F; at 15 pounds, it's 250°F. The standard of 15psi is the most important setting because it is used by most recipes. Read the owner's manual to find out the pressure settings of your particular brand. To complicate matters, some nonstandard pressure cookers operate at a maximum setting ranging from 11 to 13psi, which means that recipes will have to be adjusted for increased time to compensate for the lower pressure setting.

A modern pressure cooker has a three-ply base for even heat distribution. Once the heat is properly adjusted to maintain a stable pressure during the cooking process, it will require very little heat, and no further heat adjustments should be neces-sary. Use the test drive (see page 55) to determine which setting on your stove will produce the best results.

Tips for Using Pressure Cookers on Glass-Top Stoves

Induction or glass-top stoves use an electromagnetic coil beneath a ceramic cooking surface that creates a magnetic field. This magnetic field passes through the cooking surface to ferrous (iron or steel) cookware, heating the pan and cooking the contents, so cookware needs to have magnetic properties. Nonmagnetic metal such as aluminum cannot be used on induction ranges. These stoves tend to cook at a very high heat, cycling on and off repeatedly—even as frequently as every few sec-onds—but the only heat generated is to the cook-ware itself; the cooktop remains relatively cool.

Be sure to read the owner's manual. Although most glass-top-stove manufacturers approve stain-less steel cookware, it's a good idea to check with the company about which pressure cookers are

Pressure to Temperature Conversion Table			
Pressure Settings	Pounds Per Square Inch (PSI)	Temperature Equivalent	Usage
Low	5psi	228°F	Rarely used—occasionally some delicate types of fish, seafood, or tender-crisp vegetables
Medium	Can vary from 8 to 10psi, check owner's manual	234° to 240°F	Sometimes used for rice, steamed puddings, or custards
High	15psi	250°F	Unless stated otherwise, this is the standard pressure setting used in most recipes.

safe for use. As with electric stovetops, a two-step method is useful; set one heating element to high and the second one to medium or low, depending on the results of your test drive (see page 55). Bring the pressure cooker to 15psi on the first burner using the high-heat setting. As soon as the cooker is pressurized, move it to the second heating element with the lower temperature and begin timing. If you are having problems with food burning on your glass-top stove, despite your best efforts to lower or adjust the heat, then call for service and have the heat calibrated and adjusted.

Tips for Using Pressure Cookers on Electric Stoves

If you are using an electric stove, it will be somewhat more difficult to adjust the pressure cooker, because electric burners are notoriously slow to respond to temperature-control changes. It will help to heat two elements, one set to high and the second set to medium or low, depending on the results of your test drive (see page 55). Bring the pressure cooker to 15psi on the first burner using the high-heat setting. As soon as the cooker is pressurized, move it to the second heating element with the lower temperature and begin timing.

Tips for Owners of Electric Pressure Cookers

Unlike modern stovetop pressure cookers, the digital or electronic appliances are limited in their capabilities. They aren't practical to use in recipes or with foods that require very short cooking times, or with the cold water release method (see page 30). Some of the more advanced pressure-cooking techniques, such as the interrupted cooking method (see page 38), may prove to be quite challenging with many of these models.

There is no generally accepted standard among the makers of electric pressure cookers, so choose carefully and select a unit that adheres to the 15psi standard pressure setting, or a corresponding temperature setting. Operating instructions vary widely, even between models made by the same manufacturer, so it's important to follow the directions in your owner's manual for basic operating instructions. In general, you can use the "brown" setting to do the initial sautéing and browning. Program the appliance for high pressure and set the timer for the amount of time recommended in the recipe. If the recipe calls for a cold water release, use the quick release mechanism instead, keeping in mind that the results may be less than expected. Use the "brown" setting to do any finish cooking after pressure is released.

Pressure Cookers with a Weighted Regulator, or Jiggle Top

If your pressure cooker uses a pressure regulator weight, or the old-style "jiggle top," then it's necessary to expel the air from the inside of the cooker *before* placing the weight on the vent pipe. Set your heat at high and wait until you see steam flowing from the vent pipe. Now place the pressure regulator weight on top. Continue cooking at high heat until the regulator weight begins to rock rapidly and lots of steam is escaping. You may see some water droplets escaping from under the weight, and hissing and spitting is normal for this type of pressure cooker. Now is the time to immediately lower the heat on your stove to the setting you determined by using the test drive (see page 55). At this point, the pressure regulator should be rocking three to five times per minute and there will be a slight hissing of escaping steam during cooking. If the regulator is rocking continuously, the heat setting is too high and must be lowered. Once pressure as been achieved and you have lowered the heat, use a timer set for the length of time indicated in your recipe. It may be necessary to make several small adjustments to the heat setting over the length of the cooking time to maintain the desired pressure.

Releasing Pressure

There are three methods for releasing the pressure in a modern stovetop pressure cooker. Recipes and the Pressure-Cooking Time Charts (see page 83) will indicate which release method to use at the end of the cooking process.

Cold Water Release Method

This is the fastest method to stop the cooking process by lowering the temperature and the pressure. This method is often used for foods with very short cooking times, or when it is essential to stop the cooking process as quickly as possible. Use this method for serving fresh, tender-crisp vegetables or delicate seafood. The pressure cooker is carried to the sink and tilted at a slight angle to allow cold water to run over the outer edge of the lid so that it runs down the side of the pot and across the top of the lid, but not directly over the vent or valve. If your faucet is too short to allow water to run over the top of the cooker, then use the sprayer attachment, if available. Otherwise, sit the pressure cooker in the sink filled with a couple of inches of cold water until the pressure drops.

When using the cold water release method, there are a couple of safety concerns to keep in mind. All modern pressure cookers should have two handles for easier lifting and carrying, but be careful when carrying any large, heavy pot full of hot food. Always check to see that you have a clear path with nothing underfoot, such as children or pets. People of small stature, or those with physical limitations, may find it easier to slide the pressure cooker along the countertop from the stove to the sink.

Never run water directly over the pressure release vent or valve when using the cold water release method. Remember those old schoolroom physics demonstrations that created a vacuum by condensation? If you inadvertently run water directly over the venting mechanism during the cold water release, you may have a real-world demonstration of physics in action, much as I did. Once—and only once—I didn't pay attention and allowed water to run straight over the pressure regulator on a stainless steel cooker. I heard a "POP" and the lid suddenly caved in—the metal was actually dished-in with a depression in the middle that made it completely unusable. When a pressure cooker is heated, the air inside expands. When the cooker is removed from heat, the air molecules inside begin to cool and contract rapidly. If the vent or valve opening is blocked by a stream of water, the air molecules cannot get inside the cooker fast enough to replace the volume and there will be less air pressure inside the pot than outside. Those condensing air molecules then start pulling a vacuum, creating a powerful suction that can actually cause the lid, or the weakest area of the cooker, to collapse. If the vacuum is strong enough, it can actually pull the metal down into the pot. Usually there is no warning before this occurs; even in my case there was only a popping sound as a result of the lid caving in.

Quick Release Method

People often confuse the quick release with the cold water release, but these are two distinctly different methods. The quick release mechanism is found on modern pressure cookers, and while not as fast as the cold water release, this special valve rapidly releases pressure with just the turn of a knob or the push of a button. The quick release is used to drop the pressure without lowering the temperature of the food. This method is suggested if you wish to interrupt the cooking process to add some further ingredients or check food for doneness. When you're finished, the pressure cooker can be returned to pressure very quickly.

Do not use the quick release method for foods that increase in volume, or froth or foam, or those that are mostly liquids, like soup or broth. The quick release method may cause foods that have a tendency to foam to boil up and vent through the release valve. This happens when the pressure drops rapidly, and you can actually hear the food begin to boil when the temperature drops back to the normal boiling point.

Natural Release Method

This is the slowest, and the most often used method of releasing pressure. The pressure cooker is removed from the heat source and the pressure is allowed to subside naturally. This gradual drop in pressure and temperature allows the food to finish cooking throughout the slow cool-down process. Use this method for most cuts of meat, and foods like beans, potatoes, or apples that have a skin or peel that you wish to remain intact. The natural release method is preferred for foods that increase in volume, and froth or foam, and those that are mostly liquids, like soup or broth, to prevent clogging the valve system. There is no hard-and-fast rule to determine how long the cooling process will take before the cooker is depressurized. Factors such as the construction of the cooker and the volume and type of foods being cooked will affect the amount of time it takes for the pressure to drop. Be patient; an appropriate length of time would be about 15 minutes. After that, if you are in a hurry or can't wait any longer, then use the cold water release method to completely drop the remaining pressure.

Basic Pressure-Cooking Techniques

I F YOU'RE SKEPTICAL ABOUT PRESSURE COOKING, you probably think that tossing some food in the cooker, drowning it under a huge amount of water, and then standing back while it cooks the ingredients to death, only to serve up globs of nondescript baby food is not your idea of fun. Well, have I got news for you! The pressure cooker is capable of a wide variety of cooking techniques for almost every kind of food. Beginners and pressure-cooker novices, even long-time users, should become familiar with these simple and easy basic pressure-cooking techniques before moving on to the more advanced methods.

Infusion Pressure Cooking

There is no secret to infusion cooking; all pressure cookers infuse the flavors if food is placed directly into a well-seasoned, flavorful broth or marinade rather than just plain water. The tasty combination of herbs, spices, seasonings, and flavor-enhancing liquids are forced into the food. In using the infusion method, or super marinating, the cooking liquid will penetrate deep inside foods, not just sit on the outside, and create a richer-tasting sauce or gravy. Infusion cooking is appropriate for thinner cuts of meat like chicken pieces, chops, steaks, cut fruits and vegetables, and even polenta and risottos, but it is not as effective on thicker cuts of meat, like a roast.

Pressure-Cooker Steaming

Steaming is the most often used method in pressure cooking, and, not surprisingly, it is one of the healthiest ways to cook because no additional fat is necessary for cooking. The pressure cooker excels as a first-class steamer, and, by using a rack, fats drain away from food. Pressure-cooker steaming takes only a few minutes for most foods, minimizing the loss of nutrients while preserving the vibrant colors and textures of even the most delicate foods. Steaming is often used for Asian recipes, fluffy rice and other grains, fresh, tender-crisp vegetables, and delicate fish or seafood. Serve up everything from hot, buttery garlic bread to traditional English molded puddings by using this method. In all cases, plain water is used to produce steam, and foods are elevated above the water line.

Pressure-Cooker Stewing

Stewing, not to be confused with a recipe for a stew, is a moist-heat cooking method much like infusion cooking, except that, generally, plain water is used instead of a flavoring liquid, although it certainly possible to use any combination of liquids that will enhance or complement the food. Stewing is the ideal cooking method for small cubes of meat from the toughest cuts of beef, such as the round, flank, plate, and shank. Stewing is also used for vegetables like stewed tomatoes and fruits such as stewed prunes. A rack is not typically used in this cooking method, and the liquid should cover the ingredients.

Boiling in a Pressure Cooker

Boiling is the cooking method of choice to turn otherwise inedible bones, such as a turkey carcass, into a rich, nutrient-dense broth or stock. Boiling tough meats such as tongue and heart, or smoked, salt-cured, or brined or pickled meats makes them more palatable and digestible.

It takes longer to bring the cooker to pressure when using the boiling method. A rack may be used as desired, and the meat is covered with plain water and any appropriate seasonings.

Packet Pressure Cooking

Similar to PIP cooking (see page 37), this method is quick and easy but is used primarily for preparing individual servings, or for separating small amounts of individual foods without intermingling flavors, and even reheating foods that might dry out in an oven. In packet cooking, the ingredients are centered on a square of heavy-duty aluminum foil, and then the foil is tightly sealed and placed on a rack above the water level for steaming. Several layers of packets can be stacked or layered in this manner.

Braising in a Pressure Cooker

You may be familiar with braising in ordinary cooking recipes for dishes like the classic osso buco. This moist-heat cooking method is often used to cook tough cuts of meat, and sometimes fish, seafood, or vegetables. The pressure cooker teams up beautifully with braising recipes, turning out very tender dishes with full-bodied sauces.

In braising, meats and vegetables are usually cut into larger serving-size portions, rather than small cubes as in stewing. Meats can be dusted with seasoned flour, which will thicken the sauce, and then browned in a small amount of hot fat in the pressure cooker. The amount of liquid, which can be anything from water or stock to wine, beer, or tomato juice, covers only about half of the item to be braised.

At the end of cooking, the braising vegetables can either be removed or puréed and incorporated into the sauce.

Precooking in a Pressure Cooker

A pressure cooker can really be a timesaver in the kitchen when used to precook large cuts of pork, beef, lamb, chicken, ham, or turkey that would normally take hours to cook by traditional means. Precook a "roast chicken" in the pressure cooker, and then pop it in a hot oven with a glaze, or baste with butter to brown and crisp the skin. Use a pressure cooker to precook roasts, and then use the meat for shredded barbecue sandwiches, tacos, fajitas, burritos, pita bread fillings, or salads. For falling-off-the-bone, tender barbecued ribs, precook them in the pressure cooker and finish up on the grill or under the broiler. Precook several pounds of chicken wings in the pressure cooker, brush on your favorite barbecue sauce, and put them in the oven for a party-size platter of hot wings.

Poaching in a Pressure Cooker

Poaching allows certain foods to retain their natural tenderness, texture, and delicate flavor. The pressure cooker does an outstanding job with this very healthy cooking method because no additional fat is required. Always use small or thin cuts of food for poaching so that they can finish cooking very quickly. Foods are cooked directly in a small amount of liquid; water is used most often but other ingredients can be added to provide additional flavor. When the poaching process is completed, the liquid can be saved as a broth for later use, or reduced to intensify the flavors and then served with the poached food.

Advanced Pressure-Cooking Techniques

THESE ADVANCED PRESSURE-COOKING techniques require a little more experience, but you can discover a wealth of new recipes by using these little known and often overlooked secrets of pressure cookery. The techniques include interrupted cooking, tiered cooking, steam roasting or baking, and PIP (pan in pot) pressure cooking.

PIP (Pan in Pot) Pressure Cooking

A PIP recipe calls for placing food in a separate pan and then inserting that pan into the pressure cooker, leaving sufficient space between the insert and the side of the cooker to allow steam to move freely. This method has the added benefit of eliminating any accidentally burned or scorched foods. It is an excellent way to prepare casseroles, one-pot meals, a perfect bowl of rice, or even a scrumptious cheesecake.

When using PIP recipes, do not fill the insert pan more than two-thirds full, or only half full for foods that foam, froth, or expand. Use the natural release method (page 31), and avoid the sudden drop in temperature caused by using the quick or cold water release methods (page 30), which may cause the foods to boil over.

Many pressure cookers already come with an assortment of inserts such as steamer baskets, trays, and other stackable pans. Acceptable substitutions may be found right in your kitchen, or accessory items can be ordered from any manufacturer, as long as the diameter will fit loosely inside your pressure cooker. A rack is necessary with this cooking method, and plain water is used to produce steam. Foil helper handles (see page 42) make it easier to position the insert and remove the pan from the cooker.

Interrupted Pressure Cooking

In this method, the longest cooking ingredients are started first, and then the cooking is interrupted to add shorter cooking ingredients using the quick release method (page 30) to drop the pressure rapidly without losing heat. The modern pressure cookers with the quick release mechanisms make it easier than ever to use the interrupted cooking method to prepare more recipes than ever before.

When making beef stew, for example, the beef takes 15 minutes to cook, but the vegetables need only 5 minutes. Many cooks will add everything to the pressure cooker at the same time, only to end up with mushy vegetables. The correct method is to partially cook the meat for 10 minutes, remove the pot from the heat, and use the quick release to drop the pressure without lowering the temperature. The lid is then removed, the shorter-cooking vegetables are added, and the pressure lid is then locked back in place. The pressure cooker is returned to pressure for the last 5 minutes of cooking time for tender meat and perfectly cooked vegetables. It's quite possible to use the interrupted cooking method more than once in preparing a recipe that uses several different ingredients with varying cooking times.

Tiered Pressure Cooking

This advanced pressure-cooking method is a variation of the PIP cooking technique, using more than one pan inside the pressure cooker to cook several different foods, or even an entire two- or three-course meal at the same time. The secret of this method is to select foods or recipes with the same, or very close, cooking times and have a pressure cooker of a large enough size to accommodate everything on your menu. Alternately, this technique can be combined with the interrupted cooking technique for foods with very different cooking times

A trivet or rack is used to raise the insert pans above the water level. The bottom tier is for meat or the longest-cooking ingredient, with the side dish(s) placed on top. Depending on the size of your pressure cooker, pans can be stacked in two or more tiers. Stainless steel, aluminum, or tightly sealed aluminum foil packets can all be used inside the pressure cooker. Glass, ceramic, or other clay-fired bowls are the least acceptable, as they require extra cooking time because of their poor heat-conducting properties.

Steam Roasting or Baking in a Pressure Cooker

Steam roasting is a moist-heat cooking method that results in tender and flavorful meats, breads, and cakes, pressure-cooker "baked" potatoes, and casserole-type dishes. It is different than oven roasting in that there is less moisture lost and meats do not shrink as much. Meats should be seared in hot fat and quickly browned on all sides before steam roasting. Foods are placed on a rack or steaming basket, well above the water level and cooked in superheated steam.

Accessory Items

IF YOUR COOKER DOES NOT COME with any accessories, it's quite all right to use products from a different manufacturer as long as the diameter is slightly smaller than the inside of your pressure cooker. Search your kitchen; you may already have several pans or dishes on hand that can be used inside the pressure cooker. Look around the cooking section of local stores and on the Internet for additional items such as mini Bundt pans, small springform pans, mini loaf pans, ramekins or custard cups, pudding basins and molds, tube pans, and small cake pans. Metal pans are preferred over glass or ceramic because of their superior heating properties.

In a pinch, doubled aluminum foil can be shaped to form a pan, or folded and sealed into individual cooking packets. In the early days of pressure cookery, resourceful cooks gathered a collection of wide, short, and tall empty food cans that could be easily arranged inside the cooker. Boston Brown Bread, for example, an old-time pressure-cooker recipe, is traditionally made in a can.

The Material Difference

Any type of heatproof dish can be used in the pressure cooker; remember the inside temperature at 15psi is 250°F, well below that of an oven. Some materials heat better than others, and choosing just the right dish for use as a PIP (Pan in Pot) insert can affect the cooking time as well as the results of the finished recipe.

Metal containers will heat faster than any other material, and may provide a slight amount of browning to make a more appealing presentation. Glass or ceramic containers will absorb heat more slowly and heat unevenly, which means foods will take longer to cook. When using nonmetallic dishware, plan to increase the cooking time by 5 to 10 percent to allow for the extra thickness and slower heating properties. Avoid using fired clay bowls, especially foreign imports, where the applied glazes may not be food safe.

Racks and Trivets

Most modern pressure cookers come with an indispensable stainless steel or aluminum rack or trivet. In a pinch, use canning rings, or a heavy heatproof ceramic, stoneware, or earthenware saucer, bowl, or small plate. You can purchase a round, 7-inch wire cake rack in most kitchen shops, or use a collapsible, stainless steel steamer basket in place of a rack. Extra racks can be purchased from most pressure-cooker manufacturers, and they are

Pan Sizes and Volume

Pan Size	Approximate Volume	Pan Size	Approximate Volume
ROUND PAN		**CHARLOTTE MOLD**	
5" × 2"	2 ⅔ cups	6 × 4¼	7½ cups
6" × 2"	3 ¾ cups	**CUSTARD CUP**	
7" × 1¼"	2 cups	2¾" × 1½"	½ cups
8" × 1½"	4 cups	3" × 1¼"	⅝ cups
CASSEROLE DISH		**LOAF PAN**	
1 quart	4 cups	5½" × 3" × 2½"	2 cups
1½ quart	6 cups	6" × 4½" × 3"	3 cups
2 quarts	8 cups	**TUBE PAN OR RING MOLD**	
2½ quarts	10 cups	7½" × 2"	4 cups
SPRINGFORM PAN		7½" × 3"	6 cups
8" × 3"	6 cups	8" × 3"	9 cups
BUNDT PAN			
7½" × 3"	6 cups		

Quick Guide to Accessories and Their Heat Conduction Properties

Metal Type	Heat Properties	Notes
BEST CHOICES FOR HEAT CONDUCTION		
Copper: bowls, molds, pans, pudding basins, Bundt pan	Accepts heat faster than any other metal; heats evenly; loses heat quickly	Best are coated or lined with tin; can be reactive with some foods; not very durable
Aluminum: trivets and racks, bowls; molds; tube, small cake, springform, mini loaf and Bundt pans; steamers; separators or dividers; pudding basins; egg poachers	Heats quick and evenly	Can discolor easily, but easily cleaned; reacts with some foods; hand washing required for some
Stainless: trivets and racks, steel bowls, molds, pans, steamers, separators or dividers, pudding basins, pasta steamer baskets	Heats quickly	Durable and nonreactive
SECOND CHOICE FOR HEAT CONDUCTION		
Recycled substitutes: disposable aluminum pans, foil packets or shaped bowls, 1-pound coffee cans, cookie tins, assorted empty food cans	Heats quickly	Readily available, toss after use, no cleanup; foil can be shaped for small or odd shapes; aluminum reacts with some foods
Wood: trivets, bamboo steamer baskets, skewers	Does not transfer heat when wet	Inexpensive; must be soaked before using; porous; may be difficult to clean; not very durable
THIRD CHOICE FOR HEAT CONDUCTION		
Ceramics, vitrified ceramic, porcelain, other heatproof glassware: ramekins, custard cups, pudding basins, soufflé dishes, mini Bundt pans, quiche, tart, and flan pans, Corningware™, Pyrex™	Heats slowly and unevenly; matte finishes increase heat absorption slightly; retains heat extremely well	Can chip or break; may be the only choice available with certain shapes or sizes
Stoneware, Earthenware, fired clay: ramekins, custard cups, pudding basins, soufflé dishes	Heats slowly and evenly, but retains its temperature for a long time	Avoid glazes that are not food safe; follow manufacturer's guidelines for allowed safe uses and care

easily interchangeable between brands as long as the diameter does not exceed the width of your cooker.

The main purpose of a rack is to raise foods or pan inserts above the waterline for steaming. A rack can be placed on top of bulky foods like greens or cabbage to keep them away from the underside of the lid as they quickly wilt and diminish in volume. By raising foods off the bottom of the cooker, you can minimize the chance of scorching foods. A rack can be used when several items need to be stacked or arranged in layers. When using individual custard cups, for example, a rack is placed on the bottom of the cooker to elevate the ramekins, and then a second rack is placed on top of the first layer to serve as a stable platform for the second tier of cups. Racks can also be used to separate foods, such as a three-course meal of pork chops, baked potatoes, and stuffed apples, making it easier to remove them when the cooking process is completed.

Some foods require a longer steaming time, requiring more than the usual amount of water, and the regular rack won't raise food above the waterline.

Lids for Insert Pans

Some recipes will require a dish with a lid, turning the covered dish into a miniature oven inside the pressure cooker. A lid might be used to contain the steam in the dish, transferring heat from the steam vapor, both inside and outside the dish, to the food. A lid can also protect the food from condensation that may drip from the lid during the cool-down phase. Some accessory pans, like a pudding mold, come with a convenient lid, but a square of aluminum foil, tightly crimped over the top of the pan, makes a reasonable substitute. Use cooking spray, or lightly butter the inside of the pan as well as the inside of the lid or foil covering, to prevent food from sticking.

Foil Helper Handles

To make a foil helper handle, tear off a length of heavy-duty aluminum foil long enough to center the dish, and fold the ends over the top of it. Begin by folding the sheet of foil in half lengthwise, and then fold it in half again, ending up with a long, double-folded narrow strip of foil. With the dish placed in the center of the strip, bring the ends up over the top of the dish to use as a helper handle. Now the insert can be easily lowered into the pressure cooker; just fold or tuck the ends down so they will not interfere with the lid. When the dish has finished cooking, use the handy helper handles to lift the hot dish out of the cooker. Use two helper handles with large cuts of meat like roasts and whole chicken, or for lifting heavy dishes.

Pressure-Cooker Cleaning and Maintenance

AS WITH ANY VALUABLE PIECE of cookware, you'll want to take good care of your pressure cooker to ensure many years of trouble-free use.

Cleaning an Aluminum Pressure Cooker

If your cooker is aluminum or has an applied nonstick coating or anodized finish, check the owner's manual for the recommended cleaning methods. Many manufacturers advise hand washing because harsh dishwasher detergents may discolor or damage the finish. When washing the pressure-cooker pot by hand, use hot, soapy water and a sponge or cloth for general cleaning. Do not use abrasive cleansers or scrubbing pads, as they may damage the finish.

Removing Dark Discolorations from Aluminum

In localities with hard water, the minerals and alkalis may be deposited on the inside surface of aluminum pans, causing dark stains and discoloration. Common household products containing alkalis, like baking soda, ammonia, washing soda (also called sal soda), or sodium carbonate will also stain aluminum. High-acid foods, such tomatoes, will also react with aluminum cookware. While unsightly, this type of stain does not affect the use of the utensil nor the food prepared in it. These discolorations can usually be removed by boiling a solution of 2 to 3 tablespoons of cream of tartar, lemon juice, or vinegar to each quart of water in the open cooker for five to ten minutes. Rinse, and scour lightly with a soap-filled nonabrasive scouring pad. Wash and dry as usual. To prevent stains in aluminum, add a tablespoon of vinegar or lemon juice to the water during steaming.

Removing Calcium Deposits from Stainless Steel or Aluminum

Sometimes the minerals in hard water may react with the fats left behind from cooking and combine with soap residue or dishwasher detergents to produce a chalky, white calcium deposit on the pot. These milky white stains, sometimes called milkstone, can be removed by a acid-based cleaner, or by filling the cooker with water and adding ⅓ cup white vinegar per quart. Bring the pot to a boil without a lid. Remove from the heat and allow it to cool, and then scrub thoroughly with the vinegar solution, followed by washing in hot, soapy water.

Cleaning a Stainless Steel Pressure Cooker

Most stainless steel pressure-cooker pots can be washed in the dishwasher unless the manufacturer states otherwise. When washing by hand, use hot water, mild dishwashing soap, and a sponge or cloth to clean the pot. Do not use any type of corrosive or abrasive cleaners, or metal or steel wool scouring pads, as they will mar and scratch the surface. For more intensive cleaning, use a nonabrasive cleanser such as Bon Ami™, and a plastic, non-scratching cleaning pad to remove stubborn spots. To shine the outside of stainless steel and restore the mirror-bright finish, use a stainless steel polish or Barkeeper's Friend™.

Removing Burnt or Scorched Food

Whenever possible, try to remove burned-on foods while the pot is still hot. Even the worst, crusty burned-on mess can be cleaned by heating the pot and adding 1 cup of water. The water will instantly boil and produce clouds of steam vapor, so don't be surprised. If this doesn't happen, then the pot isn't hot enough and you'll need to begin all over again. As the liquid boils rapidly, the heat and steam will begin to loosen and dissolve the really stubborn deposits that have crusted and burned on the bottom of the pot. With a stainless steel pressure cooker, use a straight-edged spatula to scrape the bottom of the pan as the burned-on crust loosens. In my experience, it seldom takes more than a few minutes to remove even the worst burned-on mess by using this method. Continue boiling and scraping as needed until the majority of the burned-on deposits are dissolved. Follow up with a good soap-and-water cleaning, and use a stainless steel polish to restore the mirror bright finish.

Cleaning the Pressure-Cooker Lid

A pressure-cooker lid should not be washed in the dishwasher or left to soak in water. Remove the gasket and wash the lid, valves, and mechanical parts by hand in hot, soapy water. After cooking any food that foams or froths, disassemble the valve and quick release mechanism according to the owner's manual and clean all the component parts in hot, soapy water using a small brush. Air dry and reassemble before putting the cooker away.

Cleaning the Gasket

The gasket is the most important part on any pressure cooker. The gasket must be removed from the lid and washed separately after every use. Do not put the gasket in the dishwasher. Do not soak or use harsh cleaners or bleach. Take care not to stretch or twist the gasket, and pay close attention to cleaning deep grooves as you wash it. While cleaning the gasket, always examine it closely for any signs of wear, cracking, or tears, and replace it when necessary.

How Do I Care for Gaskets?

Most gaskets today are made of silicon or other polymers and not rubber. This material is less likely to retain food odors and is far more durable than rubber products. There is no need to do anything special to a new gasket other than give it a quick wash. The old wives' tales about soaking in water are a fallacy; neither silicon nor rubber absorbs water, so this does nothing to improve the gasket. Don't pull or stretch the gasket or it may not seat properly in the lid.

How Do I Install the Gasket in the Lid?

Some gaskets have a right side and a wrong side and they must be installed with the right side up. Look for any kind of printing on your gasket and install the gasket in the lid so the words are facing up toward you when you look down at the lid. If you are having trouble getting your pressure cooker to pressurize, the problem can often be resolved by simply flipping the gasket over.

Do I Need to Lubricate My Gasket?

No; oils can retain unpleasant odors, and when exposed to high heat they can become as sticky as shellac and fuse the gasket material to the metal. New gaskets are designed to fit snugly into the rim inside the lid and do not require any kind of lubricant. If your gasket is old, stretched, stiff, or hard to fit, you may get a few more uses out of it by applying a very thin film of plain Vaseline, which is very heat tolerant, and will make opening and closing the lid less difficult while awaiting a replacement.

Keep a Spare on Hand

How often a gasket needs to be replaced depends on how the pressure cooker is used, and quite naturally one that is in heavy use will require a new gasket more often. Other factors that will shorten the expected lifespan of gaskets are exposure to excessive or prolonged overheating, frequent overpressuring, and damage caused by hot fats and oils. Often the first indication that your gasket needs to be replaced is when the pot refuses to pressurize. If you use your pressure cooker frequently, then it's a good idea to keep an extra gasket on hand so that you will not be inconvenienced with ordering a new one and waiting for it to arrive. Always keep a record of the address of where you can purchase replacement parts for your pressure cooker.

Cleaning the Valve Mechanisms

It's important to ensure that all the valves on the pressure lid are clean and the mechanisms move freely. Use a small brush to clean the small over-pressure valve. The quick release valve and the pressure regulator valve units should be periodically disassembled as a part of regular maintenance, and the component pieces washed by hand using a small brush in hot, soapy water. The valve, or vent pipe in the case of old-style units, should also be deep cleaned after cooking any foods that foam or froth to be sure that no small food particles have gotten trapped inside the assembly. Follow the directions in your owner's manual for instructions on how to remove and disassemble the valve assembly for your particular brand. After the parts have been cleaned and inspected, they should be allowed to dry thoroughly before reassembly. Spring-valve assemblies that are attached with a screw need to be checked from time to time and the screw tightened when necessary. If the valve is sticking or is difficult to move, it should be disassembled and washed by hand in hot, soapy water.

General Pressure-Cooker Maintenance

Pressure-cooker handles that are attached with a screw need to be checked occasionally and the screws tightened when necessary. Valves are attached to the underside of the lid with screws that can loosen over time. These screws should be checked occasionally and tightened with a small screwdriver when necessary. Some brands have detachable handles for easier cleaning; follow the disassembly instruction provided in the instruction manual.

Storing the Pressure Cooker

Make sure the inside of the pot and the lid are dry before putting it away. If you use your cooker several times a week, invert the lid and place it on top of the pot to protect the valve or vent pipe. Leave the gasket loose on the lid, but not fitted into the groove. Do not store the cooker with the lid closed because odors will build up and the gasket will become compressed, shortening its usefulness. For pressure cookers using the old-style regulator weights, the weights should be removed from the lid and stored loose in the pot to minimize the chance of loss.

For long-term storage or infrequent use, place the detachable pressure regulator and gasket loosely inside the cooker and sprinkle 2 tablespoons of baking soda inside the pot to absorb moisture and odors. Invert the lid and place it on top of the cooker to protect the valve or vent pipe from accidental damage.

Common Mistakes in Pressure Cookery

MANY VINTAGE PRESSURE COOKERS had inherent mechanical problems, but those conditions no longer exist in today's modern pressure cookers. Yet, many pressure-cooker users make common mistakes that often get blamed on the pressure cooker, rather than on simple user error. Let's examine the most common mistakes in pressure cookery and the solutions for how to avoid them.

Overcooking

Overcooking is a common mistake made by novices and longtime pressure-cooker users alike. A pressure cooker requires accurate timing to produce high-quality results. An extra minute or two may not affect a roast that takes 30 minutes, but it will definitely ruin fresh green beans that only take three minutes to cook. Overcooking can negatively alter the taste, appearance, and texture of your food. There may be a loss in the nutritional value of your food as well.

Meats especially can become dried out from overcooking. It sounds odd, but even when meat is cooked in a broth, it can become dried out, tough, and stringy, because the longer the meat cooks, the more the muscle fibers shorten in both length and width and eventually squeeze out the juices they normally hold.

Vegetables that are overcooked turn into soft and mushy baby food and lose much of their vitamins and minerals in the process.

> Solution: Always follow recipe directions, or refer to the Cooking Time Charts (page 83) for best results, and don't guess about cooking times. Use the timer on your stove, an inexpensive wind up timer, or a digital timer on a lanyard or clip so you won't forget to turn off the heat and depressurize the cooker.

Overheating and Overpressuring

Overheating is a common problem for novices as well as many longtime pressure cooker users, and it's the main reason why foods burn or scorch on the bottom of the pressure cooker.

Overheating leads to overpressuring, which will trigger the safety release system. The first sign of overpressurization is indicated by a steady stream of audible and visible escaping steam. This will alert you to the problem so you can immediately lower the heat. The type of heat source used can play a part in overheating. Overheating can cause a heat tint on stainless steel, leaving a permanent, iridescent blue discoloration, and while this doesn't damage the cookware, it is unsightly.

> Solution: Remember to reduce the heat to the lowest possible setting that will stabilize and maintain that pressure. Do the test drive (see page 55); it will help you learn the best combination of settings for your stove and pressure cooker.

Overfilling the Pressure Cooker

Overfilling can delay or prevent the pressure cooker from achieving sufficient pressure, which increases the possibility of overcooking and scorching food. Overfilling may also trigger the safety system should the valves become blocked by food particles.

> Solution: The pressure cooker should only be filled two-thirds full for most cooking purposes, but only half full when cooking foods that are mostly liquids, or foods that foam, froth, or expand during cooking. The pressure cooker needs the remaining space to generate steam and build pressure.

Using an Incorrect Amount of Liquid

A pressure cooker requires a minimum amount of water to build pressure, and a sufficient amount to last throughout the cooking process. Use too little liquid and the pressure cooker can run dry, leading to overheating and overpressuring, which will burn the food and engage the safety systems. Using too much liquid makes it difficult for the cooker to generate enough steam to come to pressure and could result in scorched food. Excessive cooking times will destroy more nutrients and increase fuel costs.

Another problem is using the wrong kind of liquid. Thick sauces like tomato sauce, oils, oil-based sauces like salad dressing, and condiments such as ketchup or barbecue sauce should not be considered as part of the cooking liquid. When these ingredients are included in a recipe, always add an additional amount of cooking liquid, such as water, broth, juice, or wine, to generate the necessary steam.

> Solution: All pressure cookers must have a minimum amount of liquid, as recommended by the manufacturer, to build pressure. Do not exceed the maximum full levels for the type of foods being cooked. Use the Test Drive (see page

55) to determine how much liquid your cooker will need. Use the appropriate cooking method for the ingredients used.

Improper Food Preparation

Many pressure-cooker owners are under the mistaken belief that they can throw everything into the pot all at one time and deliver a delicious meal a few minutes later. However, basic rules of good cooking apply to pressure-cooker recipes just the same as they do to any other cooking methods.

> **Solution:** A pressure cooker is a wonderful appliance and a great addition to any kitchen, but don't skip the basic rules of good cooking. Foods must be properly prepared for the best results. Most meats should be at least partially thawed and browned or sautéed or they will be tasteless, blanched-looking, and unappealing. Food needs to be cut to a uniform size or the pieces will cook unevenly. To cook mixed foods that have different cooking times, you can "fudge" a little by varying the size of the pieces—larger pieces for the quicker-cooking foods and smaller pieces for the foods needing a little longer cooking times. Use the interrupted cooking method (see page 38) for foods that have very different cooking times.

Incorrect Cooking Method

Many people are surprised learn there are several different methods used in pressure cookery. Just as in regular cooking, foods may be cooked by using any of several different methods, depending on personal preference and the desired outcome for a particular dish.

> **Solution:** Become familiar with all the cooking methods and carefully follow the recipe instructions.

Incorrect Pressure Settings

Be careful when using heirloom or shared pressure-cooker recipes that may have incorrect cooking times or be designed for a nonstandard pressure cooker using less than the standard 15psi. Nonstandard pressure cookers, those with a maximum operating pressure of less than 15psi, will require longer cooking times when using a recipe designed for the 15psi standard, and that will affect the quality of the finished dish.

> **Solution:** As discussed in A Buyer's Guide to Modern Pressure Cookers (see page 13), not all pressure cookers are created equal. Unless stated otherwise, the recipes in this book, as well as the majority of other books and recipes for pressure cookery, use the accepted standard of 15psi. You can make adjustments to cooking times, but it only makes sense to purchase a pressure cooker that is capable of cooking standard recipes.

Incorrect Pressure Release Methods

Different foods require different release methods. Foods inside a pressure cooker will remain hot and continue cooking even after removing the pot from the stove. While this is excellent for finishing large cuts of meat, delicate vegetables will be overcooked. Recipes will the state the correct way to depressurize the cooker before opening the lid.

> **Solution:** Understand the three methods of pressure release as described in Pressure: Getting It, Keeping It, Releasing It (see page 27), and follow recipe directions.

Adapting Recipes to the Pressure Cooker

SWITCHING FROM ORDINARY cooking methods to pressure cooking will save you an incredible amount of time, but don't skip the basics of good cooking. When cooking meat, first heat a little oil in the pressure cooker and brown the pieces on all sides. Sauté onions and garlic to develop their flavor. Use flavoring liquids (see page 58) such as stock or wine in place of all or part of the water. The final procedure in any recipe should be to adjust seasoning to your taste, altering and adapting the seasoning ingredients to your personal preferences.

Apply the Ten Golden Rules of Pressure Cookery (see page 23). Taking care not to exceed the appropriate fill levels and selecting the correct pressure release method for the ingredients used in the recipe are important considerations in adapting. Keep notes as you go, including comments about:

1. The amount of liquid: was it adequate, or does it need to be adjusted higher or lower?

2. Were the seasonings appropriate, or do they need to be modified?

3. Was the pressure-cooking method correct, or would a different method work better?

4. Did all the ingredients finish cooking at the same time, or will adjustments need to be made?

5. Was the cooking time correct, or will refinements improve the recipe?

It may take a couple of tries to get the adjustments just right, but a little extra effort spent in converting a recipe will save a great deal of cooking time.

What Kind of Recipes Can Be Adapted to the Pressure Cooker?

Many recipes that are cooked by ordinary cooking methods on top of the stove, in the oven, or in a slow cooker can be easily adapted for use in a pressure cooker. Recipes that cook by simmering, stewing, poaching, boiling, braising, or steaming, such as soups, stews, casseroles, curries, risotto, pasta dishes, roasts, dried beans, desserts, fruits, and vegetables, can be cooked to perfection in a pressure cooker. Recipes that require long cooking times—tough cuts of meats like pot roasts and round steaks—can be turned into sumptuous meals in just a third of the time required by conventional cooking methods. Unless noted, use the standard pressure setting of 15psi.

Amount of Liquid

Because the modern pressure cooker is tightly sealed, there is very little evaporation, and depending on the type of recipe, the amount of liquid used in a conventional recipe can be decreased. Foods release their own juices during pressure cooking, adding to the volume of liquid and increasing the flavor of the dish. However, do not use less than the minimum amount of liquid as recommended by the pressure-cooker manufacturer.

Applying Pressure-Cooking Techniques

When deciding to convert a standard recipe to the pressure cooker, you'll need to choose the correct pressure-cooking technique that will produce the desired results. A simple way to do this is to find a pressure-cooking recipe with similar ingredients and duplicate the directions. Test the recipe and make adjustments accordingly.

Converting Ordinary Cooking Times to Pressure Settings

As a general rule, reduce the cooking time by two-thirds when cooking at 15psi, or use the Pressure-Cooking Time Charts (see page 83), but be prepared to make adjustments.

Methods of Depressurizing the Cooker

Choosing the best pressure release method for your recipe is key to success. First, check the Ten Golden Rules of Pressure Cooking (see page 23); the pressure release method to use depends on the type of food being prepared. The information in the Pressure-Cooking Time Charts (see page 83) also lists the recommended pressure release method for many kinds of food. Another option would be to find a similar pressure-cooker recipe and apply the directions to your version. Be sure to refer to Releasing Pressure (see page 30).

Pressure Cooking at High Altitudes

At high altitude (3,500 feet and above), cooks really have to plan ahead to do some of the same things the rest of us take for granted, because the boiling point of water decreases with altitude. A pressure cooker is the perfect solution to high-altitude cooking, and a necessity for anyone living or camping in the mountains.

Using a little basic physics, we know that water boils at 212°F at sea level, which is arbitrarily defined as zero. As altitude increases, the temperature at which water boils decreases at the rate of about 1.9°F for each 1,000 feet. Even though foods will appear to be at a bubbling boil, their temperature will be several degrees cooler than when the same foods are cooked at sea level. On top of the 14,000-foot Pike's Peak, for example, the boiling point of water is only 187°F, and even though the water is boiling, it is not very hot, and therefore food takes longer to finish cooking. By increasing the pressure, the temperature at which water boils is raised, and food cooks more quickly.

Various opinions exist as to whether timing adjustments are needed when pressure cooking at high altitudes. In my experience, no changes in cooking times need to be made when using a pressure cooker for high-altitude cooking. It will take a little longer to reach 15psi, because at high altitudes, the contents will boil at a lower temperature until the cooker is fully pressurized. After the cooker is at 15psi, the temperature inside the tightly sealed pot is no different than it would be at sea level, so the food is still cooking at 250°F.

Test Drive Your Pressure Cooker

WHY SHOULD YOU DO THIS? When you buy a new pressure cooker, or if you're about to try pressure cooking for the first time, you may be in a rush to see the results as quickly as possible. However, by first taking the pressure cooker for a test drive, you can determine how your particular brand works in conjunction with your stove without putting your dinner at risk. A test drive will give you a good idea of how your cooker operates, and show you how long it takes for the pressure cooker to reach pressure and how much heat is needed to maintain it.

How to Begin the Test Drive

Before starting, be sure that the pressure cooker is clean and that the seal or gasket is properly positioned. Check that all the vents, valves, and safety mechanisms are in good working order. You'll need a watch, clock, or timer, as well as a measuring cup, paper and pencil, and some tape and a marking pen, or one of those little colored sticky dots from the office-supply store.

Begin by adding 2 cups of water to the pressure cooker, and then lock the lid in place. Bring to high pressure over high heat, and then immediately adjust the heat to the lowest possible setting to maintain that pressure. This is the point when timing begins for all pressure-cooker recipes. It may take several attempts before you find just the right heat setting to stabilize the pressure.

Once the cooker has maintained that pressure for ten minutes, make a note of the actual heat position of your stove by marking the setting with a piece of tape or placing a colored sticky dot as a reminder. Keep a written record of how long it took to reach that stage. If your cooker has more than one pressure setting, repeat the process with the other settings.

To determine how much water your cooker will use during the test, use the cold water release method (page 30), which will immediately stop the cooking process and quickly lower the pressure. When the pressure cooker has completely returned to normal pressure, carefully remove the lid. Measure the water remaining in the cooker and make a note of it. There should be at least ½ cup of water remaining, or no less than the minimum recommended by the manufacturer.

Water and Other Liquids

ALL PRESSURE COOKERS need some type of liquid to operate, and the most common choice is water. Water is fine for steaming food on the rack, or when the food does not require any additional flavor, or sauce. There are all kinds of liquids or combinations of liquids that can be used to enhance the flavor, taste, and aroma of foods, as well as improve the visual appeal of foods cooked in a pressure cooker.

Soft drinks, fruit juices and nectars, vegetable juice, beer and wine, stocks and broth, many varieties of vinegar (especially a good-quality balsamic), and soy sauce are all good choices to use as all or part of the required liquid. Experiment with your pressure cooker. Combine several complementary flavoring liquids, or mix them with water.

How Much Liquid Is Needed?

The recipes in this book specify the amount of water necessary to cook with modern, spring-valve pressure cookers. The Pressure-Cooking Time Charts (see page 83) will also list the minimum amount of water required. Check the owner's manual of your pressure cooker and never use less than the minimum amount of liquid required by your brand and model. The amount of liquid needed depends on the cooking method, the recipe ingredients, and the length of the cooking time. In general, a modern spring-valve pressure cooker will need about ½ cup of liquid per 15 minutes of cooking time, but do use the test drive (see page 55) to find out how much liquid is needed for longer cooking times. Do not exceed the maximum fill rules.

What Isn't a Liquid?

There are many choices of ingredients that can be used as all or part of the minimal required cooking liquids for the pressure cooker, but the ingredients listed below should not be considered as cooking liquids.

* Oils, fats, or grease: ¼ cup is usually the maximum. Check your owner's manual, and never use more oil than the manufacturer recommends.

* Thick sauces: Steak, BBQ, mustard, ketchup, tomato sauce, etc., should not be considered as part of the required cooking liquid. If using, add water to thin and minimize burning.

* Salad dressings: French, Catalina, Russian, Italian, etc., are good as flavor enhancers but should not be counted as a cooking liquid.

* Milk, cream, or other dairy products: Do not use during pressure cooking, as the high heat will make dairy products separate and look curdled. Add dairy products after the pot is depressurized.

* Condensed soups: These should not be counted as part of the cooking liquid.

Going Beyond Water	
Food	**Flavoring Liquids**
Poultry	Use lighter flavorings for most poultry dishes. Chicken stock or broth is always a good choice. Tropical juices of all kinds, including lemon, lime, orange, and pineapple juice, complement many poultry recipes. White wine and lemon-lime soft drinks are other possibilities. Small amounts of balsamic or wine vinegar will enhance many flavors.
Beef and veal	Beef stands up to strong flavors like beer, cola, Dr. Pepper™, coffee, red wine, and stock and broth. Small amounts of balsamic or wine vinegar will enhance many flavors, and dark-colored fruit juices such as cranberry or raspberry, or vegetable juices like tomato, are other good choices.
Beans	A good, well-seasoned, hearty meat or vegetable broth will add more flavor to beans than any other ingredient.
Pork	Pork goes well with apple juice or cider, beer and wine, citrus, fruit and vegetable juices, and many kinds of cola. Vinegar, especially good-quality balsamic vinegar, is an excellent addition to most pork recipes. Chicken stock or broth can be added or mixed in combination as needed.
Fish and Seafood	Fresh lemon or lime juice, fish or chicken stock, white wine, and lemon-lime soft drinks add flavor to delicate foods.

Troubleshooting

Q. Why is my meat so dry and tough?

A. In ordinary cooking methods, meat becomes more tender the longer it cooks, but as odd as it sounds, quite the opposite happens in the pressure cooker. When meats are pressure cooked at the appropriate pressure, for the correct length of time, and with the correct release method, they are tender, moist, and flavorful. However, when meats are overcooked under high heat and pressure, or when the incorrect method is used to depressurized the cooker, the muscle fibers will shorten in both length and width, forcing the fat and juices out of the meat. When this occurs, the meat passes from fork-tenderness, to dry, tough, and taste-less as cooking continues.

Using the quick-release or cold water release rather than the recommended natural release method results in dry, tough meats. The rapid depressurization causes the meat fibers to contract. Although the meat fibers relax somewhat after a 10-minute resting period, the meat is never as tasty and tender as when the pressure comes down naturally.

To avoid this problem, check the Pressure-Cooking Time Charts (see page 83) or follow a recipe, and use the natural release method when cooking larger cuts of meat.

Meat that has been overcooked in the pressure cooker can be salvaged by continuing to cook the meat. This will eventually break down the tough, dried-out fibers until the meat finally becomes tender again.

Q. The valve stem seems to stick, and sometimes I have to "help" it rise. Does this mean it needs to be replaced?

A. No, not necessarily; this problem can usually be corrected with a good cleaning, which should be a part of periodic pressure-cooker maintenance. Occasionally a valve will become sticky and not rise properly, especially after cooking foods that foam or froth, because a sticky build-up of fats or food residue has collected inside the valve housing. The solution is to dismantle the valve mechanism and wash the component parts thoroughly in hot, soapy water, using a small brush to get into hard-to-reach places. If the valve still seems sluggish, lubricate it with a drop or two of high-heat-tolerant cooking oil like sunflower or peanut oil. If this doesn't solve the problem then consider a replacement, but start with just the spring mechanism before replacing the entire valve unit.

Q. My stainless steel pressure cooker has developed a dark, bluish or mottled rainbow-like discoloration. How do I clean this off?

A. The iridescent or bluish-purple discoloration is called a heat tint and is caused by excessive heat. In mild cases, the discoloration may fade over time, but heat tint is permanent and cannot be removed. While it may be unsightly, the heat tint will not affect the pot or its usefulness.

Q. I can't locate a replacement part—what can I do?

A. Pressure cookers, just like other pieces of cookware, are eventually discontinued and the manufacturer no longer carries needed replacement parts. It might be impossible to locate replacement parts for little-known brands, foreign imports, and marketing fads that come and go. If you have the misfortune of owning an orphan pressure cooker, one that you can no longer obtain parts for, then it is unusable except as an ordinary stockpot using a regular lid. For safety reasons, never attempt to use any type of homemade gasket material or substitute a gasket intended for a different make or model.

Q. How can I prolong the life of my gasket?

A. Always wash the gasket after every use. Keep the gasket clean and dry between use. Wipe the rim of the pot with a clean, damp cloth to remove any grains of salt or other spices, fats, oils, or other bits of food and drips before locking the lid in place. This will prevent the gasket from sticking to the food and tearing when you try to open the lid. Do not twist, knot, fold, or stretch the gasket, and don't let the kids (or the puppy—yes, that happens too) play with the gasket. Always use sufficient water or other cooking liquids. If you let your cooker run dry, the heat increases and shortens the life of the gasket material. Do not cook with large amounts of oil, because oil gets far hotter than water or other liquid. Gasket materials that are designed to work well at 250°F may fail at 400°F, the temperature of boiling oil. Even small amounts of oil will splatter, and that can damage the gasket material.

Q. What should I do if a lot of steam is leaking around the rim or from beneath the lid?

A. With any signs of excess steam, first check the gasket to make sure that it is in good condition, clean, and correctly positioned. Some gaskets must be seated rightside-up, with the printing readable as you look down at it. In rare cases, leaks around the lid are not the fault of the gasket, but of structural damage to the cooker or the lid caused by dropping, warping, or misuse. Damage to the rim of the cooker can occur by using harsh, abrasive cleaners or steel wool scouring pads. Rapping cooking utensils against the rim can cause dents, deep scratches, or nicks.

Q. How do I know when to replace the gasket?

A. There's no hard-and-fast rule about when to replace a pressure-cooker gasket. Gaskets vary in their life expectancy. The durability depends on the gasket material, the frequency of use, the care, and even the foods cooked. Some gaskets can last many years, while others may not last a year. Sometimes there is no advance warning before a gasket fails. The first indication you may notice is steam escaping from a certain spot(s) beneath the lid. Depressurize the pot and carefully remove the lid. Closely examine the gasket at the point where you noticed the escaping steam, and you will find a tear or crack in the gasket. Even a very minute defect is enough to prevent the cooker from properly coming to pressure.

Replace gaskets as they become stretched, cut, gummy, or brittle. An old-fashioned thumbnail test is a good way to check: press your thumbnail against the gasket, and if leaves a permanent dent, then the gasket should be replaced. If it is difficult to settle the gasket in the lid or if the lid is hard to open and close, it's probably a good time to replace the gasket as well as all the soft sealing parts. I recommend keeping a spare gasket in stock at all times.

Q. Help! My gasket has melted and stuck to the metal! What can I do?

A. This may happen to old gaskets that need to be replaced or have been exposed to a prolonged or too high heat source. If oils or fats have been used on the gasket, the heat can create a sticky, shellac-like coating that may bond the gasket to the metal.

If the gasket is stuck to the pot, use warm water and liquid dish soap to soak and loosen it and remove as much as possible. Do not use abrasives, sandpaper, scrapers, or anything that may damage the metal sealing surfaces of the pot or the lid. If the gasket has melted or bonded to the metal, try a solvent like Goo-Gone™ or Gum Out™ (check the housewares or automotive sections of your neighborhood store). Use these products only as a last resort, taking care to follow directions and use only on the metal surfaces.

Q. Water droplets are leaking out from the valve assembly. Is this dangerous?

A. During the course of building pressure, there might be a slight leakage of water around the valve, or the vent pipe in old-style pressure cookers. A few water droplets are normal, but this should stop once full pressure is achieved. If it persists, examine the valve or vent pipe for any debris. Disassemble the valve and clean all the components in hot, soapy water.

Q. A lot of steam is coming from the valve mechanism. Is this normal?

A. Some steam will be visible as the pressure cooker exhausts all the air out during pressurization. This is common, and will stop once pressure is achieved. Pay close attention to any unusually loud sputter, hissing, or large amounts of escaping steam, which indicates a problem with the gasket.

Q. Why does food burn on the bottom of the pressure cooker, and how can I avoid it?

A. Remember to bring the cooker to pressure over high heat, and then immediately reduce the heat to the lowest possible setting to stabilize and maintain that setting. Do not cook on high BTU burners or use hobs that are bigger than the base of the pot. Do not overfill the pot. If you load the pressure cooker to the maximum fill level, it will take more time to come to pressure, and that may increase the possibility of burning some foods. Thick soups, stews, and sauces are more prone to burning. To avoid this problem, first bring the food to a boil in the cooker using only a regular lid, stirring often to avoid burning. When the contents reach a rapid boil, lock the pressure lid in place, and the cooker will rise to pressure very quickly. This will enable you to lower the heat sooner. Do not add flour, cornstarch, or other thickeners at the start of cooking; instead, wait until the food is done and then add thickeners after pressure cooking.

Tips and Tricks

∗ When the pressure cooker is filled at or near the maximum two-thirds capacity, it will take longer to reach full pressure. This may be a problem when cooking thick sauces or stews and cause scorching on the bottom. To reduce the time it will take to pressurize the cooker, start simmering the liquid while chopping the rest of the ingredients. Bring it to a boil, stirring occasionally, and then lock the lid in place.

∗ When cooking breads or puddings with a leavening agent (baking powder, baking soda), remember that it must have room to rise, so do not fill the mold more than two-thirds full.

∗ If you don't have a suitable insert pan, simply use a bowl of the appropriate size to shape a double layer of heavy-duty aluminum foil into a bowl. Leave the top of the foil bowl open, unless stated otherwise in the recipe. Always place the foil bowl on a rack and not in direct contact with the bottom of the cooker. Make sure to leave enough space between the bowl and the sides of the pressure cooker for steam to move freely.

∗ When chopping foods to be cooked together, be sure they are of similar size so they will cook in the same amount of time.

∗ You can always cook small items in a large pressure cooker, but not the reverse. Never exceed the maximum fill rules, and always use at least the minimum amount of liquid as recommended by the manufacturer and required by the length of cooking.

* Do not allow the liquid to touch the food when steaming or the food will boil and overcook.

* When cooking in tiers, place meats, fish, or juicy foods in the bottom tiers so they cannot drip onto foods below. Place the larger or longer-cooking foods on the bottom where they are closest to the heat source. Foods cooked in upper tiers cook slower because they are farther away from the heat, so plan ahead and place the most delicate ingredients on top. Always leave space around the insert pans to allow steam to circulate and to cook more efficiently.

* When cooking whole potatoes, use the natural release method to keep the skin intact. To make it easier to remove the skin for peeling, use the cold water release method.

* Foods that rise, such as cakes and puddings, require a preliminary steaming period before the cooker is pressurized. There are several methods to use: (1) For pressure cookers with a spring valve, use a regular lid or leave the pressure lid ajar and not in the locking position. (2) For a pressure cooker with a removable or weighted regulator, simply remove it from the vent pipe and let the steam escape freely, or leave the pressure lid ajar and not in the locking position.

Kitchen Shortcuts and Frugal Tips

* If you don't have all the fresh vegetables called for, by all means substitute frozen vegetables.

* Be a frugal cook and save and freeze vegetable trimmings, meat and bone scraps, and other leftover ingredients that might otherwise be tossed for making a great pot of free stock.

* I love garlic, but I'm always running out, so I keep a large jar of prepared minced garlic in the fridge. It eliminates all that peeling, chopping, crushing, or mincing when you're short on time.

* Fresh herbs are available all year long, and they are a quick way to transform ordinary meals into extraordinary meals. As a general guideline when exchanging fresh herbs for dried for use in a pressure cooker, use three times as much of the fresh variety as you would use of a dried herb. Herbs are great to have on hand, but they do not keep. The good news is they freeze rather well, and in the process the flavor and aroma intensifies. To freeze fresh herbs, wash, drain, and pat dry with paper towels. Fill the sections of an ice-cube tray about half full with chopped herbs, cover with water, and freeze. Transfer the frozen cubes to a freezer bag, and then they are ready to drop into soups, stews, and sauces as needed. Be aware that frozen herbs are not suitable for garnish, as they become wilted and darker in color after thawing.

* To remove the last bit of fat from stew or broth, drop a lettuce leaf in the pot to absorb excess grease.

* *Mise en place*—this French term (pronounced MEEZ ahn plahs) translates as "everything in its place," or premeasured and ready to use. Cooking a great meal begins with proper planning, and this means organizing yourself, your recipe ingredients, and the accompanying side dishes for the meal. An important first step in cooking is simply to have all the needed equip-

ment and utensils on hand and all the recipe ingredients prepared, measured, and ready to go *before* you start cooking. Read each step of the recipe directions and cooking techniques before starting! Using this technique will save time and lessen the chance of leaving something out of the recipe.

✳ Out of whipped cream? Partially freeze evaporated milk in a shallow pan. Chill a mixing bowl and beaters by filling with ice water until the evaporated milk is frozen. Empty the bowl and wipe it and the beaters dry before adding the semi-frozen evaporated milk. Whip the evaporated milk on high until soft peaks form, and serve immediately.

✳ To keep your hands from getting greasy when making meatloaf, put all the ingredients in a large food storage bag. Seal tightly and mix the ingredients together by squeezing the bag. Use a stand mixer to combine meatloaf ingredients to make a densely textured mix that will retain its shape.

✳ To cut down on the greasiness of inexpensive ground beef, rinse under cool water in a colander after cooking.

✳ Stock up on several varieties of canned chopped or diced tomatoes and you'll never have to do the messy and time-consuming chore of cutting up fresh tomatoes again.

✳ A trick for saving tomato paste: On a small plate, divide a 3-ounce can of tomato paste in little mounds of 2 tablespoons each. Freeze, and then pop off the portions and store them in a plastic freezer container, ready for use.

✳ Frozen foods can really cut down the prep work and get you out of the kitchen in record time. Frozen chicken, for example, comes in a wide variety of choices, and I stock up on large bags of boneless and skinless chicken breasts and thighs. If you don't want to go to the trouble of cutting up a round steak, then by all means buy the stew meat already cut. If you don't have time for all that peeling, chopping, and dicing when it comes to preparing vegetables, then stock up on an assortment of frozen vegetables for another great way to cut your workload.

✳ Many fresh vegetables can be quickly prepared and frozen in convenient serving portions. Take advantage of sales to stock up on fresh vegetables and herbs like onions, celery, carrots, carrots, and my favorite, fresh cilantro. After a little slicing and dicing, just measure them out in convenient amounts, seal them up in a plastic freezer bag, and tuck them into the freezer for use whenever needed.

✳ Stock your pantry with an assortment of non-perishable foods like dry and condensed soups, pasta sauces, canned fruits and juices, broth, pasta, rice, and dried beans. Many wonderful vinegars, mustards, cooking sauces and condiments, spices, and seasoning packets are available to enhance the taste and aroma of foods. These shortcuts will increase your productivity and decrease your workload.

Kitchen Equipment That Will Save You Time

Using a pressure cooker is so fast that the preparation time actually takes longer than the cooking process in many cases. Don't be afraid to cut corners to save time in the prep work. I think one of the most important appliances that should be in every kitchen is a food processor to handle much of the chopping, mixing, puréeing, dicing, shredding, and grating work. If you don't have one, it's really worth the investment and will definitely cut short the time and the workload of preparing many recipe ingredients.

Another handy item to add to your kitchen equipment is a hand blender. I use this to mix and blend ingredients, or hot sauces and gravies, right in the cooker—no more lumpy gravy.

By all means, invest in a couple of good-quality knives, and a chopper, for chopping and slicing. Instead of a rigid cutting boad, try flexible plastic cutting mats; these are great for chopping vegetables and then easily transferring them to the pot.

Sets of measuring cups and spoons are a necessity. Little custard cups are not just for desserts; use them to set out all the premeasured recipe ingredients to save time.

Using a tall pressure cooker requires the use of long-handled cooking utensils to transfer foods in and out of the pot. At a minimum, I recommend at least one set of locking tongs, a spatula, a mixing spoon, and a ladle of reasonably good-quality stainless steel for strength and durability.

For the cost of one can of cooking spray, buy an oil spritzer and simply fill it with your own oil and save money every time you refill it.

25 Important Do's and Don'ts

1. Pressure cooking is really fairly simple once you become familiar with how the cooker operates. The best place to start is always the owner's manual. Do read it thoroughly and make sure you understand all the new terms and processes for this exciting method of cooking.

2. Do not use oils, fats, or grease in any quantity beyond ¼ cup or exceed the amount recommended by the pressure-cooker manufacturer.

3. Do not cook thick sauces, such as spaghetti or pasta-type sauces, without thinning them first with ½ cup of liquid for every 2 cups of sauce. Thick sauces take much longer to heat up, and that means the pot takes longer to pressurize, increasing the possibility of scorching the sauce.

4. Do not overcook; remember that pressure-cooker timing depends on the size of the individual pieces of food, not the quantity.

5. As a general rule, do not add milk, cream, cheese, or other dairy products at the beginning of pressure cooking because they tend to scorch, and high heat causes the milk solids to separate and curdle.

6. Do not add too much salt when pressure cooking. Everyone has personal or dietary preferences for the amount of salt used in their food; wait until the food has cooked and adjust to taste.

7. Do read the recipe from start to finish before you began. Make sure you understand the cooking processes and methods used. Make sure that you have all the necessary ingredients and equipment required to complete the recipe.

8. Do not use a pressure cooker without setting a timer.

9. Do not use a pressure cooker as a pressure fryer. Never, ever.

10. Just as you would not leave a broiler or grill unsupervised, do not leave your pressure cooker unattended.

11. When combining several different ingredients with slightly different cooking times, do cut foods that cook more quickly into

slightly larger pieces, and those that cook with longer cooking times into smaller pieces.

12. Do cut the same foods into pieces of uniform size to promote even cooking.

13. Do remember to brown meats first. This important step not only improves the visual appearance, but also adds increased flavor and improves the taste.

14. When a recipe calls for frozen vegetables, do not allow them to thaw before putting them in the pressure cooker. Thawing will affect the cooking time and result in the vegetables being overcooked.

15. When a recipe calls for frozen vegetables, break up any solid clumps to assure uniform cooking, but do not allow them to thaw.

16. Do not add thickeners such as flour or cornstarch at the start of pressure cooking, because they can thicken the sauce to the point where it begins to burn. Instead, wait until the pot is pressurized and thicken the sauce as desired

17. To minimize foaming and frothing, do add a spoonful of cooking oil.

18. Do not use less cooking liquid than the minimum amount recommended by the manufacturer.

19. To mingle the flavors of different foods in a pressure cooker, do let them come into contact with the cooking liquid, which will transmit the flavors.

20. To keep the flavors of different foods separate in a pressure cooker, do place the foods on a rack or steamer basket well above the water level. Steam does not transmit, blend, or mix flavors.

21. When pressure cooking breads or cakes that contain a leavening agent such as baking powder or baking soda, a 15-minute period of steaming is required to allow the recipe to rise before the cooker is pressurized. With a pressure cooker that uses a removable regulator, just remove the weight for the steaming. For a modern pressure cooker with a spring-loaded valve, use a regular lid instead of the locking pressure lid. Check the water level, replenishing with boiling water if necessary, before locking the lid in place.

22. A pressure cooker with a three-ply base is the best defense against scorched foods. One old-fashioned trick is to layer the ingredients in such a way that foods with high sugar or starch content are not placed near the bottom of the cooker.

23. Do not alter the cooking times when multiplying or dividing a recipe. The amount of food in the pressure cooker has no bearing on the cooking time. For example, a dozen pork chops will cook just as quickly as one.

24. If using a pressure cooker with an electric or glass-top stove do set one burner on high and a second one on a lower heat. Bring the cooker up to pressure on the high-heat burner, and then move it to the second burner for the rest of cooking.

25. Do remember to perform routine maintenance on your pressure cooker, and periodically check the screws that hold handles and valve assemblies in place, tightening them as needed.

The Best-Kept Cooking Secret

MANY PEOPLE ARE INTERESTED in learning how to use a pressure cooker, and just as with any other piece of cookware, basic cooking skills apply to pressure cookery. One of the best-kept cooking "secrets" you'll ever learn is browning. This first step is essential for serving up great-tasting food that is not only full of flavor, but it smells as delicious as it looks. This is why recipe instructions say to brown the meat, developing the flavor and aroma and a deep rich color.

The Maillard reaction, a scientific term for browning, requires that the pan is hot enough to quickly sear and brown the surface of the meat without cooking the interior. Today's modern pressure cooker, with its heavy, encapsulated base, is ideal for browning meat, and the high sides keep spattering to a minimum. Before browning, wipe the meat dry with paper towels to reduce moisture, which can cause spattering.

Adding Oil to the Pan

A good way to check that the pan is properly heated is to add a few droplets of water to the hot pan. The drops should immediately begin to sizzle and dance across the surface. At this point, it's time to add a couple of tablespoons of cooking oil, just enough to coat the bottom of the pan with a light film of oil. The oil must be heated before any food is added, and this may take another minute. The oil is there to transfer heat; as long as it is hot when the meat is added, very little will be absorbed.

Choose Cooking Oil with a High Smoke Point

Cooking oils that can tolerate a high temperature before they begin to smoke are best for browning. Canola, peanut, sunflower, and safflower oils are good choices because their high smoke points allow you to heat the pan to a higher degree of heat so that you can sear and brown meats very quickly.

When Is the Oil Hot Enough?

When you see wisps of vapor, it's time to see if the pan is hot enough. Hold a piece of meat with a pair of tongs and touch one edge to the bottom of the hot pan. If the oil is hot enough, the meat will slide easily on the light film of oil, but if it sticks, then the pan needs to be hotter.

Browning the Meat

Do not overfill the pan when browning or the temperature will drop and the meat will begin cooking rather than browning. Brown the meat in small batches—no poking or peeking, please—turning until all sides have a nicely browned crust. Use long-handled stainless steel tongs to turn the meat; never use a fork because it pierces the meat and lets the juices escape. As a rule of thumb, the deeper the color, the more flavorful the meat and the richer the gravy, broth, or sauce. Add additional oil as needed, and drain the browned meat on paper towels.

Deglazing—Or, What's with All Those Browned Bits?

Once your meats are browned, you'll find all those lovely browned bits of food stuck to the bottom of the pan, and that's where all the rich flavor is hiding and just waiting to be released. "Deglazing" is just chef talk describing the simple process of adding a little bit of liquid to the hot pan and then scraping up and dissolving all those crusty, dark brown flavor bits.

Drain off any excess oil and set the pan over medium-high heat. Add about a cup of deglazing liquid, such as wine or beer, stock, broth, or even water to the hot pan. Scrape the pan with a flat spatula as the heat begins to loosen and dissolve those browned deposits, incorporating them into the liquid, which will become the broth or gravy.

Thickening Sauces and Gravies

A pressure cooker creates wonderful, full-bodied, flavorful sauces even without thickening agents. To make a sauce or gravy thicker, wait until after the pot is depressurized to avoid scorching during pressure cooking. Sauces can be thickened using a variety of ingredients and methods. In the most common method, a starch such as flour or cornstarch is mixed with a little cold water into a slurry and then stirred into the sauce until the desired thickness is reached. The reduction method, if you have time, will result in natural thickening by simply continuing to cook the sauce over medium-high heat until much of the liquid evaporates and the sauce reduces in volume to the desired thickness. Using the reduction method also concentrates the flavors in the sauce.

Using Flour to Thicken Sauces

Flour can be used to thicken a sauce in three ways:

1. *Beurre manié:* This is one of those unpronounceable French chef terms, but don't give up yet. It just means that for each cup of liquid in the pot, blend 1 tablespoon each of softened butter and flour with a fork until it looks like a smooth paste. Slowly stir the mixture into the simmering sauce, whisking until the sauce is smooth and thickened to the desired consistency. The butter-flour mixture may be stored in the freezer for use when needed. Just pinch off little balls, and whisk one or two into your sauce. Bring the sauce to a simmer, adding more balls until the sauce reaches the desired consistency. Do not boil; the high heat will cause it to thin out.

2. **Roux:** This is just a fancy name for mixing equal amounts of fat (butter, oil, margarine, shortening, drippings, lard, etc.) and flour, and then cooking the mixture over medium heat to remove the starchy taste of the flour. Remove the roux from the heat and slowly whisk it into the liquid, stirring until smooth, and then return it all to the heat, bringing the sauce to a boil until thickened. A roux can be called white, blond, or brown, depending on how long it is cooked. The old adage "the browner the sauce, the richer the flavor," definitely applies to a dark roux, which will increase the flavor and color of your sauce or gravy.

   * **For a thicker sauce:** 3 tablespoons prepared roux per 1 cup liquid

   * **For a medium sauce:** 2 tablespoons prepared roux per 1 cup liquid

   * **For a thinner sauce:** 1 tablespoon prepared roux per 1 cup liquid

3. **Slurry:** This is often used to thicken gravies for roasted meats. Slurries are made by mixing a small amount of starch into cold water, and then pouring the mixture a little at a time into the simmering sauce, whisking constantly as it thickens. Slurries can be made with flour, cornstarch, arrowroot, or potato starch (instant potato flakes), stirring 1 or 2 tablespoons into an equal amount of cold water until smooth. Pour the mixture into the simmering liquid, whisking until the sauce has thickened but taking care not to boil the sauce, or it will thin out again.

The Best Cuts of Meat for Pressure Cooking

ONE OF THE MOST IMPORTANT benefits of pressure cooking is turning a tough cut of meat into a tender, flavorful meal in just minutes. This is very economical, allowing cooks to take advantage of sales, buy cheaper cuts of meat, and be energy smart by saving fuel used to cook the meat.

Meat is made up of lean muscle tissue, proteins, fats, collagen, and 75 percent water. Collagen exists in flesh, bone, and connective tissue and is very important to us as we cook, because the amount of collagen in a piece of meat will determine the length of time it should be cooked. The higher the level of connective tissue, the tougher the meat, so the first thing to look at when deciding which cut of meat to buy is to recognize which part of the animal it came from.

Which Cuts of Beef Are the Most Tender?

Cuts of beef that come from the center of the animal, such as the loin and rib area, are the most tender, but also the most expensive. They are suspension muscles and do not move as much as the muscles in the front and rear portions of the animal, which are responsible for locomotion, making them very lean cuts. The most highly prized steaks come from the short loin, and include the porterhouse and T-bone, rib roasts, rib eyes, tri-tips, and sirloins. These cuts are tender, but lack the flavor of the tougher cuts that contain more connective tissue, and they are often cooked with dry-heat cooking methods such as grilling, broiling, or roasting. Not surprisingly, they can also easily be cooked in the pressure cooker.

Which Cuts of Beef Are the Least Tender?

The more a muscle is used, the less tender it is. Weight-bearing muscles that are constantly used, like the legs, chest, and rump, are best cooked in moist heat, like in a pressure cooker. The chuck includes the shoulder blade and upper arm, and such cuts as chuck, brisket, plate, flank, and shank. These are some of the most exercised muscles, and hence they are among the toughest cuts of beef, but also the most flavorful.

Beef cuts from the round are located in the rear portion of the animal, which includes the top of the leg, or hind shank, and the rump. Cuts from the round, including top and bottom rounds, rump roasts, and round steaks, are lean but not tender. The limited amount of marbling makes them best suited for moist-heat cooking methods such as braising, pot-roasting, stewing, and steaming, and they are a perfect match for the pressure cooker.

The Pros and Cons of Cooking Thawed vs. Frozen Meats

Thawed	Frozen
Thawed or partially thawed meat can be browned, and that develops flavor, taste, aroma, and color, which add to the visual appeal.	Frozen meats, or any meat that is not browned, will have less flavor, taste, and aroma. Red meats will be unappetizingly gray, and white meats will look pale and blanched.
Thawing ground beef and then browning the meat allows it to be evenly distributed throughout the dish, and the grease can be drained off.	Frozen ground meat will end up as solid blocks of gray cooked ground meat that add grease to the food and take extra time to break up.
Don't try cooking large pieces of frozen meat such as a roast, because they may not get cooked through the thickest part. Always use a meat thermometer to check for doneness when cooking larger cuts of meat.	Extended cooking times destroy vitamins and minerals the body needs for good nutrition. The results may vary when cooking large pieces of frozen meat, with the outside being overcooked and the inside not cooked enough.
Thawed meats absorb marinades and seasonings better, so you'll have a more flavorful end result.	Since the frozen parts can't absorb flavors from cooking liquids, seasonings, or herbs, you end up with a very bland piece of meat.
Scrape up all the little browned bits before locking the lid for a richer gravy, broth, or sauce. The browner the meat, the richer the broth.	Without browning, there is no flavor to gravy or broth. The pan juices used for the gravy or sauce will be less flavorful and look anemic.

Grades of Beef and Veal

Prime grade is produced from young, well-fed beef cattle. It has abundant marbling and is generally sold to the restaurant and hotel trades. Prime roasts and steaks are excellent for dry-heat cooking (i.e., roasting, broiling, and grilling).

Choice grade is high quality, but has less marbling than Prime. Choice roasts and steaks from the loin and rib will be very tender, juicy, and flavorful and are, like Prime, suited to dry-heat cooking. Many of the less tender cuts, such as those from the rump, round, and blade chuck, are best for moist-heat cooking methods, and do especially well in the pressure cooker.

Select grade is uniform in quality and normally leaner than the higher grades. It is tender, but, because it has less marbling, it lacks the juiciness and flavor of the higher grades. Only the most tender cuts (loin, rib, sirloin) should be cooked with dry heat. Other cuts should be cooked with moisture to obtain maximum tenderness and flavor.

Why Does Red Meat Sometimes Turn Brown?

The color of red meats is not an indication of freshness. Some prime meats are aged for added tenderness, and they will appear darker than meats that are not aged. Freshly cut meat is normally a dark color. However, when it is exposed to air, it will "bloom" and turn red again.

New, modern packaging methods of vacuum sealing remove air to preserve freshness, and meats packaged this way will appear darker than meats in regular plastic packaging. When you open the meat package and let it stand for a short while, the meat will begin to turn red again. When choosing hamburger, look for the medium-to-deep color that signifies a low-fat content (a light pink color is a warning that excess fat has been ground

in with the meat). Ground beef should contain no more than 15 percent fat.

Pork and Ham

Pork and ham are not graded with USDA quality grades like beef because pigs are usually slaughtered at a younger age than cows. Pork is generally more tender and their muscles are less developed than those of cows, and pigs are bred and fed to produce a leaner and more uniformly tender meat. Appearance is an important guide in buying fresh pork. Look for cuts with a relatively small amount of fat over the outside and with meat that is firm and pale in color. Pork's consistency makes it especially suitable for pressure-cooker recipes.

Lamb

Lamb is produced from animals less than a year old. There are five grades for lamb, but only the top two grades are found at the retail level—Prime and Choice. Prime grade is very tender, juicy, and flavorful. Choice grade has slightly less marbling, but still is of very high quality. Most cuts of lamb are very tender and can be cooked by dry-heat methods. The less tender cuts, from the breast, riblets, neck, and shank, should be cooked by moist-heat methods and are best for pressure cooking.

Poultry

The USDA grades poultry, and only the highest-quality, grade A poultry is seen at the retail level. All kinds of poultry do well in pressure-cooker recipes.

Pressure Cooking Frozen Meats

Q: Can I cook frozen meat in my pressure cooker?

This is one of the most frequently asked questions about pressure cooking. Yes, it's possible to cook frozen meat in the pressure cooker. However, if you toss a block of frozen ground beef into the pressure cooker, it will end up as a solid block of tasteless, greasy, gray ground beef. It's cooked, but it's certainly not very appealing or appetizing.

A pressure cooker is not a substitute for eliminating the basics of good cooking. It's not that hard to defrost, or at least partially thaw, meats before cooking. Remember, the secret to flavor, taste, and aroma begins with browning the meat.

Larger cuts of frozen meat, such as a roast or whole chicken, will require increased cooking times, up to one-third more than usual, and that extra cooking time will often produce a dry, colorless, tasteless, and tough piece of meat, so my advice is, just thaw it.

Somewhat better results can be obtained when using separate, individual cuts of frozen meat up to 1 inch thick, such as chicken pieces, chops, patties, and other thin cuts. The cooking time does not need to be altered; however, it will take longer for the cooker to pressurize. Again, the results will be inferior compared to meats that were at least partially thawed and browned before cooking. Cooking frozen meat in a hearty, colorful, and flavor-filled sauce can help hide the "boiled" appearance of meat cooked without browning.

Pressure-Cooker Barbecuing

Using a pressure cooker will allow you to skip the marinating process. The result will be meat that is moist and tender. It takes just a few minutes in the pressure cooker, so there's no reason not to serve up a rack of ribs any day of the week.

Barbecuing by the Infusion Method

The infusion cooking method works with smaller cuts like chicken, steaks or chops, and sausages.

Use a recipe or refer to the Pressure-Cooking Time Charts (see page 94), cooking the meat directly in the pressure cooker, or in an insert pan, with the barbecue sauce with a minimal amount of added cooking liquid.

Using the Pressure Cooker to Precook Meats for Barbecuing

Use the pressure cooker to partially cook and tenderize any kind of meat using the precooking method. Use only the minimum amount of water and the cooking rack to keep the meat above the water level. Use a recipe, or the Pressure-Cooking Time Charts (see page 94). Use the cold water release method to open the lid when precooking to stop the cooking and prevent overcooking, or the meat will be so tender it will fall off the bones. Finish the meat on the grill or under the broiler, basting with your favorite barbecue sauce.

Special Directions for Precooking Ribs

To precook slabs of ribs, stand them up in a tall pressure cooker and bend the rack around in a circle. For larger amounts, depending on the size of the cooker, cut each rack into smaller sections and stand them up vertically or stack them horizontally in layers. Do not overcook ribs or the meat will be falling off the bone before you get it to the table. To cook beef ribs, a tall pressure cooker is required to accommodate the length of the bones. Arrange the ribs so that they lean at an angle that will fit the most ribs, but do not overcrowd them. Again, the ribs are steamed and not boiled. Precooked ribs can be finished up on the grill or broiler with your favorite barbecue sauce.

Dried Beans, Peas, and Legumes

BEANS ARE AN INEXPENSIVE SOURCE of protein. Pound for pound they are equal to a good cut of meat, but cost only pennies. No matter how much food prices have increased, dried beans have remained at or near the top of the USDA's list of foods that provide the most protein per dollar. Sometimes called the "poor man's meat," legumes are nutritious and low in fat, and provide a good source of fiber. Dried beans can be used in endless recipes for soups, salads, casseroles, dips, and many other dishes, and they are easy to cook in a pressure cooker. A pound of dried beans measures about 2 cups, and yields about nine servings of cooked beans. Chemical changes occur within old beans, so always check the expiration date when purchasing dried beans. Old or improperly stored beans are difficult, if not impossible, to cook, even in a pressure cooker; they will be as hard as rocks.

Adding Taste and Flavor to Beans

The secret to great-tasting beans is in the broth. Using plain water, even with added seasonings, will not make beans as tasty as using a good broth. Start with either a rich, meaty broth or a hearty vegetable broth, and everyone will rave about your next pot of beans.

Sort the Beans

Spread the beans out on a large, flat pan or baking sheet and discard any shriveled, broken, misshapen, or discolored beans. Remove any loose skins, and look closely for stones, grit, and other debris.

Do I Have to Soak Beans?

When it comes to bean cookery, nothing is more controversial than whether beans should be soaked before cooking or not. Perhaps, as many cooks do, you've been cooking dried beans for years without soaking, but if you skip this step, it can take up to five times longer to cook unsoaked dried beans until they are soft enough to eat. In the process, much of the vital nutrients in the beans are lost to the heat, not to mention that longer cooking time wastes time and increases energy expenses. Dried beans contain only about 15 percent moisture, and they must first rehydrate before they get soft enough to eat, which means they need to soak up a lot of water.

For many people, eating beans causes gas and intestinal discomfort because it is difficult for them to digest the complex sugars. Soaking dried beans will help to break down the indigestible sugars that cause gas, making the beans more digestible.

Unsoaked beans also have a tendency to split open because the exterior cooks first, often leaving the inside hard and uncooked. Water initially enters the bean through a small opening where the bean was attached to the stem and slowly soaks through the seed coat to penetrate the interior. Soaked beans have a significantly shorter cooking time, which preserves the maximum amount of nutrients.

How to Soak Beans

Mung beans, black-eyed peas, split peas, and lentils are thin skinned and low in sugars. They are softer than other dried beans and can be cooked without soaking. Other varieties of dried beans need to be soaked for several hours prior to cooking so they can absorb enough water to cook evenly. Place the beans on a baking sheet and pick

Soaking Methods for Beans

As a general rule, use 3 cups of cold water to soak each cup of dried beans.

Long-Soak Method	Quick-Soak Method	Pressure-Soak Method
Soak beans according to the Pressure-Cooking Time Chart (see page 101)—a minimum of 4 hours, but preferably 8 hours or overnight. Drain and discard the soaking water, rinse the beans, and proceed with the recipe of choice.	Bring water and beans to a boil, cover, and boil for 2 minutes. Remove from the heat and let stand for at least 1 hour, but preferably 4 hours or more. Drain and discard the soaking water, rinse the beans, and proceed with the recipe of choice.	Bring the water and beans to pressure and cook for 5 minutes. Remove from the heat and let the pressure drop naturally. Drain and discard the soaking water, rinse the beans, and proceed with the recipe of choice.

out any broken or blemished beans, and then place them in a large nonreactive bowl and cover with water, removing any foreign matter or beans that float to the surface. Depending on the variety of bean, they should be soaked for a minimum of four hours or overnight. During hot weather, or for longer soaking times, put the beans in the refrigerator to avoid sprouting or fermentation. Always discard the soaking water and thoroughly rinse the beans in cold water before cooking.

Fats and Oils

Dried beans or legumes tend to froth and foam. To minimize foaming when cooking beans in the pressure cooker, add 1 to 2 tablespoons of a pure fat, such as cooking oil, bacon drippings, butter, or lard. The choice of fat can also add flavor to beans.

Pressure Cooking Dried Beans and Legumes

Review the Ten Golden Rules of Pressure Cookery (see page 23) and the Five Formulas for Foods that Foam (see page 24). Use a large pressure cooker and do not exceed the half-full rule when cooking any type of dried bean or legume. For best results, always use a recipe or the Pressure-Cooking Time Charts (see page 101) as a guide. After cleaning and soaking, drain and rinse the beans in cold running water. Place the beans in the cooker with the other ingredients, seasonings, and the fat or oil. Add water, a combination of other liquids, or a flavorful broth to cover the beans by at least 2 inches. Lock the lid in place. Bring to 15psi over high heat. Reduce the heat to maintain and stabilize that pressure and cook according to the recipe or the directions in the Pressure-Cooking Time Charts (see page 101). Always use the natural re-

lease method when pressure cooking any type of dried bean or legume. Check for doneness, and if necessary return the beans to pressure for an additional 3 minutes, or until they can be easily mashed with a fork.

Adding Other Ingredients

A good broth is the best flavor enhancer for dried beans. Dried or fresh herbs and spices, and aromatic vegetables like onions, garlic, and peppers, can be added at the start of cooking.

Salt

Adding salt to beans before cooking tends to make them tougher and extend the cooking times. For best results, taste the beans and add salt after they have finished cooking.

For Thicker, Creamy Beans

For creamier, richer, and thicker beans, remove about 2 cups of cooked beans and a little broth. Purée with a blender or mash with a fork to release the starch in the beans. Stir the puréed beans back into the pot, simmering gently over a low heat as the starch thickens the bean broth.

Flavor Enhancers

Commonly used acidic flavorings such as chile sauce, ketchup, lemon juice, pickled hot peppers, hot sauce, tomato, wine, or vinegar should not be added during the cooking process. Acid seals the tiny hole where water enters the bean, and that means it will take longer for the beans to cook. Add these flavorings after the cooking process so you can better adjust the amounts to taste.

Pressure Cooking Pasta

I N THE HEYDAY OF PRESSURE COOKING, recipes using pasta were commonplace, but over time, the technique was almost lost and nearly forgotten. Today's modern pressure cooker makes it easier than ever to cook casseroles and one-pot-meal-type dishes with macaroni, noodles, and pasta. For best results, use a modern pressure cooker with a three-ply base for recipes containing pasta. Always add just enough liquid or sauce to cover the pasta, and use the natural release method.

Measuring Pasta

Dried pasta doubles in volume when cooked. The general rule is that 1 pound of dry pasta will serve four as a main course. In casseroles or one-pot meals, I've found that 3 cups of dry pasta will provide five generous servings or six smaller amounts. To measure short pasta, use a liquid measuring cup (one with a spout), and do not fill past the 8-ounce line. Follow the Ten Golden Rules of Pressure Cooking (see page 23) and the Five Formulas for Foods that Foam, Froth, or Expand (see page 24) when cooking any recipe containing pasta. Pasta releases a starch that foams during cooking. A spritz of oil around the rim of the pot, on the inside of the lid, and 1 to 2 tablespoons of oil added to the cooking water will help minimize this.

Pasta Shapes

Dried pasta is available in many shapes and sizes with varying cooking times. The larger, bulkier types of dry pasta shapes have a longer cooking time and better withstand the rigors of pressure cooking than the smaller or thinner types. Wide egg noodles, bow-ties or spirals, elbow macaroni, penne, and ziti pasta are all good choices for pressure cooker recipes. Read the pasta label carefully. The best varieties are made from 100 percent semolina durum wheat. They retain their shape and firmness during cooking. Imported Italian brands of pasta are generally thicker and more substantial than American-made brands. Fresh or refrigerated pastas cook much faster than the dried varieties, making them unsuitable for pressure cooking.

It is important to match the shapes of pasta to the sauce. Flat pastas are best with thin sauces, and shapes with nooks and crannies are better for chunkier sauces. To cook long strands of pasta, like spaghetti, in the pressure cooker, first bring the required amount of water to a boil, and then place the ends of the pasta in the water until they bend, pressing down until they will fit. Alternately, break the lengths into shorter pieces to fit the size of your cooker.

Pressure-Cooking
Time Charts

DON'T RELY ON GUESSWORK when it comes to using a pressure cooker. Even a mistake of just a few minutes can ruin your dinner, so follow a recipe with instructions, or use these cooking time charts for best results.

Pressure-Cooking Time Chart for Vegetables

All times are for 15psi, steaming with a steamer basket or rack. Use the cold water release method (see page 30) for fresh, tender-crisp vegetables, or the natural release method (see page 31) for more well-done vegetables, according to personal preference. Adjust liquid minimums and quantity to comply with manufacturer's directions if different.

Vegetables	Minimum Water	Cooking Times	Suggested Release Method
Artichokes, medium whole, trimmed	½ cup	6 to 8 minutes	Natural
Artichokes, large whole, trimmed	½ cup	9 to 11 minutes	Natural
Artichokes, hearts	½ cup	2 to 3 minutes	Cold water
Asparagus, thick whole (fresh or frozen)	½ cup	1 to 2 minutes	Cold water
Asparagus, thin whole	½ cup	1 to 1½ minutes	Cold water
Beans, green, wax, or Italian (fresh or frozen)	½ cup	2 to 3 minutes	Cold water
Beets, small whole	½ cup	12 minutes	Natural
Beets, large whole	1 cup	20 minutes	Natural
Beets, ¼-inch slices	½ cup	4 minutes	Natural
Broccoli, florets (fresh or frozen)	½ cup	3 minutes	Cold water
Broccoli, spears	½ cup	3 minutes	Cold water
Broccoli stalks, ¼-inch slices	½ cup	4 minutes	Cold water
Brussels sprouts, large (fresh)	½ cup	4 to 5 minutes	Natural
Brussels sprouts, small (fresh or frozen)	½ cup	3 minutes	Cold water
Cabbage, red or green, ¼-inch shreds	½ cup	3 minutes	Cold water
Cabbage, red or green, quartered	½ cup	4 minutes	Natural
Cabbage, red or green, coarsely shredded	½ cup	1 to 1½minutes	Cold water
Cabbage, savoy or napa, quartered	½ cup	3 minutes	Natural
Carrots, whole	½ cup	4 minute	Natural
Carrots, 1-inch chunks	½ cup	3 minutes	Cold water

Vegetables	Minimum Water	Cooking Times	Suggested Release Method
Carrots, ¼-inch slices	½ cup	2 minute	Cold water
Cauliflower, florets	½ cup	2 minutes	Cold water
Cauliflower, whole	½ cup	5 minutes	Cold water
Celery, 1-inch slices	½ cup	3 minute	Cold water
Corn, kernels (fresh or frozen)	½ cup	1 minute	Cold water
Corn on the cob (fresh or frozen)	½ cup	3 minutes	Cold water
Eggplant, ⅛- to ¼-inch slices	½ cup	2 minutes	Cold water
Eggplant, ½-inch chunks	½ cup	3 minutes	Cold water
Escarole, coarsely chopped	½ cup	1 minute	Cold water
Greens, beet, coarsely chopped	½ cup	4 minutes	Natural
Greens, collard, coarsely chopped	½ cup	5 minutes	Natural
Greens, kale, coarsely chopped	½ cup	2 minutes	Cold water
Greens, kohlrabi, cut in pieces	½ cup	4 minutes	Natural
Greens, mustard, cut in pieces	½ cup	4 minutes	Natural
Greens, Swiss chard, coarsely chopped	½ cup	2 minutes	Natural
Greens, turnip, coarsely chopped	½ cup	4 minutes	Natural
Leeks, sliced, both green and white parts	½ cup	4 minutes	Natural
Leeks, sliced, white parts only	½ cup	2 minutes	Cold water
Mixed vegetables, frozen	½ cup	2 minutes	Cold water
Okra, small pods or thick slices	½ cup	2 to 3 minutes	Cold water
Onions, whole	½ cup	7 to 9 minutes	Natural
Onions, quartered	½ cup	4 minutes	Natural
Parsnips, ¼-inch cubes or sliced	½ cup	2 minutes	Natural

Pressure-Cooking Time Chart for Vegetables (continued)

Vegetables	Minimum Water	Cooking Times	Suggested Release Method
Peas, green (fresh or frozen)	½ cup	1 minute	Cold water
Peppers, sweet or bell (green, red, yellow), Mexican mild or hot pepper types, whole	½ cup	3 minutes	Cold water
Potatoes, new or small (about 2 oz.), whole	½ cup	5 to 6 minutes	Natural
Potatoes, red, large, whole	1 cup	10 minutes	Natural
Potatoes, red, large, halved	½ cup	8 minutes	Natural
Potatoes, red, cubed	½ cup	4 to 5 minutes	Natural
Potatoes, russet (baking type), large, whole	1 cups	18 minutes	Natural
Potatoes, russet, peeled, quartered	½ cup	8 minutes	Natural
Potatoes, russet, peeled, 1½-inch chunks	½ cup	6 minutes	Natural
Potato, sweet, sliced or chunks	½ cup	5 minutes	Natural
Potatoes, sweet, whole	1 cup	15 minutes	Natural
Potatoes, white, whole	1 cup	16 minutes	Natural
Potatoes, white, halved	½ cup	8 minutes	Natural
Potatoes, white, cubed	½ cup	5 minutes	Natural
Pumpkin, 2-inch chunks	½ cup	4 minutes	Natural
Rutabagas, peeled, 1-inch chunks	¾ cup	4 minutes	Natural
Rutabagas, peeled, 2-inch chunks	½ cup	6 minutes	Natural
Spinach, fresh or frozen, coarsely chopped	½ cup	1 minute	Cold water
Spinach, fresh, whole leaves	½ cup	3 minutes	Cold water
Squash, acorn, halved	½ cup	8 minutes	Natural
Squash, banana, peeled, cubed	½ cup	3 minutes	Natural
Squash, butternut, peeled, 1-inch chunks	½ cup	4 minutes	Natural
Squash, hubbard, peeled, 1-inch chunks	½ cup	5 minutes	Natural

Pressure-Cooking Time Chart for Vegetables *(continued)*

Vegetables	Minimum Water	Cooking Times	Suggested Release Method
Squash, patty pan, sliced or cubed	½ cup	2 minutes	Cold water
Squash, spaghetti, 2 pounds, halved	½ cup	10 minutes	Natural
Squash, summer or crookneck, ½-inch slices	½ cup	2 minutes	Cold water
Squash, zucchini, 1½-inch slices	½ cup	2 minutes	Cold water
Tomatoes, quartered	½ cup	2 minutes	Cold water
Tomatoes, whole	½ cup	3 minutes	Natural
Turnips, small, quartered	½ cup	6 minutes	Natural
Turnips, ½-inch chunks	½ cup	5 minutes	Natural
Yams, ½-inch slices	½ cup	6 minutes	Natural
Yams, whole	½ cup	16 minutes	Natural

Pressure-Cooking Time Chart for Fresh, Frozen, and Dried Fruits

All times are for 15psi, steaming with a steamer basket or rack. The cold water release method (see page 30) is recommended for fresh or frozen fruits, and the natural release method (see page 31) for dried fruit. Adjust liquid minimums and quantity to comply with manufacturer's directions if different.

Fresh and Dried Fruit	Liquid	Cooking Time
Apples, fresh, sliced or chunks	½ cup	3 minutes
Apples, dried, slices	½ cup	3 minutes
Apricots, dried	½ cup	4 minutes
Apricots, fresh, whole or halved	½ cup	2 to 3 minutes
Bananas	½ cup	0 minutes*
Berries, fresh	½ cup	0 minutes*
Blueberries, fresh or frozen	½ cup	0 minutes

Pressure-Cooking Time Chart for Fresh, Frozen, and Dried Fruits *(continued)*

Fresh and Dried Fruit	Liquid	Cooking Time
Cherries, fresh or frozen	½ cup	0 minutes*
Cranberries, dried	½ cup	0 minutes
Cranberries, fresh or frozen	½ cup	4 to 5 minutes
Dates	½ cup	6 minutes
Figs, dried (presoak tough-skinned varieties)	½ cup	6 minutes
Figs, fresh	½ cup	2 minutes
Grapes, for jelly making	½ cup	4 minutes
Lemons	½ cup	2 minutes
Oranges	½ cup	2 minutes
Peaches, dried	½ cup	4 minutes
Peaches, halved, fresh or frozen	½ cup	3 minutes
Peaches, whole	½ cup	2 minutes
Pears, dried	½ cup	4 minutes
Pears, fresh, halved	½ cup	3 to 4 minutes
Pears, fresh, whole	½ cup	5 minutes
Pineapple, sliced or chunks	½ cup	3 minutes
Plums, fresh	½ cup	0 minutes*
Plums, dried (prunes)	½ cup	4 to 5 minutes
Quince, fresh, quartered	½ cup	4 minutes
Raisins	½ cup	0 minutes
Raspberries, fresh or frozen	½ cup	0 minute
Strawberries, for jelly making	½ cup	0 minute

*0 minutes = rapidly bring to 15psi over high heat and then immediately use the cold water release method to open the lid.

Pressure-Cooking Time Chart for Rice

All times are for 15psi, following the directions given below. To avoid sticking, long-grain white rice and wild rice is rinsed several times to remove the starch. For creamier rice, risottos, Asian sticky rice, or brown rice, use unrinsed short-grain rice. Adjust liquid minimums and quantity to comply with manufacturer's directions if different.

PIP (Pan in Pot) Method for Perfect Fluffy Rice

For foolproof rice in a pressure cooker, use my PIP (Pan in Pot) method for perfect, fluffy rice. Add 1 cup water to the pressure cooker and position the rack in the cooker. Rinse white rice until water runs clear. Use the ratio of grain to water from the table and place the given amounts in a small metal bowl that fits inside the cooker. Use foil helper handles (see page 42) to make it easier to move the bowl. Lock the lid in place. Bring to 15psi over high heat, and then reduce the heat to the lowest setting that will maintain and stabilize that pressure. Cook according to the chart below. Remove from the heat and let the pressure drop naturally (see page 31). Open the lid. Remove the bowl from the cooker and fluff the rice with a fork before serving.

Rice Variety	Rice to Water	Cooking Time	Description
White rice, long grain: basmati, jasmine, Texmati	1:1½	4 minutes	Basmati is aged, aromatic rice imported from India. Jasmine is aromatic rice grown in Thailand and is similar to basmati. Texmati is basmati grown in Texas. Cooked grains are separate, light, and fluffy.
White rice, short grain: Arborio, Vialone, Carnaroli, Baldo	1:1½	7 minutes	Short-grain white rice is characterized by round grains. After cooking, the rice is plump and slightly sticky. Look for it in better supermarkets and specialty markets. Medium-grain rices may work as a substitute.
White rice, medium grain: Cal-Rose	1:1½	7 minutes	Medium-grain rice has a shorter, wider kernel than long-grain rice. Cooked grains are more moist and tender, and have a greater tendency to cling together than long grain.

Pressure-Cooking Time Chart for Rice *(continued)*

Rice Variety	Rice to Water	Cooking Time	Description
Brown rice, short grain: basmati, Texmati, sweet brown	1:2	15 minutes	Brown rice is more nutritious than white rice because it is packed with vitamins E and B and minerals, as well as fiber and protein because it retains the oil-rich germ and bran. Brown rice has a chewier texture than white rice.
Brown rice, medium grain	1:2	15 minutes	Medium-grain brown rice yields a lighter, fluffier dish than short grain.
Brown rice, long grain	1:2	12 minutes	This rice has a nutty flavor and cooks up fluffier and drier than medium- or short-grain rices.
Wild rice, Manomen, "Water Grass"	1:4	20 to 22 minutes	Wild rice was a staple for Native Americans, but it's not really rice at all, being more closely related to corn. Found in North America, wild rice is low in fat and high in B vitamins and has more protein than other rice.

1 cup uncooked white rice = 3 cups cooked
1 cup uncooked brown rice = 4 cups cooked

Except where noted, use 15psi and the natural release method (see page 31) to finish steaming grains. When pressure drops, open the lid, remove the bowl, and fluff with a fork before serving. Use the PIP cooking method (see page 37) for best results. Adjust liquid minimums and quantity to comply with manufacturer's directions if different.

Grain	Grain to Water	Cooking Time	Instructions and Ideas
Amaranth	1:3	9 minutes	Ancient Aztec grain with superior nutrition. Nutty, slightly spicy, and sticky gelatinous texture.
Barley, flakes	1:2	9 minutes	Barley flakes are made by heating whole, lightly toasted barley until soft and then pressing it flat with steel rollers.
Barley, pearl	1:4½	18 to 20 minutes	Pearled means the grain is lightly milled to remove part or all of the germ and bran, but it retains its endosperm.
Barley, whole	1:3	20 minutes	Whole barley is very chewy because it is a whole grain, retaining its germ, bran, and endosperm.
Buckwheat, kasha	1:2	12 minutes	These chestnut-colored fruit seeds belong to a plant related to rhubarb. Available toasted (brown) and untoasted (white), which has a milder flavor.
Corn, hominy; pozole meal; samp, grits, masa harina	1:4	10 minutes	These are hulled corn kernels that have been stripped of their bran and germ. White hominy is made from white corn kernels and is sweeter; yellow hominy is made from yellow corn kernels. Samp is coarsely ground or broken hominy, and hominy grits are more finely ground.

Grain	Grain to Water	Cooking Time	Instructions and Ideas
Corn, dried cracked, cornmeal, matzo meal	1:2	12 to 15 minutes	Dried yellow corn has a rich, nutty flavor, very different from fresh.
Kamut, whole	1:3	10 to 12 minutes	Recently rediscovered ancient Egyptian wheat with a rich, buttery flavor and chewy texture.
Millet	1:3	9 minutes	Mild and very digestible, and often used in wheat-free diets because it is a high-quality protein. It is also high in B vitamins.
Oats, quick	1:2	2 minutes	Quick oats are steel cut into pieces, then flattened by steel rollers. Less texture and less chewy than rolled oats.
Oats, rolled or "old fashioned"	1:2	5 minutes	Rolled oats are steamed whole oats pressed flat with steel rollers.
Oats, steel cut, Scotch, Irish	1:4	10 minutes	These are whole oat groats that are steamed and sliced with steel blades.
Oats, whole; oat groats	1:3	15 to 18 minutes	Oat groats are the hulled whole oat kernels with their bran and germ intact. Presoaking reduces cooking time.
Quinoa (pronounced KEEN wah)	1:2	6 minutes	Uncooked, these tiny yellow seeds look like the vermiculite used to pot plants. It has the highest protein and fat of all the grains, more calcium than milk, and it is a good source of iron, phosphorous, B vitamins, and vitamin E. Rinse several times before cooking to remove bitter-tasting coating. For an extra-nutty flavor, toast grain before cooking
Rye berries	1:2	15 to 20 minutes	High-protein grain with high fiber.

Pressure-Cooking Time Chart for Grains (continued)

Grain	Grain to Water	Cooking Time	Instructions and Ideas
Spelt berries; farro; dinkel	1:3	15 minutes	Spelt has a light and nutty flavor, and is tolerated by many people who are sensitive to wheat.
Teff berries	1:3	5 minutes	Common Ethiopian grain with a sweet malt flavor, it's the smallest grain in the world. The name means "lost." Lightly toast before cooking for a richer flavor.
Triticale berries (prounounced tri ti KAY lee)	1:4	20 to 25 minutes	A cross between rye and wheat. Nutty flavor, richer than wheat but less assertive than rye.
Wheat, berries	1:3	30 to 40 minutes	A hard, red winter wheat with short rounded kernels.
Wheat, bulgur, cracked	1:3	8 to 10 minutes	Whole wheat berries cracked into small pieces between steel rollers to reduce cooking time. Bulgur is the star of the Middle Eastern dish tabbouleh.
Wheat, couscous (rhymes with moose-moose)	1:2	3 minutes	It's not a grain, but a grain product made from semolina wheat flour that's been rolled into thin strands, crumbled into tiny pieces, steamed, and dried. Use cold water release.
Wheat, flakes	1:3	8 to 10 minutes	These flakes are steam pressed from wheat berries. Combine with other grains for extra fiber and nutrients.

Just like any other cooking method, pressure-cooker times for meats can vary depending on personal preferences, as well as the grade, cut, and thickness of the meat. A heavier flat roast will cook faster than a small chunkier cut, so use these cooking times as a general guide, but make adjustments as needed. All times given are for fresh or thawed meat cooked at 15psi. Use an instant-read digital thermometer to accurately check for doneness. Adjust liquid minimums and quantity to comply with manufacturer's directions if different.

Meat Variety	Brown Meat	Minimum Liquid	Cooking Time	Release
Beef, brisket, corned; 2 to 4 inches thick		Cover completely	45 to 50 minutes	Natural
Beef, brisket, fresh; 3 to 4 inches thick	Yes	1½ to 2 cups	55 to 65 minutes	Natural
Beef, cube steak	Yes	½ cup	6 minutes	Natural
Beef, flank steak	Yes	1 cup	30 minutes	Natural
Beef, ground, coarse or patties less than 1 inch thick	Yes	½ cup	6 minutes	Natural
Beef, heart, 3 to 4 lbs.		Cover completely	50 to 75 minutes	Natural
Beef, kidney		Cover completely	8 to 10 minutes	Natural
Beef, liver, sliced		½ cup	4 minutes	Natural
Beef, neck bones	Yes	Cover completely	45 minutes	Natural
Beef, oxtails	Yes	Cover completely	40 to 45 minutes	Natural
Beef, pot roast, round, blade, chuck, or rump, 3 to 4 lbs.	Yes	1½ to 2 cups	35 to 45 minutes	Natural
Beef, rolled or rib roast, 3 to 4 lbs.	Yes	1½ to 2 cups	35 to 45 minutes	Natural
Beef, roast, round, chuck, blade, or rump, 2 to 3 inches thick	Yes	1½ to 2 cups	25 minutes	Natural
Beef, short ribs	Yes	1½ to 2 cups	25 minutes	Natural

Pressure-Cooking Time Chart for Meat, Poultry, Game, and Eggs *(continued)*

Meat Variety	Brown Meat	Minimum Liquid	Cooking Time	Release
Beef steak, round, chuck, blade, 2 inches thick	Yes	1½ to 2 cups	20 minutes	Natural
Beef steak, tri-tip, sirloin, triangle	Yes	½ cup	12 minutes	Natural
Beef, stew meat 1½- to 2-inch cubes	Yes	½ to 1 cup	15 minutes	Natural
Beef, tongue, fresh or smoked, 2 to 3 lbs.		Cover completely	75 minutes	Natural
Chicken, breasts, boneless, whole	Yes	½ cup	8 minutes	Natural
Chicken, breasts with bone	Yes	½ cup	10 minutes	Natural
Chicken, breasts, boneless, cut up	Yes	½ cup	4 minutes	Quick or cold water
Chicken, breasts or thighs, frozen, boneless	Yes	½ cup	8 minutes	Natural
Chicken, ground	Yes	½ cup	3 minutes	Quick or cold water
Chicken, legs	Yes	½ cup	6 minutes	Natural
Chicken, livers		½ cup	2 minutes	Quick or cold water
Chicken, quarters, bone in	Yes	½ cup	12 minutes	Natural
Chicken, stewing, 4 to 5 lbs.		Cover completely	30 minutes	Natural
Chicken, whole, steam roasted (3 to 4 lbs.)	Yes	1 cup	20 to 25 minutes	Natural
Cornish hen, whole, steam roasted	Yes	1 cup	8 minutes	Natural

Meat Variety	Brown Meat	Minimum Liquid	Cooking Time	Release
Duck, pieces	Yes	½ cup	8 to 10 minutes	Natural
Duck, whole or breast, steam roasted	Yes	½ cup	30 minutes	Natural
Eggs, hard boiled in shell		Cover completely; must use a rack	5 minutes	Cold water
Eggs, shirred, poached, soft cooked, scrambled		Use ramekins on a rack	3 minutes	Cold water
Ham hocks, smoked		Cover completely	45 minutes	Natural
Ham, picnic or shoulder, uncooked, 3 to 5 lbs.		2 cups	45 minutes	Natural
Ham, shank or butt, fully cooked, 3 to 5 lbs.		2 cups	25 minutes	Natural
Ham, shank or butt, not fully cooked, 3 to 5 lbs.		2 to 2½ cups	35 minutes	Natural
Ham, fully cooked, ½-inch-thick slices		½ cup	4 minutes	Natural
Ham, fully cooked, 1-inch-thick slices		½ cup	6 minutes	Natural
Ham, fully cooked, 2-inch-thick slices		½ cup	10 minutes	Natural
Lamb, breast, under 2 lbs.	Yes	1 to 1½ cups	35 minutes	Natural
Lamb, chops, ½ inch thick	Yes	½ cup	5 minutes	Quick or cold water
Lamb, chops, ¼ inch thick	Yes	½ cup	2 minutes	Quick or cold water
Lamb, leg, 3 lbs., steam roasted	Yes	1 to ½ cups	35 minutes	Natural
Lamb, shoulder; 3 to 6 lbs., steam roasted	Yes	1 to ½ cups	35 to 45 minutes	Natural

Pressure-Cooking Time Chart for Meat, Poultry, Game, and Eggs *(continued)*

Meat Variety	Brown Meat	Minimum Liquid	Cooking Time	Release
Lamb, steaks, ½ inch thick	Yes	½ cup	9 minutes	Natural
Lamb, stew meat, 1-inch cubes	Yes	1 to ½ cups	15 minutes	Natural
Lamb, mutton roast; 4 to 6 lbs., steam roasted	Yes	1½ to 2 cups	45 minutes	Natural
Pheasant, whole, steam roasted	Yes	1 to 1½ cups	30 minutes	Natural
Pigeon (squab), whole, steam roasted	Yes	1½ cups	12 to 15 minutes	Natural
Pork, chops, thicker than 1 inch, or stuffed	Yes	½ cup	12 minutes	Natural
Pork, chops, thinner than 1 inch	Yes	½ cup	10 minutes	Natural
Pork, loin, 3 to 4 lbs., steam roasted	Yes	1½ cups	40 minutes	Natural
Pork, pig's feet		Cover completely	45 minutes	Natural
Pork ribs, spareribs		1 to 1½ cups	10 minutes	Natural
Pork ribs, baby back ribs		1 to 1½ cups	10 minutes	Natural
Pork ribs, country-style ribs		1 to 1½ cups	12 minutes	Natural
Pork, roasts, any cut, 3 to 4 lbs., steam roasted	Yes	1 to 1½ cups	40 minutes	Natural
Pork sausage, Italian, Polish, kielbasa, steamed on a rack	Yes	½ cup	8 minutes	Quick or cold water
Pork, shanks	Yes	1 to 1½ cups	35 minutes	Natural
Pork, shoulder, steam roasted	Yes	1 to 1½ cups	35 minutes	Natural

Pressure-Cooking Time Chart for Meat, Poultry, Game, and Eggs *(continued)*

Meat Variety	Brown Meat	Minimum Liquid	Cooking Time	Release
Pork, smoked neck bones		Cover completely	45 to 55 minutes	Natural
Rabbit, parts	Yes	½ cup	12 to 15 minutes	Natural
Turkey, breast, boneless or rolled, steam roasted	Yes	1½ cups	20 minutes	Natural
Turkey, breast, whole or half with bone in, steam roasted (5 to 6 lbs.)	Yes	1½ cups	30 minutes	Natural
Turkey, legs		1½ cups	15 minutes	Natural
Turkey, wings		½ cup	12 minutes	Natural
Veal, chops or steak; less than 1 inch thick	Yes	½ cup	5 minutes	Quick or cold water
Veal, leg, 3 to 4 lbs., steam roasted	Yes	1½ cups	40 minutes	Natural
Veal, roast, 3 to 4 lbs., steam roasted	Yes	1½ cups	40 minutes	Natural
Veal, shanks	Yes	1½ cups	25 minutes	Natural
Veal, stew meat, 1- to 1½-inch cubes	Yes	1½ cups	8 minutes	Natural
Venison, roast, any cut with bone, 3 to 4 inches thick, steam roasted	Yes	1½ cups	30 to 40 minutes	Natural
Venison, chops or steaks, up to 1 inch thick	Yes	1½ cups	12 minutes	Natural
Venison, stew meat, 1- to 1½-inch cubes	Yes	1½ cups	10 minutes	Natural
Venison, ground	Yes	½ cups	9 minutes	Natural

Pressure-Cooking Time Chart for Fish and Seafood

All times given are for 15psi using fresh or thawed fish. Adjust liquid minimums and quantity to comply with manufacturer's directions if different.

Fish Variety	Liquid	Cooking Time	Release
Clams	½ cup	5 minutes	Cold water
Cod, fillet, 1 inch thick	½ cup	5 minutes	Cold water
Crab, legs	½ cup	2 minutes	Cold water
Flounder, fillet, 1 inch thick	½ cup	3 minutes	Cold water
Frog's legs	½ cup	8 minutes	Cold water
Haddock, fillet, 1 inch thick	½ cup	5 minutes	Cold water
Haddock, 2 inches thick	½ cup	6 minutes	Cold water
Halibut, 1 inch thick	½ cup	4 minutes	Cold water
Halibut, 2 inches thick	½ cup	6 minutes	Cold water
Lobster, tail, 12 to 16 ounces, steamed on a rack	½ cup	8 minutes	Cold water
Lobster, tail, 6 to 8 ounces, steamed on a rack	½ cup	5 minutes	Cold water
Lobster, whole, steamed on a rack	½ cup	12 minutes	Cold water
Mackerel	½ cup	6 minutes	Cold water
Perch, ocean, 6 inches long	½ cup	3 minutes	Cold water
Pike	½ cup	8 minutes	Cold water
Salmon, steak, 2 inches thick	½ cup	8 minutes	Cold water
Scallops, large, steamed on a rack	½ cup	2 minutes	Cold water
Scallops, small, steamed on a rack	½ cup	1 minutes	Cold water
Shrimp, large (prawns), steamed on a rack	½ cup	3 minutes	Cold water
Shrimp, medium, steamed on a rack	½ cup	2 minutes	Cold water
Shrimp, small, steamed on a rack	½ cup	1 minutes	Cold water

Pressure-Cooking Time Chart for Fish and Seafood (continued)

Fish Variety	Liquid	Cooking Time	Release
Sole, fillet, 1 inch thick	½ cup	3 minutes	Cold water
Trout, 1 inch thick	½ cup	4 minutes	Cold water
Trout, 2 inches thick	½ cup	8 minutes	Cold water
Whitefish, 1 to 2 inches thick	½ cup	8 minutes	Cold water

Pressure-Cooking Time Chart for Dry Pasta

Amounts are given for 15psi using a 5-quart or larger pressure cooker, followed by the natural release method (see page 31). Do not exceed the half-full rule (see Five Formulas for Foods that Foam, Froth, or Expand, page 24). Adjust liquid minimums and quantity to comply with manufacturer's directions if different.

Long-shaped pasta: To use long strands in the pressure cooker, first bring the required amount of water to a boil and then place the ends of the spaghetti in the water until it will bend, pressing down until they are completely covered; otherwise, break the spaghetti into shorter lengths to fit your pot.

Pasta Type	Uncooked Amount	Cooked Yield	Cooking Time
Spaghetti (thick)	8 oz.	5 cups	6 minutes
Spaghetti (thin)	8 oz.	4½ cups	Unsuitable
Vermicelli	8 oz.	4½ cups	Unsuitable
Linguine (flat)	8 oz.	4¼ cups	6 minutes
Fettuccine (flat)	8 oz.	3¼ cups	6 minutes
SMALL-SHAPED PASTA			
Ditalini	2 cups (8 oz.)	4 cups	4 minutes
Orzo	1⅓ cups (8 oz.)	3 cups	2 minutes
Alphabets	1⅓ cups (8 oz.)	4⅔ cups	2 minutes
Tubetti	1⅓ cups (8 oz.)	3 cups	4 minutes

Pressure-Cooking Time Chart for Dry Pasta (*continued*)

Pasta Type	Uncooked Amount	Cooked Yield	Cooking Time
SHORT-SHAPED PASTA			
Rigatoni	3 cups (8 oz.)	4½ cups	7 minutes
Ziti, penne	3 cups (8 oz.)	4½ cups	7 minutes
Rotini	3 cups (8 oz.)	4 cups	7 minutes
Elbows (small)	2 cups (8 oz.)	4 cups	6 minutes
(large)			7 minutes
Shells	3 cups (8 oz.)	4 cups	5 minutes
Egg noodles	3 cups (8 oz.)	5 cups	5 minutes
Bows	3 cups (8 oz.)	5 cups	5 minutes

Pressure-Cooking Time Chart for Dried Beans

Many factors influence cooking times—use this information as a guideline, but the actual cooking times may vary depending on the quality of the beans. As a rule, beans should be soaked at least 4 hours before cooking to preserve nutrients and allow even cooking. Rinse beans, put them in the pressure cooker, and add enough water to cover by 2 inches. Add 1 to 2 tablespoons of fat (cooking oil, butter, lard, bacon drippings) to minimize foaming. Do not exceed the half-full rule (see Five Formulas for Foods that Foam, Froth, or Expand, page 24). Adjust liquid minimums and quantity to comply with manufacturer's directions if different. Bring to 15psi over high heat, and then reduce the heat to the lowest setting that will maintain and stabilize that pressure. Use the natural release method (see page 31), except where noted.

Name of Legume	Minimal Soaking	Minimal Cooking Time	Legume Characteristics and Description
Adzuki, aduki	Optional	10 to 12 minutes	Adzuki are small, vivid red beans with a slightly sweet flavor, originally from Asia. Their name means "little bean" in Japanese. They are easier to digest than most beans due to a very low fat content.

Name of Legume	Minimal Soaking	Minimal Cooking Time	Legume Characteristics and Description
Anasazi	4 hours	10 to 12 minutes	This revived ancient heirloom bean is related to, and similar in size and shape to, pinto beans, but sweeter and more flavorful. Use in any recipe that calls for pinto beans. It holds its shape when cooked. Very digestible. Mottled burgundy/white markings fade when cooked.
Black turtle bean, Venezuelan, Mexican black, Spanish	4 hours	18 to 20 minutes	A staple of Latin American and Tampico, Caribbean cuisine, these beans have a strong, earthy, almost mushroom-like flavor and soft, floury texture. They're best combined with assertive flavorings
Black-eyed pea	No	8 to 10 minutes	Black-eyed peas have a good aroma, creamy texture, and distinctive flavor. These beans are characterized by a small black eye and they are really a type of pea originally from Africa. No presoaking needed, as they are easily digested. Traditionally served with rice and greens. Celebrate New Year's with a dish called Hoppin' John.
Cannellini, fazolia, kidney bean	4 hours	10 to 12 minutes	These taste like the great Northern white or navy bean but are longer and fatter. Excellent in bean salads, Italian minestrone, soups with tomato, or simply served warm with a splash of olive oil, fresh minced rosemary, and a dash of black pepper.
Cranberry bean, borlotti bean, shell bean, Christmas bean	4 hours	10 to 12 minutes	Cranberry beans are rounded with red specks, which disappear on cooking, similar to the pinto bean but with a more delicate, nutty flavor. Commonly used in Italian soups and stews.

Name of Legume	Minimal Soaking	Minimal Cooking Time	Legume Characteristics and Description
Flageolet	4 hours	10 to 12 minutes	The French make good use of this small, creamy bean, often serving it with lamb. Substitutes: great Northern beans
Fava, broad bean, butterbean, Windsor bean, English bean	8 hours; preferably overnight	6 to 8 minutes Cook these beans at 8 to 10psi and use the natural release method	A huge, substantial bean with tough outer skin. Peel off and discard skins after soaking. Creamy texture; nutty, sweet, earthy flavor. Use in soups, or purée into paté-like hummus with rosemary, olive oil, garlic, lemon, and fresh herbs. Try with blanched cauliflower pieces, chopped red onion, olive oil, and balsamic vinegar. Use caution when pressure cooking because of the loose skins. Always use oil with these beans and place the rack on TOP of the beans to help keep loose skins from floating up.
Garbanzo, chickpea	8 hours; preferably overnight	14 to 18 minutes	Garbanzo beans or chickpeas are the most widely consumed legume in the world. Originating in the Middle East, they have a firm texture with a flavor somewhere between chestnuts and walnuts. These round beans are high in fat and keep their unique shape when cooked. They are usually pale yellow in color, but they can also be red, black, or brown. Mild and sweet flavor with good protein and iron. Add to salads, soups, and pasta dishes. Purée into hummus with tahini, garlic, lemon juice, sea salt, and olive oil.
Great Northern	4 hours	14 minutes	Also called white kidney beans, these beans have a smooth texture and delicate flavor and can be substituted for cannellini or navy beans. Use in Italian-style soups and pasta dishes. Substitute for garbanzo beans in hummus.

Name of Legume	Minimal Soaking	Minimal Cooking Time	Legume Characteristics and Description
Lentils, green, French, Spanish brown, Dal lentil, black Beluga lentil; colors include green, brown, white, yellow, red, coral, black	No	5 to 7 minutes (turn mushy if overcooked)	Very versatile lentils have a mild, often earthy, flavor, and they're best if cooked with assertive flavorings or other foods in combination with robust, zesty sauces. Unlike dried beans and peas, there's no need to soak them. Lentils are rich in protein, carbohydrates, and fiber, and low in fat. Before cooking, always rinse lentils and pick out stones and other debris. The most delicate lentils are the peppery French green lentils. The mild brown lentils are the most common variety and hold their shape well after cooking.
Kidney, rajma, Mexican bean	4 hours	10 to 12 minutes	A large, kidney-shaped bean with a subtle sweet flavor and soft texture that keeps its shape during cooking. Used in Southwestern dishes and bean salads.
Lima Bean, Madagascar bean	8 hours; better overnight	3 to 5 minutes, cook these beans at 8 to 10psi and use the natural release method	Large beans with a buttery flavor and starchy texture. Caution: loose, large skins can clog pressure cookers; remove loose skins before cooking. Always use oil with these beans and place the rack on TOP of the beans to help keep loose skins from floating up.
Mung, mungo, mung pea	4 hours	8 to 10 minutes, cook these beans at 8 to 10psi	A major player in Indian and Chinese dishes. Easy to digest, these beans do not hold their shape well, but they are great in stews or served over rice.
Navy, Yankee bean, pearl haricot, Boston navy bean	4 hours	9 to 12 minutes	Small white ovals; mild flavor with powdery texture, these beans were named for their large role in the diet aboard U.S. Navy ships during the late 19th century. Makes great soup, chowders, and beanpot recipes.

Name of Legume	Minimal Soaking	Minimal Cooking Time	Legume Characteristics and Description
Peas, whole	Min. 4 hours	16 minutes	Dried garden peas. Called soup peas in the U.S., and mushy peas in Great Britain. Use in soups and stews.
Peas, split green and yellow	No	10 to 13 minutes	Yellow peas are milder than green; both have a grainy texture and do not hold their shape. Great for soups—purée half of the cooked peas for a creamier texture.
Pigeon pea, gandule	4 hours	7 to 9 minutes	Most often found in dried form, but delicious fresh. They have been discovered in Egyptian tombs, and are important to the cuisines of India, where the bean is known as arhar, tur, toor, or tuvaram. Color includes red, white, brown, and black. Interestingly, pigeon peas have a reputation for being slightly narcotic . . . possibly accounting for especially deep naps after dinner. . . .
Pink, chile bean	4 hours	10 to 12 minutes	Small, pale, pink-colored; rich, meaty flavor with a slightly powdery texture, these are related to the kidney bean. Turns reddish brown when cooked. Used in Mexican-American dishes, and often featured in chili and Western barbecues.
Pinto bean	4 hours	10 to 12 minutes	Pintos are medium ovals with an earthy flavor and powdery texture. They tend to be mushier when cooked than pink or red beans. Their dappled, bicolor appearance changes to brown when cooked. A favorite for Mexican dishes.

Name of Legume	Minimal Soaking	Minimal Cooking Time	Legume Characteristics and Description
Rattlesnake bean	4 hours	10 to 12 minutes	A pinto bean hybrid, the rattlesnake bean gets its name from the way its bean pods twist and snake around the vines and poles. These beans are great for chile, refried beans, soups, and casseroles. Substitutes: pinto bean, chile bean, or red kidney bean.
Red bean	4 hours	10 to 12 minutes	Used in traditional Southern cooking, and often combined with rice. Also complements the flavor and color of corn pasta, either plain and simple or hot and spicy.
Scarlet, white, black runner bean	4 hours	10 to 12 minutes	These large beans are very flavorful, and they work well in salads or as a side dish.
Small red bean, Mexican red bean	4 hours	10 to 12 minutes	These dark red beans hold their shape and firmness when cooked. Similar to red kidney, but smoother in taste and texture. They can be substituted for any of the red colored varieties and used in soups, salads, chili, and Creole dishes.
Soy, soya beans: beige or black	8 hours, preferably overnight	30 to 35 minutes	They come in two kinds, beige and black. Sweet, nutty flavor, and touted for health benefits, these beans are hard to digest, and they are the hardest of all dried beans. Soak in the refrigerator.

Manufacturers and Suppliers

ONE OF MY ORIGINAL GOALS in creating the Web site missvickie .com was to provide easy access to information on replacement parts for pressure cookers. This is a very small listing of some of the brands that people ask about most often. To see the complete listing for replacement parts suppliers online, see http://missvickie.com/resources/parts.html.

All-American
Chef's Design
Wisconsin Aluminum Foundry Co., Inc.
Consumer Products Division
838 South 16th Street
P.O. Box 246
Manitowoc, WI 54221-0246 USA
1-920-682-8627
Fax: 1-920-682-4090
http://www.wafco.com/
customerrelations@wafco.com

Fagor
Fagor America, Inc
P.O. Box 94
Lyndhurst, NJ 07071
1-800-207-0806
http://www.fagoramerica.com/
info@fagoramerica.com

Kuhn Rikon
Kuhn Rikon
1-415-924-1125
http://www.kuhnrikon.com/

Magafesa
North American Promotions, Ltd.
P.O. Box 328
Prospect Heights, IL 60070
1-888-787-9991 or 1-888-705-8700
http://www.magefesausa.com/index.htm

Mirro
Regal
Wearever
The WearEver Company
519 N. Pierce Avenue
Lancaster, OH 43130
1-800-527-7727
ConsumerAffairs@Wearever.com
http://www.wearever.com/

Presto
National Presto Industries, Inc.
http://www.gopresto.com/
contact@gopresto.com

T-Fal
T-Fal Consumer Service
2121 Eden Road
Millville, NJ 08332
1-800-395-8325
Fax: 1-973-736-9267
http://www.t-falusa.com/tefal/

**Companies that Carry Parts
for Several Brands**

Cooking and Canning
12629 S. Tithill RD.
Buckeye, AZ 85326
http://www.pressurecookerparts.net/
info@cookingandcanning.net

Goodman's Parts
13130 SW 128 Street, # 3
Miami, FL 33186
1-888-333-4660
1-305-278-8822
Fax: 1-305-278-1884
http://www.goodmans.net/

Pressure Cooker Outlet
1035 Sylvatus Highway
Hillsville, Va. 24343, USA
http://www.pressurecooker-outlet.com/index.htm
1-800-251-8824

Beef

BEEF IS EVERYONE'S FAVORITE main dish, and the pressure cooker excels in cooking it. Cuts from the center of the animal—the loin and rib—are suspension muscles getting little exercise, so they are naturally tender. Popular cuts include the T-bone, porterhouse, rib-eye, rib, and tenderloin.

More economical cuts come from the front and rear of the animal, where the heavily exercised muscles are less tender. The moist-heat cooking environment of the pressure cooker is the perfect choice for these cuts. The chuck and round come from these areas, including the tri-tip, round tip, rump, bottom round and eye round, top sirloin, chuck eye, and round tip—all good candidates for pressure cooking.

Ground beef is inexpensive and always a good buy because it's so versatile and can be used in a great number of pressure-cooker recipes. Lean-to-fat ratios vary, so be sure to check the label. Base your purchase decision on price, personal preference, and the type of dish you will be cooking.

Italian Beef Stew

Does the world need another beef stew recipe? Well, if you're tired of the same old meat-and-potato versions, this recipe fits the bill. I cobbled this recipe together in a pinch one day, and since then it underwent several transformations before I was happy with the final results. I use the interrupted cooking method (see page 38) to prepare the meat and broth first, and then add the vegetables so they do not get overcooked or lose their texture and color.

1 tablespoon mixed pickling spice
5 black peppercorns
1 bay leaf
2 tablespoons olive oil
2 pounds beef round steak, cut into
    1½-inch cubes
2 onions, cut into wedges
½ cup red wine
1 (14-ounce) can beef broth
1 (28-ounce) can diced tomatoes, with juice
1 (14-ounce) can kidney beans, drained
    and rinsed
4 carrots, cut into ¼-inch slices
2 teaspoons dried basil
2 teaspoons dried oregano
1 teaspoon garlic powder
1 teaspoon dried rosemary
¼ teaspoon red pepper flakes
1 teaspoon salt
4 cups tomato-vegetable juice
    (V8 or similar brand)
2 zucchini, cut into ½-inch slices
1 small bunch fresh spinach, washed and
    stems removed

2 tablespoons all-purpose flour
6 slices day-old Italian bread, toasted
Grated Parmesan cheese, for garnish

Place the pickling spice, peppercorns, and bay leaf in the center of a piece of cheesecloth (use a coffee filter or a tea ball as an alternative) and tie it tightly with a piece of string.

Heat the oil in a large pressure cooker over medium high heat. Add the meat, cook until well browned on all sides, and set aside. Add the onions to the cooker and cook, stirring, until clear, about 3 minutes. Deglaze the cooker with the wine, scraping up all those crusty, brown bits from the bottom. Return the meat to the cooker and add the broth, tomatoes, beans, carrots, basil, oregano, garlic powder, rosemary, red pepper flakes, and salt. Add the tomato-vegetable juice and 2 cups water and stir. Lock the lid in place. Bring to 15psi over high heat, immediately reduce the heat to the lowest possible setting to stabilize and maintain that pressure, and cook for 12 minutes. Remove from the heat and use the quick release method (see page 30) to depressurize and remove the lid. Remove and discard the spice bag. Skim off any excess fat from the surface of the broth.

Add the zucchini and spinach and lock the lid back in place. Return to 15psi over high heat, immediately reduce the heat to the lowest possible setting to stabilize and maintain that pressure, and cook for an additional 3 minutes. Remove from the heat and use the natural release method (see page 31) to depressurize. Carefully open the lid after the pressure drops. To thicken the broth, make a slurry with the flour mixed with ½ cup water, and then stir it into the broth, simmering gently over medium heat until it reaches the desired consistency. Place 1 slice of toasted bread in the bottom of each soup bowl and spoon the stew mixture over the bread just before serving. Serve the

Parmesan cheese at the table, and be sure to include plenty of buttery garlic toast or some crusty bread on the side. ✳ **Serves 6 generously**

Pepper Bellies

This is a popular recipe in California, where it's dished up at county fairs and school cafeterias. There are many variations, but it's always a big hit with kids.

  1 pound ground beef
  1 onion, diced
  1 green bell pepper, seeded and diced
  1 (10-ounce) can kidney beans, drained and
      rinsed
  1 (14-ounce) can tomato sauce
  1 (6-ounce) can diced green chiles
  1 tablespoon minced garlic
  1 tablespoon chili powder
  1 (16-ounce) package corn chips, such as Fritos
      or Doritos
  2 cups shredded jalapeño jack cheese
  1 cup sour cream
  1 cup prepared guacamole
  1 cup sliced black olives

Heat the pressure cooker over medium heat. Add the ground beef and cook until browned and crumbly. Add the onion and green pepper to the cooker and cook, stirring, until soft, about 3 minutes. Divide the beans and mash half with a fork or potato masher, then add all the beans to the cooker. Add the tomato sauce, green chiles, garlic, chili powder, and ½ cup water, stirring well. Lock the lid in place. Bring to 15psi over high heat, immediately reduce the heat to the lowest possible setting to stabilize and maintain that pressure, and cook for 8 minutes. Remove from the heat and use the natural release method (see page 31) to depressurize. Carefully open the lid after the pressure drops. Adjust the seasonings to taste. To serve, place a mound of crushed corn chips in 4 individual bowls and ladle about 1 cup chili mixture on top of each serving. Add a generous amount of shredded cheese, and top with the sour cream, guacamole, and olives, as desired. ✳ **Serves 4**

Italian Seasoned Veal Tortellini Stew

A good, hearty dinner for a cold winter night, perfect served with lots of warm, crusty, Italian bread for dunking into the broth. In answer to that eternal question, "What's for dinner?," this dish delivers plenty of taste and aroma. I use the interrupted cooking method (see page 38) to prepare the broth and meat, and then add the more delicate vegetables and tortellini so they do not overcook.

½ cup all-purpose flour

1 teaspoon freshly ground black pepper

½ teaspoon salt

2 pounds veal stew meat, trimmed and cut into 1-inch chunks

3 tablespoons olive oil

1 onion, chopped

1 green bell pepper, seeded and chopped

2 tablespoons minced garlic

1 tablespoon dried oregano

1 tablespoon dried basil

1 teaspoon dried rosemary

½ teaspoon crushed fennel seeds

½ teaspoon red pepper flakes

2 bay leaves

½ cup red wine

2 (28-ounce) cans stewed Italian-style tomatoes, with juice

1 (14-ounce) can beef broth

½ cup chopped fresh parsley

2 tablespoons minced capers

3 zucchini, cut in ¼-inch slices

3 cups fresh or 1 (16-ounce) bag frozen Italian green beans

2 cups (1 [10-ounce] package) frozen chopped spinach

8 ounces uncooked dry or frozen cheese tortellini

In a plastic bag, mix together the flour, ½ teaspoon of the black pepper, and the salt. Add the meat to the bag and shake gently until each piece is lightly coated. Heat the oil in a large pressure cooker over medium heat. Add the meat and cook, in small batches, until well browned on all sides, setting each batch aside on paper towels until finished. Add the onion, green pepper, and garlic and cook, stirring, until slightly softened, about 3 minutes. Add the oregano, basil, rosemary, fennel, red pepper flakes, remaining ½ teaspoon of black pepper, and bay leaves, and cook, stirring, for a minute, until they begin to sizzle. Deglaze the pot with the wine, scraping up all those crusty, brown bits from the bottom.

Add tomatoes, the broth, parsley, and capers to the cooker. Return the meat to the cooker. Stir, and then lock the lid in place. Bring to 15psi over high heat, immediately reduce the heat to the lowest possible setting to stabilize and maintain that pressure, and cook for 15 minutes. Remove from the heat and use the quick release method (see page 30) to depressurize. Carefully open the lid after the pressure drops. Skim off any excess fat from the surface of the broth.

Add the zucchini, green beans, spinach, and tortellini, pushing them beneath the level of the broth. Return to 15psi over high heat, immediately reduce the heat to the lowest possible setting to stabilize and maintain that pressure, and cook for an additional 3 minutes. Remove from the heat and use the quick or cold water release method (see page 30) to depressurize. Carefully open the lid after the pressure drops. Discard the bay leaves. If desired, thicken the broth by making a slurry with 2 tablespoons of the flour-pepper-salt mixture combined with ½ cup water; stir the slurry into the broth, and simmer gently over medium heat until it reaches the desired consistency. Adjust the seasonings to taste and serve.

✳ Serves 6 generously

Good and Plenty Beef Stew

When I was growing up, my grandmother told stories about the food shortages during World War II. Despite rationing, resourceful people made the best of what was available. Neighbors often traded ingredients, and it was common for several families to share a pressure cooker to conserve cooking fuel. Many foods were rationed, so in addition to the all-important Victory Gardens, many households kept a cow, a few milk goats, or chickens in the backyard. Stews were popular because with just a little meat and some vegetables, a hearty dinner was quickly on the table. With a few modern adjustments, this is still essentially my grandmother's basic recipe, but I use the interrupted cooking method (see page 38) to preserve the texture of the vegetables.

½ cup all-purpose flour

½ teaspoon salt

½ teaspoon ground black pepper

1½ pounds boneless beef chuck, cut into 1½-inch cubes

2 tablespoons butter or oil

2 onions, halved and quartered

2 (16-ounce) cans beef broth

1 bay leaf

1 teaspoon ground sage

4 potatoes, peeled and cut into 1-inch cubes

3 carrots, peeled and cut into ¼-inch slices

2 stalkss celery, cut into 1-inch slices

In a plastic bag, mix the flour, salt, and pepper. Add the meat to the bag, shaking gently until each piece is lightly coated. Heat the oil in a large pressure cooker over medium heat. Add the meat and cook, in small batches, until well browned on all sides, setting each batch aside on paper towels until finished. Add the onions to the cooker and cook, stirring, until soft, about 3 minutes. Deglaze the cooker with the broth, scraping up all those crusty, brown bits from the bottom. Add the bay leaf, sage, and 2 cups water, stirring the contents to blend. Return the meat to the cooker and lock the lid in place. Bring to 15psi over high heat, immediately reduce the heat to the lowest possible setting to stabilize and maintain that pressure, and cook for 12 minutes. Remove from the heat and use the quick or cold water release method (see page 30) to depressurize. Carefully open the lid after the pressure drops. Skim off any excess fat from the surface of the broth. Add the potatoes, carrots, celery, and enough water to cover the ingredients by 1 inch, if necessary. Stir and lock the lid in place again. Return to 15psi over high heat, immediately reduce the heat to the lowest possible setting to stabilize and maintain that pressure, and cook for 4 minutes longer. Remove from the heat and use the natural release method (see page 31) to depressurize. Carefully open the lid after the pressure drops. Discard the bay leaf. Thicken the broth by making a slurry with 2 tablespoons of the flour-salt-pepper mixture combined with ½ cup water; stir the slurry into the broth, and simmer gently over medium heat until it reaches the desired consistency. Adjust the seasonings to taste and serve. ✳ Serves 6

Brisket of Beef with Vegetables in Chili Sauce

This is a tastier version of the traditional Colonial Boiled Dinner, with tender beef cooked in an infusion of spicy chili sauce and beer instead of plain water, so the rich gravy adds a flavorful accompaniment. I'm using the interrupted method (see page 38) to cook lots of vegetables.

  1 (12-ounce) bottle beer
  1 (8-ounce) bottle chili sauce
  1 onion, chopped
  ½ teaspoon garlic powder
  ¼ teaspoon pepper
  3 pounds fresh beef brisket
  8 to 10 small unpeeled red potatoes, halved
  2 cups fresh or frozen sliced carrots
  2 small turnips, peeled and sliced
  1 head cabbage, cut in 6 to 8 wedges
  2 tablespoons flour

Place the beer, chili sauce, onion, garlic powder, and pepper in a large pressure cooker and mix well. Place beef brisket fat-side down in the pressure cooker. Lock the lid in place. Bring to 15psi over high heat, immediately reduce the heat to the lowest possible setting to stabilize and maintain that pressure, and cook for 35 minutes. Remove from the heat and use the quick release method (see page 30) to depressurize. Carefully open the lid after the pressure drops. Add the potatoes, carrots, turnips, and cabbage wedges. Lock the lid in place, return to 15psi over high heat, immediately re-duce the heat to the lowest possible setting to stabilize and maintain that pressure, and cook for 3 more minutes. Remove from the heat and use the natural release method (see page 31) to depressur-ize. Carefully open the lid after the pressure drops.

Transfer the cabbage to a serving bowl. Place the brisket on a large serving platter and slice very thin. Arrange the root vegetables around the meat. To thicken the sauce, make a slurry with the 2 tablespoons of flour mixed into ½ cup water. Stir the slurry into the broth and simmer gently over medium heat until it reaches the desired consis-tency. Serve the sauce in gravy boat to be passed at the table. ✳ Serves 4.

Cook's Note: If you have two pressure cookers, use the small one for the meat, adjusting the cooking time to 40 minutes. Place the vegetables on a rack in the largest one and add ½ cup water. Lock the lid in place. Bring to 15psi over high heat, immedi-ately reduce the heat to the lowest possible setting to stabilize and maintain that pressure, and cook for 3 minutes. Remove from the heat and use the natural release method (see page 31) to depressur-ize. Carefully open the lid after the pressure drops.

Steak Sandwiches with Honeyed Red Onions

What! Sandwiches from the pressure cooker? Absolutely, and if you are tired of the usual cold cuts, what could be better—or more delicious—than a big, two-handed, man-sized sandwich with some sweet onions and peppers that's a meal in itself. For more variety, use any type of bread rolls that appeal to you, and include some crisp dill pickles, pepperoncini, or cherry peppers and the beverage of your choice to feed the hungry meat lovers in your family.

1½ pound sirloin steak, about 1 inch thick,
    trimmed of fat
2 tablespoons red wine vinegar
2 tablespoons balsamic vinegar
2 tablespoons soy sauce
½ teaspoon ground ginger
½ teaspoon red pepper flakes
1 red onion, thinly sliced
1 red bell pepper, seeded and cut into thin strips
½ teaspoon cracked black pepper
3 tablespoons honey
6 store-bought sub rolls, split, buttered, and
    lightly toasted

Place the meat in the freezer for about 20 minutes, or until it is partially frozen, for easier cutting. Stir the vinegars, soy sauce, ginger, red pepper flakes, and ½ cup water together in the pressure cooker. Separate the onion slices into rings and layer them on the bottom of the pressure cooker; add the bell pepper strips, letting them marinate in the vinegar mixture while preparing the meat. Sprinkle both sides of the steak with the cracked pepper, pressing the pepper into the surface of the meat, and then slice the meat as thinly as possible. Arrange the meat slices on top of the vegetables in the pressure cooker. Lock the lid in place. Bring to 15psi over high heat, immediately reduce the heat to the lowest possible setting to stabilize and maintain that pressure, and cook for 6 minutes. Remove from the heat and use the natural release method (see page 31) to depressurize. Carefully open the lid after the pressure drops. Use a slotted spoon to transfer the steak slices, bell peppers, and onions from the pressure cooker to a plate. Over high heat, bring the broth to a boil and cook, uncovered, until it is reduced by half. Stir in the honey and return the meat, bell peppers, and onions to the cooker, stirring to coat with the sauce. Pile up a generous amount of the steak and vegetables on one side of each of the sub rolls, and spoon a little of the sauce over each just before serving. Serve any remaining sauce on the side for dipping. ✳ Serves 6

Yankee Pot Roast with Vegetables and Gravy

"The meat falls off the bone . . .": how many times have you heard that and wanted to serve up a roast that was so tender it practically melts in your mouth? The pressure cooker makes the meat fork-tender in this amazingly simple, old-time favorite dish. All the deep flavors are concentrated in a rich-tasting gravy—the *pièce de résistance*, in my opinion—and that's always a big hit with the 'meat and potatoes' lovers in your family. As a side benefit, since everything is cooked in one pot, there's little cleanup afterward. Cooked in one pot using the interrupted cooking method (see page 38), the roast and broth for the gravy are prepared first; next the vegetables are added to retain their texture and color.

Step One: The Beef

3 to 4 pounds beef chuck or round roast

4 cloves garlic, peeled and thinly sliced

½ cup all-purpose flour

½ teaspoon salt

½ teaspoon freshly ground black pepper

3 tablespoons oil

2 onions, chopped

½ cup red wine

1 (28-ounce) can beef broth

1 (28-ounce) can chopped tomatoes, with juice

1 teaspoon ground thyme

2 bay leaves

Make 1-inch-deep, evenly distributed incisions in the roast and push 1 slice of garlic into each. In a plastic bag, mix the flour, salt, and pepper, add the meat, and shake gently until it is lightly coated. Heat the oil in a large pressure cooker over medium-high heat. Add the meat, cook until well browned on all sides, and set aside. Add the onions to the cooker and cook, stirring, until clear, about 3 minutes. Remove half of the onions and cook the other half, stirring, until soft. Deglaze the cooker with the wine, scraping up all those crusty, brown bits from the bottom. Add the remaining onions, the broth, tomatoes, thyme, bay leaves, and 1½ cups water and stir. Return the meat to the cooker and lock the lid in place. Bring to 15psi over high heat, immediately reduce the heat to the lowest possible setting to stabilize and maintain that pressure, and cook for 35 minutes. Remove from the heat and use the quick release method (see page 30) to depressurize. Carefully open the lid after the pressure drops. Check for doneness. If the meat is not sufficiently tender, lock the lid back in place. Return to 15psi over high heat, immediately reduce the heat to the lowest possible setting to stabilize and maintain that pressure, and cook for another 5 minutes, then check again using the quick release method.

Step Two: The Vegetables and Gravy

4 carrots, peeled, halved lengthwise, and quartered

3 stalks celery, cut into 1-inch pieces

6 red potatoes, scrubbed and quartered if large or halved if small

3 parsnips, peeled and cut into 2-inch pieces

Add the carrots, celery, potatoes, and parsnips to the cooker, arranging the pieces to fit around the roast. Lock the lid back in place. Return to 15psi over high heat, immediately reduce the heat to the lowest possible setting to stabilize and maintain that pressure, and cook for an additional 4 minutes. Remove from the heat and use the natural release method (see page 31) to depressurize. Carefully open the lid after the pressure drops. Transfer the meat to a carving board, cover with a sheet of aluminum foil, and let it rest while making the gravy. Transfer the vegetables to a large serving bowl. Skim off any excess fat from the surface of the broth and discard the bay leaves. Thicken the broth by making a slurry with 2 tablespoons of the flour-salt-pepper mixture combined with ½ cup water; stir the slurry into the broth, and simmer gently over medium heat until it reaches the desired consistency. Adjust the seasonings to taste. Slice the meat across the grain and serve the gravy separately to pour over the meat and vegetables at the table. ✳ **Serves 6 generously**

Zesty Mexican Shredded Beef Sandwiches

I love everything about Mexican food; the zesty, complex flavors and aroma from all the robust spices makes my mouth water. It's the fastest-growing food segment in the Western world, a twentieth-century phenomenon with many variations that appeals to people from coast to coast. The best way to judge a good sandwich is by the number of napkins used, and with all that spicy shredded beef, make sure you stock up.

1 onion, quartered
1 mild chile pepper (poblano, pasilla, Anaheim), seeded and halved
1 cup packed cilantro stems and leaves
3 tomatillos, papery skins removed and cut in half
1 cup bottled salsa
1 teaspoon ground cumin
2 pounds boneless beef roast
6 store-bought hamburger buns or onion rolls, lightly toasted
1 (4-ounce) can frozen guacamole, thawed
Sliced tomatoes, for garnish

Using a food processor, puree the onion, chile pepper, cilantro, and tomatillos to a smooth consistency, adding a little water if necessary until the mixture resembles pesto sauce. Pour the mixture into the pressure cooker. Add the salsa, cumin, and 1 cup water, stirring well. Add the beef. Lock the lid in place and bring to 15psi over high heat, immediately reduce the heat to the lowest possible setting to stabilize and maintain that pressure, and cook for 45 minutes. Remove from the heat and use the natural release method (see page 31) to depressurize. Carefully open the lid after the pressure drops. Check for doneness using a fork; the meat should shred easily. If necessary, lock the lid back in place, return to 15psi over high heat, immediately reduce the heat to the lowest possible setting to stabilize and maintain that pressure, cook for an additional 5 minutes, and check for doneness again. Remove the beef to a carving board and shred it with 2 forks. Skim off any excess fat from the surface of the remaining broth, and reserve the broth to freeze for later use. Spoon a generous amount of the shredded beef onto the rolls and add a spoonful of guacamole and a tomato slice before serving. ✳ **Serves 6**

Peppered Beef Marsala

I enjoy cooking with a variety of spirits—the deep flavors of beers, wines, and liquors improve the taste of many foods while enhancing the accompanying broth or gravy. Marsala, a dark-amber-colored fortified wine, is Italy's version of sherry or Madeira. It has a rich, smoky flavor, and that's what gives this dish a distinctive flavor and turns an ordinary ho-hum round steak into a gourmet entrée. Serve with mounds of mashed potatoes or cooked noodles.

2 pounds round steak

2 teaspoons coarsely ground black pepper

½ cup all-purpose flour

½ teaspoon salt

2 tablespoons butter

1 onion, finely chopped

½ pound fresh mushrooms, washed and
    thickly sliced

1 green bell pepper, seeded and thinly sliced

½ cup Marsala (substitutes: Madeira, or equal
    parts sherry and sweet vermouth)

2 tablespoons tomato paste

Cut the steak into serving portions. One at a time, place each steak on a cutting board between 2 pieces of plastic wrap. Using the flat part of a meat mallet or the bottom of a heavy pan, pound the meat out to about ¼ inch thick. Rub and press the coarsely ground black pepper into both sides of each piece of meat. In a plastic bag, mix the flour and salt. Add the meat, shaking gently until each piece is lightly coated. Heat the butter in the pressure cooker over medium-high heat. Add the meat, cook until well browned on all sides, and set aside. Add the onions, mushrooms, and peppers to the cooker and cook, stirring, for about 3 minutes. Deglaze the cooker with the wine, scraping up all those crusty, brown bits from the bottom. Add the tomato paste and 1 cup water, stirring to blend. Return the meat to the cooker and lock the lid in place. Bring to 15psi over high heat, immediately reduce the heat to the lowest possible setting to stabilize and maintain that pressure, and cook for 15 minutes. Remove from the heat and use the natural release method (see page 31) to depressurize. Carefully open the lid after the pressure drops. Transfer the meat to a serving platter. Skim off any excess fat from the surface of the broth and pour into a gravy boat to serve at the table.

✳ Serves 4 generously

Braised Beef Brisket with Horseradish Sauce

Not many people want to cook a brisket because it takes hours and hours using conventional cooking methods. Of course, the pressure cooker cuts the time down to under an hour, making one of the most delicious pot roasts you can imagine. The horseradish enhances the meat and sauce without being overwhelming, and the sour cream mellows it completely. Serve this with either mashed or baked potatoes, which can be quickly prepared in the last few minutes that the brisket is cooking, or use a second pressure cooker if you have one.

Step One: The Beef

½ cup all-purpose flour
½ teaspoon salt
½ teaspoon freshly ground black pepper
4 pounds beef brisket
2 tablespoons olive oil
2 onions, thinly sliced
2 cups dry red wine
⅓ cup prepared horseradish
2 tablespoons minced garlic
1 teaspoon dried thyme
2 bay leaves

In a plastic bag, mix the flour, salt, and pepper and add the meat, shaking gently until it is uniformly coated. Heat the oil in the pressure cooker over medium-high heat. Add the meat, cook until well browned on all sides, and set aside. Add the onions to the cooker and cook, stirring, until golden brown, about 8 minutes. Deglaze the cooker with the wine, scraping up all those crusty, brown bits from the bottom. Add the horseradish, garlic, thyme, bay leaves, and 1½ cups water, stirring to blend. Return the meat to the cooker and lock the lid in place. Bring to 15psi over high heat, immediately reduce the heat to the lowest possible setting to stabilize and maintain that pressure, and cook for 55 minutes. Remove from the heat and use the natural release method (see page 31) to depressurize. Carefully open the lid after the pressure drops. Transfer the brisket to a cutting surface and cover loosely with foil while you make the sauce. When ready to serve, thinly slice the brisket, cutting against the grain, and arrange the slices on a serving platter.

Step Two: The Horseradish Sauce

1 cup sour cream
1 tablespoon snipped fresh chives,
   for garnish

Discard the bay leaves. Skim off any excess fat from the surface of the broth. Mix the sour cream into the broth over low heat, stirring until well blended and heated through. Pour the sauce into a small bowl, sprinkle the chives on top, and serve at the table. ✳ Serves 6

Italian Beef Simmered in Tomato-Garlic Sauce (Braciole Alla Pizzaiola)

When one of my aunts sent me her special pressure cooker recipe for this Italian entrée, I couldn't wait to try it. There are many variations of this dish, but this is the braciole I've always had in mind. The beef is tender, and the well seasoned tomato sauce is full of flavor and goes well with your choice of rotini pasta (sometimes called spirals or twists), mashed potatoes, or polenta, and a simple antipasto salad.

> 2 tablespoons olive oil
> 2 pounds round steak, trimmed of fat
> ½ cup red wine
> 1 (28-ounce) can diced or chopped tomatoes, with juice
> ⅓ cup grated Parmesan cheese
> 3 tablespoons minced garlic
> 1 tablespoon dried oregano
> 1 teaspoon dried basil

Heat the oil in the pressure cooker over medium-high heat. Add the meat, cook until well browned on all sides, and set aside. Pour off any remaining fat and deglaze the cooker with the wine, scraping up all those crusty, brown bits from the bottom. Add the tomatoes, cheese, garlic, oregano, and basil, stirring to mix. Return the meat to the cooker and lock the lid in place. Bring to 15psi over high heat, immediately reduce the heat to the lowest possible setting to stabilize and maintain that pressure, and cook for 15 minutes. Remove from the heat and use the natural release method (see page 31) to depressurize. Carefully open the lid after the pressure drops. Transfer the meat to a serving platter and pour the sauce into a serving bowl. ✳ Serves 6

Curried Beef with Dried Fruits and Chilled Cucumber-Yogurt Sauce

Curry can be quite complex, not only in the sheer number of ingredients, but also in the many flavors and steps involved. What's the point in having a great recipe if you can't find the ingredients and it takes forever to prepare? After a lot of trial and error, I finally found a combination of ingredients that worked well, and, most importantly, could be easily found in the local supermarket. Despite the ingredient list, most of the prep work involves simple measuring and not a lot of cutting and chopping, so it is quick and easy to get started. I like to serve this wonderfully fragrant and delicious curry over hot, fluffy rice, but you can also use mashed potatoes or noodles.

Step One: Cucumber-Yogurt Sauce

1 cup plain yogurt

2 cucumbers, peeled, seeded, and chopped

1 teaspoon minced garlic

1 teaspoon minced fresh ginger

¼ teaspoon ground ginger

¼ teaspoon ground nutmeg

In a small glass bowl, mix all the ingredients. Cover and chill for several hours before serving.

Step Two: The Beef

2 tablespoons oil

2 pounds boneless beef chuck, trimmed of fat and cut into 2-inch cubes

1 onion, sliced

2 tablespoons garam masala

2 tablespoons curry powder

1 teaspoon freshly ground black pepper

2 bay leaves

1 red bell pepper, seeded and chopped

1 green bell pepper, seeded and chopped

1 small jalapeño chile, seeded and minced

½ cup packed finely minced cilantro leaves

1 piece fresh ginger, about 2 inches long, peeled and minced

8 cloves garlic, peeled and minced

1 (14-ounce) can beef broth

½ cup dried apricots, cut in half

¼ cup raisins

2 tablespoons cornstarch

1 cup unsweetened coconut milk

⅓ cup coarsely chopped cilantro leaves, for garnish

Heat the oil in the pressure cooker over medium-high heat. Add the meat, cook until well browned on all sides, and set aside. Add the onions and cook, stirring, until clear, about 3 minutes. Add the garam masala, curry powder, black pepper, and bay leaves and cook, stirring, until the aromas are released, 2 to 3 minutes. Stir in the bell peppers, jalapeño, cilantro, ginger, and garlic. Add the beef broth, apricots, and raisins and return the beef to the cooker, stirring to mix. Lock the lid in place. Bring to 15psi over high heat, immediately reduce the heat to the lowest possible setting to stabilize and maintain that pressure, and cook for 15 minutes. Remove from the heat and use the natural release method (see page 31) to depressurize. Carefully open the lid after the pressure drops. Thicken the sauce by making a slurry with the cornstarch mixed with the coconut milk. Stir the slurry into the sauce and simmer over medium heat, stirring often as it thickens, but do not boil. Place the curried beef mixture in a large serving bowl and garnish with the chopped cilantro. Serve topped with a big spoonful of the chilled Cucumber-Yogurt Sauce. ✳ Serves 4

Columbian Roast Beef

Eavesdropping on a conversation at the next table during lunch at a local café, I listened as two women described a fabulously delicious beef roast cooked in coffee. Coffee, I thought, how intriguing and what a marvelous blend of unique flavors. After some experimentation, I came up with the following recipe for a very tender roast with a flavorful gravy, and since then, no coffee ever goes to waste in my house. Make sure to use a good coffee with robust flavor; don't try to make the coffee stronger by omitting water or increasing the grounds, this only will make it bitter. Serve with lots of mashed potatoes with this roast; you'll need something for all that delicious gravy after all.

> 2 tablespoons oil
> 1 onion, finely chopped
> 3 pounds boneless pot or chuck roast
> 1 cup strong black coffee
> 1 (3-ounce) can tomato paste
> 2 tablespoons minced garlic
> 2 tablespoons all-purpose flour

Heat the oil in the pressure cooker over medium-high heat. Add the onions and cook, stirring, until clear, about 3 minutes. Add the beef and cook until well browned on all sides. Deglaze the cooker with the coffee, scraping up all those crusty, brown bits from the bottom. Add the tomato paste and garlic, and stir in 1 cup water. Lock the lid in place.

Bring to 15psi over high heat, immediately reduce the heat to the lowest possible setting to stabilize and maintain that pressure, and cook for 40 minutes. Remove from the heat and use the natural release method (see page 31) to depressurize. Carefully open the lid after the pressure drops. Transfer the roast to serving platter and cover with foil while you make the gravy. Thicken the broth by making a slurry with the flour combined with ½ cup water; stir the slurry into the broth and simmer gently over medium heat until it reaches the desired consistency. Adjust the seasonings to taste. Slice the meat across the grain and serve the gravy separately to pour over the meat at the table.

✳ **Serves 6**

Teriyaki Steaks with Fresh Mango Salsa

Whenever possible, prepare the salsa a day ahead, which really makes a big impact on the flavors. There's something about the taste of teriyaki that has a special appeal for kids, but don't be fooled—this dish has a gourmet touch with the addition of the fresh fruit salsa. The meat is so tender that no one would ever guess that it was an inexpensive round steak. I serve this dish with steamed broccoli and white rice.

Step One: Fresh Mango Salsa
2 ripe mangos, peeled, seeded, and diced
1 small red onion, diced
2 Roma tomatoes, seeded and diced

⅓ cup packed finely chopped cilantro leaves

2 tablespoons fresh lime juice

1 tablespoon sugar

1 teaspoon salt

½ teaspoon red pepper flakes

Combine all the ingredients in a glass or ceramic bowl. Taste and adjust the seasonings. Cover the bowl with plastic wrap and refrigerate for at least 4 hours before serving, or overnight if possible.

Step Two: The Steaks

2 tablespoons oil

2 pounds round steak, cut into serving portions

½ cup teriyaki sauce

2 tablespoons balsamic vinegar

2 tablespoons minced garlic

Heat the oil in the pressure cooker over high medium-heat. Add the meat, and cook until browned on both sides. Add the teriyaki sauce, vinegar, garlic, and ½ cup water. Lock the lid in place. Bring to 15psi over high heat, immediately reduce the heat to the lowest possible setting to stabilize and maintain that pressure, and cook for 20 minutes. Remove from the heat and use the natural release method (see page 31) to depressurize. Carefully open the lid after the pressure drops. Place the meat on a serving platter. Pass the bowl of Fresh Mango Salsa at the table.

❊ **Serves 4 generously**

So, So Simple Barbecued Beef Ribs

My pressure cooker is the best barbecue "grill" I have ever owned. It only takes a few minutes in the pressure cooker to precook the ribs until the meat is very tender, but not quite falling off the bone. The ribs are then ready to be basted with your favorite barbecue sauce and popped under the broiler, or onto the grill if you're a purist.

4 pounds beef ribs, trimmed of visible fat

1 cup of your favorite barbecue sauce

Place the ribs in the pressure cooker, leaning them at an angle if necessary to fit, and add ½ cup water. Lock the lid in place. Bring to 15psi over high heat, immediately reduce the heat to the lowest possible setting to stabilize and maintain that pressure, and cook for 12 minutes. Remove from the heat and use the natural release method (see page 31) to depressurize. Carefully open the lid after the pressure drops. Preheat the broiler. Using long-handled tongs, remove the ribs and place them on a broiler pan. Set aside ½ cup of the barbecue sauce for serving at the table. Pour the remaining ½ cup of barbecue sauce into a small bowl and baste the ribs. Place the ribs under the broiler and baste often, watching closely until the first side is nicely browned. Turn the ribs, basting again, and broil the other side until browned. Serve the ribs with the reserved barbecue sauce on the side.

❊ **Serves 4 generously**

Mesquite Lime-Marinated Shredded Beef Sandwiches

I enjoy a good barbecue, but summer temperatures here can reach 110°F or more, so who wants to go stand outside over a hot grill and barbecue . . . not me, 'cause I'm comfortably parked near the air conditioner. What a dilemma! Years ago, I came up with the idea of an indoor barbecue, something with all the benefits of a backyard barbecue without any of the inconvenience, and right in my own kitchen too. Enter my trusty pressure cooker and the infusion cooking method (see page 33). All the wonderful flavors will penetrate the meat and infuse the sauce, until the beef is tender and tastes remarkably like it has been cooked all day over a mesquite fire. Serve with your favorite coleslaw and some beans for a fun inside barbecue any time of year, and any day of the week.

4 pounds boneless beef chuck or rump roast
1 (12-ounce) can lemon-lime soft drink
   (regular, not diet)
3 tablespoons frozen limeade concentrate
1 tablespoon sugar
1 tablespoon mesquite-flavored liquid smoke
6 store-bought poppy seed or onion rolls,
   split and lightly toasted

Pat the roast dry with a paper towel and place it in the center of the pressure cooker. Add the remaining ingredients (except the rolls) and lock the lid in place. Bring to 15psi over high heat, immediately reduce the heat to the lowest possible setting to stabilize and maintain that pressure, and cook for 30 minutes. Remove from the heat and use the natural release method (see page 31) to depressurize. Carefully open the lid after the pressure drops. Check for doneness; the meat should shred easily with the tines of a fork. If necessary, lock the lid back in place, return to 15psi over high heat, immediately reduce the heat to the lowest possible setting to stabilize and maintain that pressure, and cook for an additional 10 minutes. Remove from the heat and use the natural release method (see page 31) to depressurize. Remove the roast to a cutting board and let it rest until cool enough to handle. Meanwhile, bring the sauce in the cooker to a simmer over medium heat, uncovered, stirring occasionally as the sauce is reduced and begins to thicken. Shred the beef with 2 forks, pulling in opposite directions until it's all torn into bite-size pieces. Place the shredded beef in the simmering sauce, heating it through. Serve the shredded beef piled high on the rolls. ✳ Serves 6

Shredded Barbecued Beef Sandwiches

As anyone knows, the secret to great-tasting barbecue is the sauce. It must have the right combination of tangy sweetness to really pop, and this recipe has been a family favorite for over 35 years. There's an added attraction, of course, in the ease of preparation, since everything is simply tossed in the pressure cooker. Serve with coleslaw and French fries.

1 (12-ounce) can Dr. Pepper (regular, not diet)
1 (3-ounce) can tomato paste
½ cup cider vinegar
3 tablespoons Worcestershire sauce
3 tablespoons molasses
1 teaspoon liquid smoke
1 cup chopped onion
¼ cup dark brown sugar
1 tablespoon chili powder
1 teaspoon garlic powder
1 teaspoon ground cumin
1 teaspoon freshly ground black pepper
2 pounds eye of the round roast
6 store-bought sandwich rolls (your choice)
Red onion slices, for topping
Dill pickle slices, for topping

Combine the first 12 ingredients in the cooker, stirring to mix. Add the roast and lock the lid in place. Bring to 15psi over high heat, immediately reduce the heat to the lowest possible setting to stabilize and maintain that pressure, and cook for 40 min-utes. Remove from the heat and use the natural release method (see page 31) to depressurize. Carefully open the lid after the pressure drops. Check for doneness; the meat should shred easily with a fork. If needed, lock the lid back in place, return to 15psi over high heat, immediately reduce the heat to the lowest possible setting to stabilize and maintain that pressure, and cook for an additional 5 minutes. Remove from the heat and use the natural release method (see page 31) to depressurize. Carefully open the lid after the pressure drops. Remove the roast to a cutting board and let it rest until cool enough to handle. Taste the sauce and adjust the seasonings to taste. Bring the sauce in the cooker to a simmer over medium heat, uncovered, stirring occasionally as the sauce is reduced and thickens. Meanwhile, shred the beef with 2 forks, pulling in opposite directions until it's all torn into bite-size pieces. Place the shredded beef in the simmering sauce, heating it through. Spoon about ½ cup beef mixture onto the bottom half of each roll; top with onion and pickles, if desired. Cover with tops of rolls. ✳ Serves 6

Kalbi Beef: Korean-Style Short Ribs with Horseradish Butter

This is my version of a popular Korean dish in which beef is cooked in a seasoned marinade until the meat is so tender it falls from the bones. Ideal for the pressure cooker, the wonderful sauce is thick with flavor. Serve with steamed white rice and sliced tomatoes for the perfect accompaniments.

Step One: The Horseradish Butter

4 tablespoons (½ stick) butter, at room temperature
2 tablespoons drained prepared horseradish
⅛ teaspoon salt

Combine all the ingredients in a glass bowl. Cover and refrigerate several hours in advance so the flavors blend.

Step Two: The Toasted Sesame Seeds

4 tablespoons sesame seeds

Heat the pressure cooker over medium heat, and add the seeds in a thin layer. Stir the seeds until they begin to lightly brown and become fragrant. Watch closely or they will go from toasted to burned in seconds. Remove the toasted seeds to a plate until ready to use.

Step Three: The Beef

2 pounds beef short ribs
2 tablespoons peanut oil

1 onion, chopped
½ cup soy sauce
2 carrots, coarsely grated
¼ cup dry sherry
3 tablespoons toasted (not plain) sesame oil
¼ cup packed dark brown sugar
2 tablespoons creamy peanut butter
2 tablespoons minced garlic
1-inch piece of fresh ginger, peeled and minced
½ teaspoon dried red pepper flakes
Sliced green onion tops, for garnish

Trim any excess fat from the meat. Heat the oil in the pressure cooker over medium heat. Add the ribs, cook until browned on all sides, then set the ribs aside on paper towels. Add the onions to the cooker and cook, stirring, in the remaining oil for about 3 minutes, or until soft. Deglaze the cooker with the soy sauce, scraping up all those crusty, brown bits from the bottom. Add ½ cup water and the remaining ingredients except for the green onion tops, mixing well. Add the ribs, using long-handled tongs to turn each piece, coating with the marinade. Lock the lid in place. Bring to 15psi over high heat, immediately reduce the heat to the lowest possible setting to stabilize and maintain that pressure, and cook for 30 minutes. Remove from the heat and use the natural release method (see page 31) to depressurize. Carefully open the lid after the pressure drops. The meat should be practically falling off the bones; if not, lock the lid back in place, bring to 15psi over high heat, immediately reduce the heat to the lowest possible setting to stabilize and maintain that pressure, and cook for an additional 5 minutes. Remove from the heat and use the natural release method (see page 31) to depressurize. Carefully open the lid after the pressure drops. Using long-handled tongs, remove the ribs to a serving platter. Dot each rib with Horseradish Butter. Sprinkle the toasted sesame seeds and sliced green onion tops over the ribs. Serve the remaining Horseradish Butter on the side. ✳ Serves 4 generously

Beer-Braised Garlicky Beef Short Ribs

Benjamin Franklin once said, "Beer is living proof that God loves us and wants us to be happy." In the pursuit of that happiness, what could be better than meaty ribs braised in beer! The secret ingredient of this recipe is malt liquor, which contains a higher percentage of fermentable sugars, making it slightly sweeter and less bitter than regular beer. Under the high heat of pressure cooking, the alcohol burns away, but the taste remains, and the garlic is infused into the meat.

3 tablespoons olive oil

4 pounds beef short ribs, trimmed of excess fat

1 onion, chopped

1 cup beef broth

1 (12-ounce) bottle malt liquor

1 (28-ounce) can diced tomatoes, with juice

2 carrots, grated

3 tablespoons minced garlic

1 tablespoon sweet paprika (not hot)

1 teaspoon curry powder

1 teaspoon ground cumin

1 teaspoon coarsely ground black pepper

1 teaspoon dry mustard

2 bay leaves

2 tablespoons cornstarch

Heat the oil in the pressure cooker over medium heat. Add the ribs, and cook until browned on all sides. Set the ribs aside on paper towels. Add the onions to the cooker and cook, stirring, for about 3 minutes, or until soft. Deglaze the cooker with the beef broth, scraping up all those crusty, brown bits from the bottom. Add the remaining ingredients except for the cornstarch, mixing well. Return the ribs to the cooker and lock the lid in place. Bring to 15psi over high heat, immediately reduce the heat to the lowest possible setting to stabilize and maintain that pressure, and cook for 30 minutes. Remove from the heat and use the natural release method (see page 31) to depressurize. Carefully open the lid after the pressure drops. The meat should be practically falling off the bones; if not, lock the lid back in place, return to 15psi over high heat, immediately reduce the heat to the lowest possible setting to stabilize and maintain that pressure, and cook for an additional 5 minutes. Remove from the heat and use the natural release method (see page 31 to depressurize. Carefully open the lid after the pressure drops. Using long-handled tongs, carefully remove the short ribs to a serving platter. Discard the bay leaves. Skim off any excess fat from the surface of the sauce. To thicken, mix the cornstarch with ⅓ cup cold water and whisk into the sauce. Simmer gently over medium-low heat as it thickens, but do not boil.

✳ Serves 6

Serving Suggestion: Serve over egg noodles or mashed potatoes.

Mexican Steak Burritos

Another treasure from my box of favorite recipes, and this one features mild Mexican chile peppers, which add spice without being remarkably hot or overwhelming the rest of the ingredients. The infusion cooking method (see page 33) is used to blend all the complex flavors of this dish. I like to arrange all the toppings in a smorgasbord-type setting, letting everyone pick and choose whatever combination they want for their own burritos.

Step One: The Meat

2 tablespoons oil

2 pounds sirloin steak, cut into
    1 × 4-inch strips

1 onion, halved and quartered

2 poblano, pasilla, or Anaheim chiles,
    seeded and cut into strips

1 green bell pepper, seeded and cut into strips

1 cup bottled salsa, hot or mild

1 cup packed chopped cilantro stems and leaves

1 tablespoon chili powder

1 teaspoon ground cumin

Heat the oil in the pressure cooker over medium heat. Add the meat, cook in small batches until browned on all sides, and set each batch aside on paper towels until finished. Add the onion to the cooker and cook, stirring, for about 3 minutes. Add ½ cup water and return the meat to the cooker, along with the chiles, peppers, salsa, cilantro, chili powder, and cumin, stirring to mix. Lock the lid in place. Bring to 15psi over high heat, immediately reduce the heat to the lowest possible setting to stabilize and maintain that pressure, and cook for 8 minutes. Remove from the heat and use the quick release method (see page 30) to depressurize. Carefully open the lid after the pressure drops. Strain, reserving the broth for soups or stews, if desired. Arrange the beef mixture on a serving platter and keep in a warm oven until ready to serve.

Step Two: The Burritos

12 (10- to 12-inch) flour tortillas

2 cups shredded cheddar cheese

2 cups shredded lettuce

3 Roma tomatoes, chopped

1 cup fresh or thawed frozen guacamole

1 cup sour cream

To warm the tortillas, wrap one at a time in a in a damp paper towel and microwave for 20 seconds, or until soft and warm. To serve, spoon ½ cup of the beef mixture in the center of each tortilla, add your choice of toppings, and fold up the bottom and then each side. ✳ Serves 6 generously

Sirloin Tips in Mushroom Gravy Over Wide Noodles

Never has so little time produced something quite so good! Tender sirloin braised with flavorful onions and mushrooms that makes a rich-tasting gravy in this super easy and inexpensive recipe. Best of all, it's one of my popular one-pot meals, which means a fast dinner and a quick cleanup. Serve with a crisp green salad on the side for a complete meal.

½ cup all-purpose flour
½ teaspoon salt
½ teaspoon freshly ground black pepper
1 pound sirloin tips, thinly sliced and cut
    into 2-inch strips
3 tablespoons olive oil
1 onion, chopped
½ pound fresh button mushrooms, washed
    and sliced
1 tablespoon minced garlic
1 cup red wine
3 cups uncooked wide egg noodles
1 (14-ounce) can beef broth

In a plastic bag, mix the flour, salt, and pepper, and add the meat, shaking gently until each piece is lightly coated. Heat the oil in the pressure cooker over medium heat. Add the meat and cook in small batches until browned on all sides, setting each batch aside on paper towels until finished. Add the onions, mushrooms, and garlic to the cooker and cook, stirring, for about 3 minutes. Deglaze the cooker with the wine, scraping up all those crusty, brown bits from the bottom. Return the meat to the cooker; add the uncooked noodles and broth, and stir. Add enough water to cover all the ingredients by 1 inch, pushing the noodles beneath the surface. Lock the lid in place. Bring to 15psi over high heat, immediately reduce the heat to the lowest possible setting to stabilize and maintain that pressure, and cook for 6 minutes. Remove from the heat and use the natural release method (see page 31) to depressurize. Carefully open the lid after the pressure drops. Adjust the seasonings to taste before serving. ❋ Serves 4

Cube Steaks and Gravy with Carrots and Potatoes

This is another one of those old heirloom recipes that has been passed from family to family over the years. The popular cube steak is a speedy, inexpensive main course that's perfect for those hectic weekdays when everybody's got to be somewhere in a hurry.

½ cup all-purpose flour

½ teaspoon salt

½ teaspoon freshly ground black pepper

2 pounds cube steaks

2 tablespoons butter

1 onion, chopped

2 cups beef broth

5 carrots, peeled and thinly sliced

4 potatoes, peeled and cut into ½-inch cubes

In a plastic bag, mix the flour, salt, and pepper, and add the meat, shaking gently until each piece is lightly coated. Heat the butter in the pressure cooker over medium heat, add the meat, and cook in small batches until browned on all sides, setting each batch aside until finished. Add the onions to the cooker and cook, stirring, for about 3 minutes. Deglaze the cooker with the broth, scraping up all those crusty, brown bits from the bottom. Return the meat to the cooker; place the carrots evenly on top of the meat. Place the potatoes in steamer tray, or in a foil packet with the top left open, on top of the carrots. Lock the lid in place. Bring to 15psi over high heat, immediately reduce the heat to the lowest possible setting to stabilize and maintain that pressure, and cook for 6 minutes. Remove from the heat and use the natural release method (see page 31) to depressurize. Carefully open the lid after the pressure drops. Carefully remove the potatoes and prepare the Basic Mashed Potatoes recipe (see page 400). Using a slotted spoon, remove the carrots to a serving bowl and transfer the meat to a serving platter. Skim off any excess fat from the surface of the broth. To thicken, make a slurry with 2 tablespoons of the flour-salt-pepper mixture combined with ½ cup water. Stir the slurry into the broth, simmering gently over medium heat until it reaches the desired consistency. Adjust the seasonings to taste. Serve the gravy in a separate bowl to spoon over the meat and potatoes.

✳ Serves 6

Beef Brisket with Winter Vegetables and Pan Gravy

I use the interrupted cooking method (see page 38) to turn out this extraordinarily tender, slightly spicy brisket with lots of sauce, without overcooking the vegetables. Vary the vegetables to your tastes, or take advantage of whichever varieties are in season.

Step One: The Beef
½ cup all-purpose flour
½ teaspoon salt
½ teaspoon freshly ground black pepper
3 to 4 pounds beef brisket
2 tablespoons oil
1 onion, chopped
1 cup dry red wine
1 (16 ounce) can beef broth
2 tablespoons minced garlic
1 teaspoon ground cinnamon
¼ teaspoon ground nutmeg

In a plastic bag, mix the flour, salt, and pepper, and add the meat, shaking gently until coated. Heat the oil in the pressure cooker over medium heat. Add the meat, cook until browned on both sides, and set aside. Add the onions to the cooker and cook, stirring, for about 3 minutes. Deglaze the cooker with the wine, scraping up all those crusty, brown bits from the bottom. Add the garlic, cinnamon, nutmeg, and stir in the broth. Return the meat to the cooker. Lock the lid in place. Bring to 15psi over high heat, immediately reduce the heat to the lowest possible setting to stabilize and maintain that pressure, and cook for 40 minutes. Remove from the heat and use the quick or cold water release method (see page 30) to depressurize. Carefully open the lid after the pressure drops. Skim the excess fat from the surface of the broth.

Step Two: The Vegetables and Gravy
4 carrots, peeled and sliced 1 inch thick
2 stalks celery, sliced 1 inch thick
2 rutabagas, peeled and sliced 1 inch thick
1 butternut or acorn squash, peeled and
    cut into 1-inch cubes
6 parsnips, peeled and sliced 1 inch thick

Add the vegetables to the pressure cooker. Lock the lid in place. Bring to 15psi over high heat, immediately reduce the heat to the lowest possible setting to stabilize and maintain that pressure, and cook for 5 minutes. Remove from the heat and use the natural release method (see page 31) to depressurize. Carefully open the lid after the pressure drops. Remove the brisket to a large serving platter. Remove the vegetables with a slotted spoon to a large serving bowl. Skim the excess fat from the surface of the broth. To thicken the broth, make a slurry using 2 tablespoons of the flour-salt-pepper mixture combined with ½ cup water. Stir the slurry into the broth, simmering gently over medium heat until it reaches the desired consistency. Adjust the seasonings to taste. Slice the brisket across the grain. Serve the gravy in a separate bowl.

✳ Serves 6

Braised Flank Steak in Mushroom and Onion Gravy

Many years ago, when flank steak was considered a cheap, inexpensive cut of meat, I had several recipes that were regularly cycled through my dinner menus. Now that this cut has become more popular, and more expensive, I developed this recipe from a conglomeration of some of the others. Make the Basic Mashed Potatoes recipe (see pages 400–401) or egg noodles while the meat is cooking in the pressure cooker, add a dinner salad, and in just about 30 minutes, give a shout out to all the hungry people in your family

½ cup all-purpose flour
½ teaspoon salt
½ teaspoon freshly ground black pepper
1 to 2 pounds flank steak
2 tablespoons oil
2 cups coarsely chopped onion
1 (28-ounce) can chopped tomatoes with juice
½ pound fresh mushrooms, washed and thickly
    sliced
1 (1-ounce) packet dried onion soup mix

In a plastic bag, mix the flour, salt, and pepper, and add the meat, shaking gently until coated. Heat the oil in the pressure cooker over medium heat. Add the meat, cook until browned on both sides, and set aside. Add the onions to the cooker and cook, stirring, for about 3 minutes. Deglaze the cooker with 1 cup water. Add the tomatoes, mushroom slices, and soup mix, stirring to mix. Return the meat to the cooker and lock the lid in place. Bring to 15psi over high heat, immediately reduce the heat to the lowest possible setting to stabilize and maintain that pressure, and cook for 35 minutes. Remove from the heat and use the natural release method (see page 31) to depressurize. Carefully open the lid after the pressure drops. Skim off any excess fat from the surface of the broth. Remove the meat to a large serving platter and slice across the grain. To thicken the mushroom gravy, make a slurry using 2 tablespoons of the flour-salt-pepper mixture combined with ½ cup water. Stir the slurry into the broth, simmering gently over medium heat until it reaches the desired consistency. Adjust the seasonings to taste.

Serve the mushroom gravy in a separate bowl.

❊ Serves 4

Braised Dijon Flank Steak in Tomato Gravy

Tomato gravy is a familiar Southern favorite, and there are as many different variations as there are cooks, that will tempt you into tasting this family tradition. This rich gravy is a great complement to the fork-tender and well-seasoned steak. Serve with cooked noodles or use the Basic Mashed Potatoes recipe (see page 400), and a pan of homemade biscuits would go nicely.

2 pounds flank steak

2 tablespoons Dijon-style mustard

1 tablespoon paprika

½ cup all-purpose flour

½ teaspoon salt

½ teaspoon freshly ground black pepper

2 tablespoons olive oil

1 onion, chopped

1 (12-ounce) bottle dark beer

1 cup grated potato

2 teaspoons beef bouillon granules

1 (15-ounce) can crushed tomatoes

Cut the steak into serving portions. Mix the mustard and paprika together and "butter" both sides of each piece. In a plastic bag, mix the flour, salt, and pepper. Add the meat to the flour, coating well. Heat the oil in the pressure cooker over medium heat. Add the meat, cook until browned on both sides, and set aside. Add the onions to the cooker and cook, stirring, until clear, about 3 minutes. Deglaze the cooker with the beer, scraping up all those crusty, brown bits from the bottom. Stir in the potatoes, bouillon, and tomatoes. Return the meat to the cooker and lock the lid in place. Bring to 15psi over high heat, immediately reduce the heat to the lowest possible setting to stabilize and maintain that pressure, and cook for 35 minutes. Remove from the heat and use the natural release method (see page 31) to depressurize. Carefully open the lid after the pressure drops. Remove the meat to a serving platter and keep warm in a low oven until ready to serve. Skim off any excess fat from the surface of the broth, and use a hand blender to puree it, or strain and use a food processor to puree the vegetables and then return them to the broth. Adjust the seasoning to taste. Serve the tomato gravy in a separate bowl. ✳ Serves 4

Brisket of Beef Steamed in Irish Stout

Served either as a main dish or on kaiser rolls for man-sized sandwiches, the beef is melt-in-the-mouth tender.

1 (12-ounce) bottle Irish stout beer, such as Guinness

2 large onions, thickly sliced

1 tablespoon dried Italian herb blend

1 tablespoon coarsely ground black pepper

1 teaspoon sweet paprika

6 fresh basil leaves

2 bay leaves

4 pounds beef brisket

Prepared horseradish, for garnish

Pour the beer into the cooker and add the onions, herb blend, pepper, paprika, basil, and bay leaves, stirring to mix. Place the meat in the cooker and lock the lid in place. Bring to 15psi over high heat, immediately reduce the heat to the lowest possible setting to stabilize and maintain that pressure, and cook for 55 minutes. Remove from the heat and use the natural release method (see page 31) to depressurize. Carefully open the lid after the pressure drops. Place the brisket on a cutting board, letting it rest for about 5 minutes, and then slice thinly across the grain. Serve with prepared horseradish. ✳ Serves 6 generously

Corned Beef Brisket in Irish Stout with Traditional Vegetables

When I was newly married, the butcher at my market gave me precise instructions on how to cook a corned beef, insisting that the only proper way was to braise it in a good-quality beer. I followed his instructions carefully, and some four hours later, I thought I'd better adapt the recipe to the pressure cooker. If you have two pressure cookers, this is the time to use them both, otherwise cook the meat first, and then the bulky vegetables separately.

Step One: The Beef
4 pounds lean corned beef brisket
1 cup dark brown sugar
2 onions, quartered
1 (12-ounce) bottle Irish stout beer, such as Guinness

Rinse the beef, discard the included pickling spices, and pat dry. Rub the brown sugar into the beef, coating the entire surface. Place the rack in the cooker and pour in the beer. Add the onions and lay the corned beef brisket on top sprinkling any remaining brown sugar over the meat. Lock the lid in place. Bring to 15psi over high heat, immediately reduce the heat to the lowest possible setting to stabilize and maintain that pressure, and cook for 45 minutes. Remove from the heat and use the natural release method (see page 31) to depressur-

ize. Carefully open the lid after the pressure drops. Remove the meat to a serving platter and keep warm in a low oven until ready to serve. Slice the corned beef across the grain just before serving.

Step Two: The Vegetables
1 head cabbage, cored and cut into wedges
8 red potatoes, unpeeled and quartered
5 carrots, cut lengthwise and quartered
Prepared horseradish, for garnish

Add rack or steamer tray to the pressure cooker and poor in 1 cup water. Add the cabbage, potatoes, and carrots and lock the lid in place. Bring to 15psi over high heat, immediately reduce the heat to the lowest possible setting to stabilize and maintain that pressure, and cook for 5 minutes. Remove from the heat and use the quick or cold water release method (see page 30) to depressurize. Carefully open the lid after the pressure drops. Using a slotted spoon, remove the vegetables to a large serving bowl. Pass the horseradish at the table.

✳ Serves 6 generously

Swiss Steak

A vintage recipe, and certainly a comfort food, this dish is associated with a pleasant childhood memory of visits to Grandma's house. With just a few stock cupboard items, a humble round steak, and a pressure cooker, this tender entrée is sure to please. Serve this over the Basic Mashed Potatoes recipe (see page 400), try the Horseraddish or Garlic versions, or even wide egg noodles.

1½ to 2 pounds round steak
½ cup all-purpose flour
½ teaspoon salt
½ teaspoon freshly ground black pepper
2 tablespoons olive oil
1 onion, chopped
½ cup red wine
1 (28-ounce) can chopped tomatoes, with juice
1 (3-ounce) can tomato paste
2 green bell peppers, seeded and chopped
2 tablespoons minced garlic
1 tablespoon dried oregano
1 tablespoon dried basil
1 teaspoon crushed dried rosemary
Pinch of red pepper flakes
2 tablespoons cornstarch

Cut the steak into serving portions. In a plastic bag, mix the flour, salt, and pepper, and add the meat, shaking gently until coated. Heat the oil in the pressure cooker over medium heat. Add the meat, cook until browned on both sides, and set aside. Add the onions to the cooker and cook, stirring, for about 3 minutes. Deglaze the cooker with the wine, scraping up all those crusty, brown bits from the bottom. Add the tomatoes, tomato paste, bell pepper, garlic, oregano, basil, rosemary, and red pepper flakes, stirring well. Return the meat to the cooker and lock the lid in place. Bring to 15psi over high heat, immediately reduce the heat to the lowest possible setting to stabilize and maintain that pressure, and cook for 18 minutes. Remove from the heat and use the natural release method (see page 31) to depressurize. Carefully open the lid after the pressure drops. Carefully open the lid after the pressure drops. Remove the meat to a serving plate. Thicken the sauce by making a slurry with the cornstarch mixed with ⅓ cup cold water; stir the slurry into the broth and simmer gently over medium heat, stirring often as it thickens, but do not boil. Adjust the seasonings to taste. Pour the gravy into a separate serving bowl.

✳ Serves 4

Italian-Style Beef Roast Braised in Red Wine with Gravy

Tender and full of Italian seasonings with flavorful gravy, the roast can be served as an entrée with your choice of side dishes, or simply sliced for sandwiches.

½ cup all-purpose flour
½ teaspoon salt
½ teaspoon freshly ground black pepper
3 pounds boneless beef rump or chuck roast
2 tablespoons olive oil
2 medium-size onions, chopped
½ cup Chianti or other light red wine
1 cup beef stock
1 (28-ounce) can Italian-style stewed tomatoes, with juice
1 cup grated carrots
1 cup finely chopped fresh parsley stems and leaves
2 tablespoons minced garlic
1 tablespoon dried oregano
1 tablespoon dried crushed rosemary
1 tablespoon dried thyme
2 bay leaves

In a plastic bag, mix the flour, salt, and pepper, and add the meat, shaking gently until it is lightly coated. Heat the oil in the pressure cooker over medium-high heat. Add the meat, cook until well browned on all sides, and set aside. Add the onions to the cooker and cook, stirring, until clear, about 3 minutes. Deglaze the cooker with the wine, scraping up all those crusty, brown bits from the bottom. Add the beef stock, tomatoes, carrots, parsley, garlic, oregano, rosemary, thyme, and bay leaves, stirring to mix. Lock the lid in place. Bring to 15psi over high heat, immediately reduce the heat to the lowest possible setting to stabilize and maintain that pressure, and cook for 35 minutes. Remove from the heat and use the natural release method (see page 31) to depressurize. Carefully open the lid after the pressure drops. Remove the roast to a serving platter and slice across the grain. Remove the bay leaves and skim off any excess fat from the surface of the broth. Use a hand blender to puree the broth, or strain and use a food processor to puree the vegetables and then return them to the broth. To thicken the broth, make a slurry using 2 tablespoons of the flour-salt-pepper mixture mixed with ½ cup water. Stir the slurry into the broth, simmering gently over medium heat until it reaches the desired consistency. Adjust the seasonings to taste. Pour the gravy into a separate serving bowl to accompany the meat. ✳ Serves 4

Beef Stroganoff with Noodles

A classic Russian recipe in a pressure cooker? Who knew! Leave it to good old American ingenuity to come up with a faster means to an end by adapting this popular favorite to the pressure cooker. I use the interrupted cooking method (see page 38) to serve up succulent, tender beef and noodles that are not overcooked. There's the added bonus that it's not only quick and simple to prepare, but it's also loaded with oodles of flavor. Of course, the fact that it's a one-pot meal is another big attraction, because it gets me out of the kitchen all the faster.

Step One: The Beef
2 tablespoons butter
1 onion, finely chopped
½ pound fresh mushrooms, washed and sliced
1½ pounds beef round steak, cut into 3 × ½-inch strips
½ cup red wine
2 (14-ounce) cans beef broth
1 tablespoon Worcestershire sauce
1 (1-ounce) packet dried onion soup mix
½ teaspoon freshly ground black pepper

Heat the butter in a pressure cooker over medium heat. Add the onions and mushrooms and cook, stirring, for about 3 minutes, then set aside. Add the meat, cook until well browned on all sides, and set aside. Deglaze the cooker with the wine, scraping up all those crusty, brown bits from the bottom. Return the meat, mushrooms, and onions to the cooker and add the broth, Worcestershire sauce, soup mix, and pepper, and stir. Lock the lid in place. Bring to 15psi over high heat, immediately reduce the heat to the lowest possible setting to stabilize and maintain that pressure, and cook for 8 minutes. Remove from the heat and use the quick or cold water release method (see page 30) to depressurize. Carefully open the lid after the pressure drops.

Step Two: The Noodles and Gravy
3 cups uncooked wide egg noodles
1 cup sour cream

Add the noodles and enough water to cover all the ingredients, pushing the noodles under the liquid. Lock the lid in place. Bring to 15psi over high heat, immediately reduce the heat to the lowest possible setting to stabilize and maintain that pressure, and cook for 6 minutes. Remove from the heat and use the natural release method (see page 31) to depressurize. Carefully open the lid after the pressure drops. Gently stir in the sour cream, mixing thoroughly, and serve. ❈ **Serves 4 generously**

Mexican Roast Beef with Vegetables and Roasted Chiptole-Salsa Sauce

Olé! Add some spicy flavor to an ordinary pot roast and go Mexican style with this recipe using traditional south-of-the-border ingredients. This is an entire meal with a roast, vegetables, and uniquely flavored gravy all from one pot and in record-breaking time, so your cleanup time will be greatly reduced.

Step One: The Roasted Salsa

4 (¼- to ½-ounce) dried chipotle chiles, or
 1 (7-ounce) can chipotle chiles in adobo sauce
1 small head of garlic, unpeeled
6 medium-size tomatillos, husked, rinsed, and
 halved
½ cup finely chopped cilantro stems and leaves

If using dried chiles, heat a heavy (cast iron works best) skillet over medium heat. Cut open the chiles and remove the stems and seeds. Cut the larger chiles in smaller pieces and place them in the hot skillet to toast, pressing flat with a spatula until they darken slightly and release their aromas. Watch closely, as this only takes about 60 seconds. Do not over-toast the chiles or they will have a bitter taste. In a small bowl, cover the toasted chiles with boiling water and let them soak for 30 minutes. Drain, and discard the water. While the chiles

are soaking, preheat the broiler. Cut off the tip of the garlic head, slicing through the top of the cloves. Place the head of garlic on a plate, cut side up, and cover tightly with microwave-safe plastic wrap. Microwave for about 5 minutes, or until the cloves of garlic have softened. Remove the plate from the microwave. Remove the plastic wrap and let stand until cool enough to handle. Pull the cloves apart and squeeze out the garlic. Roast the tomatillos on a baking sheet 4 inches below the broiler until blackened on one side, about 5 minutes. Use long-handled tongs to turn and roast the other side. Put the tomatillos and any juice, the chiles, garlic, and cilantro into a food processor or blender and process to a fine-textured puree.

Step Two: The Roast

3 to 4 pounds boneless beef round, chuck,
 or rump roast
½ cup all-purpose flour
1 to 2 tablespoons vegetable oil
2 Spanish onions, thickly sliced into rings
1 (12-ounce) bottle Mexican beer
2 teaspoons ground cumin
½ teaspoon salt
½ teaspoon freshly ground black pepper
2 medium-size pasilla, poblano, or Anaheim
 chiles, seeded and cut into strips
4 medium-size carrots, peeled and cut into
 ½-inch rounds
2 chayote squash, peeled, pitted, and cut into
 1-inch cubes
6 medium-size red potatoes, scrubbed and
 quartered
2 cups frozen whole-kernel corn

Dry the meat on paper towels and dredge in the flour. Heat the oil in the pressure cooker over medium-high heat. Add the meat, cook until well browned on all sides, and set aside. Add the onions and cook, stirring, until they are deeply browned and well caramelized, about 8 minutes. Deglaze the cooker with the beer, scraping up all the browned bits. Stir in the salsa mixture, cumin, salt, and pepper. Return the roast to the cooker and lock the lid in place. Bring to 15psi over high heat, immediately reduce the heat to the lowest possible setting to stabilize and maintain that pressure, and cook for 35 minutes. Remove from the heat and use the natural release method (see page 31) to depressurize. Carefully open the lid after the pressure drops. Turn the meat over and add the chiles, carrots, chayotes, potatoes, and corn, distributing them evenly. Lock the lid in place. Bring to 15psi over high heat, immediately reduce the heat to the lowest possible setting to stabilize and maintain that pressure, and cook for 5 minutes more. Remove from the heat and use the quick or cold water release method (see page 30) to depressurize. Carefully open the lid after the pressure drops. Transfer the roast to a serving platter and slice across the grain. Scoop out the vegetables with a slotted spoon, transfer to a large serving bowl. Skim off any excess fat from the surface of the sauce. Adjust the seasoning to taste. Pour the salsa sauce into a serving bowl to ladle over the meat and vegetables. ✳ Serves 6

Cook's Note: Substitute a pork roast for the beef for an interesting variation to this recipe.

Steak Pizzaiola

Anyone remember this old-fashioned Italian-American recipe? Combine steak and pasta with the flavors of pizza, and here is a decep-

tively simple but excellent alternative way to serve a flank steak.

2 pounds flank steak
2 tablespoons olive oil
1 onion, sliced
½ pound of fresh mushrooms, washed and sliced
1 green bell pepper, seeded and chopped
1 red bell pepper, seeded and chopped
2 tablespoons minced garlic
1 tablespoon dried basil
1 (14-ounce) can crushed tomatoes

If possible, ask the butcher to tenderize the flank steak at the meat counter. To do this yourself, place the meat between 2 pieces of plastic wrap and use a mallet, pounding both sides until the meat is thin. Cut the steak into serving portions. Heat the oil in the pressure cooker over medium-high heat. Add each portion of meat, cook until browned on both sides, and set aside. Add the onions to the cooker and cook, stirring, until clear, about 3 minutes. Add the mushrooms, peppers, garlic, basil, and crushed tomatoes to the cooker, return the meat to the cooker, and stir. Lock the lid in place. Bring to 15psi over high heat, immediately reduce the heat to the lowest possible setting to stabilize and maintain that pressure, and cook for 12 minutes. Remove from the heat and use the natural release method (see page 31) to depressurize. Carefully open the lid after the pressure drops. Transfer the meat to a platter and pour the sauce into a separate bowl for serving. ✳ Serves 6

Serving Suggestion: Serve the sauce over cooked spaghetti or any pasta of choice, or use mashed potatoes.

Beef Short Ribs with Potatoes and Carrots in Mushroom Gravy

In my opinion, the pressure cooker is the only way to prepare short ribs, and this recipe is *the* best! The ribs are so quick and easy to fix, not to mention so tender and delicious, that you'll want to serve them often.

Step One: The Beef

½ cup all-purpose flour
½ teaspoon salt
½ teaspoon freshly ground black pepper
3 pounds beef short ribs
2 tablespoons oil
1 onion, coarsely chopped
½ cup red wine
1 (1-ounce) packet dried onion soup mix

In a plastic bag, mix the flour, salt, and pepper, and add the meat, shaking gently until coated. Heat the oil in the pressure cooker over medium heat. Add the meat, cook until browned on both sides, and set aside. Add the onions to the cooker and cook, stirring, for about 3 minutes. Deglaze the cooker with the wine, scraping up all those crusty, brown bits from the bottom. Add the soup mix and 2 cups water, stirring to mix. Return the meat to the cooker and lock the lid in place. Bring to 15psi over high heat, immediately reduce the heat to the lowest possible setting to stabilize and maintain that pressure, and cook for 25 minutes. Remove from the heat and use the quick or cold water release method (see page 30) to depressurize. Carefully open the lid after the pressure drops.

Step Two: The Vegetables and Gravy

1 (10-ounce) can condensed mushroom soup
6 potatoes, peeled and quartered
4 carrots, peeled and quartered
½ pound fresh mushrooms, washed and
 thickly sliced
2 tablespoons cornstarch

Stir in the mushroom soup. Add the potatoes, carrots, and mushrooms and stir. Lock the lid in place. Bring to 15psi over high heat, immediately reduce the heat to the lowest possible setting to stabilize and maintain that pressure, and cook for 5 minutes more. Remove from the heat and use the natural release method (see page 31) to depressurize. Carefully open the lid after the pressure drops. Using a slotted spoon, remove the vegetables to a serving bowl, and place the short ribs on a platter. Thicken the sauce by making a slurry with the cornstarch mixed with ⅓ cup cold water; stir the slurry into the broth and simmer gently over medium heat, stirring often as it thickens, but do not boil. Adjust the seasonings to taste and serve the gravy in a separate bowl. ❋ **Serves 6**

Steak and Cheesy Macaroni Dinner

Unearthed from the family-heirloom recipe shoebox, the original version of this recipe was handwritten on the back of a letter dating from shortly after World War II. The original instructions included home-canned tomatoes, so there have been a few minor adjustments in keeping with more modern times.

Step One: The Beef
2 tablespoons oil
1 pound round steak, sliced into
    3 × ½-inch strips
1 onion, chopped
1 (28-ounce) can chopped tomatoes,
    with juice
1 (3-ounce) can tomato paste
1 green bell pepper, seeded and chopped
2 tablespoons mild paprika
1 tablespoon minced garlic

Heat the oil in the pressure cooker over medium heat, add the meat, cook until browned on all sides, and set aside. Add the onions to the cooker and cook, stirring, for about 3 minutes. Deglaze the cooker with ½ cup water, scraping up all those crusty, brown bits from the bottom. Add the tomatoes, tomato paste, bell pepper, paprika, and garlic, stirring to mix. Lock the lid in place. Bring to 15psi over high heat, immediately reduce the heat to the lowest possible setting to stabilize and maintain that pressure, and cook for 8 minutes. Remove from the heat and use the natural release method (see page 31) to depressurize. Carefully open the lid after the pressure drops.

Step Two: The Macaroni
3 cups large elbow macaroni
2 cups grated sharp cheddar cheese

Add the macaroni and enough water to cover all the ingredients, pushing the macaroni under the liquid. Lock the lid in place. Bring to 15psi over high heat, immediately reduce the heat to the lowest possible setting to stabilize and maintain that pressure, and cook for 6 minutes. Remove from the heat and use the natural release method (see page 31) to depressurize. Carefully open the lid after the pressure drops. Gently stir in the cheese. Cover with a regular lid and let stand for about 5 minutes, or until the cheese has melted and any excess liquid is absorbed. ※ Serves 4

Old-Fashioned German Sauerbraten

Given my grandmother's German heritage, this recipe has been in our family for as long as anyone can remember, and the notes say it was made with venison when beef was scarce. I'm sure the original recipe has a long history, and probably an equally long cooking time until somewhere over the years it was adapted to the pressure cooker. Serve this spicy dish with cooked cabbage and potatoes and some dark rye bread.

Step One: The Marinade
3 to 4 pounds rump roast
2 teaspoons freshly ground black pepper
1 small lemon, sliced
2 cloves garlic, peeled and crushed
8 whole cloves
3 bay leaves
10 whole black peppercorns

½ cup dry red wine
½ cup malt vinegar
¼ cup balsamic vinegar
1 onion, coarsely chopped
⅓ cup packed dark brown sugar
2 teaspoons salt

Rinse the roast and pat dry with a paper towel. Rub the meat with the ground pepper and place it in a large glass bowl. Tie the sliced lemon, garlic, cloves, bay leaves, and peppercorns in a small square of cheesecloth for easy removal. Combine the spice bag, 1 cup water, the wine, vinegars, onions, sugar, and salt in a small sauce pan and bring to a rapid boil over high heat, stirring to dissolve the sugar. Immediately remove from the heat and let the marinade cool to room temperature before pouring the mixture over the meat. Cover the bowl tightly with plastic wrap and refrigerate for 48 hours, turning the meat every 8 hours.

Step Two: The Beef
2 tablespoons vegetable oil
1 onion, coarsely chopped
4 carrots, coarsely chopped
2 stalks celery, coarsely chopped
¾ cup finely crushed gingersnap cookies

Heat the oil in the pressure cooker over medium-high heat. Remove the meat from the marinade and cook until well browned on all sides, and set aside. Add the onions to the cooker and cook, stirring, until clear, about 3 minutes. Place the carrots and celery on the bottom of the cooker, pour in the marinade, and add the spice bag. Place the meat on top and lock the lid in place. Bring to 15psi over high heat, immediately reduce the heat to the lowest possible setting to stabilize and maintain that pressure, and cook for 40 minutes. Remove from the heat and use the natural release method (see page 31) to depressurize. Carefully open the lid after the pressure drops. Remove the beef to a serving platter and keep in a warm oven; slice across the grain just before serving. Discard the spice bag. Skim off any excess fat from the surface of the broth. Using a hand blender, puree the broth and vegetables to a fine texture, or place the vegetables in a food processor, blend until smooth, and return to the broth. Bring the broth to a boil over medium heat. Reduce the heat, and slowly stir in the gingersnap crumbs. Continue stirring as the sauce thickens. Serve in a separate bowl to ladle over the meat. ✳ Serves 6

Veal Osso Buco

This is a well-known dish that's popular in pressure cookery because it cuts hours off the cooking time. Serve over almost anything, including polenta, orzo, or spaghetti, or even potatoes. A crunchy bread is a must . . . you'll need something for all that tasty sauce, after all.

4 pounds veal shanks, cut 1 inch thick
½ cup all-purpose flour
½ teaspoon salt
½ teaspoon freshly ground black pepper
3 tablespoons olive oil
1 onion, coarsely chopped
½ cup dry red wine
1 (28-ounce) can chopped tomatoes,
   with juice
1 (14-ounce) can beef broth
2 tablespoons tomato paste
2 tablespoons balsamic vinegar
2 carrots, coarsely chopped
1 stalk celery, thinly sliced
8 ounces fresh mushrooms, sliced
3 tablespoons minced garlic
1 tablespoon dried basil
1 tablespoon dried oregano
¼ teaspoon ground nutmeg

Rinse the veal shanks, and pat dry with paper towels. In a plastic bag, mix the flour, salt, and pepper, and add the meat, shaking gently until coated. Heat the oil in the pressure cooker over medium heat. Add the meat, cook until browned on both sides, and set aside. Add the onions to the cooker and cook, stirring, until soft, about 3 minutes. Deglaze the cooker with the wine, scraping up all those crusty, brown bits from the bottom. Add the tomatoes, broth, tomato paste, vinegar, carrots, celery, mushrooms, garlic, basil, oregano, and nutmeg, and stir. Lock the lid in place. Bring to 15psi over high heat, immediately reduce the heat to the lowest possible setting to stabilize and maintain that pressure, and cook for 20 minutes. Remove from the heat and use the natural release method (see page 31) to depressurize. Carefully open the lid after the pressure drops. Remove the shanks to a serving platter. Adjust the seasonings to taste and serve the sauce in a gravy boat. ✳ Serves 6

Beef Tagine

Many years ago, I went to a charity function based on the theme of a Persian bazaar, where several food stalls supplied Middle Eastern cuisine. After trying one dish in particular, I couldn't wait to get home and apply a little reverse engineering to come up with my own version. This exotic stew tastes as delicious as it smells, with wonderful aromas of garlic, cinnamon, lemons, and honey. Serve with plain white rice, couscous, or a rice pilaf.

2 tablespoons ground cinnamon

2 tablespoons paprika

1 tablespoon ground turmeric

1 teaspoon freshly ground black pepper

1 teaspoon ground ginger

½ teaspoon cayenne pepper

2 pounds round steak, cut into 2-inch cubes

½ cup all-purpose flour

2 tablespoons olive oil

2 onions, diced

1 cup tomato juice

1 (28-ounce) can diced or chopped tomatoes, with juice

1 cup grated carrots

½ cup dried apricots, cut in half

½ cup pitted dates, cut in half

½ cup raisins

½ cup pitted green olives, sliced

½ cup packed coarsely chopped cilantro stems and leaves

3 tablespoons minced garlic

½ teaspoon red pepper flakes

Zest of 1 lemon

Juice of 1 lemon

1 (14-ounce) can beef broth

1 teaspoon saffron stamens soaked in 2 tablespoons cold water

2 tablespoons honey

⅓ cup flaked or slivered almonds, toasted

Mix the cinnamon, paprika, turmeric, black pepper, ginger, and cayenne pepper in a small bowl. Rinse the beef and pat dry with paper towels. On a sheet of waxed paper, rub the ground spices into the meat and then dredge in the flour. Heat the oil in the pressure cooker over medium-high heat. Add the meat and any remaining spice rub, cooking until well browned on all sides, and set aside. Add the onions and cook, stirring, until clear, about 3 minutes. Deglaze the cooker with the tomato juice, scraping up all those crusty, brown bits from the bottom. Add the tomatoes, carrots, apricots, dates, raisins, olives, cilantro, garlic, red pepper flakes, and lemon zest. Stir in the lemon juice, beef broth, and the saffron and its soaking water. Return the meat to the cooker and lock the lid in place. Bring to 15psi over high heat, immediately reduce the heat to the lowest possible setting to stabilize and maintain that pressure, and cook for 20 minutes. Remove from the heat and use the natural release method (see page 31) to depressurize. Carefully open the lid after the pressure drops. Skim off any excess fat from the surface of the broth. To thicken the broth, make a slurry using 2 tablespoons of the flour and ½ cup water. Stir the slurry into the broth, simmering gently over medium heat until it reaches the desired consistency. Add the honey and almonds. Place in a large serving bowl. ✳ Serves 6

Serving Suggestion: Serve over cooked rice, orzo, noodles, or the traditional couscous.

Old-Fashioned Pot Roast with Potatoes, Carrots, and Gravy

Flavorful and oh so tender, this pot roast has plenty of onions and a rich brown gravy with a touch of sage; this is the best pot roast ever, and guaranteed to please. Don't mention that it wasn't simmering in the oven all day, and take credit for all your "hard" work in serving a wonderful dinner.

Step One: The Beef

½ cup all-purpose flour
½ teaspoon salt
½ teaspoon freshly ground black pepper
2 to 3 pounds beef chuck or round roast
3 tablespoons oil
2 onions, cut in half and then quartered
½ cup red wine
1 (3-ounce) can tomato paste
2 tablespoons minced garlic
2 teaspoons ground sage
1 teaspoon dried thyme leaves
2 bay leaves

In a plastic bag, mix the flour, salt, and pepper, and add the meat, shaking gently until each piece is lightly coated. Heat the oil in the pressure cooker over medium-high heat. Add the meat, cook until well browned on all sides, and set aside. Add the onions to the cooker and cook, stirring, until clear, about 3 minutes. Deglaze the cooker with the wine, scraping up all those crusty, brown bits from the bottom. Add the tomato paste, garlic, sage, thyme, bay leaves, and 2 cups water, stirring to blend. Lock the lid in place. Bring to 15psi over high heat, immediately reduce the heat to the lowest possible setting to stabilize and maintain that pressure, and cook for 30 minutes. Remove from the heat and use the quick or cold water release method (see page 30) to depressurize. Carefully open the lid after the pressure drops.

Step Two: The Vegetables and Gravy

4 potatoes, peeled and quartered
6 carrots, peeled, halved, and then quartered
2 stalks celery, cut into 1-inch slices

Arrange the potatoes, carrots, and celery around the meat. Lock the lid in place, return to 15psi over high heat, immediately reduce the heat to the lowest possible setting to stabilize and maintain that pressure, and cook for an additional 4 minutes. Remove from the heat and use the natural release method (see page 31) to depressurize. Carefully open the lid after the pressure drops. Use a slotted spoon to transfer the vegetables to a serving bowl. Remove the roast to a serving plate. Discard the bay leaves. Skim off any excess fat from the surface of the broth. To thicken the broth, make a slurry using 2 tablespoons of the flour-salt-pepper mixture mixed with ½ cup water. Stir the slurry into the broth, simmering gently over medium heat until it reaches the desired consistency. Adjust the seasonings to taste. Pour the gravy into a separate serving bowl to ladle over the meat and vegetables as desired. ❋ Serves 6

Apple Cider-Braised Beef Pot Roast with Sour Cream Gravy

This recipe is easy to make and always pleases. The combination of sweet cider and vinegar adds a delicate sweet-sour taste to this deliciously tender pot roast. Try serving it with mashed sweet potatoes instead of mashed white potatoes.

2 tablespoons oil
3 to 4 pounds boneless beef round or
    chuck roast
1 onion, thinly sliced
1 cup sweet apple cider
½ cup malt or cider vinegar
¼ cup packed brown sugar
1 teaspoon freshly ground black pepper
1 teaspoon ground allspice
½ teaspoon ground cinnamon
2 bay leaves
2 tablespoons cornstarch
1 cup sour cream

Heat the oil in the pressure cooker over medium-high heat. Add the meat, cook until well browned on all sides, and set aside. Add the onions to the cooker and cook, stirring, until clear, about 3 minutes. Deglaze the cooker with the apple cider, scraping up all those crusty, brown bits from the bottom. Add the vinegar, brown sugar, pepper, allspice, cinnamon, and bay leaves and stir. Return the meat to the cooker and lock the lid in place. Bring to 15psi over high heat, immediately reduce the heat to the lowest possible setting to stabilize and maintain that pressure, and cook for 35 minutes. Remove from the heat and use the natural release method (see page 31) to depressurize. Carefully open the lid after the pressure drops. Lift the meat to a serving platter and let stand for about 10 minutes before slicing across the grain. Discard the bay leaves. Skim off any excess fat from the surface of the broth. To thicken the broth, make a slurry using the cornstarch mixed with ½ cup water. Stir the slurry into the broth, simmering gently over medium heat until it reaches the desired consistency. Add the sour cream, blending well, and adjust the seasonings to taste. Pour the gravy into a sauce boat. ✳ Serves 6

Serving Suggestion: Serve with mashed or boiled potatoes.

Swiss Steak with Potatoes and Onion Gravy

This vintage recipe is a longtime family favorite, and it was a frequent main dish on our table because it was not only very tasty, but it was easy on the budget as well. It comes with plenty of rich tomato gravy, so plan on serving this dish with either mashed potatoes or egg noodles.

Step One: The Beef

½ cup all-purpose flour

½ teaspoon salt

½ teaspoon freshly ground black pepper

2 pounds round steak, cut into serving portions

2 tablespoons oil

1 onion, diced

1 (14-ounce) can beef broth

1 (28-ounce) can chopped tomatoes, with juice

2 tablespoons tomato paste

2 stalks celery, sliced

¼ pound fresh mushrooms, washed and sliced

1 bell pepper, seeded and diced

1 (1-ounce) packet dried onion soup mix

2 tablespoons dried oregano

1 tablespoon dried basil

2 teaspoons minced garlic

Generous pinch of red pepper flakes

In a plastic bag, mix the flour, salt, and pepper, and add the meat, shaking gently until coated. Reserve the excess flour mixture. Heat the oil in the pressure cooker over medium heat. Add the meat, cook until browned on both sides, and set aside. Add the onions to the cooker and cook, stirring, until clear, about 3 minutes. Deglaze the cooker with the broth, scraping up all those crusty, brown bits from the bottom. Add the tomatoes, tomato paste, celery, mushrooms, and bell peppers. Stir in the soup mix, oregano, basil, garlic, and red pepper flakes. Return the meat to the cooker and lock the lid in place. Bring to 15psi over high heat, immediately reduce the heat to the lowest possible setting to stabilize and maintain that pressure, and cook for 16 minutes. Use the quick or cold water release method (see page 30) to depressurize. Carefully open the lid after the pressure drops.

Step Two: The Potatoes and Gravy

4 to 5 medium-size potatoes, peeled and halved

Add the potatoes, arranging them around the roast. Lock the lid in place and return to 15psi over high heat, immediately reduce the heat to the lowest possible setting to stabilize and maintain that pressure, and cook for an additional 5 minutes. Remove from the heat and use the natural release method (see page 31) to depressurize. Carefully open the lid after the pressure drops. Arrange the meat and potatoes on a serving platter. Skim off any excess fat from the surface of the broth. To thicken the broth, make a slurry using 2 tablespoons of the flour-salt-pepper mixture mixed with ½ cup water. Stir the slurry into the broth, simmering gently over medium heat until it reaches the desired consistency. Serve the gravy in a separate bowl. ※ **Serves 4 generously**

Fajita Beef Platter

This is a fun meal that kids just love. I like to arrange all the toppings on the table in a buffet style, and let everyone pass by and help themselves to the ones they like best. It's great for a light dinner or lunch, or just for munching in front of the TV when friends drop by.

2 tablespoons olive oil
2 pounds boneless round or chuck steak,
    cut in strips about ½ inch wide by
    3 inches long
1 onion, sliced
1 cup bottled salsa
2 green bell peppers, seeded and chopped
2 tablespoons minced garlic
2 tablespoons chili powder
2 teaspoons ground cumin
1 small bunch cilantro, leaves only, chopped
1 (14-ounce) can refried beans
2 cups coarsely shredded iceberg lettuce
3 to 4 Roma tomatoes, chopped
½ cup chopped green onion tops
1 (15.5-ounce) package of your favorite
    tortilla chips
1 (14-ounce) can pitted black olives, drained
    and sliced
1 cup sour cream
1 cup fresh or thawed frozen guacamole
2 cups shredded jalapeño Jack cheese

Heat the oil in the pressure cooker over medium-high heat. Add the meat and cook until well browned on all sides. Add the onions to the cooker and cook, stirring, until clear, about 3 minutes. Add the salsa, green peppers, garlic, chili powder, cumin, and cilantro and stir. Lock the lid in place. Bring to 15psi over high heat, immediately reduce the heat to the lowest possible setting to stabilize and maintain that pressure, and cook for 12 minutes. Remove from the heat and use the natural release method (see page 31) to depressurize. Carefully open the lid after the pressure drops. Bring the contents to a boil over medium heat, uncovered, stirring occasionally, until reduced by half. Stir in the refried beans, and simmer until thoroughly heated. To serve, mound the beef and bean mixture in the center of a large serving platter. Arrange the shredded lettuce around the outer edge, and place the chopped tomatoes on top of the lettuce. Sprinkle the chopped green onions on top of the meat mixture. Place the tortilla chips in a large bowl, and the black olives, sour cream, guacamole, and cheese in separate bowls for individual selections. To serve, mound a handful of tortilla chips on a plate and add a helping of the beef and bean mixture, topping with some lettuce and tomatoes. Add other toppings according to taste. ✳ Serves 6

Beef Ragoût
with Mushrooms
and Olives

While you're waiting the 15 minutes for this recipe, put a Bocelli CD on the stereo, pop the cork on a nice red wine, and enjoy a little aromatherapy as this fabulous dish cooks.
I like serving this ragoût over any variety of pasta—penne, rotini, and even spinach linguine are all good choices—and include lots of garlic toast, of course.

1 tablespoon olive oil

1½ to 2 pounds beef round or chuck steak, trimmed of fat and cut into 1-inch cubes

1 onion, chopped

1 (28-ounce) can crushed tomatoes, with juice

1 (3-ounce) can tomato sauce

1 green bell pepper, seeded and chopped

2 stalks celery, sliced

½ pound fresh mushrooms, washed and thickly sliced

1 (14-ounce) can pitted black olives, drained and sliced

2 tablespoons minced garlic

Zest of 1 orange

2 teaspoons ground tarragon

½ teaspoon red pepper flakes

2 tablespoons cornstarch

Heat the oil in the pressure cooker over medium-high heat. Add the meat and cook until well browned on all sides. Add the onions to the cooker and cook, stirring, until clear, about 3 minutes.

Add the tomatoes, tomato sauce, peppers, celery, mushrooms, olives, and garlic. Add 1 cup of water, stirring to mix, and then add all the remaining ingredients except the cornstarch. Lock the lid in place. Bring to 15psi over high heat, immediately reduce the heat to the lowest possible setting to stabilize and maintain that pressure, and cook for 15 minutes. Remove from the heat and use the natural release method (see page 31) to depressurize. Carefully open the lid after the pressure drops. Skim off any excess fat from the surface of the broth. Thicken the sauce by making a slurry with the cornstarch mixed with ⅓ cup cold water; stir the slurry into the sauce and simmer gently over medium heat, stirring often as it thickens, but do not boil. Adjust the seasonings to taste and serve. ✳ Serves 4

Shredded Salsa Beef Sandwiches

Tender beef, fragrant with garlic, gets piled high on these big, man-sized sandwiches. Add sliced pepper Jack cheese, lettuce, and sliced tomatoes for variety.

2 to 3 pounds brisket, trimmed of fat and
    cut into 4 pieces
2 tablespoons butter or margarine
1 onion, chopped
2 tablespoons minced garlic
1 cup bottled salsa
½ cup packed finely minced cilantro leaves
2 tablespoons chili powder
2 teaspoons ground cumin
6 kaiser, hoagie, or onion rolls, lightly toasted
3 green onion tops, sliced

Place the rack in the bottom of the pressure cooker. Add 2 cups water. Arrange the chunks of beef on the rack and lock the lid in place. Bring to 15psi over high heat, immediately reduce the heat to the lowest possible setting to stabilize and maintain that pressure, and cook for 50 minutes. Remove the cooker from the heat and use the natural release method (see page 31) to depressurize. Carefully open the lid after the pressure drops. Check the meat for doneness; it should shred easily with a fork. If needed, lock the lid back in place, return to 15psi over high heat, immediately reduce the heat to the lowest possible setting to stabilize and maintain that pressure, and cook for an additional 5 minutes, or until fork-tender. Remove

from the heat and use the natural release method (see page 31) to depressurize. Carefully open the lid after the pressure drops. Remove the meat from the cooker and shred with a fork. Discard the water in the cooker. Heat the butter in the cooker over medium heat, add the onions and garlic, and cook, stirring, until clear, about 3 minutes. Add ½ cup water and the salsa, cilantro, chili powder, and cumin. Return the shredded beef to the cooker, stirring to mix well. Lock the lid in place. Bring to 15psi over high heat, immediately reduce the heat to the lowest possible setting to stabilize and maintain that pressure, and cook for 3 minutes. Remove from the heat and use the natural release method (see page 31) to depressurize. Carefully open the lid after the pressure drops. Divide the shredded salsa beef between the rolls, sprinkle some of the green onions on top of each sandwich, and serve hot.

❋ Serves 6

Barbecued Beef Sandwiches

In the summertime when it's too hot to cook, who wants to go outside and fuss with a smoky grill? Certainly not me, and that's why I came up with the idea of the indoor barbecue machine—the pressure cooker! This is the perfect solution for those hot days of summer when you want to barbecue, but don't want to heat up the kitchen or spend hours tending the grill.

**2 to 3 pounds brisket, trimmed of fat and
cut into 4 pieces**
1½ cups barbecue sauce
6 kaiser, hoagie, or onion rolls
1 onion, sliced into thin rings

Place the rack in the bottom of the pressure cooker. Add 2 cups water. Arrange the chunks of beef on the rack and lock the lid in place. Bring to 15psi over high heat, immediately reduce the heat to the lowest possible setting to stabilize and maintain that pressure, and cook for 50 minutes. Remove the cooker from the heat and use the natural release method (see page 31) to depressurize. Carefully open the lid after the pressure drops. Check the meat; it should shred easily with a fork. If needed, lock the lid back in place, return to 15psi over high heat, immediately reduce the heat to the lowest possible setting to stabilize and maintain that pressure, and cook for an additional 5 minutes, or until the beef is fork-tender. Remove from the heat and use the natural release method (see page 31) to depressurize. Carefully open the lid after the pressure drops. Remove the meat from the cooker and shred with a fork. Discard the water in the cooker. Return the beef to the cooker and stir in the barbecue sauce, simmering over medium heat until heated through. Split the rolls, and butter and toast them if desired. Divide the shredded barbecued beef among the rolls, and top each sandwich with some of the onion rings before serving. ✳ Serves 6

Mushroom Smothered Beef Roast

This super-easy recipe is no work at all—I promise—and in almost no time at all, you'll be sitting down to a generous portion of sliced beef served with loads of smothered mushrooms. Add the Basic Mashed Potatoes recipe (see page 400) and a green salad to complete the meal.

½ cup all-purpose flour

½ teaspoon salt

½ teaspoon freshly ground black pepper

3 pounds boneless beef rump, round, or
    chuck roast

3 tablespoons oil

1 cup dry red wine

1 (14-ounce) can beef broth

2 tablespoons Worcestershire sauce

1 large onion, coarsely chopped

1 tablespoon minced garlic

1/2 pound sliced fresh white mushrooms

2 ounces dried shitake mushrooms,
    break up the larger pieces

2 tablespoons cornstarch

Mix the flour, salt, and pepper, and dredge the meat, coating all sides. Heat the oil in the pressure cooker and brown the meat on both sides. Deglaze the pot with wine, scraping up all those crusty, brown bits from the bottom. Stir in the broth, Worcestershire sauce, onions, garlic and mushrooms. Lock the lid in place. Bring to 15psi over high heat, immediately reduce the heat to the lowest possible setting to stabilize and maintain that pressure, and cook for 25 minutes. Remove from the heat and use the quick or natural release method (see page 31) to depressurize. Carefully open the lid after the pressure drops. Remove the meat to a serving platter and slice across the grain just before serving. Thicken the pan juices by making a slurry with the cornstarch mixed with ⅓ cup cold water, and stir the slurry into the broth. Simmer over medium heat as the gravy thickens, stirring occasionally and taking care that it does not boil. Pour the mushroom gravy into a separate bowl to be ladled over the meat at the table.

✳ Serves 6 generously

Shredded Beef Burritos

If you love Mexican cuisine, this is the hands-down best burrito recipe ever! The pressure cooker is used to first precook and infuse the meat with all the distinct flavors of Mexico, from the mild chile peppers and tomatillos to the pungent spices.

Step One: Precooking
1 sweet Vidalia onion, quartered
2 poblano, pasilla, or Anaheim mild chile
    peppers, seeded and quartered
1 green bell pepper, seeded and quartered
4 tomatillos, husked, washed, and halved
1 small bunch cilantro, leaves only
2 tablespoons chili powder
1 teaspoon ground cumin
3 pounds brisket, trimmed of fat

Using a food processor, blend the onions, chile peppers, tomatillos, cilantro, chili powder, and cumin into a smooth consistency resembling pesto sauce, and pour into the pressure cooker. Add the enchilada sauce, stirring to mix. Add ½ cup water. Place the beef in the cooker and lock the lid in place. Bring to 15psi over high heat, immediately reduce the heat to the lowest possible setting to stabilize and maintain that pressure, and cook for 45 minutes. Remove from the heat and use the natural release method (see page 31) to depressurize. Carefully open the lid after the pressure drops. Check the meat for doneness; it should shred easily with a fork. If needed, lock the lid back in place, return to 15psi over high heat, immediately reduce the heat to the lowest possible setting to stabilize and main-

tain that pressure, and cook for an additional 5 minutes, or until it can be shredded into small pieces with a fork. Remove from the heat and use the natural release method (see page 31) to depressurize. Carefully open the lid after the pressure drops.

Step Two: The Burritos
12 (10-inch) flour tortillas
2 cups shredded cheddar cheese
2 cups shredded lettuce
1 cup chopped tomato
1 cup sour cream, for topping
1 avocado, sliced, for topping
1 cup bottled salsa, for topping

Shred the beef into small pieces. Return to the sauce in the cooker and bring to a simmer over medium heat, uncovered, heating through. To prepare the burritos, use a slotted spoon to put some of the meat onto the center of each flour tortilla and the cheese, lettuce, and tomatoes. Fold up both ends of the tortilla, and then fold the sides over to close the burrito. Top each serving with a dollop of sour cream and a slice of avocado, and pass the salsa at the table. ✳ Serves 6

Balsamic-Braised Sirloin Tips in Mushroom Gravy

I admit that I adore the flavor of balsamic vinegar, and I use it often in recipes that I create because it complements so many foods. Talk about an easy recipe—this one could easily pass for a gourmet meal. I serve this ladled over wide egg noodles or garlic mashed potatoes.

1 teaspoon freshly ground black pepper
2 pounds beef sirloin tips, all fat removed
    and cut into 2-inch cubes
2 tablespoons oil
1 onion, finely chopped
1 (14-ounce) can beef broth
¼ cup good-quality balsamic vinegar
½ pound fresh mushrooms, washed
    and sliced
2 tablespoons minced garlic
2 tablespoons cornstarch

Sprinkle the pepper on the meat, coating all sides. Heat the oil in the pressure cooker over medium-high heat. Add the meat, cook until well browned on all sides, and set aside. Add the onions to the cooker and cook, stirring, until clear, about 3 minutes. Deglaze the cooker with the broth, scraping up all those crusty, brown bits from the bottom. Return the meat to the cooker. Add the vinegar, mushrooms, and garlic and stir. Lock the lid in place. Bring to 15psi over high heat, immediately reduce the heat to the lowest possible setting to stabilize and maintain that pressure, and cook for 15 minutes. Remove from the heat and use the natural release method (see page 31) to depressurize. Carefully open the lid after the pressure drops. Place the meat in a serving bowl. Thicken the sauce by making a slurry with the cornstarch mixed with ⅓ cup cold water; stir the slurry into the broth and simmer over medium heat, stirring often as it thickens, but do not boil. Pour the mushroom gravy over the meat and serve.

✳ **Serves 4 generously**

Asian Beef and Vegetables

This recipe is based on a dish my mother made over 30 years ago. To be sure those vegetables stay tender-crisp, I use the interrupted cooking method (see page 38), cooking the meat in the first stage and then finishing with the vegetables during the last few minutes of cooking time. The secret of tender-crisp vegetables is the cold water release method (see page 30) which must be used promptly to completely stop the cooking process. As soon as the cooker depressurizes, the lid must be removed immediately and the vegetables transferred to a serving dish or they will continue cooking and lose their color and crispness. I serve this over steamed white rice or chow mein noodles, and it's always a big hit in my house. For variety, try substituting chicken or pork.

1 pound sirloin steak, about ½-inch thick
2 tablespoons butter
1 small onion, chopped
¼ pound fresh mushrooms, washed and sliced
1 carrot, peeled and sliced
2 plum tomatoes, chopped
⅓ cup teriyaki sauce
3 tablespoons creamy peanut butter
2 tablespoons soy sauce
½ teaspoon ground ginger
3 cups fresh snow peas, washed and trimmed
1 (4-ounce) can whole water chestnuts, drained and sliced
2 tablespoons cornstarch

The steak will slice easier if it is partially frozen. Cut it across the grain into thin strips about 2 inches long. Heat the butter in the pressure cooker over medium-high heat. Add the meat in small batches and cook until browned on all sides. Add the onions to the cooker and cook, stirring, until soft, about 3 minutes. Add the mushrooms, carrots, tomatoes, teriyaki sauce, peanut butter, soy sauce, and ginger. Add ⅓ cup water and blend well. Lock the lid in place. Bring to 15psi over high heat, immediately reduce the heat to the lowest possible setting to stabilize and maintain that pressure, and cook for 8 minutes. Remove from the heat and use the quick or cold water release method (see page 30) to depressurize. Carefully open the lid after the pressure drops. Add the snow peas and water chestnuts and stir. Lock the lid back in place, return to 15psi over high heat, immediately reduce the heat to the lowest possible setting to stabilize and maintain that pressure, and cook for an additional 2 minutes. Immediately remove from the heat and use the cold water release method (see page 30) to depressurize. Carefully open the lid after the pressure drops. Using a slotted spoon, remove the meat and vegetables to a large serving bowl. Thicken the sauce by making a slurry with the cornstarch mixed with ⅓ cup cold water; stir the slurry into the sauce and simmer over medium heat, stirring often as it thickens, but do not boil. Pour the sauce into a separate serving bowl. ✳ Serves 4

Teriyaki Beef and Broccoli Bowls

Pineapple and crunchy cashews give beef and broccoli a delicious Asian-style flair, and the delicate scent of the sesame oil reminds me of an Asian restaurant. I serve this in individual bowls over hot, fluffy rice, adding extra teriyaki sauce as desired. The interrupted cooking method (see page 38) ensures that the vegetables are not overcooked, and the cold water release method (see page 30) keeps them colorful and tender-crisp. Using the cold water release method promptly after the cooking time is up will completely stop the cooking process by rapidly depressurizing the cooker.

Step One: The Beef
2 tablespoons butter
1 tablespoon sesame oil
1 pound boneless beef sirloin steak, sliced
   into thin strips about 3 inches long
1 medium-size onion, chopped
½ cup teriyaki sauce
2 tablespoons soy sauce
1 tablespoon minced garlic
½ teaspoon ground ginger

Heat the butter and oil in the pressure cooker over medium-high heat. Add the meat and cook until well browned on all sides. Add the onions to the cooker and cook, stirring, until soft, about 3 minutes. Add the teriyaki and soy sauces, garlic, ginger, and ½ cup water and stir. Lock the lid in place. Bring to 15psi over high heat, immediately reduce the heat to the lowest possible setting to stabilize and maintain that pressure, and cook for 6 minutes. Remove from the heat and use the quick or cold water release method (see page 30) to depressurize. Carefully open the lid after the pressure drops.

Step Two: The Vegetables
3 cups broccoli florets
1 carrot, peeled and thinly sliced
1 cup canned pineapple chunks, drained
⅓ cup cashew halves, for garnish

Add the broccoli, carrots, and pineapple to the cooker and stir. Lock the lid back in place, return to 15psi over high heat, immediately reduce the heat to the lowest possible setting to stabilize and maintain that pressure, and cook for 3 minutes longer. Immediately remove from the heat and use the cold water release method (see page 30) to depressurize. Carefully open the lid immediately after the pressure drops. Drain the beef and broccoli mixture, transfer to a serving bowl, and sprinkle the cashews on top. Serve the teriyaki sauce in a separate serving bowl. ✳ Serves 4

Jerked Beef Barbecue

Using the pressure cooker to precook a tough round steak will make it tender enough to cut with a fork. This is a fast and easy summertime dish that would go perfectly with steamed corn on the cob and a plate of thick-sliced beefsteak tomatoes.

Step One: The Rub
3 pounds boneless beef round steak
¼ cup fresh lime juice
3 tablespoons jerk seasoning mix
2 teaspoons sugar
1 teaspoon coarsely ground black pepper
½ teaspoon salt

Score the meat on both sides, making a crosshatch pattern. Working over a plate, brush the lime juice on both sides of the meat. Mix all the spices in a small bowl. Rub the mixture into both sides of the meat, pressing it into the cuts. Reserve any excess spice mixture and lime juice.

Step Two: The Meat
½ cup onion, thinly sliced
1 Scotch bonnet chile, seeded and finely chopped
4 tablespoons minced garlic
2 teaspoons beef bouillon granules
1 cup beer
½ cup ketchup
2 tablespoons soy sauce

Cut the steak into serving portions, add to the cooker. Add the onions, all the remaining ingredients, stir in any remaining spice mixture and lime juice. Lock the lid in place. Bring to 15psi over high heat, immediately reduce the heat to the lowest possible setting to stabilize and maintain that pressure, and cook for 18 minutes. Remove from the heat and use the natural release method (see page 31) to depressurize. Carefully open the lid after the pressure drops. Preheat the broiler. Transfer the meat to a broiler pan, baste with the sauce from the pressure cooker, and place under the broiler. Baste often, and when the meat begins to crisp and has achieved the desired color, turn it over and repeat with the other side. This can also be done on the grill if it's more convenient. ✳ Serves 6

Cook's Note: Scotch bonnet peppers are very hot, and it's a good idea to wear plastic gloves when handling them.

Cola Beef Roast with Sweet Onion au Jus

Back in the '60s, it was all the rage to cook with various brands of soda pop. Ladies' magazines were filled with recipes, newspapers offered discount coupons for famous-brand colas featuring similar recipes, and supermarkets handed out little cards with still more cola recipes. I found one of those promotional recipes from a local supermarket chain tucked into an old recipe book as a bookmark. Although the supermarket has long since faded into history, its original recipe took on a second life after I adapted it to the pressure cooker. The meat is very juicy and melt-in-your-mouth tender. There is lots of pan gravy to be ladled over mashed potatoes for a filling meal.

- 4 tablespoons (½ stick) butter
- 2 sweet Vidalia onions, cut into ¼-inch slices
- 1 (3- to 4-pound) boneless beef roast: rump, pot roast, or bottom round
- 1 (12-ounce) can cola soft drink (regular, not diet)
- ¼ cup soy sauce
- 1 (1-ounce) packet dried onion soup mix
- 1 tablespoon minced garlic

Heat the butter in the pressure cooker over medium-high heat. Add the onion slices and cook, stirring, until lightly browned on all sides. Place the roast on top of the onions. Add the cola, soy sauce, soup mix, and garlic to the cooker and stir. Lock the lid in place. Bring to 15psi over high heat, immediately reduce the heat to the lowest possible setting to stabilize and maintain that pressure, and cook for 30 minutes. Remove from the heat and use the natural release method (see page 31) to depressurize. Carefully open the lid after the pressure drops. Remove the roast and allow to rest for 5 minutes before carving, slicing across the grain. Skim off any excess fat from the surface of the broth, and pour the onion *au jus* into a small serving bowl to be ladled over the sliced beef.

✳ Serves 6

Variation: Butter and toast 6 sub rolls. Slice the meat thinly and pile a generous amount on each roll. Serve with small bowls of the *au jus* sauce for dipping.

French Dip Sandwiches with au Jus Dipping Sauce

Everyone loves French dip sandwiches, and this pressure-cooker version is so quick and easy, you'll be serving this popular dish in just a few minutes. I've made sure that there will be plenty of *au jus* broth for dipping by adding beer to this recipe, which gives the sauce a distinctive taste that really goes well with beef.

1 (2- to 3-pound) boneless beef roast: rump, pot roast, or bottom round
2 tablespoons butter
2 onions, cut into rings
12 ounces beer
1 (14-ounce) can beef broth
1 (1-ounce) packet dried onion soup mix
1 teaspoon finely crushed, dried rosemary
½ teaspoon garlic powder
8 French or sub rolls, sliced lengthwise

If possible, have the butcher thinly slice the roast at the meat counter. Otherwise use meat that is still partially frozen, so that it is easier to slice very thinly before placing it in the cooker. Heat the butter in the pressure cooker over medium-high heat. Add the onions, and cook, stirring, until they began to turn brown and caramelize, about 8 minutes. Deglaze the cooker with the beer, scraping up all those crusty, brown bits from the bottom. Add the broth, soup mix, rosemary, and garlic powder, stirring to mix. Layer the sliced meat in the cooker and lock the lid in place. Bring to 15psi over high heat, immediately reduce the heat to the lowest possible setting to stabilize and maintain that pressure, and cook for 10 minutes. Remove from the heat and use the natural release method (see page 31) to depressurize. Carefully open the lid after the pressure drops. Toast the French rolls if desired. Using long-handled tongs, remove the beef from the cooker and divide the slices among the French rolls. Include a small bowl of *au jus* dipping sauce with each sandwich and add a big crispy dill pickle on the side. ✳ **Serves 6 generously**

Sloppy Joes

This is a kid favorite, and who doesn't like Sloppy Joes? You'll never go back to the canned version once you've used the pressure cooker to make this homemade recipe.

1 pound lean ground beef
1 onion, finely chopped
1 green bell pepper, seeded and finely chopped
¾ cup ketchup
2 tablespoons vinegar
2 tablespoons Worcestershire sauce
¼ cup packed brown sugar
1 tablespoon minced garlic
¼ teaspoon freshly ground black pepper
6 hamburger buns

Heat the pressure cooker over high heat and brown the ground beef until crumbly. Drain off the fat. Sauté the onions and green peppers until soft. Add the ketchup, vinegar, Worcestershire sauce, brown sugar, garlic, pepper, and ½ cup water. Stir to mix and lock the lid in place. Bring to 15psi over high heat, immediately reduce the heat to the lowest possible setting to stabilize and maintain that pressure, and cook for 8 minutes. Remove from the heat and use the natural release method (see page 31) to depressurize. Carefully open the lid after the pressure drops. Drain off any excess liquid. Place about ½ cup of the meat mixture onto the bottom half of each bun and top with the other half. ✳ Serves 6

Philly Cheese Steak Sandwiches

When I talk to people about pressure cooking, it surprises me how few of them ever think of making sandwiches. Thinly sliced meat, oodles of melted cheese, and tasty veggies tucked into some warm bread—what else could you possibly want? These are big, delicious, and filling sandwiches, and take very little time to prepare, which makes this recipe a real plus for the harried cook. The caramelized onions and peppers give the sandwiches a great flavor. Serve them with a relish tray of crispy dill pickles, pepperoncini, and cherry peppers.

2 tablespoons butter

2 onions, cut into rings

1 tablespoon paprika

1 tablespoon chili powder

1 teaspoon garlic powder

½ teaspoon salt

½ teaspoon freshly ground black pepper

2 green bell peppers, seeded and cut into strips

1 (2-pound) boneless beef roast: rump,
    pot roast, or bottom round

6 French or sub rolls, sliced lengthwise

6 to 8 slices provolone cheese (try the smoked
    variety if available in your supermarket
    deli department)

Heat the butter in the pressure cooker over medium-high heat. Add the onions and cook, stirring, until lightly browned, about 3 minutes. Add the paprika, chili powder, garlic powder, salt, and pepper. Add the peppers and 1 cup water, stirring to mix. Place the meat in the cooker and lock the lid in place. Bring to 15psi over high heat, immediately reduce the heat to the lowest possible setting to stabilize and maintain that pressure, and cook for 30 minutes. Remove from the heat and use the natural release method (see page 31) to depressurize. Carefully open the lid after the pressure drops. Place the meat on a carving board and let it rest for 10 minutes. Using a slotted spoon, remove the cooked onions and green peppers from the broth and place on paper towels to absorb any remaining liquid. If desired, freeze the broth for later use in soups, stews, etc. Preheat the broiler. Carve the meat into thin slices and divide between the bottom halves of the rolls, add some of the onions and green peppers, then top with slices of cheese. Place the open sandwiches on a cookie sheet, and pop under the broiler until the cheese is melted. Cover with tops of rolls and serve. ✳ Serves 6

Sesame-Ginger Beef Steak with Ginger-Pecan Butter

Can you imagine using a tough round steak in a delicate Asian dish? The pressure cooker is world renowned for transforming tough but flavorful cuts of meat into tender delicacies, and in this recipe it certainly lives up to that reputation. This recipe evolved into its present form over a period of time, with many alterations and adjustments along the way. I wanted a dish that was packed with Asian flavors, with the amazing taste and aroma of a double snap of ginger combined with garlic and a hint of sesame. This recipe can be served over steamed jasmine rice or stuffed into your favorite bakery rolls for sandwiches.

Step One: Ginger-Pecan Butter

8 tablespoons (1 stick) butter at room temperature
¼ cup crushed pecans
1 tablespoon minced crystallized ginger
1 tablespoon packed brown sugar
¼ teaspoon ground allspice

Mix all the ingredients together several hours in advance and store in the refrigerator until ready to serve.

Step Two: The Beef

2 teaspoons sesame oil
2 tablespoons butter
2 pounds boneless beef top or bottom round roast
2 tablespoons soy sauce
2 tablespoons dry sherry
2 tablespoons rice wine vinegar
1 cup ginger ale
3 medium-size bell peppers (use different colors, green, red, or yellow), seeded and cut into strips
1 onion, cut into thin strips
3 tablespoons minced garlic
2 tablespoons grated fresh ginger
½ teaspoon ground ginger
⅛ teaspoon red pepper flakes

Heat the oil and butter in the pressure cooker over medium heat. Add the meat and cook until browned on all sides. Add all the remaining ingredients, stir, and lock the lid in place. Bring to 15psi over high heat, immediately reduce the heat to the lowest possible setting to stabilize and maintain that pressure, and cook for 20 minutes. Remove from the heat and use the natural release method (see page 31) to depressurize. Carefully open the lid after the pressure drops. Transfer the meat to a cutting board and let it rest for 5 minutes before slicing thinly across the grain. Arrange the meat on a serving platter and top with the onions and peppers. Pass the Ginger-Pecan Butter at the table.

✳ Serves 6

Variation: To make sandwiches, spread the Ginger-Pecan Butter on 6 sliced sesame rolls and lightly toast them under the broiler. Pile on a generous amount of the beef, onions, and peppers, and serve hot.

Braised Beef Shanks with Tomatoes and Orzo

This is another old recipe that came to me via the coveted family-recipe shoebox. It was carefully written on a well-worn sheet of pale blue stationery, but who wrote the recipe remains a mystery. I have used the interrupted cooking method (see page 38), cooking the meat first, and then the tiny orzo pasta is added last. Look for orzo in the dry pasta section of the supermarket, or substitute the Basic Mashed Potatoes recipe (see page 400) if you prefer.

Step One: The Beef
2 tablespoons olive oil

4 cross-cut beef shanks, about 1 inch thick

1 onion, chopped

1 (28-ounce) can chopped tomatoes, with juice

1 (14-ounce) can beef broth

1 (3-ounce) can tomato paste

½ cup red wine

½ cup packed minced cilantro or fresh parsley leaves

2 tablespoons minced garlic

1 tablespoon dried basil

1 tablespoon dried oregano

1 teaspoon crushed fennel seed

½ teaspoon red pepper flakes

½ teaspoon coarsely ground black pepper

Juice of 1 lemon

Zest of 1 lemon

Heat the oil in the pressure cooker over medium-high heat. Add the meat, cook until well browned on all sides, and set aside. Add the onions to the cooker and cook, stirring, until clear, about 3 minutes. Add all the remaining ingredients and 3 cups water, stirring well. Return the meat to the cooker and lock the lid in place. Bring to 15psi over high heat, immediately reduce the heat to the lowest possible setting to stabilize and maintain that pressure, and cook for 20 minutes. Remove from the heat and use the quick or cold water release method (see page 30) to depressurize. Carefully open the lid after the pressure drops.

Step Two: The Vegetables and Orzo
½ cup uncooked orzo

1 cup diced celery

1 cup grated carrots

2 zucchini, sliced ½ inch thick

½ cup grated Parmesan cheese

Add the orzo, pushing the pasta beneath the surface of the sauce, and then add the celery, carrots, and zucchini to the cooker. Lock the lid back in place, return to 15psi over high heat, immediately reduce the heat to the lowest possible setting to stabilize and maintain that pressure, and cook for 3 minutes longer. Remove from the heat and use the cold water release method (see page 30) to depressurize. Carefully open the lid after the pressure drops. Place the meat on a serving plate, and spoon the orzo, broth, and vegetables into a bowl, sprinkle with the Parmesan cheese, and toss gently.

❋ Serves 6

Beef Short Ribs with Potato Wedges, Carrots, Corn on the Cob, and Gravy

Beef short ribs are generally inexpensive, very versatile, and easily customized for many different menu applications. Cooks are often put off from trying short ribs because they are unbelievably tough and stringy, which means they have a tremendous flavor but require hours of long, slow cooking before they are tender enough to eat. Pressure cooking is the ideal method to quickly tenderize short ribs. Like many people, I enjoy the convenience of one-pot meals. I'm always looking for ways to combine foods and serve a two- or three-course meal with as little fuss and cleanup as possible.

Step One: The Beef

2 tablespoons oil

4 pounds beef short ribs, cut into serving-size portions

1 onion, chopped

2 tablespoons minced garlic

1 teaspoon dried marjoram

1 teaspoon ground thyme

Juice of 1 lemon

Zest of 1 lemon

1 (14-ounce) can beef broth

2 tablespoons tomato paste

Heat the oil in the pressure cooker over medium-high heat. Add the meat, cook until well browned on all sides, and set aside. Add the onions to the cooker and cook, stirring, until clear, about 3 minutes. Add the garlic, marjoram, thyme, lemon juice and zest, broth, and tomato paste, stirring well. Return the meat to the cooker and lock the lid in place. Bring to 15psi over high heat, immediately reduce the heat to the lowest possible setting to stabilize and maintain that pressure, and cook for 25 minutes. Remove from the heat and use the quick release method (see page 30) to depressurize. Carefully open the lid after the pressure drops.

Step Two: The Vegetables and Gravy

6 potatoes, scrubbed and cut lengthwise into 8 thin wedges

6 carrots, scrubbed, halved, and then quartered

6 ears fresh or thawed frozen corn on the cob, cut into 4-inch lengths

2 tablespoons all-purpose flour

Salt and freshly ground black pepper to taste

Arrange the potatoes, carrots, and corn in the cooker. Lock the lid back in place, return to 15psi over high heat, immediately reduce the heat to the lowest possible setting to stabilize and maintain that pressure, and cook for 4 minutes longer. Remove from the heat and use the natural release method (see page 31) to depressurize. Carefully open the lid after the pressure drops. Use a slotted spoon to transfer the vegetables and ribs to a serving platter. Skim off any excess fat from the surface of the broth. To thicken the broth, make a slurry using the flour mixed with ½ cup water. Stir the slurry into the broth, simmering gently over medium heat until it reaches the desired consistency. Add salt and pepper to taste. Pour the gravy into a separate serving bowl. ✳ **Serves 6**

Veal Marengo

This is my version of the classic Provençal stew, with chunks of veal in a sauce of tomatoes, wine, herbs, and mushrooms. Serve over mashed potatoes or pasta, with a big loaf of crunchy bread from the bakery.

½ cup all-purpose flour

½ teaspoon salt

½ teaspoon freshly ground black pepper

2 pounds veal stew meat, cut into 1-inch chunks

2 tablespoons olive oil

3 tablespoons butter

2 onions, diced

½ pound fresh mushrooms, washed and sliced

2 tablespoons minced garlic

1 cup white wine

1 (28-ounce) can chopped tomatoes, with juice

1 (14-ounce) can beef broth

2 tablespoons tomato paste

⅓ cup minced fresh parsley

2 teaspoons dried thyme leaves

¼ teaspoon ground cloves

1 bay leaf

Zest of 1 orange

Juice of 1 orange

In a plastic bag, mix the flour, salt, and pepper, and add the meat, shaking gently until coated. Heat the oil in the pressure cooker over medium heat. Add the meat, cook until browned on both sides, and set aside. Add the butter to the cooker, add the onions, and cook, stirring, until clear, about 3 minutes. Add the mushrooms and garlic and cook, stirring, for about 3 minutes more. Deglaze the cooker with the wine, scraping up all those crusty, brown bits from the bottom. Return the meat to the cooker, add all the remaining ingredients, and stir to mix thoroughly. Lock the lid in place. Bring to 15psi over high heat, immediately reduce the heat to the lowest possible setting to stabilize and maintain that pressure, and cook for 12 minutes. Use the quick or cold water release method (see page 30) to depressurize. Carefully open the lid after the pressure drops. Discard the bay leaf. To thicken the broth, make a slurry using 2 tablespoons of the flour-salt-pepper mixture combined with ½ cup water. Stir the slurry into the broth, simmering gently over medium heat until it reaches the desired consistency. Adjust the seasonings to taste and serve. ✳ Serves 4 generously

Veal Scaloppini

In this recipe, the pressure cooker is used to quickly precook the veal, which is then finished in the oven just long enough to melt the cheese. It's simple enough to prepare for a quick weekday dinner, yet it's full of flavor and sophisticated enough for company.

½ cup all-purpose flour

1 teaspoon paprika

½ teaspoon freshly ground black pepper

½ teaspoon salt

4 veal cutlets, about ½ inch thick

1 large egg, beaten

1 cup bread crumbs

2 tablespoons olive oil

1 onion, chopped

½ pound fresh mushrooms, washed and sliced

1 tablespoon minced garlic

1 (28-ounce) can Italian-style stewed tomatoes,
with juice
2 tablespoons tomato paste
1 tablespoon balsamic vinegar
1 teaspoon beef bouillon granules
½ cup grated Parmesan cheese
8 slices mozzarella cheese

In a plastic bag, mix the flour, paprika, pepper, and salt and add the meat, shaking gently until coated. Dip the flour-coated cutlets into the egg, and then press into the bread crumbs, coating both sides. Heat the oil in the pressure cooker over medium heat. Add the meat, cook until well browned on all sides, and set aside on paper towels. Add the onions to the cooker and cook, stirring, until clear, about 3 minutes. Add the mushrooms and garlic and cook, stirring, for about 3 minutes more. Add the tomatoes, tomato paste, vinegar, ⅓ cup water, and bouillon, stir well, and return the meat to the cooker. Lock the lid in place. Bring to 15psi over high heat, immediately reduce the heat to the lowest possible setting to stabilize and maintain that pressure, and cook for 5 minutes. Remove from the heat and use the quick or cold water release method (see page 30) to depressurize. Carefully open the lid after the pressure drops. Preheat the oven to 350°F. Using long-handled tongs, carefully remove the cutlets and place them side by side in a heatproof oven dish. Sprinkle the Parmesan cheese over the cutlets, and slowly pour in the sauce. Cover with the mozzarella slices and bake for 15 minutes, or until the cheese is melted. ✳ Serves 4

Serving Suggestion: Serve this with cooked linguine, garlic toast, and a nice salad.

Variation: Serve on your choice of rolls as sandwiches, adding just a little sauce and using the remainder for dipping as desired.

Hamburger Stroganoff

Another of my favorite recipes from the bottomless shoebox of family heirloom recipes! Quick, easy, tasty—this is what hamburger stroganoff should be—and it's a hit with the kids, too. What more could you ask for?

1 pound lean ground beef
1 onion, chopped
1 (14-ounce) can beef broth
1 (10-ounce) can cream of mushroom soup
2 (6-ounce) cans mushrooms slices, drained
3 cups uncooked wide egg noodles
2 cups sour cream
Milk, if needed

Heat the pressure cooker over medium heat, add the meat, and cook until it is browned and well crumbled. Add the onions to the cooker and cook, stirring, until clear, about 3 minutes. Add the broth, soup, mushrooms, and egg noodles and stir. Add just enough water to cover the ingredients, pushing the noodles beneath the liquid. Lock the lid in place. Bring to 15psi over high heat, immediately reduce the heat to the lowest possible setting to stabilize and maintain that pressure, and cook for 8 minutes. Remove from the heat and use the natural release method (see page 31) to depressurize. Carefully open the lid after the pressure drops. Stir in the sour cream and simmer over medium heat, uncovered, until heated through. Thin with a little milk if the sauce becomes too thick. Serve immediately. ✳ Serves 6

Shredded Beef Tacos

Actually, this is quite a versatile recipe that serves as the basic meat mixture for burritos as well as tacos, Tex-Mex sandwiches, or even in a big Mexican-style salad with a guacamole dressing. For variety, try substituting a pork roast for the beef.

Step One: The Beef
2 pounds boneless beef chuck or round roast, trimmed of fat and cut into 4 portions
2 cups bottled salsa, hot or mild
2 mild Mexican chiles, such as Anaheim, poblano, or pasilla, seeded and chopped
1 jalapeño chile, seeded and chopped
1 onion, chopped
½ cup packed finely minced cilantro leaves
1 tablespoon minced garlic
1 tablespoon chili powder
2 teaspoons ground cumin

Place the roast in a pressure cooker and add the salsa, chiles, onions, cilantro, garlic, chili powder, and cumin, and stir. Lock the lid in place. Bring to 15psi over high heat, immediately reduce the heat to the lowest possible setting to stabilize and maintain that pressure, and cook for 30 minutes. Remove from the heat and use the natural release method (see page 31) to depressurize. Carefully open the lid after the pressure drops. The meat should shred easily with a fork; if necessary, lock the lid back in place, return to 15psi over high heat, immediately reduce the heat to the lowest possible setting to stabilize and maintain that pressure, and cook for an additional 5 minutes. Remove from the heat and use the natural release method (see page 31) to depressurize. Carefully open the lid after the pressure drops. Transfer the meat to a cutting board and use 2 forks to pull the meat across the grain into shreds. Mix the shredded beef back into the sauce in the pressure cooker and bring to a simmer over medium heat. Continue simmering, uncovered, to reduce any excess liquid.

Step Two: The Toppings
12 (8-inch) flour tortillas
2 cups shredded cheddar cheese
2 cups shredded lettuce
1 cup chopped tomatoes
1 cup bottled salsa
1 cup prepared guacamole
1 cup sour cream

To prepare the tacos, heat the tortillas according to the package directions. Place about ½ cup of shredded beef in the center of each tortilla. Pass the toppings at the table and let everyone choose the ones they like. ✳ Serves 6

Stuffed Cabbage Rolls

Yes, lots of ingredients, but thankfully most of the prep work is just measuring, so this dish is actually quite simple and easy to make. Serve with garlic toast, and mashed potatoes or polenta as a bed for all the tasty sauce.

Step One: The Cabbage
1 head green cabbage

Boil 3 cups of water in the pressure cooker using a regular lid. Cut out the core from the head of cabbage and place the cabbage in the boiling water with the bottom facing up. Using long-handled tongs, remove each leaf from the boiling water as it becomes soft. Repeat until all the large leaves are removed. Cut out the hard center rib from each leaf. Drain the cooker.

Step Two: The Sauce

2 tablespoons butter

1 onion, minced

1 (28-ounce) can diced or chopped tomatoes, with juice

1 (8-ounce) can tomato sauce

¼ cup white vinegar

1 tablespoon Italian herb blend, or 1 teaspoon each of dried basil, oregano, and marjoram

2 teaspoons instant beef bouillon

½ teaspoon garlic powder

½ teaspoon onion powder

½ teaspoon coarsely ground black pepper

½ teaspoon red pepper flakes

1 cup sour cream for garnish

Heat the butter in the pressure cooker over medium-high heat. Add the onions and cook, stirring, until they are a nice golden brown color. Add the tomatoes, tomato sauce, vinegar, Italian herbs, bouillon, garlic and onion powder, black pepper, and red pepper flakes, and mix with ½ cup water. Pour the sauce into a large bowl while you prepare the cabbage rolls.

Step Three: The Stuffing

½ pound lean ground beef

1 cup cooked white rice

⅓ cup Italian-style bread crumbs

2 tablespoons chopped fresh dill

1 large egg, slightly beaten

In a large bowl, combine the beef, rice, bread crumbs, dill, and egg, mixing until well blended. Place about ⅓ cup of the meat-rice mixture at the stem end of a cabbage leaf. Roll toward the top of the leaf, folding in the sides just before the end, sealing in the meat. Use a toothpick if necessary to hold the leaf closed. Make all the cabbage rolls. Place the rack is the pressure cooker and add ½ cup water. Chop up any remaining cabbage and spread it over the rack. Place each cabbage roll seam side down in the first layer and ladle in just enough tomato sauce to cover. Arrange 2 or more layers as needed, turning the rolls in the opposite direction with each new layer and ladling in more sauce until all the sauce is added. Lock the lid in place. Bring to 15psi over high heat, immediately reduce the heat to the lowest possible setting to stabilize and maintain that pressure, and cook for 4 minutes. Remove from the heat and use the natural release method (see page 31) to depressurize. Carefully open the lid after the pressure drops. Gently transfer the cabbage rolls to a serving platter and pour the tomato sauce into a separate serving bowl to be passed at the table. Top each portion with a dollop of sour cream. ✳ Serves 6

8-Minute Chili

When I was learning to cook, this was one of the first recipes I made in the pressure cooker, and almost 40 years later it's still one of my favorites. Not only is it super fast and easy, it also cooks in one pot for easy cleanup. Serve with saltine crackers or your favorite style of Mexican corn chips. If you're lucky, there might be just enough leftover for lunch the following day.

    1 pound lean ground beef
    1 onion, chopped
    2 (14-ounce) cans kidney beans, drained
        and rinsed
    1 (28-ounce) can crushed tomatoes
    1 (3-ounce) can tomato paste
    1 mild Mexican chile, such as Anaheim,
        poblano, or pasilla, seeded and
        chopped
    ½ cup packed minced cilantro leaves
    2 tablespoons chili powder
    1 tablespoon minced garlic
    1 teaspoon ground cumin
    ½ teaspoon red pepper flakes
    2 tablespoons masa harina or
        all-purpose flour

Heat the pressure cooker over medium-high heat. Add the meat and cook until it is browned and well crumbled. Add the onions and cook, stirring, until clear, about 3 minutes. Add the remaining ingredients, except the masa harina, and stir in 2 cups water, mixing well. Lock the lid in place. Bring to 15psi over high heat, immediately reduce the heat to the lowest possible setting to stabilize and maintain that pressure, and cook for 8 minutes. Remove from the heat and use the natural release method (see page 31) to depressurize. Carefully open the lid after the pressure drops. To thicken, make a slurry using the masa harina mixed with ½ cup water. Stir the slurry into the chili, simmering gently over medium heat as it thickens to the desired consistency, and serve. ※ Serves 4 generously

Salisbury Steaks with Mushroom Gravy and Dilled New Potatoes

If you're old enough, you might remember when Salisbury steak with potatoes and gravy was staple fare at lunch counters from the main street Woolworth's to bustling downtown cafeterias. I've added dilled potatoes, but if you're partial to mashed, that's a good substitute for this a complete one-pot meal.

1 pound lean ground beef

1 onion, finely chopped

½ cup dry cracker crumbs

1 large egg, slightly beaten

2 tablespoons oil

½ pound fresh mushrooms, washed and sliced

1 (14-ounce) can beef broth

2 tablespoons Worcestershire sauce

1 (1-ounce) packet dried onion soup mix

6 to 8 small red potatoes, scrubbed

2 tablespoons butter, melted

2 tablespoons finely chopped fresh dill

2 tablespoons cornstarch

In a large bowl, mix the ground beef, onions, cracker crumbs, and egg with your hands until all the ingredients are thoroughly blended.* Shape the meat mixture into 4 oval patties about 1 inch thick. Heat the oil in the pressure cooker over medium-high heat, and cook each patty until browned on both sides. Set aside to drain on paper towels. Add the mushrooms to the cooker and cook, stirring, for about 3 minutes. Deglaze the cooker with the broth, scraping up all those crusty, brown bits from the bottom. Add the Worcestershire sauce and stir in the soup mix. Pare a thin strip from around the center of each potato and place the potatoes in the bottom of the pressure cooker. Place the rack on top of the potatoes and carefully arrange the ground beef patties, making sure they are well above the liquid. Lock the lid in place. Bring to 15psi over high heat, immediately reduce the heat to the lowest possible setting to stabilize and maintain that pressure, and cook for 8 minutes. Use the quick or cold water release method (see page 30) to depressurize. Carefully open the lid after the pressure drops. Carefully remove each patty to a serving plate and keep warm in the oven. Remove the potatoes to a warmed serving bowl. Mix the melted butter and dill and drizzle over the potatoes, turning gently to coat. Keep warm until ready to serve. Thicken the mushroom gravy by making a slurry with the cornstarch mixed with ⅓ cup cold water; stir the slurry into the broth and simmer over medium heat, stirring often as it thickens, but do not boil. Adjust the seasonings to taste and pour the gravy into a separate serving dish. ✳ Serves 4

Miss Vickie Says

Place the ground beef and other ingredients in a 1-gallon plastic food bag and zip it closed. Knead the meat mixture through the bag until the ingredients are thoroughly mixed, and your hands will stay clean.

Gourmet Blue Cheese–Stuffed Burgers

There was a fabulous little family-owned diner that specialized in all manner of interesting, gourmet-quality hamburgers. While it's all but faded from memory, there was one item on the menu that was my particular favorite, and I was determined to re-create it and adapt it to the pressure cooker. I hit the jackpot with my first attempt, and the gourmet burgers were just as delicious as I remembered. I usually serve these burgers as a main dish with a baked potato and simple tomato vinaigrette, but they are equally at home on a bun.

1 pound lean ground beef
½ teaspoon garlic powder
½ teaspoon freshly ground black pepper
4 tablespoons crumbled blue cheese
4 hamburger buns, split and toasted
4 lettuce leaves, for topping
1 tomato, sliced, for topping
1 red onion, sliced, for topping
Mustard or ketchup, for topping

Mix the beef, garlic powder, and pepper in a medium-size bowl and shape the mixture into 8 thin oval patties. Place 1 tablespoon of blue cheese in the center of 4 of the meat patties. Place the 4 remaining patties on top of the other patties and pinch the edges to seal in the filling. Place the rack in the cooker and add 1 cup water. Arrange the 4 stuffed meat patties on the rack and lock the lid in place. Bring to 15psi over high heat, immediately reduce the heat to the lowest possible setting to stabilize and maintain that pressure, and cook for 6 minutes. Remove from the heat and use the quick release method (see page 30) to depressurize. Carefully open the lid after the pressure drops. Place each patty on a bun and serve with toppings as desired. ※ **Serves 4**

Variation: Instead of blue cheese, substitute 2 tablespoons chopped capers mixed into ⅔ cup sour cream for the stuffing.

Beefy Cheesy Mexi-Mac

This recipe has a lot going for it . . . it's cheap, fast, and very tasty, just the thing when you are short on time and have to serve something that will please everyone. This very easy one-pot meal goes beyond the traditional kid-friendly dish you may remember from childhood, with just enough chile to make it interesting, but not overwhelming. Choose a really sharp cheddar or the cheese will get lost in all the other ingredients.

1 pound lean ground beef
1 onion, chopped

1 mild Mexican chile, such as Anaheim, poblano, or pasilla, seeded and chopped

2 cups bottled salsa, mild or hot

1 (3-ounce) can tomato paste

2 tablespoons chili powder

1 tablespoon minced garlic

3 cups uncooked ziti or penne

2 cups shredded sharp cheddar cheese

Heat the pressure cooker over medium-high heat. Add the meat and cook until it is browned and well crumbled. Add the onions and chiles to the cooker and cook, stirring, for about 3 minutes. Add the salsa, tomato paste, chili powder, and garlic, stirring to blend. Add the pasta and enough water to cover all the ingredients, pushing the noodles beneath the liquid. Lock the lid in place. Bring to 15psi over high heat, immediately reduce the heat to the lowest possible setting to stabilize and maintain that pressure, and cook for 6 minutes. Remove from the heat and use the natural release method (see page 31) to depressurize. Carefully open the lid after the pressure drops. Stir in the cheddar cheese, mixing gently. Cover until the cheese melts, and then transfer to a large serving bowl.

✳ Serves 6

Italian Meatball Subs

True, Italians eat meatballs, but when they are tucked inside a sub roll, it's purely an American invention. These are hearty, man-sized sandwiches that are sure to please all the hungry people at your table.

1 pound lean ground beef

1 large egg, beaten

½ cup minced onion

½ cup Italian-style bread crumbs

2 tablespoons grated Parmesan cheese

2 teaspoons dried oregano

1 teaspoon garlic powder

1 teaspoon dried basil

1 teaspoon salt

½ teaspoon freshly ground black pepper

½ teaspoon red pepper flakes

½ teaspoon crushed fennel seed

1 (28-ounce) jar marinara sauce, any variety

6 sub or hoagie-style rolls, buttered and lightly toasted

2 cups shredded mozzarella cheese

Use a stand mixer to combine the ground beef, egg, onions, bread crumbs, Parmesan cheese, oregano, garlic powder, basil, salt, black pepper, red pepper flakes, and fennel. Alternately, keep your hands clean by placing the ingredients in a large plastic freezer bag and kneading until it is thoroughly mixed. Shape the meat mixture into ping-pong-size balls—use a small ice-cream scoop to make them all the same size. Add the meatballs to the pressure cooker and pour the marinara sauce. Lock the lid in place. Bring to 15psi over high heat, immediately reduce the heat to the lowest possible setting to stabilize and maintain that pressure, and cook for 5 minutes. Remove from the heat and use the natural release method (see page 31) to depressurize. Carefully open the lid after the pressure drops. Lay out the sub rolls and cut the meatballs in half. Place the meatball halves on the sub rolls and ladle on the marinara sauce. Top each sandwich with some of the mozzarella cheese. Serve the extra marinara sauce in a separate bowl to be passed at the table. ✳ Serves 6

Twice-Cooked Meat Loaf with French Mashed Potatoes

This PIP (Pan in Pot) recipe (see page 37) uses a springform pan to cook the meat loaf, which is then covered with the French Mashed Potatoes and popped into the oven to complete this great-tasting and fabulous-looking dish. French Mashed Potatoes is a uniquely Southern recipe, hence the French reference, I suppose, but I can't explain why the addition of a little baking powder is related to French cooking. Regardless of the mystery, the baking powder does make for a difference, so vive la difference, I say!

Step One: The Meat Loaf
1 pound lean ground beef
1 cup saltine cracker crumbs
½ cup chopped onion
½ cup minced green bell pepper
1 (8-ounce) can tomato sauce
2 large eggs, slightly beaten
1 teaspoon ground sage
½ teaspoon freshly ground black pepper
½ teaspoon garlic powder

In a large bowl, mix the beef, cracker crumbs, onions, green pepper, tomato sauce, eggs, and the spices with your hands until all the ingredients are thoroughly blended. Pack all the ingredients into a springform pan that will fit in your pressure cooker. Place the rack in the cooker and add 1 cup water. Use foil helper handles (see page 42) to lower the springform pan inside the cooker. Lock the lid in place. Bring to 15psi over high heat, immediately reduce the heat to the lowest possible setting to stabilize and maintain that pressure, and cook for 20 minutes. Remove the cooker from the heat and use the quick release method (see page 30) to depressurize. Carefully open the lid after the pressure drops.

Miss Vickie Says: I use a stand mixer to quickly and thoroughly blend all the ingredients into a smooth and uniform consistency that makes a very finely textured meat loaf. As an alternative, place the ground beef and other ingredients in a 1-gallon plastic food bag and zip it closed. Knead the meat mixture through the bag until the ingredients are thoroughly mixed, and your hands will stay clean.

Step Two: The French Mashed Potatoes
4 russet potatoes, peeled and cubed
4 tablespoons buttermilk
6 tablespoons (3/4 stick) butter
2 tablespoons chopped chives
1 teaspoon baking powder
1 teaspoon salt
½ teaspoon freshly ground black pepper

Place the potatoes on a second rack on top of the meatloaf pan, or in a steamer pan. Bring to 15psi over high heat, immediately reduce the heat to the lowest possible setting to stabilize and maintain that pressure, and cook for 4 minutes. Remove from the heat and use the quick release method (see page 30) to depressurize. Carefully open the lid after the pressure drops. Transfer the potatoes to a mixing bowl and mash using your preferred method, adding the, butter, buttermilk, chives, salt and pepper, and baking powder, mixing until fluffy.

1 (6-ounce) can French's French Fried Onions, coarsely chopped

Preheat the oven to 325°F. Carefully remove the meat loaf from the cooker and release the springform pan. Slide the meat loaf off the base of the springform pan and center it on a pie plate. Mound the French Mashed Potatoes on top of the meat loaf, and spread the potatoes over the side, like icing on a cake. Sprinkle the fried onion bits on top. Bake until the onions start to brown. Slice the meat loaf into wedges just as you would cut a cake, and serve. ✳ Serves 6

Southern-Style Meatballs in Buttermilk Gravy

Woo-Hoo! Homemade buttermilk meatballs star in this typically Southern recipe. Serve with mashed potatoes or rice, a big helping of greens, and buttermilk biscuits.

Step One: The Meatballs

1 pound lean ground beef
¾ cup buttermilk
2 large eggs, lightly beaten
⅔ cup dry bread crumbs
½ teaspoon freshly ground black pepper
½ teaspoon ground cinnamon
3 tablespoons butter

Combine the beef, buttermilk, eggs, bread crumbs, pepper, and cinnamon in a large bowl and mix thoroughly with your hands until well blended. Form the mixture into about 16 small meatballs. Heat the butter in the pressure cooker over medium-high heat. Add the meatballs, cook until well browned on all sides, and set aside. Place the rack in the cooker and add ½ cup water. Arrange the meatballs in layers a steamer tray, and use foil helper handles to position it on the rack. Lock the lid in place. Bring to 15psi over high heat, immediately reduce the heat to the lowest possible setting to stabilize and maintain that pressure, and cook for 6 minutes. Remove from the heat and use the natural release method (see page 31) to depressurize. Carefully open the lid after the pressure drops. Remove the meatballs from the cooker.

Step Two: The Buttermilk Gravy

3 tablespoons butter
2 cups buttermilk
¼ cup all-purpose flour
2 teaspoons sugar
1 teaspoon salt
½ teaspoon freshly ground black pepper
½ teaspoon Louisiana-style hot sauce

Empty the cooker, and wipe dry with paper towels. Heat the butter over medium heat. Blend the buttermilk and flour into a slurry and add it to the hot butter. Add the sugar, salt, pepper, and hot sauce, stirring constantly with a wire whisk as the gravy thickens, but do not boil. Return the meatballs to the sauce and reduce the heat to low, simmering slowly until meatballs are heated through. Adjust the seasonings to taste, and serve. ✳ Serves 4

Monster Meatballs and "Baked" Potatoes with Sour Cream-Onion Gravy

I was in a hurry when I came up with the idea for this recipe, which was limited to what was available in my cupboard at that moment. Think of these giant meatballs as small round meat loaves. Kids go nuts over these big meatballs, and with the addition of baked potatoes and gravy, this is a meal big enough to satisfy anyone with a hearty appetite.

Step One: The Potatoes and Monster Meatballs

1¼ pounds ground beef

1 large egg, lightly beaten

½ cup saltine cracker crumbs

¾ teaspoon salt

½ teaspoon freshly ground black pepper

½ teaspoon garlic powder

½ cup all-purpose flour

2 tablespoons oil

1 (1-ounce) packet dried onion soup mix

1 (16-ounce) can beef broth

4 medium-size russet potatoes, scrubbed and halved

Place the ground beef, egg, cracker crumbs, salt, pepper, and garlic powder in a large bowl and mix thoroughly with your hands. Form the mixture into 4 large meatballs and gently roll in the flour, coating well. Heat the oil in the pressure cooker over medium-high heat. Add the meatballs, cook until browned on all sides, and set aside. Add the soup mix and stir in the broth. Place the rack in the cooker and arrange the potatoes on top of the rack. Place the meatballs in a steamer tray on top of the potatoes, using foil helper handles if needed. Lock the lid in place. Bring to 15psi over high heat, immediately reduce the heat to the lowest possible setting to stabilize and maintain that pressure, and cook for 12 minutes. Remove from the heat and use the natural release method (see page 31) to depressurize. Carefully open the lid after the pressure drops. Remove the pan with the meatballs, transfer them to a serving platter and place in a low oven to keep warm.

Step Two: The Sour Cream–Onion Gravy

¼ cup all-purpose flour

1 cup sour cream

To thicken the soup make a slurry with the flour mixed in cup ½ water; stir the slurry into the broth, and simmer gently over medium heat until it reaches the desired consistency. Add the sour cream and stir until blended and heated through. Adjust the seasonings to taste and serve the gravy in a separate bowl to ladle over the meatballs and potatoes. ※ Serves 4

Variation: Prepare the Monster Meatballs according to directions, but instead of using the Sour Cream–Onion Gravy, substitute marinara sauce and serve with your choice of pasta and plenty of garlic toast.

Party Beef Nachos

Served as an appetizer, this is an absolute hit for a party! Don't limit this recipe to parties, though; it makes a nice weekend lunch or a light supper to munch in front of the TV. While the pressure cooker is cooking the meat mixture, you'll have just barely enough time to prepare all the toppings—yes, it's that fast.

Step One: The Meat Mixture
1 pound lean ground beef
½ cup minced onion
1 cup bottled salsa
1 (14-ounce) can refried beans
1 mild Mexican chile, such as Anaheim, poblano, or pasilla, seeded and chopped
1 cup packed cilantro leaves
1 tablespoon chili powder
1 teaspoon ground cumin

Heat the pressure cooker over medium heat, add the beef, and cook until crumbly and browned. Add the onions and cook, stirring, until soft, about 3 minutes. Add ½ cup water, the salsa, refried beans, chile, cilantro, chili powder, and cumin, stirring to mix. Lock the lid in place. Bring to 15psi over high heat, immediately reduce the heat to the lowest possible setting to stabilize and maintain that pressure, and cook for 6 minutes. Remove from the heat and use the natural release method (see page 31) to depressurize. Carefully open the lid after the pressure drops. If necessary, simmer the open pot over medium heat to reduce any excess liquid.

Step Two: The Toppings
1 (15-ounce) bag of your favorite tortilla chips
2 cups shredded lettuce
2 cups shredded cheddar cheese
2 cups finely chopped tomatoes
1 cup chopped green onions
1 cup fresh or thawed frozen guacamole
1 cup sour cream
Chopped jalapeño chiles, if desired

I serve this on a community platter, but it's just as easy to prepare individual plates, if you prefer. Arrange the tortilla chips on a large platter and spread the meat mixture on top. Add the lettuce, cheese, tomatoes, and onions. Serve the guacamole and sour cream separately, and garnish with the chopped jalapeños, if desired. ✳ Serves 4

Mexicali Hamburger Pasta Pot

This is a spicy twist on the usual boring boxed macaroni dish. One of the best things I like about pressure cooking is the fact that once the lid is locked in place, there's no more stirring. While dinner is cooking, prepare a Mexican salad consisting of shredded lettuce, chopped tomatoes, and sliced black olives with a dressing of mashed avocados and salsa. Now all you have to do is stand back and watch as the whole family tucks into this dish with gusto.

1 pound ground beef

1 onion, chopped

1 green bell pepper, seeded and chopped

1 mild chile, such as Anaheim, poblano, or pasilla, seeded and chopped

2 (10-ounce) cans Rotel (or similar brand) chopped tomatoes with chiles

1 (10-ounce) can whole-kernel corn

1 (3-ounce) can tomato paste

½ cup packed cilantro leaves

2 tablespoons chili powder

1 teaspoon garlic powder

3 cups uncooked ziti or penne

2 cups shredded jalapeño Jack cheese

Heat the pressure cooker over medium heat. Add the ground beef and cook until crumbly and browned. Add the onions, bell peppers, and chile and cook, stirring, until slightly softened, about 3 minutes. Pour off any remaining fat. Add the tomatoes, corn, tomato paste, cilantro, chili powder, and garlic powder, stirring well to mix thoroughly. Add the pasta and enough water to cover the ingredients, pushing the pasta beneath the surface of the liquid. Lock the lid in place. Bring to 15psi over high heat, immediately reduce the heat to the lowest possible setting to stabilize and maintain that pressure, and cook for 8 minutes. Remove from the heat and use the natural release method (see page 31) to depressurize. Carefully open the lid after the pressure drops. Stir in the cheese and mix thoroughly before serving. ❋ Serves 6

8-Minute Beef Goulash

This is a favorite family recipe that my mother always made for us when we were kids. A hearty and comforting meal with the added bonus that it's easy to prepare, easy on the budget, and quickly finished in the pressure cooker. I serve this with garlic bread sticks and a crunchy Waldorf salad of apples, celery, walnuts, and sweetened mayonnaise.

1 pound lean ground beef

1 onion, chopped

1 green bell pepper, seeded and chopped

1 (28-ounce) can chopped tomatoes, with juice

1 (14-ounce) can kidney beans, drained and rinsed

1½ cups frozen corn

1 (3-ounce) can tomato paste

2 tablespoons sweet Hungarian paprika

2 tablespoons chili powder

1 tablespoon minced garlic

3 cups uncooked ziti or penne

2 cups shredded cheddar cheese

Heat the pressure cooker over medium heat. Add the meat and cook until crumbled and browned. Add the onions and bell peppers and cook, stirring, for about 3 minutes. Pour off the fat. Add the tomatoes, beans, corn, tomato paste, paprika, chili powder, and garlic, and stir. Add the pasta and enough water to cover the ingredients, pushing the pasta beneath the surface of the liquid, taking care not to exceed the half-fill rule for pasta. Lock the lid in place. Bring to 15psi over high heat, immediately reduce the heat to the lowest possible setting to stabilize and maintain that pressure, and cook for 8 minutes. Remove from the heat and use the natural release method (see page 31) to depressurize. Carefully open the lid after the pressure drops. Add the cheese, stirring to mix. Cover with a regular lid until the cheese melts, then serve.

✳ **Serves 6**

Beef and Bean Tacos

This is a recipe that the frugal cook will appreciate, since it uses refried beans to stretch the yield, making this a real penny pincher for an economical meal.

1 pound ground beef

1 (14-ounce) can refried beans

1 cup bottled salsa

1 onion, chopped

1 mild chile, such as Anaheim, poblano, or pasilla, seeded and chopped

1 cup packed cilantro leaves

2 tablespoons chili powder

1 tablespoon minced garlic

1 tablespoon ground cumin

12 (6-inch) corn tortillas

Toppings

1½ cups shredded lettuce

1 cup chopped tomatoes

2 cups grated cheddar cheese

Heat the pressure cooker over medium heat. Add the ground beef and cook until crumbly and browned. Add the refried beans, salsa, onions, chile, cilantro, chili powder, garlic, and cumin to the pressure cooker. Stir in ½ cup water, mixing thoroughly. Lock the lid in place. Bring to 15psi over high heat, immediately reduce the heat to the lowest possible setting to stabilize and maintain that pressure, and cook for 6 minutes. Remove from the heat and use the natural release method (see page 31) to depressurize. Carefully open the lid after the pressure drops. While the meat mixture is in the pressure cooker, prepare the tortillas according to package directions for either crisply fried or soft tacos. Fill each tortilla with a scoop of the meat and bean mixture and add the toppings of your choice. ✳ **Serves 4**

Meat-Stuffed Green Pepper Boats

If tender bell pepper halves stuffed with Italian seasoned ground beef good to you, then this recipe should be at the top of the list. Serve with rice or potatoes.

1 large egg, slightly beaten
½ pound lean ground beef
1½ cups Italian-style bread crumbs
6 fresh mushrooms, washed and finely chopped
½ cup minced onion
½ cup sliced black olives
½ cup ketchup
¼ cup grated Parmesan cheese
1 tablespoon minced garlic
1 teaspoon dried basil
1 teaspoon dried oregano
¼ teaspoon crushed red pepper flakes
2 green bell peppers, seeded and halved lengthwise
1 cup shredded mozzarella cheese

Combine the egg, beef, bread crumbs, mushrooms, onions, olives, ketchup, Parmesan cheese, garlic, basil, oregano, and red pepper flakes in a large bowl and mix thoroughly with your hands until well blended. Stuff each pepper half with the meat mixture, mounding the top slightly. Place the rack in a pressure cooker and add 1 cup water. Arrange the stuffed peppers in a steamer tray, and place the tray on the rack in the pressure cooker. Place a sheet of aluminum foil loosely over the top of the peppers and lock the lid in place. Bring to 15psi over high heat, immediately reduce the heat to the lowest possible setting to stabilize and maintain that pressure, and cook for 5 minutes. Remove from the heat and use the natural release method (see page 31) to depressurize. Carefully open the lid after the pressure drops. Lift out the steamer tray, carefully set the stuffed peppers on a serving platter, and quickly top with the shredded cheese.

✳ **Serves 4**

Zesty Salsa Mini Meat Loaves

Even those who claim they don't like meat loaf will love this absolutely delicious recipe with its Mexican-inspired sauce! This is a PIP (Pan in Pot) recipe (see page 37) using individual mini loaf pans. As a substitute, consider using squares of aluminum foil formed into a similar pan configuration. Serve with mashed potatoes or pasta. If you're lucky enough to have any leftovers, this makes a great meat loaf sandwich the next day.

1 pound lean ground beef
1½ cups crushed Mexican-style tortilla chips
1 onion, diced
1 mild chile, such as Anaheim, poblano, or pasilla, seeded and chopped
½ cup packed finely minced cilantro leaves
1 tablespoon minced garlic
2 teaspoons ground cumin
1 cup bottled salsa
1 large egg, beaten

Combine all the ingredients in a 1-gallon plastic food bag and zip it closed. Knead the meat mixture through the bag until the ingredients are thoroughly mixed. Place the rack in the cooker and add 1 cup water. Using 4 mini loaf pans, generously pack the meat mixture into each pan and arrange them on top of the rack in the pressure cooker in two layers. Lock the lid in place. Bring to 15psi over high heat, immediately reduce the heat to the lowest possible setting to stabilize and maintain that pressure, and cook for 15 minutes. Remove from the heat and use the natural release method (see page 31) to depressurize. Carefully open the lid after the pressure drops. Lift out the steamer tray and place the mini-meat loaves on a serving plate.

✳ **Serves 4**

Serving Suggestion: Serve with mashed potatoes and steamed fresh green beans.

Cook's Note: Substitute any metal pan if you don't have the mini loaf pan accessories.

Gourmet Patty Melt Cheeseburgers

It required a trip to my favorite diner to indulge a craving for patty melts before I decided to explore the possibility of creating a pressure-cooker version. This is the final result, and, I must say, my version tastes every bit as good as the restaurant variety, without the fuss and expense of dining out.

1 pound ground beef
1 tablespoon prepared horseradish

1 tablespoon minced garlic
1 tablespoon oil
1 green bell pepper, seeded and cut in rings
2 red onions, sliced into thin rings
4 slices rye or pumpernickel bread, buttered and
  lightly toasted
4 thick slices deli-style Swiss cheese
Dill pickle spears, for garnish
Any style bottled mustard, as desired

In a medium-size bowl, mix the ground beef, horseradish, and garlic. Shape the meat mixture into 4 oval patties of equal size, shaped to fit the bread. Heat the oil in the pressure cooker over medium-high heat. Add the patties, cook until well browned on all sides, and set aside. Place the rack in the cooker and add 1 cup water. Arrange two patties on the rack, add a square of aluminum foil and stack a second layer on top. Top each patty with slices of pepper and onion and lock the lid in place. Bring to 15psi over high heat, immediately reduce the heat to the lowest possible setting to stabilize and maintain that pressure, and cook for 4 minutes. Remove from the heat and use the quick or cold water release method (see page 30) to depressurize. Carefully open the lid after the pressure drops. Place a patty on a slice of toasted bread and top with a slice of Swiss cheese. Repeat for each of the patties and serve with dill pickle spears and mustard, if desired. ✳ **Serves 4**

Beef and Eggplant Strata

This PIP recipe (see page 37) uses a deep, straight-sided metal pan, or a springform pan, that will fit loosely inside the pressure cooker. The aroma will make your kitchen smell like an Italian restaurant, and your family will be lined up waiting for dinner! Add a simple salad of crisp romaine lettuce and a crusty baguette or garlic toast for a perfect meal.

1 pound lean ground beef

1 onion, chopped

⅔ cup Italian-style bread crumbs

⅓ cup grated Parmesan cheese

1 tablespoon minced garlic

1 tablespoon dried basil

½ teaspoon crushed fennel seed

¼ teaspoon red pepper flakes

1 eggplant, peeled and thinly sliced

1 (16-ounce) jar marinara sauce—your choice

1 cup shredded mozzarella cheese

Heat the pressure cooker over medium heat. Add the ground beef, cook until crumbly and browned, and set aside. Add the onions to the cooker and cook, stirring, until slightly softened, about 3 minutes. In a large bowl, combine the cooked meat, onions, bread crumbs, Parmesan cheese, garlic, basil, fennel, and red pepper flakes. Lightly butter a flat-bottomed metal pan that will fit loosely within the pressure cooker. Arrange alternating layers of eggplant and the ground beef mixture in the pan, starting with a layer of eggplant and ending with a layer of ground beef. Pour the ragu sauce over the top, making sure it penetrates all the layers, and reserve the remaining sauce to serve at the table. Save any extra to be heated in a microwave and served in a separate bowl. Place the rack in the pressure cooker and add 1 cup of water. Using foil helper handles (see page 42), place the dish in the pressure cooker and lay a square of aluminum foil lightly over the top of the dish—do not crimp the edges or seal. Lock the lid in place. Bring to 15psi over high heat, immediately reduce the heat to the lowest possible setting to stabilize and maintain that pressure, and cook for 20 minutes. Remove from the heat and use the natural release method (see page 31) to depressurize. Carefully open the lid after the pressure drops. Add the cheese to the top of the meat and replace the lid, waiting until the cheese is melted. Using the foil helper handles, remove the pan from the pressure cooker. Spoon portions onto individual plates. Quickly heat the remaining sauce in the microwave and ladle over each portion. ✳ Serves 4

Beef-Stuffed Acorn Squash in the Half Shell

The colorful acorn squash, which is named for its shape, not flavor, grows prolifically in my garden. I'm always looking for ways to utilize the current crop, and so the acorn squash is the star of this very tasty dish. Served in the half shell, it makes a lovely presentation.

Step One: The Squash

2 medium-size acorn squash, halved lengthwise and seeded

Place the rack in the cooker and add ½ cup water. Arrange the squash halves on the rack, cut side down. Lock the lid in place. Bring to 15psi over high heat, immediately reduce the heat to the lowest possible setting to stabilize and maintain that pressure, and cook for 4 minutes. Remove from the heat and use the quick or cold water release method (see page 30) to depressurize. Carefully open the lid after the pressure drops and remove the squash halves, setting aside to cool. When the squash can be handled, carefully scoop out the insides, leaving the shell about ¼ inch thick in order to retain its shape. Cut the squash flesh into bite-size pieces.

Step Two: The Beef

½ pound lean ground beef
½ cup minced onion
⅓ cup minced packed cilantro leaves
1 tablespoon minced garlic
½ teaspoon freshly ground black pepper
¼ teaspoon ground nutmeg

Heat the pressure cooker over medium heat. Add the ground beef and cook until crumbly and browned. Add the onion and cook, stirring, for about 3 minutes. Add the cilantro, garlic, pepper, and nutmeg and ½ cup water, stirring to mix. Lock the lid in place. Bring to 15psi over high heat, immediately reduce the heat to the lowest possible setting to stabilize and maintain that pressure, and cook for 6 minutes. Remove from the heat and use the natural release method (see page 31) to depressurize. Carefully open the lid after the pressure drops. Drain well.

Step Three: The Finish

1 cup herb-seasoned croutons, slightly crumbled if large
4 slices Swiss cheese

Preheat the oven to 350°F. Gently mix the croutons, squash and the beef mixture and divide between the hollowed-out squash shells. Place the filled squash shells on a baking dish and top each with a slice of Swiss cheese. Place the pan in the oven for about 15 minutes, or just until the cheese is melted. Remove the finished stuffed squash from the oven and serve in the shell. ✳ Serves 4

Three-Meat Bolognese Sauce

Traditionally, this popular Italian sauce is cooked for several hours. An incredibly flexible sauce, this is one of my favorite pressure-cooker recipes because it's so easy and really delivers great taste in a fraction of the time. Spaghetti is too thin for this rich and hearty sauce, so I recommend linguine, or you can also try it with ziti, penne, rigatoni, or radiatore.

Step One: The *Bouquet Garni*
1 sprig fresh rosemary, about 3 inches in length
1 bay leaf
½ teaspoon whole black peppercorns

Wrap all of the ingredients together in a square of cheesecloth and tie tightly.

Step Two: The Sauce
1 pound mild or hot Italian sausages, casings removed
1 pound lean ground beef
½ pound coarsely ground pork
1 onion, diced
4 tablespoons minced garlic
1 tablespoon dried basil
½ teaspoon crushed fennel seed
Pinch of red pepper flakes
½ cup red wine
1 (14-ounce) can chicken broth
1 carrot, coarsely grated
1 stalk celery, diced
1 (28-ounce) can crushed tomatoes
2 (28-ounce) cans chopped tomatoes, with juice
⅓ cup heavy cream or half-and-half

Heat a large pressure cooker over medium heat. Add the sausage meat, cook until it is nicely crumbled and browned, and set aside on paper towels to drain. Add the ground beef to any fat that remains in the cooker and cook until it is nicely crumbled and browned, and then set aside on paper towels. Repeat the browning step with the ground pork. To remove as much grease as possible, place all the meat in a colander, rinse in cold water, and drain thoroughly. If there is any fat remaining in the cooker, pour off all but about 1 tablespoon. Add the onions and garlic to the cooker, and cook, stirring, until slightly softened, about 3 minutes. Add the basil, fennel, and red pepper flakes, frying until the spices begin to sizzle, and then deglaze the cooker with the wine, scraping up all those crusty, brown bits from the bottom. Return all the meat to the cooker and add the broth, *bouquet garni*, carrots, celery, and all the tomatoes. Stir to mix and lock the lid in place. Bring to 15psi over high heat, immediately reduce the heat to the lowest possible setting to stabilize and maintain that pressure, and cook for 8 minutes. Remove from the heat and use the natural release method (see page 31) to depressurize. Carefully open the lid after the pressure drops. Stir in the cream; if you want a lighter-colored and creamier-tasting sauce, increase the amount of cream to your taste. Simmer, uncovered, over medium heat until the sauce is heated through. ✳ Serves 6 generously

Chili con Carne

Although I had made this chili recipe for years and years, I never really wrote down the ingredients until it came down to write this cookbook. I use plenty of Mexican spices and mild chile peppers, ingredients that add flavor and a little heat without being overwhelmingly hot. Serve with warm flour tortillas or your favorite tortilla chips.

2 tablespoons olive oil
½ pound ground pork
1½ pounds lean ground beef
2 onions, chopped
4 tablespoons chili powder
1 tablespoon ground cumin
½ teaspoon ground cinnamon
¼ teaspoon red pepper flakes, or more to taste
1 large green bell pepper, seeded and chopped
2 large poblano, Anaheim, or pasilla chile, seeded and chopped
3 tomatillos, husked and minced
1 cup packed chopped cilantro leaves
4 (14-ounce) cans kidney beans, drained and rinsed
1 (28-ounce) can chopped tomatoes, with juice
2 (8-ounce) cans Mexican-style chopped tomatoes with green chiles
2 (3-ounce) cans tomato paste
1 (12-ounce) bottle Mexican beer
¼ cup cornmeal

Heat the oil in the pressure cooker over medium heat. Add the pork, cook until it's nicely browned and crumbly, and set aside on paper towels to absorb any excess fat. Repeat with the ground beef. Add the onions to the cooker and cook, stirring, until slightly softened, about 3 minutes. Add the chili powder, cumin, cinnamon, and red pepper flakes, frying until the spices begin to sizzle. Return the meat to the cooker, and add all the remaining ingredients except the cornmeal. Stir, mixing well. Lock the lid in place. Bring to 15psi over high heat, immediately reduce the heat to the lowest possible setting to stabilize and maintain that pressure, and cook for 10 minutes. Remove from the heat and use the natural release method (see page 31) to depressurize. Carefully open the lid after the pressure drops. To thicken the chili, make a slurry by mixing the cornmeal with ½ cup water, and stir the slurry into the chili. Simmer, uncovered, over medium heat until it reaches the desired consistency. Adjust the seasonings to taste and serve. ✷
Serves 6

Bacon-Wrapped Beef Birds with Chipotle Butter

The original version of this old-fashioned recipe was popular during World War II, although it requires a considerable stretch of the imagination to think these tasty little oval-shaped beef patties actually resemble "birds." I've kept the original recipe for the meat mixture that my grandma used, but added the bacon wraps and a bit of upscale pizzazz with a flavorful butter sauce.

Step One: The Chipotle Butter

8 tablespoons (1 stick) butter, at room temperature

3 tablespoons minced shallots

1 tablespoon minced fresh cilantro leaves

1 tablespoons minced chipotle peppers in adobo sauce

1 tablespoon fresh lime juice

Combine all of the ingredients and beat until light and fluffy at least 4 hours in advance. Cover and refrigerate until ready to serve.

Step Two: The Beef Birds

1 pound lean ground beef

1 onion, minced

1 green bell pepper, seeded and minced

1 cup fine bread crumbs

½ teaspoon ground sage

½ teaspoon garlic powder

Juice of 1 lemon

½ cup milk

1 large egg, slightly beaten

4 thick slices bacon

Using a stand mixer for the best results, combine all of the ingredients except the bacon and thoroughly blend all the ingredients. Divide the mixture into 4 equal parts, and form into thick oval-shaped patties. Wrap each beef bird in a strip of bacon, securing the bacon with toothpicks. Heat the pressure cooker over medium heat, add the bacon-wrapped rolls, cook until browned on both sides, and transfer to paper towels to drain. Pour off all the fat. Place the rack in the cooker and add ½ cup water. Carefully arrange the beef birds on the rack using long-handled tongs. Lock the lid in place. Bring to 15psi over high heat, immediately reduce the heat to the lowest possible setting to stabilize and maintain that pressure, and cook for 6 minutes. Remove from the heat and use the natural release method (see page 31) to depressurize. Carefully open the lid after the pressure drops. Transfer the beef birds to a serving plate. Using a melon baller, place a small round ball of the chilled Chipotle Butter on each bird.

✳ Serves 4

Gourmet Beef Patties in Balsamic Cream Sauce

Balsamic vinegar enhances the flavor of food, and this is a delicious way to elevate a rather ordinary hamburger patty into the stratosphere of fine gourmet dining. Using the pressure cooker, the cooking time zooms into light-speed, and you'll have dinner on the table in record time.

Step One: The Beef Patties
1 pound lean ground beef
1 cup grated Parmesan cheese
1 small onion, finely minced
½ cup fine bread crumbs
1 large egg, slightly beaten
½ teaspoon freshly ground black pepper
½ teaspoon garlic powder
¼ teaspoon ground nutmeg
2 tablespoons butter
½ cup white wine

In a medium-size bowl, thoroughly mix the ground beef, Parmesan cheese, half of the onions, the bread crumbs, egg, pepper, garlic, and nutmeg, and shape into 4 thick patties. Heat the butter in the pressure cooker, add the patties, cook until browned on both sides, and set aside. Add the remaining onions to the cooker and cook, stirring, until soft and golden brown, about 3 minutes. Pour in the wine, scraping up all the crusty, brown bits, and add the rack in the bottom of the cooker. Arrange the beef patties on top of the rack and lock the lid in place. Bring to 15psi over high heat,

immediately reduce the heat to the lowest possible setting to stabilize and maintain that pressure, and cook for 8 minutes. Remove from the heat and use the natural release method (see page 31) to depressurize. Carefully open the lid after the pressure drops. Carefully transfer the patties to a plate and cover with foil. Remove the rack from the pressure cooker.

Step Two: The Balsamic Cream Sauce
4 tablespoons balsamic vinegar
2 tablespoons cornstarch
½ cup heavy cream
4 thick slices French bread, lightly buttered and toasted

Add the balsamic vinegar to the sauce and simmer, uncovered, over medium-low heat. To thicken the sauce, make a slurry with the cornstarch mixed into the cream and add it to the sauce, slowly stirring as it thickens, but do not allow the sauce to boil. To serve, top each slice of bread with a beef patty and spoon the cream sauce over the top.

✳ Serves 4

Basic Kitchen Stock

Soup is prime comfort food, and nothing is better on a chilly day than a hot, steaming bowl of home-made soup. Cherished by everyone, soup is a cultural mainstay in every cook's kitchen. Today, with a pressure cooker and a few staple ingredients, it takes mere minutes to create a great-tasting home-made soup, but a richly flavored stock is the key.

Free Stock-Making Kit

With a little advance planning, you can have "free" stock. Be a frugal cook and save everything. Freeze all those vegetable parings, the dry fibrous stalks and tough leaves—all the stuff that you would ordinarily toss out—as the start of a great soup base. Freeze bones, meat trimmings, leftover meat and vegetables—almost anything can go into your stock-making kit. Once you've gathered up your saved ingredients, you're ready to proceed.

This is not so much a recipe as a do-it-yourself guide to creating wonderful homemade stock, and once you have tried it, you will never want to go back to the commercial stuff. One of the best things about stock is the infinite variety of ingredients that can be used. You'll find dozens of ways to vary the proportions or ingredients, so feel free to experiment, using any combination of ingredients that you like or have on hand. You will need a 7-quart or larger pressure cooker, or divide the ingredients and make two batches.

Root Vegetables: Use vegetables that are in season. Start with 1 pound of coarsely chopped mixed root vegetables. Carrots are a must, but use at least one other, such as: parsnips, turnips, rutabagas, or celery root, but no potatoes of any kind, as the starch acts as a thickener.

Aromatic Vegetables: Gather up 3 cups of coarsely chopped aromatic vegetables. Onions are a must (any variety or mixture of white, brown, green, purple, red, etc.), and use at least two others, such as: garlic, shallots, celery stalks and leaves, parsley, leeks, fennel, or cilantro stems and leaves.

Leafy Vegetables: You'll need ½ pound of coarsely chopped leafy vegetables, but don't overdo it, because most leafy vegetables tend to have a stronger taste. Use at least two different varieties, such as the greens from beets, mustard greens, turnip greens, kale, collards, or chard. Cabbage, spinach, and even lettuce can be tossed into the stockpot. Wilt bulky leaves so that they take up less room by steaming them in the pressure cooker using the regular lid.

Herbs and Spices: Use the ones that you have on hand, or the ones that appeal to you most when making up your bouquet garni. Tie the ingredients up in a little cheesecloth bag, or try using a convenient tea ball for easy removal. No salt in the stock, please; wait to add the salt when using your homemade stock in a favorite recipe, but always taste first. You will need twice as much fresh herbs as dried, so plan accordingly. Choose at least five items, measured at 1 teaspoon each: 2 bay leaves (counts as one item), 10 whole black peppercorns (counts as one item), thyme, rosemary, oregano, basil, sage, marjoram. Other additions you may want to consider are whole cinnamon sticks, cloves, fresh or candied ginger, whole cardamom and nutmeg, star anise—there are so many to choose from, so let your creativity shine!

Meat and Bones: Use any combination of meat and bones that will equal 2 pounds, but use more bones than meat. If you have been saving bones and meat scraps in the freezer as part of your Free Stock-Making Kit, then you're off to a great start.

For a beefy or meaty stock, it's perfectly acceptable to mix a variety of bones if you don't have enough of any one particular kind. Use bones from beef, veal, venison, or lamb. If buying bones for stock, consider shanks, marrow bones, neck bones, oxtails, calves foot, or knuckle (soup) bones, and have the butcher cut or split them into smaller sections. For poultry-based soups, a meaty chicken or turkey carcass is a wonderful foundation, but if you are buying the meat, use the cheapest bony parts such as wings, necks, and backs for stock. Remember, it's the bones that count.

Them Bones, Them Bones, Them Dry Bones

Bones for stock need to be browned first to develop a better flavor. Heat the oven to 400°F. Oil the bones, and place a layer of coarsely chopped onions and carrots on a greased roasting pan, adding the bones on top of the vegetables. Place the pan in the oven and cook until they are nicely browned, about 40 minutes. Don't worry if the vegetables get a little browned or begin to caramelize, but if they start to get too blackened, scoop them into the pressure cooker. When the bones are finished, add them to the cooker as well. Deglaze the roasting pan with about 1 cup water, scraping up the bits and pieces in the bottom, and then pour all of that into the cooker, too.

Into the Pot!

When all the bones for your stock are in the pressure cooker, add all the other ingredients you've collected and enough water to cover the ingredients, taking care not to exceed the maximum ⅔-full level of your pressure cooker. Stir and lock the lid in place. Bring to 15psi over high heat, immediately reduce the heat to the lowest possible setting to stabilize and maintain that pressure, and cook for 30 minutes. Remove from the heat and use the natural release method (see page 31) to depressurize. Carefully open the lid after the pressure drops. Strain the stock through a fine sieve or several layers of cheesecloth in a colander, and discard all the solid ingredients. Refrigerate the stock for several hours or overnight so that the fat will congeal at the top and can be easily removed. The best, and the richest, most nutritious stock will have a thick, gelatin-like consistency, but a stock that is less firm will still be wonderfully delicious. Your stock is now ready for use in soups, stews, and other recipes. If you don't plan on using the stock within a couple of days, divide it into 1-cup portions and freeze in plastic containers or self-closing plastic bags. ✳ **Serves 6**

Beef and Barley Soup

This soup comes from my grandmother's shoebox of recipes. Perfect in the winter, it makes a hearty and filling meal when served with plenty of warm, crusty bread. This makes a huge pot of soup, with enough to pack in lunches the next day or freeze in portion sizes to have on hand for a quick bowl of hot soup. Not only is this fast in the pressure cooker, but once the ingredients are assembled, it's very easy to make.

- ½ cup all-purpose flour
- ½ teaspoon salt
- ½ teaspoon freshly ground black pepper
- 2 pounds beef round or chuck, trimmed of excess fat and cut into 2-inch cubes
- 2 tablespoons oil
- 1 onion, chopped
- 2 (14-ounce) cans beef broth
- ½ cup dry red wine
- ⅓ cup pearl barley
- 1 (8-ounce) can mushroom slices, drained
- ½ teaspoon dried thyme leaves
- 1 herb bouquet consisting of 1 bay leaf, the peel from 1 orange, 4 whole cloves, 10 whole peppercorns, 1 sprig fresh rosemary, 3 celery tops with leaves, and 2 cloves crushed garlic, all tied in cheesecloth
- 3 stalks celery, cut into 1-inch slices
- 2 carrots, peeled and cut into 1-inch slices

In a plastic bag, mix the flour, salt, and pepper, and add the meat, shaking gently until coated. Heat the oil in a large pressure cooker over medium heat. Add the meat, cook until browned on both sides, and set aside. Add the onions to the cooker and cook, stirring, for about 3 minutes. Deglaze the cooker with the wine. Add the broth barley, mushrooms, thyme, and basil, and add the herb bouquet. Return the meat to the cooker. Add the celery and carrots, and enough additional water, if needed, to cover the ingredients by at least 3 inches. Lock the lid in place. Bring to 15psi over high heat, immediately reduce the heat to the lowest possible setting to stabilize and maintain that pressure, and cook for 16 minutes. Remove from the heat and use the natural release method (see page 31) to depressurize. Carefully open the lid after the pressure drops. Adjust the seasonings to taste and serve. ✳ Serves 6

Cook's Note: Barley has a tendency to continue to absorb liquid, so before refrigerating any leftovers, stir in some additional water or broth.

Beefy French Onion Soup

The traditional onion soup is a rich beef broth dense with onions, crowned with cheese-laden toast, and so filling it's often served as a main dish. Here's a recipe that takes this popular soup up a step with the addition of a rich, made-from-scratch beefy broth. To round out the meal, all this soup needs is a loaf of crusty bread and a robust red wine. The broth can be prepared a day or more in advance.

Step One: The Beef and Stock

4 tablespoons (½ stick) butter

1 tablespoon oil

3½ pounds beef shanks

1 onion, quartered

2 stalks celery with leaves, cut into 2-inch pieces

2 tablespoons minced garlic

2 carrots, cut into 2-inch lengths

1 teaspoon whole black peppercorns

5 sprigs fresh parsley or cilantro

1 bay leaf

½ cup red wine

Heat the butter and oil in a large pressure cooker over medium heat. Add the beef shanks, cook until well browned on all sides, and set aside. Add the onions, celery, and garlic to the cooker and cook, stirring, until softened, about 3 minutes. Add the carrots. Make a *bouquet garni* with the peppercorns, parsley, and bay leaf, tying the ingredients in a little square of cheesecloth, or use a convenient tea ball for easy removal, and add to the cooker. Add 2 quarts water and the wine and stir. Lock the lid in place. Bring to 15psi over high heat, immediately reduce the heat to the lowest possible setting to stabilize and maintain that pressure, and cook for 30 minutes. Remove from the heat and use the natural release method (see page 31) to depressurize. Carefully open the lid after the pressure drops. Remove the beef and set aside to cool. Strain the stock through a colander lined with cheesecloth into a large bowl, and discard the herbs and vegetables. Skim off any excess fat from the top of the stock. Remove the meat from the bones, shred or cut into very small pieces, and set aside.

Step Two: The Toast

6 thick slices French bread

1 cup shredded Swiss cheese

½ cup grated Parmesan cheese

Paprika to taste

Meanwhile, preheat the broiler. Make the cheese toast by topping each slice of bread with a portion of the Swiss and Parmesan cheeses. Place the bread under the broiler, about 5 inches from the heat, watching closely until the cheese is melted and lightly browned. Remove from the oven as soon as the cheese is melted, dust lightly with paprika, and set aside.

Step Three: The Soup

4 tablespoons (½ stick) butter

8 yellow onions, halved and thinly sliced

2 tablespoons minced garlic

2 teaspoons beef bouillon granules

Chopped chives or green onion tops,
     for garnish

Heat the butter in the pressure cooker over medium heat. Add the onions and garlic in batches and cook, stirring, until they are all slightly softened, about 3 minutes per batch. Add all the onions, garlic, the stock, bouillon, and the meat to the cooker and stir. Lock the lid back in place. Return to 15psi, over high heat, immediately reduce the heat to the lowest possible setting to stabilize and maintain that pressure, and cook for an additional 5 minutes. Remove from the heat and use the natural release method (see page 31) to depressurize. Carefully open the lid after the pressure drops. Adjust the seasonings to taste. To serve, place each piece of cheese toast in the bottom of a large soup bowl and ladle the soup on top. Garnish with a sprinkling of chives. ✳ Serves 6

Cook's Note: For variety, use a mix of different onions, and cut them in different ways—rings, half rings, wedges, coarsely and finely chopped, etc.

Tender Beef Noodle Soup

I think a lot of people avoid making soup because it takes hours and hours to cook by conventional cooking methods, but use a pressure cooker and a lovely, delicious, and nutritious homemade soup can be on the table in less than 30 minutes. This is a simple recipe that even picky eaters will enjoy.

Step One: The Beef and Broth
½ cup all-purpose flour
½ teaspoon salt
1 teaspoon freshly ground black pepper
1 ½ pounds boneless beef, cut into 2-inch cubes
2 to 4 tablespoons butter
2 onions, halved and then quartered
2 tablespoons minced garlic
2 (14-ounce) cans beef broth
2 bay leaves

In a plastic bag, mix the flour, salt, and ½ teaspoon of the pepper, and add the meat, shaking gently until coated. Heat the butter in a large pressure cooker over medium-high heat. Add the meat, cook until well browned on all sides, and set aside. Add the onions and garlic to the cooker and cook, stirring, until soft, about 3 minutes. Deglaze the cooker with some of the broth, scraping up all those crusty, brown bits from the bottom. Add the remaining pepper, the bay leaves, and remaining broth, return the meat to the cooker, and lock the lid in place. Bring to 15psi over high heat, immediately reduce the heat to the lowest possible setting to stabilize and maintain that pressure, and cook for 12 minutes. Remove from the heat and use the natural release method (see page 31) to depressurize. Carefully open the lid after the pressure drops. Remove the bay leaves and skim off any excess fat.

Step Two: The Noodles
3 cups uncooked twisted egg noodles

Add the uncooked egg noodles to the cooker, pushing them beneath the surface of the broth. If necessary, add more water so there are about 2 inches of liquid above the level of the combined ingredients. Do not exceed the ⅔-full level. Lock the lid back in place, return to 15psi over high heat, immediately reduce the heat to the lowest possible setting to stabilize and maintain that pressure, and cook for an additional 5 minutes. Remove from the heat and use the natural release method (see page 31) to depressurize. Carefully open the lid after the pressure drops. Stir gently and adjust the seasonings to taste before serving. ✳ Serves 6

Irish Oxtail Soup

There are a lot of things to like about soup: it's easy to cook, easy on your tummy, and easy on your wallet, too. Nothing takes away the winter chill quite like a big steaming bowl of hot soup. Making a great-tasting soup is simple, and you can't go wrong in this meaty oxtail soup with a variety of hearty vegetables.

Step One: The Beef and Stock

2 tablespoons oil

2 pounds beef oxtails, cut into 1½- to 2-inch sections

1 onion, halved and then quartered

2 stalks celery, cut into ½-inch pieces

2 sprigs celery leaves

3 cloves garlic, crushed

1 teaspoon whole black peppercorns

2 bay leaves

1 tablespoon dried thyme leaves

1 tablespoon ground sage

1 teaspoon dried marjoram

2 (12-ounce) bottles stout beer (Guinness or any dark beer)

Heat the oil in a large pressure cooker over medium-high heat. Add the meat, cook until well browned on all sides, and set aside. Add the onions and celery to the cooker and cook, stirring, until soft, about 3 minutes. To make the bouquet garni, place the celery leaves, garlic, peppercorns, and bay leaves in the center of a square of cheesecloth and tie the top very tightly to make a spice bag, then add it to the cooker. Add the thyme, sage, and marjoram and return the meat to the cooker. Pour in the beer and add 3 cups water, stirring to mix. Lock the lid in place. Bring to 15psi over high heat,

immediately reduce the heat to the lowest possible setting to stabilize and maintain that pressure, and cook for 35 minutes. Remove from the heat and use the natural release method (see page 31) to depressurize. Carefully open the lid after the pressure drops. Remove the oxtails and set aside to cool. Strain the stock through a colander lined with cheesecloth, and discard the herbs and vegetables. Skim off any excess fat from the top of the stock and return the stock to the pressure cooker. Remove the meat from the bones and add it back to the stock.

Step Two: The Soup

2 potatoes, peeled and diced

2 parsnips, peeled and diced

2 carrots, peeled and diced

2 stalks celery, chopped

Add the vegetables to the stock and lock the lid back in place. Return to 15psi over high heat, immediately reduce the heat to the lowest possible setting to stabilize and maintain that pressure, and cook for an additional 4 minutes. Remove from the heat and use the natural release method (see page 31) to depressurize. Carefully open the lid after the pressure drops. Adjust the seasonings to taste. Pour into a heated soup tureen and serve.

✳ Serves 6

Cook's Note: If you don't like these vegetables or don't have them on hand, use what you like or substitute frozen mixed vegetables.

Chicken

WHEN YOU NEED SOMETHING that tastes good and offers a huge variety of recipes, chicken is a standout. Whether it's for a barbecue, a quick meal on the run, or a special dinner, chicken can be prepared in so many ways. America loves chicken, and with our fast-paced lifestyle it is a popular choice that is quick and easy to prepare.

The way we cook may have changed from the early days of pressure cooking, but we still want to prepare nutritious, homemade meals. At the same time, we also want to spend less time in the kitchen. For most people who do not own a pressure cooker, the definition of cooking has gone from scratch cooking to the mechanics of meal assembly from assorted cans and packages of commercially prepared foods.

For a healthy, delicious alternative to traditional fast food, choose from a variety of chicken dishes for quick meals. Chicken practically guarantees a good result no matter how it's prepared, and from spicy chicken wing appetizers to a whole roast chicken, the modern pressure cooker is one of the most versatile pieces of cookware in your kitchen. Use it to prepare creative and tasty chicken recipes in just minutes, choosing from a variety of recipes designed to satisfy a wide range of tastes.

After-the-Fact Fried Chicken and Buttermilk Gravy

Everyone knows that you can't use a pressure cooker as a pressure fryer because it is too dangerous. Here is a method that first uses the pressure cooker to precook the chicken to make it moist and tender, and then the chicken is quickly fried to a crisp golden brown.

Step One: The Precooked Chicken
6 boneless, skinless chicken breasts

Rinse the chicken pieces and pat dry. Place the rack in the cooker, add ½ cup water, and arrange the chicken pieces on the rack. Lock the lid in place. Bring to 15psi over high heat, immediately reduce the heat to the lowest possible setting to stabilize and maintain that pressure, and cook for 6 minutes. Remove from the heat and use the quick or cold water release method (see page 30) to depressurize. Carefully open the lid after the pressure drops.

Step Two: The Fried Chicken
1 cup buttermilk
1 large egg, slightly beaten
1 cup flour
1 (.7-ounce) package dried Italian-style salad dressing mix
1 teaspoon ground sage
½ teaspoon salt
½ teaspoon freshly ground black pepper
½ cup peanut oil, for frying

Mix the buttermilk and egg together in a small bowl. In a large resealable plastic bag, combine the flour, Italian dressing mix, sage, salt, and pepper. Remove from heat and use the natural release method before opening the lid. Remove the chicken from the pressure cooker and use paper towels to pat the pieces dry. Dip each piece in the buttermilk mixture. One at a time, add the chicken pieces to the seasoned flour mixture and shake gently to coat each piece, dip again in buttermilk, and then shake in the seasoned flour bag. Pour ½ inch of oil in a large skillet and heat to approximately 350°F. If you do not have a thermometer available, test the temperature by placing a small cube of bread into the oil. When it is hot enough, the bread cube turns golden brown within 30 seconds. Add several pieces chicken and fry in batches until golden brown on both sides. This only takes a couple of minutes, so watch closely and do not overcook. Place the fried chicken on paper towels to drain. Transfer the cooked chicken to a roasting pan with a rack and place cooked chicken in 325°F oven to keep warm while finishing remaining chicken.

Step Three: The Buttermilk Gravy
3 tablespoons pan drippings
¼ cup of the seasoned flour
3 cups buttermilk
1 teaspoon paprika
½ teaspoon salt
½ teaspoon freshly ground black pepper
⅛ teaspoon cayenne pepper

After all the chicken has been cooked, pour off all of the oil except 3 tablespoons, keeping any of the remaining crispy bits, to make the gravy. Heat the skillet with the oil over medium-low heat, whisk in the seasoned flour and stir until it becomes a smooth browned paste. Gradually whisk in the buttermilk, add the paprika, salt and pepper, and the cayenne pepper, and then simmer, stirring constantly until thickened and bubbly, about 3 minutes. Serve the gravy in a separate bowl. ✳ **Serves 6**

Russian Apricot Chicken

An easy chicken recipe braised in apricot nectar with dried apricots and a surprising burst of tangy flavor provided by the addition of Russian salad dressing. This goes particularly well with mashed potatoes, but fluffy rice or egg noodles are good choices as well.

½ **cup all-purpose flour**
½ **teaspoon salt**
½ **teaspoon freshly ground black pepper**
6 boneless, skinless chicken breasts
3 tablespoons oil
1 onion, minced
1 (12-ounce) can apricot nectar
1 green bell pepper, seeded and finely chopped
½ **cup dried apricots, chopped**
½ **cup bottled Russian salad dressing**
2 tablespoons cornstarch

In a large resealable plastic bag, mix the flour, salt, and pepper, and add the chicken, shaking gently until each piece is lightly coated. Heat the oil in the pressure cooker over medium heat. Add the chicken pieces, cook until golden brown on all sides, and set aside. Add the onions to the cooker and cook, stirring, until clear, about 3 minutes. Drain off all the oil. Deglaze the cooker with the apricot nectar, scraping up all those crusty, brown bits from the bottom. Add the bell pepper, apricots, Russian dressing, and ⅓ cup water, stirring to mix. Return the chicken pieces to the cooker and lock the lid in place. Bring to 15psi over high heat, immediately reduce the heat to the lowest possible setting to stabilize and maintain that pressure, and cook for 8 minutes. Remove from the heat and use the natural release method (see page 31) to depressurize. Carefully open the lid after the pressure drops. Transfer the chicken to an oven-safe platter and place in a low oven to keep warm. Bring the sauce to a simmer over medium heat. Thicken the apricot sauce by making a slurry with the cornstarch mixed into ⅓ cup cold water; stir the slurry into the sauce and stir frequently until it begins to thicken, but do not boil. Serve the apricot sauce in a separate bowl. ✳ **Serves 6**

Chicken in Orange Sauce

There are a million and one ways to cook chicken, so there is no reason to settle for ordinary when a tangy citrus sauce will transform it into something delicious.

> 6 boneless, skinless chicken breasts
> 2 tablespoons butter or margarine
> 1 onion, chopped
> ½ teaspoon freshly ground black pepper
> ½ cup sugar
> 1/4 teaspoon salt
> 1 1/4 cups orange juice
> 1/4 cup lemon juice
> 2 tablespoons cornstarch
> 1 tablespoon grated orange zest
> 1 tablespoon grated lemon zest
> 1 small orange, sliced, for garnish

Heat the butter in the pressure cooker over medium-high heat. Add the chicken pieces, cook until golden brown on all sides, and set aside. Add the onions to the cooker and stir in ½ cup water. Place the cooking rack in the bottom and return the chicken pieces to the pressure cooker and lock the lid in place. Bring to 15psi over high heat, immediately reduce the heat to the lowest possible setting to stabilize and maintain that pressure, and cook for 8 minutes. Remove from the heat and use the natural release method (see page 31) to depressurize. Carefully open the lid after the pressure drops. Transfer the chicken to a serving plate and garnish with the orange slices. To make the sauce, skim off any excess fat from the pan juices and stir in the sugar and lemon juice. Mix the orange juice and cornstarch all together and pour it into the pan juices, cooking over medium heat, stirring constantly, until the mixture boils and thickens. Remove from heat and stir in the orange and lemon zest. Adjust the seasonings to taste. Pour the orange sauce in a gravy boat to serve at the table.

❋ Serves 6

Blushing Chicken

Chicken breasts are briefly sautéed, then simmered in a tangy sauce of cranberries and orange juice, giving the chicken a lovely pink blush and a sweet, tangy taste. This is a dish with minimal preparation, but it's big on taste.

> 2 tablespoons oil
> 6 boneless, skinless chicken breasts
> 1 onion, chopped
> 2 cups fresh or frozen whole cranberries
> ½ can frozen orange juice concentrate, thawed
> 2 tablespoons grated orange zest
> 1 teaspoon pumpkin pie spice
> ½ teaspoon red pepper flakes
> ⅓ cup sugar, or to taste

Heat the oil in the pressure cooker over medium heat. Add the chicken pieces, cook until golden brown on all sides, and set aside. Add the onions to the cooker and cook, stirring, until clear, about 3 minutes. Add the cranberries, orange juice concentrate, orange peel, pumpkin pie spice, and red pepper flakes. Stir in ½ cup water, mixing well, and return the chicken pieces to the cooker. Lock the lid in place. Bring to 15psi over high heat, immediately reduce the heat to the lowest possible setting to stabilize and maintain that pressure, and cook for 8 minutes. Remove from the heat and use the natural release method (see page 31) to depressurize. Carefully open the lid after the pressure drops. Transfer the chicken to an oven-safe platter and place in a low oven to keep warm. Stir the sugar into the sauce and bring to a boil over high heat, stirring frequently until it begins to thicken. Taste after the sugar has dissolved and adjust as desired, but leave the sauce tangy. Serve the sauce in a separate bowl. ✳ Serves 6

Chicken à la King

In need of some comfort food, what could be nicer than this old-fashioned dish? This is basically chicken pot pie without the crust, so it's perfect served over hot-from-the-oven split biscuits, or toast points. My grandma's version was made on Monday, using leftover chicken from Sunday's supper, and served over waffles.

3 tablespoons butter or margarine
1 teaspoon salt
⅛ teaspoon freshly ground black pepper
3 boneless, skinless chicken breasts cut into
   1-inch pieces
⅓ cup minced onion
1 cup frozen peas
1 (4-ounce) can mushroom stems and pieces,
   drained
1 (2-ounce) jar pimientos, drained
   and chopped

1 (14-ounce) can chicken broth
¼ cup all-purpose flour
1 cup half-and-half
Toast points or biscuits

Heat the butter in the pressure cooker over high heat. Rub the salt and pepper into both sides of the chicken pieces. Add the chicken to the cooker, cook until golden brown on both sides, and set aside. Add the onion and cook, stirring, until tender, about 3 minutes. Add the peas, mushrooms, pimientos, and broth, mixing well. Return the chicken to the cooker. Lock the lid in place. Bring to 15psi over high heat, immediately reduce the heat to the lowest possible setting to stabilize and maintain that pressure, and cook for 5 minutes. Remove from the heat and use the natural release method (see page 31) to depressurize. Carefully open the lid after the pressure drops. Thicken the broth by making a slurry with the flour combined with the half-and-half; stir the slurry into the broth and simmer gently over medium heat until it's the desired consistency. Adjust the seasonings to taste and serve over toast points or split biscuits. ✳ Serves 4

Cook's Note: Use 3 cups diced, cooked, leftover chicken in place of the breasts, and reduce the cooking time to just 3 minutes.

Variations

Substitute 3 cups diced, cooked leftover turkey for Turkey à la King.

Substitute 2 (6½-ounce) cans tuna, flaked, with packing juice, for Tuna à la King.

Chicken Breasts Romano

This pasta dish is easy to put together and features a tangy tomato sauce. It makes such a pretty presentation when served over pasta that it works just as well for company as it does for a family meal.

½ cup all-purpose flour
½ teaspoon salt
½ teaspoon freshly ground black pepper
6 boneless, skinless chicken breasts
2 tablespoons oil
1 onion, minced
1 (10-ounce) can tomato sauce
1 teaspoon vinegar
1 (4-ounce) can mushroom slices, drained
1 tablespoon sugar
1 tablespoon garlic, minced
1 tablespoon dried oregano
1 teaspoon dried basil
1 teaspoon chicken bouillon granules
1 cup grated Romano cheese

In a large resealable plastic bag, mix the flour, salt, and pepper and add the chicken, shaking gently until each piece is lightly coated. Heat the oil in the pressure cooker over medium heat. Add the chicken, cook until well browned on all sides, and set aside. Add the onions to the cooker and cook, stirring, until clear, about 3 minutes. Add the tomato sauce, vinegar, mushrooms, sugar, garlic, oregano, basil, and bouillon. Add ½ cup water, stirring until well blended. Return the chicken to the pressure cooker and lock the lid in place. Bring to 15psi over high heat, immediately reduce the heat to the lowest possible setting to stabilize and maintain that pressure, and cook for 8 minutes. Remove from the heat and use the natural release method (see page 31) to depressurize. Carefully open the lid after the pressure drops. Transfer the chicken breasts to a serving plate and top each piece with a mound of grated cheese. Pour the tomato sauce into a serving bowl. ✻ Serves 6

Serving Suggestion: Serve over cooked spaghetti or other pasta, or try it over mashed potatoes.

Chicken Scampi

This is a chicken and garlic recipe to be served with pasta. Lots of succulent chicken bites in a creamy garlic sauce that I like to serve over linguine or hot buttered egg noodles.

Step One: The White Sauce
1 tablespoon butter
2 tablespoons all-purpose flour
¾ cup hot milk

Melt the butter in a small heavy-bottomed saucepan. Add the flour and cook for 2 minutes on medium-high heat, stirring constantly until it forms a smooth paste. Slowly add the hot milk, stirring until it is thick and smooth. Set aside, keeping warm.

Step Two: The Chicken
2 tablespoons butter
3 boneless, skinless chicken breasts
1 onion, minced
¼ cup dry white wine
2 tablespoons minced garlic
2 tablespoons mixed Italian herbs
1 tablespoon dried parsley flakes

½ teaspoon red pepper flakes

½ teaspoon freshly ground black pepper

1 cup chicken broth

3 tablespoons fresh lemon juice

⅓ cup grated Parmesan cheese

Heat the butter in the pressure cooker over high heat. Add the chicken, cook until golden brown on both sides, and set aside. Add the onions to the cooker and cook, stirring, until clear, about 3 minutes. Deglaze the cooker with the wine, scraping up all those crusty, brown bits from the bottom. Add the garlic, Italian herbs, parsley, red pepper, black pepper, broth, and lemon juice, return the chicken pieces to the cooker, and stir. Lock the lid in place. Bring to 15psi over high heat, immediately reduce the heat to the lowest possible setting to stabilize and maintain that pressure, and cook for 4 minutes. Remove from the heat and use the natural release method (see page 31) to depressurize. Carefully open the lid after the pressure drops. Remove the chicken breasts, cut them into bite-size cubes, and set aside. Make sure that the white sauce is hot, and then whisk it into the broth in the pressure cooker. Stir until the sauce is slightly thickened. Add the Parmesan cheese and the cut-up chicken, stirring to blend. ✳ Serves 4

Chicken Fricassee

Chicken fricassee became popular with frugal cooks during the Depression because it stretched a single chicken into a hearty meal that served a family of four to six. If the chicken happened to be a little tough, the long simmering made the meat tender. I remember this dish from childhood, but in this updated version, I've substituted chicken breasts for a quick and easy weekday meal.

6 boneless, skinless chicken breasts, cut into bite-size pieces

½ pound fresh mushrooms, washed and sliced

1 onion, sliced

½ cup white wine

1 (14-ounce) can chicken broth

1 tablespoon minced garlic

¼ teaspoon cayenne pepper

1 cup heavy cream

½ cup sour cream

2 tablespoons cornstarch

2 tablespoons chopped fresh parsley leaves, for garnish

Toast points or biscuits, for serving

Heat the butter in the pressure cooker over high heat. Add the mushrooms and onions to the cooker and cook, stirring, until soft, about 3 minutes. Deglaze the cooker with the wine, scraping up all those crusty, brown bits from the bottom. Add the broth, garlic, and cayenne pepper, and stir in the chicken pieces to the cooker. Lock the lid in place. Bring to 15psi over high heat, immediately reduce the heat to the lowest possible setting to stabilize and maintain that pressure, and cook for 5 minutes. Remove from the heat and use the natural release method (see page 31) to depressurize. Carefully open the lid after the pressure drops. Bring the sauce to a simmer over medium-low heat, and stir in the heavy cream and the sour cream. Thicken the sauce by making a slurry with the cornstarch mixed with ⅓ cup cold water; stir the slurry into the sauce and simmer, stirring often as it thickens, but do not boil. Taste and correct seasonings. Transfer to a serving bowl and sprinkle on the chopped parsley as a garnish. Spoon over toast points or biscuits. ✳ Serves 6

Glazed Teriyaki Chicken Strips

Adding teriyaki sauce adds bold flavors and really pumps up the taste of plain chicken. Served with fluffy hot rice, this recipe will enliven your taste buds, and your next meal.

> 2 tablespoons butter
> 4 boneless, skinless chicken breasts
> 1 onion, sliced into thin rings
> ¼ cup teriyaki sauce
> ¼ cup soy sauce
> ¼ cup dry sherry
> 2 tablespoons good-quality balsamic vinegar
> 2 tablespoons minced garlic
> ½ teaspoon freshly ground black pepper
> ½ teaspoon ground ginger
> ⅓ cup minced green onion tops, for garnish

Heat the butter in the pressure cooker over medium heat. Add the chicken, cook until golden brown on both sides, cut into 1-inch strips, and set aside. Add the onions to the cooker and cook, stirring, until clear, about 3 minutes. Arrange the chicken strips on the bottom of the pressure cooker. In a small bowl, combine the teriyaki sauce, soy sauce, sherry, vinegar, garlic, pepper, and ginger, stirring to mix. Pour the teriyaki mixture into the cooker and lock the lid in place. Bring to 15psi over high heat, immediately reduce the heat to the lowest possible setting to stabilize and maintain that pressure, and cook for 4 minutes. Remove from the heat and use the quick or cold water release method (see page 30) to depressurize. Carefully open the lid after the pressure drops. Remove the chicken pieces to a roasting pan and pour the sauce over the chicken. Meanwhile, preheat the broiler and place the pan under the broiler, about 6 inches from the heat, until the chicken just begins to crisp and brown. Turn once, again basting the chicken strips, and remove them after they have slightly browned. Transfer the chicken strips to a serving plate and drizzle any remaining glaze over the top. Sprinkle the chopped green onions just before serving. ✳ Serves 4

Serving Suggestion: Serve over hot fluffy rice or ramen-style noodles.

Chicken with Peachy Jalapeño Salsa

One year when my peach tree kicked into overdrive, I found myself with more peaches than I could possibly use. On a whim, I came up with the idea of adding fresh peaches to my usual salsa recipe, instead of tomatoes. It was such a hit that the recipe has become an annual favorite during the summer, when fresh peaches are plentiful. Serve with wild rice for a great accompaniment.

Step One: The Salsa
> 2 large, ripe peaches, peeled, pitted, and diced, with any accumulated juice
> ½ cup minced red onion
> 1 medium-size jalapeño chile, seeded and minced
> ⅓ cup minced cilantro leaves
> 2 teaspoons powdered sugar, or to taste
> 1 tablespoon fresh lime juice

Several hours in advance, combine all the ingredients for the salsa in a small nonreactive glass bowl and cover tightly with plastic wrap. Refrigerate until ready to serve.

Step Two: The Chicken
1 tablespoon sweet paprika
½ teaspoon coarsely ground black pepper
⅛ teaspoon cayenne pepper
4 boneless, skinless chicken breasts
2 tablespoons oil

Mix together the paprika, black pepper, and cayenne pepper, and rub them into both sides of the chicken. Heat the oil in the pressure cooker over medium heat. Add the chicken pieces, cook until golden brown on both sides, and set aside. Place the rack in the cooker and add ½ cup water. Arrange the chicken on top of the rack and lock the lid in place. Bring to 15psi over high heat, immediately reduce the heat to the lowest possible setting to stabilize and maintain that pressure, and cook for 8 minutes. Remove from the heat and use the natural release method (see page 31) to depressurize. Carefully open the lid after the pressure drops. Transfer the chicken to a serving plate and serve the salsa on the side. ✳ **Serves 4**

Pecan Apricot Chicken

Tender chicken cooked in a delicious sauce of sweet apricots topped with crunchy pecans makes for a wonderful combination of flavors and textures that come together for this delicious chicken dish. Serve the flavorful sauce with a side dish of white or brown rice.

4 boneless, skinless chicken breasts
½ cup chopped pecans
3 tablespoons butter
1 small red onion, minced
¼ cup apricot preserves
¼ cup bourbon
2 tablespoons tomato paste
1 teaspoon spicy brown or Dijon mustard
1 tablespoon minced garlic
2 tablespoons cornstarch

To toast the pecans, place them in the cooker or use a skillet, but don't overcrowd the nuts. Cook over medium heat for about 10 minutes, or until fragrant and lightly browned, stirring frequently to prevent burning. Transfer to a plate. Heat the butter in the pressure cooker over medium heat. Add the chicken pieces, cook until golden brown, cut into strips and set aside. Add the onions to the cooker and cook, stirring, until soft, about 3 minutes. Add the apricot preserves, bourbon, tomato paste, mustard, and garlic, plus ⅓ cup water, stirring to blend. Return the chicken pieces to the cooker. Lock the lid in place. Bring to 15psi over high heat, immediately reduce the heat to the lowest possible setting to stabilize and maintain that pressure, and cook for 5 minutes. Remove from the heat and use the natural release method (see page 31) to depressurize. Carefully open the lid after the pressure drops. Transfer the chicken pieces to a serving platter and top with the toasted pecans. Thicken the sauce by making a slurry with the cornstarch mixed with ⅓ cup cold water; stir the slurry into the sauce and simmer over medium heat, stirring often as it thickens, but do not boil. Serve the sauce separately, to be spooned over each portion at the table. ✳ **Serves 4**

Honey-Lime Chicken

I first used this recipe and the pressure cooker when a planned outdoor grilling session went by the wayside during a thunderstorm. I've added pineapple to the robust honey-lime sauce, which really penetrates the tender chicken pieces in this almost instant entrée that uses the infusion cooking method (see page 33). Serve with rice if desired.

2 tablespoons butter

4 boneless, skinless chicken breasts

3 tablespoons minced garlic

⅓ cup pineapple juice

¼ cup fresh lime juice

2 tablespoons soy sauce

1 teaspoon grated lime zest

4 red onion slices, about ¼ inch thick

4 pineapple slices

2 tablespoons chopped cilantro leaves, for garnish

2 tablespoons cornstarch

¼ cup honey

Heat the butter in the pressure cooker over medium heat. Add the chicken pieces, cook until golden brown on both sides, and set aside. Add the garlic, pineapple juice, lime juice, soy sauce, and lime zest, stirring to mix. Return the chicken pieces to the cooker, turning over once or twice to coat both sides with the sauce. Place 1 onion slice and 1 pineapple slice on top of each chicken breast and secure with a toothpick. Lock the lid in place. Bring to 15psi over high heat, immediately reduce the heat to the lowest possible setting to stabilize and maintain that pressure, and cook for 8 minutes. Remove from the heat and use the natural release method (see page 31) to depressurize. Carefully open the lid after the pressure drops. Transfer the chicken pieces to a serving platter, remove the toothpicks, and sprinkle with cilantro leaves. Thicken the sauce by making a slurry with the cornstarch mixed with ⅓ cup cold water; stir the slurry into the sauce and simmer over medium heat. Add the honey, stirring often as it thickens, but do not boil. Serve the sauce separately, to be spooned over each portion at the table. ✳ **Serves 4**

Walnut Chicken Braised in Pomegranate Juice

To give an interesting edge to this recipe, chicken simmers in tart pomegranate juice, mellowed with sweet honey and balsamic vinegar. Using the infusion cooking method (see page 33), the wonderful combination of flavors penetrates deeply into the meat, not only adding taste, but a beautiful visual presentation.

½ cup unsweetened pomegranate juice, or
    2 whole pomegranates for juice
1 cup walnuts, finely chopped
3 tablespoons butter
4 boneless, skinless chicken breasts
1 sweet Maui onion, finely chopped
3 tablespoons honey
2 tablespoons balsamic vinegar
½ teaspoon ground cinnamon
2 tablespoons cornstarch

If using whole pomegranates, halve them and save some seeds for garnish. Juice the halves using a citrus juicer. Strain and measure the juice to get as close to ½ cup as you can, adding water if needed. To toast the walnuts, place them in the cooker or use a skillet, but don't overcrowd the nuts. Cook over medium heat for about 10 minutes or until fragrant and lightly browned, stirring frequently to prevent burning. Transfer to a plate. Heat the butter in the pressure cooker over medium heat. Add the chicken pieces, cook until golden brown on both sides, and set aside. Add the onions to the cooker and cook, stirring, until clear, about 3 minutes. Add the honey, vinegar, cinnamon, and the ½ cup pomegranate juice and stir. Return the chicken pieces to the cooker and lock the lid in place. Bring to 15psi over high heat, immediately reduce the heat to the lowest possible setting to stabilize and maintain that pressure, and cook for 8 minutes. Remove from the heat and use the natural release method (see page 31) to depressurize. Carefully open the lid after the pressure drops. Transfer the chicken pieces to a serving platter and sprinkle on a few of the pomegranate seeds, if using, for garnish. Add the walnuts to the sauce. Thicken the sauce by making a slurry with the cornstarch mixed with ⅓ cup cold water; stir the slurry into the sauce and simmer over medium heat, stirring often as it thickens, but do not boil. Taste the sauce and, if you find it a little too tart, add more honey or sugar to taste. Serve the pomegranate sauce in a separate bowl to be ladled over the chicken at the table. ✳ Serves 4

Serving Suggestion: This recipe goes very well with fluffy white rice or couscous.

Chicken and Pepperoni Pasta

It you like Italian, this pressure cooker casserole recipe is an easy weekday dinner. Everything cooks together and you can be sitting down to eat with practically no effort.

  1 (28-ounce) can chopped tomatoes, with juice
  1 (3-ounce) can tomato paste
  1 teaspoon dried basil
  1 teaspoon dried oregano
  ½ teaspoon red pepper flakes
  1 red bell pepper, seeded and cut into thin strips
  1 green bell pepper, seeded and cut into thin strips
  1 onion, thinly sliced
  1 tablespoon minced garlic
  3 cups uncooked farfalle (bow ties or butterflies)
  4 boneless, skinless chicken breasts cut into bite-sized pieces
  1 cup thinly sliced pepperoni
  1½ cups shredded mozzarella cheese

Combine the chopped tomatoes, tomato paste, basil, oregano, and red pepper flakes in a large pressure cooker, stirring to mix. Add the chicken pieces bell peppers, onions, and garlic, and then the pasta. Add enough water to cover the ingredients completely, pushing the pasta beneath the surface. Place the pepperoni on top and lock the lid in place. Bring to 15psi over high heat, immediately reduce the heat to the lowest possible setting to stabilize and maintain that pressure, and cook for 5 minutes. Remove from the heat and use the natural release method (see page 31) to depressurize. Carefully open the lid after the pressure drops. Transfer the chicken breasts to a serving bowl. Add the mozzarella cheese to the cooker and stir. When the cheese has melted, transfer the pasta to the bowl and toss gently. ✳ Serves 4

Chinese Ginger-Orange Chicken

Cooked by the infusion cooking method (see page 33), this tasty, tangy dish packs a real ginger-and-orange-flavored wallop. Serve with crisp Chinese noodles, ramen or Asian-style noodles, or hot rice. Many years ago, I made this recipe to serve at a gourmet dinner group, and, not surprisingly, everyone was amazed that I used a pressure cooker. Over the next several days, I received several phone calls asking for more information about pressure cookery, and I daresay more than a few of my guests were convinced enough to go and buy their own cookers.

  2 tablespoons oil
  4 boneless, skinless chicken breasts
  ½ cup frozen orange juice concentrate, thawed
  ¼ cup hoisin sauce
  3 tablespoons fresh lemon juice
  ¼ teaspoon hot Chinese-style mustard
  3 tablespoons freshly grated ginger
  2 tablespoons minced garlic

2 tablespoons firmly packed brown sugar
½ teaspoon ground ginger
¼ teaspoon ground cinnamon
1 orange, cut in ½-inch slices, for garnish

Heat the oil in the pressure cooker over medium heat. Add the chicken pieces and cook until golden brown on both sides. Add all of the remaining ingredients except the orange slices and lock the lid in place. Bring to 15psi over high heat, immediately reduce the heat to the lowest possible setting to stabilize and maintain that pressure, and cook for 8 minutes. Remove from the heat and use the natural release method (see page 31) to depressurize. Carefully open the lid after the pressure drops. Transfer the chicken pieces to a serving platter. Simmer the orange sauce over high heat, uncovered, for about 10 minutes longer, or until it is reduced and slightly thickened. Slice the chicken breasts lengthwise, cutting thin strips that are still attached at one end. Arrange the sliced breasts on serving plates, fanning out the slices. Drizzle a little orange sauce over the chicken and top with the orange slices. Pass the extra sauce at the table.

✳ Serves 4

Mango Chicken

Most people think mangos are only eaten fresh, but they're also delicious cooked, as in this recipe. When cooked, the mangos create their own fruity sauce, absolutely wonderful when combined with tender pieces of chicken. Serve with either white or brown rice, or try it in a salad of cool, crisp greens.

2 tablespoons olive oil
2 tablespoons minced garlic
1 tablespoon mild or spicy curry powder, according to taste
¼ teaspoon cayenne pepper
4 boneless, skinless chicken breasts
2 to 3 mangos, skinned and cubed, including any accumulated juice
1 green bell pepper, seeded and chopped
1 cup diced red or purple onion
3 tablespoons soy sauce
¼ cup fresh lemon juice

Heat the oil in the pressure cooker over medium heat and add the garlic, curry powder, and cayenne pepper, stirring constantly as the curry powder fries and begins to release its aroma, taking care that it doesn't burn. Add the chicken, turning several times to coat with the fried curry. Cook the chicken pieces until golden brown on both sides, and set aside. Add the mango, bell pepper, and red onion, return the chicken to the cooker, add the soy sauce and lemon juice, pour in ¼ cup water, and stir. Lock the lid in place. Bring to 15psi over high heat, immediately reduce the heat to the lowest possible setting to stabilize and maintain that pressure, and cook for 8 minutes. Remove from the heat and use the natural release method (see page 31) to depressurize. Carefully open the lid after the pressure drops. Using a slotted spoon, transfer the chicken pieces to a serving platter and top with the mango, onion, and green pepper mixture. Tent with a square of aluminum foil to keep warm. Simmer the remaining sauce over high heat, uncovered, for about 10 minutes longer, or until it is reduced and slightly thickened. Before serving, drizzle a little sauce over the chicken, and pass the extra sauce at the table. ✳ Serves 4

Chicken Braised in Pineapple-Orange Sauce

Braised in orange juice, this chicken is quick and easy but full of flavor. Serve with either white rice or mashed potatoes.

Step One: The Sauce

¼ cup frozen orange juice concentrate,
  thawed
2 tablespoons soy sauce
1 teaspoon ground ginger
⅛ teaspoon ground cloves

Combine all of the ingredients in the pressure cooker, and bring to a simmer over medium-high heat. Cook, stirring frequently, for about 10 minutes, or until the sauce begins to thicken. Transfer to a small bowl and set aside.

Step Two: The Chicken

6 boneless, skinless chicken breasts
1 tablespoon paprika
½ teaspoon freshly ground black ground pepper
2 tablespoons butter
1 red onion, cut into ½-inch rings
2 tablespoons cornstarch
1½ cups pineapple chunks
2 navel oranges, peeled and sectioned,
  including any accumulated juice
Very thin orange peel slivers, for garnish

Rub the chicken breasts with the paprika and pepper. Heat the butter in the pressure cooker over high heat. Add the chicken, cook until browned on both sides, and set aside. Add the onions to the cooker and cook, stirring, until clear, about 3 minutes. Place the rack in the pressure cooker and arrange the chicken pieces and onions on top. Add ½ cup water and lock the lid in place. Bring to 15psi over high heat, immediately reduce the heat to the lowest possible setting to stabilize and maintain that pressure, and cook for 8 minutes. Remove from the heat and use the natural release method (see page 31) to depressurize. Carefully open the lid after the pressure drops. Transfer the chicken and onions to a serving platter and drain the pressure cooker. Cut the chicken pieces into strips across the grain. Add the orange sauce to the pressure cooker, add the chicken strips and onion rings, and bring to a simmer over medium heat. Thicken the sauce by making a slurry with the cornstarch mixed with ¼ cup cold water; stir the slurry into the sauce and simmer gently over medium heat. Add the pineapple chunks and navel oranges, simmering over medium heat and stirring often as the sauce thickens, but do not boil. Garnish with the orange peel. ✳ Serves 6

Dilled Sour Cream Chicken and Vegetables

The dilled sauce really makes a difference to plain chicken. Serve this meal with a crusty bread so you don't leave anything on your plate.

1 tablespoon paprika

½ teaspoon freshly ground black pepper

6 boneless, skinless chicken breasts

2 tablespoons oil

1 onion, sliced into rings

¼ pound fresh mushrooms, washed and
　　sliced

1 (10-ounce) can condensed cream of
　　mushroom soup

1 (1-ounce) packet dried onion soup mix

3 tablespoons fresh dill, chopped

6 to 8 small red potatoes, scrubbed and halved

2 cups small baby carrots

2 tablespoons cornstarch

1 cup sour cream

Mix together the paprika and pepper and rub the mixture on both sides of the chicken breasts. Heat the oil in the pressure cooker over medium heat. Add the chicken, cook until well browned on all sides, and set aside. Add any remaining spice mixture, frying until the spice begins to sizzle. Add the onions and mushrooms to the cooker and cook, stirring, until slightly softened, about 3 minutes. Add the canned soup, soup mix, 2 tablespoons of the dill, and 1 cup water, mixing well. Add the potatoes, carrots, and chicken, and lock the lid in place. Bring to 15psi over high heat, immediately reduce the heat to the lowest possible setting to stabilize and maintain that pressure, and cook for 8 minutes. Remove from the heat and use the natural release method (see page 31) to depressurize. Carefully open the lid after the pressure drops. Transfer the chicken pieces, carrots, potatoes, mushrooms, and onions to a heatproof serving plate, cover with aluminum foil, and keep warm in a low oven. Thicken the sauce by making a slurry with the cornstarch mixed with ⅓ cup cold water; stir the slurry into the sauce and simmer gently over medium heat. Add the sour cream and simmer over medium heat, stirring often as it thickens, but do not boil. Serve the sour cream sauce separately to be spooned over the chicken and vegetables at the table. Garnish with the remaining 1 tablespoon dill. ✳ Serves 6

Chinese Red-Cooked Chicken Thighs

The soy sauce imparts loads of delicious flavor and aroma, but it also gives the chicken a deep, dark reddish-brown color that gives this dish its name. Serve over hot, fluffy rice.

- ¼ cup sherry
- ¼ cup soy sauce
- Juice of 1 orange
- 3 tablespoons sugar
- 1 (2-inch) piece of fresh ginger, peeled and cut into ¼-inch slices
- Rind of 1 orange, cut into strips
- 2 (3-inch) cinnamon sticks
- 1 teaspoon fennel seeds, crushed
- ½ teaspoon red pepper flakes
- ¼ teaspoon ground cloves
- 8 skinless chicken thighs

Combine the sherry, soy sauce, orange juice, sugar, ginger, orange rind, cinnamon sticks, fennel seeds, red pepper flakes, and cloves in the pressure cooker and bring to a boil over high heat. Reduce the heat and simmer, uncovered, for about 10 minutes. Add the chicken thighs and ½ cup water, stirring to mix. Lock the lid in place. Bring to 15psi over high heat, immediately reduce the heat to the lowest possible setting to stabilize and maintain that pressure, and cook for 6 minutes. Remove from the heat and use the natural release method (see page 31) to depressurize. Carefully open the lid after the pressure drops. Discard the cinnamon sticks and orange rind. ✳ Serves 4 generously

Honey-Mustard Chicken

With traditional cooking methods, we are accustomed to spending more time cooking the dish than preparing it, but the opposite is true in pressure cooking. Because the cooking times are so short, often the the prep time takes longer than the actual pressure cooking. This dish offers the best of both worlds because the prep time is just about as short as the cooking time.

- 2 tablespoons olive oil
- 6 boneless, skinless chicken breasts
- 1 onion, finely chopped
- 1 cup chicken broth
- 2 tablespoons Dijon mustard (or any spicy mustard of choice)
- ½ teaspoon freshly ground black pepper
- 2 tablespoons honey
- ⅓ cup minced green onion tops, for garnish

Heat the oil in the pressure cooker over medium heat. Add the chicken pieces, cook until golden brown on both sides, and set aside. Add the onions to the cooker and cook, stirring, until clear, about 3 minutes. Add the broth, mustard, and pepper, stirring to mix. Return the chicken to the pressure cooker and lock the lid in place. Bring to 15psi over high heat, immediately reduce the heat to the lowest possible setting to stabilize and maintain that pressure, and cook for 8 minutes. Remove from the heat and use the natural release method (see page 31) to depressurize. Carefully open the lid after the pressure drops. Transfer the chicken to a serving platter. Add the honey and simmer the sauce over high heat, uncovered, for about 10 minutes longer, or until it is reduced and begins to thicken. Return the chicken pieces to the sauce and continue cooking, turning the chicken occasionally as the mixture begins to caramelize—usually just a few minutes more. Place the chicken on a serving platter, drizzle with some of the sauce, and sprinkle with the green onions just before serving. Pass any remaining sauce at the table. ✳ Serves 6

Old-Fashioned Chicken Salad

Nothing is better than homemade chicken salad. This is a versatile recipe that can be made into wonderful sandwiches served on buttery croissants. Try it as an hors d'oeuvre on assorted crackers, or use in almost any kind of green salad. As a bonus, you'll have some richly flavorful broth to freeze for later use in soups or stews.

Step One: The Chicken

2 pounds boneless, skinless chicken thighs
2 stalks celery with leaves, cut into
    3-inch pieces
1 small onion, quartered
2 tablespoons minced garlic
1 teaspoon salt
½ teaspoon freshly ground black pepper
2 sprigs fresh rosemary
Zest of 1 lemon
Juice of 1 lemon

Put the chicken thighs in the pressure cooker and add of the remaining ingredients. Add 4 cups water, stir, and lock the lid in place. Bring to 15psi over high heat, immediately reduce the heat to the lowest possible setting to stabilize and maintain that pressure, and cook for 15 minutes. Remove from the heat and use the natural release method (see page 31) to depressurize. Carefully open the lid after the pressure drops. Using a slotted spoon, transfer the chicken pieces to a cutting board and, when cool enough to handle, pull the meat from the bones, cutting it into bite-size pieces. Save the chicken stock if desired: Strain the stock, discarding the solid ingredients. Use a fat separator, or skim the excess fat from the surface of the stock. Freeze in tightly sealed containers for later use in soups and stews.

Step Two: The Salad

2 stalks celery, thinly sliced
½ cup diced red onion
½ cup slivered almonds
1 teaspoon sugar
1 teaspoon dried tarragon leaves
3 tablespoons capers, drained
3 tablespoons mayonnaise
3 tablespoons sour cream
Juice of 1 lemon

In a large bowl, combine the chicken and other salad ingredients, and mix well. Taste, and adjust the seasonings as needed. ✳ Serves 6

Chicken with Lemon Herb Sauce

Say goodbye to plain chicken—the zing of lemon and fresh herbs add a finishing touch to this elegant sauce. Serve over hot rice or mashed potatoes.

> 2 tablespoons olive oil
> 4 boneless, skinless chicken breasts, cut into small cubes
> ½ cup white wine
> 2 tablespoons fresh lemon juice
> 1 tablespoon minced garlic
> 1 tablespoon chicken bouillon granules
> 1 teaspoon Dijon mustard
> 2 tablespoons chopped mixed fresh herbs such as basil, rosemary, or oregano

Heat the oil in the pressure cooker over medium heat. Add the chicken pieces and cook until golden brown on both sides. Add all of the remaining ingredients and mix well. Lock the lid in place. Bring to 15psi over high heat, immediately reduce the heat to the lowest possible setting to stabilize and maintain that pressure, and cook for 8 minutes. Remove from the heat and use the natural release method (see page 31) to depressurize. Carefully open the lid after the pressure drops. Transfer the chicken to a serving plate. Simmer the sauce over high heat, uncovered, for about 10 minutes longer, or until it is reduced and slightly thickened. Drizzle the sauce over the chicken. ✳ **Serves 4**

Lemony Chicken Piccata

Always looking for ways to duplicate the fine dishes I find in various restaurants, this is another "tweaked till true" recipe that I designed for the pressure cooker. This tangy yet delicate entrée is not only quick and easy, but it's also very tasty with the addition of lemon and capers. Serve with mashed potatoes, if desired.

> 1 tablespoon paprika
> 1 teaspoon freshly ground black pepper
> ½ teaspoon garlic powder
> ½ teaspoon onion powder
> 6 boneless, skinless chicken breasts
> 2 teaspoons butter
> 1 teaspoon lemon zest
> 1 cup dry white wine
> 1 tablespoon capers
> 2 lemons, thinly sliced

Mix together the paprika, pepper, garlic powder, and onion powder and rub the spice mixture into both sides of the chicken breasts. Heat the butter in the pressure cooker over high heat. Add the chicken, cook until well browned on all sides, and set aside. Add any remaining spice mixture and the lemon zest to the cooker, frying until the spices begin to sizzle. Deglaze the cooker with the wine, scraping up all those crusty, brown bits from the bottom. Add the capers and a layer of lemon slices on the bottom of the cooker. Top with the chicken pieces and another layer of lemon slices. Lock the lid in place. Bring to 15psi over high heat, immediately reduce the heat to the lowest possible setting to stabilize and maintain that pressure, and cook for 8 minutes. Remove from the heat and use the natural release method (see page 31) to depressurize. Carefully open the lid after the pressure drops. Transfer the chicken pieces to a serving plate. Bring the sauce to a boil, reduce the heat, and simmer, uncovered, for about 10 minutes, or until the liquid reduces by about half. Return the chicken to the cooker, turning once to coat with the sauce, and heat through. Transfer the chicken to a serving plate and pass the sauce at the table.

✳ **Serves 6**

Warm Mandarin Chicken Salad

"Crunch" is one of the most popular characteristics in my favorite foods list. That's why the crunchy ingredients in this recipe make it an easy winner for lunch or a summertime meal. The sweet, tangy dressing goes well with salad greens.

Step One: The Honey-Mustard Dressing
1 cup plain yogurt
⅓ cup honey
⅓ cup mayonnaise
2 tablespoons Dijon mustard
2 tablespoons rice wine vinegar

Prepare the Honey-Mustard Dressing several hours before serving. Whisk all of the ingredients together in a small bowl. Cover and chill thoroughly to develop the flavors.

Step Two: The Chicken
2 tablespoons butter
4 boneless, skinless chicken breasts
    and/or thighs
2 cups frozen sugar snap peas
1 (10-ounce) package prepared
    romaine lettuce
1 red onion, diced
1 (11-ounce) can mandarin oranges,
    drained and chilled
1 (5-ounce) can sliced water chestnuts
1 cup crispy chow mein noodles

Heat the butter in the pressure cooker over medium heat. Add the chicken pieces, and cook until golden brown on all sides. Transfer to a cutting board and cut into large bite-size pieces. Add the chicken pieces, frozen sugar snap peas, and just enough water to barely cover the ingredients to the cooker, and stir. Lock the lid in place. Bring to 15psi over high heat, immediately reduce the heat to the lowest possible setting to stabilize and maintain that pressure, and cook for 4 minutes. Remove from the heat and use the quick release method (see page 30) to depressurize. Carefully open the lid after the pressure drops. In a large bowl, stir together the chicken, sugar snap peas, romaine, onions, mandarin oranges, and water chestnuts. Add the dressing and toss to mix. Top each serving with a sprinkle of crispy chow mein noodles. ✳ **Serves 4**

Almost Instant Creamy Chicken Alfredo

A quick and easy shortcut to a hot, hearty, and complete meal—without sacrificing any of the home-style goodness—that will solve your "what's for dinner?" dilemma.

> 4 boneless, skinless chicken breasts, cut into
>   large bite-size pieces
> 3 cups frozen mixed vegetables of your choice
> 2 cups uncooked ditalini (little thimbles)
> 1 (14-ounce) can chicken broth
> 1 teaspoon onion powder
> ¼ teaspoon freshly ground black pepper
> 1 (16-ounce) jar Alfredo sauce

Place all of the ingredients except the Alfredo sauce in the pressure cooker. Add enough additional water to just barely cover all the ingredients, and stir. Lock the lid in place. Bring to 15psi over high heat, immediately reduce the heat to the lowest possible setting to stabilize and maintain that pressure, and cook for 6 minutes. Remove from the heat and use the natural release method (see page 31) to depressurize. Carefully open the lid after the pressure drops. Add the Alfredo sauce, stirring to mix, and simmer over medium heat until hot and bubbly. If necessary, thin the sauce with a little milk until it reaches the desired creamy consistency. Transfer to a serving bowl and serve. ❊ Serves 4

Raspberry Balsamic Chicken with Spinach Tortellini

Sweet and succulent, tart and tantalizing. Raspberry preserves and balsamic vinegar are the perfect contrasts in this delicious chicken main dish.

> 2 tablespoons olive oil
> 6 boneless, skinless chicken breasts
> ½ red onion, chopped
> 1 (11-ounce) package frozen spinach or
>   cheese tortellini
> 1 cup fresh or frozen raspberries
> ⅓ cup raspberry preserves
> 3 tablespoons good-quality balsamic vinegar
> ½ teaspoon freshly ground black pepper
> Pinch of red pepper flakes

Heat the oil in the pressure cooker over medium heat. Add the chicken pieces, cook until golden brown on both sides, and transfer to a cutting board. Cutting across the grain, slice the chicken into strips. Add the onions to the cooker and cook, stirring, until slightly softened, about 3 minutes. Add the frozen tortellini, chicken strips, and just enough water to barely cover the ingredients, and stir. Lock the lid in place. Bring to 15psi over high heat, immediately reduce the heat to the lowest possible setting to stabilize and maintain that pressure, and cook for 4 minutes. Remove from the heat and use the natural release method (see page 31) to depressurize. Carefully open the lid after the pressure drops. Drain into a colander and then transfer to a serving bowl. Add the raspberries, preserves, vinegar, black pepper, and red pepper flakes to the cooker and bring to a simmer, uncovered, over medium-high heat. Stir constantly until the sauce is well blended and bubbly. Adjust the seasonings to taste. Drizzle the raspberry sauce over the chicken and tortellini and serve immediately. ✳ Serves 6

Chinese Chicken with Duck Sauce

When I was very much younger, I ordered a menu item with this name at a very upscale restaurant. Naturally, I expected to be served "duck" sauce with actual duck in it. I was sure I had been shorted when my plate arrived without the expected "duck." Years later, I learned that duck sauce, or plum sauce, as it is also called, is a sweet-and-sour sauce made with plums and apricots. This popular Chinese dish for the pressure cooker uses the infusion cooking method (see page 33) so that all the flavors of the apricot preserves and balsamic vinegar will sink into the chicken and make the sweet and tangy sauce that gives this dish great distinction. Serve over hot white rice.

Step One: The Chicken
1 tablespoon paprika
½ teaspoon freshly ground black pepper
½ teaspoon curry powder

6 boneless, skinless chicken breasts
1 tablespoon olive oil
1 tablespoon dried marjoram
½ cup chicken broth

Mix together the paprika, pepper, and curry powder, and rub the spice mixture on both sides of the chicken breasts. Heat the oil in the pressure cooker over medium heat. Add the chicken, and cook until well browned on all sides. Add any remaining spice mixture and the marjoram, frying until the spices begin to sizzle. Deglaze the cooker with the broth, scraping up all those crusty, brown bits from the bottom. Lock the lid in place. Bring to 15psi over high heat, immediately reduce the heat to the lowest possible setting to stabilize and maintain that pressure, and cook for 8 minutes. Remove from the heat and use the natural release method (see page 31) to depressurize. Carefully open the lid after the pressure drops. Transfer the chicken to a serving dish, and drain the pressure cooker.

Step Two: The Duck Sauce
¼ cup apricot preserves
¼ cup plum preserves
2 tablespoons balsamic vinegar
½ teaspoons crushed red pepper flakes
1½ teaspoons minced fresh ginger
¼ cup finely minced green onion tops,
    for garnish
¼ cup finely chopped cashews, for garnish

Add the preserves, vinegar, honey, and ginger to the pressure cooker and bring to a boil. Reduce the heat and simmer, uncovered, until the sauce has reduced into a thick and syrupy consistency. Taste, adding more vinegar for a tangier sauce if desired. Drizzle the sauce over the chicken pieces. Garnish the top of the chicken with a sprinkle of green onions and chopped cashews. ✳ Serves 6

Sesame Pear Chicken

Indulging a fondness for toasted sesame seeds, I really like incorporating them into my recipes. They add the unique, nutty taste of sesame oil to enhance the delicate taste of fresh pears. The chicken is simmered in pear nectar to really enhance the fruity taste. Serve over white or brown rice.

1 tablespoon sesame seeds
2 tablespoons sesame oil
4 boneless, skinless chicken breasts
4 fresh Bosc pears, peeled and halved
½ cup chopped green onions
½ cup pear nectar
2 tablespoons soy sauce

To toast the sesame seeds, heat the pressure cooker over high heat. When a droplet of water dances and sizzles across the bottom of the cooker, add the sesame seeds and cook, stirring continuously, until they turn a light golden color. Transfer the toasted seeds to a small plate. Heat the sesame oil in the pressure cooker over medium heat. Add the chicken pieces, cook until golden brown on both sides, and transfer to a cutting board. Slice the chicken pieces lengthwise into strips and return to the cooker. Add the pears, green onions, pear nectar, and soy sauce and stir. Lock the lid in place. Bring to 15psi over high heat, immediately reduce the heat to the lowest possible setting to stabilize and maintain that pressure, and cook for 4 minutes. Remove from the heat and use the quick release method (see page 30) to depressurize. Carefully open the lid after the pressure drops. Using a slotted spoon, transfer the chicken pieces, pears, and onions to a serving bowl and sprinkle with the toasted sesame seeds. ✳ Serves 4

Balsamic Peppered Chicken

Another one of my favorite recipe ingredients is good-quality balsamic vinegar. I just can't get enough of the sweet, tangy flavor, and it complements so many different foods. And in this richly flavored and peppery spiced sauce, tender chicken perks up. Serve over a bed of rice, noodles, or mashed potatoes.

6 boneless, skinless chicken breasts
2 teaspoons coarsely ground lemon pepper seasoning
2 tablespoons olive oil
⅓ cup chicken broth
⅓ cup good-quality balsamic vinegar
2 tablespoons minced garlic

One at a time, place each piece of chicken on a cutting board between sheets of plastic wrap. Flatten the chicken with a meat mallet, or use a small heavy pan, pounding until the meat is ¼-inch thick. Press and rub the lemon pepper seasoning evenly on both sides. Heat the oil in the pressure cooker over medium heat, add the chicken pieces, cook until golden brown on both sides, and set aside. Deglaze the cooker with the broth, scraping up all those crusty, brown bits from the bottom. Add the vinegar and garlic, stir, and return the chicken pieces to the pressure cooker, one at a time, turning once to coat both sides with the sauce. Lock the lid in place. Bring to 15psi over high heat, immediately reduce the heat to the lowest possible setting to stabilize and maintain that pressure, and cook for 5 minutes. Remove from the heat and use the natural release method (see page 31) to depressurize. Carefully open the lid after the pressure drops. Transfer the chicken to a serving plate. Bring the sauce in the pressure cooker to a boil; reduce the heat and simmer, uncovered, for about 10 minutes, or until the mixture is reduced and syrupy. Spoon the sauce over the chicken and serve.

✳ Serves 6

Sweet and Sour Pineapple Chicken

This recipe features a well-seasoned and full-bodied sauce made with sweet onions and juicy pineapple. Using the infusion cooking method (see page 33), the sweet and sour flavors really penetrate the chicken. Serve over hot white rice or crispy Chinese noodles.

2 tablespoons oil

6 boneless, skinless chicken breasts

2 cups celery pieces sliced diagonally

1 green bell pepper, seeded and cut into strips

1 sweet Vidalia or Maui onion, chopped

1 (14-ounce) can unsweetened pineapple tidbits, with juice

⅓ cup vinegar

¼ cup soy sauce

⅔ cup brown sugar

1 carrot, thinly sliced

2 tablespoons cornstarch

Heat the oil in the pressure cooker over medium heat. Add the chicken pieces, cook until golden brown on both sides, and set aside. Add the celery, bell peppers, and onions and cook, stirring, until slightly softened, about 3 minutes. Measure the pineapple juice, adding additional water if needed to equal ½ cup. Add the pineapple juice, vinegar, soy sauce, brown sugar, carrots, and chicken to the pressure cooker and stir. Lock the lid in place. Bring to 15psi over high heat, immediately reduce the heat to the lowest possible setting to stabilize and maintain that pressure, and cook for 8 minutes. Remove from the heat and use the natural release method (see page 31) to depressurize. Carefully open the lid after the pressure drops. Using a slotted spoon, transfer the chicken and vegetable pieces to a serving plate. Add the pineapple tidbits to the broth in the cooker. Thicken the sauce by making a slurry with the cornstarch mixed with ⅓ cup cold water; stir the slurry into the sauce and simmer over medium heat, stirring often as it thickens, but do not boil. Simmer, uncovered, for about 10 minutes, or until the mixture is reduced and syrupy. Serve the sauce in a separate bowl.

✳ Serves 6

Chicken in Tomato-Basil Sauce

Home-cooked flavor, with tomatoes, basil, onion, and garlic, simmered not for the traditional 2 hours, but just 8 minutes for an authentic Italian taste. Serve with your choice of pasta, and add a fresh salad and a nice bottle of red wine for a lovely, no-fuss meal.

½ teaspoon salt
¼ teaspoon freshly ground black pepper
4 boneless, skinless chicken breasts
2 tablespoons oil
1 onion, finely chopped
1 (28-ounce) can Italian stewed tomatoes
1 tablespoon minced garlic
¼ cup fresh basil, chopped
¼ cup sliced black olives, for garnish

Press and rub the salt and pepper on both sides of the chicken pieces. Heat the oil in the pressure cooker over medium heat. Add the chicken, cook until golden brown on both sides, and set aside. Add the onions to the cooker and cook, stirring, until clear, about 3 minutes. Add the tomatoes, garlic, basil, and the chicken pieces and stir. Lock the lid in place. Bring to 15psi over high heat, immediately reduce the heat to the lowest possible setting to stabilize and maintain that pressure, and cook for 8 minutes. Remove from the heat and use the natural release method (see page 31) to depressurize. Carefully open the lid after the pressure drops. Transfer the chicken to a serving plate and garnish with the olives; serve the sauce separately.

✳ Serves 4

Sweet and Spicy Chicken Curry

Tender chicken cooked with sweet onions, apples, and apricots is the foundation of this simple curry recipe. For a quick and easy midweek meal, this dish will get you in and out of the kitchen in record time.

2 tablespoons oil
6 boneless, skinless chicken breasts
1 red bell pepper, seeded and finely chopped
1 sweet Vidalia or Maui onion, finely chopped
1 tablespoon minced garlic
1 cup chicken stock
2 Gala or Fuji apples, peeled and diced
⅓ cup currants
⅓ cup dried apricot pieces
3 tablespoons chopped cilantro
1 tablespoon curry powder
¼ teaspoon red pepper flakes
Cilantro leaves, for garnish

Heat the oil in the pressure cooker over medium heat. Add the chicken pieces and cook until golden brown. Transfer the chicken to a cutting board and cut into bite-size pieces. Add the bell peppers, onions, and garlic to the cooker and cook, stirring, until soft, about 3 minutes. Add the stock, apples, currants, apricots, cilantro, curry powder, and red pepper flakes, return the chicken pieces to the cooker, and stir. Lock the lid in place. Bring to 15psi over high heat, immediately reduce the heat to the lowest possible setting to stabilize and maintain that pressure, and cook for 5 minutes. Remove from the heat and use the natural release method (see page 31) to depressurize. Carefully open the lid after the pressure drops. Transfer the chicken, fruit, and vegetables to a serving bowl. Bring the sauce in the pressure cooker to a boil; reduce the heat and simmer, uncovered, for about 10 minutes, or until the mixture is reduced and syrupy, and pour over the chicken mixture just before serving. Sprinkle with a few cilantro leaves for garnish.

✳ Serves 6

Serving Suggestion: Serve over fluffy white rice or couscous.

Chicken Wings in Honeyed Sesame Sauce

Toasted sesame seeds garnish these chicken wings, cooked in a spicy dipping sauce with honey and sherry. While I chose to use wings for this appetizer recipe, you can certainly substitute other chicken parts and use it as a main-dish recipe by increasing the cooking time according to the Pressure-Cooking Time Charts (see page 95).

2 tablespoons sesame seeds

¼ cup sesame oil

2 pounds chicken wings, cut apart at joints

½ cup chicken broth

¼ cup soy sauce

2 tablespoons sherry

2 cloves garlic, crushed

½ teaspoon red pepper flakes

½ teaspoon ground ginger

¼ cup honey

Chopped green onions, for garnish

To toast the sesame seeds, heat the pressure cooker over high heat. When a droplet of water dances and sizzles across the bottom of the cooker, add the sesame seeds and cook, stirring continuously, until they turn a light golden color. Transfer the toasted seeds to a small plate. Heat the oil in the pressure cooker over medium heat. Add the chicken and cook until browned on all sides. Combine the broth, soy sauce, sherry, garlic, red pepper flakes, and ginger in the pressure cooker; stir well. Turn the chicken to coat both sides, and lock the lid in place. Bring to 15psi over high heat, immediately reduce the heat to the lowest possible setting to stabilize and maintain that pressure, and cook for 5 minutes. Remove from the heat and use the natural release method (see page 31) to depressurize. Carefully open the lid after the pressure drops. Transfer the chicken wings to a broiler pan. Simmer the sauce over high heat, uncovered, for about 10 minutes longer, or until it is reduced and slightly thickened. Stir in the honey. Preheat the broiler. Generously baste the chicken wings with the sauce and place under the broiler, about 6 inches from the heat, until they just begin to crisp and brown. Turn once, again basting the chicken, and remove after they are slightly browned. Transfer the chicken wings to a serving plate and sprinkle with toasted sesame seeds and green onions. Serve any remaining sauce separately for dipping.

✳ Serves 4 to 5

Cherry Buffalo Wings

For a new twist on the traditional Buffalo wings, try my version made with a surprising burst of cherry flavor. Serve this easy recipe either as a finger food for a terrific snack with your favorite dipping sauce, or as a main dish with French fries and sliced cucumbers and tomatoes.

> 2 tablespoons oil
> 24 chicken wings
> 1 red onion, minced
> 1 cup fresh or frozen cherries, minced
> 1 cup bottled barbecue sauce
> 3 tablespoons frozen cherry juice concentrate
> Bottled ranch dressing, for dipping

Heat the oil in the pressure cooker over medium heat. Add the chicken wings, cook until golden brown on all sides, and set aside. Combine the onions, cherries, barbecue sauce, and cherry juice in the pressure cooker, mixing well. Return the chicken wings to the cooker and lock the lid in place. Bring to 15psi over high heat, immediately reduce the heat to the lowest possible setting to stabilize and maintain that pressure, and cook for 5 minutes. Remove from the heat and use the quick release method (see page 30) to depressurize. Carefully open the lid after the pressure drops. Serve the extra sauce at the table, along with the ranch dressing. ✳ Serves 4 to 5

Chicken and Potatoes in Sweet Onion Sauce

A one-pot meal that is so quick and easy, it will soon become a menu favorite for those days when time and energy are in short supply. Check the produce department at your grocery store for the many new varieties of sweet onions that are now available.

> 2 tablespoons oil
> 6 boneless, skinless chicken breasts
> 2 sweet Vidalia or Maui onions, chopped
> 1 (10-ounce) can cream of mushroom soup
> 6 potatoes, peeled and sliced ½ inch thick

Heat the oil in the pressure cooker over medium heat. Add the chicken pieces, cook until golden brown on both sides, and set aside. Add the onions to the cooker and cook, stirring, until slightly softened, about 3 minutes. Add the mushroom soup and 1 cup water, stirring to mix. Add the potatoes, return the chicken pieces to the cooker, and stir. Lock the lid in place. Bring to 15psi over high heat, immediately reduce the heat to the lowest possible setting to stabilize and maintain that pressure, and cook for 8 minutes. Remove from the heat and use the natural release method (see page 31) to depressurize. Carefully open the lid after the pressure drops. Using a slotted spoon, transfer the potatoes to a serving bowl. Place the chicken pieces on a serving plate. Serve the sauce separately to be spooned over the potatoes at the table. ✳ Serves 6

Quick Barbecued Chicken and Potato Wedges

Some people wait all year long for barbecuing season to come along. With a pressure cooker, there's certainly no waiting, and that means no excuse for not making up a barbecue any time the mood strikes you.

> 2 tablespoons oil
> 2 pounds mixed chicken breasts, thighs, and
>   drumsticks
> 1 onion, minced
> 1 green bell pepper, seeded and diced
> 6 potatoes, cut lengthwise into quarters
> 2 cups bottled barbecue sauce
> ½ cup cola soft drink (regular, not diet)

Heat the oil in the pressure cooker over medium heat. Add the chicken pieces and cook until golden brown on all sides. Add the onions and bell peppers, and top with the potato wedges. In a small bowl, mix the barbecue sauce with the cola, and pour the mixture over the ingredients in the pressure cooker. Lock the lid in place. Bring to 15psi over high heat, immediately reduce the heat to the lowest possible setting to stabilize and maintain that pressure, and cook for 8 minutes. Remove from the heat and use the natural release method (page 31) to depressurize. Carefully open the lid after the pressure drops. Transfer the chicken and potato wedges to a serving platter, and serve the barbecue sauce separately. ❋ Serves 6

Doctored Barbecued Chicken Sandwiches

If you are old enough, you might remember a unique '60s dining fad that had homemakers cooking everything from canapés to cakes with various brands of soft drinks. At that time the pressure-cooker was in almost every kitchen, so it was a perfect match for shredded chicken in a tangy sweet barbecue sauce. Serve on lightly toasted buns for big two-handed sandwiches everyone will enjoy.

> 2½ pounds boneless, skinless chicken thighs
> 1 (12-ounce) can Dr. Pepper soft drink
> 1 cup bottled barbecue sauce
> 6 hamburger buns, lightly buttered and toasted

Add the chicken thighs and Dr. Pepper to the pressure cooker and lock the lid in place. Bring to 15psi over high heat, immediately reduce the heat to the lowest possible setting to stabilize and maintain that pressure, and cook for 12 minutes. Remove from the heat and use the natural release method (see page 31) to depressurize. Carefully open the lid after the pressure drops. Shred the meat with a fork. Discard the cooking liquid and return the meat to the cooker. Add the barbecue sauce and simmer over medium heat, stirring, until hot and bubbly. Pile a generous amount of barbecued chicken on each bun and serve immediately. ❋ Serves 5 to 6

Whole Roasted Chicken

Simple though it may be, nothing quite beats the appearance of a succulent, golden-skinned chicken for dinner.

1 (2- to 3-pound) whole young chicken
3 cloves garlic, crushed
3 sprigs fresh rosemary
1 tablespoon paprika
½ teaspoon seasoned salt
½ teaspoon freshly ground black pepper
½ teaspoon garlic powder

Place the rack in the pressure cooker and add 1 cup of water. Remove the neck and giblets from the chicken and freeze for making chicken stock later. Trim the chicken of any excess fat around the cavity openings. Rinse and pat dry with paper towels. Stuff the cavity of the chicken with the garlic and rosemary. Mix the paprika, salt, pepper, and garlic powder in a small bowl and rub the mixture over the chicken. To truss the chicken, tie the legs together with string and tuck the wings under. Use two foil helper handles (see page 42) under the chicken, and place it on the rack in the pressure cooker. Lock the lid in place. Bring to 15psi over high heat, immediately reduce the heat to the lowest possible setting to stabilize and maintain that pressure, and cook for 20 minutes. Remove from the heat and use the natural release method (see page 31) to depressurize. Carefully open the lid after the pressure drops. The chicken is done if a thermometer into the middle of the thigh meat reads 170°F, or when the juices run clear when the leg is pricked with a fork. If the juice is pink, return to the pressure cooker and lock the lid back in place. Return to 15psi over high heat, immediately reduce the heat to the lowest possible setting to stabilize and maintain that pressure, and cook for an additional 5 minutes. Remove from the heat and use the quick or cold water release method (see page 30) to depressurize. Carefully open the lid after the pressure drops. Preheat the oven to 450°F. Use the foil helper handles to transfer the chicken to a roasting pan with a rack and place in the oven to roast for about 15 minutes, or until the skin is golden brown and beginning to crisp. Transfer the cooked chicken to a large serving platter and let it rest for 10 to 15 minutes before carving at the table. ✳ Serves 4 to 5

Chicken Ratatouille

Ratatouille is a southern French dish made from eggplant, zucchini, onions, peppers, tomatoes, and garlic. There are many different variations of this popular recipe, and it can be served over pasta or potatoes. In my pressure cooker adaptation, I pound the chicken breasts flat so they will cook in the same time as the vegetables.

4 boneless, skinless chicken breasts
2 tablespoons olive oil
2 zucchini, about 7 inches long, unpeeled and
    sliced ¼ inch thick
1 narrow Japanese eggplant, peeled and
    sliced ½ inch thick
1 onion, thinly sliced
1 green bell pepper, seeded and chopped
½ pound fresh mushrooms, washed and sliced
1 (28-ounce) can chopped tomatoes,
    with juice
3 tablespoons tomato paste
1 tablespoon minced garlic
2 teaspoons dried basil
½ teaspoon red pepper flakes
Freshly grated Parmesan cheese, for garnish

One at a time, place each piece of chicken on a cutting board between sheets of plastic wrap. Flatten the chicken with a meat mallet, or use a small heavy pan, pounding until the meat is thin, and then cut each piece into two portions. Heat the oil in the pressure cooker over high heat. Add the chicken pieces and cook until golden brown on both sides. Add the zucchini, eggplant, onions, bell peppers, mushrooms, tomatoes, tomato paste, garlic, basil, and red pepper flakes and stir in ½ cup water. Lock the lid in place. Bring to 15psi over high heat, immediately reduce the heat to the lowest possible setting to stabilize and maintain that pressure, and cook for 5 minutes. Remove from the heat and use the quick or cold water release method (see page 30) to depressurize. Carefully open the lid after the pressure drops. Adjust the seasonings and transfer the chicken mixture to a serving dish. Pass the Parmesan cheese at the table. ✳ **Serves 4**

Chicken with Mixed Vegetables and Country Gravy

Everything you need for dinner is right here in one pot. Tender, juicy chicken breasts, potatoes, carrots, and fresh green beans served with creamy chicken gravy . . . what more could you ask for in just 8 minutes?

2 tablespoons oil

4 boneless, skinless chicken breasts

1 onion, coarsely chopped

1 (14-ounce) can chicken broth

4 potatoes, peeled and halved

4 carrots, peeled and cut into chunks

1 teaspoon ground sage

1 pound green beans, trimmed and cut into
    1-inch pieces

2 tablespoons cornstarch

1 cup cold milk

Heat the oil in the pressure cooker over medium heat. Add the chicken pieces, cook until golden brown on both sides, and set aside. Add the onions to the cooker and cook, stirring, until slightly softened, about 3 minutes. Add the broth, potatoes, carrots, and sage, return the chicken pieces to the pressure cooker, and stir. Lock the lid in place. Bring to 15psi over high heat, immediately reduce the heat to the lowest possible setting to stabilize and maintain that pressure, and cook for 5 minutes. Remove from the heat and use the quick or cold water release method (see page 30) to depressurize. Carefully open the lid after the pressure drops. Add the green beans and lock the lid back in place. Return to 15psi over high heat, immediately reduce the heat to the lowest possible setting to stabilize and maintain that pressure, and cook for an additional 3 minutes. Remove from the heat and use the cold water release method (see page 30) to depressurize. Carefully open the lid immediately after the pressure drops. Remove the meat and vegetables to a platter and keep warm in a low oven. Bring the broth to a boil, uncovered, and simmer over medium heat. Thicken the sauce by making a slurry with the cornstarch mixed with the cold milk, stir the slurry into the sauce and simmer over medium heat, stirring often as it thickens, but do not boil. Pour into a gravy boat to ladle over the potatoes at the table. ✳ Serves 4

Salsa Chicken and Potatoes

In this recipe, I added a little south-of-the-border flair by including salsa as the flavoring liquid. Use the infusion cooking method (see page 33) to super-marinate the chicken. The potatoes are cooked above the flavoring liquid so that they do not share the same flavors.

1 tablespoon paprika

½ teaspoon freshly ground black pepper

4 boneless, skinless chicken breasts

2 tablespoons butter

½ cup bottled salsa

6 red potatoes, quartered

Mix together the paprika and pepper and rub the spice mixture on both sides of the chicken breasts, saving any remainder. Heat the butter in the pressure cooker over medium heat. Add the chicken pieces, cook until golden brown on both sides, remove to a cutting board, and cut the chicken into bite-size pieces. Add the chicken, salsa, and any remaining spice mixture to the pressure cooker, stirring well until the chicken pieces are well coated with the salsa. Place the rack on top of the chicken and add the potatoes, making sure they are above the level of the flavoring liquid. Lock the lid in place. Bring to 15psi over high heat, immediately reduce the heat to the lowest possible setting to stabilize and maintain that pressure, and cook for 5 minutes. Remove from the heat and use the natural release method (see page 31) to depressurize. Carefully open the lid after the pressure drops. Transfer the potatoes and chicken to a serving bowl. Pour the sauce into a separate bowl to ladle over the chicken and potatoes at the table.

✳ Serves 4

Chicken in Plum Sauce

Using a combination of sweet plums and plum jam to intensify the fruit flavors, this recipe gets an added boost from a pungent mixture of fragrant spices. Using the infusion cooking method (see page 33) intensifies the flavor. Serve with rice.

1 tablespoon paprika
1 teaspoon curry powder
½ teaspoon freshly ground black pepper
½ teaspoon cinnamon
Dash of cayenne pepper
6 boneless, skinless chicken breasts
2 tablespoons butter
1 (8-ounce) can blue plums, with juice
½ cup plum jam
¼ cup soy sauce
¼ cup vinegar
¼ cup dry sherry
2 tablespoons cornstarch

Mix together the paprika, curry powder, black pepper, cinnamon, and cayenne pepper, and rub the mixture on both sides of the chicken breasts, saving any remainder. Heat the butter in the pressure cooker over medium heat. Add the chicken pieces, cook until golden brown on both sides, and set aside. Pit the plums if necessary and mash them in their juice, then pour into the pressure cooker. Add the plum jam, soy sauce, vinegar, sherry, and the remaining spice mixture, stirring to blend, and return the chicken pieces to the pressure cooker. Lock the lid in place. Bring to 15psi over high heat, immediately reduce the heat to the lowest possible setting to stabilize and maintain that pressure, and cook for 8 minutes. Remove from the heat and use the natural release method (see page 31) to depressurize. Carefully open the lid after the pressure drops. Thicken the sauce by making a slurry with the cornstarch mixed with ⅓ cup cold water; stir the slurry into the sauce and simmer over medium heat, stirring often as it thickens, but do not boil.

✳ Serves 6

Normandy Chicken

One of my grandmother's favorite recipes was this dish featuring tender chicken served in a creamy mushroom sauce. This is her original version dating from the mid-1940s, rich with farm-fresh butter and cream from the family cow. The boneless, skinless chicken pieces are my substitution for the chicken thighs used in the original version.

    1 tablespoon paprika
    ½ teaspoon freshly ground black pepper
    ½ teaspoon salt
    4 boneless, skinless chicken breasts
    2 tablespoons butter
    2 cups fresh mushrooms, washed and sliced
    1 onion, chopped
    2 leeks
    1 cup chicken stock or broth
    ½ cup white wine
    1 tablespoon spicy brown mustard
    2 tablespoons cornstarch
    ½ cup heavy cream

Mix together the paprika, pepper, and salt, and rub the spice mixture on both sides of the chicken breasts. Heat the butter in the pressure cooker over medium heat. Add the chicken pieces, cook until golden brown on both sides, remove to a cutting board, and cut the chicken into large bite-size chunks. Add the mushrooms and onions to the cooker and cook, stirring, until slightly softened, about 3 minutes. Trim the coarse green ends from the leeks. Slit the leeks lengthwise and fan the leaves open under cold running water to remove all the dirt, and then cut crosswise into ½-inch slices and add to the cooker. Combine the stock, wine, and mustard in the pressure cooker and stir. Return the chicken pieces to the pressure cooker and lock the lid in place. Bring to 15psi over high heat, immediately reduce the heat to the lowest possible setting to stabilize and maintain that pressure, and cook for 5 minutes. Remove from the heat and use the natural release method (see page 31) to depressurize. Carefully open the lid after the pressure drops. Transfer the chicken and vegetables to a serving dish. Thicken the sauce by making a slurry with the cornstarch mixed with the cream; stir the slurry into the sauce and simmer over medium heat, stirring often as it thickens, but do not boil. Adjust the seasonings to taste and pour over the chicken. ✳ Serves 4

Serving Suggestion: Serve over hot rice or egg noodles.

Chicken Maque Choux

Maque choux is a Cajun side dish made with corn, cream, bell peppers, and tomatoes, but I've added chunks of tender chicken and transformed it into a meal. Serve over hot fluffy rice or split buttermilk biscuits.

    2 tablespoons oil
    4 boneless, skinless chicken breasts
    2 onions, finely chopped
    1 green bell pepper, seeded and finely chopped
    2 ears fresh corn, kernels removed

1 (14-ounce) can chopped tomatoes, with juice
2 sprigs fresh rosemary, minced
½ cup heavy cream

Heat the oil in the pressure cooker over medium heat. Add the chicken pieces, cook until golden brown on both sides, then cut into bite-size pieces and set aside. Add the onions and bell peppers to the cooker and cook, stirring, until slightly softened, about 3 minutes. Add the corn kernels, tomatoes, rosemary, and chicken pieces to the pressure cooker, stirring to mix. Bring to 15psi over high heat, immediately reduce the heat to the lowest possible setting to stabilize and maintain that pressure, and cook for 4 minutes. Remove from the heat and use the natural release method (see page 31) to depressurize. Carefully open the lid after the pressure drops. Transfer the chicken to a serving dish. Bring the broth to a simmer over medium-high heat, uncovered, and add the cream, stirring briefly. Pour the vegetable mixture and sauce into a separate serving bowl. ✳ Serves 4

Cook's Note: Substitute boneless pork cut into bite-size pieces for the chicken.

Artichoke Chicken

This is an easy dish, but packed with flavor and visual appeal. Serve over cooked egg noodles with a Caesar salad and crusty bread.

½ cup all-purpose flour
½ teaspoon freshly ground black pepper
½ teaspoon salt
4 boneless, skinless chicken breasts

2 tablespoons olive oil
1 (14-ounce) can artichoke hearts, drained and halved
Juice of 1 lemon
1 cup chicken broth
¼ cup vermouth or sherry
1 teaspoon spicy brown mustard
1 tablespoon minced garlic
Zest of 1 lemon
1 teaspoon dried basil
1 bay leaf

In a plastic bag, mix the flour, pepper, and salt, and add the chicken, shaking gently until each piece is lightly coated. Heat the oil in the pressure cooker over medium heat. Add the chicken pieces, cook until golden brown on both sides, and set aside. Add the artichokes, lemon juice, broth, vermouth, mustard, garlic, lemon zest, basil, and bay leaf to the cooker, stirring to mix. Return the chicken pieces to the pressure cooker. Lock the lid in place. Bring to 15psi over high heat, immediately reduce the heat to the lowest possible setting to stabilize and maintain that pressure, and cook for 8 minutes. Remove from the heat and use the natural release method (see page 31) to depressurize. Carefully open the lid after the pressure drops. Transfer the chicken and artichokes to a serving plate. Remove the bay leaf and bring the sauce to a boil. Reduce the heat and simmer, uncovered, for about 10 minutes, or until the liquid reduces by about half. Pass the sauce at the table. ✳ Serves 4

Chicken and Penne Pasta with Walnut Pesto Sauce

During a dinner with my gourmet cooking group, the host provided the recipe for the walnut pesto sauce served, and I fell in love on the spot. Of course, I couldn't wait to put together a pressure-cooker recipe that would incorporate my latest culinary find, and this is the marvelous yet very simple recipe built around that delicious walnut pesto sauce.

Step One: The Walnut Pesto Sauce
½ cup walnuts

2 cups tightly packed fresh basil leaves

¼ cup grated Parmigiano-Reggiano cheese

1 tablespoon minced garlic

⅓ cup olive oil

Spread the walnuts in a small skillet and heat over medium-low to medium heat, stirring often until the walnuts are lightly toasted. Remove from the heat and cool slightly. Combine the walnuts, basil, cheese, and garlic in a food processor. Process until the mixture is finely chopped. With the processor running, add the olive oil in a thin, steady stream until blended and smooth.

Step Two: The Chicken and Pasta
2 tablespoons olive oil

4 boneless, skinless chicken breasts

1 onion, chopped

3 cups uncooked penne

Heat the oil in the pressure cooker over medium heat. Add the chicken pieces, cook until golden brown on both sides, and set aside. Add the onions to the cooker and cook, stirring, until slightly softened, about 3 minutes. Add the pasta and enough water to cover, pushing the ingredients below the surface. Place the chicken pieces on top and lock the lid in place. Bring to 15psi over high heat, immediately reduce the heat to the lowest possible setting to stabilize and maintain that pressure, and cook for 8 minutes. Remove from the heat and use the natural release method (see page 31) to depressurize. Carefully open the lid after the pressure drops. Transfer the chicken pieces to a carving board and cut into bite-size pieces. Thoroughly drain the pasta and return to the cooker, then add the chicken pieces. Heat slowly until hot and bubbly. Serve immediately. ✳ Serves 4

Quick Chicken Pilaf

What a tasty pilaf to make on a day that you don't have much time to spend in the kitchen. Chunky pieces of chicken cook with white rice and just a hint of Indian spices, making it a perfect meal that the kids will enjoy, but tasty enough to tempt adult taste buds.

2 tablespoons oil

4 boneless, skinless chicken breasts

1 onion, chopped

1 cup uncooked long-grain white rice

2 cups frozen mixed vegetables
  (peas, carrots, corn)
1 (14-ounce) can chicken broth
1 teaspoon curry powder
Half of a cinnamon stick
1 bay leaf

Heat the oil in the pressure cooker over medium heat. Add the chicken pieces, cook until golden brown on both sides, transfer to a cutting board, and cut the chicken into large bite-size pieces. Add the onions to the cooker and cook, stirring, until slightly softened, about 3 minutes. Add the rice, stirring until coated with oil and translucent. Add the frozen vegetables, chicken pieces, broth, curry powder, cinnamon stick, bay leaf, and 1½ cups water, stirring to mix. Lock the lid in place. Bring to 15psi over high heat, immediately reduce the heat to the lowest possible setting to stabilize and maintain that pressure, and cook for 5 minutes. Remove from the heat and use the natural release method (see page 31) to depressurize. Carefully open the lid after the pressure drops. Remove the cinnamon stick and bay leaf and fluff with a fork before serving. ✳ Serves 4

Chicken Hash

This old-fashioned recipe was usually made with leftover chicken and potatoes. Since I don't often have enough leftovers, this version uses fresh ingredients. Everything you need is in the pot, plus it's easy and simple, and it only takes 4 minutes to cook. Best of all, there's hardly any preparation and only one pot to wash. You can't beat that!

2 tablespoons vegetable oil
4 boneless, skinless chicken thighs
1 onion, minced
1 red bell pepper, seeded and chopped
2 cups diced potatoes

Heat the oil in the pressure cooker over medium heat. Add the chicken pieces, cook until golden brown on both sides, transfer to a cutting board, and cut into bite-size pieces. Add the onions and peppers to the cooker and cook, stirring, until slightly softened, about 3 minutes. Add the potatoes and ½ cup water. Lock the lid in place. Bring to 15psi over high heat, immediately reduce the heat to the lowest possible setting to stabilize and maintain that pressure, and cook for 4 minutes. Remove from the heat and use the natural release method (see page 31) to depressurize. Carefully open the lid after the pressure drops. Drain off any excess liquid. Adjust the seasonings to taste and serve hot.
✳ Serves 4

Chicken Loaf

Another recipe from the family recipe coffers, this was a popular meatloaf some 50 years ago. Try this Chicken Loaf recipe for either hot or cold sandwiches or as a main dish with mashed potatoes and a tossed green salad. This recipe uses my PIP cooking technique to cook the loaf in mini loaf pans, a plain ring mold, or a round or spring-form pan.

    1½ pounds ground turkey or chicken
    1 onion, minced
    1 stalk celery, minced
    1 carrot, coarsely grated
    ½ cups saltine cracker crumbs
    2 tablespoons minced garlic
    ½ teaspoon dried basil
    ½ teaspoon salt
    ¼ teaspoon freshly ground black pepper
    1 large egg, slightly beaten
    3 tablespoons ketchup

Combine all of the ingredients in a large bowl and mix by hand until uniformly blended. Pack the meat mixture into the insert pan of your choice. Place the rack in the pressure cooker, add 1 cup water and place the pan on the rack using foil helper handles (see page 42). Lock the lid in place. Bring to 15psi over high heat, immediately reduce the heat to the lowest possible setting to stabilize and maintain that pressure, and cook for 20 minutes. Remove from the heat and use the natural release method (see page 31) to depressurize. Carefully open the lid after the pressure drops. Using oven mitts, carefully lift the pan out of the cooker and transfer the meatloaf to serving plate. Serve hot or cold as desired. ✳ Serves 5 to 6

Curried Chicken Sandwiches

There are many different lovely textures and mouthwatering flavors to these out-of-the-ordinary chicken sandwiches. I serve them on croissant rolls, stuffed into pita bread, or as a wrap in a flour tortilla. The chicken mixture is also excellent as a brunch or light lunch when served on a bed of crisp salad greens.

    Step One: The Chicken
    1 teaspoon curry powder
    ½ teaspoon lemon pepper
    ½ teaspoon garlic powder
    ½ teaspoon onion powder
    4 boneless, skinless chicken breasts
    1 tablespoon oil

Mix together the curry, lemon pepper, garlic powder, and onion powder, and rub the mixture into both sides of the chicken breasts, reserving any extra spice mix. Heat the oil in the pressure cooker over medium heat. Add the chicken pieces and cook until golden brown on both sides. Add the remaining spice mixture to the oil, frying until the spices begin to sizzle. Turn the chicken pieces over, coating with the spices, then remove the chicken. Place the rack in the cooker and arrange the chicken pieces on top. Add ½ cup water and lock the lid in place. Bring to 15psi over high heat, immediately reduce the heat to the lowest possible setting to stabilize and maintain that pressure, and cook for 15 minutes. Remove from the heat and use the natural release method (see page 31) to depressurize. Carefully open the lid after the pressure drops. Transfer the chicken pieces to a cutting board and shred with a fork.

Step Two: The Sandwich Filling

¾ cup mayonnaise

1 tablespoon fresh lemon juice

1 tablespoon honey

½ cup minced celery

½ cup halved green grapes

⅓ cup toasted slivered almonds

¼ cups minced onion

½ to 1 teaspoon curry powder, or to taste

Lettuce leaves

6 large croissant rolls, split

Mix the mayonnaise, lemon juice, honey, celery, grapes, almonds, onions, and curry powder in a bowl. Adjust the seasonings to taste. Fill each croissant with some of the mixture, add lettuce leaves and the chicken, and serve immediately.

✳ **Serves 6**

Teriyaki Chicken

Using the pressure cooker to precook the chicken, super-marinating the meat in a spicy and flavorful teriyaki-based sauce takes only 8 minutes. Pop the chicken under the broiler to finish for a sticky, sweet glaze.

6 boneless, skinless chicken breasts

⅓ cup teriyaki sauce

⅓ cup soy sauce

2 tablespoons sherry

1 tablespoon brown sugar

1 tablespoon minced garlic

1 teaspoon ground ginger

¼ teaspoon red pepper flakes

2 tablespoons sliced green onions, for garnish

Place the chicken in the pressure cooker. In a small bowl, combine the remaining ingredients except for the green onions, stir briefly to blend, and pour the mixture over the chicken. Lock the lid in place. Bring to 15psi over high heat, immediately reduce the heat to the lowest possible setting to stabilize and maintain that pressure, and cook for 8 minutes. Remove from the heat and use the natural release method (see page 31) to depressurize. Carefully open the lid after the pressure drops. Transfer the chicken pieces to a plate. Bring to the sauce to a boil, uncovered; reduce the heat to a simmer, and cook for about 10 minutes, stirring occasionally, or until the sauce is reduced and slightly sticky. Preheat the broiler. Return the chicken pieces to the cooker, turning once to coat with the sauce. Transfer the chicken pieces to a roasting pan, generously baste with sauce, and place about 6 inches under the broiler. Watch closely, and once the chicken just begins to brown, turn the pieces and baste again. Broil just until the pieces are brown, and then transfer to a serving plate. Garnish with a sprinkling of green onions.

✳ **Serves 6**

The Fastest Chicken Pot Pie Ever

Do you remember homemade chicken pot pies? Doesn't it make your mouth water just thinking about all the ingredients in that creamy filling hidden inside a flaky pie crust? In this recipe, the pressure cooker is used to precook the chicken, vegetables, and creamy sauce before adding it to a prepared pie crust.

Step One: The Chicken Pie Filling

2 boneless, skinless chicken breasts, cut into 1-inch cubes

1 onion, finely chopped

1 large potato, peeled and diced

2 cups frozen peas and carrots

1 teaspoon chicken bouillon granules

½ teaspoon ground sage

½ teaspoon freshly ground black pepper

½ cup chicken stock

2 tablespoons cornstarch

Place all of the ingredients except for the cornstarch in a pressure cooker. Lock the lid in place. Bring to 15psi over high heat, immediately reduce the heat to the lowest possible setting to stabilize and maintain that pressure, and cook for 4 minutes. Remove from the heat and use the quick release method (see page 30) to depressurize. Carefully open the lid after the pressure drops. Drain the chicken and vegetables into a colander, reserving ½ cup of the broth. Bring the broth to a simmer over medium heat. Thicken the broth by making a slurry with the cornstarch mixed with ¼ cup cold water; stir the slurry into the sauce and simmer gently over medium heat, uncovered, stirring often as it thickens, but do not boil. Return the chicken and vegetable mixture to the thickened sauce, stirring gently to mix.

Step Two: The Pie

Preheat the oven to 400°F. Use ready-made pie crusts or your own recipe—enough for both the bottom and top crusts. Line the bottom of a 10-inch pie pan with 1 pie crust and pour in the chicken pie filling mixture. Add a crust on top and crimp the edges to seal. Make several small cuts in the top crust with a sharp knife. Place the pie on a baking sheet to catch any spills. Bake for about 10 minutes, or until the crust is golden brown. Remove from the oven and let rest for a few minutes before serving. ✳ Serves 4

Brandied Chicken Liver Pâté

Serve this richly flavored pâté with assorted crackers as a gourmet treat for your next party, or just spread it on a slice of crusty bread for a fabulous lunchtime sandwich.

Step One: The *Bouquet Garni*
3 sprigs fresh parsley
2 sprigs fresh rosemary
2 cloves garlic, crushed
2 teaspoons dried oregano
1 teaspoon whole black peppercorns
½ teaspoons whole cloves garlic
1 bay leaf

Tie all of the ingredients up in a square of cheesecloth.

Step Two: The Chicken Livers
2 pounds chicken livers
2 tablespoons butter
2 medium-size onions, finely diced
2 tablespoons minced garlic
½ cup beef broth
½ teaspoon salt
½ teaspoon freshly ground black pepper

Rinse the chicken livers in cold water. Trim away any visible fat and bits of tough sinews. Heat the butter in the pressure cooker over medium heat. Add the onions and garlic and cook, stirring, until translucent, about 3 minutes. Add the chicken livers, broth, salt, pepper, and *bouquet garni*, and lock the lid in place. Bring to 15psi over high heat, immediately reduce the heat to the lowest possible setting to stabilize and maintain that pressure, and cook for 2 minutes. Remove from the heat and use the natural release method (see page 31) to depressurize. Carefully open the lid after the pressure drops. Press the *bouquet garni* against the side of the cooker with the back of a spoon to squeeze out all liquid, and then discard.

Step Three: The Pâté
⅓ cup butter, softened to room temperature
2 tablespoons brandy or Cognac
Parsley leaves, for garnish

Transfer the entire contents of the pressure cooker to a food processor. Add the butter and brandy and pulse briefly until the desired thick-creamy texture is achieved. Be careful not to overprocess the pâté or it will become a puree. Lightly spritz a decorative mold of your choice with nonstick cooking spray and transfer the liver mixture, smoothing out the top with a rubber spatula. Tightly wrap the entire mold in plastic wrap and place in the refrigerator overnight to age and set. To unmold and serve, fill the sink with very hot water and set the mold in it for 30 seconds, or just long enough to loosen the sides, taking care not to let the water go over the rim of the mold. Unwrap the mold, place a serving plate over the top, and invert the mold. The pâté will now be upside down on the plate, and you are good to go. ✳ Serves 6

Serving Suggestion: Garnish the serving plate with a few fresh parsley leaves, and serve with your choice of crackers or crusty, thinly sliced bread. Complete the presentation with bowls of finely minced red and green onions, and sliced black and green olives as garnishes, if desired.

Chicken Tacos with Avocado Salsa

The pressure cooker makes quick work of the chicken mixture for homemade tacos. Cooking the chicken only takes a few minutes, but if you hurry, you just might be able to cut up all the toppings for the tacos before the chicken is finished.

Step One: The Avocado Salsa
2 large ripe but firm avocados, peeled and pitted
4 ripe Roma tomatoes, diced
½ cup chopped Vidalia or Maui onions
1 fresh jalapeño chile, seeded and minced
⅓ cup packed cilantro leaves, minced
½ teaspoon garlic powder
3 tablespoons fresh lime juice

Prepare the salsa just before serving. Cut the avocados into small cubes and gently mix with the remaining salsa ingredients in a small bowl. Cover with plastic wrap and refrigerate until ready to serve.

Step Two: The Chicken
4 boneless, skinless chicken breasts
4 teaspoons ground cumin
1 tablespoon chili powder
1 tablespoon vegetable oil

Pat the chicken dry with paper towels. Combine the cumin and chili powder and rub the mixture into both sides of the chicken breasts, reserving any extra spice mix. Heat the oil in the pressure cooker over medium heat. Add the chicken pieces, cook until golden brown on both sides, and set aside. Add the remaining spices to the oil, frying until they begin to release their aroma. Place the rack in a pressure cooker, add ½ cup water, and arrange the chicken pieces on top of the rack. Lock the lid in place. Bring to 15psi over high heat, immediately reduce the heat to the lowest possible setting to stabilize and maintain that pressure, and cook for 8 minutes. Remove from the heat and use the natural release method (see page 31) to depressurize. Carefully open the lid after the pressure drops. Transfer the chicken to a carving board, and slice into very thin strips.

Step Three: The Toppings
1 package 6- to 8-inch flour tortillas, warmed
　　according to package directions
2 cups shredded lettuce
1½ cups shredded cheddar cheese
1 cup sour cream

Keep the soft tortillas warm in a covered dish. Arrange the chicken pieces, lettuce and shredded cheese on a large serving platter. Pass the sour cream and Avocado Salsa at the table and let everyone assemble the chicken tacos according to their personal preferences. ✳ Serves 4 to 5

Cranberry-Braised Turkey Breast with Gravy

If you never bother to cook turkey because it's too much trouble to cook a whole bird, you'll change your mind after trying this recipe using just the whole turkey breast. Of course, the pressure cooker really delivers when it comes to cooking large pieces of meat, and it will only take 25 minutes.

Step One: The Turkey
2 cups cranberry juice
1 cup fresh or frozen whole cranberries
2 onions, chopped
1 (2- to 3-pound) whole turkey breast
2 tablespoons butter, at room temperature

Place the rack in the pressure cooker and add the cranberry juice, cranberries, and onions. Rinse the turkey breast and pat dry with paper towels. Using foil helper handles (see page 42), lower the turkey breast onto the rack. Lock the lid in place. Bring to 15psi over high heat, immediately reduce the heat to the lowest possible setting to stabilize and maintain that pressure, and cook for 25 minutes. Remove from the heat and use the natural release method (see page 31) to depressurize. Carefully open the lid after the pressure drops.

To present the bird to be carved at the table for the main course, I recommend browning in a hot oven before serving, but if the turkey is to be sliced for sandwiches or other recipes you can skip this step. Preheat the oven to 450°F. Transfer the turkey breast to a roasting pan and rub the butter over the entire surface. Place the turkey breast in the oven to crisp and brown the skin. Baste frequently with the drippings, and watch closely so that the skin turns golden but does not burn. When the skin is nicely colored, remove the turkey breast to a carving board and let it rest for about 10 minutes before carving.

Step Two: The Gravy
¼ cup all-purpose flour
1 teaspoon salt
½ teaspoon freshly ground black pepper

In a small bowl, dissolve the flour in ½ cup water and add the salt and pepper, mixing until smooth. Remove the rack from the pressure cooker. Using a hand blender, puree the cranberry and onion pieces in the turkey broth to a smooth consistency. Bring the broth in the pressure cooker to a boil, uncovered, over medium-high heat. Gradually whisk the flour mixture into the simmering broth. Reduce the heat, and simmer for about 10 minutes, or until thickened. Taste and adjust the seasonings as desired. Pour the gravy into a sauce boat and serve with the turkey. ✳ Serves 5 to 6

Coconut Drumsticks with Pineapple-Jalapeño Salsa

This dish is a little spicy, a little sweet, and very delicious. The sweetness comes from coconut, pineapple, and sweet onion and helps temper the hot chiles. It's a combination that pairs well together and adds a complex blend of flavors to the chicken.

Step One: The Pineapple-Jalapeño Salsa

2 cups canned pineapple chunks

1 mild chile, such as poblano, pasilla, or Anaheim, seeded and minced

1 jalapeo chile, seeded and minced

½ cup sweet Vidalia or Maui onion, minced

1 (4-ounce) jar pimientos, drained and coarsely chopped

3 tablespoons cilantro leaves, finely chopped

1 tablespoon fresh lime juice

1 teaspoon sugar

Combine all of the ingredients for the salsa in a medium-size bowl. Adjust the seasonings to taste. Cover and refrigerate for several hours or overnight before serving.

Step Two: The Chicken

⅓ cup unsweetened flaked coconut

2 tablespoons butter

2 tablespoons soy sauce

1 teaspoon chicken bouillon granules

12 chicken legs

½ cup unsweetened coconut milk

To toast the coconut, heat the pressure cooker over medium-high heat. Spread the coconut on the bottom and stir as it begins to color, taking care that it does not burn. Remove the toasted coconut to a small plate and set aside. Heat the pressure cooker over medium heat and melt the butter. Add the soy sauce, bouillon granules, and ½ cup water, and stir. Add the chicken pieces, turning to coat all sides. Lock the lid in place. Bring to 15psi over high heat, immediately reduce the heat to the lowest possible setting to stabilize and maintain that pressure, and cook for 6 minutes. Remove from the heat and use the natural release method (see page 31) to depressurize. Carefully open the lid after the pressure drops. Transfer the chicken to a heatproof serving platter and keep warm in a low oven. Add the coconut milk to the cooker and simmer until the liquid reduces by about half and begins to thicken, taking care not to boil. Drizzle the sauce over the chicken pieces. Pass the salsa at the table.

✳ Serves 6

Naked Hens and Vegetables in Cream Gravy

Growing up, our kitchen filled with squeals of childish laughter whenever Mom made her "naked" chicken recipe. She gave this old-fashioned recipe the odd name because almost everything in the dish is white. The delicate Cornish game hens are so tender the meat will melt in your mouth. Using the interrupted cooking method (see page 38), the hens are partially cooked and then the vegetables added so that they remain tender-crisp and everything finishes at the same time.

Step One: The Cornish Game Hens and Vegetables
1 (14-ounce) can chicken broth
2 tablespoons minced garlic
1 teaspoon salt
½ teaspoon freshly ground black pepper
½ teaspoon ground sage
1 bay leaf
2 Cornish game hens
6 parsnips, peeled and cut into ¼-inch slices
4 small turnips, peeled and diced
4 small red potatoes, peeled and diced
4 small boiling onions, peeled and chopped
4 leeks, whites only, cut into ¼-inch slices

Place the rack in a large pressure cooker. Add the broth, garlic, salt, pepper, sage, and bay leaf. To truss the hens, tie the legs together with string and tuck the wings under. Using foil helper handles (see page 42), place the birds on the rack. Lock the lid in place. Bring to 15psi over high heat, immediately reduce the heat to the lowest possible setting to stabilize and maintain that pressure, and cook for 4 minutes. Remove from the heat and use the quick release method (see page 30) to depressurize. Carefully open the lid after the pressure drops. Arrange all of the vegetables around the hens, and lock the lid back in place. Return to 15psi over high heat, immediately reduce the heat to the lowest possible setting to stabilize and maintain that pressure, and cook for an additional 4 minutes. Remove from the heat and use the natural release method (see page 31) to depressurize. Carefully open the lid after the pressure drops. Transfer the Cornish hens to a large, heatproof serving platter and arrange the vegetables around them. Keep warm in a low oven. Pour the broth into a large bowl and set aside.

Step Two: The Cream Gravy
2 tablespoons butter
¼ cup all-purpose flour
1 cup heavy cream

Heat the butter in the pressure cooker until melted. Stir in the flour and cook over medium heat until it is the consistency of a thick paste. Slowly stir in the reserved broth, whisking continuously to blend with the flour mixture. Bring to a boil, stirring as the sauce thickens. Lower the heat and add the cream, stirring until well blended and heated through, but do not allow the gravy to boil. Taste and adjust the seasoning. Pour into a gravy boat to serve at the table. ✳ Serves 4

Stuffed Chicken Rolls with Gravy

The wonderful aroma of these stuffed chicken rolls contain a delicious surprise—savory herbed stuffing mix—so it's like eating a mini stuffed chicken.

Step One: The Chicken Rolls
4 large boneless, skinless chicken breasts
1 tablespoon paprika
1 teaspoon freshly ground black pepper
½ teaspoon garlic powder
½ teaspoon onion powder
1 package prepared chicken stuffing mix (such as Stove Top)
2 tablespoons butter or margarine
¼ cup diced onion
Half of a 14-ounce can chicken broth

One at a time, place each piece of chicken on a cutting board between sheets of plastic wrap. Flatten the chicken with a meat mallet, or use a small heavy pan, pounding until the meat is thin and about doubled in area. Mix together the paprika, pepper, garlic powder, and onion powder, and rub the spice mixture into both sides of the chicken breasts, reserving any remaining spice mixture. Add just enough prepared stuffing mix to still allow the edges of the chicken to be brought together and secured with one or two toothpicks. Heat the butter in the pressure cooker over medium heat, onions to the cooker and cook, stirring, until slightly softened, about 3 minutes. Add the remaining spice mixture and half of the broth. Place the rack in the cooker and arrange the stuffed chicken rolls on the rack. Lock the lid in place. Bring to 15psi over high heat, immediately reduce the heat to the lowest possible setting to stabilize and maintain that pressure, and cook for 5 minutes. Remove from the heat and use the natural release method (see page 31) to depressurize. Carefully open the lid after the pressure drops. Using long-handled tongs, transfer the chicken rolls to a heatproof serving platter and place the remaining stuffing mix in the center. Cover the platter with aluminum foil and keep warm in a low oven until ready to serve.

Step Two: The Gravy
¼ cup all-purpose flour
Half of a 14-ounce can chicken broth
1 teaspoon salt
½ teaspoon freshly ground black pepper

In a small bowl, dissolve the flour in the remaining chicken broth and add the salt and pepper, mixing until smooth. Remove the rack from the pressure cooker. Bring the broth in the pressure cooker to a boil, uncovered, over medium-high heat. Gradually whisk the flour mixture into the simmering broth. Reduce the heat, and simmer for about 10 minutes, or until thickened. Taste and adjust the seasonings as desired. Pour the gravy into a sauce boat and serve with the chicken rolls. ✳ **Serves 4**

Wine-Braised Turkey Breast with Mushroom Gravy

Elegant but hearty, the turkey breast is braised in a sweet wine and seasoned with a blend of savory herbs and garlic, with plenty of mushrooms.

Step One: The Turkey

2 tablespoons oil

1 (2-pound) boneless rolled turkey breast

1 pound fresh button mushrooms, washed and sliced

1 onion, chopped

1 (14-ounce) can chicken broth

½ cup sweet Port or Madeira

2 tablespoons minced garlic

1 teaspoon ground thyme

1 bay leaf

Heat the oil in the pressure cooker over medium heat. Add the turkey, cook until golden brown on all sides, and set aside. Add the mushrooms and onions to the cooker and cook, stirring, until slightly softened, about 3 minutes. Add the broth, wine, garlic, thyme, and bay leaf and stir. Place the rack in the cooker and return the turkey to the cooker using foil helper handles (see page 42). Lock the lid in place. Bring to 15psi over high heat, immediately reduce the heat to the lowest possible setting to stabilize and maintain that pressure, and cook for 25 minutes. Remove from the heat and use the natural release method (see page 31) to depressurize. Carefully open the lid after the pressure drops. Transfer the turkey to a large serving platter and let it rest for about 10 minutes before carving. Remove the rack and discard the bay leaf. Skim off any excess fat from the surface of the broth and transfer the broth to a separate bowl.

Step Two: The Gravy

2 tablespoons butter

¼ cup all-purpose flour

Melt the butter in the pressure cooker. Add the flour, mixing into a smooth paste. Slowly pour in the reserved broth, whisking to keep a smooth consistency. Bring to a boil, uncovered, and then reduce the heat, simmering for about 10 minutes or until thickened. Taste and adjust the seasonings as desired. Pour the gravy into a sauce boat to be passed at the table. ✳ Serves 4 to 5

California Pulled Turkey Wraps

Fun wraps with a fresh California flavor, a nice dish to serve for lunch or as a light meal during the heat of summer.

1 large onion, chopped

½ cup packed cilantro stems and leaves

2 cloves garlic, crushed

½ teaspoon red pepper flakes

½ teaspoon whole black peppercorns

1 bay leaf

1 (2-pound) boneless half turkey breast

10 to 12 (10-inch) flour tortillas, warmed according to package directions

1 cup sour cream

Whole lettuce leaves

2 cups chopped Roma tomatoes

1 (5-ounce) package alfalfa sprouts, rinsed and well drained

1 red onion, sliced into very thin rings

2 large avocados, peeled and sliced

1 cup grated sharp cheddar cheese

Place the onions, cilantro, garlic, red pepper flakes, peppercorns, and bay leaf in the pressure cooker, add 2 cups water, and stir to mix. Place the rack in the pressure cooker and position the turkey breast on top. Lock the lid in place. Bring to 15psi over high heat, immediately reduce the heat to the lowest possible setting to stabilize and maintain that pressure, and cook for 15 minutes. Remove from the heat and use the natural release method (see page 31) to depressurize. Carefully open the lid after the pressure drops. Check for doneness; the meat should easily pull apart with a fork. If necessary, lock the lid back in place, return to 15psi over high heat, immedi-

ately reduce the heat to the lowest possible setting to stabilize and maintain that pressure, and cook for an additional 5 minutes. Remove from the heat and use the quick or cold water release method (see page 30) to depressurize. Carefully open the lid after the pressure drops, and check for doneness again. Transfer the turkey to a carving board and slice thinly. Strain the broth, discarding all the solids, and freeze for later use in soups and stews. Lay the warmed tortillas on a work surface and spread with some sour cream. Cover each tortilla with lettuce leaves and then a layer of sliced turkey. Add a few chopped tomatoes, alfalfa sprouts, and the onion rings. Top with avocado slices and some cheese. Carefully roll up the wraps, jelly-roll fashion. Using a sharp knife, cut each wrap in half before serving.

✳ Serves 6

Chicken in Red Wine Sauce

This is my version of the classic *coq au vin* recipe that was popular in many old pressure cooker recipes.

½ pound bacon

1 onion, chopped

6 cloves garlic, sliced into slivers

16 small fresh mushrooms, washed and sliced

4 boneless, skinless chicken breasts

1 (14-ounce) can chicken broth

2 cups red wine

2 teaspoons dried thyme

Cook the bacon in the open pressure cooker until crisp, and then set aside on paper towels to drain. Add the onions and garlic to the hot bacon fat and cook, stirring, until they just begin to brown, and then set aside on paper towels to drain. Add the mushrooms and cook, stirring, until slightly softened, and set aside on paper towels to drain. Add the chicken breasts to the cooker, cook until golden brown on both sides, and set aside. Drain the fat from the cooker. Return the bacon pieces, onions and garlic, mushrooms, and chicken pieces to the pressure cooker. Add the broth, wine, and thyme and stir. Lock the lid in place. Bring to 15psi over high heat, immediately reduce the heat to the lowest possible setting to stabilize and maintain that pressure, and cook for 10 minutes. Remove from the heat and use the natural release method (see page 31) to depressurize. Carefully open the lid after the pressure drops. Transfer the chicken and mushrooms to a serving plate using a slotted spoon. Reduce the sauce by boiling, uncovered, over high heat until thick enough to coat a spoon, about 15 minutes. Adjust the seasonings to taste. Serve the sauce separately. ✳ Serves 4

Serving Suggestion: This is especially good served over garlic mashed potatoes.

Kung Pao Chicken

Spicy chicken in a piquant sauce and crunchy peanuts are the stars in this recipe. With no hard-to-find ingredients, this is a dish that is quick and easy enough to prepare for a weeknight meal with a wonderful combination of flavors. Serve with rice.

Step One: The Chicken
1 tablespoon oil
6 boneless, skinless chicken breasts
1 onion, chopped

2 tablespoons minced garlic
2 teaspoons fresh ginger, minced

Heat the oil in the pressure cooker over medium heat. Add the chicken pieces and cook until golden brown on both sides. Add the onions to the cooker and cook, stirring, until slightly softened, about 3 minutes. Add the garlic, ginger, and ½ cup water. Lock the lid in place. Bring to 15psi over high heat, immediately reduce the heat to the lowest possible setting to stabilize and maintain that pressure, and cook for 8 minutes. Remove from the heat and use the natural release method (see page 31) to depressurize. Carefully open the lid after the pressure drops. Discard the liquid and cut the chicken into bite-size pieces. Transfer the chicken, onion, garlic, and ginger to a bowl.

Step Two: The Sauce
¼ cup soy sauce
1 tablespoon sherry
1 tablespoon rice wine vinegar
5 dashes of hot pepper sauce
2 tablespoons cornstarch
1 tablespoon sugar
1 cup chopped green onions
½ cup dry-roasted peanuts

Heat the pressure cooker over medium heat and add the soy sauce, sherry, vinegar, hot sauce, cornstarch, and sugar. Cook and stir until the sauce is thick and bubbly. Add the chicken, onion, garlic, ginger, green onions, and peanuts to the sauce, stirring to coat, and cook 1 to 2 minutes more or until heated through, stirring frequently so that it doesn't burn. Adjust the seasonings to taste. ✳ Serves 6

Asian Chicken with Tender-Crisp Vegetables

Cooking tender-crisp vegetables in a pressure cooker is not an impossible feat. The secret is using the cold water release method (see page 30) to stop the cooking process immediately, and then opening the lid and promptly removing the vegetables.

Step One: The Chicken

1 tablespoon butter
1 tablespoon sesame oil
4 boneless, skinless chicken breasts
1 onion, cut into thin strips
1½ cups sliced fresh mushrooms
2 cloves garlic, minced
1 cup chicken stock

Heat the butter and oil in the pressure cooker over medium heat. Add the chicken pieces, cook until golden brown on both sides. Add the onions and mushrooms to the cooker and cook, stirring, until slightly softened, about 3 minutes. Add the garlic and stock, and return the chicken strips to the cooker. Lock the lid in place. Bring to 15psi over high heat, immediately reduce the heat to the lowest possible setting to stabilize and maintain that pressure, and cook for 5 minutes. Remove from the heat and use the cold water release method (see page 30) to depressurize. Carefully open the lid after the pressure drops.

Step Two: The Vegetables

2 cups broccoli florets
2 cups cabbage cut into thin strips
2 cups fresh or frozen snow peas
1 red bell pepper, seeded and thinly sliced
1 cup cauliflower florets
1 cup pineapple tidbits
½ cup coarsely shredded carrots

Add all of the ingredients to the cooker and lock the lid back in place. Return to 15psi over high heat, immediately reduce the heat to the lowest possible setting to stabilize and maintain that pressure, and cook for an additional 3 minutes. Remove from the heat and use the cold water release method (see page 30) to depressurize. Carefully open the lid immediately after the pressure drops. Drain the meat and vegetable mixture, reserving the broth. Cut the chicken into thin strips and transfer the meat and vegetables to a serving bowl.

Step Three: The Sauce

2 teaspoons sugar
¼ cup fresh lemon juice
¼ cup packed cilantro leaves, finely chopped
1 teaspoon grated lemon zest
2 tablespoons cornstarch
¼ cup soy sauce

Return ½ cup of the reserved broth to the cooker and add the sugar, lemon juice, cilantro, and lemon zest. Bring to a boil over high heat for 3 minutes, or until it begins to thicken. Mix the cornstarch into the soy sauce. Lower the heat and add the soy sauce mixture, stirring as the sauce thickens. Pour a little sauce over the top of the chicken and vegetable mixture. Pour the rest of the sauce into a serving bowl and pass at the table.

✳ Serves 4

Serving Suggestion: This is great served with rice and egg rolls.

Chicken in Orange Cream Sauce

Fragrant with the scent of oranges and tarragon, tender pieces of chicken are served in a creamy sour cream sauce.

¼ cup plus 2 tablespoons all-purpose flour
1 teaspoon salt
⅛ teaspoon freshly ground black pepper
6 boneless, skinless chicken breasts
2 tablespoons butter or margarine
½ cup dry white wine or apple juice
1½ tablespoons frozen orange juice concentrate
1 tablespoon minced garlic
1 teaspoon grated orange zest
1 teaspoon dried tarragon leaves
½ teaspoon dried thyme leaves
1½ tablespoons thinly sliced green onions,
    for garnish
Orange wedges, for garnish
2 teaspoons sugar
½ cup sour cream

In a plastic bag, mix ¼ cup of the flour with the salt and pepper, and add the chicken, shaking gently until each piece is lightly coated. Heat the butter in the pressure cooker over medium heat. Add the chicken pieces, cook until golden brown on both sides, and set aside. Deglaze the pot with the wine, scraping up all those crusty, brown bits from the bottom. Add the orange juice, garlic, orange zest, tarragon, and thyme and mix well. Add the chicken, turning once to coat, and lock the lid in place. Bring to 15psi over high heat, immediately reduce the heat to the lowest possible setting to stabilize and maintain that pressure, and cook for 8 minutes. Remove from the heat and use the natural release method (see page 31) to depressurize. Carefully open the lid after the pressure drops. Transfer the chicken pieces to a serving plate and sprinkle with the green onions. Add the orange wedges to the plate to squeeze over individual portions. Simmer the broth, uncovered, over medium-high heat. Mix the remaining 2 tablespoons of flour and the sugar with the sour cream to make a smooth mixture. Whisk the sour cream mixture into the simmering broth, lower the heat, and continue stirring until it thickens to the desired consistency. Adjust the seasonings to taste. Pour the gravy in a separate bowl to serve at the table. ✳ Serves 6

Apricot- and Tea-Braised Chicken

This is a delicious dish, redolent with the flavors of apricots and curry, and pungent spices all mingled together with the subtle flavor of tea. Serve over rice or cooked oriental noodles.

2 tablespoons canola oil
6 boneless, skinless chicken breasts
2 cups sliced carrots
1 onion, sliced
1 green bell pepper, seeded and cut into strips
½ cup dried apricots, chopped
1 tablespoon minced garlic
1 teaspoon ground cumin
1 teaspoon curry powder
½ teaspoon red pepper flakes
1 teaspoon salt
¼ teaspoon freshly ground black pepper
1 (12-ounce) can apricot nectar
1 tablespoon rice vinegar
2 tea bags (choose English Breakfast,
    Earl Grey, or another full-bodied tea)
2 tablespoons cornstarch

Heat the oil in the pressure cooker over medium heat. Add the chicken pieces, cook until golden brown on both sides, transfer to a cutting board, and cut into large bite-size pieces. Add the carrots, onions, bell peppers, apricots, garlic, cumin, curry, red pepper flakes, salt, black pepper, apricot nectar, vinegar, and ⅓ cup water to the cooker, and bring to a boil. Add the tea bags, cover with a regular lid, and let steep for 5 minutes. Remove the tea bags and add the chicken pieces, stirring to mix. Lock the lid in place. Bring to 15psi over high heat, im-mediately reduce the heat to the lowest possible setting to stabilize and maintain that pressure, and cook for 4 minutes. Remove from the heat and use the natural release method (see page 31) to depres-surize. Carefully open the lid after the pressure drops. Thicken the sauce by making a slurry with the cornstarch mixed with ⅓ cup cold water; stir the slurry into the sauce and simmer over medium heat, stirring often as it thickens, but do not boil.

✳ Serves 6

Tangy Key Lime Chicken with Cool Cucumber Salsa

The tangy lime juice and refreshing cucumber salsa add a touch of Caribbean spiciness to plain chicken breasts for an interesting con-trast of hot and spicy flavors with creamy and cool tastes.

Step One: The Salsa
2 medium-size cucumbers, peeled, seeded,
    and chopped
½ cup chopped green bell pepper
1 jalapeño chile, seeded and minced
1 small red onion, minced
2 tablespoons minced cilantro leaves
1 tablespoon minced garlic
½ teaspoon salt
2 tablespoons fresh key lime juice

In a medium-size glass bowl, stir together all of the ingredients. Cover and refrigerate for several hours before serving.

Step Two: The Chicken

2 tablespoons oil

6 boneless, skinless chicken breast halves

½ cup key lime juice

1 tablespoon honey

½ cup chopped cilantro

2 tablespoons minced garlic

½ teaspoon red pepper flakes

½ teaspoon freshly ground black pepper

Cilantro sprigs, for garnish

Heat the oil in the pressure cooker over medium heat. Add the chicken pieces and cook until golden brown on both sides. Add the lime juice, honey, cilantro, garlic, red pepper flakes, and black pepper to the pressure cooker, turning the chicken once to coat both sides. Lock the lid in place. Bring to 15psi over high heat, immediately reduce the heat to the lowest possible setting to stabilize and maintain that pressure, and cook for 8 minutes. Remove from the heat and use the natural release method (see page 31) to depressurize. Carefully open the lid after the pressure drops. Preheat the broiler. Transfer the chicken to a broiler pan and baste with some of the sauce. Place the pan about 6 inches from the heat, turning and basting with the reserved marinade until both sides look crisp and brown. Garnish with cilantro sprigs and serve with the Cool Cucumber Salsa on the side. ✳ **Serves 6**

Chicken in Tarragon Cream Sauce

Fast, easy, and elegant, the tarragon cream sauce with white wine adds a wonderful flavor to this chicken dish. Make sure to serve this with steamed rice or plain noodles to take advantage of the lovely sauce.

4 thick slices bacon

4 boneless, skinless chicken breasts

Salt and freshly ground black pepper to taste

1 onion, finely chopped

2 tablespoons minced garlic

½ cup dry white wine

2 tablespoons fresh tarragon, coarsely chopped

1 cup heavy cream

Fresh tarragon leaves, for garnish

Fry the bacon in the pressure cooker over medium heat until crispy, then set aside on paper towels. Season the chicken pieces with salt and pepper, add to the cooker, cook until golden brown on both sides, and set aside. Add the onions and garlic to the cooker and cook, stirring, until slightly softened, about 3 minutes. Pour off the remaining fat. Deglaze the cooker with the wine, scraping up all those crusty, brown bits from the bottom. Return the chicken pieces to the cooker, add the chopped tarragon, and stir. Lock the lid in place. Bring to 15psi over high heat, immediately reduce the heat to the lowest possible setting to stabilize and maintain that pressure, and cook for 8 minutes. Remove from the heat and use the natural release method (see page 31) to depressurize. Carefully open the lid after the pressure drops. Transfer the chicken to a serving platter. Quickly add the cream to the hot pan juices and whisk until the mixture is smooth. Spoon the sauce over the chicken pieces. Sprinkle on the crumbled bacon and a few tarragon leaves for garnish. ✳ **Serves 4**

Black Peppered Chicken and Potatoes with Gravy

Plenty of pungent black pepper is what makes this simple chicken dish so good. It not only has a fabulous flavor and texture, but also just enough kick to make every bite an absolute delight. Using the tiered cooking method (see page 38), this one-pot meal includes potatoes cooked in a separate pan and a creamy buttermilk gravy.

Step One: The Chicken

1 teaspoon cracked or coarsely ground black pepper
1 teaspoon spicy paprika
6 boneless, skinless chicken breast halves
2 tablespoons olive oil
1 onion, chopped
1 tablespoon minced garlic
1 (14-ounce) can chicken broth
4 potatoes, scrubbed and halved
¼ cup chopped green onion tops, for garnish

Mix together the cracked pepper and the paprika, and rub and press the mixture into both sides of the chicken breasts, coating each piece. Save any remaining pepper mixture. Heat the oil in the pressure cooker over medium heat. Add the chicken pieces, cook until golden brown on both sides, and set aside. Add the onions to the cooker and cook, stirring, until slightly softened, about 3 minutes.

Add the garlic and any of the remaining pepper mix, frying until the spices begin to release their aroma. Add the broth and stir. Spritz the rack with oil or nonstick cooking spray and place it in the cooker; it must be higher than the chicken broth. Arrange the chicken breasts on the rack, taking care not to disturb the pepper coating. Spritz both sides of a second rack, and lay it on top of the chicken pieces. As an alternative, use a steamer tray or butter both sides of a sheet of heavy-duty aluminum foil. Place the potatoes on top of the second rack or tray and lock the lid in place. Bring to 15psi over high heat, immediately reduce the heat to the lowest possible setting to stabilize and maintain that pressure, and cook for 8 minutes. Remove from the heat and use the natural release method (see page 31) to depressurize. Carefully open the lid after the pressure drops. Transfer the potatoes to a serving bowl. Remove the top rack and carefully transfer the chicken pieces to a serving platter, sprinkling with the chopped green onions for garnish.

Step Two: The Gravy

4 tablespoons (½ stick) butter or margarine
¼ cup all-purpose flour
1 cup milk
1 cup buttermilk

Use a fat separator, or skim the fat from the surface of the broth with a spoon, and freeze the broth for later use in soups and stews. Melt the butter in the cooker over medium heat. Add the flour and stir until it becomes a smooth, brown paste. Gradually add the milk and buttermilk, stirring constantly, until thickened and bubbly. Adjust the seasonings to taste. Serve the milk gravy in a separate bowl.

❋ Serves 6

Swiss Chicken on a Shingle with Mushrooms in Wine Sauce

Here's a good old-fashioned chicken recipe reminiscent of lunch at the neighborhood diner. My version is slightly more elegant, with chicken breasts served on slices of French bread, topped with melting Swiss cheese and loads of sliced mushrooms in a delicate wine sauce.

1 teaspoon ground cumin
1 teaspoon paprika
¼ teaspoon freshly ground black pepper
4 boneless, skinless chicken breast halves
2 tablespoons olive oil
1 onion, sliced
½ pound fresh mushrooms, washed and sliced
½ cup white wine
½ cup chicken broth
2 tablespoons all-purpose flour
4 (½-inch-thick) slices French bread
6 (⅛-inch-thick) slices Swiss cheese

Mix together the cumin, paprika, and pepper, and rub the spice mixture into both sides of the chicken breasts. Save any remaining spice mixture. Heat the oil in the pressure cooker over medium heat. Add the chicken pieces, cook until golden brown on both sides, and set aside. Add the onions and mushrooms to the cooker and cook, stirring, until slightly softened, about 3 minutes. Add the remaining spice mix, frying until the spices begin to release their aroma. Add the wine and broth and stir, and return the chicken to the cooker. Lock the lid in place. Bring to 15psi over high heat, immediately reduce the heat to the lowest possible setting to stabilize and maintain that pressure, and cook for 8 minutes. Remove from the heat and use the natural release method (see page 31) to depressurize. Carefully open the lid after the pressure drops. Remove the chicken from the cooker. Thicken the broth by making a slurry with the flour mixed with ¼ cup water; stir the slurry into the broth and simmer gently over medium heat until the sauce reaches the desired consistency. Adjust the seasonings to taste. Preheat the broiler. Top each bread slice with a slice of cheese and pop them under the broiler until the cheese starts to melt. Place a chicken breast on top of each bread slice and top with mushroom sauce. ❊ Serves 4

Chicken Breasts
in Riesling
with Grapes

Something fresh, and a perfect light meal for summertime eating. The chicken is cooked in a colorful combination of red onions and bright orange carrots. Served with green grapes in a subtle white wine sauce, it goes well over jasmine rice or noodles.

Step One: The Chicken

2 tablespoons oil

4 boneless, skinless chicken breast halves

1 red onion, minced

½ cup chicken broth

1 cup shredded carrots

2 teaspoons minced garlic

1 teaspoon dried thyme leaves

Heat the oil in the pressure cooker over medium heat. Add the chicken pieces, cook until golden brown on both sides, and set aside. Add the onions to the cooker and cook, stirring, until slightly softened, about 3 minutes. Add the broth, carrots, garlic, and thyme and stir. Lock the lid in place. Bring to 15psi over high heat, immediately reduce the heat to the lowest possible setting to stabilize and maintain that pressure, and cook for 8 minutes. Remove from the heat and use the quick release method (see page 30) to depressurize. Carefully open the lid after the pressure drops. Transfer the chicken pieces to a serving plate. Pour the broth into a small bowl and skim off any visible fat from the surface.

Step Two: The Sauce

2 tablespoons butter

2 teaspoons all-purpose flour

½ cup Riesling

1 cup halved seedless green grapes

Melt the butter in the pressure cooker over medium heat. Stir in the flour until smooth. Slowly add the Riesling, whisking in until it is nice and smooth. Simmer over medium heat, adding the reserved broth until the sauce reaches the desired consistency. Adjust the seasonings to taste. Return the chicken to the cooker with any juices that have accumulated on the plate and add the grapes, stirring occasionally until heated through. Serve the chicken in the sauce. ✳ Serves 4

Chicken Fajitas

This dish is zesty, colorful, and satisfying, easy to make but even more fun to assemble. Chicken pieces are cooked with assorted bell peppers, onions, Mexican chiles, and spices, and then folded into tortillas and topped with an assortment of fresh vegetables. Everyone at the table can make their very own personalized fajitas, selecting the toppings that most appeal to individual tastes.

2 tablespoons oil

4 boneless, skinless chicken breasts

2 onions, cut into rings

2 mild chiles, such as poblano, pasilla, or
    Anaheim, seeded and cut into strips

1 green bell pepper, seeded and cut into strips

1 red bell pepper, seeded and cut into strips

2 tablespoons minced garlic

1 tablespoon chili powder

1½ teaspoons ground cumin

1 teaspoon dried oregano

½ teaspoon red pepper flakes

¼ cup fresh lime juice

¼ cup white wine

½ cup packed cilantro leaves, chopped

2 limes, cut into wedges, for garnish

16 flour tortillas, warmed according to package
    directions

Toppings: chopped avocados, chopped tomatoes,
    sliced black olives, shredded lettuce,
    shredded cheese, salsa, sour cream, and
    anything else you desire

Heat the oil in the pressure cooker over medium heat. Add the chicken pieces, cook until golden brown on both sides, and transfer to a cutting board. Cutting across the grain, slice the chicken breasts into strips. Add the onions, chiles, and bell peppers to the cooker and cook, stirring, until slightly softened, about 3 minutes. Add the garlic, chili powder, cumin, oregano, and red pepper flakes, frying until the spices begin to release a wonderful spicy aroma. Combine the lime juice and wine and deglaze the cooker, scraping up all those crusty, brown bits from the bottom. Add the cilantro leaves, return the chicken pieces to the cooker, and stir. Lock the lid in place. Bring to 15psi over high heat, immediately reduce the heat to the lowest possible setting to stabilize and maintain that pressure, and cook for 6 minutes. Remove from the heat and use the quick or cold water release method (see page 30) to depressurize. Carefully open the lid after the pressure drops. Transfer the meat and vegetables to a serving platter using a slotted spoon, add the lime wedges around the outside, and bring it to the table, along with the warm tortillas. For do-it-yourself fajitas: take a flour tortilla and lay it flat on the plate. Place a big spoonful of the chicken and vegetable mixture in the middle and add small amounts of any other toppings you like, leaving enough room to close up the tortilla. Fold the bottom third of the tortilla up over the filling, and next fold over the sides, leaving the top end open. ✳ Serves 4 to 5

Chicken and Potatoes

This dish is so easy and delicious that it will become a regular in your collection of favorite recipes. Everything you need for dinner cooks in one pot, making this a great midweek meal that can help get you in and out of the kitchen fast.

1 teaspoon paprika
½ teaspoon freshly ground black pepper
½ teaspoon garlic powder
½ teaspoon onion powder
4 boneless, skinless chicken breasts
2 tablespoons butter
3 large potatoes, sliced about 1 inch thick

Combine the paprika, pepper, garlic powder, and onion powder in a small bowl. Rub the mixture into both sides of the chicken breasts. Heat the butter in the pressure cooker over high heat. Add the chicken, cook until browned on both sides, and set aside. Add the rack to the pressure cooker, and pour in ½ cup water. Layer the potatoes on the rack and arrange the chicken on top of the potatoes. Lock the lid in place. Bring to 15psi over high heat, immediately reduce the heat to the lowest possible setting to stabilize and maintain that pressure, and cook for 8 minutes. Remove from the heat and use the cold water release method (see page 30) to depressurize. Carefully open the lid after the pressure drops. Using long-handled tongs, transfer the chicken pieces to a serving platter and arrange the sliced potatoes beside them.

✳ Serves 4

Chicken Cacciatore Subs

"Cacciatore" refers to food prepared "hunter-style," with mushrooms, onions, tomatoes, various herbs, and wine. You've probably had it served over pasta, but this version is for man-sized sandwiches.

8 boneless, skinless chicken thighs
2 tablespoons olive oil
2 onions, sliced into rings
2 cups thinly sliced fresh mushrooms
1 (16-ounce) jar chunky-style pasta sauce
½ cup sliced black olives
2 tablespoons minced garlic
1 tablespoon dried mixed Italian herbs
1 teaspoon dried basil
6 store-bought sub rolls, buttered and lightly toasted
2 cups shredded mozzarella cheese

One at a time, place each piece of chicken on a cutting board between sheets of plastic wrap. Flatten the chicken with a meat mallet, or use a small heavy pan, pounding until the meat is thin. Heat the oil in the pressure cooker over medium heat. Add the chicken pieces, cook until golden brown on both sides, and set aside. Add the onions and mushrooms to the cooker and cook, stirring, until slightly softened, about 3 minutes. Add the pasta sauce, olives, garlic, Italian herbs, and basil and stir. Lock the lid in place. Bring to 15psi over high heat, immediately reduce the heat to the lowest possible setting to stabilize and maintain that pressure, and cook for 5 minutes. Remove from the heat and use the natural release method (see page 31) to depressurize. Carefully open the lid after the pressure drops. Place the chicken on the rolls and, using a slotted spoon, add some of the vegetables, and spoon on a little sauce. Divide the cheese evenly between the sandwiches. Serve the extra sauce on the side for dipping. ✳ Serves 6

Rainy Day Barbecued Chicken

What's that you say—you can't cook BBQ chicken in a pressure cooker? When the weather isn't cooperative, or you're just pressed for time, this recipe will deliver great taste without any fuss, and you don't have to go outside and stand over a hot grill. The prep work is mostly just measuring the ingredients for the custom barbecue sauce, and this can be prepared a day or so in advance if you are pressed for time.

Step One: The Barbecue Sauce
1 cup ketchup
¼ cup Worcestershire sauce
¼ cup malt vinegar
¼ cup soy sauce
2 tablespoons fresh lemon juice
1 teaspoon liquid smoke
Tabasco sauce to taste
¼ cup packed dark brown sugar
1 onion, minced
1 tablespoon minced garlic
2 teaspoons chili powder
½ teaspoon onion powder

Mix all of the ingredients in a glass bowl.

Step Two: The Chicken
2 to 3 pounds chicken parts (breasts, thighs, and drumsticks)
2 tablespoons oil

Wash the chicken pieces and pat dry. Heat the oil in the pressure cooker over medium heat. Add the chicken pieces and cook until golden brown on all sides. Arrange the chicken skin side up in the cooker, and add the barbecue sauce. Lock the lid in place. Bring to 15psi over high heat, immediately reduce the heat to the lowest possible setting to stabilize and maintain that pressure, and cook for 8 minutes. Remove from the heat and use the natural release method (see page 31) to depressurize. Carefully open the lid after the pressure drops. Transfer the chicken to a serving dish or platter, and serve the sauce on the side. ✳ Serves 6

Caribbean Spice-Rubbed Chicken Breasts with Tropical Fruit Salsa

I can almost hear the steel drums of a calypso band when I smell the wonderful aroma of this colorful and spicy dish. A lot of ingredients, but the prep work is mostly measuring and only takes a few minutes, and the end results are well worth it. The spicy rub coats the chicken pieces, and they are precooked in the pressure cooker before finishing either under the broiler or on a grill, basted with a gingery orange marmalade glaze. Serve the chicken with the cool, sweet tropical fruit salsa and rice.

Step One: The Tropical Fruit Salsa
1 firm banana, sliced
1 cup pineapple chunks
1 cup diced papaya or mango
1 small jalapeño chile, seeded and finely minced
¼ cup minced green onion tops
¼ cup packed cilantro leaves, coarsely chopped
1 (4-ounce) jar pimientos, drained and chopped
2 tablespoons minced crystallized ginger
1 tablespoon minced garlic

Several hours before serving, combine all of the ingredients in a small bowl; mix well and refrigerate.

Step Two: The Orange Marmalade Glaze
¼ cup orange marmalade
1 tablespoon fresh lime juice
½ teaspoon minced fresh ginger

Combine all of the ingredients in a small bowl and heat in a microwave just until the marmalade melts.

Step Three: The Spice Rub
½ teaspoon ground ginger
½ teaspoon salt
¼ teaspoon ground allspice
¼ teaspoon cayenne pepper

Mix all of the ingredients in a small bowl, and then spread the mixture out on a plate.

Step Four: The Chicken
¼ cup flaked unsweetened coconut for garnish
4 boneless, skinless chicken breasts
2 tablespoons butter

To toast the coconut, heat the pressure cooker over medium-high heat. Spread the coconut on the bottom and stir as it begins to color, taking care that it does not burn. Remove the toasted coconut to a small plate and set aside. One at a time, place the chicken breasts in the spice rub mixture, pressing and rubbing until both sides are evenly coated. Heat the butter in the pressure cooker over medium heat. Add the chicken pieces, cook until golden brown on both sides, and set aside. Place the rack in the pressure cooker and add ½ cup water. Arrange the chicken breasts on top of the rack and lock the lid in place. Bring to 15psi over high heat, immediately reduce the heat to the lowest possible setting to stabilize and maintain that pressure, and cook for 8 minutes. Remove from the heat and use the natural release method (see page 31) to depressurize. Carefully open the lid after the pressure drops. Preheat the broiler. Transfer the chicken pieces to a roasting pan and baste with the glaze. Put the chicken under the broiler, about 6 inches from the heat, until the skin begins to crisp. Baste frequently, taking care that the skin does not burn.

Turn once, basting again, and cook the other side until browned. Transfer the chicken pieces to a serving platter, drizzle any remaining glaze over the top, and sprinkle with the toasted coconut. Pass the salsa at the table. ✳ **Serves 4**

Honeyed Chicken Drumettes

This is a great way to get some fantastic-tasting chicken without spending a lot of time. Using just the meatiest part of the chicken wing, these little drumettes are cooked in a flavored sauce and given a honey glaze. These half-wings can be dished up as a terrific finger-food appetizer, or add a side dish of rice and serve them as a main course.

¼ cup Worchestershire sauce
½ cup cilantro leaves, chopped
2 tablespoons minced garlic
1 (1-inch) piece fresh ginger, peeled and grated
2 pounds chicken wing drumettes
⅓ cup honey
¼ cup brown sugar

Combine the Worchestershire sauce, cilantro, garlic, and ginger in the pressure cooker, mixing well. Add the chicken wings, 1¼ cup water, and lock the lid in place. Bring to 15psi over high heat, immediately reduce the heat to the lowest possible setting to stabilize and maintain that pressure, and cook for 5 minutes. Remove from the heat and use the natural release method (see page 31) to depressurize. Carefully open the lid after the pressure drops.

Remove the wings and set aside. Stir the honey and brown sugar into the sauce. Reduce the sauce by boiling, uncovered, until it is thick enough to coat a spoon, about 10 minutes. Return the wings to the cooker, turning once or twice to coat with the sticky sauce. Transfer to a serving plate and serve the extra sauce on the side.

✳ **Serves 4 to 5**

Cook's Note: It's okay to use frozen chicken drumettes in this recipe.

Chicken and Vegetables with Linguine in Alfredo Sauce

This recipe is so easy and delicious, and best of all, the cooking time is under 10 minutes, but your family will think you spent all day cooking. Using the interrupted cooking method (see page 38), the chicken is partially cooked before the delicate Chinese vegetables are added so everything finishes cooking at the same time and the vegetables remain tender-crisp.

Step One: The Ridiculously Easy Alfredo Sauce
¾ cup grated Parmesan cheese
8 tablespoons (1 stick) butter, at room temperature
1 cup heavy cream

Using a deep bowl to minimize splattering, mix the Parmesan cheese and butter with a hand blender until light and fluffy. Add the cream slowly, blending with the butter and cheese until the mixture is smooth. Set aside.

Step Two: The Chicken
2 tablespoons olive oil
4 boneless, skinless chicken breasts
1 onion, chopped
1 red bell pepper, seeded and diced

¼ pound fresh mushrooms, washed and sliced
2 tablespoons minced garlic
1 tablespoon dried basil
1 teaspoon dried thyme leaves
¼ teaspoon ground nutmeg
¼ teaspoon freshly ground black pepper
1 (14-ounce) can chicken broth
8 ounces linguine

Heat the oil in a large pressure cooker over medium heat. Add the chicken pieces, cook until golden brown on both sides, and set aside. Add the onions, bell peppers, and mushrooms to the cooker and cook, stirring, until slightly softened, about 3 minutes. Add the garlic, basil, thyme, nutmeg, and pepper, frying until they begin to sizzle. Deglaze the cooker with the broth, scraping up all those crusty, brown bits from the bottom. Measure the linguine (see note below), break the pieces in half, and add them to the cooker. Add more water if necessary to just barely cover all the ingredients. Return the chicken pieces to the pressure cooker, arranging them on top of the other ingredients, and lock the lid in place. Bring to 15psi over high heat, immediately reduce the heat to the lowest possible setting to stabilize and maintain that pressure, and cook for 3 minutes. Remove from the heat and use the quick or cold water release method (see page 30) to depressurize. Carefully open the lid after the pressure drops.

Step Three: The Vegetables
¼ pound fresh Chinese pea pods, sliced diagonally
3 cups frozen vegetables (carrots, broccoli, and cauliflower)

Add the vegetables to the pressure cooker, arranging them on top of all the other ingredients, and lock the lid back in place. Return to 15psi over high heat, immediately reduce the heat to the lowest possible setting to stabilize and maintain that pressure, and cook for 3 minutes longer. Use the cold water release method (see page 30) to depressurize, and carefully open the lid immediately after the pressure drops. Remove the chicken pieces to a cutting board. Add the Ridiculously Easy Alfredo Sauce to the pasta and vegetables in the pressure cooker and heat gently until heated through. Transfer the linguine mixture to a shallow serving pan or large platter. Slice the chicken breasts across the grain and fan the pieces over top of the pasta and vegetables. Serve immediately.

❋ Serves 4

Cook's Note: Eight ounces of long pasta shapes (spaghetti, linguine, etc.) = a 1½-inch-diameter bunch = 4 cups cooked.

Chicken Rarebit

This is an updated variation on an old-fashioned recipe my grandmother used to make. Her version originated in the lean years of World War II, when people had to stretch the luxury of chicken during food rationing.

> 2 tablespoons butter
> 6 boneless, skinless chicken thighs, cut into 1-inch pieces
> 1 (10-ounce) can condensed tomato soup
> ½ cup chicken broth
> ½ teaspoon freshly ground black pepper
> ¼ teaspoon garlic powder
> 6 thick slices French bread, lightly buttered and toasted
> 1½ cups shredded cheddar cheese
> ¼ cup grated Parmesan cheese, for garnish

Heat the butter in the pressure cooker over medium heat. Add the chicken pieces, cook until golden brown on all sides, and pour off the excess fat. Stir in the soup, broth, pepper, and garlic and lock the lid in place. Bring to 15psi over high heat, immediately reduce the heat to the lowest possible setting to stabilize and maintain that pressure, and cook for 6 minutes. Remove from the heat and use the natural release method (see page 31) to depressurize. Carefully open the lid after the pressure drops. Transfer the chicken pieces to the toasted bread slices. Bring the sauce to a simmer over medium heat and add the cheddar cheese, stirring continuously until the cheese is melted and well blended into the sauce. Spoon the sauce over the chicken and bread slices and garnish with a sprinkling of Parmesan cheese. Serve immediately.

❋ Serves 6

Wine-Braised Chicken with Potatoes Romanoff

This upscale recipe with chicken breasts cooked in a sweet white wine sauce is good enough to impress company. Choose a good Chablis or Chardonnay, although a nice Gewürztraminer, Riesling, or Chenin Blanc is eminently more drinkable—in my opinion—if you serve wine with dinner. The recipe includes mashed potatoes in sour cream with cheese and green onions. Add crisp salad greens and a crunchy loaf of bread to complete this scrumptious meal.

2 tablespoons butter
4 boneless, skinless chicken breasts
½ cup sweet white wine
4 potatoes, peeled and cut into eighths
1½ cups shredded sharp cheddar cheese
1 cup sour cream
4 green onions, sliced
1 teaspoon salt
½ teaspoon freshly ground black pepper
Paprika, for garnish

Heat the butter in the pressure cooker over medium heat. Add the chicken pieces and cook until golden brown on both sides. Pour in the wine and place the rack on top of the chicken. Add the potatoes on top of the rack and lock the lid in place. Bring to 15psi over high heat, immediately reduce the heat

to the lowest possible setting to stabilize and maintain that pressure, and cook for 8 minutes. Remove from the heat and use the natural release method (see page 31) to depressurize. Carefully open the lid after the pressure drops. Drain off the liquid and transfer the chicken to a serving plate. Use your preferred method to whip the potatoes with the cheese, sour cream, green onions, salt, and pepper. Dust the top of the chicken pieces and the potatoes with paprika before serving. ❋ Serves 4

Cook's Note: Use a handheld electric mixer and whip the potatoes right in the pressure cooker to cut down on cleanup.

Italian Chicken and Mushrooms in White Wine Sauce

This recipe is as easy as can be, but is sophisticated and elegant enough to serve for company or as a special-occasion meal. Chicken and mushrooms simmered in wine with onions and garlic are served in a creamy sauce with Parmesan cheese. Serve over cooked pasta or with mashed potatoes.

2 tablespoons olive oil
4 boneless, skinless chicken breasts,
    sliced into strips
1 pound fresh mushrooms, washed,
    caps sliced and stems chopped
1 onion, finely chopped
3 to 4 tablespoons minced garlic
1 tablespoon dried mixed Italian herbs

½ cup white wine

¼ cup heavy cream

¼ cup grated Parmesan cheese

2 tablespoons chopped fresh parsley

Heat the oil in the pressure cooker over medium heat. Add the chicken pieces and cook until golden brown on all sides. Add the mushrooms, onions, and garlic to the cooker and cook, stirring, until slightly softened, about 3 minutes. Add the Italian herbs and deglaze the pot with the wine, scraping up any crusty, brown bits from the bottom. Lock the lid in place. Bring to 15psi over high heat, immediately reduce the heat to the lowest possible setting to stabilize and maintain that pressure, and cook for 6 minutes. Remove from the heat and use the natural release method (see page 31) to depressurize. Carefully open the lid after the pressure drops. Transfer the chicken and mushrooms to a serving plate. Finish the sauce by adding the cream, Parmesan cheese, and parsley, simmering just until it begins to bubble, and then remove from the heat. Taste and adjust the seasonings. Return the chicken and mushrooms to the sauce, tossing gently to coat before serving. ✳ Serves 4

Chicken and Sausage Gumbo

This easy-to-make main dish has everything— tender chicken, spicy sausage, and plenty of vegetables. Serve over rice, if desired.

2 tablespoons olive oil

⅓ pound smoked andouille sausage or kielbasa, cut into ¼-inch slices

4 boneless, skinless chicken breasts

2 onions, thinly sliced

2 tablespoons minced garlic

1½ teaspoons dried thyme leaves

1 teaspoon filé powder

¼ teaspoon red pepper flakes

½ teaspoon freshly ground black pepper

¼ teaspoon cayenne pepper

¼ teaspoon ground sage

3 large bay leaves

½ cup white wine

2 stalks celery, cut into ½-inch slices

1 green bell pepper, seeded and diced

½ pound fresh okra, trimmed and sliced, or one 10-ounce package frozen sliced okra

½ cup packed cilantro leaves

1 (14-ounce) can diced tomatoes, with juice

1 (14-ounce) can chicken broth

Heat the oil in the pressure cooker over medium heat. Add the sausage and chicken pieces and cook until browned on all sides. Remove the chicken to a cutting board, cut into large bite-size chunks, and add the chicken back to the cooker. Add the onions to the cooker and cook, stirring, until slightly softened, about 3 minutes. Pour off all but about 1 teaspoon of fat and add the garlic and all of the spices, stirring constantly as they began to release their aroma. Deglaze the cooker with the wine, scraping up all those crusty, brown bits from the bottom. Add the celery, bell peppers, okra, cilantro, tomatoes, and broth and stir. Lock the lid in place. Bring to 15psi over high heat, immediately reduce the heat to the lowest possible setting to stabilize and maintain that pressure, and cook for 5 minutes. Remove from the heat and use the natural release method (see page 31) to depressurize. Carefully open the lid after the pressure drops. Remove the bay leaf and adjust the seasonings to taste before serving in large shallow bowls. ✳ Serves 4

Chicken and Vegetables with Pasta in Italian Ragu Sauce

Everyone will enjoy this satisfying one-pot meal. It's easy and convenient to prepare and uses ingredients you probably have on hand.

>   4 boneless, skinless chicken breasts and/or
>   thighs, cut into large bite-size pieces
>   2 tablespoons minced garlic
>   ½ teaspoon freshly ground black pepper
>   2 tablespoons dried mixed Italian herbs
>   3 cups uncooked spiral pasta
>   3 cups frozen mixed vegetable succotash
>   1 (30-ounce) jar Ragu pasta sauce, any variety
>   1½ cups shredded mozzarella cheese

Place all of the ingredients except for the cheese in the pressure cooker in the order above. Add enough water to just barely cover all the ingredients, and push the pasta under the surface, but do not stir. Lock the lid in place. Bring to 15psi over high heat, immediately reduce the heat to the lowest possible setting to stabilize and maintain that pressure, and cook for 6 minutes. Remove from the heat and use the natural release method (see page 31) to depressurize. Carefully open the lid after the pressure drops. Add the cheese, tossing gently to mix. Replace the lid, but do not lock it in place, and wait 5 minutes, or until the cheese has melted, before transferring to a large serving bowl. ✳ Serves 4

Chicken and Mushrooms in Creamy Parmesan Cheese Sauce

Easy to make and pleasing on the palate, this recipe features tender chicken breast and fresh mushrooms served in a creamy Parmesan cheese sauce with a hint of tarragon and white wine. Serve over your choice of hot, split biscuits, pasta, mashed potatoes, or rice.

>   2 tablespoons butter
>   4 boneless, skinless chicken breast halves
>   ½ pound fresh mushrooms, washed and sliced
>   1 onion, chopped
>   ½ cup white wine
>   2 teaspoons dried tarragon
>   2 tablespoons all-purpose flour
>   1 teaspoon salt
>   ½ teaspoon freshly ground black pepper
>   1 cup milk
>   ½ cup grated Parmesan cheese

Heat the butter in the pressure cooker over medium heat. Add the chicken, cook until browned on both sides, and set aside. Add the mushrooms and onions to the cooker and cook, stirring, until slightly softened, about 3 minutes. Deglaze the cooker with the wine, scraping up all those crusty, brown bits from the bottom. Add the tarragon and stir. Lock the lid in place. Bring to 15psi over high heat, immediately reduce the heat to the lowest possible setting to stabilize and maintain that pressure, and cook for 6 minutes. Remove from the heat and use the natural release method (see page 31) to depressurize. Carefully open the lid after the pressure drops. Transfer the chicken, onions, and mushrooms to a serving plate and tent with aluminum foil to keep warm. Bring the pan juices to a boil, uncovered, and reduce the volume by half. To thicken the broth, make a slurry by mixing the flour, salt, and pepper into the milk; stir the slurry into the broth, add the Parmesan cheese, and simmer gently over medium heat until it reaches the desired consistency. ✳ Serves 4

Creamy White Chicken Soup

A half-century ago, it was considered very elegant and chic to serve dishes that were nearly all white in color. This is a recipe taken from the secret family-recipe file, representative of a dish of tender chicken pieces and white vegetables that was served when my mother's lady friends dropped by for an elegant luncheon.

2 leeks, white parts only, sliced
4 tablespoons butter or margarine, at room
    temperature
4 boneless, skinless chicken breasts
1 onion, chopped
1 (8-ounce) can cream-style corn
1 (10-ounce) can cream of celery soup
1 teaspoon dried marjoram
1 teaspoon dried thyme leaves
½ teaspoons ground black pepper
2 large potatoes, peeled and diced

3 parsnips, peeled and sliced ¼ inch thick
2 tablespoons all-purpose flour
1 cup milk

Discard the green ends from the leeks and slit them lengthwise, fanning the leaves open under cold running water to remove all the dirt. Cut the leeks crosswise into ½-inch slices. Heat 2 tablespoons of the butter in the pressure cooker over medium heat. Add the chicken pieces, cook until golden brown on both sides, and set aside. Add the onions and leeks to the cooker and cook, stirring, until slightly softened but not browned, about 3 minutes. Stir in the corn, soup, and 2 cups water. Add the spices and return the chicken pieces to the cooker. Add the potatoes and parsnips and give the mixture a stir. Lock the lid in place. Bring to 15psi over high heat, immediately reduce the heat to the lowest possible setting to stabilize and maintain that pressure, and cook for 6 minutes. Remove from the heat and use the natural release method (see page 31) to depressurize. Carefully open the lid after the pressure drops. Remove the chicken, chop it into small pieces, and then return it to the cooker. Bring the soup to a simmer over medium heat, uncovered. Mix the remaining 2 tablespoons of butter and the flour together, blending until smooth, and then slowly whisk in the milk, again blending until the mixture is smooth. Slowly stir the milk mixture into the simmering soup, and continue stirring as it begins to thicken. Adjust the seasonings to taste. Transfer the soup to a serving tureen or individual soup bowls. ✳ Serves 4 to 5

✳ ONE-POT MEAL

Mexican-Style Chicken Stew

Not for the timid, this hearty, well-seasoned Mexican-style chicken stew comes with plenty of vegetables cooked in a richly flavored and pungent sauce made from salsa and green chiles. Served with a crusty baguette and a dry red wine, this is a wonderful dish for anyone who enjoys spicy Mexican foods.

2 tablespoons butter
4 boneless, skinless chicken breasts
4 potatoes, peeled and coarsely shredded
2 cups frozen cut green beans
1 cup frozen whole kernel corn
1 (15-ounce) can black beans, drained and rinsed
1 (4-ounce) can diced green chiles, with juice
2 cups bottled salsa
1 (8-ounce) can tomato sauce
2 tablespoons fresh lime juice
1 tablespoon chili powder
2 teaspoons ground cumin
½ teaspoon red pepper flakes

Heat the butter in a large pressure cooker over medium heat. Add the chicken pieces, cook until golden brown on both sides, and transfer to a cutting board. Cut the chicken into 1-inch pieces and return to the cooker. Add the potatoes, green beans, corn, black beans, chiles, salsa, tomato sauce, lime juice, and spices and mix well. Lock the lid in place. Bring to 15psi over high heat, immediately reduce the heat to the lowest possible setting to stabilize and maintain that pressure, and cook for 6 minutes. Remove from the heat and use the natural release method (see page 31) to depressurize. Carefully open the lid after the pressure drops. Taste, and adjust the seasonings. Transfer to a covered tureen or serving bowl and serve immediately.

✳ **Serves 4 to 5**

Italian Chicken Soup

There's nothing better than a home-cooked, hearty bowl of hot soup. This is a simple recipe using chicken and fresh vegetables in a tomato broth seasoned with Italian herbs and spices. Add some crusty garlic toast to complete the meal.

2 tablespoons olive oil
6 boneless, skinless chicken thighs
2 onions, coarsely chopped
1 green bell pepper, seeded and chopped
1 cup sliced fresh mushrooms
1 tablespoon minced garlic
1 tablespoon dried mixed Italian herbs
½ teaspoon red pepper flakes
2 (14-ounce) cans diced tomatoes, with juice
1 (14-ounce) can chicken broth
2 zucchini, cubed
2 cups sliced carrots
Grated Parmesan cheese, for garnish

Heat the oil in the pressure cooker over medium heat. Add the chicken pieces, cook until golden brown on all sides, and set aside. Add the onions, green peppers, and mushrooms to the cooker and cook, stirring, until slightly softened, about 3 minutes. Add the garlic, Italian herbs, and red pepper flakes, frying until the spices begin to sizzle. Add the tomatoes and chicken broth, stirring to mix. Add the chicken pieces, zucchini, carrots, and 6 cups of water and stir. Lock the lid in place. Bring to 15psi over high heat, immediately reduce the heat to the lowest possible setting to stabilize and maintain that pressure, and cook for 6 minutes. Remove from the heat and use the natural release method (see page 31) to depressurize. Carefully open the lid after the pressure drops. Remove the chicken pieces, chop them into small pieces, and return them to the cooker. Adjust the seasonings to taste. Transfer the soup to a heated serving tureen or individual soup bowls, and garnish with a sprinkling of Parmesan cheese. ✳ Serves 6

Tomato Soup with Chicken and Macaroni

This is a quick and inexpensive soup recipe made with ingredients that are almost always on hand. Bite-size pieces of chicken breast are cooked in an herb-seasoned, creamy tomato broth with pasta. Serve with soft bread sticks hot from the oven.

2 tablespoons butter
3 boneless, skinless chicken breasts
1 onion, minced
2 tablespoons minced garlic
1 tablespoon dried basil

1 teaspoon dried oregano
1 teaspoon salt
½ teaspoon freshly ground black pepper
½ teaspoon red pepper flakes
2 (14-ounce) cans chicken broth
1 (14-ounce) can crushed tomatoes
1 (3-ounce) can tomato paste
1 cup uncooked small pasta (ditalini, small elbows, or shells)
1 cup sour cream
Seasoned croutons, for garnish

Heat the butter in the pressure cooker over medium heat. Add the chicken pieces, cook until golden brown on all sides, transfer to a cutting board, and cut into bite-size pieces. Add the onions to the cooker and cook, stirring, until slightly softened, about 3 minutes. Add the garlic, basil, oregano, salt, black pepper, and red pepper flakes, frying until the spices begin to sizzle. Add the chicken pieces, broth, crushed tomatoes, tomato paste, and pasta, plus 4 cups water, stirring well. Lock the lid in place. Bring to 15psi over high heat, immediately reduce the heat to the lowest possible setting to stabilize and maintain that pressure, and cook for 4 minutes. Remove from the heat and use the natural release method (see page 31) to depressurize. Carefully open the lid after the pressure drops. Slowly stir in the sour cream a little at a time until it's well blended. Adjust the seasonings to taste. Ladle into soup mugs and top with the seasoned croutons. ✳ Serves 4 to 5

Variation: Use leftover cooked turkey or beef as a substitute for the chicken.

Miss Vickie Says: What You Need to Know about Chicken Stock and Broth

Homemade stocks and broth are a healthy and economical alternative to the canned variety or powdered bouillon. Be creative when making stock and don't limit your choice of ingredients to just the basic recipe. Be frugal and toss in some assorted vegetable scraps, those chicken backs that no one will eat, or that chicken carcass you've been saving in the freezer. All the additional ingredients will make for a more flavorful, richer, and nutritious stock. When preparing a pot of stock or broth, I recommend using a large, 7- to 8-quart or larger, pressure cooker to accommodate all the ingredients.

Stock. This is the liquid extracted from an assortment of meat, vegetables, herbs, and spices that are simmered in water and/or wine. Stock is used as a foundation for soup and many other recipes. There are two types of chicken stock. "Brown" stock is made from roasted chicken bones, and "white" stock is not. Both types rely on the protein in the bones and meat scraps, which causes a good stock to congeal. So if your stock has the consistency of egg whites, you did it right and have made a great pot of stock. If your stock resembles loosely set Jell-O, you have the really good stuff. The recipes you make with your homemade chicken stock will be full of flavor and very nutritious. Stock congeals when it is chilled because of the proteins that come out of the bones.

Broth. If just the meat is simmered in water to extract the flavor, the liquid is called broth. Usually this liquid is reduced or concentrated to further enhance the flavor, or it can be used as is. Broth is used either as a foundation for soup or as a simple soup itself. A refrigerated broth remains liquid even when chilled.

Removing the Fat. You can skim some of the visible fat from the surface of stock or broth with a spoon, or use a fat separator cup. To get all of the fat removed, you'll need to chill the stock in the refrigerator for several hours or overnight. The cold will solidify the fat on top, where it's easy to lift off and remove.

Storage. Stock and broth can be frozen in ice-cube trays, and then the cubes packed into freezer containers or bags to use as needed. Larger quantities of 2 cups may be frozen in tightly sealed freezer containers or plastic freezer bags.

Homemade Chicken Stock from Scratch

Chicken is a "white" stock, and it is very easy to make, a good thing since it's the foundation of so many recipes. Why make chicken stock from scratch? Besides the obvious taste differences, homemade chicken stock contains gelatin that comes from bones and cartilage. It's this gelatin that imparts the silkiness and texture to stock.

> 3 pounds chicken parts, wings, backs, and necks
> Bouquet garni consisting of 3 bay leaves,
>   10 whole black peppercorns, and
>   2 cloves crushed garlic, tied up in a
>   square of cheesecloth
> 2 onions, quartered
> 2 stalks celery with leaves, cut into
>   3 or 4 pieces
> ½ bunch fresh parsley or cilantro
> 1 carrot, cut into 3 or 4 pieces

Rinse the chicken and place the pieces on a rack in a large pressure cooker. Add the *bouquet garni*, onions, celery, parsley, and carrot and cover completely with water. Lock the lid in place. Bring to 15psi over high heat, immediately reduce the heat to the lowest possible setting to stabilize and maintain that pressure, and cook for 20 minutes. Remove from the heat and use the cold water release method (see page 30) to depressurize. Carefully open the lid after the pressure drops. Strain the stock through a sieve or cheesecloth-lined colander. Since the meat has given up its flavor to the broth, discard the solid material. Refrigerate the stock overnight, and then remove the layer of fat that has hardened on top. Portion out the stock in 2-cup measurements poured into freezer containers or plastic freezer bags. Freeze the bags flat so they're easier to store and don't take up so much room in your freezer. ✳ **Makes about 2 quarts**

Alphabet Chicken Soup

Nothing spells out comfort food better than homemade chicken soup, and when the fun shapes of little alphabet noodles are added, this becomes a kid-pleasing meal. Easy to prepare, with a superfast cooking time, this is a good soup to serve for a rainy day weekend lunch.

> 2 tablespoons oil
> 2 boneless, skinless chicken breasts
> 2 stalks celery, diced
> 1 onion, diced
> 1 tablespoon minced garlic
> 1 teaspoon ground sage
> 1 teaspoon dried rosemary
> 1 teaspoon dried marjoram
> 3 cups frozen mixed vegetables (corn, peas, and carrots)
> 1 cup uncooked alphabet-shaped pasta
> 1 quart homemade chicken stock, or 2 (14-ounce) cans chicken broth

Heat the oil in the pressure cooker over medium heat. Add the chicken pieces and cook until golden brown on both sides. Transfer the chicken to a cutting board and dice into small chunks. Add the celery and onions to the cooker and cook, stirring, until slightly softened, about 3 minutes. Pour off all but about 1 teaspoon of fat and add the garlic, sage, rosemary, and marjoram, stirring until they began to sizzle. Add the diced chicken, vegetables, alphabet pasta, stock, and 2 cups water, stirring to mix. Lock the lid in place. Bring to 15psi over high heat, immediately reduce the heat to the lowest possible setting to stabilize and maintain that pressure, and cook for 2 minutes. Remove from the heat and use the natural release method (see page 31) to depressurize. Carefully open the lid after the pressure drops. Ladle into soup mugs and serve.

❋ Serves 4

Thai Coconut Chicken Soup

A truly unique mix of flavors, with the sweetness of coconut contrasting nicely with the tartness of limes. A wonderfully flavored soup that I often serve as a first course in an Asian dinner.

> 2 tablespoons peanut oil
> 4 boneless, skinless chicken breasts and/or thighs
> 1 onion, chopped
> 2 jalapeño chiles, seeded and chopped
> 1 red bell pepper, seeded and chopped
> 1 green bell pepper, seeded and chopped
> ½ cup packed cilantro leaves, chopped, plus extra for garnish
> ¼ cup unsweetened flaked coconut
> 2 tablespoons minced garlic
> 2 tablespoons grated fresh ginger
> 2 tablespoons brown sugar
> 2 (14-ounce) cans chicken broth
> 2 tablespoons oyster sauce
> 2 tablespoons fresh lime juice
> 1 (14-ounce) can unsweetened coconut milk

Heat the oil in the pressure cooker over medium heat. Add the chicken pieces and cook until golden brown on all sides. Transfer the chicken to a cutting board and cut it into large bite-size pieces. Add the onions to the cooker and cook, stirring, until slightly softened, about 3 minutes. Return the chicken to the pressure cooker and add the jalapeños, bell peppers, cilantro, coconut, garlic, ginger, brown sugar, broth, oyster sauce, and lime juice. Stir to mix and lock the lid in place. Bring to 15psi over high heat, immediately reduce the heat to the lowest possible setting to stabilize and maintain that pressure, and cook for 6 minutes. Remove from the heat and use the natural release method (see page 31) to depressurize. Carefully open the lid after the pressure drops. Add the coconut milk and simmer for a few minutes over medium heat until heated through, but do not let it come to a boil. Taste and adjust the seasonings, ladle the soup into bowls, and garnish with chopped cilantro just before serving. ✳ Serves 4 to 5

Rotisserie Roasted Chicken Carcass Soup

What's left after you serve one of those nice rotisserie chickens from the take-out or grocery store? Probably not much more than the wings, the back, and a bunch of bones, which more often than not gets tossed out with the garbage. Stop! Save everything for the classic beginnings of "brown" stock and an almost free pot of soup with that delicious rotisserie taste.

1 rotisserie chicken carcass and any leftover pieces, skin, bones, and congealed broth in the bottom of the package
1 (10-ounce) can condensed cream of mushroom soup
1 onion, chopped
3 cups frozen mixed vegetables (corn, carrots, and green beans)
2 cups uncooked bowtie pasta
2 teaspoons dried thyme
½ teaspoon garlic powder
½ teaspoon freshly ground black pepper

Break up the rotisserie chicken carcass if needed to make it fit, put all the chicken pieces and parts in a large pressure cooker, and cover with 10 cups water. Lock the lid in place. Bring to 15psi over high heat, immediately reduce the heat to the lowest possible setting to stabilize and maintain that pressure, and cook for 20 minutes. Remove from the heat and use the natural release method (see page 31) to depressurize. Carefully open the lid after the pressure drops. Strain the chicken and broth, and when the chicken pieces are cool enough, separate the meat from the skin and bones. Skim the fat from the broth or use the fat separator to remove as much as possible. Put the meat and the broth back into the pressure cooker. Stir in the can of soup, mixing completely. Add the onions, frozen vegetables, pasta, thyme, garlic powder, and pepper and stir. Lock the lid back in place. Return to 15psi over high heat, immediately reduce the heat to the lowest possible setting to stabilize and maintain that pressure, and cook for an additional 4 minutes. Remove from the heat and use the natural release method (see page 31) to depressurize. Carefully open the lid after the pressure drops. Adjust the seasonings to taste, and serve at once.

✳ Serves 4 to 5

Chicken and Dumplings from Scratch

When my mom made chicken and dumplings from scratch, the wonderful aroma filled the house. I especially love the light, tender dumplings, which are still my most favorite part of this dish.

Step One: The Stock
1 large fryer chicken, cut into pieces
1 onion, diced
1 (14-ounce) can chicken broth
2 tablespoons dried parsley
2 teaspoons chicken bouillon granules
1½ teaspoons salt
1 teaspoon freshly ground black pepper

Combine all of the ingredients in a large pressure cooker. Add enough water fill the pressure cooker to the maximum ⅔-full capacity and stir. Lock the lid in place. Bring to 15psi over high heat, immediately reduce the heat to the lowest possible setting to stabilize and maintain that pressure, and cook for 30 minutes. Remove from the heat and use the natural release method (see page 31) to depressurize. Carefully open the lid after the pressure drops. Use a slotted spoon to transfer the chicken pieces to a large platter to cool. When cool enough to handle, discard the skin, pull the meat from the bones, and cut it into bite-size pieces. Strain the stock, discarding the solids. Use a fat separator, or skim the excess fat and then return the stock to the cooker.

Step Two: The Soup
3 stalks celery, cut into ¼-inch slices

2 carrots, cut into ¼-inch slices

Add the celery, carrots, and chopped chicken to the stock, taking care not to exceed the ⅔-full capacity. Freeze any remaining stock for later use. Lock the lid in place. Bring to 15psi over high heat, immediately reduce the heat to the lowest possible setting to stabilize and maintain that pressure, and cook for 4 minutes. Remove from the heat and use the natural release method (see page 31) to depressurize. Carefully open the lid after the pressure drops. Bring the soup to a simmer over medium heat while preparing the dumplings.

Step Three: The Dumplings
2 cups all-purpose flour
4 teaspoons baking powder
1 teaspoon salt
¾ cup milk
4 tablespoons oil

Combine all of the ingredients in a bowl and mix to form a stiff dough. Drop by tablespoonfuls into the simmering soup. Cover with a regular lid and simmer for about 15 minutes, or until a toothpick inserted into one of the dumplings comes out clean. Ladle the chicken soup into individual serving bowls, and include 1 or 2 dumplings in each serving.

✳ Serves 6

Turkey Carcass Soup

Any good pot of soup begins with the stock, because that's where the flavor comes from. Even if you don't have a turkey carcass, save up all those bones until you've accumulated enough in the freezer to make a pot of stock. Using the remains of a cooked bird for stock adds more flavor and aroma, plus it has the added bonus of costing absolutely nothing.

Step One: The Stock

1 roasted turkey carcass, skin and fat discarded
2 stalks celery with leaves
2 carrots, coarsely chopped
1 onion, coarsely chopped
2 cloves garlic, peeled and smashed with a
    blade of a knife
1 small bunch fresh parsley or cilantro
2 bay leaves
10 whole black peppercorns

Wrap the carcass in a clean, dampened towel and pound with a meat mallet or heavy skillet to break apart the bones. Place all of the ingredients into a large pressure cooker and cover with water. Lock the lid in place. Bring to 15psi over high heat, immediately reduce the heat to the lowest possible setting to stabilize and maintain that pressure, and cook for 35 minutes. Remove from the heat and use the natural release method (see page 31) to depressurize. Carefully open the lid after the pressure drops. Strain and reserve the stock and discard the vegetables. When cool enough to handle, pick the meat off the bones and return it to the cooker, discarding the bones. Pour the strained stock back into the cooker.

Step Two: The Soup

1 onion, diced
2 stalks celery, diced
2 cups frozen mixed vegetables (peas, corn, and
    carrots)
½ cup tiny conchiglie (shells) pasta
1 tablespoon minced garlic
1 teaspoon ground thyme
1 teaspoon ground sage
Salt and freshly ground black pepper to taste
2 tablespoons cornstarch (optional)

Add all of the ingredients except for the cornstarch to the cooker, add more water if needed to cover, and stir. Lock the lid in place. Bring to 15psi over high heat, immediately reduce the heat to the lowest possible setting to stabilize and maintain that pressure, and cook for 6 minutes. Remove from the heat and use the natural release method (see page 31) to depressurize. Carefully open the lid after the pressure drops. If you like your soup a little thicker, stir 2 tablespoons cornstarch into ½ cup cold water and add to the soup. Simmer over medium heat as it thickens. Adjust the seasonings as needed.

✳ Serves 6

Pork and Ham

PORK IS THE MOST POPULAR MEAT in the world, and there are many cuts available to fit any budget. Your grocery meat section is stocked with an astonishing selection of fresh pork from lean ground pork, economical chops, and meaty ribs for the grill, to mouth-watering roasts, as well as cured pork including ham and bacon. Most cuts of pork are an excellent choice for pressure cooking, from a traditional main dish to something with a zippy sauce that pleases the taste buds.

Pork today compares favorably with other meats, and many cuts are as lean as or leaner than chicken. Cuts from the loin—like pork chops and pork roast—are leaner than skinless chicken thighs, and according to the U.S. Department of Agriculture, today's pork has an average of 31 percent less fat than the pork your parents and grandparents ate when they were young.

Pork Chops in Garlic Sauce with Mashed Potatoes

This is one of my favorite ways to serve pork chops because it's very easy, and even nicer that it's a one-pot meal with very little cleanup. The pork chops are fork-tender, and if you like garlic, this sauce is quite garlicky and really makes those mashed potatoes delicious.

2 tablespoons oil
4 pork chops, ½ inch thick
4 tablespoons minced garlic
1 teaspoon beef bouillon granules
1 teaspoon dried rosemary, crushed
⅓ teaspoon freshly ground black pepper
4 potatoes, peeled and cubed
Butter, for mashed potatoes
Milk, for mashed potatoes
½ cup sour cream

Heat the oil in the pressure cooker over medium heat. Add the chops, cook until browned on both sides, and set aside. Add the garlic to the cooker and cook, stirring, until slightly softened, about 3 minutes. Deglaze the cooker with 1 cup water, scraping up all those crusty, brown bits from the bottom, and stir in the bouillon. Return the chops to the cooker and sprinkle with the rosemary and pepper. Place the cubed potatoes in a metal bowl, or use a double aluminum foil packet that is left

open. Set the potatoes on top of the chops and lock the lid in place. Bring to 15psi over high heat, immediately reduce the heat to the lowest possible setting to stabilize and maintain that pressure, and cook for 8 minutes. Remove from the heat and use the natural release method (see page 31) to depressurize. Carefully open the lid after the pressure drops. Transfer the potatoes to a mixing bowl and mash, adding butter first, and then milk as needed to reach the desired consistency. Adjust the seasonings to taste. Transfer the chops to a serving plate. Bring the sauce in the cooker to a simmer over medium heat and add the sour cream, whisking until the sauce is smooth and heated through. Pass the sauce at the table to spoon over the chops and mashed potatoes. ✳ Serves 4

Pork Chops with Apples and Yams

Sometimes, unexpectedly delicious results can result from a happy accident. Apples and sweet onions combine with sweet potatoes for something a little different with in this easy two-course meal. Use the yellow variety of sweet potato as the texture is much like a russet potato.

2 tablespoons oil
4 pork chops, ½ inch thick
2 sweet potatoes, peeled and sliced
   ½ inch thick
2 McIntosh or Fuji apples, peeled, cored,
   and sliced ½ inch thick
1 sweet onion, chopped
½ cup sweet apple cider
2 teaspoons spicy mustard
½ cup brown sugar
½ teaspoon ground cinnamon

Heat the oil in the pressure cooker over medium heat. Add the chops and cook until browned on both sides. Add alternating layers of sweet potatoes, onions, and apples on top of the pork chops. In a small bowl, stir together the apple cider, mustard, brown sugar, and cinnamon, and pour the mixture into the pressure cooker. Lock the lid in place. Bring to 15psi over high heat, immediately reduce the heat to the lowest possible setting to stabilize and maintain that pressure, and cook for 8 minutes. Remove from the heat and use the natural release method (see page 31) to depressurize. Carefully open the lid after the pressure drops. Arrange the mixture of apples and potatoes on a serving platter next to the pork chops. If desired, bring the broth in the cooker to a rolling boil, uncovered, and reduce by half. Drizzle the apple reduction sauce over the apples, potatoes, and pork chops. ⁂ Serves 4

Pork, Beans, and Sweet Potato Stew with Chipotle Sour Cream Topping

Filled with a heady mixture of Mexican flavors, this is a fabulous stew that looks as good as it tastes. In this recipe, use the interrupted cooking method (see page 38) to keep the sweet potatoes from overcooking. The addition of the spicy sour cream topping is a definite bonus that really enlivens this dish.

Step One: The Chipotle Sour Cream Topping

1 cup sour cream
2 tablespoons canned chipotle chiles in adobo
   sauce, drained and minced
¼ cup minced fresh cilantro
1 tablespoon minced garlic

In a medium-size bowl, combine the sour cream, chipotle chiles, cilantro, and garlic; mix until well blended. Cover and refrigerate for at least several hours or overnight to marry the flavors.

Step Two: The Pork Stew

1 pound dried pink beans, soaked for a
   minimum of 4 hours or overnight
1 tablespoon olive oil
1½ pounds boneless pork, cut into
   2-inch chunks
2 onions, sliced

2 mild poblano chiles, seeded and chopped
1 jalapeño chile pepper, seeded and chopped
2 tablespoons minced garlic
2 (10-ounce) cans Rotel (or similar brand)
   diced tomatoes with chiles
½ cup cilantro leaves, chopped
1 tablespoon ground cumin
2 tablespoons fresh lime juice

Drain and rinse the beans. Heat the oil in a large pressure cooker over medium heat. Add the meat, cook until browned on both sides, and set aside. Add the onions, poblano and jalapeño chiles, and garlic to the cooker and cook, stirring, until slightly softened, about 3 minutes. Return the meat to the pressure cooker and add the beans, tomatoes, cilantro, cumin, and lime juice and stir. Add enough water or flavoring liquids to cover all the ingredients by 2 inches. Lock the lid in place. Bring to 15psi over high heat, immediately reduce the heat to the lowest possible setting to stabilize and maintain that pressure, and cook for 12 minutes. Remove from the heat and use the quick or cold water release method (see page 30) to depressurize. Carefully open the lid after the pressure drops.

Step Three: The Sweet Potatoes

4 cups sweet potatoes, peeled and cut into
   1-inch cubes

Add the potatoes to the cooker, stir, and lock the lid back in place. Return to 15psi over high heat, immediately reduce the heat to the lowest possible setting to stabilize and maintain that pressure, and cook for an additional 4 minutes. Remove from the heat and use the natural release method (see page 31) to depressurize. Carefully open the lid after the pressure drops. Serve the stew in individual serving bowls with a dollop of the prepared sour cream topping. ✳ Serves 4

Double Pork and Black Bean Chili

For me, cooking is a very relaxing, fun, and creative process. I wanted to create a recipe that would add some oomph to black beans, and this combination of two kinds of pork simmered in Mexican spices had the perfect flavor combination that I was looking for. The aroma is reason enough to make it over and over again, and, should you have any leftovers, they freeze well for later use.

2 tablespoons olive oil

1 pound boneless pork, cut into 2-inch cubes

1 pound coarsely ground pork

1 onion, chopped

2 mild pasilla, poblano, or Anaheim chiles, seeded and chopped

4 tablespoons minced garlic

2 tablespoons chili powder

1 tablespoon ground cumin

½ teaspoon red pepper flakes

¼ teaspoon ground cinnamon

2 (28-ounce) cans chopped tomatoes, with juice

1 (3-ounce) can tomato paste

1 cup chopped cilantro

1 pound dried black beans, soaked for a minimum of 4 hours or overnight

1 cup sour cream

Heat the oil in the pressure cooker over medium heat. Add the cubes of pork, cook until browned on all sides, and set aside to drain on paper towels. Next, add the ground pork to the cooker, cook until it is nicely crumbled and browned, and set aside to drain on paper towels. Add the onions, chiles, and garlic to the cooker and cook, stirring, until slightly softened, about 3 minutes. Add the chili powder, cumin, red pepper flakes, and cinnamon, frying until the spices begin to sizzle. Return the meat to the cooker and add the chopped tomatoes, tomato paste, cilantro, and beans and stir. Add enough water or flavoring liquids to cover the contents by 2 inches. Lock the lid in place. Bring to 15psi over high heat, immediately reduce the heat to the lowest possible setting to stabilize and maintain that pressure, and cook for 15 minutes. Remove from the heat and use the natural release method (see page 31) to depressurize. Carefully open the lid after the pressure drops. Ladle the beans into individual serving bowls and top each with a dollop of sour cream. ✳ Serves 6

Pork Steaks with Potatoes and Sour Cream Gravy

The beer gives this dish a rich, mellow flavor, and the darker the beer, the better the taste. It combines with the pan juices to make excellent gravy, just perfect to ladle over the potatoes. What could be better than a quick and easy one-pot meal with hardly any cleanup!

Step One: The Pork and Potatoes
½ cup all-purpose flour
½ teaspoon salt
½ teaspoon freshly ground black pepper
4 boneless pork steaks
2 tablespoons oil
2 onions, chopped
2 tablespoons minced garlic
1 cup dark beer, at room temperature
4 potatoes, peeled and sliced ¼ inch thick

In a plastic bag, mix the flour, salt, and pepper, and add the meat, shaking gently until each piece is lightly coated. Heat the oil in the pressure cooker over medium heat. Add the meat, cook until browned on both sides, and set aside. Add the onions and garlic to the cooker and cook, stirring, until slightly softened, about 3 minutes, then add the beer. Layer the potatoes in the pressure cooker and place the pork on top. Lock the lid in place. Bring to 15psi over high heat, immediately reduce the heat to the lowest possible setting to stabilize and maintain that pressure, and cook for 8 min-

utes. Remove from the heat and use the natural release method (see page 31) to depressurize. Carefully open the lid after the pressure drops. Transfer the pork steaks to a serving plate and the potatoes to a separate bowl. Skim off any excess fat from the surface of the broth.

Step Two: The Gravy
1 cup sour cream
3 tablespoons all-purpose flour
¼ teaspoon freshly ground black pepper
½ cup milk

Bring the broth in the pressure cooker to a boil. Combine the sour cream, flour, and pepper in a small bowl, mixing to a smooth consistency. Stir into the sauce and reduce the heat to medium. Slowly stir in the milk, and continue stirring until the sauce has thickened to the desired consistency. Adjust the seasonings to taste. Serve the gravy in a separate bowl to be spooned over the meat and potatoes. ✳ Serves 4

Classic Roast Pork with Creamy Dijon Sauce

This absolutely delicious sauce with Dijon mustard adds just the right amount of zing without being overpowering, transforming the pork loin into something special. The roast will be moist and so tender, and goes perfectly with mashed potatoes or noodles.

2 tablespoons oil
1 tablespoon butter
2½ pounds boneless pork loin
1 onion, chopped
¾ cup white wine
2 tablespoons country-style Dijon mustard
1 cup sour cream
2 tablespoons all-purpose flour

Heat the oil and butter in the pressure cooker over medium heat. If the pork roast is in netting or is tied, do not remove. Add the roast to the cooker, cook until browned on all sides, and set aside. Add the onions to the cooker and cook, stirring, until slightly softened, about 3 minutes. Add the wine and mustard to the cooker, stirring to mix. Return to the roast to the cooker using foil helper handles (see page 42) to make it easier to move. Lock the lid in place. Bring to 15psi over high heat, immediately reduce the heat to the lowest possible setting to stabilize and maintain that pressure, and cook for 40 minutes. Remove from the heat and use the natural release method (see page 31) to depressurize. Carefully open the lid after the pressure drops. Transfer the roast to a cutting board. Skim off any excess fat from the surface of the broth. Bring the broth in the pressure cooker to a boil. Combine the sour cream and flour and stir the mixture into the broth. Reduce the heat and continue stirring as the sauce thickens. Adjust the seasonings to taste and serve in a separate bowl. ✳ **Serves 4 to 5**

Easiest Ever Braised Pork Loin Roast

This simple, easy recipe delivers a tender and juicy dish of braised pork roast, and takes hardly any time to prepare and even less time to clean up. The perfect solution at the end of a busy day, it can be served as a main dish with your choice of sides, or sliced thinly for big, meaty sandwiches.

2 tablespoons oil
1 (2- to 3-pound) boneless pork loin roast

Heat the oil in the pressure cooker over medium heat. Add the meat and cook until browned on all sides. Add 1½ cups water and lock the lid in place. Bring to 15psi over high heat, immediately reduce the heat to the lowest possible setting to stabilize and maintain that pressure, and cook for 25 minutes. Remove from the heat and use the natural release method (see page 31) to depressurize. Carefully open the lid after the pressure drops. Transfer the roast to a serving plate and let it rest for 5 minutes before carving. ✳ **Serves 4 to 5**

ABC Pork Chops with "Baked" Potatoes and Fruit Sauce

A is for apple, B is for balsamic vinegar, and C is for cranberries. This recipe is loaded with flavor and aroma. The unique blend of sweet apples combined with the tangy sweetness of balsamic vinegar in the sauce really perks up the pork chops.

> 1 teaspoon freshly ground black pepper
> 4 boneless center-cut pork chops,
>   1 to 1½ inches thick
> 1 tablespoon oil
> 1 onion, chopped
> 1 tablespoon minced garlic
> 1 cup apple juice
> 1 red or yellow Delicious apple, peeled, cored,
>   and chopped
> ½ cup whole fresh or frozen cranberries
> ¼ cup balsamic vinegar
> 4 large potatoes, scrubbed

Rub the pepper into the chops. Heat the oil in the pressure cooker over medium heat. Add the meat, cook until browned on both sides, and set aside. Add the onions and garlic to the cooker and cook, stirring, until slightly softened, about 3 minutes. Deglaze the cooker with the apple juice, scraping up all those crusty, brown bits from the bottom. Add the apples, cranberries, and vinegar, stirring

to mix. Return the chops to the cooker, arranging them on top of the fruit mixture. Place the rack on top of the chops and arrange the potatoes on the rack. Lock the lid in place. Bring to 15psi over high heat, immediately reduce the heat to the lowest possible setting to stabilize and maintain that pressure, and cook for 15 minutes. Remove from the heat and use the natural release method (see page 31) to depressurize. Carefully open the lid after the pressure drops. Remove the potatoes and chops to a serving plate. Use a hand blender to puree the broth and fruit to a smooth consistency. Pour into a serving bowl to spoon over the chops and potatoes at the table. ※ Serves 4

Cinnamon Apple Pork Chops

Succulent pork chops topped with spicy hot applesauce deliver a bright, mouthwatering medley of flavors. Cooked to perfection in the pressure cooker, the thick boneless pork chops are topped with a sweet, cinnamon-spiced red applesauce to create a main dish that really makes an impressive entrée. The secret ingredient is red-hot cinnamon candies, but don't give away the surprise.

> **Step One: The Sauce**
> ½ cup chunky applesauce
> 1 tablespoon red-hot cinnamon candies

In a small saucepan, combine the applesauce and candies, and stir over medium heat until the candies are melted. Keep warm until ready to serve.

Step Two: The Pork Chops

4 boneless pork chops, less than 1 inch thick
1 teaspoon coarsely ground black pepper
2 tablespoons oil

Sprinkle the chops with the pepper, pressing into both sides of the meat. Heat the oil in the pressure cooker over medium heat. Add the meat, cook until browned on both sides, and set aside. Add ½ cup water to the cooker, place the rack in the cooker, and arrange the chops on the rack. Lock the lid in place. Bring to 15psi over high heat, immediately reduce the heat to the lowest possible setting to stabilize and maintain that pressure, and cook for 12 minutes. Remove from the heat and use the natural release method (see page 31) to depressurize. Carefully open the lid after the pressure drops. Transfer the chops to a serving dish and top with the warm applesauce mixture.

✳ Serves 4

✳ ONE-POT MEAL

Pork Chops with Red Potatoes and Country-Style Gravy

Thick pork chops and potatoes in country gravy come together in this satisfying, homey one-dish meal. Big, meaty pork chops paired with little red potatoes are cooked in a full-flavored sauce in this no-fuss entrée.

Step One: The Chops and Potatoes

2 tablespoons olive oil
6 pork chops, 1 inch thick

1 onion, chopped
2 tablespoons minced garlic
6 red potatoes, with a strip peeled off around the middle
2 teaspoons dried oregano

Heat the oil in the pressure cooker over medium heat. Add the meat, cook until browned on both sides, and set aside. Add the onions and garlic to the cooker and cook, stirring, until slightly softened, about 3 minutes. Deglaze the pot with ½ cup water, scraping up all the crusty, brown bits from the bottom. Return the chops to the cooker, add the potatoes, and sprinkle the oregano on top. Lock the lid in place. Bring to 15psi over high heat, immediately reduce the heat to the lowest possible setting to stabilize and maintain that pressure, and cook for 15 minutes. Remove from the heat and use the natural release method (see page 31) to depressurize. Carefully open the lid after the pressure drops. Transfer the chops and potatoes to a serving platter. Pour the broth into a medium-size glass bowl, and skim off the fat from the surface.

Step Two: The Country-Style Gravy

4 tablespoons (½ stick) butter
4 tablespoons all-purpose flour

Melt the butter in the pressure cooker over medium heat and stir in the flour, cooking until the flour is a beautiful chocolate brown color. Measure the broth, and, if necessary, add hot water to equal 2 cups liquid. Heat the broth in the microwave. Slowly add it to the butter and flour mixture in the cooker, stirring and scraping the pan until it has thickened to the desired consistency. Adjust the seasonings to taste and serve the gravy in a separate bowl to pour over the chops and potatoes.

✳ Serves 6

Cranberry-Braised Pork Chops with Gravy

Make an everyday dinner into a holiday feast with succulent pork chops simmering in a well-seasoned saucy gravy of tart cranberries, and onions. The bright and colorful, sweet and tangy sauce adds to the wonderful flavor and transforms ordinary pork chops into a gourmet-quality main dish. With its dark, sweet flavor, a good-quality balsamic vinegar will quickly become one of your favorite ingredients.

    2 tablespoons oil
    4 boneless pork loin chops, 1½ inches thick
    1 sweet Vidalia or Maui onion, diced
    1 cup whole cranberry sauce
    1 cup chunky applesauce
    ½ cup apple juice
    ½ teaspoon coarsely ground black pepper
    ¼ teaspoon ground allspice
    2 tablespoons cornstarch

Heat the oil in the pressure cooker over medium heat. Add the meat, cook until browned on both sides, and set aside. Add the onions to the cooker and cook, stirring, until slightly softened, about 3 minutes. Combine the cranberry sauce, applesauce, apple juice, pepper, and allspice in the pressure cooker, mixing well. Return the chops to the cooker, turning once to coat. Lock the lid in place. Bring to 15psi over high heat, immediately reduce the heat to the lowest possible setting to stabilize and maintain that pressure, and cook for 15 min-

utes. Remove from the heat and use the natural release method (see page 31) to depressurize. Carefully open the lid after the pressure drops. Transfer the chops to a serving plate. Thicken the sauce by making a slurry with the cornstarch mixed with ⅓ cup cold water; stir the slurry into the sauce and simmer over medium heat until it reaches the desired consistency, stirring often as it thickens, but do not boil. Serve the sauce at the table.

✳ Serves 4

Serving Suggestion: Mashed potatoes or egg noodles will round out the meal.

Pork Chops and Mushroom Gravy

Short on time, but still want an inexpensive, flavorful home-cooked meal? This recipe for pork chops and fresh mushrooms in a rich gravy is a satisfying main dish with a tempting aroma that will bring everyone to the table. Serve with mashed potatoes and buttered broccoli spears for a wonderful family dinner.

    2 tablespoons butter
    4 pork chops, up to 1 inch thick
    1 medium-size onion, peeled and thinly sliced
    ½ pound fresh mushrooms, washed and sliced
    1 teaspoon dried thyme leaves
    ½ teaspoon garlic powder
    1 (10-ounce) can condensed golden
       mushroom soup

Heat the butter in the pressure cooker over medium heat. Add the meat, cook until browned on both sides, and set aside. Add the onions and mushrooms to the cooker and cook, stirring, until slightly softened, about 3 minutes. Add the thyme, garlic powder, and soup, mixing well. Return the chops to the cooker, pushing them beneath the liquid. Lock the lid in place. Bring to 15psi over high heat, immediately reduce the heat to the lowest possible setting to stabilize and maintain that pressure, and cook for 12 minutes. Remove from the heat and use the natural release method (see page 31) to depressurize. Carefully open the lid after the pressure drops. Transfer the chops to a serving dish and pour the mushroom gravy into a separate bowl. ✳ Serves 4

✳ ONE-POT MEAL

Pork Chops with Steam-Roasted Potatoes and Salsa Gravy

Here's very good and easy-to-assemble recipe that packs a lot of flavor using simple ingredients. Depending on whether you choose to use mild or hot salsa, the taste can be mild or bold; either way, it creates a fabulous sauce for melt-in-your-mouth pork chops.

2 tablespoons butter
1 tablespoon oil
4 large russet potatoes, peeled and halved
   lengthwise
Freshly ground black pepper to taste
Paprika to taste
6 pork chops, less than 1 inch thick
1 cup of your favorite fresh or bottled salsa

Heat the butter and oil in the pressure cooker over medium heat. Add the potatoes, turning to coat all sides, then remove to a plate. Grind a generous amount of black pepper over the potatoes, and lightly dust with paprika. Add the chops to the cooker, cook until browned on both sides, and add the salsa plus ⅓ cup water. Turn the meat once or twice to coat both sides with the salsa. Arrange the chops in layers as necessary, and lay the rack on top. Using long-handled tongs, arrange the potato halves on top of the rack and lay a square of aluminum foil over the top. Lock the lid in place. Bring to 15psi over high heat, immediately reduce the heat to the lowest possible setting to stabilize and maintain that pressure, and cook for 12 minutes. Remove from the heat and use the natural release method (see page 31) to depressurize. Carefully open the lid after the pressure drops. Remove the aluminum foil and transfer the potatoes and chops to a serving platter. Pour the salsa gravy into a small bowl to be passed at the table and spooned over the chops and potatoes as desired.

✳ Serves 4

Pork Chops in Tart Cherry Sauce

Succulent pork chops are simmered with tart red cherries and sweet balsamic vinegar to create a rich and flavorful sauce that transforms a simple meal into a taste sensation with a delicious combination of flavors.

Step One: The Tart Cherry Sauce
2 cups canned tart red pie cherries
¼ cup balsamic vinegar
2 tablespoons sugar
1 teaspoon orange zest
½ teaspoon ground cinnamon
1½ teaspoons cornstarch

Place the cherries, vinegar, sugar, zest, and cinnamon in the pressure cooker and bring to a simmer over medium heat, stirring constantly. Dissolve the cornstarch in 1 tablespoon cold water, add it to the cherries, and continue stirring. As soon as the sauce thickens, remove from the heat and scoop the sauce into a small bowl.

Step Two: The Pork Chops
2 tablespoons oil
6 boneless center-cut loin pork chops,
    1½ inches thick
½ cup orange juice

Heat the oil in the pressure cooker over medium heat. Add the meat, cook until browned on both sides, and add the orange juice. Lock the lid in place. Bring to 15psi over high heat, immediately reduce the heat to the lowest possible setting to stabilize and maintain that pressure, and cook for 12 minutes. Remove from the heat and use the natural release method (see page 31) to depressurize. Carefully open the lid after the pressure drops. Transfer the chops to a serving plate and drain the cooker. Pour the Tart Cherry Sauce into the cooker and simmer gently over medium heat, but do not boil. Return the chops to the cooker and turn once or twice to coat with the sauce. Arrange the pork chops on plates and serve the Tart Cherry Sauce on the side. ✳ Serves 6

Orange Marmalade Pork Chops with Sauce

If you're adventurous, this elegant, but incredibly easy, mouthwatering recipe combines the crisp taste of orange juice with sweet onions. Pork chops are braised in an orange marmalade pan sauce, but do experiment on your own and try other fruit marmalades or preserves.

2 tablespoons olive oil
6 boneless pork loin chops, about ¾ inch thick
1 sweet Vidalia or Maui onion, diced
1 green bell pepper, seeded and finely chopped
½ cup orange juice
¼ cup orange marmalade
1 orange, thinly sliced, for garnish

Heat the oil in the pressure cooker over medium heat. Add the meat, cook until browned on both sides, and set aside. Add the onions and bell peppers to the cooker and cook, stirring, until slightly softened, about 3 minutes. Deglaze the cooker with the orange juice, scraping up all those crusty, brown bits from the bottom. Mix in the marmalade, and return the chops to the pressure cooker, turning once to coat and arranging them in layers to fit. Lock the lid in place. Bring to 15psi over high heat, immediately reduce the heat to the lowest possible setting to stabilize and maintain that pressure, and cook for 12 minutes. Remove from the heat and use the natural release method (see page 31) to depressurize. Carefully open the lid after the pressure drops. Remove the chops and sauce to a serving platter and garnish with the orange slices. ✳ Serves 6

Serving Suggestion: Serve these chops with mashed potatoes and a salad.

Pulled Pork Sandwiches with au Jus Dipping Sauce

Au jus describes serving meat with its own natural juices, and the pressure cooker deserves all the credit for making the meat so tender that it can be easily shredded with a fork. This is a simple recipe for delicious pulled pork sandwiches, with the meat simmered with flavorful onions and green peppers, which are added to the sandwiches and which also flavor the delicious sauce used for dipping. Make the sandwiches big, two handed, he-man size, for a filling dinner or weekend lunch.

2 tablespoons butter
2 onions, chopped
2 green bell peppers, seeded and chopped
2 tablespoons minced garlic
1 (1-ounce) packet dried onion soup mix
½ teaspoon red pepper flakes
½ cup red wine
3 pounds pork roast
6 store-bought French rolls, split and lightly toasted

Heat the butter in the pressure cooker over medium heat. Add the onions, bell peppers, and garlic, and cook, stirring, until slightly softened, about 3 minutes. Add the soup mix, red pepper flakes, wine, and 1 cup water, stirring to mix. Place the rack in the cooker and put the roast on top. Lock the lid in place. Bring to 15psi over high heat, immediately reduce the heat to the lowest possible setting to stabilize and maintain that pressure, and cook for 25 minutes. Remove from the heat and use the natural release method (see page 31) to depressurize. Carefully open the lid after the pressure drops. Check for doneness; the pork should shred easily with a fork. If needed, lock the lid back in place, return to 15psi over high heat, immediately reduce the heat to the lowest possible setting to stabilize and maintain that pressure, and cook for an additional 8 minutes. Remove from the heat and use the natural release method (see page 31) to depressurize. Carefully open the lid after the pressure drops. Transfer the roast to a cutting board and let rest for about 10 minutes. In the meantime, return the sauce in the cooker to a boil and boil, uncovered, until the liquid reduces by half. Pull the pork to shreds using 2 forks. Pile a generous amount of shredded pork on each roll, and top with some of the onions and bell peppers. Serve the remaining broth in small bowls for dipping at the table. ✳ Serves 6

Pork and Vegetables Stewed in Ale

Pork is simmered in ale for this distinctive and flavorful dish that is so tasty it will disappear before your very eyes. The stew celebrates the season, taking on an autumn orange color from the sweet potatoes and carrots. You'll taste the subtle flavor of ale, so be sure to use a decent-quality brand. Serve this with homemade cornbread or polenta.

2 tablespoons oil

2 pounds pork shoulder, cut into 2-inch cubes

1 onion, chopped

2 tablespoons minced garlic

½ teaspoon freshly ground black pepper

½ teaspoon red pepper flakes

¼ teaspoon ground cinnamon

2 (14-ounce) cans chicken broth

2 (12-ounce) bottles ale or dark beer, at room temperature

2 small sweet potatoes, peeled and cubed

2 carrots, peeled and sliced

1 bunch greens, such as collards, mustard, or turnip, coarsely chopped

Heat the oil in a large pressure cooker over medium heat. Add the meat in small batches, cook until browned, and set aside. Add the onions to the cooker and cook, stirring, until slightly softened. Add the garlic, black pepper, red pepper flakes, and cinnamon, frying until they begin to sizzle. Add the pork, broth, and ale, plus 4 cups water, stirring

to mix. Lock the lid in place. Bring to 15psi over high heat, immediately reduce the heat to the lowest possible setting to stabilize and maintain that pressure, and cook for 12 minutes. Remove from the heat and use the quick or cold water release method (see page 30) to depressurize. Carefully open the lid after the pressure drops. Add the sweet potatoes, carrots, and greens. Lock the lid back in place, return to 15psi over high heat, immediately reduce the heat to the lowest possible setting to stabilize and maintain that pressure, and cook for 5 minutes longer. Remove from the heat and use the natural release method (see page 31) to depressurize. Carefully open the lid after the pressure drops. Adjust the seasonings as desired, and serve.

✳ Serves 4 to 5

Sweet Caramel Apple Pork Chops

A recipe that would take hours in the oven will be center stage on your dinner table in just a few minutes in the pressure cooker. Apples are the perfect accompaniment to pork chops, and they simmer in a combination of sweet flavors and spices for an unforgettable taste.

2 tablespoons butter

2 tart red apples, cored and sliced into ½-inch wedges

½ cup orange juice

2 tablespoons balsamic vinegar

2 tablespoons molasses

2 tablespoons brown sugar

¼ teaspoon ground cinnamon

⅛ teaspoon ground nutmeg

4 boneless pork chops, ¾ inch thick

3 tablespoons finely chopped pecans,
   for garnish

Heat the butter in the pressure cooker over medium heat. Add the apples, orange juice, vinegar, molasses, brown sugar, cinnamon, and nutmeg, stirring to mix. Add the pork chops, turning once or twice to coat with the sauce mixture. Use a slotted spoon to arrange the apple pieces on top of the pork chops. Lock the lid in place. Bring to 15psi over high heat, immediately reduce the heat to the lowest possible setting to stabilize and maintain that pressure, and cook for 10 minutes. Remove from the heat and use the natural release method (see page 31) to depressurize. Carefully open the lid after the pressure drops. Remove the chops and apple pieces to a serving plate and keep warm in a low oven. Bring the sauce in the pressure cooker to a simmer over medium-high heat and continue cooking, uncovered, until the sauce thickens slightly. Spoon the sauce over the apples and chops and sprinkle with the pecans. ✳ Serves 4

Pork Chops with Horseradish Sauce

This recipe works well on a budget, and it's fast and easy to make. The robust taste of horseradish is mellowed with sour cream in a deliciously creamy gravy to accompany the tender pork chops.

2 tablespoons oil

6 pork chops, less than 1 inch thick

2 tablespoons prepared horseradish

1 teaspoon chicken bouillon granules

1 tablespoon cornstarch

½ cup sour cream

Heat the oil in the pressure cooker over medium heat. Add the chops, cook until browned on both sides, and set aside. Add the horseradish, bouillon granules, and 1 cup water to the cooker and stir. Return the chops to the cooker and lock the lid in place. Bring to 15psi over high heat, immediately reduce the heat to the lowest possible setting to stabilize and maintain that pressure, and cook for 10 minutes. Remove from the heat and use the natural release method (see page 31) to depressurize. Carefully open the lid after the pressure drops. Transfer the chops to a serving plate. Thicken the sauce by making a slurry with the cornstarch mixed with ⅓ cup cold water; stir the slurry into the sauce and simmer over medium heat, uncovered, stirring often as it thickens, but do not boil. Slowly add the sour cream, stir, and heat through. Serve the horseradish sauce separately to spoon over the chops. ✳ Serves 6

Pork-N-Pop Roast with Gravy

No one will ever know that this embarrassingly easy recipe takes only a few minutes in the pressure cooker. Don't give away the secret ingredient, but the root beer gives this tender roast a rich color and pleasant sweetness.

> 2 tablespoons oil
> 1 (4-pound) pork roast
> 1 (10-ounce) can golden cream of
>   mushroom soup
> 1 (12-ounce) can root beer (regular, not diet)
> 1 (1-ounce) packet dried onion soup mix

Heat the oil in the pressure cooker over medium heat. Add the meat, cook until browned on all sides, and set aside. Add the soup, root beer, and soup mix, stirring to mix. Return the roast to the cooker and lock the lid in place. Bring to 15psi over high heat, immediately reduce the heat to the lowest possible setting to stabilize and maintain that pressure, and cook for 40 minutes. Remove from the heat and use the natural release method (see page 31) to depressurize. Carefully open the lid after the pressure drops. Transfer the roast to a cutting board and let it sit for 5 minutes or so before slicing. Serve the gravy in a separate bowl to be passed at the table. ✳ Serves 6

Garlicky Pork Chops with Balsamic Vinegar and Potatoes

The balsamic vinegar combined with garlic makes this simple recipe taste and smell like a gourmet dish. Don't stint on the balsamic vinegar; use a good-quality brand for a wonderful combination of sweetness and tangy tartness that gives these chops that extra zing.

> 6 bone-in pork chops, about ½ inch thick
> 1 tablespoon lemon pepper
> 2 tablespoons olive oil
> 1 onion, diced
> ⅓ cup red wine
> ¼ cup balsamic vinegar
> 2 tablespoons minced garlic
> 4 large potatoes, scrubbed and halved lengthwise

Rub both sides of the chops with the lemon pepper. Heat the oil in the pressure cooker over medium heat. Add the meat, cook until browned on both sides, and set aside. Add the onions to the cooker and cook, stirring, until slightly softened, about 3 minutes. Deglaze the cooker with the wine, scraping up all those crusty, brown bits from the bottom. Add the vinegar, garlic, and ½ cup water and stir. Return the chops to the cooker and add the potato halves, placing them on top of the pork chops. Lock the lid in place. Bring to 15psi over high heat, immediately reduce the heat to the lowest possible setting to stabilize and maintain that pressure, and cook for 8 minutes. Remove from the heat and use the natural release method (see page 31) to depressurize. Carefully open the lid after the pressure drops. Transfer the chops and potatoes to a serving platter and cover with aluminum foil to keep warm. Bring the sauce to a boil, uncovered, and continue to boil until the liquid is reduced by half, 2 to 3 minutes. Adjust the seasonings to taste, and then spoon the sauce over the chops. ✳ Serves 6

✳ ONE-POT MEAL

Pork Chops with Winter Squash and Spiced Raisin Sauce

Cool weather signals the start of the winter squash season. Also known as hard squash, winter squash is available in a variety of shapes, colors, and sizes and is an especially good complement to pork.

Step One: The Pork and Squash

1 (2-pound) hard winter squash, such as
    hubbard, acorn, butternut, golden nugget,
    turban, or banana (see preparation
    directions below)

2 tablespoons butter or margarine

½ teaspoon ground cinnamon

½ teaspoon coarsely ground black pepper

¼ teaspoon ground cloves

¼ teaspoon ground allspice

4 bone-in pork chops, about ½ inch thick

½ cup orange juice

1 teaspoon grated lemon zest

Cut each squash in half and remove all the seeds and fibrous material. Pare the squash and cut it in quarter sections that will fit easily into the pressure cooker. Heat the butter in the pressure cooker over medium heat. Add the cinnamon, pepper, cloves, and allspice, stirring and frying until they begin to sizzle and release a pungent aroma. Add the chops, and cook until browned on both sides. Add the orange juice and lemon zest. Arrange the chops in 2 or more layers and lay the squash pieces on top of the chops. Lock the lid in place. Bring to 15psi over high heat, immediately reduce the heat to the lowest possible setting to stabilize and maintain that pressure, and cook for 8 minutes. Remove from the heat and use the natural release method (see page 31) to depressurize. Carefully open the lid after the pressure drops. Using a slotted spoon, transfer the squash to a large bowl and mash according to your preferred method, adding a little of the pan juices until the squash is at the desired consistency. Arrange the pork chops on a large serving platter and keep warm in a low oven.

Step Two: The Spiced Raisin Sauce

¾ cup brown sugar

½ cups raisins

2 tablespoons maple syrup

1 tablespoon cornstarch

½ cup apple juice

Skim off any visible fat from the surface of the broth. Add the brown sugar, raisins, and maple syrup to the broth and bring to a boil over high heat. To thicken the sauce, make a slurry by mixing the cornstarch and apple juice. Lower the heat, stir the slurry into the sauce, and continue cooking and stirring as the sauce thickens, but do not boil. Pour the sauce into a gravy boat or small bowl to be spooned over the pork chops and mashed squash at the table. ✳ Serves 4

Sweet and Sour Pork

Looking for a quick and easy meal to throw together when you get home? This recipe tastes like you put a lot of time into making this really delicious sweet and sour dish. Serve with hot fluffy rice or crisp Chinese noodles.

½ cups all-purpose flour
1 teaspoon salt
½ teaspoon freshly ground black pepper
1½ pound boneless pork chops, cut
    into 1-inch cubes
1 tablespoon sesame oil
1 tablespoon olive oil
1 sweet Vidalia or Maui onion, minced
2 tablespoons minced garlic
1 tablespoon minced fresh ginger
1 cup ketchup
½ cup soy sauce
¼ cup red wine vinegar
¼ cup honey
¼ cup sugar
½ teaspoon red pepper flakes
1 carrot, thinly sliced on the diagonal
1 stalk celery, diced
1 red bell pepper, seeded and chopped
1 green bell pepper, seeded and chopped
1 (14-ounce) can pineapple chunks, drained
2 tablespoons cornstarch

In a plastic bag, mix the flour, salt, and pepper, and add the meat, shaking gently until each piece is lightly coated. Heat the sesame and olive oils in the pressure cooker over medium heat. Add the meat in small batches, cook until browned on all sides, and set aside. Add the onions, garlic, and ginger to the cooker and cook, stirring, until slightly softened, about 3 minutes. Add the ketchup, soy sauce, vinegar, honey, sugar, and red pepper flakes to the pressure cooker and blend with a wire whisk. Return the pork pieces to the pressure cooker. Add the carrots, celery, red and green bell peppers, and pineapple chunks, in that order. Lock the lid in place. Bring to 15psi over high heat, immediately reduce the heat to the lowest possible setting to stabilize and maintain that pressure, and cook for 6 minutes. Remove from the heat and use the natural release method (see page 31) to depressurize. Carefully open the lid after the pressure drops. Strain, reserving the broth. Place the pork and vegetable mixture in a large serving bowl. Return the broth to the pressure cooker. Thicken the sauce by making a slurry with the cornstarch mixed with ⅓ cup cold water; stir the slurry into the sauce and simmer over medium heat, stirring often as it thickens, but do not boil. Adjust the seasonings to taste and pour over the meat and vegetables, tossing gently to coat. ✳ **Serves 4**

Mexican Pork Carnitas

Carnitas is a very popular Mexican dish that consists of braised pork in plenty of pungent and aromatic spices. It's a very versatile recipe and can be served in a variety of different ways: as a main dish over noodles, potatoes, or rice or with tortillas as a filling in tacos, taquitos, or burritos.

2 tablespoons oil
2 pounds boneless pork shoulder or butt,
    cut into 1-inch cubes or ½ × 2-inch strips
1 onion, chopped

2 mild poblano chiles, seeded and chopped

2 tablespoons minced garlic

1 teaspoon ground cumin

1 teaspoon dried oregano

½ teaspoon freshly ground black pepper

¼ teaspoon cayenne pepper

Heat the oil in the pressure cooker over medium heat. Add the meat, cook until browned on both sides, and set aside. Add the onions and chiles to the cooker and cook, stirring, until slightly softened, about 3 minutes. Add the garlic, cumin, oregano, black pepper, and cayenne pepper, frying until they begin to sizzle. Return the pork roast to the pressure cooker and add 1 cup water. Lock the lid in place. Bring to 15psi over high heat, immediately reduce the heat to the lowest possible setting to stabilize and maintain that pressure, and cook for 16 minutes. Remove from the heat and use the natural release method (see page 31) to depressurize. Carefully open the lid after the pressure drops. Remove the pork with a slotted spoon and use in the intended recipe (above). Skim off any remaining fat from the surface of the broth and portion into freezer containers for later use in other pork recipes. ✳ Serves 4 to 5

Pork Roast with Mushroom-Dill Sauce

Nothing could be better than a savory, well-seasoned, succulent pork roast, and this recipe fills the kitchen with wonderful aromas. Cooked quickly in the pressure cooker, the meat is flavorful and very tender.

4 tablespoons (½ stick) butter

1 onion, chopped

½ pound fresh mushrooms, washed and sliced

2 tablespoons minced garlic

2 tablespoons minced fresh dill

1½ teaspoons coarsely ground black pepper

1 teaspoon beef bouillon granules

1 (14-ounce) can beef broth

3 to 4 pounds boneless pork shoulder roast, trimmed of fat

2 tablespoons all-purpose flour

½ cup sour cream

Heat the butter in the pressure cooker over medium heat. Add the onions and mushrooms and cook, stirring, until slightly softened, about 3 minutes. Add the garlic, dill, pepper, and bouillon granules, frying until they begin to sizzle and release a pungent aroma. Deglaze the cooker with the broth, scraping up all those crusty, brown bits from the bottom. Place the rack in the cooker and use foil helper handles (see page 42) to position the roast on the rack. Lock the lid in place. Bring to 15psi over high heat, immediately reduce the heat to the lowest possible setting to stabilize and maintain that pressure, and cook for 35 minutes. Remove from the heat and use the natural release method (see page 31) to depressurize. Carefully open the lid after the pressure drops. Use the helper handles to transfer the pork to a serving platter, and let it rest for a few minutes before carving. Skim off any excess fat from the surface of the broth. Mix the flour into ⅓ cup cold water to make a smooth paste, and blend it into the broth in the pressure cooker. Bring to a simmer over medium heat, stirring until the sauce is smooth and thickened. Taste and adjust the seasonings. Stir in the sour cream and heat through, but do not boil. Serve the sauce separately to be spooned over the pork.

✳ Serves 4 to 5

Caraway Pork Roast with Pan Gravy

Preparing a good pork roast is relatively easy and surprisingly fast in the pressure cooker! This tender and juicy pork roast is simmered with caraway, a flavor that really stars with any pork recipe.

> 1 tablespoon caraway seeds
> 2 teaspoons dried marjoram
> 1 teaspoon ground sage
> 1 teaspoon coarsely ground black pepper
> 2 to 3 pounds pork shoulder
> 2 tablespoons olive oil
> 1 onion, diced
> 1 (14-ounce) can beef broth
> 2 tablespoons cornstarch

In a small bowl, combine the caraway seeds, marjoram, sage, and pepper. Rub the mixture all over the pork, saving any remaining spice mixture. Heat the oil in the pressure cooker over medium heat. Add the meat, cook until browned on both sides, and set aside. Add the onions to the cooker and cook, stirring, until slightly softened, about 3 minutes. Add the remaining spices, frying until they begin to sizzle. Deglaze the cooker with the broth, scraping up all those crusty, brown bits from the bottom. Using foil helper handles (see page 42), place the roast in the pressure cooker. Lock the lid in place. Bring to 15psi over high heat, immediately reduce the heat to the lowest possible setting to stabilize and maintain that pressure, and cook for 35 minutes. Remove from the heat and use the natural release method (see page 31) to depressurize. Carefully open the lid after the pressure drops. Transfer the roast to a serving platter to be carved at the table. Drain the pressure cooker, reserving 2 cups of the broth and adding it back to the pressure cooker; simmer over medium-high heat. Thicken the sauce by making a slurry with the cornstarch mixed with ⅓ cup cold water; stir the slurry into the sauce and simmer, stirring often, but do not boil. Serve in a separate bowl to be passed with the pork roast. ✳ Serves 6

Serving Suggestion: Serve with creamy garlic mashed potatoes and sweet honeyed carrots for a wonderful meal.

Posole: Mexican Pork and Green Chile Stew

Posole is traditionally served at Christmastime in Mexico, but you can enjoy this thick and hearty stew any time of the year. Filled with succulent chunks of pork, hominy, corn, and tomatoes that are simmered in a robust and zesty seasoned broth, this has just enough heat to keep it interesting. Serve with plenty of warmed buttered flour tortillas, crushed tortilla chips, or crusty bread.

1 tablespoon vegetable oil
2 pounds boneless pork sirloin or shoulder, cubed
1 onion, chopped
1 green bell pepper, seeded and chopped
2 teaspoons ground cumin
1 teaspoon dried basil
1 teaspoon dried oregano
½ teaspoon red pepper flakes
2 carrots, diced
½ cup packed cilantro leaves, chopped
1 (32-ounce) can chopped tomatoes, with juice
2 (14-ounce) cans chicken broth
1 (14-ounce) can hominy, drained
1 (12-ounce) can whole kernel corn, drained
2 (4-ounce) cans diced green chiles, with juice

Heat the oil in the pressure cooker over medium heat. Add the meat, cook until browned on all sides, and set aside. Add the onions and bell peppers to the cooker and cook, stirring, until slightly softened, about 3 minutes. Add the cumin, basil, oregano, and red pepper flakes, frying until they begin to sizzle and release their pungent aromas. Add the carrots, cilantro, tomatoes, broth, hominy, corn, chiles, and 2 cups water. Return the pork to the cooker, stirring to mix. Lock the lid in place. Bring to 15psi over high heat, immediately reduce the heat to the lowest possible setting to stabilize and maintain that pressure, and cook for 15 minutes. Remove from the heat and use the natural release method (see page 31) to depressurize. Carefully open the lid after the pressure drops. Adjust the seasonings to taste. Serve the soup in a tureen or individual soup bowls. ✳ Serves 6

Asian Pork Stew

Let me introduce you to bok choy, the white Chinese cabbage. Don't let this curious vegetable that looks like celery on steroids remain a mystery. With lovely white and dark green leaves, it's easy to prepare—just coarsely shred the leaves and enjoy the slight mustard taste that makes bok choy a perfect complement to pork recipes.

1 tablespoon vegetable oil
1 pound boneless pork loin, cut into
   ¼-inch-thick strips
1 cup diced celery
1 cup chopped green onion tops
1 cup diced carrots
1 jalapeño chile, seeded and minced
2 tablespoons minced garlic
½ teaspoon red pepper flakes
¼ cup soy sauce
1 (14-ounce) can chicken broth
1 small head bok choy, coarsely shredded
1 (3½-ounce) package crumbled ramen
   noodles, or 1 cup broken vermicelli

Heat the oil in the pressure cooker over medium heat. Add the meat, cook until browned on both sides, and set aside. Add the celery and green onions to the cooker and cook, stirring, until slightly softened, about 3 minutes. Return the pork to the cooker and add the carrots, jalapeño, garlic, red pepper flakes, soy sauce, and chicken broth and stir. Lock the lid in place. Bring to 15psi over high heat, immediately reduce the heat to the low-est possible setting to stabilize and maintain that pressure, and cook for 4 minutes. Remove from the heat and use the quick release method (see page 30) to depressurize. Carefully open the lid after the pressure drops. Add the cabbage and vermicelli, pushing them beneath the surface of the liquid. Add water if needed to cover and lock the lid back in place. Return to 15psi over high heat, immediately reduce the heat to the lowest possible setting to stabilize and maintain that pressure, and cook for an additional 3 minutes. Remove from the heat and use the natural release method (see page 31) to depressurize. Carefully open the lid after the pressure drops. Adjust the seasonings to taste and serve. ❋ Serves 4

Seasoned Pork Cutlets with Capers in Sauce

When I first envisioned this quick pork recipe, I wanted an entrée that was elegant with a sophisticated spin, but still exceptionally easy to prepare. I thought of pork cutlets or medallions—thin, boneless slices that work perfectly as an easy, cook-in-minutes supper. These tender pork cutlets are served with a flavorful, delicious caper sauce that really makes this a memorable meal. Serve this with garlicky mashed potatoes and green beans.

4 boneless pork cutlets or medallions
2 teaspoons ground thyme
½ teaspoon freshly ground black pepper
2 tablespoons all-purpose flour
2 tablespoons butter
1 small red onion, diced
2 tablespoons minced garlic
½ cup white wine
Grated zest of 1 lemon
2 tablespoons nonpareil capers, drained and
    chopped
Lemon slices, for garnish

Wipe the cutlets dry with a paper towel. Combine the thyme and black pepper in a small bowl and rub the mixture into both sides of the cutlets. Heat the butter in the pressure cooker over medium heat. Add the meat, cook until browned on both sides, and set aside. Add the onions and garlic to the cooker and cook, stirring, until slightly soft-ened, about 3 minutes. Add the white wine, capers and lemon zest. Place the cooking rack in the cooker, arranging the cutlets on top. Lock the lid in place. Bring to 15psi over high heat, immediately reduce the heat to the lowest possible setting to stabilize and maintain that pressure, and cook for 5 minutes. Remove from the heat and use the natural release method (see page 31) to depressurize. Carefully open the lid after the pressure drops. Use tongs to remove the cutlets to a serving plate and keep warm in a low oven. Using a hand blender, puree the sauce until smooth. Bring the sauce to a boil, uncovered, and cook for about 10 minutes, stirring gently until most of the liquid is reduced and slightly thicker. Spoon the caper sauce over the cutlets, garnish with lemon slices, and serve immediately. ✳ **Serves 4**

Pork with Potatoes, Carrots, and Cabbage

Hot and chunky cubes of tender pork with vegetables make for a good supper on a cold, blustery night. Serve this quick-cooking main dish plain, or spoon it over noodles or mashed potatoes. Crusty rye bread is a must.

> 2 tablespoons oil
> 1½ pounds boneless pork, cut into 1-inch cubes
> 2 onions, halved and cut into strips
> 3 tablespoons minced garlic
> 4 potatoes, peeled and cubed
> 3 carrots, peeled and sliced
> 1 head cabbage, cored and cut into wedges
> ½ teaspoon poppy seeds, for garnish

Heat the oil in the pressure cooker over medium heat. Add the meat, cook until browned on both sides, and set aside. Add the onions and garlic to the cooker and cook, stirring, until slightly softened, about 3 minutes. Place the rack in the pressure cooker and pour in ½ cup water. Place the meat and onions on the rack. Add layers of potatoes, carrots, and cabbage, and lock the lid in place. Bring to 15psi over high heat, immediately reduce the heat to the lowest possible setting to stabilize and maintain that pressure, and cook for 6 minutes. Remove from the heat and use the natural release method (see page 31) to depressurize. Carefully open the lid after the pressure drops. Use tongs to transfer the meat and vegetables to a serving dish. Garnish with a sprinkle of poppy seeds.

❋ Serves 4

❋ ONE-POT MEAL

Pork Chops with Stewed Tomatoes and Potatoes

Pork is very versatile, and this savory dish of pork chops and potatoes is smothered in old-time stewed tomatoes for a new twist. Green chiles add a snappy, south-of-the-border flavor that really pumps up the taste of this quick and easy dish.

> 2 tablespoons olive oil
> 4 pork chops, less than 1 inch thick
> 1 onion, chopped
> 2 tablespoons minced garlic
> 4 potatoes, peeled and quartered
> 1 (14-ounce) can Mexican-style stewed tomatoes, with juice
> 1 (7-ounce) can diced green chiles, with juice
> 2 teaspoons dried oregano, crushed
> ½ teaspoon coarsely ground black pepper
> 1 tablespoon cornstarch

Heat the oil in the pressure cooker over medium heat. Add the chops, cook until browned on both sides, and set aside. Add the onions and garlic to the cooker and cook, stirring, until slightly softened, about 3 minutes. Return the chops to the cooker and add the potatoes, tomatoes, chiles, oregano, and pepper. Lock the lid in place. Bring to 15psi over high heat, immediately reduce the heat to the lowest possible setting to stabilize and maintain that pressure, and cook for 10 minutes. Remove from the heat and use the natural release method (see page 31) to depressurize. Carefully open the lid after the pressure drops. Transfer the potatoes and chops to a serving dish. Thicken the stewed tomatoes by making a slurry with the cornstarch mixed with ⅓ cup cold water; stir the slurry into the tomatoes and simmer over medium heat, stirring often as the sauce thickens, but do not boil. Serve the stewed tomatoes separately.

✳ **Serves 4**

Berried Treasure Pork Chops

Tangy and sweet fruit is an excellent way of adding flavor to lean meats like pork. Here, I'm using cranberries to add a fruity chutney, which adds a yummy twist to a weekday supper. It will bump plain pork chops up a notch or two with this very simple and very tasty dish. To complete the meal I would add a green vegetable and dinner salad with a sharp French or Russian dressing.

> 1 teaspoon freshly ground black pepper
> 6 bone-in pork chops, ¾ inch thick
> 2 tablespoons butter
> ½ cup cranberry juice
> 1 (16-ounce) can whole cranberry sauce
> ¼ cup balsamic vinegar
> ¼ cup fresh lemon juice
> 2 to 3 sweet potatoes, peeled and cut into
>   1-inch cubes

Rub and press the pepper into both sides of the chops. Heat the butter in the pressure cooker over medium heat. Add the chops, cook until browned on both sides, and set aside. Deglaze the cooker with the cranberry juice, scraping up all those crusty, brown bits from the bottom. Add the cranberry sauce, vinegar, and lemon juice, stirring to mix. Add the sweet potatoes, and place the chops on top. Lock the lid in place. Bring to 15psi over high heat, immediately reduce the heat to the lowest possible setting to stabilize and maintain that pressure, and cook for 8 minutes. Remove from the heat and use the natural release method (see page 31) to depressurize. Carefully open the lid after the pressure drops. Transfer the meat and sweet potatoes to a serving platter and serve the sauce in a separate bowl. ✳ **Serves 6**

Jiffy Pork Chops with Sawmill Gravy

Depending on what part of the country you're from, it might be called "white gravy," or it's also known as "country gravy," but on my aunt's Kentucky farm, it was called "sawmill gravy." This was part of her everyday breakfast, but its just as satisfying as the main dish on the dinner table. You'll want to serve this with hot biscuits, mashed potatoes, corn on the cob, and sliced tomatoes for dinner; or try it with biscuits and eggs for breakfast.

2 tablespoons oil
½ pound bulk breakfast sausage
6 bone-in pork chops, ¾ inch thick
½ ground black pepper or more to taste
½ teaspoon ground sage
¼ cup all-purpose flour
2 cups half-and-half

Heat the oil in the pressure cooker over medium heat. Add the pork chops and cook until browned on both sides, then set aside. Add the sausage, and cook until it's crumbly. Add the pepper, sage, and ½ cup water and stir to mix. Return the pork chops to the cooker Lock the lid in place. Bring to 15psi over high heat, immediately reduce the heat to the lowest possible setting to stabilize and maintain that pressure, and cook for 8 minutes. Remove from the heat and use the natural release method (see page 31) to depressurize. Carefully open the lid after the pressure drops. Transfer the chops to a serving platter and pop it into a low 200°F oven to keep warm. Drain the sausage in a colander, pouring off all but 2 tablespoons of fat. Heat the fat over medium heat and be sure to scrape up any brown bits that might be stuck to the bottom of the pan. Whisk the flour into the fat, and cook for about 1 minute, stirring constantly. Whisk in the half-and-half a little at a time as the gravy comes to a simmer. Add the cooked sausage to the gravy, stirring as it thickens and becomes hot and bubbly. Taste, adding more pepper if desired. Serve in a separate bowl to be passed at the table. ✳ Serves 6

EZ Pork Chops with Potatoes au Gratin

I am the queen of comfort foods, and the recipes nearest and dearest to my heart come from my mother's and grandmothers' kitchens. After a particularly long day, this is one of those old-fashioned recipes that makes me feel like I'm back at the dinner table with my parents, shoveling in comfort by the forkful.

Step One: The Cheddar Cheese Sauce
2 tablespoons butter
2 tablespoons all-purpose flour
¼ teaspoon salt
Louisiana-style hot sauce, to taste
1 cup milk
1 cup shredded sharp cheddar cheese

Melt the butter in the pressure cooker over medium heat. Add the flour, salt, and hot sauce, blending to a smooth paste. Slowly stir in the milk, and continue stirring constantly as it thickens. Add the cheese, stirring until melted. Adjust the seasonings to taste and transfer the sauce to a bowl. Rinse the cooker before proceeding to the next phase.

Step Two: The Chops and Potatoes

2 tablespoons butter

6 pork chops, ½ inch thick

1 onion, thinly sliced

2 tablespoons minced garlic

1 teaspoon dried thyme

½ cup dark beer

6 potatoes, peeled and halved

¼ cup sliced green onion tops, for garnish

Heat the butter in the pressure cooker over medium heat. Add the meat, cook until browned on both sides, and set aside. Add the onions and garlic to the cooker and cook, stirring, until slightly softened, about 3 minutes, then sprinkle with the thyme. Deglaze the cooker with the beer, scraping up all those crusty, brown bits from the bottom. Place the chops on the bottom of the cooker and layer the potatoes on top. Lock the lid in place. Bring to 15psi over high heat, immediately reduce the heat to the lowest possible setting to stabilize and maintain that pressure, and cook for 6 minutes. Remove from the heat and use the natural release method (see page 31) to depressurize. Carefully open the lid after the pressure drops. Drain the potatoes and chops into a colander, reserving the broth. Transfer the chops to a serving dish. Return the cheese sauce to the pressure cooker and heat over medium heat. Thin the sauce if necessary with a little of the reserved broth. Slice the potatoes ½ inch thick and add to the cooker, mixing gently with the sauce to heat thoroughly. Transfer the potatoes and cheese sauce to a serving bowl and garnish with the green onions. ✳ Serves 6

Smokey Chinese Barbecued Ribs

Five-spice powder is a mixture of spices often used in Chinese cooking. Although combinations may vary, the fragrant powder usually includes cinnamon, aniseed, fennel, black or Szechwan pepper, and cloves, flavors that complement pork to a tee. Served either as a main course or an appetizer, these are great-tasting ribs.

¾ cup ketchup

¼ cup soy sauce

2 tablespoons balsamic vinegar

1 tablespoon liquid smoke

⅓ cup brown sugar

2 teaspoons ground ginger

1 teaspoon Chinese five-spice powder

1 teaspoon garlic powder

4 pounds baby back pork ribs, cut
    into single ribs

Lime wedges, for garnish

Combine all of the ingredients except for the liquid smoke and the lime wedges in the pressure cooker and add ½ cup water, mixing well. Lock the lid in place. Bring to 15psi over high heat, immediately reduce the heat to the lowest possible setting to stabilize and maintain that pressure, and cook for 10 minutes. Remove from the heat and use the natural release method (see page 31) to depressurize. Carefully open the lid after the pressure drops. Transfer the ribs to a serving plate, garnish with lime wedges. Stir the liquid smoke into the sauce and serve it in a separate bowl to be passed at the table. ✳ Serves 6

Two-Meat California Chili with All the Fixin's

We all have a favorite chili recipe, and this one is loaded with plenty of extras that will allow everyone to customize this main dish with the topping they like best. This is a fun meal, and a sure kid-pleaser, or great for munching in front of the TV when that big game is on.

Step One: The Peppers
3 dried ancho chiles
3 dried New Mexico red chiles
1 small bunch cilantro, leaves only
2 teaspoons ground cumin
2 tablespoons chili powder

The chiles used in this recipe are not really hot, but you can adjust the amount to taste if you prefer a milder version. Cover the chiles with hot water and let them stand for 30 minutes to soften. Remove and discard the seeds and stems. Place the chiles, cilantro, and cumin in a food processor and blend, adding water a little at a time to form a smooth puree.

Step Two: The Chili
1 tablespoon oil
1 pound coarsely ground beef
1 pound coarsely ground pork
1 onion, chopped
1 green bell pepper, seeded and chopped
1 tablespoon minced garlic
1 (28-ounce) can chopped tomatoes, with juice
2 (10-ounce) cans kidney beans, drained and rinsed

1 (3-ounce) can tomato paste

Heat the oil in a large pressure cooker over medium heat. Add the beef and pork, and cook until the meat is browned and nicely crumbled. Add the onions, green peppers, and garlic and cook, stirring, until slightly softened, about 3 minutes. Pour off all the excess grease. Add the chile puree, tomatoes, kidney beans, tomato paste, and 3 cups water, stirring until well blended. Lock the lid in place. Bring to 15psi over high heat, immediately reduce the heat to the lowest possible setting to stabilize and maintain that pressure, and cook for 8 minutes. Remove from the heat and use the natural release method (see page 31) to depressurize. Carefully open the lid after the pressure drops.

Step Three: The Fixin's
2 cups shredded pepper Jack cheese
1 cup salsa, any variety
1 cup sour cream
2 avocados, diced
1 cup sliced black olives
1 cup sliced green onions
Corn tortilla chips, any variety

Serve the chili in individual bowls with all the fixin's arranged on the table to add as desired.

✳ Serves 6

Cook's Note: Chile peppers come in a staggering assortment of flavors and burn levels, from mild to call-the-hospital-that's-hot and everything in between. The trick is to find the right chile pepper to add flavor, not just heat. Dried red chiles are sold whole and vary in size from ½ to 5 or 6 inches in length, often the smallest peppers are the hottest. Dried chiles are usually soaked in hot water for 1 hour and drained, and then the hotter ribs and seeds are removed. When chopping hot chiles, it's best to wear rubber or latex gloves because the oils can be quite irritating. Be very careful not to touch your eyes or mouth when working with hot chiles. Wash your hands, knives, and cutting boards with soap and hot water after use; water alone will not remove the burning oils and may in fact spread them, making it worse. An old remedy that will quickly neutralize the hot oils on your skin, or in your mouth, is to use dairy fats such as cream, butter, sour cream, whole milk, or even ice cream to ease the burn.

Easy, Anytime Barbecued Baby Back Ribs

On those rare occasions when you don't want to use an outdoor grill, the pressure cooker makes the tenderest ribs you will ever eat. Given the added bonus that you don't have to go outside in the heat and sweat over a flaming grill while being bitten by bugs, you might find this recipe a welcome solution. Not only is this one of my summertime favorites, but now there's no excuse for not serving up barbecued ribs on a snowy day in mid-January.

2 pounds baby back ribs
2 cups of your favorite barbecue sauce

Prepare a gas or charcoal grill, or preheat the broiler. Place the metal rack in the cooker and add ½ cup water. If your cooker is large enough, you can bend the racks of ribs around in a circle. Otherwise, cut the racks into sections and stand them upright in the cooker. Lock the lid in place. Bring to 15psi over high heat, immediately reduce the heat to the lowest possible setting to stabilize and maintain that pressure, and cook for 12 minutes. Remove from the heat and use the quick or cold water release method (see page 30) to depressurize. Carefully open the lid after the pressure drops. Carefully remove the ribs from the cooker using long-handled tongs so as not to tear them apart. Pour the barbecue sauce into a shallow pan, dip each section of ribs in the sauce, and place them on the grill to glaze. If using the broiler, place the ribs on a broiling pan and position about 6 inches away from the heat source until glazed. Baste the meat frequently, and turn the ribs over when they brown. Baste again, watching carefully until the second side is brown. Serve the ribs with the remaining barbecue sauce on the side. ✳ Serves 4

Spareribs, Potatoes, and Kraut

Homey and comforting, here's a classic combination of ribs and sauerkraut with potatoes, a combination that makes a fast and easy one-pot meal. The earthy scent of caraway provides a robust aroma, and a little brown sugar and apple juice mellows the kraut and infuses a subtle flavor into the ribs.

1 (28-ounce) package or jar deli or refrigerated sauerkraut, drained
1 onion, chopped
¼ cup packed brown sugar
1 teaspoon caraway seeds, crushed
3 to 4 pounds spareribs, cut into sections that fit in the pressure cooker
4 potatoes, scrubbed and halved
1 cup apple juice

In a large bowl, mix the sauerkraut, onions, brown sugar, and caraway seeds. Layer the spareribs in a large pressure cooker first, and next add the sauerkraut mixture, and then place the potatoes on top. Add the apple juice and lock the lid in place. Bring to 15psi over high heat, immediately reduce the heat to the lowest possible setting to stabilize and maintain that pressure, and cook for 10 minutes. Remove from the heat and use the natural release method (see page 31) to depressurize. Carefully

open the lid after the pressure drops. Using long-handled tongs, remove the potatoes and ribs to a serving plate. Drain the sauerkraut and transfer to a serving bowl. ✳ Serves 4

Cook's Note: Rinse the sauerkraut in cold water before cooking to minimize the sourness.

Caesar's Ribs and Potatoes

The few extra minutes it takes to brown the pork are well spent, because it brings out the flavor of the meat and adds appealing color. Cooked with potatoes, these meaty, thick and juicy, boneless pork ribs are braised in an infusion sauce featuring robust Italian seasonings.

3 tablespoons olive oil
2 to 3 pounds country-style boneless pork ribs
1 (1¼-ounce) packet dried Caesar dressing mix
1 tablespoon dried mixed Italian herbs
1 teaspoon garlic powder
½ teaspoon red pepper flakes
½ cup white wine
4 large baking potatoes, scrubbed and halved lengthwise

Heat the oil in the pressure cooker over medium heat. Add the ribs, cook until browned on all sides, and set aside. Combine the Caesar dressing mix, Italian herbs, garlic powder, red pepper flakes, and wine in the pressure cooker, mixing well. Return the pork to the pressure cooker, turning once to coat with the sauce. Arrange the potato halves on top of the pork, cut side down, and lock the lid in place. Bring to 15psi over high heat, immediately reduce the heat to the lowest possible setting to stabilize and maintain that pressure, and cook for 10 minutes. Remove from the heat and use the natural release method (see page 31) to depressurize. Carefully open the lid after the pressure drops. Transfer the potatoes and ribs to a large serving platter, and serve the sauce separately to be spooned over the meat and potatoes.

❋ Serves 4 to 5

Old-Fashioned Luncheon Loaf

This heirloom recipe for "sandwich meat" was very common back in the days before supermarkets and packaged, processed lunch meats. Most households had their own favorite combination of ingredients, but it was just as often made from whatever leftover meats were available after Sunday dinner. I've updated my grandmother's original version, taking advantage of ground chicken or turkey, although you can certainly use whatever cooked leftovers you have on hand.

1 pound smoked ham, coarsely ground in a meat
    grinder or food processor
½ pound ground chicken or turkey
1 cup dry bread crumbs or saltine cracker crumbs

½ cup minced onion
½ cup seeded and finely chopped green bell
    pepper
1 tablespoon paprika
1 teaspoon garlic powder
½ teaspoon freshly ground black pepper
2 large eggs, slightly beaten
4 tablespoons ketchup
2 tablespoons Worcestershire sauce
2 to 3 dashes Tabasco sauce
1 cup whole pimiento-stuffed green olives

Combine all of the ingredients except for the stuffed green olives in the bowl of a stand mixer, and blend thoroughly until they are uniformly mixed. If you don't have a stand mixer, place everything in a large plastic freezer bag, and knead it until the ingredients are well blended. If necessary, increase the amount of ketchup to make the mixture workable. When the mixture is thoroughly blended, gently stir in the olives so that they are well distributed throughout. Place the rack in the pressure cooker and add 1 cup water. Pack the meat mixture into mini loaf pans, or a springform pan. Lock the lid in place. Bring to 15psi over high heat, immediately reduce the heat to the lowest possible setting to stabilize and maintain that pressure, and cook for 30 minutes. Remove from the heat and use the natural release method (see page 31) to depressurize. Carefully open the lid after the pressure drops. Using oven mitts, carefully lift the loaf pan out of the cooker and let it rest for about 10 minutes before removing the loaf from the pan. Cover tightly with plastic wrap and refrigerate until completely chilled, giving the flavors time to develop. Serve the loaf warmed or chilled, sliced to make sandwiches with your choice of breads and condiments. ❋ Serves 6

Country Ham Steak with Redeye Gravy

When I was growing up, my mom was fond of repeating an old adage popular with Southern cooks: "The darker the roux, the richer the flavor," and its very true. A dark roux has a wonderful roasted nutty flavor and aroma, and this very easy recipe is still popular. Traditionally, serve with mounds of creamy buttermilk mashed potatoes, some collard greens, and enough cornbread to soak up all that redeye gravy.

Step One: The Roux
2 tablespoons butter
2 tablespoons all-purpose flour

Melt the butter in a pressure cooker over medium heat. Add the flour, stirring constantly until the flour is smooth and about the color of peanut butter; but be careful not to let it burn. Scoop the roux into a small bowl and set aside.

Step Two: The Ham and Gravy
1 pound country ham steak, trimmed of fat
    and thickly sliced
1½ cups chicken broth
1 onion, chopped
½ teaspoon coarsely ground black pepper
¼ teaspoon cayenne pepper, or to taste
1 cup strong black coffee
⅓ cup Kentucky bourbon

Add the broth, the coffee, onions, black pepper, and cayenne pepper to the pressure cooker, and stir to mix. Add the ham and lock the lid in place. Bring to 15psi over high heat, immediately reduce the heat to the lowest possible setting to stabilize and maintain that pressure, and cook for 6 minutes. Remove from the heat and use the quick release method (see page 30) to depressurize. Carefully open the lid after the pressure drops. Remove the ham steak to a serving platter and pop it into a low oven to keep warm. Skim off any fat from the surface of the broth. Pour the broth into a bowl. Return the roux to the pressure cooker and heat over medium-high heat. Slowly add the broth and the bourbon, whisking constantly as the gravy thickens. Adjust the amount of liquid, adding more if necessary to reach the desired consistency. Serve the gravy in a separate bowl.

✳ Serves 4

Scalloped Potatoes and Ham

As far as I'm concerned, the pressure cooker is the only way to make tender scalloped potatoes, ham, and a wonderful creamy sauce. This is simply old-fashioned comfort food, the sort of meal that will remind you of home. Serve with a crisp green salad.

> 1 cup milk
> 2 tablespoons butter
> Generous dash of Louisiana-style hot sauce
> ½ teaspoon freshly ground black pepper
> 2 tablespoons all-purpose flour
> ½ teaspoon baking soda
> ½ cup heavy cream
> 4 potatoes, peeled and thinly sliced
> 1 onion, diced
> 1 cup saltine cracker crumbs
> 2 cups diced cooked or leftover ham
> 1 teaspoon dried parsley

Place the rack in the bottom of the cooker. Heat the milk, cream, butter, hot sauce, and pepper in a microwave-safe bowl until the butter is melted and the milk is beginning to boil and bubble around the edges. Whisk the flour and baking soda into the milk mixture, and slowly stir in the sour cream. Butter a shallow, round metal pan with a flat bottom, such as a cake pan, that will fit loosely inside the pressure cooker. If your pressure cooker came with a similarly shaped steamer tray, just line it with a square of aluminum foil to block the steam holes, and butter the foil. Beginning with a layer of potatoes, fill the pan with alternating layers of potatoes, onions, cracker crumbs, and ham, reserving some cracker crumbs for the top. Pour in the milk mixture and top with the reserved cracker crumbs. Insert a knife blade around the edge of the pan to allow the milk to get down through all the layers. Sprinkle the parsley on top. Lay a sheet of aluminum foil over the top of the dish, but do not seal or crimp the edges. Use foil helper handles (see page 42) to lower the dish into the pressure cooker. Add enough water to reach halfway up the side of the pan, and lock the lid in place. Bring to 15psi over high heat, immediately reduce the heat to the lowest possible setting to stabilize and maintain that pressure, and cook for 25 minutes. Remove from the heat and use the natural release method (see page 31) to depressurize. Carefully open the lid after the pressure drops. ✳ Serves 4 to 5

Variation: For Cheesy Scalloped Potatoes and Ham, add 1½ cups grated sharp cheddar cheese, layering the cheese on top of each layer of potatoes.

Cola-Cooked Ham with Yams

Cooking a ham in the pressure cooker has the added benefit of draining much of the unwanted fat. Back in the '50s, a popular cooking fad called for flavored soft drinks to be added to many recipes. My frugal Southern relatives zealously saved their faded old newspaper clippings featuring recipes using soda pop. This one has handwritten instructions on the margin about how to choose the right kind of yams: "choose the red, narrowish ones for sweetness."

 ½ cup brown sugar
 1 tablespoon prepared horseradish
 1 teaspoon dry mustard
 ½ teaspoon ground cloves
 1 (12-ounce) can cola soft drink (regular, not diet)
 1 (3- to 4- pound) precooked ham
 4 small yams, scrubbed

Combine the brown sugar, horseradish, mustard, and cloves in a small bowl and add just enough cola to make a smooth, spreadable paste; reserve the remaining cola. Rub the mixture over the entire ham. Place the rack in the pressure cooker and pour in the remaining cola. Use foil helper handles (see page 42) to place the ham in the pressure cooker. Arrange the yams around the ham and lock the lid in place. Bring to 15psi over high heat, immediately reduce the heat to the lowest possible setting to stabilize and maintain that pressure, and cook for 25 minutes. Remove from the heat and use the natural release method (see page 31) to depressurize. Carefully open the lid after the pressure drops. Transfer the ham to a serving plate and slice thinly. Cut the yams in quarters and arrange them on the same platter. ✳ **Serves 6**

Baked Ham with Pineapple-Raisin Sauce

A traditional Southern recipe for ham includes raisin sauce, but I've gone one step further in adding pineapple, a flavor that goes remarkably well with ham. This simple recipe can deliver a gorgeous ham to grace the center of your holiday table, but, even better, because it's so quick and easy, you can serve ham any day of the week.

 Step One: The Ham
 1 (4-pound) ready-to-eat ham
 1 teaspoon whole cloves
 1 cup apple juice
 ¼ cup packed brown sugar
 ½ teaspoon ground ginger
 ½ teaspoon ground cinnamon
 1 onion, sliced into rings

Score through the fat on top of the ham in a decorative diamond pattern and stud with the cloves. Combine the apple juice, brown sugar, ginger, and cinnamon in the pressure cooker, stir to mix, and add the onions. Place the rack in the bottom of the pressure cooker. Use foil helper handles (see page

42) under the ham to position it on the rack. Lock the lid in place. Bring to 15psi over high heat, immediately reduce the heat to the lowest possible setting to stabilize and maintain that pressure, and cook for 20 minutes. Remove from the heat and use the natural release method (see page 31) to depressurize. Carefully open the lid after the pressure drops. Transfer the ham to a large serving platter and keep warm in a low oven until ready to slice. Remove the rack from the cooker and skim off any excess fat from the surface of the broth. Bring the broth to a boil, uncovered, and reduce to about 1 cup, watching that it does not scorch on the bottom.

Step Two: The Sauce
½ cup raisins
1 (14-ounce) can pineapple chunks, drained
½ cup apple butter
½ cup maple syrup
2 tablespoons balsamic vinegar

Reduce the heat and add the raisins to the simmering sauce. Stir in the pineapple chunks, apple butter, maple syrup, and vinegar, and simmer until bubbly. Serve separately, spooning over the sliced ham at the table. ✳ Serves 6

✳ ONE-POT MEAL

Kielbasa Sausage Supper

Here's just the ticket for a quick, hearty weekday meal. This fast, easy, and delicious recipe smells, looks, and tastes wonderful, and there's very little mess. Kielbasa sausages, potatoes, and cabbage are cooked together so fast that you'll barely have time to set the table.

2 pounds kielbasa sausage, any variety
2 tablespoons butter
1 onion, chopped
½ cup apple juice
2 teaspoons mustard, any variety
4 carrots, sliced ¼ inch thick
4 potatoes, peeled and sliced ¼ inch thick
1 head cabbage, cored and cut into wedges

Cut the kielbasa into serving-size portions. Heat the butter in the pressure cooker over medium heat. Add the sausage and cook until browned on all sides. Add the onions and cook, stirring, until slightly softened, about 3 minutes. Mix the apple juice and mustard in the pressure cooker. Add the carrots, potatoes, and cabbage, in that order. Lock the lid in place. Bring to 15psi over high heat, immediately reduce the heat to the lowest possible setting to stabilize and maintain that pressure, and cook for 4 minutes. Remove from the heat and use the natural release method (see page 31) to depressurize. Carefully open the lid after the pressure drops. Transfer the vegetables and sausage to a serving dish with a slotted spoon. ✳ Serves 4 to 5

Smoked Kielbasa Sausage Cassoulet

Kielbasa, a smoked pork sausage, comes in chubby precooked links and is often labeled as smoked Polish sausage. Traditionally a cassoulet, a classic French peasant dish, is simmered for hours, but my pressure-cooker version slashes the cooking time to just 8 minutes. I've used a robust blend of Mexican-inspired ingredients to create this "International" version of a thick and hearty soup. Serve with a nice crusty bread to mop the bowl.

    1 onion, thinly sliced
    ⅓ cup packed cilantro leaves, minced
    2 tablespoons minced garlic
    2 tablespoons chili powder
    1 teaspoon dried rosemary
    1 teaspoon ground sage
    1 teaspoon ground cumin
    1 (14-ounce) can chicken broth
    1 (3-ounce) can tomato paste
    1 pound smoked kielbasa-style sausage,
        cut into serving portions
    1 (28-ounce) can diced tomatoes, with juice
    1 (14-ounce) can hominy, drained
    1 (14-ounce) can black beans, drained and rinsed
    1 (12-ounce) can whole kernel corn, drained
    1 cup Italian-style croutons, for garnish

Add the onions, cilantro, garlic, chili powder, rosemary, sage, cumin, broth, and tomato paste to a large cooker, and 2 cups of water, stirring until well mixed. Place the sausage in the bottom of pot, add all of the remaining ingredients except for the croutons, and stir. Lock the lid in place. Bring to 15psi over high heat, immediately reduce the heat to the lowest possible setting to stabilize and maintain that pressure, and cook for 8 minutes. Remove from the heat and use the natural release method (see page 31) to depressurize. Carefully open the lid after the pressure drops. Serve in a tureen or individual soup bowls, and top each serving with a few croutons. ✳ Serves 4

Italian Sausage Casserole

There is nothing timid about Italian flavors, and this great Italian one-pot meal certainly doesn't skimp on flavor. It doesn't require a lot of work, either. You'll get all the wonderful flavors of Italy with this quick classic featuring Italian sausage and pasta cooked in a thick and well-seasoned tomato sauce.

    1 tablespoon oil
    1 pound sweet Italian sausage, casings removed
    1 onion, chopped
    3 cups uncooked small pasta shells
    2 cups frozen green beans
    3 tablespoons tomato paste
    1 tablespoon dried mixed Italian herbs
    1 (28-ounce) can chopped tomatoes, with juice
    1½ cups shredded mozzarella cheese

Heat the oil in the pressure cooker over medium heat. Add the meat, cook until it's browned and nicely crumbled, and set aside. Add the onions to the cooker and cook, stirring, until slightly softened, about 3 minutes. Add the pasta, green beans, tomato paste, and Italian herbs, stir, and return the meat to the pressure cooker. Add the tomatoes and enough water to cover all the ingredients, pushing the pasta beneath the surface of the liquid. Lock the lid in place. Bring to 15psi over high heat, immediately reduce the heat to the lowest possible setting to stabilize and maintain that pressure, and cook for 6 minutes. Remove from the heat and use the natural release method (see page 31) to depressurize. Carefully open the lid after the pressure drops. Add the mozzarella cheese, tossing to mix. Cover with a regular lid, and let the pressure cooker sit until the cheese has melted. Transfer to a serving bowl. ✳ Serves 6

Serving Suggestion: Add some garlic toast and a salad with vinaigrette dressing to complete the meal.

✳ ONE-POT MEAL

Italian Sausage, Peppers, and Pasta in Ragu Sauce

For an extra kick, I recommend using half sweet sausage and half hot sausage. Removed from its casing, the sausage breaks up into bits—like ground beef—during cooking, and what a difference just a couple of hot Italian sausages will make when added to this sauce! This one-pot recipe with pork, peppers, pasta, and Parmesan is quick and easy, but accented with plenty of wonderful Italian flavors and aroma for a terrific one-pot meal.

2 pounds Italian sausage (sweet, hot, or a combination of the two)
1 onion, chopped
1 red bell pepper, seeded and coarsely chopped
1 green bell pepper, seeded and coarsely chopped
2 tablespoons minced garlic
1 (28-ounce) can Italian-style stewed tomatoes, with juice
1 (16-ounce) jar of your favorite Italian-style tomato sauce
8 ounces uncooked penne
2 large zucchini, cut into 2-inch pieces
2 tablespoons dried mixed Italian herbs
Grated Parmesan cheese, for garnish

Remove the casings from the sausages, add the meat to the cooker, and cook over medium heat until nicely crumbled and browned. Drain off all but 2 tablespoons fat. Add the onions, bell peppers, and garlic to the cooker and cook, stirring, about 3 minutes. Add the tomatoes, pasta sauce, pasta, zucchini, and Italian herbs and stir. Add enough water to just barely cover all the ingredients, pushing the pasta beneath the surface. Lock the lid in place. Bring to 15psi over high heat, immediately reduce the heat to the lowest possible setting to stabilize and maintain that pressure, and cook for 8 minutes. Remove from the heat and use the natural release method (see page 31) to depressurize. Carefully open the lid after the pressure drops. Transfer to a serving bowl, add the Parmesan cheese, and toss gently just before serving. ✳ Serves 4 to 5

Collard Greens and Sausage Soup

Who knew collard greens could be so wonderful? The pressure cooker makes the tough leaves a dark, rich green color and very tender. Combined with the spicy sausage and other ingredients, it makes a flavorful dish with plenty of bold taste. A big pan of cornbread goes perfectly with this soup.

2 tablespoons bacon drippings or other fat
1 pound andouille or kielbasa sausage, diced
1 onion, chopped
1 red bell pepper, seeded and chopped
4 tablespoons minced garlic
2 tablespoons pickled jalapeño chiles, minced
1 tablespoon packed dark brown sugar
½ teaspoon red pepper flakes
2 tablespoons balsamic vinegar
1 to 2 bunches collard greens, washed, trimmed, and chopped into 1-inch pieces
3 cups cubed fresh butternut squash
2 carrots, finely chopped
1 cup frozen whole kernel corn
2 (14-ounce) cans chicken broth
2 (10-ounce) cans stewed tomatoes, with juice

Heat the bacon drippings in a large pressure cooker over medium heat. Add the sausage and cook until browned on all sides. Add the onions, bell peppers, and garlic and cook, stirring, until slightly softened, about 3 minutes. Add the jalapeños, brown sugar, red pepper flakes, and vinegar and mix well. When cooking a large amount of greens, wilt them first to reduce their volume before pressurizing the cooker. Add 2 cups of water to the pressure cooker and bring to a boil, using a regular lid. Add all the greens and cook over medium heat until they have slightly wilted. Add the squash, carrots, corn, broth, and tomatoes and stir. Lock the lid in place. Bring to 15psi over high heat, immediately reduce the heat to the lowest possible setting to stabilize and maintain that pressure, and cook for 4 minutes. Remove from the heat and use the cold water release method (see page 30) to depressurize. Carefully open the lid after the pressure drops. Adjust the seasonings to taste. Ladle into soup bowls and serve hot. ❊ Serves 4 to 5

Ragu Sauce with Italian Sausage

This well-seasoned, thick, and meaty sauce with spicy Italian sausages delivers lots of flavor and aroma with minimal effort. This is a very versatile recipe that works well when served over a variety of sides; besides the obvious pasta, consider mashed potatoes, assorted steamed Italian-type vegetables, or even rice. Serve with crusty bread for mopping the last of the sauce off the plate, and add a tossed salad.

2 pounds Italian sausage, a combination of
   mild and hot varieties
2 tablespoons olive oil
2 onions, chopped
½ pound fresh mushrooms, washed and sliced
1 green bell pepper, seeded and chopped
4 tablespoons minced garlic
1 (28-ounce) can chopped or diced tomatoes,
   with juice
1 (28-ounce) can crushed or pureed tomatoes
1 (14-ounce) can black olives, drained
   and sliced
2 (3-ounce) cans tomato paste
1 tablespoon dried oregano
1 teaspoon ground sage
1 teaspoon dried marjoram
½ teaspoon fennel seed, crushed
½ teaspoon red pepper flakes
2 bay leaves

Remove the casings from the sausages. Heat the oil in a large pressure cooker over medium heat. Add the sausage, cook until the meat is nicely crumbled and browned, and set aside on paper towels to drain. Add the onions, mushrooms, green peppers, and garlic to the cooker and cook, stirring, until slightly softened, about 3 minutes. Return the sausage meat to the cooker and add the chopped and crushed tomatoes, the olives, tomato paste, and all the spices, plus 4 cups water, and stir. Lock the lid in place. Bring to 15psi over high heat, immediately reduce the heat to the lowest possible setting to stabilize and maintain that pressure, and cook for 8 minutes. Remove from the heat and use the natural release method (see page 31) to depressurize. Carefully open the lid after the pressure drops. Remove the bay leaves, adjust the seasonings to taste, and serve. ✳ **Serves 6**

Lamb

LAMB AND MUTTON are popular in many ethnic cuisines, particularly Mediterranean and Middle Eastern cooking. In the U.S., tender spring lamb under six months of age is usually available in supermarkets all year long. Yearling lamb is another good choice, as it provides slightly larger cuts of meat. When choosing lamb, look for a bright color—the darker the flesh, the older and less tender the cut. The most common cuts are chops, ribs, roasts, and steaks.

Americans tend to shy away from lamb, associating it with a strong or gamey taste. I raised sheep for about 30 years, and both lamb and mutton were mainstays of my weekly menu planning. Prepared correctly, lamb, and even mutton, are sweet and mild-tasting meats. What's the trick, you ask skeptically with a raised eyebrow? Simple: it's the fat on lamb that has the strong taste, not the meat itself. Take the time to remove all the fat from the surface of the meat, give it a quick rinse, and it's ready for cooking. Occasionally you will find a thin but tough membrane on some cuts of lamb. This is called the "fell," and it too should be removed before cooking or it will add that undesirable gamey taste.

Lamb Stew

With a pressure cooker, it's great to have a whole meal in one carefree operation. This stew is so delicious and so easy to make that it's often on the menu. I like to serve it with mashed potatoes since it makes its own gravy. Crusty bread comes in handy, too.

2 tablespoons oil
2 pounds boneless lamb shoulder, cut into
    1½-inch cubes
2 onions, sliced
2 tablespoons minced garlic
1 teaspoon ground sage
2 bay leaves
½ teaspoon freshly ground black pepper
3 tablespoons tomato paste
4 turnips, peeled and cut into 1-inch cubes
4 carrots, peeled and sliced
4 potatoes, peeled and cut into 1-inch cubes
2 tablespoons cornstarch

Heat the oil in the pressure cooker over medium heat. Add the meat, cook until browned on all sides, and set aside. Add the onions and garlic to the cooker and cook, stirring, until slightly softened, about 3 minutes. Return the meat to the cooker and add the sage, bay leaves, pepper, and tomato paste; pour in 1½ quarts water and stir well. Lock the lid in place. Bring to 15psi over high heat, immediately reduce the heat to the lowest possible setting to stabilize and maintain that pressure, and cook for 10 minutes. Remove from the heat and use the quick or cold water release method (see page 30) to depressurize. Carefully open the lid after the pressure drops. Add the turnips, carrots, and potatoes to the cooker, pushing them beneath the surface of the broth, and lock the lid back in place. Return to 15psi over high heat, immediately reduce the heat to the lowest possible setting to stabilize and maintain that pressure, and cook for an additional 5 minutes. Remove from the heat and use the natural release method (see page 31) to depressurize. Carefully open the lid after the pressure drops. Thicken the broth by making a slurry with the cornstarch mixed with ⅓ cup water; stir the slurry into the broth and simmer over medium heat, stirring often as it thickens to the desired consistency, but do not boil. Ladle into bowls and serve hot. ※ Serves 4 to 5

Braised Lamb Shanks with Vegetables

Lamb shanks are inexpensive and very flavorful, but very tough because that part of the animal gets a lot of movement, and that makes the meat tough. Typically shanks are one of those dishes that you might remember your mother or grandmother cooking in the oven or in that big pot on the stove all day. When it was finished, the meat was falling-off-the-bone tender, and the sauce was thick and full of flavor. A crunchy loaf of bread is a good addition to this rustic dish.

Step One: The *Bouquet Garni*

10 whole black peppercorns

3 stalks' worth of celery leaves

1 sprig fresh rosemary

Place all of the ingredients in a small square of cheesecloth and tie it closed with a piece of string or a doubled length of white sewing thread.

Step Two: The Lamb and Vegetables

2 tablespoons olive oil

4 pounds lamb shanks, trimmed of excess fat

2 onions, chopped

3 tablespoons minced garlic

1 (28-ounce) can chopped tomatoes, with juce

⅓ cup packed cilantro stems and leaves, chopped

2 teaspoons dried basil

1 teaspoon dried oregano

1 (14-ounce) can chicken broth

2 carrots, peeled and chopped

1 stalk celery, chopped

6 new potatoes, quartered

Heat the oil in the pressure cooker over medium heat. Add the meat, cook until browned on both sides, and set aside. Add the onions and garlic to the cooker and cook, stirring, until slightly softened, about 3 minutes. Add the tomatoes, cilantro, basil, oregano, and the *bouquet garni*. Add the chicken broth and the lamb shanks, stirring to mix well. Lock the lid in place. Bring to 15psi over high heat, immediately reduce the heat to the lowest possible setting to stabilize and maintain that pressure, and cook for 20 minutes. Remove from the heat and use the natural release method (see page 31) to depressurize. Carefully open the lid after the pressure drops. Check for doneness; the meat should be fork-tender. If needed, lock the lid back in place, return to 15psi over high heat, immediately reduce the heat to the lowest possible setting to stabilize and maintain that pressure, and cook for an additional 5 minutes. Remove from the heat and use the natural release method (see page 31) to depressurize. Carefully open the lid after the pressure drops. Skim off any excess fat from the surface of the broth. Add the carrots, celery, and potatoes, stir, and lock the lid in place. Bring to 15psi over high heat, immediately reduce the heat to the lowest possible setting to stabilize and maintain that pressure, and cook for 5 minutes. Remove from the heat and use the natural release method (see page 31) to depressurize. Carefully open the lid after the pressure drops. Remove the *bouquet garni*. Place the lamb on a serving platter and serve the vegetables in a separate bowl to be passed at the table. ✳ Serves 4 to 5

Rustic Lamb in Garlic Sauce

Combined with succulent lamb, this is a sauce that garlic lovers will appreciate. Don't be put off by the amount of garlic used in this recipe; the end result is delicious. Serve over wide egg noodles, and don't forget to add a nice baguette or some other crusty artisan bread, and maybe a dish of sliced cucumbers and green onions with a splash of fresh lemon juice.

½ cup plus 2 tablespoons all-purpose flour
½ teaspoon salt
1 teaspoon freshly ground black pepper
2 pounds boneless lamb, cut into
　　2-inch chunks
2 tablespoons olive oil
2 onions, chopped
4 tablespoons minced garlic
½ cup dry white wine
1 (14-ounce) can beef broth
¼ cup white vinegar
1 teaspoon fresh rosemary, chopped
2 tablespoons butter

In a plastic bag, mix ½ cup of the flour, the salt, and ½ teaspoon of the pepper and add the lamb pieces, shaking gently until each piece is lightly coated. Heat the oil in the pressure cooker over medium heat. Add the meat, cook until browned on both sides, and set aside. Add the onions and garlic to the cooker and cook, stirring, until slightly softened, about 3 minutes. Deglaze the cooker with the wine, scraping up all those crusty, brown bits from the bottom. Add the lamb, broth, vinegar, rosemary, and the remaining ½ teaspoon pepper to the cooker. Stir to mix and lock the lid in place. Bring to 15psi over high heat, immediately reduce the heat to the lowest possible setting to stabilize and maintain that pressure, and cook for 10 minutes. Remove from the heat and use the natural release method (see page 31) to depressurize. Carefully open the lid after the pressure drops. Skim off any excess fat from the surface of the broth. In a small bowl, mix the remaining 2 tablespoons flour and the butter until smooth. Stir the mixture into the broth. Simmer, stirring often, over medium heat for about 5 minutes, or until the sauce thickens. Adjust the seasonings to taste, and serve.

✳ Serves 4

Moroccan Lamb

I admit it, I'm a spice junkie! Middle Eastern recipes use an abundance of aromatic spices and fragrant herbs. Since it's well known that the pressure cooker intensifies and enhances flavors, it's the perfect marriage of Old World cuisine and modern cooking convenience.

2 tablespoons olive oil
2 pounds leg of lamb, cut into 2-inch cubes
1 onion, quartered
½ cup chopped cilantro
3 tablespoons minced garlic
1 tablespoon ground cumin
1 tablespoon paprika
½ teaspoon ground ginger
½ teaspoon freshly ground black pepper

Dash teaspoon cayenne pepper

3 tablespoons fresh lemon juice

Sour cream or plain yogurt, for garnish

Heat the oil in the pressure cooker over medium heat. Add the meat, cook until browned on all sides, and set aside. In a food processor fitted with the metal blade, place the onion, cilantro, garlic, cumin, paprika, ginger, black pepper, cayenne pepper, and lemon juice, and puree. Add the pureed mixture and the broth to the pressure cooker and stir in ½ cup water. Return the meat to the pressure cooker and lock the lid in place. Bring to 15psi over high heat, immediately reduce the heat to the lowest possible setting to stabilize and maintain that pressure, and cook for 12 minutes. Remove from the heat and use the natural release method (see page 31) to depressurize. Carefully open the lid after the pressure drops. Transfer the lamb to a serving bowl. Serve the sour cream or yogurt separately, to be passed at the table. ✳ Serves 4

Serving Suggestion: Serve over couscous, rice, or noodles.

Lamb Cacciatore

This is a fairly easy recipe yielding an absolutely delicious entrée with Mediterranean-inspired ingredients. I like to serve this with a salad of sliced cucumbers and tomatoes dressed with a little dilled sour cream. Serve over hot rice or pasta, and you'll want to have plenty of fresh, crusty bread on hand to mop up the last of the sauce.

1 pound boneless lamb, cut into 1-inch cubes

½ cups all-purpose flour

2 tablespoons olive oil

1 onion, coarsely chopped

2 tablespoons minced garlic

2 (14-ounce) cans chicken broth

1 (28-ounce) can chopped tomatoes, with juice

1 (3-ounce) can tomato paste

1 cup white wine

½ cup white vinegar

2 zucchini, sliced ½ inch thick

2 cups sliced fresh mushrooms

⅓ cup packed cilantro

1 tablespoon crushed dried rosemary

2 teaspoons ground sage

½ teaspoon freshly ground black pepper

½ teaspoon dried basil

Dredge the meat in the flour. Heat the oil in the pressure cooker over medium heat. Add the meat, cook until browned on all sides, and set aside. Add the onions and garlic to the cooker and cook, stirring, until slightly softened, about 3 minutes. Add all of the remaining ingredients, return the meat to the cooker, and add 2 cups water, stirring well. Lock the lid in place. Bring to 15psi over high heat, immediately reduce the heat to the lowest possible setting to stabilize and maintain that pressure, and cook for 12 minutes. Remove from the heat and use the natural release method (see page 31) to depressurize. Carefully open the lid after the pressure drops. Adjust the seasonings to taste, and serve. ✳ Serves 4

Lamb with Chunky Rhubarb Sauce

My grandmother grew rhubarb in her garden, and she held that the deeper the red, the more flavorful the stalks were likely to be. Rhubarb is a tangy complement to the lamb.

Step One: The Rhubarb Sauce

4 cups sliced (1 inch thick) fresh or frozen
   rhubarb

1 jalapeño chile, seeded and minced

½ cup strawberry nectar

2 tablespoons balsamic vinegar

½ cup honey

Combine all of the ingredients in a metal bowl. Place the rack in the pressure cooker and add ½ cup water. Place the bowl on the rack. Lock the lid in place. Bring to 15psi over high heat, immediately reduce the heat to the lowest possible setting to stabilize and maintain that pressure, and cook for 3 minutes. Remove from the heat and use the natural release method (see page 31) to depressurize. Carefully open the lid after the pressure drops. Add more honey if desired, until it's the right combination of tangy sweetness to suit your taste. The sauce can be made ahead and refrigerated for up to 2 days in a covered container.

Step Two: The Lamb

2 tablespoons olive oil

2 to 3 pounds leg of lamb

1 onion, chopped

3 tablespoons minced garlic

½ teaspoon freshly ground black pepper

½ teaspoon ground sage

½ teaspoon ground cardamom

1 (14-ounce) can chicken broth

Heat the oil in the pressure cooker over medium heat. Add the meat, cook until browned on all sides, and set aside. Add the onions and garlic to the cooker and cook, stirring, until slightly softened, about 3 minutes. Add the pepper, sage, and cardamom and fry until the spices begin to sizzle. Deglaze the cooker with the broth, scraping up all those crusty, brown bits from the bottom. Return the meat to the cooker using foil helper handles (see page 42) and lock the lid in place. Bring to 15psi over high heat, immediately reduce the heat to the lowest possible setting to stabilize and maintain that pressure, and cook for 25 minutes. Remove from the heat and use the natural release method (see page 31) to depressurize. Carefully open the lid after the pressure drops, remove the lamb to a serving platter, and keep warm in a low oven until ready to serve. Bring the broth to a boil, uncovered, over medium heat, and continue cooking until it's reduced by half. Slowly stir the rhubarb sauce into the broth, heating through. Serve the sauce separately, to be spooned over the lamb at the table. ✳ Serves 4 to 5

Armenian Lamb Stew

"If you are going to have stew lamb, do it the Armenian way!" So said Bev, a lady I worked with, when she shared this recipe with me. A Middle Eastern favorite, this dish is packed with six different vegetables and uses the interrupted cooking method (see page 38) to make sure they are not overcooked. Serve with a nice artisan bread.

½ cup all-purpose flour

½ teaspoon salt

1 teaspoon freshly ground black pepper

2 pounds leg of lamb, cut into 1-inch cubes

2 tablespoons olive oil

1 onion, sliced

2 tablespoons minced garlic

1 tablespoon paprika

1 teaspoon ground cumin

½ teaspoon dried mint

1 (14-ounce) can chicken broth

1 (14-ounce) can chopped tomatoes, with juice

1 teaspoon chicken bouillon granules

1 eggplant, cut into 1-inch cubes

1 green bell pepper, seeded and chopped

2 carrots, sliced

2 zucchini, sliced ½ inch thick

6 small okra pods, sliced

¼ cup fresh lemon juice

Sour cream or plain yogurt, for garnish

In a plastic bag, mix the flour, salt, and ½ teaspoon of the pepper and add the lamb pieces, shaking gently until each piece is lightly coated. Heat the oil in the pressure cooker over medium heat. Add the meat, cook in small batches until browned on all sides, and set aside. Add the onions and garlic to the cooker and cook, stirring, until slightly softened, about 3 minutes. Add the paprika, cumin, the remaining ½ teaspoon pepper, and the mint, frying until the spices begin to sizzle. Deglaze the cooker with the broth, scraping up all those crusty, brown bits from the bottom. Return the lamb to the cooker and add the tomatoes, 2 cups water, and the bouillon, stirring to mix. Lock the lid in place. Bring to 15psi over high heat, immediately reduce the heat to the lowest possible setting to stabilize and maintain that pressure, and cook for 10 minutes. Remove from the heat and use the quick or cold water release method (see page 30) to depressurize. Carefully open the lid after the pressure drops.

Add all the vegetables and the lemon juice to the cooker, stir, and lock the lid back in place. Return to 15psi over high heat, immediately reduce the heat to the lowest possible setting to stabilize and maintain that pressure, and cook for an additional 5 minutes. Remove from the heat and use the natural release method (see page 31) to depressurize. Carefully open the lid after the pressure drops. Adjust the seasonings to taste. Ladle the stew into bowls and pass the sour cream at the table. ✳ Serves 4

Lamb Paprikash with Noodles

When you're in a hurry for a fast but fancy feast, this entrée should definitely be on your short list of recipes. Don't be put off by cooking pasta in a pressure cooker; it cooks up very nicely, and this dish is absolutely fantastic.

> 2 tablespoons olive oil
> 2 pounds leg of lamb, cut into 1-inch cubes
> 1 onion, chopped
> 2 tablespoons minced garlic
> 1 tablespoon paprika, plus more for garnish
> 2 teaspoons chili powder
> 2 teaspoons dried parsley flakes
> ½ teaspoon freshly ground black pepper
> 1 (28-ounce) can chopped tomatoes, with juice
> 3 cups uncooked wide egg noodles
> 1 cup sour cream

Heat the oil in the pressure cooker over medium heat. Add the meat, cook until browned on all sides, and set aside. Add the onions and garlic to the cooker and cook, stirring, until slightly softened, about 3 minutes. Add the paprika, chili powder, parsley, and pepper, frying until the spices begin to sizzle. Return the meat to the cooker and add the tomatoes and egg noodles, and pour in enough water to barely cover the ingredients. Stir to mix and lock the lid in place. Bring to 15psi over high heat, immediately reduce the heat to the lowest possible setting to stabilize and maintain that pressure, and cook for 8 minutes. Remove from the heat and use the natural release method (see page 31) to depressurize. Carefully open the lid after the pressure drops. Stir in the sour cream and heat through over medium heat. Transfer the noodles and lamb to a serving platter and dust with a little paprika. ✳ **Serves 4 to 5**

Lamb Mulligatawny

There are endless variations of this easy and flavorful Indian soup recipe. This is the result of many different trials over the years, adding and changing the ingredients until it came down to this final version. Play around with the ingredients if you want, and make it as spicy as you like.

> 2 tablespoons butter
> 1 pound lamb stew meat, trimmed of fat and finely diced
> 1 onion, minced
> 2 tablespoons minced garlic
> 1 tablespoon curry powder
> 1 teaspoon grated lemon zest
> ½ teaspoon ground mace
> ½ teaspoon freshly ground black pepper to taste
> ½ teaspoon ground cloves
> 1 bay leaf
> 2 (14-ounce) cans chicken broth
> 2 tart apples, peeled and diced
> 1 green bell pepper, seeded and diced
> 2 stalks celery, diced
> 2 carrots, diced
> ½ cup uncooked long-grain white rice
> 1 cup unsweetened coconut milk

Heat the butter in a large pressure cooker over medium heat. Add the meat and cook until browned on all sides. Add the onions and garlic to the cooker and cook, stirring, until slightly softened, about 3 minutes. Add the curry powder, lemon zest, mace, pepper, cloves, and bay leaf, frying until the spices begin to sizzle. Deglaze the cooker with the broth, scraping up all those crusty, brown bits from the bottom. Add the apples, bell peppers, celery, carrots, rice, and 4 cups water. Stir to mix and lock the lid in place. Bring to 15psi over high heat, immediately reduce the heat to the lowest possible setting to stabilize and maintain that pressure, and cook for 8 minutes. Remove from the heat and use the natural release method (see page 31) to depressurize. Carefully open the lid after the pressure drops. Add the coconut milk and heat through over medium heat, but do not boil. Adjust the seasonings to taste. Ladle into soup bowls and serve. ✳ Serves 4

Lamb Ragu with Peppers

The delicious sauce really complements the lamb. For variety, try a mix of red, yellow, and green peppers for a dish that looks as good as it tastes. I like to serve this over mashed potatoes or pasta with a simple salad of halved cherry tomatoes, sliced green onions, and some crumbled feta cheese tossed with a drizzle of good olive oil and balsamic vinegar. Add some nice artisan bread for a complete meal.

2 pounds leg of lamb, cut into 1-inch cubes
½ cup all-purpose flour
2 tablespoons olive oil
2 onions, halved and thinly sliced
2 cups fresh mushrooms, washed and thickly sliced
2 tablespoons minced garlic
½ cup red wine
1 red bell pepper, seeded and chopped
1 green bell pepper, seeded and chopped
1 (28-ounce) can chopped tomatoes, with juice
¼ cup balsamic vinegar
2 tablespoons tomato paste
2 teaspoons sweet paprika
1½ teaspoons dried thyme leaves
½ teaspoon freshly ground black pepper
2 bay leaves

Dredge the lamb in the flour. Heat the oil in the pressure cooker over medium heat. Add the meat, cook until browned on all sides, and set aside. Add the onions, mushrooms, and garlic to the cooker and cook, stirring, until slightly softened, about 3 minutes. Deglaze the cooker with the wine, scraping up all those crusty, brown bits from the bottom. Return the meat to the cooker and add all of the remaining ingredients. Stir to mix and lock the lid in place. Bring to 15psi over high heat, immediately reduce the heat to the lowest possible setting to stabilize and maintain that pressure, and cook for 12 minutes. Remove from the heat and use the natural release method (see page 31) to depressurize. Carefully open the lid after the pressure drops. Remove the bay leaves, adjust the seasonings to taste, and serve. ✳ Serves 4 to 5

Persian Lamb Tagine

This is one of my own variations of a favorite Middle Eastern dish. The preparation is streamlined, and of course the cooking time is superfast. The recipe has a wonderful blend of spicy flavors that taste great served over couscous or rice with a cool cucumber and tomato salad, and plenty of crusty bread to scoop up the last of the sauce.

3 tablespoons butter

2 pounds boneless lamb, cut into 2-inch cubes

1 large onion, chopped

1 (28-ounce) can chopped tomatoes, with juice

1 (14-ounce) can chicken broth

2 tablespoons tomato paste

2 carrots, sliced

2 stalks celery, sliced

½ cup golden raisins

½ cup dried apricots, chopped

2 tablespoons minced garlic

2 tablespoons curry powder

1 tablespoon brown sugar

1 tablespoon grated fresh ginger

½ teaspoon freshly ground black pepper

1 bay leaf

Heat the butter in the pressure cooker over medium heat. Add the meat, cook until browned on both sides, and set aside. Add the onions to the cooker and cook, stirring, until slightly softened, about 3 minutes. Return the meat to the cooker and add all of the remaining ingredients, plus 2 cups water. Stir to mix and lock the lid in place. Bring to 15psi over high heat, immediately reduce the heat to the lowest possible setting to stabilize and maintain that pressure, and cook for 15 minutes. Remove from the heat and use the natural release method (see page 31) to depressurize. Carefully open the lid after the pressure drops. Adjust the seasonings to taste, and serve. ✳ Serves 4 to 5

Lamb Chops with Port Wine Mushroom Sauce

It takes only a few minutes to put together the ingredients for this luscious combination of delicate lamb in a sweet wine sauce with plenty of mushrooms. Served with egg noodles or fluffy rice, this is a speedy but gourmet-quality supper.

2 teaspoons coarsely ground black pepper

1 teaspoon garlic powder

8 bone-in lamb loin chops, ¾ inch thick

2 tablespoons olive oil

1 onion, halved and thinly sliced

½ pound fresh mushrooms, washed and thickly sliced

1 cup Port wine

¼ cup balsamic vinegar

⅓ cup thinly sliced green onion tops, for garnish

In a small bowl, combine the pepper and garlic powder. Rub the mixture into both sides of the chops. Heat the oil in the pressure cooker over medium heat. Add the meat, cook until browned on both sides, and set aside. Add the onions and mushrooms to the cooker and cook, stirring, until slightly softened, about 3 minutes. Return the meat to the cooker, add the wine and vinegar, and stir to mix. Lock the lid in place. Bring to 15psi over high heat, immediately reduce the heat to the lowest possible setting to stabilize and maintain that pressure, and cook for 6 minutes. Remove from the heat and use the natural release method (see page 31) to depressurize. Carefully open the lid after the pressure drops. Transfer the chops to a serving platter. Pour the mushroom sauce into a bowl and sprinkle with the green onions. ✳ Serves 4

Lamb Shanks Braised in Fruit

This recipe uses the interrupted cooking method (see page 38) to serve up some very tender lamb with lots of aromatic spices and the sweet taste of fresh fruits. Served over rice, couscous, mashed potatoes, or noodles for a memorable dish.

2 tablespoons butter

1½ to 2 pounds lamb shanks

1 onion, minced

2 tablespoons minced garlic

1 tablespoon ground turmeric

1 teaspoon dried thyme leaves

½ teaspoon red pepper flakes

1 bay leaf

½ cup white wine

1 cup chicken broth

¼ cup balsamic vinegar

2 peaches, peeled, pitted, and coarsely chopped, with any accumulated juices

2 nectarines, pitted and coarsely chopped, with any accumulated juices

2 plums, pitted and coarsely chopped, with any accumulated juices

Heat the butter in the pressure cooker over medium heat. Add the meat, cook until browned on all sides, and set aside. Add the onions to the cooker and cook, stirring, until slightly softened, about 3 minutes. Add the garlic, turmeric, thyme, red pepper, and bay leaf, frying until the spices begin to sizzle. Deglaze the cooker with the wine, scraping up all those crusty, brown bits from the bottom. Add the broth, vinegar, and fruit and return the lamb to the cooker. Stir to mix and lock the lid in place. Bring to 15psi over high heat, immediately reduce the heat to the lowest possible setting to stabilize and maintain that pressure, and cook for 25 minutes. Remove from the heat and use the natural release method (see page 31) to depressurize. Carefully open the lid after the pressure drops. Check for doneness; the meat should be tender enough to be pulled away from the bone. If needed, lock the lid back in place, return to 15psi over high heat, immediately reduce the heat to the lowest possible setting to stabilize and maintain that pressure, and cook for an additional 5 minutes. Remove from the heat and use the natural release method (see page 31) to depressurize. Carefully open the lid after the pressure drops. Skim off any excess fat from the surface of the broth. Transfer the shanks to a cutting board and pull or cut the meat from the bones. Return the meat to the sauce and heat through over medium heat. ✳ Serves 4

Lamb Chops with Carrots, New Potatoes, and Creamy Dijon Gravy

With a very pleasing, rich-tasting sauce, this is a three-course meal of lamb and two vegetables that is ready for the table in just a few minutes. What could be easier or faster?

1 teaspoon lemon pepper

2 tablespoons oil

6 loin lamb chops, ½ inch thick

1 onion, sliced

2 tablespoons minced garlic

1 (14-ounce) can chicken broth

1 (14-ounce) can chopped tomatoes, with juice

2 teaspoons Dijon mustard

1 teaspoon dried rosemary

1 teaspoon dried basil

2 carrots, sliced

6 small red potatoes, quartered

2 tablespoons cornstarch

1 (6-ounce) container plain yogurt

Rub the lemon pepper on both sides of the chops. Heat the oil in the pressure cooker over medium heat. Add the meat, cook until browned on both sides, and set aside. Add the onions and garlic to the cooker and cook, stirring, until slightly softened, about 3 minutes. Deglaze the cooker with the broth, scraping up all those crusty, brown bits from the bottom. Stir in the tomatoes, mustard,

rosemary, and basil, mixing well. Return the chops to the pressure cooker and place the carrots and potatoes on top. Lock the lid in place. Bring to 15psi over high heat, immediately reduce the heat to the lowest possible setting to stabilize and maintain that pressure, and cook for 6 minutes. Remove from the heat and use the natural release method (see page 31) to depressurize. Carefully open the lid after the pressure drops, and transfer the vegetables and chops to a large serving platter. Bring the sauce to a simmer, uncovered, over medium heat. Thicken the sauce by making a slurry with the cornstarch mixed with ⅓ cup cold water; stir the slurry into the sauce and simmer over medium heat, stirring often as it thickens to the desired consistency, but do not boil. Serve the sauce and the plain yogurt separately, to be spooned over the meat and vegetables at the table. ❋ Serves 6

Seasoned Lamb Chops with Green Beans in a Garlicky Tomato Sauce

I raised sheep for about 30 years. The freezer was always well stocked with lamb. Indulging my creative spirit and spurred on by economic necessity, I created many recipes along the way. This is one of my favorite recipes because it's so good and easy to make.

2 tablespoons olive oil

6 thinly cut lamb chops or steaks

1 onion, diced

4 tablespoons minced garlic

1 tablespoon grated lemon zest

1 teaspoon dried oregano

½ teaspoon ground cinnamon

½ teaspoon freshly ground black pepper

½ teaspoon crushed fennel seed

½ cup red wine

1 (14-ounce) can chopped tomatoes, with juice

3 cups frozen Italian green beans

Heat the oil in the pressure cooker over medium heat. Add the meat, cook until browned on both sides, and set aside. Add the onions and garlic to the cooker and cook, stirring, until slightly softened, about 3 minutes. Add the lemon zest, oregano, cinnamon, pepper, and fennel seed, frying until the spices begin to sizzle. Deglaze the cooker with the wine, scraping up all those crusty, brown bits from the bottom. Return the chops to the cooker and add the tomatoes and green beans. Lock the lid in place. Bring to 15psi over high heat, immediately reduce the heat to the lowest possible setting to stabilize and maintain that pressure, and cook for 5 minutes. Remove from the heat and use the natural release method (see page 31) to depressurize. Carefully open the lid after the pressure drops. Transfer the chops to a serving plate, and serve the green beans and tomato sauce in a separate bowl. ✳ Serves 6

Zippy Lamb Rib Chops

Using lamb rib chops, sometimes called lamb riblets, this recipe is a great way to enjoy lamb.

2 tablespoons olive oil

6 to 8 lamb rib chops

1 (14-ounce) can chopped tomatoes, with juice

¼ cup balsamic vinegar

¼ cup apple butter

¼ cup molasses

2 tablespoons minced garlic

1 teaspoon spicy brown mustard

1 (1-ounce) packet dried onion soup mix

Heat the oil in the pressure cooker over medium heat. Add the meat, cook until browned on both sides, and set aside. Add all of the remaining ingredients and ½ cup water to the cooker, stirring well. Return the chops to the cooker, turning once to coat with the sauce. Lock the lid in place. Bring to 15psi over high heat, immediately reduce the heat to the lowest possible setting to stabilize and maintain that pressure, and cook for 4 minutes. Remove from the heat and use the natural release method (see page 31) to depressurize. Carefully open the lid after the pressure drops. Transfer the chops to a serving plate and keep warm in a low oven. Skim off any excess fat from the surface of the sauce. Bring the sauce to a boil, uncovered, and cook, stirring, until reduced by half. Spoon the sauce over the chops and serve. ✳ Serves 4

Lamb Chops with au Gratin Potatoes

Mouthwatering! Just writing this recipe makes me drool as I remember how delicious it was the last time.

Step One: The Cheddar Cheese Sauce
2 tablespoons butter
2 tablespoons all-purpose flour
¼ teaspoon salt
Louisiana hot sauce to taste
1 cup milk
1 cup shredded sharp cheddar cheese

Melt the butter in the pressure cooker over medium heat. Add the flour, salt, and hot sauce, blending to a smooth paste. Slowly stir in the milk, and continue stirring constantly as the sauce thickens. Add the cheese, stirring until melted. Adjust the seasonings to taste and transfer the sauce to a serving dish. Rinse the cooker before proceeding to the next step.

Step Two: The Chops and Potatoes
2 tablespoons butter
6 loin lamb chops
1 onion, halved and thinly sliced
2 tablespoons minced garlic
¼ teaspoon ground nutmeg
½ cup dark beer
6 potatoes, peeled and sliced ½ inch thick
¼ cup sliced green onion tops, for garnish

Heat the butter in the pressure cooker over medium heat. Add the meat, cook until browned on both sides, and set aside. Add the onions and garlic to the cooker and cook, stirring, until slightly softened, about 3 minutes. Sprinkle with the nutmeg. Deglaze the cooker with the beer, scraping up all those crusty, brown bits from the bottom. Place the chops on the bottom of the cooker and layer the potatoes on top. Lock the lid in place. Bring to 15psi over high heat, immediately reduce the heat to the lowest possible setting to stabilize and maintain that pressure, and cook for 6 minutes. Remove from the heat and use the natural release method (see page 31) to depressurize. Carefully open the lid after the pressure drops. Drain the potatoes and chops into a colander, reserving the broth. Transfer the chops to a serving dish. Return the cheese sauce to the pressure cooker and heat over medium heat. Thin the sauce if necessary with a little of the reserved broth. Return the potatoes to the cooker, mixing gently with the sauce, and heat thoroughly. Transfer the potatoes and cheese sauce to a serving bowl and garnish with the green onions.

✳ Serves 4

Tangy Lemon-Curried Lamb Chops with Steamed Rice

These make a perfect weeknight meal that's fast, flavorful, and easy. This is a simple recipe with sensational flavors that will appeal even to people who think they do not like lamb.

> 2 tablespoons butter
> 6 lamb chops, ½ inch thick
> ⅓ cup fresh lemon juice
> ⅓ cup balsamic vinegar
> ¼ cup soy sauce
> 1 tablespoon curry powder
> 1 teaspoon sugar
> 1 cup uncooked long-grain white rice
> Lemon wedges, for garnish

Heat the butter in the pressure cooker over medium heat. Add the meat, cook until browned on both sides, and set aside. Add the lemon juice, vinegar, soy sauce, curry powder, and sugar and stir. Return the chops to the cooker, turning once to coat. Rinse the rice in cold water to remove the starch. Place the rice in a metal pan that will fit loosely inside the pressure cooker and add 1½ cups water. Use foil helper handles (see page 42) to place the pan on top of the chops, adjusting the position so it's as level as possible. Lock the lid in place. Bring to 15psi over high heat, immediately reduce the heat to the lowest possible setting to stabilize and maintain that pressure, and cook for 6 minutes. Remove from the heat and use the nat-ural release method (see page 31) to depressurize. Carefully open the lid after the pressure drops. Transfer the rice to a serving dish and fluff with a fork. Arrange the chops on a plate with the lemon wedges. Skim off any excess fat from the surface of the sauce. Bring the sauce to a boil, uncovered, and let it reduce by half, stirring frequently to avoid burning. Serve the curry sauce in a small bowl to be spooned over the chops. ❋ **Serves 4**

Lamb Stifado

This is my version of a popular Greek stew, a dish that traditionally is made with braised meat and small whole onions. I use a variety of chopped onions to add a mild sweetness to the sauce. The mouthwatering aroma of this stew more than lives up to the promise of great taste.

Step One: The Spices
2 bay leaves
1 (1-inch) cinnamon stick
6 allspice berries
10 whole cloves
10 whole black peppercorns
1 teaspoon fennel seed

Make up a spice bag using all of the ingredients, tying them in a square of cheesecloth or putting them in a tea ball.

Step Two: The Meat and Sauce
2 tablespoons butter
2 pounds boneless lamb, cut into 2-inch cubes
4 onions, mixed varieties if possible, chopped
2 tablespoons minced garlic
1 teaspoon ground cumin
½ teaspoon ground nutmeg
½ cup red wine
1 (28-ounce) can chopped tomatoes, with juice
1 (3-ounce) can tomato paste
¼ cup red wine vinegar

Heat the butter in the pressure cooker over medium heat. Add the meat, cook until browned on both sides, and set aside. Add the onions and garlic to the cooker and cook, stirring, until slightly softened,

about 3 minutes. Add the cumin and nutmeg, frying until the spices begin to sizzle. Deglaze the cooker with the wine, scraping up all those crusty, brown bits from the bottom. Add the tomatoes, tomato paste, vinegar, and 1 cup water, stirring to mix. Return the meat to the cooker, pushing the pieces to the bottom of the sauce, and lock the lid in place. Bring to 15psi over high heat, immediately reduce the heat to the lowest possible setting to stabilize and maintain that pressure, and cook for 12 minutes. Remove from the heat and use the natural release method (see page 31) to depressurize. Carefully open the lid after the pressure drops. ✳ Serves 4 to 5

Serving Suggestion: Serve over hot cooked rice, noodles, or couscous.

Lamb Vindaloo

This is a lovely, warming, spicy curry, and it's one of my favorite recipes because it's so easy to make, but still full of all the wonderfully complex flavors associated with Indian cooking. Depending on my mood of the moment, I serve this over plain rice, boiled potatoes, or a rice pilaf, which can be prepared in a second pressure cooker at the same time that the main dish is cooking.

Step One: The Spices
1 tablespoon ground coriander
1 tablespoon ground cumin
1 tablespoon ground turmeric
2 teaspoons paprika
½ teaspoon ground cinnamon
¼ teaspoon cayenne pepper
1 (1-inch) piece fresh ginger, peeled
    and minced

Heat the pressure cooker over medium heat and add all of the ingredients, stirring constantly until they begin to release their oils and turn slightly darker, about 2 minutes. Take care that the spices do not burn. Remove the spices to a small bowl and set aside.

Step Two: The Lamb and Sauce
3 tablespoons butter
2 pounds boneless lamb, cut into 2-inch cubes
2 onions, chopped
1 green bell pepper, seeded and chopped
4 tablespoons minced garlic
½ cup red wine
⅓ cup red wine vinegar

Heat the butter in the pressure cooker over medium heat. Add the meat, cook until browned on both sides, and set aside. Add the onions, green peppers, and garlic to the cooker and cook, stirring, until slightly softened, about 3 minutes. Deglaze the cooker with the wine, scraping up all those crusty, brown bits from the bottom. Add the vinegar and ½ cup water, stirring to mix. Return the meat and spices to the cooker and lock the lid in place. Bring to 15psi over high heat, immediately reduce the heat to the lowest possible setting to stabilize and maintain that pressure, and cook for 15 minutes. Remove from the heat and use the natural release method (see page 31) to depressurize. Carefully open the lid after the pressure drops, transfer to a serving bowl, and serve. ✳ Serves 4 to 5

Fish and Seafood

HEARD ANY GOOD FISH STORIES LATELY? Well, here's one: fish is not only good for your health, but also easy to prepare in a pressure cooker. Did you know that there are so many varieties of fish and seafood that if you ate one variety daily for 4½ months, you still wouldn't have tried them all? With today's modern pressure cooker, flaky and delicate fish can be cooked in just a few minutes. Because it cooks in steam, without any flipping and turning, each piece of fish remains perfectly intact. Even shrimp and scallops can find a place in pressure cookery.

Several kinds of white-meat fish have a very light, delicate flavor and flaky, tender texture. These include cod, haddock, and yellowtail snapper. Catfish, sea trout, and whiting also have white meat, and a slightly stronger flavor. Fish with light meat and a richer flavor with moderately firm texture include Alaskan pollock, giant sea bass, mahi mahi, ocean perch, rainbow trout, red snapper, and walleye. For fish with darker meat with moderate flavor and a moderately firm texture, try pink or silver salmon, lake trout, freshwater perch, striped bass, mackerel, tuna, shark, and swordfish.

Clams, mussels, and oysters, and even lobster, can be steamed in the pressure cooker. Keep in mind that shellfish cooks much faster than finfish. Scallops and shrimp usually take 3 to 5 minutes, depending on the size. When fully cooked, scallops will be firm and white, and shrimp will turn pink.

You can cook many kinds of fish and seafood confidently in the pressure cooker by keeping a few basic tips in mind. First, remember that leaner, white-meat fish work best with moist-heat cooking methods, which enable the fish to maintain moisture and tenderness. For fattier fish, use the rack so the oils can drain away as the fish cooks. Leaving the skin on one side of the fillet and cooking it skin side down will help hold the meat together. If one end is thinner than the other, fold it under for more uniform cooking. As a rule of thumb, I generally allow about 3 minutes minimum cooking time for every inch of thickness. When fully cooked, fish will be opaque and will flake easily with a fork. One of the best things about pressure cooking fish is that it can be cooked straight from the freezer, as long as the fish is in individual pieces and not all clumped together.

Salmon Croquettes with Lemon Cheese Sauce

When I was a child, this was served when my mother invited her lady friends for luncheon. They arrived en masse, fashionably attired in prim pillbox hats, white gloves, and handbags that matched their shoes. Banned from the festivities, all of us kids waited expectantly for the ladies to depart so that we could fall

upon any remaining Salmon Croquettes and gobble them up with gusto. I serve this with Lemon Rice (page 372) and steamed peas (see Pressure-Cooking Time Charts, page 86).

Step One: Prepare the Ramekins

Butter for the bowls
⅔ cup very fine cheese cracker crumbs
½ teaspoon ground turmeric
½ teaspoon paprika
¼ teaspoon freshly ground black pepper

Generously butter the insides of 4 (6-ounce) ramekins. In a small bowl, combine the cracker crumbs, turmeric, paprika, and pepper. Evenly press and pat the seasoned cracker crumbs around the inside of the buttered ramekins. Reserve the remaining cracker mixture.

Step Two: The Croquettes

1 (16-ounce) can salmon, drained and liquid reserved
1 cup fine dry bread crumbs
½ cup minced onion
½ cup finely chopped green bell pepper
¼ cup minced cilantro
Freshly ground black pepper to taste
2 large eggs, well beaten

Remove the bones and any pieces of dark skin from the salmon. Flake the salmon and mix all of the ingredients together in a large bowl, adding some of the reserved liquid if needed, until it is a smooth consistency. Spoon the salmon mixture into the buttered ramekins, mounding the tops so they are rounded. Place the rack in the cooker and add 1 cup water. Arrange the ramekins on the rack and lock the lid in place. Bring to 15psi over high heat, immediately reduce the heat to the lowest possible setting to stabilize and maintain that pressure, and cook for 8 minutes. Remove from the heat and use the natural release method (see page 31) to depressurize. Carefully open the lid after the pressure drops. Use long-handled tongs to remove the ramekins from the cooker. Run a thin knife around the inside of each ramekin and unmold to individual serving plates.

Step Three: The Lemon Cheese Sauce

2 large egg yolks
2 tablespoons butter
2 tablespoons all-purpose flour
1 cup scalded milk (heated just until bubbles
  form around the edge of the pan)
Dash of Tabasco sauce
Freshly ground black pepper to taste
1/2 cup shredded cheddar cheese
2 tablespoons fresh lemon juice
Cilantro leaves, for garnish

Beat the egg yolks in a small bowl and set aside. Mix the butter and flour into a smooth paste in a small heavy skillet and cook over medium heat for about 2 minutes, stirring to make a smooth consistency. Add the hot milk, Tabasco sauce, and pepper, stirring as it thickens. Whisk ¼ cup of the hot milk mixture into the egg yolks until smooth, and then slowly add the egg yolk mixture to the remaining milk mixture in the skillet, stirring constantly until smooth. Add the cheese and lemon juice and stir until hot and bubbly, about 2 minutes. Pour the sauce over the salmon croquettes, add a dusting of the reserved cracker mixture, and top each with a perfect cilantro leaf. ✳ Serves 4

Cook's Note: Cook the ramekins in 2 batches, or use 2 pressure cookers, if they will not fit in your cooker.

Tuna and Rice

Remember your mama serving this dish? It's just plain and simple comfort food, and, best of all, it's quick and easy to prepare, cooking in just 4 minutes and in just one pot—what could be better, faster, or easier?

2 tablespoons butter
1 onion, chopped
1 cup chopped celery
1 (4-ounce) can mushrooms, drained
1 (10-ounce) can cream of mushroom soup
2 (6-ounce) cans tuna
1 cup frozen green peas
1 cup uncooked long-grain rice

Heat the butter in a pressure cooker over medium heat. Add the onions, celery, and mushrooms, and cook, stirring, for about 3 minutes. Add the remaining ingredients and 2 cups water, mixing thoroughly. Lock the lid in place. Bring to 15psi over high heat, immediately reduce the heat to the lowest possible setting to stabilize and maintain that pressure, and cook for 4 minutes. Remove from the heat and use the natural release method (see page 31) to depressurize. Carefully open the lid after the pressure drops. Fluff with a fork before serving. ✳ Serves 4 to 5

New England Clam Chowder

It's cold out there! Warm up with a big, steaming bowl of homemade New England clam chowder, a dish that's definitely soup-as-a-meal. Serve with big chunks of crusty bread slathered with butter, and dig in.

> 1 quart shucked clams, or 3 (10-ounce) cans minced clams, with juice
> ½ pound thickly sliced bacon
> 1 onion, minced
> 3 stalks celery, sliced
> 1 (8-ounce) bottle clam juice
> 2 potatoes, diced
> 1 teaspoon salt
> ½ teaspoon freshly ground black pepper
> ½ teaspoon ground thyme
> ¼ teaspoon cayenne pepper
> 1 bay leaf
> 2 cups milk
> 2 cups cream or half-and-half
> ½ cup instant potato flakes
> Chopped green onion tops, for garnish
> Paprika, for garnish

If using fresh clams, drain and chop the clams, reserving the liquid. Heat the pressure cooker over medium heat and fry the diced bacon until it is crisp and the fat is rendered. Remove the bacon and set aside. Drain off all but 2 tablespoons of the bacon fat. Add the minced onions and the celery to the hot bacon fat in the cooker and cook, stirring, until softened, about 3 minutes. Add the clams, clam juice, potatoes, salt, black pepper, thyme, cayenne pepper, and bay leaf. Stir to mix and lock the lid in place. Bring to 15psi over high heat, immediately reduce the heat to the lowest possible setting to stabilize and maintain that pressure, and cook for 5 minutes. Remove from the heat and use the natural release method (see page 31) to depressurize. Carefully open the lid after the pressure drops. Discard the bay leaf. Add the milk, cream, and most of the crumbled bacon, reserving some bacon for garnishing. Bring to a simmer over medium heat, but do not boil. Add the potato flakes a little at a time, stirring as the chowder thickens to the desired consistency. Pour into a heated soup tureen and garnish with the green onions, a dusting of paprika, and the extra crumbled bacon. ✳ Serves 4 to 5

Variation: Add ½ pound fresh fish, shrimp, crabmeat, or lobster to make seafood chowder.

California Lobster Gazpacho with Avocado and Pico de Gallo

Gazpacho is like chili—everyone has a certain way of doing it, and while there are an endless number of recipes, very few utilize the speed of pressure cooking to perfectly steam the lobster. Served with chunks of crusty bread, avocado, and the piquant flavors of spicy pico de gallo, a Mexican relish similar to fresh salsa, this makes a flavorful, cool, and delicious summer meal when it's too hot to cook. Although gazpacho is traditionally served cold, the food police will not come knocking at your door if you decide to serve it as a hot soup.

Step One: The Pico de Gallo

3 Roma tomatoes, chopped

4 green onions, green and white parts, chopped

⅓ cup chopped cilantro leaves

2 tablespoons fresh lemon juice

The night before, or at least several hours in advance, combine all of the ingredients in a small bowl. Cover and refrigerate until needed. By the way, this makes a great dip for tortilla or corn chips, too.

Step Two: The Lobster Tails

2 (6-ounce) fresh or frozen lobster tails

If the lobster tails are frozen, do not thaw. Arrange the tails on the rack of the pressure cooker and add ½ cup water. Lock the lid in place. Bring to 15psi over high heat, immediately reduce the heat to the lowest possible setting to stabilize and maintain that pressure, and cook for 5 minutes. Remove from the heat and use the cold water release method (see page 30) to depressurize. Carefully open the lid immediately after the pressure drops. The shells should be bright red, and the meat tender and white. Remove the lobsters, and, when cool enough to handle, remove and discard the shells and coarsely chop the meat. Cover and chill in the refrigerator until ready to use.

Step Three: The Gazpacho

2 (28-ounce) cans chopped tomatoes, with juice

1 onion, minced

½ cucumber, peeled, seeded, and chopped

½ green bell pepper, seeded, and chopped

1 tablespoon minced garlic

¼ cup finely chopped cilantro leaves

1 tablespoon minced fresh basil

½ teaspoon ground cumin

½ teaspoon cayenne pepper

Juice of 1 lemon

Zest of 1 lemon

2 Hass avocados, peeled and sliced,
    for garnish

Sour cream, for garnish

Working in batches, puree the tomatoes, onions, cucumber, green pepper, and garlic in a blender. Add the cilantro, basil, cumin, cayenne pepper, lemon juice, and lemon zest and blend until very smooth. Transfer everything to a large bowl, taste, and adjust the seasonings. Gently fold the lobster into the tomato mixture. Cover and chill for 4 to 8 hours to allow the flavors to blend. To serve, ladle into chilled serving bowls, garnish each with 2 slices of avocado arranged in an × pattern, add a spoonful of Pico de Gallo, and top with a dollop of sour cream. ❋ Serves 4

Variation: This soup is also delicious with prawns and clams, either instead of, or combined with, the lobster.

Halibut with Fennel, Purple Onions, and Yellow Tomatoes in Packets

Yellow tomatoes aren't grown in large commercial quantities, but a few usually appear in the specialty produce section of most supermarkets from August through late November. With a mild, somewhat sweet flavor, they are a deep, almost school-bus-yellow color and come in a variety of sizes, from the size of grapes to huge 1-pounders. The vivid white of the halibut, the bright yellow of the tomatoes, and the rich green of the fennel leaves give this dish flavor and make it visually appealing as well.

> 4 tablespoons (½ stick) butter
> 1 large yellow tomato, sliced ¼ inch thick
> 1 fennel bulb, thinly sliced
> 1 purple onion, thinly sliced
> 4 halibut fillets, up to 1 inch thick
> Lemon pepper to taste
> 4 teaspoons fresh lemon juice
> 1 lemon, sliced, for garnish
> 4 sprigs fennel fronds

Butter the centers of 4 sheets of aluminum foil. For each of the 4 packets, place 1 slice of yellow tomato and 1 slice of fennel on the buttered surface. Break apart 1 onion slice and arrange the onion rings on top of the tomato and fennel slices. Place a halibut fillet on top of the onion rings and season each with the lemon pepper and 1 teaspoon of the lemon juice. Arrange 2 lemon slices on top of each fillet and add a sprig of the fennel fronds. Fold the edges of each packet over, sealing the top, and then fold up the sides, sealing the packets tightly. Place the rack in the pressure cooker and add ½ cup water. Arrange the packets on the rack, overlapping as little as possible. Lock the lid in place. Bring to 15psi over high heat, immediately reduce the heat to the lowest possible setting to stabilize and maintain that pressure, and cook for 6 minutes. Remove from the heat and use the cold water release method (see page 30) to depressurize. Carefully open the lid immediately after the pressure drops. Use long-handled tongs to remove the packets from the pressure cooker. Use kitchen scissors to open each packet, being especially careful of escaping steam. Transfer the contents of each packet to individual serving plates. ✳ **Serves 4**

Serving Suggestion: Serve with hot rice.

Lemon Shrimp and Scallops with Fettuccine Parmesana

As unconventional as international diplomacy, this elegant entrée is a blend of complex Asian aromas, fragrant with tender, lemon-infused seafood served over creamy Italian pasta. If you're looking for a spectacular main dish for a very special occasion, this recipe is designed to impress. The key to pressure cooking delicate seafood is the cold water release method (see page 30), which immediately stops the cooking process and delivers tender and succulent results every time.

Step One: The Fettuccine
8 ounces uncooked fettuccine

While preparing the seafood and sauce below, cook the pasta according to package directions. When the seafood and sauce have finished cooking, drain the pasta, but do not rinse.

Step Two: The Seafood
2 pounds medium-size shrimp, shelled, deveined, and tails removed
½ pound small scallops of uniform size, no thicker than the shrimp
2 tablespoons butter
1 cup minced onion
2 tablespoons minced garlic
1 (8-ounce) bottle clam juice, or 1 cup fish stock
½ cup white wine
⅓ cup soy sauce
¼ cup hoisin sauce
Juice of 1 lemon
Zest of 1 lemon
2 spears lemongrass (available in the Asian section of your supermarket), bruised
¼ cup finely chopped cilantro leaves
2 teaspoons minced fresh ginger
½ teaspoon red pepper flakes
½ teaspoon ground turmeric
¼ teaspoon cayenne pepper

Rinse the seafood and pat dry. Heat the butter in the pressure cooker over medium heat. Add the onion and garlic and cook, stirring, until soft, about 3 minutes. Add the clam juice, wine, soy sauce, hoisin sauce, lemon juice, lemon zest, lemongrass, cilantro, ginger, red pepper flakes, turmeric, and cayenne pepper, stir to mix, and bring to a rapid boil. Add the shrimp and scallops and lock the lid in place. Bring to 15psi over high heat, immediately reduce the heat to the lowest possible setting to stabilize and maintain that pressure, and cook for 3 minutes. Remove from the heat and use the natural release method (see page 31) to depressurize. Carefully open the lid immediately after the pressure drops. Drain through a colander, reserving the broth. Discard the lemongrass. Add the seafood mixture to the drained fettuccine, but do not stir yet, and cover with a regular lid.

Step Three: The Parmesan Sauce
4 tablespoons (½ stick) butter
2 tablespoons all-purpose flour
1½ cups half-and-half
⅓ cup freshly grated Parmesan cheese

Melt the butter in the pressure cooker over medium heat. Add the flour and cook over medium-high heat, stirring constantly until it begins to turn a light golden color. Slowly add the reserved seafood broth, whisking with a wire whisk until the mixture begins to thicken, about 2 minutes. Slowly add the half-and-half, whisking the sauce as it continues to thicken. Remove from the heat and stir in the cheese. Add the cheese sauce to the seafood and fettuccine, tossing gently to coat. Serve hot. ✳ **Serves 6**

Teriyaki-Braised Scallops with Shoestring Vegetables

Succulent scallops in concentrated teriyaki sauce nestled on a mound of delicate and tender-crisp spring vegetables make for an elegant presentation. Add fluffy steamed rice for a more substantial meal, if desired.

Step One: The Scallops
1 pound scallops of uniform size
½ cup sliced green onions, white and
   green parts
¼ cup finely chopped cilantro leaves
½ teaspoon red pepper flakes
½ teaspoon ground turmeric
¼ teaspoon cayenne pepper
⅓ cup teriyaki sauce
¼ cup soy sauce
3 tablespoons rice wine vinegar
Juice of 1 lime
Grated zest of 1 lime

Place the scallops in the pressure cooker and add all of the remaining ingredients. Toss to coat, and let the scallops marinate in the cooker while preparing the vegetables.

Step Two: The Shoestring Vegetables
1 carrot, peeled and cut into thin sticks about 3
   inches in length
1 small red onion, sliced into half-circles
½ pound fresh green beans, trimmed
1 red bell pepper, seeded and cut into thin strips
1 yellow bell pepper, seeded and cut into
   thin strips
1 zucchini, cut into thin sticks about
   3 inches in length
1 tablespoon toasted sesame seeds,
   for garnish

Place all the cut vegetables on top of the scallops in the pressure cooker. Stir to mix and lock the lid in place. Bring to 15psi over high heat, immediately reduce the heat to the lowest possible setting to stabilize and maintain that pressure, and cook for 2 minutes. Remove from the heat and use the cold water release method (see page 30) to depressurize. Carefully open the lid immediately after the pressure drops. Drain through a colander, reserving the broth. Transfer the scallops and vegetables to a serving dish and keep warm in a low oven while making the sauce.

Step Three: The Sauce
2 tablespoons cold butter, cut into bits

Pour the reserved broth back into the cooker and boil rapidly, uncovered, until reduced to about 2 tablespoons. Whisk in the butter, bit by bit, until the sauce is smooth. Pour the sauce over the scallops and vegetables, and serve. ✳ **Serves 4**

Braised Seafood Salad with Grapefruit Salsa and Poppy Seed Dressing

Complex textures and flavors bring sophistication to this elegant seafood salad that makes a refreshing main dish for a hot summer meal, or a special light lunch or brunch. Beginning the day before, I prepare this in stages, allowing plenty of time for the flavors to mingle. Serve with a crusty loaf of fresh bread.

Step One: The Poppy Seed Dressing

½ cup mayonnaise

1 tablespoon sugar

1 tablespoon balsamic vinegar

1 teaspoon poppy seeds

1 teaspoon curry powder

¼ teaspoon cayenne pepper

Combine all of the ingredients and refrigerate in a covered container for at least 4 hours or overnight to allow the flavors to marry.

Step Two: The Seafood

10 large shrimp, shelled, deveined, and tails removed

8 scallops, quartered

⅓ pound lump crabmeat

½ cup ruby red grapefruit juice

1 tablespoon soy sauce

Rinse the seafood and pat dry. Add the seafood pieces to the pressure cooker and stir in the grapefruit juice and soy sauce. Lock the lid in place. Bring to 15psi over high heat, immediately reduce the heat to the lowest possible setting to stabilize and maintain that pressure, and cook for 3 minutes. Remove from the heat and use the cold water release method (see page 30) to depressurize. Carefully open the lid immediately after the pressure drops. Drain and refrigerate the seafood mixture in a covered container until well chilled.

Step Three: The Grapefruit Salsa

2 small ruby red grapefruits

1 Roma tomato, seeded and chopped

½ cup sliced celery

⅓ cup finely chopped walnuts

3 green onions, white and green parts, thinly sliced

2 tablespoons chopped cilantro leaves

2 tablespoons minced fresh ginger

1 teaspoon seeded and minced jalapeño chile

Cut the grapefruits in half and remove the flesh with a small sharp knife. Separate the grapefruit sections from the pith and chop into small pieces. Retain the grapefruit shells. Combine the grapefruit sections with all of the remaining ingredients. Add the chilled seafood mixture to the salsa just before serving, tossing gently and then spooning into the grapefruit shells.

Step Four: The Salad

4 cups mixed salad greens of choice

Toss the salad greens with the Poppy Seed Dressing and mound on each plate. Place the seafood-filled grapefruit shells beside the salad greens and serve.

✳ Serves 4 to 5

Curried Crab Quiche Cups

Unlike traditional quiches, these little babies have no crusts; they're cooked in ramekins.

> 3 large eggs, separated
> 1 (12-ounce) can evaporated milk
> 2 tablespoons all-purpose flour
> 1 teaspoon curry powder
> ½ teaspoon cayenne pepper
> ¼ teaspoon dry mustard
> 1 (6-ounce) can crabmeat, drained and flaked
> 1 cup shredded Swiss cheese
> ½ cup stale bread crumbs
> ¼ cup minced green onion tops
> Butter, for the ramekins
> Paprika, for garnish

Use an electric mixer to beat the egg whites until they form stiff peaks. In a large mixing bowl, combine the egg yolks, milk, flour, curry powder, cayenne pepper, and dry mustard, whisking until smooth. Stir the crabmeat, cheese, bread crumbs, and minced green onions into the milk and egg mixture. Gently fold in the stiffly beaten egg whites. Butter the ramekins and spoon the crab mixture into each one. Place the rack in the cooker and add ½ cup water. Place the ramekins directly on the steamer rack or tray. Lock the lid in place. Bring to 15psi over high heat, immediately reduce the heat to the lowest possible setting to stabilize and maintain that pressure, and cook for 5 minutes. Remove from the heat and use the cold water release method (see page 30) to depressurize. Carefully open the lid immediately after the pressure drops. Carefully lift each ramekin out of the pressure cooker using long-handled tongs. Transfer the Quiche Cups to a serving plate and dust a little paprika over the top of each. ✳ Serves 4

Packets of Scallops and Green Beans with Tarragon-Caper Butter

A super-quick and tasty dish that makes a great romantic dinner for two.

> 2 tablespoons butter
> ½ cup chopped onion
> 1 tablespoon drained capers, patted dry
> 1 tablespoon chopped fresh tarragon
> ½ pound sea scallops, rinsed and patted dry
> ½ pound fresh green beans, trimmed
> 2 teaspoons fresh lemon juice
> Lemon wedges, for garnish

Heat the butter in a pressure cooker over medium-high heat. Add the onion, capers, and tarragon and cook, stirring, for about 2 minutes. Using a slotted spoon, transfer to a small bowl. Double 2 sheets of aluminum foil for each of the packets. Spritz nonstick cooking spray on the center of each foil square. Divide the scallops and green beans on each square of foil. Divide the onion mixture between each packet, and add 1 teaspoon of lemon juice to each. Fold the foil to form 2 sealed packets, creasing the seams to make a tight closure. Place the rack in the cooker and add ½ cup water. Arrange the foil packets on the rack, leaving space around each for steaming. Lock the lid in place. Bring to 15psi over high heat, immediately reduce the heat to the lowest possible setting to stabilize and maintain that pressure, and cook for 5 minutes. Remove from the heat and use the cold water release method (see page 30) to depressurize. Carefully open the lid immediately after the pressure drops. Remove the packets with long-handled tongs and place on individual serving plates. Open each packet carefully, arrange the scallops and green bean mixture on each serving plate, and drizzle with the sauce before discarding the foil packets. Garnish with lemon wedges.

✳ Serves 2

Salmon Steaks in Smoky Maple Balsamic Glaze

Real maple syrup and good-quality balsamic vinegar are the key ingredients in giving the salmon a delightfully fragrant and delicious twist.

Step One: The Salmon Steaks
4 (6-ounce) salmon steaks, about 1 inch thick
½ cup white wine
1 tablespoon soy sauce
½ teaspoon garlic powder
½ teaspoon lemon pepper

Rinse the salmon and pat dry. Mix the wine, soy sauce, garlic powder, and lemon pepper in the pressure cooker and add the salmon steaks, turning once to coat. Lock the lid in place. Bring to 15psi

over high heat, immediately reduce the heat to the lowest possible setting to stabilize and maintain that pressure, and cook for 6 minutes. Remove from the heat and use the cold water release method (see page 30) to depressurize. Carefully open the lid immediately after the pressure drops. Transfer the salmon to a serving dish and keep warm in a low oven.

Step Two: The Maple Balsamic Glaze
2 tablespoons pure maple syrup
2 tablespoons balsamic vinegar
½ teaspoon liquid smoke, or more to taste

Add the syrup and vinegar to the broth in the pressure cooker and bring the mixture to a rapid boil, uncovered, stirring often until the sauce is reduced and slightly thickened. Stir in the liquid smoke and spoon the glaze on the salmon steaks just before serving. ✳ Serves 4

Seafood à la King

An old-fashioned dish that was quite popular in the '50s, but has all but disappeared from today's menus. You'll slip back in time with this creamy, delicate seafood dish, a delicious change from the day-to-day chicken and beef routine.

> 1½ pounds firm fish fillets, such as cod, haddock, or whiting, cut into 1½-inch pieces
> 2 cups frozen green peas
> 1 cup diced red bell pepper
> ½ cup minced onion
> ¼ cup fresh lemon juice
> 1 (10-ounce) can cream of mushroom soup

Place the fish, peas, bell peppers, onions, and lemon juice in a pressure cooker and add ¼ cup water. Stir to mix and lock the lid in place. Bring to 15psi over high heat, immediately reduce the heat to the lowest possible setting to stabilize and maintain that pressure, and cook for 3 minutes. Remove from the heat and use the cold water release method (see page 30) to depressurize. Carefully open the lid immediately after the pressure drops. Add the canned soup, stirring to blend, and simmer over low heat until heated through.

❋ Serves 4 to 5

Serving Suggestion: This is traditionally served over toast points or split biscuits, but try it with fluffy white rice or buttered noodles.

Variations

Shrimp à la King: Substitute an equal amount of shelled frozen shrimp.

Crab à la King: Substitute an equal amount of shelled fresh or frozen crabmeat.

Lobster à la King: Substitute an equal amount of shelled fresh or frozen lobster meat.

Mixed Seafood à la King: Substitute varying amounts of fish and shelled seafood according to preferences.

Seafood Gumbo

It's gumbo, you know, so add whatever turns you on, mon! Substitute oysters, scallops, chicken—anything that appeals to your taste; that's part of the fun of making gumbo. The crab boil spice mixture is the key ingredient, so do not omit it. The aroma will whet your appetite, and the added spiciness gives an uncommon punch to this popular seafood dish.

Step One: The Roux
> 8 tablespoons (1 stick) butter
> ½ cup all-purpose flour

In a cast-iron skillet, melt the butter over medium-high heat. Stir in the flour. Cook, stirring often, until the roux is deep chocolate brown in color, 15 to 20 minutes. Watch the mixture closely and adjust the heat to keep it from burning. Remove from the heat and set aside.

Step Two: The Rice
> 2 cups uncooked long-grain white rice
> 2 (14-ounce) cans chicken broth
> 1 (3-ounce) can tomato paste

Place all of the ingredients in the pressure cooker, add 2 cups water, and stir to mix. Lock the lid in place. Bring to 15psi over high heat, immediately reduce the heat to the lowest possible setting to stabilize and maintain that pressure, and cook for 4 minutes. Remove from the heat and use the natural release method (see page 31) to depressurize. Carefully open the lid after the pressure drops. If you have 2 pressure cookers, the rice can be cooked at the same time as the gumbo. If using 1 cooker, cook the rice first and transfer the rice mixture to a bowl to keep warm in a low oven.

Step Three: The Gumbo

3 tablespoons butter

1 red or purple onion, diced

2 cups sliced celery

6 cloves minced garlic

2 (28-ounce) cans chopped tomatoes, with juice

1½ cups sliced fresh or frozen okra pods

1 green bell pepper, seeded and chopped

1 cup whole kernel corn

½ pound lump crabmeat or lobster

½ pound medium-size shrimp, shelled, deveined, and tails removed

½ pound smoked ham or kielbasa, cut into ½-inch slices

2 to 3 tablespoons filé powder

2 to 3 tablespoons crab boil spice blend

½ teaspoon red pepper flakes

Heat the butter in a large pressure cooker over medium heat. Add the onions, celery, and garlic and cook, stirring, until soft, about 3 minutes. Add the remaining ingredients and 6 cups water. Stir to mix and lock the lid in place. Bring to 15psi over high heat, immediately reduce the heat to the lowest possible setting to stabilize and maintain that pressure, and cook for 3 minutes. Remove from the heat and use the cold water release method (see page 30) to depressurize. Carefully open the lid immediately after the pressure drops. Slowly add a little of the hot seafood pan juices to the roux, stirring to make a smooth paste. Simmer the gumbo over medium heat and add the roux a little at a time, stirring until thickened. Adjust the seasonings to taste. To serve, place a big mound of rice in each soup bowl and ladle on the gumbo.

✳ Serves 4 to 5

Cook's Note: Usually found in the spice section of your supermarket or at the fish counter or the butcher's case, premade seafood or crab boil seasoning is easier to use than purchasing all of the ingredients to make your own crab boil spice blend. If you can't locate crab boil spice in your local grocery, try this blend. It is quite good in any fish or seafood soup or stew.

Crab Boil Spice Blend

¼ cup pickling spices

¼ cup sea salt

2 tablespoons whole black peppercorns

2 tablespoons red pepper flakes

1 tablespoon whole mustard seeds

1 tablespoon whole celery seeds

2 teaspoons ground ginger

2 teaspoons dried oregano

5 bay leaves

Add all the ingredients to a food processor and pulse until the mixture forms a coarse powder. Store in a tightly sealed container.

Beer-Steamed Clams with Lemon-Garlic Butter Sauce

The name pretty much gives away the recipe, but this is my favorite way to eat clams (and most other seafood). Be sure to have crusty French bread on hand to soak up the excess as you dip the clams in the Lemon-Garlic Butter Sauce.

Step One: The Lemon-Garlic Butter Sauce
8 tablespoons (1 stick) butter
⅓ cup fresh lemon juice
2 teaspoons garlic powder
1 teaspoon whole cloves

Make this sauce the day before to allow plenty of time for the unique flavor of the cloves to penetrate the butter. Combine all of the ingredients in a heat-proof dish and microwave for 1 minute, or until the butter has melted. Cover with plastic wrap and refrigerate until serving time. Before serving, reheat in the microwave and scoop out the cloves with a slotted spoon. Serve in small individual bowls for each place at the table.

Step Two: The Clams
1½ to 2 pounds fresh soft-shell or littleneck
    clams in the shell
½ cup beer
⅓ cup fresh lemon juice

Wash the clams several times to remove the sand. Place the rack in the pressure cooker, add the beer and lemon juice, and stir. Add the clams to the cooker, distributing them evenly. Lock the lid in place. Bring to 15psi over high heat, immediately reduce the heat to the lowest possible setting to stabilize and maintain that pressure, and cook for 3 minutes. Remove from the heat and use the cold water release method (see page 30) to depressurize. Carefully open the lid immediately after the pressure drops. Do not overcook—the clams will be barely open; longer cooking will cause them to become tough and rubbery. Serve with the Lemon-Garlic Butter Sauce. ✳ Serves 4

Cook's Note: Because clams vary so much in size and shape, the actual amount used will depend on the size of your pressure cooker. Remember the Ten Golden Rules of Pressure Cookery (see page 23) and do not fill the cooker more than ⅔ full. If needed, cook the clams in 2 batches, using the same cooking liquid for each batch.

Quick Creamed King Crab with Crunchy Crumb Topping

Faster than you can order take-out and quicker than you can drive through the fast food line, you can use the pressure cooker to quickly precook the crab. Add the easy, creamy sauce, sprinkle on the topping, and pop under the broiler for a great meal. Serve with a wild rice pilaf, or over egg noodles, and a fresh salad.

Step One: The Crumb Topping
1½ cups bread crumbs, or 3 slices day-old white
    bread, crumbled in the food processor
4 tablespoons (½ stick) melted butter
1 teaspoon garlic powder

Combine all of the ingredients in a bowl, tossing gently, and set aside.

Step Two: The Crab
4 tablespoons (½ stick) butter
½ cup chopped red onions
1 pound king crabmeat, chopped into bite-size
    chunks
2 tablespoons fresh lemon juice
2 tablespoons soy sauce
Salt and freshly ground black pepper to taste
½ cup heavy cream

Heat the butter in the pressure cooker over medium heat. Add the onions and cook, stirring, until soft, about 3 minutes, but do not let them brown. Add the crabmeat, lemon juice, soy sauce, salt, pepper, and ⅓ cup water. Stir to mix and lock the lid in place. Bring to 15psi over high heat, immediately reduce the heat to the lowest possible setting to stabilize and maintain that pressure, and cook for 2 minutes. Remove from the heat and use the cold water release method (see page 30) to depressurize. Carefully open the lid immediately after the pressure drops. Preheat the broiler. Use a slotted spoon to transfer the crab mixture to a buttered 9 × 13-inch baking dish. Add the cream to the broth remaining in the pressure cooker, stirring until blended, and pour over the crab mixture. Top with the bread crumb mixture, spreading it evenly over the top of the crab. Place the pan under the broiler and watch closely until the topping forms a crisp crust. ✳ Serves 4

Beans and Legumes

MOST VARIETIES OF DRIED BEANS are mild tasting on their own, and even adding additional flavoring ingredients like hot peppers or vinegar does not make an appreciable difference. The secret to a great-tasting bowl of beans or legumes is the broth. Without a good broth as the foundation, dry beans will remain bland and tasteless.

I use a two-step method when preparing dry beans. The broth should be cooked first, separate from the dried beans, because of the wide differences in cooking times. For example, ham hocks require 40 minutes of cooking time in the pressure cooker, but presoaked navy beans need only about 10. Cooked at the same time, the beans would be extremely overcooked and they would lose their shape and texture long before the ham hocks were edible. Overcooking legumes destroys many of their important nutrients.

I've included two versions of my Best Bean Broth (page 342): one with smoked meat, and a meatless version as well. The broth can certainly can be prepared several days ahead of time and refrigerated to make it easier on the cook. The broth can also be packaged and frozen for later use, which makes it even more convenient. Best of all, broth is so simple to make, requiring little prep work and hardly any effort to produce a wonderfully rich and flavorful base for your next pot of beans.

Best Bean Broth with Smoked Meat

This is the universal meat broth that will add much-needed flavor to any pot of dried beans.

- 2 tablespoons oil
- 1 onion, quartered
- 3 cloves garlic, crushed
- 1 large meaty ham bone, or 2 pounds smoked meat (pork hocks, neck bones, smoked turkey legs and wings)
- 1 jalapeño chile, seeded and halved
- 1 cup packed chopped cilantro stems and leaves
- Celery leaves from about 3 stalks
- 2 bay leaves
- 10 whole black peppercorns
- ½ teaspoon red pepper flakes
- 1 teaspoon liquid smoke

Heat the oil in a large pressure cooker over medium heat. Add the onions and garlic and cook, stirring, until they are slightly browned and beginning to caramelize, about 6 minutes. Add the remaining ingredients except for the liquid smoke to the pressure cooker, add enough cold water to cover completely, and lock the lid in place. Bring to 15psi over high heat, immediately reduce the heat to the lowest possible setting to stabilize and maintain that pressure, and cook for 40 minutes. Remove from the heat and use the natural release method (see page 31) to depressurize. Carefully open the lid after the pressure drops. Strain the broth through a colander into a large bowl. Pick the meat from the bones. Discard all the leftover vegetables, bones, and pieces of fat. Skim off any excess fat from the surface of the broth, return the meat to the broth, and stir in the liquid smoke. The meaty broth is ready to use for your dried bean recipe or to freeze for later use. ✳ Serves 6

Best Bean Broth without Meat

For those who prefer a meatless version, use this rich and flavorful vegetable broth when cooking dried beans.

- 2 tablespoons olive oil
- 2 onions, quartered
- 1 green bell pepper, seeded and coarsely chopped
- 2 garlic cloves, crushed
- 8 cups coarsely chopped assorted vegetables (no potatoes or cabbage), including trimmings, such as asparagus stalks, broccoli stems, leeks, greens, winter squash, turnips, parsnips, rutabagas, etc.
- 3 carrots, split and halved
- 3 stalks celery with leaves, cut into 3-inch lengths, plus 3 additional sprigs celery leaves
- 1 jalapeño chile, seeded and halved
- 1 small bunch cilantro
- 2 bay leaves
- 10 whole black peppercorns
- ½ teaspoon red pepper flakes

Heat the oil in a large pressure cooker over medium heat. Add the onions, bell peppers, and garlic and cook, stirring, until they are nicely browned and slightly caramelized, about 6 minutes. Add ½ cup water and deglaze the pot, scraping up all those crusty, brown bits from the bottom. Throw all the remaining ingredients into the pressure cooker and add 8 cups cold water. Stir to mix and lock the lid in place. Bring to 15psi over high heat, immediately reduce the heat to the lowest possible setting to stabilize and maintain that pressure, and cook for 15 minutes. Remove from the heat and use the natural release method (see page 31) to depressurize. Carefully open the lid after the pressure drops. Strain the broth through a wire sieve into a large bowl. Discard all the vegetable pieces and skim off any visible fat from the surface of the broth. Use this broth immediately, or freeze for later use.

✳ Serves 6

Peas Porridge with Ham

Imagine a cold winter evening and a big mug of hot split pea soup. It goes together like . . . well, like two peas in a pod! My split pea soup is very thick; it's more like a hearty porridge than a thinner soup. If you prefer a thinner version, add more water or broth to get the consistency you prefer. Split peas, which do not need to be presoaked, have a tendency to thicken up after cooking, and if you're fortunate enough to have any leftovers, you may need to add a little more liquid after a night in the fridge.

1 quart Best Bean Broth (page 342) or
   2 (14-ounce) cans of chicken broth
2 tablespoons butter

1 pound dried split green peas
2 cups cubed cooked or leftover ham
1 carrot, coarsely grated
1 onion, minced
1 tablespoon minced garlic
1 teaspoon ground thyme
1 teaspoon ground sage

Add the Best Bean Broth to a large pressure cooker. Add all of the remaining ingredients and enough water to cover by 2 inches. Stir to mix, and lock the lid in place. Bring to 15psi over high heat, immediately reduce the heat to the lowest possible setting to stabilize and maintain that pressure, and cook for 10 minutes. Remove from the heat and use the natural release method (see page 31) to depressurize. Carefully open the lid after the pressure drops. Check the beans for doneness; a fully cooked bean can be easily mashed between your finger and thumb. If necessary, return to 15psi over high heat, immediately reduce the heat to the lowest possible setting to stabilize and maintain that pressure, and cook for a few more minutes. Remove from the heat and use the natural release method (see page 31) to depressurize. Carefully open the lid after the pressure drops. For a thicker, creamier porridge, transfer 2 cups of peas and broth to a blender or food processor and puree until smooth. Return the puree to the cooker and simmer over low heat until the released starches thicken the broth naturally and the porridge is heated through.

✳ Serves 6

Navy Bean Soup

The small white navy bean gets its name from the fact that it has been a primary fare served in United States Navy mess halls since the mid-1800s. There's nothing quite like a bowl of comforting homemade bean soup to satisfy a hungry appetite. It's hearty, nutritious, and very easy to make, and served with a pan of hot cornbread, this is the perfect meal for a cold-weather supper.

1 pound dried navy, great Northern, or small
    white beans, presoaked for 4 hours
2 tablespoons butter
1 onion, chopped
2 tablespoons minced garlic
1 teaspoon red pepper flakes
½ teaspoon freshly ground black pepper
4 cups Best Bean Broth (page 342), or
    2 (14-ounce) cans of chicken broth

Drain and rinse the presoaked beans and add them to a large pressure cooker. Add all of the remaining ingredients plus enough water if needed to cover the ingredients by 2 inches. Stir to mix and lock the lid in place. Bring to 15psi over high heat, immediately reduce the heat to the lowest possible setting to stabilize and maintain that pressure, and cook for 10 minutes. Remove from the heat and use the natural release method (see page 31) to depressurize. Carefully open the lid after the pressure drops. Check the beans for doneness; a fully cooked bean can be easily mashed between your finger and thumb. If necessary, return to 15psi over high heat, immediately reduce the heat to the lowest possible setting to stabilize and maintain that pressure, and cook for a few more minutes. Remove from the heat and use the natural release method (see page 31) to depressurize. Carefully open the lid after the pressure drops. For a thicker, creamier texture, remove 2 cups of the beans and a little broth and puree or mash them together, then return the puree to the remaining soup in the cooker. Adjust the seasonings to taste, and serve.
❊ **Serves 6**

Variation: Add 2 cups cooked, chopped ham or sausage to the beans before cooking, if desired.

Black-eyed Peas 'n' Greens

A genuine Southern staple, this wonderfully rich-tasting and very colorful dish comes together with black-eyed peas, greens, and some chopped ham. Serve with a pan of hot cornbread for a filling and very inexpensive meal.

2 tablespoons olive oil
1 onion, chopped
2 carrots, sliced
2 tablespoons minced garlic
1 bunch collard greens or your choice of other
    leafy greens in any combination
1 pound dried black-eyed peas
2 cups diced cooked ham or sausage
1 jalapeño chile, seeded and finely minced
2 bay leaves
4 cups Best Bean Broth (page 342), stock, or
    water

Heat the oil in a large pressure cooker over medium heat. Add the onions and garlic and cook, stirring, until soft, about 3 minutes. Prepare the collards by rinsing each leaf, cutting off the stems, and removing any blemished sections and the large central rib. Cut the leaves in half, lengthwise, cutting through the center vein. Stack the leaves on top of one another and roll them up tightly from the longest side; they should look like a long green cigar. Slice across the roll, making diagonal cuts about 1 inch apart, and then add the cut greens to the cooker. For a large quantity of greens, add a little water to the cooker and steam them with the regular lid until they begin to wilt and reduce in volume. Rinse and pick through the peas, then add them to the pressure cooker. Add all of the remaining ingredients, plus enough water if needed to cover the ingredients by 2 inches. Stir to mix and lock the lid in place. Bring to 15psi over high heat, immediately reduce the heat to the lowest possible setting to stabilize and maintain that pressure, and cook for 10 minutes. Remove from the heat and use the natural release method (see page 31) to depressurize. Carefully open the lid after the pressure drops. Check the different beans for doneness; a fully cooked pea can be easily mashed between your finger and thumb. If necessary, return to 15psi over high heat, immediately reduce the heat to the lowest possible setting to stabilize and maintain that pressure, and cook for 3 more minutes. Remove from the heat and use the natural release method (see page 31) to depressurize. Carefully open the lid after the pressure drops. Adjust the seasonings to taste, and serve. ✳ Serves 6

Zesty Pinto Beans

Enjoy a taste of south-of-the-border flavor with this zesty combination of pinto beans, snappy Mexican peppers, and pungent spices.

> 1 pound dried pinto beans, presoaked
>   for 4 hours
> 2 (10-ounce) cans Rotel tomatoes with chiles
> 1 onion, chopped
> 2 mild poblano, pasilla, or Anaheim chiles,
>   seeded and chopped
> 1 jalapeño chile, seeded and chopped
> 2 cloves garlic, crushed
> ½ cup chopped packed cilantro stems and leaves,
>   plus extra for garnish (optional)
> ½ teaspoon red pepper flakes
> 4 cups Best Bean Broth (page 342), stock,
>   or water
> Sour cream, for garnish (optional)

Drain and rinse the presoaked beans and add them to a large pressure cooker. Add all of the remaining ingredients except for the sour cream, plus enough water if needed to cover the ingredients by 2 inches. Stir to mix and lock the lid in place. Bring to 15psi over high heat, immediately reduce the heat to the lowest possible setting to stabilize and maintain that pressure, and cook for 10 minutes. Remove from the heat and use the natural release method (see page 31) to depressurize. Carefully open the lid after the pressure drops. For a thicker, creamier texture, remove 2 cups of the beans and a little broth and puree or mash them together, then return the puree to the remaining beans in the cooker. Adjust the seasonings to taste. Ladle into serving bowls and top with a spoonful of sour cream and a sprinkling of minced cilantro, if desired.

✳ Serves 6

Barbecued Beans

These barbecued beans are flavored with a tangy sauce and make the perfect accompaniment to a picnic lunch or side dish with a slab of ribs or a juicy steak.

4 slices bacon

1 onion, chopped

1 teaspoon minced garlic

1 pound small dried white (navy) beans, presoaked for 4 hours

1 cup ketchup

½ cup vinegar

½ cup firmly packed dark brown sugar

⅓ cup molasses

1 teaspoon liquid smoke

Dash of hot sauce, or more to taste

½ teaspoon dry mustard

Fry the bacon in the pressure cooker over medium heat until crisp, and set aside on paper towels to drain. Drain off all but about 2 tablespoons of the bacon fat. Add the onions and garlic to the remaining bacon fat and cook, stirring, until slightly softened, about 3 minutes. Drain and rinse the beans. Add the beans and enough water to cover the beans by 2 inches. Stir to mix and lock the lid in place. Bring to 15psi over high heat, immediately reduce the heat to the lowest possible setting to stabilize and maintain that pressure, and cook for 12 minutes. Remove from the heat and use the natural release method (see page 31) to depressurize. Carefully open the lid after the pressure drops. Check for doneness; a fully cooked bean can be easily mashed between your finger and thumb. If necessary, lock the lid back in place, return to 15psi over high heat, immediately reduce the heat to the lowest possible setting to stabilize and maintain that pressure, and cook for an additional 3 minutes, or until the beans are soft. Remove the cooker from the heat and use the natural release method (see page 31) to depressurize. Carefully open the lid after the pressure drops. Drain off any remaining liquid. Combine the ketchup, vinegar, brown sugar, molasses, liquid smoke, hot sauce, and dry mustard, stirring to mix. Simmer over low heat, uncovered, until heated through. Adjust the seasonings to taste, and serve. ✳ Serves 6

Refried Beans: Frijoles Refritos

In Spanish, the name means "well-fried," and the canned version can't compare to home-made. I really love refried beans because they are inexpensive and so versatile for use in dips, as a side dish, or in casseroles or all kinds of Mexican-style recipes. Once you've made your first batch of refried beans, you'll never go back to the canned version again. This recipe takes just a few minutes to cook, and you get to tailor the fat, sodium, and seasonings to your liking. Freeze in 2-cup portions for later use in recipes calling for refried beans.

Step One: The Basic Beans

1 pound dried pinto beans, presoaked
    for 4 hours
1 jalapeño chile, seeded and minced
½ cup chopped packed cilantro stems
    and leaves
4 cups Best Bean Broth (page 342), stock,
    or water

Drain and rinse the presoaked beans and add them to a large pressure cooker. Add all of the remaining ingredients, plus enough water if needed to cover the ingredients by 2 inches. Stir to mix and lock the lid in place. Bring to 15psi over high heat, immediately reduce the heat to the lowest possible setting to stabilize and maintain that pressure, and cook for 12 minutes. Remove from the heat and use the natural release method (see page 31) to depressurize. Carefully open the lid after the pressure drops.

Check for doneness; a fully cooked bean can be easily mashed between your finger and thumb. If necessary, return to 15psi over high heat, immediately reduce the heat to the lowest possible setting to stabilize and maintain that pressure, and cook for a few more minutes. Remove from the heat and use the natural release method (see page 31) to depressurize. Carefully open the lid after the pressure drops. Drain the beans, reserving the broth to freeze for later use. Spread the beans out on a cookie sheet and mash with a potato masher until all the beans reach the consistency you desire. Don't try to pulverize every single bean; leave some larger pieces of beans in the mash.

Step Two: The Refried Beans

¼ cup bacon drippings
2 onions, finely chopped
1 mild poblano, pasilla, or Anaheim chile,
    seeded and chopped
2 cloves garlic, crushed
1½ teaspoons ground cumin

Heat the bacon drippings in the pressure cooker over medium heat. Add the onions, chiles, and garlic and cook, stirring, until they are very soft, 8 to 10 minutes. Add the mashed beans and cumin. Stir to mix, adding a bit of bean broth if necessary to keep them at the desired consistency. Adjust the seasonings to taste, and serve as a side dish with a Mexican-style meal, or use in recipes calling for refried beans, such as tacos and burritos, or try it as a bean dip with a bag of your favorite corn chips. ✳ Serves 6

Frijoles Tostadas

This is a perfect use for your homemade Refried Beans (page 347). Tostadas are like flat tacos made with crisp corn tortillas topped with refried beans, lettuce, tomatoes, cheese, a little salsa, sour cream, and avocado slices.

> ½ cup corn oil
> 12 corn tortillas
> 3 cups Refried Beans (page 347), heated to serving temperature
> 1 cup bottled thick and chunky salsa
> 2 cups shredded sharp cheddar cheese
> 1 head lettuce, shredded
> 2 to 3 tomatoes, diced
> 1 avocado, sliced
> ½ cup chopped green onions, white and green parts
> Sour cream, for garnish

In a small frying pan, heat the oil over medium heat until a drop of water sizzles immediately when added to it. Fry each tortilla lightly on one side. Turn and fry lightly on the other side until lightly browned and crisp. Drain on paper towels. Repeat with all 12 tortillas. Spread a generous amount of refried beans on each tortilla. Add a spoonful of salsa and some cheese, and then add any of the other toppings according to taste.

※ Makes 12 tostadas

Variation: Add cooked and shredded chicken or beef, if desired.

Mexican Pinto Bean Dip

Forget all those bland canned bean dips—here's a classic that captures the flavor of Mexico without being too hot. It leaves a lingering spicy memory that will have you coming back for more!

> 2 cups Refried Beans (page 347)
> 1 cup shredded sharp cheddar cheese
> ½ cup bottled salsa, hot or mild
> 2 tablespoons minced garlic
> 1 teaspoon ground cumin
> 1 teaspoon chili powder
> ½ teaspoon red pepper flakes
> Tortilla chips, for serving

Mix all of the ingredients in a heatproof bowl and microwave until the cheese has melted, 4 to 5 minutes. Stir and adjust the seasonings to taste. Serve hot with assorted tortilla chips. ※ Serves 6

Black-Eyed Peas and Greens with Sausage

Neither a pea nor a bean, the lowly black-eyed pea is actually a lentil. Black-eyed peas, also known as cowpeas, are often associated with a New Year's Day tradition popular in the southern United States. Some people hope that eating a big bowl of black-eyed peas on New Year's Day will bring them good luck for the upcoming year. My Southern relatives say that the black-eyed peas stand for coins, which is all well and good, but greens must be added to the pot for real cash, and don't forget to add a pan of cornbread, which represents gold. Don't wait until New Year's to serve black-eyed peas; they are wonderful cold-weather food, with the bonus that they do not need to be soaked before cooking, which makes them a very quick, inexpensive, and simple choice for dinner. Here's a substantial meal, and, with just a hint of heat from the sausages, it's pleasing to a wide range of palates.

2 tablespoons olive oil

1 pound sweet or hot Italian sausages, casings removed

1 onion, chopped

2 tablespoons minced garlic

1 bunch collard greens or your choice of other leafy greens (approximately 20 leaves)

1 pound dried black-eyed peas

2 bay leaves

1 tablespoon dried basil

1 tablespoon dried oregano

¼ teaspoon crushed red pepper flakes

2 (14-ounce) cans chopped tomatoes with juice

Heat a large pressure cooker over medium heat and brown the sausage meat until crumbled. Add the onions and garlic and cook, stirring, until soft, about 3 minutes. Prepare the greens by rinsing each leaf and cutting out or paring the large rib. Cut each leaf in half lengthwise, cutting through the center vein. Stack the leaves top of one another and roll them up tightly; they should look like a long green cigar. Slice across the roll, making diagonal cuts about 1 inch apart, and then add the cut greens to the cooker. Add the black-eyed peas, bay leaves, basil, oregano, and red pepper flakes to the pressure cooker. Add the tomatoes plus enough water if needed to cover all the ingredients by 1 inch. Stir to mix and lock the lid in place. Bring to 15psi over high heat, immediately reduce the heat to the lowest possible setting to stabilize and maintain that pressure, and cook for 10 minutes. Remove from the heat and use the natural release method (see page 31) to depressurize. Carefully open the lid after the pressure drops. Check the beans for doneness; a fully cooked bean can be easily mashed between your finger and thumb. If necessary, return to 15psi over high heat, immediately reduce the heat to the lowest possible setting to stabilize and maintain that pressure, and cook for a few more minutes. Remove from the heat and use the natural release method (see page 31) to depressurize. Carefully open the lid after the pressure drops. Adjust the seasonings to taste, and serve.

✳ Serves 6

Hoppin' John

A distant cousin of the Spanish paella and Creole jambalaya, Hoppin' John, also known as Happy Jack or Happy John, can trace its origins back to Africa, and it is another popular Southern recipe served on New Year's Day. Fresh steamed greens and cornbread usually accompany this dish. This old family recipe started out with a mixture of black-eyed peas, rice, bacon, salt pork, and rice. Over time, I've updated it with smoked sausage and added some seasonings that spiced up the original version just a bit. Choose the meat you prefer based on how hot you like it.

2 tablespoons olive oil

2 cups diced cooked ham, Louisiana hot links, andouille sausage, or smoked kielbasa

1 onion, chopped

1 green bell pepper, seeded and chopped

3 stalks celery, diced

1 tablespoon minced garlic

1 pound dried black-eyed peas

1 cup uncooked long-grain white rice

1 (10-ounce) can diced tomatoes with chiles

1 jalapeño chile, seeded and minced

½ cup packed chopped cilantro leaves

1 teaspoon filé powder

1 teaspoon dried thyme leaves

1 teaspoon ground cumin

2 bay leaves

Heat the oil in a large pressure cooker over medium heat. Add the meat, cook until browned on all sides, and set aside. Add the onions, bell peppers, celery, and garlic to the cooker and cook, stirring, until softened, about 3 minutes. Add all of the remaining ingredients and enough water to cover by 3 inches. Stir to mix and lock the lid in place. Bring to 15psi over high heat, immediately reduce the heat to the lowest possible setting to stabilize and maintain that pressure, and cook for 10 minutes. Remove from the heat and use the natural release method (see page 31) to depressurize. Carefully open the lid after the pressure drops. Check for doneness; the beans should mash easily between your finger and thumb. If necessary, lock the lid back in place, return to 15psi over high heat, immediately reduce the heat to the lowest possible setting to stabilize and maintain that pressure, and cook for an additional 3 minutes. Remove from the heat and use the natural release method (see page 31) to depressurize. Carefully open the lid after the pressure drops. Discard the bay leaves, adjust the seasonings to taste, and serve. ✳ Serves 6

Rice

ICE IS RICE IS RICE, you say, but there are many varieties of rice, and each has a different shape, color, taste, and aroma.

Types of Rice

Long-grain rice: The most commonly used type in the U.S., it is available in white and brown varieties. Cooked grains are separate, and 4 to 5 times longer than they are wide. Long-grain rice is light and fluffy, perfect for plain steamed rice and pilaf dishes.

Medium-grain rice: A popular rice in Asian and Latin American recipes, it is available in white and brown varieties. It has a shorter, wider kernel than long-grain rice; the cooked grains are tender and have a tendency to cling together.

Short-grain rice: Also called Oriental, Japanese, sushi, and pudding rice, short-grain rice is almost round. It has the highest percentage of starch, making it "sticky" when cooked so that it clumps together.

Varieties of Rice

Arborio	Arborio is a starchy white rice, with a short, plump, almost round grain, grown mainly in the Po Valley of Italy. Traditionally used for cooking the Italian dish risotto, it also works well for paella and rice pudding. Arborio absorbs up to 5 times its weight in liquid as it cooks, which results in grains of a creamy consistency.
Calrose	This medium-grained white rice from California cooks up plump, moist, and tender and makes a good substitute for Arborio rice used in risottos. The texture is stickier than long-grain rice, but fluffier than short-grain rice, making this versatile rice perfect for a variety of Asian dishes, too.
Basmati	Basmati, the most famous aromatic rice, is grown in India and Pakistan. It has a distinctive buttery aroma and is sometimes called "popcorn" rice. Unlike other types of rice, the grains elongate rather than plump as they cook. It is fairly expensive, but the California version, Calmati, is an excellent substitute.
Jasmine	Jasmine is a traditional long-grain white rice grown in Thailand. It has a soft texture and is similar in flavor to basmati rice. Jasmine rice is also grown in the United States, and is available in both white and brown forms.
Brown	Brown rice retains the bran that surrounds the kernel, making it chewier, nuttier, and richer in nutrients than white rice.
Wild	Not really a rice at all, wild rice is native to North America and grows predominantly in the Great Lakes region. This large seed is in the grass family and has been eaten since prehistoric times.

Mexican Steak and Red Rice

Carne asada e rojo arroz, as some would say, is a combination of traditional bold Mexican flavors, and the pressure cooker infuses them into the meat and rice. There's little prep work involved with this one-pot recipe, which is another bonus you will appreciate. Serve this as a main dish with a side of refried beans and some warm flour tortillas. It also doubles as a filling for a Mexican tortilla wrap, rolled into warmed flour tortillas with the addition of shredded lettuce, chopped tomatoes, and grated cheese.

½ cup all-purpose flour

½ teaspoon salt

½ teaspoon freshly ground black pepper

2 pounds round or chuck steak, cut into
    serving portions

2 tablespoons oil

1 onion, chopped

2½ cups spicy tomato juice

1 green bell pepper, seeded and diced

1 (10-ounce) can Rotel (or similar brand) diced
    tomatoes with chiles

1 (3-ounce) can tomato paste

2 teaspoons ground cumin

½ teaspoon red pepper flakes

1 cup uncooked long-grain white rice,
    well rinsed

In a plastic bag, mix the flour, salt, and pepper and add the meat, shaking gently until coated. Heat the oil in the pressure cooker over medium heat. Add the meat, cook until browned on all sides, and set aside. Add the onions to the cooker and cook, stirring, until clear, about 3 minutes. Deglaze the cooker with the tomato juice, scraping up all those crusty, brown bits from the bottom. Add the green pepper, tomatoes with chiles, tomato paste, cumin, and red pepper flakes, stirring until mixed. Return the meat to the cooker, arranging the pieces in layers, if needed, on top of the other ingredients. Lock the lid in place. Bring to 15psi over high heat, immediately reduce the heat to the lowest possible setting to stabilize and maintain that pressure, and cook for 15 minutes. Remove from the heat and use the quick or cold water release method (see page 30) to depressurize. Carefully open the lid after the pressure drops. Remove the meat from the cooker. Add the rice, stirring to mix, and return the beef to the cooker, laying it on top of the rice mixture. Lock the lid back in place, return to 15psi over high heat, immediately reduce the heat to the lowest possible setting to stabilize and maintain that pressure, and cook for 4 minutes longer. Remove from the heat and use the natural release method (see page 31) to depressurize. Carefully open the lid after the pressure drops. Remove the beef to a serving plate. Fluff up the rice with a fork and serve in a separate bowl. ✴ Serves 4 to 5

Beefy Spanish Rice

When I was growing up, my family served Spanish rice all the time, but our version included ground beef and was more like a casserole dish. Much later, it surprised me to learn that when most people think of serving Spanish rice, it's just a recipe for gussied-up rice sans meat. Without apology, I like mine better and hope you will, too.

> 1 pound lean ground beef
> 1 onion, chopped
> 1 green bell pepper, seeded and diced
> 1 mild Anaheim or pasilla chile, seeded and chopped
> 1 (28-ounce) can crushed tomatoes, with juice
> 2 (10-ounce) cans Rotel (or similar brand) chopped tomatoes with chiles
> 1 (3-ounce) can tomato paste
> 1 cup packed minced cilantro leaves
> 2 tablespoons chili powder, or to taste
> 1 tablespoon minced garlic
> 2 teaspoons ground cumin
> ½ teaspoon red pepper flakes, or to taste
> 1 cup uncooked long-grain white rice, well rinsed
> Green onion tops, thinly sliced, for garnish

Heat the pressure cooker over high heat. Add the meat and cook until it is well browned and crumbled. Add the onions, bell peppers, and chiles to the cooker and cook, stirring, for about 3 minutes. Add the crushed tomatoes, tomatoes with chiles, tomato paste, cilantro, chili powder, garlic, cumin, and red pepper flakes. Rinse the rice 3 or 4 times to remove the starchy coating. Add the rice and 2 cups water, stirring to blend. Lock the lid in place. Bring to 15psi over high heat, immediately reduce the heat to the lowest possible setting to stabilize and maintain that pressure, and cook for 6 minutes. Remove from the heat and use the natural release method (see page 31) to depressurize. Carefully open the lid after the pressure drops. Sprinkle the green onions on top of each serving.

> ✳ Serves 6 generously

Variation:

> Beefy-Cheesy Spanish Rice: Prepare the recipe as above. After removing the lid, stir in 2 cups grated sharp cheddar cheese. Cover with a regular lid and serve when the cheese has melted.

Chicken and Rice with Mushrooms

The timeless one-pot chicken and rice dish is a family tradition in most American homes, and it must be the quintessential definition of a classic comfort food. Everyone's got a different recipe, but this pressure-cooker method will be ready before you can set the table.

> 2 tablespoons olive oil
> 4 boneless, skinless chicken breasts
> 1 onion, chopped

½ pound fresh mushrooms, washed and sliced

½ cup dry white wine

1 (14-ounce) can chicken broth

1 (10-ounce) can cream of chicken soup

1 cup uncooked long-grain white rice, well rinsed

1 teaspoon dried tarragon leaves

½ teaspoon freshly ground black pepper

2 tablespoons chopped fresh parsley, for garnish

Heat the oil in the pressure cooker over high heat. Add the chicken and cook until golden brown on both sides. Remove the chicken from the cooker, cut into 1-inch strips, and set aside. Add the onions and mushrooms to the cooker and cook, stirring, until soft, about 3 minutes. Deglaze the cooker with the wine, scraping up all those crusty, brown bits from the bottom. Add the broth, soup, rice, tarragon, and pepper, stirring to mix. Return the chicken to the cooker and lock the lid in place. Bring to 15psi over high heat, immediately reduce the heat to the lowest possible setting to stabilize and maintain that pressure, and cook for 5 minutes. Remove from the heat and use the natural release method (see page 31) to depressurize. Carefully open the lid after the pressure drops. Transfer the chicken and rice mixture to a serving bowl and garnish with the parsley just before serving.

❋ Serves 6

Foolproof Rice

This is a foolproof method for cooking rice in a pressure cooker. Just imagine—no more burned rice! Just use my PIP (Pan in Pot) method (see page 89) for perfect, fluffy rice, and best of all, it is so quick and easy. Before cooking, the rice must be rinsed. For perfect long-grain white rice, with each grain separate and not all clumped together, rinsing is the secret. When long-grain white rice is thoroughly rinsed before cooking, the starchy coating that causes the rice to stick together is removed. Place the rice in a large bowl and pour in cold tap water to cover. Swish the grains with your fingertips to release starches and to encourage any husks to float to the surface. Pour off the milky water and repeat. Wash two or three times, until the water runs clear. There is no need to rinse brown or wild rice, and short- and medium-grained white rice are usually not rinsed either. For sticky, Asian-style rice, omit the rinsing.

To serve 3 cups cooked rice, begin with 1 cup uncooked long-grain white rice. Rinse the rice. Position the rack in the cooker and add ½ cup water. In a small metal bowl that fits inside the cooker, mix the uncooked long-grain white rice and 1½ cups water or other cooking liquid. Use foil helper handles (see page 42) to place the bowl in the cooker. Lock the lid in place. Bring to 15psi over high heat, immediately reduce the heat to the lowest possible setting to stabilize and maintain that pressure, and cook for exactly 4 minutes. Remove from the heat and use the natural release method (see page 31) to depressurize. Carefully open the lid after the pressure drops. Remove the bowl and fluff the rice with a fork before serving.

Use the Pressure-Cooking Time Charts (see page 89) for the correct ratio of water (or other liquid) to rice and the cooking times for different varieties of rice.

Porcupine Meatballs with Mushroom Gravy

I learned to make "porcupines" with a cream sauce, although there is another school of folks that prefers them in a tomato sauce. To add another twist to this classic pressure-cooker recipe, here is an option made with mushroom gravy.

1 pound lean ground beef

1 small onion, minced

½ cup uncooked long-grain white rice,
** well rinsed**

½ teaspoon freshly ground black pepper

1 large egg, slightly beaten

2 (14-ounce) cans beef broth

1 (1-ounce) packet dried onion soup mix

½ pound fresh mushrooms, washed and sliced

3 tablespoons cornstarch

In a large bowl, mix the ground beef, onions, rice, and pepper with the beaten egg. Shape the meat mixture into ping-pong-size balls—use an ice-cream scoop to make them all the same size. Heat the pressure cooker over medium heat, add the meatballs, cook until well browned on all sides, and set aside on paper towels. Deglaze the cooker with the broth, scraping up all those crusty, brown bits from the bottom. Mix in the onion soup packet and add the mushrooms, stirring well. Return the meatballs to the pressure cooker, but don't crowd; stack them in 2 layers if necessary. The upper layer of meatballs must be completely covered with liquid; add water or more broth if necessary. Lock the lid in place. Bring to 15psi over high heat, immediately reduce the heat to the lowest possible setting to stabilize and maintain that pressure, and cook for 6 minutes. Remove from the heat and use the natural release method (see page 31) to depressurize. Carefully open the lid after the pressure drops. Remove the meatballs to a serving plate and keep warm in a low oven. Bring the broth to a gentle simmer over low heat in the open pressure cooker. Mix the cornstarch with ⅓ cup cold water and slowly stir into the simmering broth, but do not boil. Stir the broth as it thickens, and adjust the seasonings to taste. Pour the mushroom gravy into a separate serving dish to be ladled over the meatballs. ✳ Serves 4 to 5

Chicken and Rice with Baby Brussels Sprouts

This is a very colorful "one-pot meal" dinner dish that looks as good as it tastes. I use the interrupted cooking method (see page 38) to separate the longer-cooking chicken from the rest of the ingredients, which require less cooking time.

Step One: The Chicken

2 tablespoons butter or margarine

4 boneless, skinless chicken breasts

1 onion, chopped

1 red bell pepper, seeded and chopped

1 tablespoon minced garlic

Heat the butter in the pressure cooker over medium heat. Add the chicken, cook until browned on both sides, and set aside. Add the onions, bell peppers, and garlic to the cooker and cook, stirring, until slightly softened, about 3 minutes. Place the rack in the bottom of the cooker and add ½ cup water. Arrange the chicken breasts on top of the rack. Lock the lid in place. Bring to 15psi over high heat, immediately reduce the heat to the lowest possible setting to stabilize and maintain that pressure, and cook for 4 minutes. Remove from the heat and use the quick or cold water release method (see page 30) to depressurize. Carefully open the lid after the pressure drops. Transfer the chicken to a cutting board and cut into bite-size pieces. Remove the rack.

Step Two: The Rice and Sprouts

1 cup uncooked long-grain white rice, well rinsed

1 (14-ounce) can chicken broth

1 (10-ounce) can whole kernel corn, drained

1 pound small Brussels sprouts, halved lengthwise

Add the rice, broth, and corn to the cooker and stir. Return the chicken to the cooker and layer the Brussels sprouts on top. Lock the lid back in place, return to 15psi over high heat, immediately reduce the heat to the lowest possible setting to stabilize and maintain that pressure, and cook for 4 minutes. Remove from the heat and use the natural release method (see page 31) to depressurize. Carefully open the lid after the pressure drops. Fluff up the rice mixture with a fork and transfer to a serving bowl. ✳ **Serves 6**

Chicken and Saffron Rice

Saffron is the little dried stigmas of the crocus flower. It takes 70,000 flowers to produce 1 pound of saffron, and 1 acre will yield only about 10 pounds of saffron. Saffron may be the world's most expensive spice, but thankfully you only need to use a very small amount to achieve that wonderful buttery yellow color.

¼ teaspoon saffron threads, crushed

1 tablespoon olive oil

4 boneless, skinless chicken breast halves

1 onion, chopped

1 cup diced green bell pepper

1 tablespoon minced garlic

1 teaspoon paprika

½ teaspoon salt

¼ teaspoon freshly ground black pepper

¼ teaspoon dried oregano

1 bay leaf

1 cup uncooked long-grain white rice, well rinsed

⅓ cup dry white wine

1 (14-ounce) can chicken broth

1 (8-ounce) can diced tomatoes, drained

Chopped green onion tops, for garnish

Lemon wedges, for garnish

In a small bowl, combine the saffron threads and a little hot water and let them soak. Heat the oil in the pressure cooker over medium heat. Add the chicken pieces, cook until golden brown on both sides, and set aside. Add the onions and green peppers to the cooker and cook, stirring, until slightly softened, about 3 minutes. Add the garlic, paprika, salt, pepper, oregano, and bay leaf. Add the rice, stirring to coat with the oil. Add the soaked saffron threads and soaking water and deglaze the cooker, scraping up all those crusty, brown bits from the bottom. Add the wine, chicken broth, and tomatoes, stir, and return the chicken pieces to the cooker. Lock the lid in place. Bring to 15psi over high heat, immediately reduce the heat to the lowest possible setting to stabilize and maintain that pressure, and cook for 8 minutes. Remove from the heat and use the natural release method (see page 31) to depressurize. Carefully open the lid after the pressure drops. Remove and discard the bay leaf. Transfer the chicken pieces to a serving platter and mound the rice beside them. Garnish with the green onions and lemon wedges. ❄ Serves 6

Creole Chicken and Rice

This spicy one-pot meal—redolent of rosemary and garlic—looks and smells as though you slaved for hours, but don't tell anyone that it takes only 6 minutes in the pressure cooker.

2 tablespoons oil

4 boneless, skinless chicken breast halves

1 onion, chopped

1 green bell pepper, cut into ½-inch pieces

2 tablespoons minced garlic

1 teaspoon crushed dried rosemary

1 teaspoon dried thyme leaves

1 teaspoon paprika

½ teaspoon red pepper flakes

½ cup white wine

1 (28-ounce) can chopped tomatoes, with juice

1 (14-ounce) can chicken broth

2 cups frozen okra, sliced

1 cup frozen whole kernel corn

2 carrots, peeled and sliced

1 cup uncooked long-grain white rice, well rinsed

½ cup packed chopped cilantro leaves

1 bay leaf

Heat the oil in the pressure cooker over medium heat. Add the chicken pieces, cook until golden brown on both sides, and transfer to a cutting board. Cutting across the grain, slice the chicken breasts into strips. Add the onions and green peppers to the cooker and cook, stirring, until slightly softened, about 3 minutes. Add the garlic, rosemary, thyme, paprika, and red pepper flakes, frying until they begin to release their aroma. Deglaze the cooker with the wine, scraping up all those crusty, brown bits from the bottom. Add the tomatoes, broth, okra, corn, carrots, rice, cilantro, and bay leaf, and return the chicken strips to the pressure cooker. Stir to mix and lock the lid in place. Bring to 15psi over high heat, immediately reduce the heat to the lowest possible setting to stabilize and maintain that pressure, and cook for 6 minutes. Remove from the heat and use the natural release method (see page 31) to depressurize. Carefully open the lid after the pressure drops. Transfer to a serving bowl, fluffing the rice with a fork.

✳ Serves 6

Chicken Caesar Rice

This Italian-inspired dish is full of tender pieces of chicken with an array of colorful mixed vegetables, fluffy white rice, and just a touch of garlic and herbs. I use the interrupted cooking method (see page 38) to keep the vegetables tender-crisp.

2 tablespoons olive oil
4 boneless, skinless chicken breasts
1 cup uncooked long-grain white rice,
   well rinsed
1 (14-ounce) can chicken broth
½ cup bottled Caesar salad dressing
2 tablespoons minced garlic
1 tablespoon dried mixed Italian herbs
3 cups frozen mixed vegetables (broccoli,
   cauliflower, carrots)
½ cup sliced pimiento-stuffed green olives
½ cup grated Parmesan cheese

Heat the oil in the pressure cooker over medium heat. Add the chicken pieces, cook until golden brown on both sides, and transfer to a cutting board, cutting into bite-size pieces. Add the rice to the cooker, stirring to coat with the oil, and then add the chicken pieces, broth, Caesar dressing, garlic, and Italian herbs. Stir to mix and lock the lid in place. Bring to 15psi over high heat, immediately reduce the heat to the lowest possible setting to stabilize and maintain that pressure, and cook for 4 minutes. Remove from the heat and use the cold water release method (see page 30) to depressurize. Carefully open the lid after the pressure drops. Add the frozen vegetables and green olives on top of the chicken and rice mixture. Lock the lid back in place, return to 15psi over high heat, immediately reduce the heat to the lowest possible setting to stabilize and maintain that pressure, and cook for 2 minutes. Remove from the heat and use the natural release method (see page 31) to depressurize. Carefully open the lid after the pressure drops. Add the Parmesan cheese and fluff with a fork. Transfer to a serving bowl, and serve hot. ❋ **Serves 6**

Barbecued Chicken and Rice with Corn on the Cob and Peaches

Enjoy a complete Southern-style barbecue dinner in the comfort of your kitchen with a dish that really delivers the flavors. This pressure-cooker menu consists of a main dish of chicken and rice that is infused with tangy barbecue sauce, a side dish of sweet corn on the cob, and a side (or call it dessert!) of spiced peaches.

2 tablespoons oil
6 chicken drumsticks
1½ cups bottled barbecue sauce
⅓ cup peach preserves
1 (14-ounce) can peach halves, with juice
1 cup uncooked long-grain white rice,
   well rinsed
⅓ cup dark brown sugar

6 half-ears frozen corn on the cob

Ground cinnamon, for garnish (optional)

Heat the oil in the pressure cooker over medium heat. Add the chicken drumsticks, cook until golden brown on all sides, and set aside. Add the barbecue sauce, peach preserves, juice from the canned peaches, rice, and 1½ cups water to the cooker, mixing well. Add the chicken legs, pushing them slightly beneath the surface of the liquid. Place the peach halves on top, and add a spoonful of brown sugar to the center of each peach. Finally, add the corn on the cob pieces on top of the peaches. Lock the lid in place. Bring to 15psi over high heat, immediately reduce the heat to the lowest possible setting to stabilize and maintain that pressure, and cook for 5 minutes. Remove from the heat and use the natural release method (see page 31) to depressurize. Carefully open the lid after the pressure drops. Use long-handled tongs to remove the corn on the cob, peaches, and chicken drumsticks, arranging them around the edges of a large serving platter. Fluff the rice mixture with a fork, and then mound it in the center of the platter. Sprinkle the tops of the peaches with a little ground cinnamon, if desired. ✳ **Serves 4 to 5**

Red Rice and Chicken

A typically Southern-style rice recipe that's similar to a Spanish rice, this is derived from one of my grandmother's neatly printed recipes. The handwritten note in the margin says that every grain of rice must stand on its own, and every grain must be red. She goes on to caution that one "should never put a spoon in rice, but use a fork instead" to fluff it up before serving.

1 cup uncooked medium-grain white rice

4 slices bacon

6 boneless, skinless chicken thighs

1 onion, chopped

1 green bell pepper, seeded and chopped

1 (28-ounce) can stewed tomatoes, with juice

1 (14-ounce) can chicken broth

3 tablespoons tomato paste

1 tablespoon minced garlic

1 tablespoon chili powder

½ teaspoon dried thyme leaves

Place the rice in a large bowl of water and scrub the grains between your hands to wash off the starch. Keep changing the water until it is clear, and then drain off the water. Heat the pressure cooker over medium heat and add the bacon. Fry the bacon until it is crispy, and then set aside to drain on paper towels. Add the chicken pieces to the cooker and cook until golden brown on all sides. Remove the chicken to a cutting board and cut into bite-size pieces. Add the onions and bell peppers to the cooker and cook, stirring, until slightly softened, about 3 minutes. Drain off any remaining grease. Return the chicken pieces to the cooker and add the rice, stewed tomatoes, broth, tomato paste, garlic, chili powder, thyme, and 1½ cups water, stirring to mix. Lock the lid in place. Bring to 15psi over high heat, immediately reduce the heat to the lowest possible setting to stabilize and maintain that pressure, and cook for 5 minutes. Remove from the heat and use the natural release method (see page 31) to depressurize. Carefully open the lid after the pressure drops. Transfer the rice mixture to a serving dish, sprinkle the crumbled bacon across the top. ✳ **Serves 4 to 5**

Lemony Chicken and Rice Soup

A friend served this soup one chilly night and was kind enough to share the recipe, which I promptly adapted to the pressure cooker. The final result is a smooth, creamy soup made without any cream.

Step One: The Chicken
2 tablespoons butter
2 boneless, skinless chicken breasts
½ cup sliced celery
⅓ cup minced onions
1 tablespoon minced garlic
2 (14-ounce) cans chicken broth
½ cup diced carrots
⅓ cup uncooked long-grain white rice, well rinsed
1 teaspoon chicken bouillon granules

Heat the butter in the pressure cooker over medium heat. Add the chicken, cook until browned on both sides, and then remove to a cutting board and mince it. Add the celery, onions, and garlic to the cooker and cook, stirring, until slightly softened, about 3 minutes. Pour in the chicken broth and add the carrots, rice, and bouillon. Stir to mix and lock the lid in place. Bring to 15psi over high heat, immediately reduce the heat to the lowest possible setting to stabilize and maintain that pressure, and cook for 5 minutes. Remove from the heat and use the natural release method (see page 31) to depressurize. Carefully open the lid after the pressure drops.

Step Two: The Sauce
2 tablespoons butter
2 tablespoons all-purpose flour
½ teaspoon salt
½ teaspoon freshly ground black pepper
⅛ teaspoon cayenne pepper
3 tablespoons fresh lemon juice
3 large eggs
Lemon slices, for garnish
Green onions tops, sliced, for garnish

In a small heavy saucepan, melt the butter over medium heat. Stir in the flour, salt, black pepper, and cayenne pepper until smooth. Slowly add 2 cups of the hot broth from the cooker, stirring constantly until the sauce is thickened, and then add the lemon juice. Gradually stir the thickened sauce back into the cooker. In a small bowl, beat the eggs until frothy. Very slowly, add the eggs into the soup, whisking constantly. Do not add the eggs if the soup is boiling or too hot, or they will cook and separate instead of combining smoothly with the broth. Heat gently over low heat until the soup thickens enough to coat a spoon, but do not boil! Adjust the seasonings to taste, and transfer to a heated soup tureen. Garnish with the lemon slices and green onions. ✳ **Serves 4**

Cream of Chicken and Rice Soup

Bite-size pieces of tender chicken breast, rice, fresh mushrooms, and vegetables are combined in a mild and creamy soup that is sure to warm body and soul. Beyond the easy preparation, this quick meal cooks in just minutes—just long enough to bake a pan of biscuits.

1 teaspoon paprika

½ teaspoon freshly ground black pepper

½ teaspoon garlic powder

⅛ teaspoon ground nutmeg

4 boneless, skinless chicken breasts and/or thighs

2 tablespoons butter or margarine

1 onion, diced

2 cups sliced celery

2 cups sliced fresh button mushrooms

1 cup coarsely grated carrots

½ cup uncooked long-grain white rice, well rinsed

2 (14-ounce) cans chicken broth

1 (8-ounce) carton small-curd cottage cheese

1 cup light cream or half-and-half

2 tablespoons snipped fresh chives, for garnish

Mix together the paprika, pepper, garlic powder, and nutmeg and rub the spice mixture into both sides of the chicken breasts, saving any remaining spices. Heat the butter in the pressure cooker over medium heat. Add the chicken pieces, cook until golden brown on all sides, and transfer to a cutting board. Cut the chicken into bite-size pieces. Add any remaining spice mixture to the cooker, frying until the spices begin to sizzle. Add the onions, celery, mushrooms, and carrots and cook, stirring, until slightly softened, about 3 minutes. Add the rice, broth, and 4 cups water. Return the chicken pieces to the cooker and stir to mix. Lock the lid in place. Bring to 15psi over high heat, immediately reduce the heat to the lowest possible setting to stabilize and maintain that pressure, and cook for 5 minutes. Remove from the heat and use the natural release method (see page 31) to depressurize. Carefully open the lid after the pressure drops. Combine the cottage cheese and cream in a blender and mix until smooth. Stir the cream mixture into the pressure cooker and simmer over medium heat, stirring, until the soup is heated through. Adjust the seasonings to taste. Transfer the soup to a heated tureen or soup bowls and garnish with the chives just before serving. ✳ Serves 4 to 5

Mexican-Style Chicken Soup

Tired of plain old chicken soup? Try this spicy Mexican-inspired soup that's loaded with rice, corn, and beans in a rich-tasting, tomato-based broth flavored with salsa and topped with pepper Jack cheese and crushed tortilla chips.

1 tablespoon oil
4 boneless, skinless chicken breasts
1 onion, chopped
1 mild poblano chile, seeded and chopped
½ cup packed chopped cilantro leaves
1 tablespoon minced garlic
2 teaspoons chili powder
1½ teaspoons ground cumin
2 (14-ounce) cans chicken broth
1 (14-ounce) can black beans, drained and rinsed
1 (10-ounce) can whole kernel corn, drained
1 (10-ounce) can creamed corn
1 (3-ounce) can tomato paste
2 cups bottled chunky-style salsa, hot or mild
½ cup uncooked long-grain white rice,
   well rinsed
1 cup shredded pepper Jack cheese
Tortilla chips of your choice, crushed,
   for garnish

Heat the oil in a large pressure cooker over medium heat. Add the chicken pieces, cook until golden brown on both sides, transfer to a cutting board, and cut into large bite-size pieces. Add the onions, chiles, cilantro, and garlic to the cooker and cook, stirring, until slightly softened, about 3 minutes. Add the chili powder and cumin, frying until they begin to sizzle. Add the broth, beans, whole kernel and creamed corn, tomato paste, salsa, rice, and 4 cups water, stirring to mix. Lock the lid in place. Bring to 15psi over high heat, immediately reduce the heat to the lowest possible setting to stabilize and maintain that pressure, and cook for 6 minutes. Remove from the heat and use the natural release method (see page 31) to depressurize. Carefully open the lid after the pressure drops. Taste and adjust the seasonings. Ladle into soup bowls, place some of the cheese on top of each serving, and then add a handful of crushed tortilla chips.

✳ Serves 4 to 5

Jamaican Rice

Looking for something different to serve with that main dish? Try this flavorful and fruity rice side dish that goes particularly well with chicken and pork.

1 tablespoon oil
1 onion, minced
2 tablespoons minced garlic
2 cups frozen peas
1 cup uncooked long-grain white rice,
   well rinsed
1 (8-ounce) can pineapple tidbits, with juice
1 jalapeño chile, seeded and minced
¼ cup chopped cilantro
1 teaspoon brown sugar
1 teaspoon ground turmeric
1 cup chicken broth
1 tablespoon soy sauce

Heat the oil in a pressure cooker over medium heat. Add the onions and garlic and cook, stirring, until soft, about 3 minutes. Then transfer to a metal pan that will fit loosely inside the pressure cooker. Add all of the remaining ingredients to the pan and stir to mix. Place the rack in the bottom of the cooker and add 1 cup water. Use foil helper handles (see page 42) to place the rice pan on the rack. Lock the lid in place. Bring to 15psi over high heat, immediately reduce the heat to the lowest possible setting to stabilize and maintain that pressure, and cook for 4 minutes. Remove from the heat and use the natural release method (see page 31) to depressurize. Carefully open the lid after the pressure drops. Transfer the rice mixture to a serving bowl and fluff with a fork before serving.

✳ Serves 4 to 5

✳ ONE-POT MEAL

Pork Chops with Brown Rice and Pecan Cream Sauce

Add some class to ordinary chops with this one-pot recipe of pork chops and nutty brown rice in a delectable, creamy sauce that is scandalously rich.

Step One: The Chops and Brown Rice

2 tablespoons butter

4 center-cut pork loin chops,
    1 to 1½ inches thick

1 onion, minced

½ pound fresh mushrooms, washed and sliced

1 cup white wine

1 cup uncooked medium-grain brown rice

1 (14-ounce) can chicken broth

Heat the butter in the pressure cooker over medium heat. Add the meat, cook until browned on both sides, and set aside. Add the onions and mushrooms to the cooker and cook, stirring, until slightly softened, about 3 minutes. Deglaze the cooker with the wine, scraping up all those crusty, brown bits from the bottom. Return the chops to the cooker. Place the rice, broth, and ½ cup water in a metal pan that will fit loosely inside the pressure cooker. Use foil helper handles (see page 42) to place the pan on top of the chops, adjusting the position so it's as level as possible. Lock the lid in place. Bring to 15psi over high heat, immediately reduce the heat to the lowest possible setting to stabilize and maintain that pressure, and cook for 15 minutes. Remove from the heat and use the natural release method (see page 31) to depressurize. Carefully open the lid after the pressure drops. Transfer the rice to a serving bowl and fluff with a fork. Arrange the chops on a serving plate and keep warm in a low oven until ready to serve.

Step Two: The Pecan Cream Sauce

½ cup heavy cream

⅓ cup finely chopped pecans

Stir the cream and pecans into the broth in the cooker and simmer over medium-high heat. Cook, uncovered, over medium heat, stirring until the sauce thickens, about 10 minutes. Pour the sauce into a separate bowl to serve with the pork chops and rice. ✳ Serves 4

Smothered Pork Chops with Sweet Potatoes, Brown Rice, and Gravy

Stovetop braising is often referred to as "smothering" in Southern parlance. Smothered pork chops with tons of gravy are considered comfort food and are usually served with cooked rice. This recipe uses the basic PIP (Pan in Pot) cooking method (see page 37), expanded to become tiered cooking (see page 38), for a complete three-course meal.

1 tablespoon olive oil

1 tablespoon butter

2 tablespoons all-purpose flour

4 bone-in pork chops, cut 1 inch thick

½ teaspoon freshly ground black pepper

2 tablespoons olive oil

2 medium-size onions, thinly sliced

1 green bell pepper, coarsely chopped

2 tablespoons minced garlic

1 (14-ounce) can chicken broth

1 tablespoon brown sugar

3 sweet potatoes, scrubbed and halved

1 cup uncooked long-grain brown rice

Make a roux in a small skillet by melting the butter in the hot oil and adding the flour, scraping up any remaining browned bits left on the bottom. Continue cooking, stirring constantly, until the flour is medium brown in color, or about the same color as peanut butter. Set aside.

Season the pork chops with plenty of pepper. Heat the oil in a large pressure cooker over medium heat. Add the chops, cook until browned on both sides, and set aside on a plate. Add the onions, bell peppers, and garlic to the cooker and cook, stirring, until slightly softened, about 3 minutes. Add half of the chicken broth and the brown sugar to the cooker. Arrange the chops in layers and place the sweet potatoes on top of the chops, cut side up. Place the rice in a metal pan that will fit loosely inside the pressure cooker. Add the remaining half of the chicken broth plus 1 cup water to the rice pan. Use foil helper handles (see page 42) to place the pan on top of the sweet potatoes, adjusting the position so it's as level as possible. Lock the lid in place. Bring to 15psi over high heat, immediately reduce the heat to the lowest possible setting to stabilize and maintain that pressure, and cook for 15 minutes. Remove from the heat and use the natural release method (see page 31) to depressurize. Carefully open the lid after the pressure drops. Remove the rice pan and transfer the rice to a serving bowl, fluffing with a fork. Transfer the sweet potatoes and chops to a serving plate and keep warm in a low oven until ready to serve. Use a hand blender to puree the vegetables and broth in the pressure cooker. Return the cooked roux to the pressure cooker and bring to a simmer over medium heat, stirring as the roux thickens the broth, about 5 minutes. Add more water if a thinner consistency is desired. Serve the gravy in a separate bowl or gravy boat to be passed at the table. ✳ Serves 4

Plum Delicious Pork Cutlets with Steamed White Rice

Recipes should challenge the senses and wake up your taste buds, and this one has just enough of a complementary balance between tartness and sweetness that it appeals to almost every palate. I use the PIP cooking method (see page 37) to keep the fluffy white rice separate from the chops and sauce.

1 tablespoon oil

4 thin pork cutlets or boneless pork chops
    pounded to a ½-inch thickness

1 sweet Vidalia or Maui onion, minced

½ cup plum jelly or preserves

¼ cup balsamic vinegar

¼ cup soy sauce

¼ cup fresh lemon juice

1 teaspoon ground ginger

1½ cups uncooked long-grain white rice,
    well rinsed

Heat the oil in the pressure cooker over medium heat. Add the meat, cook until browned on both sides, and set aside. Add the onions to the cooker and cook, stirring, until slightly softened, about 3 minutes. Stir in all of the remaining ingredients except for the rice, mixing well. Return the cutlets to the pressure cooker. Place the rice and 3 cups water in a metal pan that will fit loosely inside the pressure cooker. Use foil helper handles (see page 42) to place the pan on top of the cutlets, adjusting the pan so it's as level as possible. Lock the lid in place. Bring to 15psi over high heat, immediately reduce the heat to the lowest possible setting to stabilize and maintain that pressure, and cook for 5 minutes. Remove from the heat and use the natural release method (see page 31) to depressurize. Carefully open the lid after the pressure drops. Carefully remove the rice pan and transfer the rice to a serving bowl, fluffing with a fork. Transfer the cutlets to a serving plate. Serve the plum sauce in a separate bowl to be passed at the table and spooned over the pork and rice. ✳ Serves 4

Pork Chops with Red Wine Risotto

Always on the lookout for easy, one-pot meals, I developed and refined this recipe for a quick and simple but elegant main dish. The only thing needed to complete the meal is a nice crisp salad.

> 2 tablespoons butter
>
> 6 bone-in pork chops, cut ½ inch thick
>
> 1 onion, minced
>
> 2 tablespoons minced garlic
>
> 1 cup uncooked Arborio rice or a medium-grain rice like Calrose
>
> ½ cup Cabernet or other red wine
>
> Zest of 1 lemon
>
> Juice of 1 lemon
>
> 1⅓ cups chicken broth
>
> ⅓ cup grated Parmesan cheese

Heat the butter in the pressure cooker over medium heat. Add the chops, cook until browned on both sides, and set aside. Add the onions and garlic to the cooker and cook, stirring, until softened, about 3 minutes. Stir in the rice, stirring to coat the grains until they are slightly translucent. Deglaze the cooker with the wine, scraping up all those crusty, brown bits from the bottom. Add the lemon zest, lemon juice, and broth, and give it a good stir. Return the chops to the cooker, placing them on top of the rice mixture. Lock the lid in place. Bring to 15psi over high heat, immediately reduce the heat to the lowest possible setting to stabilize and maintain that pressure, and cook for 7 minutes.

Remove from the heat and use the cold water release method (see page 30) to depressurize. Carefully open the lid after the pressure drops. Remove the chops to a serving plate. The rice should have a creamy consistency; add a little more broth if necessary. Stir in the Parmesan and adjust the seasonings to taste. Transfer the risotto to a serving bowl and serve with the chops. ✳ Serves 6

Best Brown Rice with Mushrooms

This dish is not only easy to make, it's also nutritious and great tasting, and when it comes to cleanup, there's only one pot to wash.

> 2 tablespoons butter
>
> ½ pound fresh mushrooms, washed, caps sliced, and stems diced
>
> 1 tablespoon minced garlic
>
> 2 cups uncooked long-grain brown rice
>
> ½ cup finely chopped green onions, white and green parts
>
> ½ cup diced red bell pepper
>
> 3 cups chicken stock or broth, canned or homemade

Heat the butter in the pressure cooker over medium heat. Add the mushrooms and garlic and cook, stirring, until tender, about 3 minutes. Add the rice, stirring until the grains are slightly translucent. Add the green onions and red peppers. Pour in the chicken stock, add 3 cups water, and stir. Lock the lid in place. Bring to 15psi over high heat, immediately reduce the heat to the lowest possible setting to stabilize and maintain that pressure, and cook for 15 minutes. Remove from the heat and use the natural release method (see page 31) to depressurize. Carefully open the lid after the pressure drops, and serve. ✳ **Serves 6**

Cook's Note: For variety and protein, add any leftover cooked or canned meat, fish, or poultry when you add the onions and peppers You can also change the flavoring liquid to whatever appeals to you—beef broth, vegetable broth or juice, or other combinations.

Caribbean Rice and Black-Eyed Pea Soup

This is a unique blend of interesting flavors with just the right amount of spices to complement the main ingredients and make this soup really stand out.

1 tablespoon olive oil
1 onion, coarsely chopped
1 green bell pepper, seeded and chopped
2 tablespoons minced garlic
1 teaspoon dried oregano
1 teaspoon ground coriander
½ teaspoon crushed dried rosemary
½ teaspoon red pepper flakes
1 cup uncooked long-grain brown rice
½ teaspoon salt
½ teaspoon freshly ground black pepper
2 bay leaves
1 (14-ounce) can stewed tomatoes, with juice
1 (14-ounce) can chicken broth
1 (6-ounce) can diced green chiles, with juice
1 cup dried black-eyed peas
½ cup unsweetened coconut milk

Heat the oil in the pressure cooker over medium heat. Add the onions, bell peppers, and garlic and cook, stirring, until slightly softened, about 3 minutes. Add the oregano, coriander, rosemary, and red pepper flakes, frying the spices until they begin to sizzle and release their aroma. Add the rice, salt, pepper, and bay leaves, stirring until the grains of rice look slightly translucent. Add the tomatoes, broth, chiles, and black-eyed peas, and pour in enough water to cover all the ingredients by at least 2 inches. Lock the lid in place. Bring to 15 psi over high heat, immediately reduce the heat to the lowest possible setting to stabilize and maintain that pressure, and cook for 10 minutes. Remove from the heat and use the natural release method (see page 31) to depressurize. Carefully open the lid after the pressure drops. Add the coconut milk and simmer over low heat until heated through. Adjust the seasonings to taste, and serve.

✳ **Serves 6**

Variation: Add 2 cups diced kielbasa, ham, or cooked sausage for a meatier version of this recipe.

Red Beans and Dirty Rice

Dirty rice, sometimes known as rice dressing, with red beans is a well-known combination in the South that can be either a hearty side dish or the main entrée. Depending on where you come from, it might be served plain or with bits of ham, sausage, shrimp, or chicken livers. In this recipe I use Louisiana hot links and ham, but you can add whatever kind of meat suits your taste. To make this with two pressure cookers, start the beans and the rice at the same time. To make this recipe with one pressure cooker, follow my directions below.

Step One: The Beans

2 tablespoons bacon drippings

1 onion, chopped

2 mild poblano, pasilla, or Anaheim chiles, seeded and chopped

2 tablespoons minced garlic

1 pound dried small red or pink beans, presoaked for 4 hours

½ pound Louisiana hot links, cut into ½-inch slices

1 cup chopped cilantro stems and leaves

2 tablespoons sweet paprika

1 tablespoon dried thyme leaves

1 teaspoon coarsely ground black pepper

½ teaspoon onion powder

Dash of cayenne pepper

Heat the bacon drippings in a large pressure cooker over medium heat. Add the onions, chiles, and gar-lic, and cook, stirring, until soft, about 3 minutes. Drain and rinse the presoaked beans and add them to the pressure cooker. Add all of the remaining ingredients and enough water to cover the ingredients by 2 inches. Stir to mix and lock the lid in place. Bring to 15psi over high heat, immediately reduce the heat to the lowest possible setting to stabilize and maintain that pressure, and cook for 10 minutes. Remove from the heat and use the natural release method (see page 31) to depressurize. Carefully open the lid after the pressure drops. Check the beans for doneness; a bean should mash easily with a fork when it's fully cooked. If necessary, return to 15psi over high heat, immediately reduce the heat to the lowest possible setting to stabilize and maintain that pressure, and cook for an additional 4 minutes, or until the beans are fully cooked. Remove from the heat and use the natural release method (see page 31) to depressurize. Carefully open the lid after the pressure drops. Remove and puree or mash 2 cups of the beans and a little broth for a thicker, creamier texture if desired, and return to the pot. Adjust the seasonings to taste.

Step Two: The Rice

2 tablespoons butter

½ pound cooked or leftover ham, diced

4 stalks celery, chopped

1 onion, chopped

1 green bell pepper, seeded and chopped

1½ cups uncooked long-grain white rice, well rinsed

1 (14-ounce) can chopped tomatoes, with juice

1 jalapeño chile, seeded and chopped

3 cups chicken or beef stock

Louisiana-style hot sauce, for garnish

Heat the butter in the pressure cooker over medium heat. Add the ham and cook until browned on all sides. Add the celery, onions, and bell peppers to the cooker and cook, stirring, until soft, about 3 minutes. Add the rice, stirring it into the butter until the grains look translucent. Add the chopped tomatoes, chile, and stock, mixing well. Lock the lid in place and bring to 15psi over high heat, immediately reduce the heat to the lowest possible setting to stabilize and maintain that pressure, and cook for 4 minutes. Remove from the heat and use the natural release method (see page 31) to depressurize. Carefully open the lid after the pressure drops. To serve, place a scoop of the dirty rice in each individual bowl and ladle on the red beans. Pass a bottle of Louisiana-style hot sauce at the table. ✳ **Serves 6**

Wild Rice and Mushroom Pilaf with Toasted Almonds

This is my pressure-cooker version of a colorful pilaf with buttery mushrooms and toasted almonds.

Step One: The Pilaf

2 tablespoons butter or margarine

½ cup uncooked medium-grain brown rice

⅓ cup uncooked wild rice

½ pound fresh button mushrooms, washed and sliced

½ cup diced green bell pepper

½ cup grated carrots

¼ cup chopped green onion, white and green parts

2 tablespoons minced garlic

1 (14-ounce) can chicken or vegetable broth

1 teaspoon salt

½ teaspoon freshly ground black pepper

Heat the butter in the pressure cooker over medium heat. Add the brown rice, wild rice, mushrooms, green peppers, carrots, green onions, and garlic and cook, stirring, until the rice looks translucent. Add the broth, salt, pepper, and 1½ cups water. Stir to mix and lock the lid in place. Bring to 15psi over high heat, immediately reduce the heat to the lowest possible setting to stabilize and maintain that pressure, and cook for 20 minutes. Remove from the heat and use the natural release method (see page 31) to depressurize. Carefully open the lid after the pressure drops. Stir in a little water if the rice seems too dry, and transfer to a serving bowl.

Step Two: The Toasted Almonds

½ cup sliced or slivered almonds

While the rice is cooking, preheat the oven to 400°F. Spread the almonds on a baking sheet and pop it into the oven, but keep a close eye on them, as they go from a nice toasty brown to burned very easily. When the almonds are golden brown in color, set them aside to cool. Add the toasted almonds to the rice, and fluff with a fork just before serving. ✳ **Serves 6**

Perfectly Steamed Long-Grain White Rice

Rinse the rice, rinse the rice again, and then rinse it one more time to remove the starchy outer coat. The water should run clear. All the rinsing is an important first step to cooking rice with each grain separate and not stuck together. Whether as a side dish, or incorporated into other recipes, this is the fastest steamed rice you'll ever make. I cook rice with the PIP cooking method (see page 37), which makes for perfect rice every time.

1 cup uncooked long-grain white rice,
    well rinsed
1 tablespoon butter

Place the rice in a metal bowl and add 1½ cups water and the butter to the rice bowl. Set the rack in the bottom of the cooker and pour in ½ cup water. Using foil helper handles (see page 42), place the rice bowl on the rack. Loosely fold the ends of the foil strip over the top of the bowl and lock the lid in place. Bring to 15psi over high heat, immediately reduce the heat to the lowest possible setting to stabilize and maintain that pressure, and cook for exactly 4 minutes. Remove from the heat and use the natural release method (see page 31) to depressurize. Carefully open the lid after the pressure drops. Remove the rice bowl and fluff the rice with a fork before serving. ✳ Serves 4

Variations

Lemon Rice: Add the juice of 1 lemon and the zest of 1 lemon to the rice bowl.

Flavored Rice: Substitute an equal amount of chicken, beef, or vegetable stock for the water.

Basic Risotto

The preparation of risotto, a thick and creamy rice dish, is a controversial matter, but don't be put off by tales of how difficult it is to make this popular Italian rice dish. What takes a laborious effort by regular cooking methods is done to perfection—tender and chewy—with no fuss in the pressure cooker in just 7 minutes. There are three key ingredients to making a great risotto: the rice, the broth, and the cheese—but the fun part is adding all the other ingredients. Never make risotto with plain water—yes, that's a rule. Always select flavor-enhancing liquids such as wine, stock, broth, juice, etc. Risotto requires a special type of rice; the regular long-grain variety stocked on supermarket shelves just won't do the job. Use Arborio rice, or substitute any plump, round-grain variety. If you have difficulty locating Arborio rice, look for it at gourmet or health food stores. Calrose rice, which is found in the Asian foods section, also makes a pretty good risotto.

1 tablespoon olive oil
1 onion, chopped
2 tablespoons minced garlic
1 cup uncooked Arborio rice
2 cups stock or broth, heated
½ cup white wine
¼ teaspoon black pepper
¼ cup grated Parmesan cheese

Heat the oil in the pressure cooker over medium heat. Add the onions and garlic and cook, stirring, until clear, about 3 minutes. Add the rice, stirring until the grains are coated with oil. Add the hot stock, wine, and pepper. Stir to mix and lock the lid in place. Bring to 15psi over high heat, immediately reduce the heat to the lowest possible setting to stabilize and maintain that pressure, and cook for exactly 7 minutes. Remove from the heat and use the quick release method (see page 30) to depressurize. Carefully open the lid after the pressure drops. Stir in the Parmesan cheese. If the risotto isn't nice and creamy, stir in a little more stock. Simmer, uncovered, over medium heat, stirring constantly, until the rice is the desired consistency. Serve immediately in shallow soup bowls.

✳ Serves 4 to 5

Variations

Add 1 cup chopped seafood, such as salmon, shrimp, or scallops, sautéed in olive oil.

Add 2 cups chopped or sliced fresh vegetables—green peas, mushrooms, greens, asparagus, artichoke hearts, tomatoes, squash—whatever you like.

Vary the cheeses and try different herbs and wines to suit your own personal preferences.

Risotto Croquettes

Make these with leftover Walnut Risotto (page 374) and serve them as a side dish or appetizer.

At least 1 cup leftover risotto
½ cup all-purpose flour
1 large egg, beaten
1 cup very fine bread crumbs
¼ cup olive oil
Soy sauce or teriyaki sauce, for dipping

Chill the risotto overnight and roll the rice into 1½-inch balls. Bread the rice balls by rolling each one first in the flour, then dipping each into the beaten egg, and then rolling them in the bread crumbs, making sure the surface is coated evenly. Heat the oil in a small skillet over medium heat. Fry the risotto croquettes until golden brown on all sides. Set aside to drain on paper towels. Serve with a choice of soy or teriyaki sauce. ✳ Serves 4

Walnut Risotto

I absolutely love risotto, and the toasted walnuts give this dish a rich aroma and crunchy taste. While risotto might seem like a difficult dish, it's actually quick and easy in the pressure cooker and can be completed in just 7 minutes. Plan on using any leftovers to make Walnut Risotto Croquettes (page 373).

Step One: The Toasted Walnuts
⅓ cup walnuts

Heat the walnuts in a heavy dry skillet over medium heat for 1 to 2 minutes, or until they're golden brown and they give off a rich, toasty fragrance. Stir frequently for even toasting, and watch closely, as it's easy to burn them. Remove from the pan to cool. Chop the nuts coarsely after they cool.

Step Two: The Risotto
2 tablespoons butter
½ cup chopped Maui onion
1 tablespoon minced garlic
1 cup uncooked Arborio rice or a medium-grain rice like Calrose
3 cups chicken broth
½ cup white wine
¼ cup grated Asiago cheese
Salt and freshly ground black pepper to taste

Heat the butter in the pressure cooker over high heat. Add the onion and garlic and cook, stirring, until soft but not brown, about 3 minutes. Add the rice, stirring until all the grains are well coated, and continue to cook, stirring, until slightly translucent. Add the broth and wine and stir to mix. Lock the lid in place, bring to 15psi over high heat, im-

mediately reduce the heat to the lowest possible setting to stabilize and maintain that pressure, and cook for 7 minutes. Remove from the heat and use the cold water release method (see page 30) to depressurize. Carefully open the lid after the pressure drops. The rice should be a creamy consistency; add a little water if necessary. Stir in the cheese and walnuts, season with salt and pepper, and serve immediately. ✳ Serves 4 to 5

Toasted Brown Rice, Barley, and Vegetable Pilaf

Brown rice and barley combine with carrots and zucchini in this healthy side dish. Using the interrupted cooking method (see page 38), the rice is partially cooked, and then the cooker is depressurized to add the vegetables so that they cook up tender-crisp.

Step One: The Rice and Barley
1 tablespoon vegetable oil
1 cup uncooked medium-grain brown rice
½ cup uncooked pearl barley
2 (14-ounce) cans chicken or vegetable broth
1 onion, cut into thin wedges
2 teaspoons dried basil
1 teaspoon dried marjoram
¼ teaspoon coarsely ground black pepper

Heat the oil in the pressure cooker over medium heat. Add the rice and barley and cook, stirring occasionally, until the grains are lightly browned.

Stir in the broth, onions, basil, marjoram, and pepper and lock the lid in place. Bring to 15psi over high heat, immediately reduce the heat to the lowest possible setting to stabilize and maintain that pressure, and cook for 15 minutes. Remove from the heat and use the natural release method (see page 31) to depressurize. Carefully open the lid after the pressure drops.

Step Two: The Vegetables
2 stalks celery, sliced
2 carrots, thinly sliced
1 zucchini, sliced
1 cup fresh or frozen corn kernels
1 cup shredded Monterey Jack cheese

Add all of the ingredients except for the cheese to the cooker and stir to mix. Lock the lid back in place, return to 15psi over high heat, immediately reduce the heat to the lowest possible setting to stabilize and maintain that pressure, and cook for exactly 3 minutes. Remove from the heat and use the cold water release method (see page 30) to depressurize. Carefully open the lid after the pressure drops. Transfer to a serving bowl, sprinkle with the cheese, fluff with a fork, and serve. ✳ Serves 6

Confetti Garden Rice

This is an old standby for me, and it's so quick and easy to make. Try this brightly colored rice dish in place of the usual plain white rice as a nutritious accompaniment to almost any entrée. Serve as a side dish, or add some leftover cooked or canned meat or fish for an almost instant main dish.

3 tablespoons butter
1 small red onion, chopped
2 tablespoons minced garlic
1 cup uncooked long-grain white rice,
    well rinsed
3 cups frozen mixed vegetables (corn, green
    beans, carrots)
1 (14-ounce) can chicken broth
¼ cup fresh lemon juice
1 tablespoon ground cumin
1 teaspoon salt
1 teaspoon freshly ground black pepper

Heat the butter in a pressure cooker over medium heat. Add the onions and garlic and cook, stirring, until soft, about 3 minutes. Add the rice, stirring until the grains look translucent. Place the rice in a metal pan that will fit loosely inside the pressure cooker. Add the vegetables, broth, lemon juice, cumin, salt, pepper, and ⅓ cup water to the pan and stir to mix. Place the rack in the bottom of the cooker and add 1 cup water. Use foil helper handles (see page 42) to place the rice pan on the rack. Lock the lid in place. Bring to 15psi over high heat, immediately reduce the heat to the lowest possible setting to stabilize and maintain that pressure, and cook for 4 minutes. Remove from the heat and use the natural release method (see page 31) to depressurize. Carefully open the lid after the pressure drops. Transfer the rice mixture to a serving bowl and fluff with a fork before serving. ✳ Serves 6

Curried Lemon Rice with Green Beans and Toasted Almonds

This beautiful and wonderfully aromatic rice dish is infused with loads of flavor, tender-crisp green beans, and crunchy almonds. It makes a great accompaniment to any main dish.

Step One: The Toasted Almonds
¼ cup sliced or slivered almonds

Preheat the oven to 400°F. Spread the almonds on a baking sheet and pop it into the oven, but keep a close eye on them, as they go from a nice toasty brown to burned very easily. When the almonds are golden brown in color, set them aside to cool.

Step Two: The Rice
1 cup uncooked long-grain white rice, well rinsed

2 cups frozen green beans

2 tablespoons minced garlic

2 tablespoons minced crystallized ginger

1 teaspoon curry powder

½ teaspoon ground turmeric

½ teaspoon freshly ground black pepper

Grated zest of 1 lemon

Juice of 1 lemon

1 (14-ounce) can chicken broth

2 tablespoons soy sauce

Place the rack in the bottom of the pressure cooker and add 1 cup water. Put the rice in a metal pan that will fit loosely inside the cooker. Add the green beans, garlic, ginger, curry powder, turmeric, pepper, lemon zest, lemon juice, broth, and soy sauce and stir to mix. Use foil helper handles (see page 42) to place the rice pan on the rack. Lock the lid in place. Bring to 15psi over high heat, immediately reduce the heat to the lowest possible setting to stabilize and maintain that pressure, and cook for 4 minutes. Remove from the heat and use the natural release method (see page 31) to depressurize. Carefully open the lid after the pressure drops. Transfer the rice mixture to a serving bowl, stir in the toasted almonds, and fluff with a fork before serving. ✳ Serves 4

Vegetables

EAT YOUR VEGETABLES! Despite the known health benefits, many people do not eat enough vegetables. From big "baked" potatoes to delicate, tender-crisp broccoli florets, the pressure cooker makes it easy to cook all kinds of vegetables, from main dishes to side dishes. If you think vegetables are boring, strive for variety in recipes, cuisines, and presentation. Always use a recipe or follow the Pressure-Cooking Time Charts (see page 84), and watch carefully that the vegetables do not overcook. There is no reason to serve mushy, overcooked veggies.

Steaming in a pressure cooker is one of the healthiest and quickest ways to cook vegetables. Since steam is hotter than boiling water, vegetables will cook faster and absorb less water. The vegetables retain their natural state, preserving the taste, texture, and color, as well as more of the vitamins and minerals that are lost through boiling or baking. Plus, pressure cooking is incredibly fast and easy.

Creamy Cheddar Vegetable Chowder

The prep work will take longer than the actual cooking time, but this is so wonderfully thick and delicious it's well worth it. I serve it with toasted garlic bread for a man-sized meal.

3 tablespoons butter
1 onion, chopped
1 tablespoon minced garlic
3 potatoes, peeled and diced
2 cups fresh broccoli florets
2 leeks, sliced lengthwise, washed, and white
    parts only cut into ½-inch slices
2 carrots, peeled and thinly sliced
2 stalks celery, sliced
½ teaspoon salt
½ teaspoon freshly ground black pepper
⅛ teaspoon cayenne pepper, or more to taste
1 (14-ounce) can chicken broth
3 cups milk
2 cups shredded sharp cheddar cheese
1 cup cream
1 cup sour cream
⅓ cup instant potato flakes

Heat the butter in the pressure cooker over medium heat. Add the onions and garlic and cook until soft, about 3 minutes. Add the potatoes, broccoli, leeks, carrots, celery, salt, black pepper, cayenne pepper, and broth. Pour in 2 cups water and stir to mix. Lock the lid in place. Bring to 15psi over high heat, immediately reduce the heat to the lowest possible setting to stabilize and maintain that pressure, and cook for 4 minutes. Remove from the heat and use the quick release method (see page 30) to depressurize. Carefully open the lid after the pressure drops. Add the milk, cheese, cream, and sour cream, and simmer, uncovered, over medium-low heat until hot and bubbly. Add the potato flakes in small amounts, stirring gently until the soup is the desired consistency. Adjust the seasonings to taste, and serve. ✳ Serves 4

Cook's Note: Add 2 cups diced cooked ham for a meatier version.

PCBs: Potatoes, Carrots, and Brussels Sprouts in a Spiced Butter Sauce

Large quantities of Brussels sprouts were cultivated near Brussels around 1587; that's how they came by the name. They were introduced in the United States in the 1800s by French settlers in Louisiana, and sometimes called the "fairy cabbage." Unlike the early varieties, modern hybrids are delicious, with a delicate, slightly sweet, nutty flavor. The poor little sprout has an undeserved bad reputation because people tend to choose the largest heads—the oldest and strongest tasting—and overcook them, and then complain about the strong cabbage-like taste and smell. When selecting fresh Brussels sprouts, choose ones of nearly the same size so they will cook evenly, and look for ones that are firm, with a bright green color and fresh aroma. Before cooking, soak the sprouts in a basin of cold water to remove any dirt that might be hidden in the leaves. Trim off the stem ends flush with the bottom of the sprouts and pull off the outer leaves.

> 6 Brussels sprouts, trimmed and halved
>   lengthwise
> 4 small red potatoes, quartered
> 1 red onion, halved and sliced
> 2 carrots, sliced ¼ inch thick
> 2 tablespoons butter
> 2 tablespoons fresh lemon juice
> 2 tablespoons balsamic vinegar
> ¼ teaspoon freshly ground black pepper
> ¼ teaspoon ground cloves
> ¼ teaspoon ground cinnamon

Place the rack in the bottom of the cooker with ½ cup water. Arrange the Brussels sprouts, potatoes, onions, and carrots in a steamer tray and place them on top of the rack in the cooker. Lock the lid in place. Bring to 15psi over high heat, immediately reduce the heat to the lowest possible setting to stabilize and maintain that pressure, and cook for 4 minutes. Remove from the heat and use the natural release method (see page 31) to depressurize. Carefully open the lid after the pressure drops. Drain the vegetables, discarding the cooking water, and then transfer them to a serving bowl to keep warm. Melt the butter in the cooker over medium-high heat and add the lemon juice, vinegar, pepper, cloves, and cinnamon, stirring until the sauce is hot and bubbly. Pour the butter sauce over the veggies and serve hot. ✳ Serves 4 to 5

Mashed Potatoes and Greens

In the South, potatoes and greens are considered comfort food. This recipe is the Southern version of the classic Irish dish colcannon, which is made with cabbage.

> 4 russet potatoes, peeled and diced
> 4 cups finely shredded greens (your choice,
>   any variety)
> 5 tablespoons butter, at room temperature,
>   plus extra for garnish
> 1 onion, diced
> ½ cup buttermilk
> ½ teaspoon Louisiana-style hot sauce
> Salt and freshly ground black pepper to taste

Place the rack in the cooker and add ½ cup water. Add the potatoes and greens, in that order, and lock the lid in place. Bring to 15psi over high heat, immediately reduce the heat to the lowest possible setting to stabilize and maintain that pressure, and cook for 5 minutes. Remove from the heat and use the quick or cold water release method (see page 30) to depressurize. Carefully open the lid after the pressure drops. Use a colander to drain the potatoes and greens, and wipe the cooker dry. Heat 2 tablespoons of the butter in the pressure cooker over medium heat. Add the onions and cook, stirring, until softened, about 3 minutes. Pour in the buttermilk, stirring until it is hot. Return the potatoes and greens to the cooker and add the remaining butter, the hot sauce, and the salt and pepper. Use a potato masher to gently mash the potatoes by hand, leaving them somewhat lumpy. Transfer to a serving bowl, and garnish with a pat of butter in the center. ✳ Serves 4 to 5

A Guide to Greens

When buying fresh greens, look for leaves that are deep green in color, with no brown or yellowing leaves. Choose leaves that are firm, not limp. Greens cook down to less than half their original volume, so be sure to buy enough. Greens must be thoroughly cleaned—put them in a sink full of cold water, stir them around with your hands, drain the water, and repeat 2–3 three times. Shake the leaves, and spread them out on a large towel. Discarding any wilted or yellowed leaves. Remove any of the large ribs or veins, which are the main culprits for the bitter taste most people associate with leafy greens. There are several ways to get the greens into bite-size pieces; one method is just to tear the leaves into small pieces. Another way is to stack 3 or 4 leaves on top of one another, roll them up tightly, cigar fashion, and slice across the roll, making cuts about 1 inch apart.

Uncooked greens can quickly fill up a pressure cooker, so allow a brief steaming time with a regular lid to wilt the leaves and reduce their volume if necessary. Ham, smoked ham hocks, bacon pieces, or sausage bits can be added to the greens if desired. Season the greens with salt and black pepper, chiles, plain or flavored vinegars, hot sauce, hot pickled peppers, or an herb butter. The frugal cook will save the discarded stems to use for stock.

All About Greens

Beet greens	Beets are two vegetables in one; not only do you get the beet root itself, but the beet greens are delicious and have a nice flavor.
Collard greens	Milder than most other greens, they can be prepared in a wide variety of ways.
Dandelion greens	A tangy and tasty addition to a salad, they can be steamed, added to soups, or sautéed.
Kale	The coarsely textured leaves have a strong cabbage flavor. The leaves hold their shape and don't wilt as much as other greens.
Kohlrabi	Sometimes called a "cabbage turnip," this funny-looking vegetable has a round white bulb with several skinny stems poking up. The bulb tastes like a mild, sweet broccoli stem. Both the bulb and root are edible.
Mustard greens	Another member of the cabbage family, these greens have a bite, with a pungent mustard flavor that adds taste to bland foods like dried beans.
Swiss chard	There are red or green varieties with leaves that taste like spinach. Unlike other greens, chard stems, which taste like celery, are eaten as well as the leaves, but they need a little more cooking time. The interesting taste complements many foods.

Turnip greens   These are the leaves of the turnip plant, which is better known for its roots. Turnip greens are smaller and more tender than their cousin, collard greens. Turnip greens are slightly sweet when young, but as they age they tend to develop a bitter taste that many people appreciate.

For more recipes featuring greens as well as other pressure cooker how-to tips, and even more recipes, visit my Web site: www.missvickie.com.

Brussels Sprouts in Parmesan Cheese Sauce

Fresh Brussels sprouts should have a mild flavor and a delicate fresh smell. The older sprouts have a strong cabbage odor. Do not wash or trim sprouts; just place them in perforated plastic bag (poke a few holes) and store in the crisper section of your refrigerator. Fresh sprouts will keep for 3 to 5 days.

2 tablespoons butter

⅓ cup minced onion

1 tablespoon minced garlic

¼ cup orange juice

1 tablespoon soy sauce

¼ teaspoon coarsely ground black pepper

1 pound Brussels sprouts, trimmed

¼ cup grated Parmesan cheese

Heat the butter in the pressure cooker over medium heat. Add the onion and garlic and cook, stirring, until softened, about 3 minutes. Stir in the orange juice, soy sauce, and pepper. Add the sprouts, tossing gently to coat, and lock the lid in place. Bring to 15psi over high heat, immediately reduce the heat to the lowest possible setting to stabilize and maintain that pressure, and cook for 4 minutes. Remove from the heat and use the cold water release method (see page 30) to depressurize. Carefully open the lid immediately after the pressure drops. Remove the Brussels sprouts using a slotted spoon and set aside. Bring the sauce in the cooker to a rapid boil over medium-high heat and cook, uncovered, for about 15 minutes, or until it is reduced by half. Add the Parmesan cheese and return the sprouts to the cooker, tossing gently to coat with the sauce. Continue to cook, stirring gently, until the sprouts are richly glazed, about 5 minutes. Transfer to a serving bowl and serve hot.

✳ Serves 4 to 5

Southern Greens with Roots and Pot "Likker"

Pot "likker" (pot liquor) is the vitamin-rich liquid left after cooking greens. I can still see my grandmother making this dish in her farmhouse kitchen, adding unmeasured ingredients according to a recipe that existed only in her memory. Although she originally used either fatback or side meat, I've modernized it a bit and substituted bacon. Some folks prefer their greens boiled to death, but I like them with just a little tooth, so I use the cold water release method (see page 30) to immediately stop the cooking process and avoid overcooking the greens. For authentic Southern cooking, corn bread must be served with greens to dip in the pot "likker"; I'm certain that must be a law somewhere, because the flavors go so well together.

6 thick slices bacon
1 onion, diced
1 red bell pepper, seeded and diced
1 jalapeño chile, seeded and finely chopped
2 tablespoons minced garlic
½ teaspoon coarsely ground black pepper
1 potato, peeled and diced
2 turnips, peeled and diced
2 parsnips, peeled and sliced
2 carrots, peeled and sliced
2 bunches turnip greens, washed and coarsely chopped
2 cups Best Bean Broth (page 342) or canned broth
Louisiana-style hot sauce, for garnish

Heat the pressure cooker over medium heat, fry the bacon pieces until crisp, and set aside to drain on paper towels. Add the onions, bell peppers, jalapeño, and garlic to the bacon drippings in the cooker and cook, stirring, until soft, about 3 minutes. Pour off all but 2 tablespoons of the bacon drippings. Crumble the bacon strips and add them to the cooker, add the black pepper, and stir to mix. Add the potatoes, turnips, parsnips, carrots, and greens, pour in the Best Bean Broth, and stir. Place the rack on top of the greens to weigh them down. Lock the lid in place. Bring to 15psi over high heat, immediately reduce the heat to the lowest possible setting to stabilize and maintain that pressure, and cook for 5 minutes. Remove from the heat and use the cold water release method (see page 30) to depressurize. Carefully open the lid immediately after the pressure drops. Transfer to a serving bowl, and pass a bottle of Louisiana-style hot sauce at the table. ✳ Serves 6

Variation: Substitute any other greens, or combination of greens, as desired.

Spaghetti Squash and Antipasto Salad

The size of a winter squash bears little relation to its flavor and tenderness, but look for ones with smooth skin and intense color. The squash should feel heavy and full; a squash that feels light for its size indicates that the inside flesh has begun to shrink and dry out. Winter squash keeps very well, and can be stored for as long as 3 months. Spaghetti squash can be used much like you would use spaghetti pasta. Select squash that will fit inside your pressure cooker when it's cut in half. Squash can be a struggle to cut, so place the squash on a folded towel on a flat surface to keep it from rolling about or moving while it's being cut. Use a large sharp knife and keep your fingers out of the way. Insert the tip of the knife into the center of the squash and cut down, and then turn the squash around and complete the cut from the other side. This method is much easier and safer than attacking a squash with the full breadth of the blade. When my brother decided to go low-carb, I suggested spaghetti squash in lieu of pasta and came up with this recipe. I recommend making this salad in advance, allowing plenty of time for the flavors to mingle and blend before serving. Serve with lots of toasted garlic bread and a nice Chianti for a filling supper.

2 spaghetti squash, halved lengthwise

1½ cups canned chickpeas, drained and rinsed

1 (6-ounce) jar marinated artichoke hearts, drained and quartered

1 red bell pepper, seeded and diced

10 to 12 grape or cherry tomatoes, halved

1 cup pitted and sliced kalamata olives (available at the supermarket deli counter)

1 cup sliced pepperoni, slices halved

½ cup thinly sliced green onion tops

¼ cup grated Parmesan cheese

⅓ cup finely chopped fresh basil leaves

1 teaspoon dried oregano

½ teaspoon coarsely ground black pepper

½ teaspoon red pepper flakes

1 (8-ounce) bottle Italian salad dressing, plus extra for serving (optional)

½ cup crumbled feta cheese

Place the rack in the pressure cooker and add ½ cup water. Place the squash halves, cut side down, in offset layers on the rack. Lock the lid in place. Bring to 15psi over high heat, immediately reduce the heat to the lowest possible setting to stabilize and maintain that pressure, and cook for 10 minutes. Remove from the heat and use the quick or cold water release method (see page 30) to depressurize. Carefully open the lid after the pressure drops. With long-handled tongs, remove the squash halves from the cooker, and use the tines of a fork to pull out the spaghetti-like strands and place them a large bowl. Add of all the remaining ingredients except for the feta cheese, tossing gently to mix. Cover tightly and refrigerate until the salad is well chilled. If needed, add additional salad dressing just before serving, and then sprinkle on the crumbled feta cheese. ✳ Serves 4 to 5

Crab and Creamy Dumpling Squash Bisque

Sweet dumpling squash is a winter variety of squash that can be found in your supermarket from September through December. You might think this plump, round little squash with the caved-in top is just another colorful gourd to be used in fall decorations, and with its cream-colored skin, striped with ivy green and hints of orange, it's certainly one of the prettiest squash. But as we all know, beauty is more than skin deep, and this little squash is so tender that it doesn't even have to be peeled. As you might guess from the name, the sweet dumpling squash has a naturally sweet flavor and creamy, pale yellow flesh; it's used in both sweet and savory dishes. Allow one squash per serving. In this recipe, I've combined the rich, sweet taste of crab with the sweet dumpling squash, a perfect mingling of tastes that's just right for a special supper.

Step One: The Crab
4 thick slices bacon
1½ cups chopped celery
½ cup chopped onion
½ cup white wine
1 teaspoon curry powder
1 teaspoon salt
¼ teaspoon freshly ground black pepper
1 pound fresh or thawed crabmeat, cut into 1-inch chunks

Heat the pressure cooker over medium heat, add the bacon, and fry until crisp. Remove the bacon to paper towels to drain, then crumble and set aside. Pour off all but 2 tablespoons of the bacon fat and return the cooker to medium-high heat. Add the celery and onions and cook, stirring, until softened, about 3 minutes. Add the wine, curry powder, salt, and pepper to the cooker and stir to mix. Place the rack on the bottom and add the crabmeat. Lock the lid in place. Bring to 15psi over high heat, immediately reduce the heat to the lowest possible setting to stabilize and maintain that pressure, and cook for 2 minutes. Remove from the heat and use the quick release method (see page 30) to depressurize. Carefully open the lid after the pressure drops. Transfer the crabmeat to a bowl and remove the rack.

Step Two: The Squash
2 (14-ounce) cans chicken broth
1 potato, peeled and diced
2 pounds sweet dumpling squash
1 cup heavy (whipping) cream
Ground nutmeg, for garnish

Add the broth, 1½ cups water, and the potatoes to the cooker. Cut the squash in half lengthwise and scoop out the fibrous pith and seeds. Layer the squash halves in the cooker, cut side down, and lock the lid in place. Bring to 15psi over high heat, immediately reduce the heat to the lowest possible setting to stabilize and maintain that pressure, and cook for 8 minutes. Remove from the heat and use the natural release method (see page 31) to depressurize. Carefully open the lid after the pressure drops. Remove the squash and scoop out the meat, cutting it into bite-size pieces and returning it to the pressure cooker. Using a hand blender, puree the ingredients in the cooker until smooth. Bring to a simmer, uncovered, over medium heat and slowly add in the heavy cream, whisking constantly until well blended. Gently stir the crabmeat and bacon into the simmering puree, heating through. Adjust the seasonings to taste and ladle into a serving bowl, adding a dash of nutmeg on the top. ✳ Serves 4

Greens 'n' Rice

Southerners love their greens, and they are a time-honored tradition in every kitchen. This recipe combines popular Southern ingredients—rice, greens, and corn—and it can be used as an easy replacement for potatoes.

2 tablespoons butter
1 onion, diced
1 jalapeño chile, seeded and finely chopped
2 tablespoons minced garlic
1 cup uncooked short- or medium-grain white rice
3 cups chopped greens (collard, mustard, turnip, or a mixture)
1 cup frozen corn kernels
½ teaspoon coarsely ground black pepper
½ teaspoon ground cumin
1 (14-ounce) can chicken broth

Heat the butter in the pressure cooker over medium heat. Add the onions, jalapeño, and garlic and cook, stirring, for about 3 minutes. Add the rice, stirring it into the butter until the grains are translucent. Add the greens, corn, pepper, cumin, and broth. Stir to mix and lock the lid in place. Bring to 15psi over high heat, immediately reduce the heat to the lowest possible setting to stabilize and maintain that pressure, and cook for 7 minutes. Remove from the heat and use the natural release method (see page 31) to depressurize. Carefully open the lid after the pressure drops. Transfer to a serving dish and fluff the rice with a fork.

✳ Serves 4 to 5

Variation: You may add 2 cups of any sort of leftover cooked meat at the start of cooking to change this recipe from a side dish to a main dish.

Savory Fresh Tomato Bread Pudding with Lemon-Caper Mayonnaise

As the story goes, the original recipe dates from the WWII years, when my grandmother made use of home-grown tomatoes from her garden. In upgrading this recipe I chose firm Roma tomatoes because they have fewer seeds and less juice than the old heirloom varieties. I also bumped up the plain mayo in Grandma's version with a zippy Lemon-Caper Mayonnaise. For this PIP recipe (see page 37), you will need a stainless steel bowl (no aluminum—it reacts with the acid in tomatoes, resulting in dark stains) that will fit loosely inside the pressure cooker.

Step One: The Tomatoes

10 Roma tomatoes, peeled and cored
   (see page 389)
2 tablespoons olive oil
1 onion, diced
½ cup diced green bell pepper
3 tablespoons minced garlic
2 tablespoons vinegar
1 teaspoon hot sauce
1 tablespoon dried basil
2 teaspoons dried oregano
1½ teaspoons salt
½ teaspoon freshly ground black pepper

Use a food processor to puree the peeled tomatoes, and then transfer them to a large mixing bowl. Heat the oil in the pressure cooker over medium heat. Add the onions, bell peppers, and garlic, and cook, stirring, until softened, about 3 minutes. Transfer to the mixing bowl and add the vinegar, hot sauce, basil, oregano, salt, and pepper, tossing until well mixed.

Step Two: The Bread

8 slices dense, finely textured white bread
⅓ cup butter

Although it's not necessary, you may trim the crust from the bread for a better appearance. The frugal cook will reserve the crusts for another use. Butter the bread, stack the slices, and cut them into 1-inch cubes.

Step Three: The Pudding

Generously butter the inside of a large stainless steel bowl. Ladle about ½ cup of tomato mixture into the bottom, and spread with a layer of bread cubes. Repeat, using alternating layers of tomatoes and bread cubes. Pour any remaining sauce from the tomatoes on top and run a knife blade around the inside of the bowl to distribute the sauce. Cover the bowl with a square of aluminum foil, crimping the edges around the rim, and let the pudding rest for about 10 minutes, or until the bread soaks up all the tomato juice. Place the rack in the bottom of the pressure cooker, add 3 cups water, and bring to a boil over high heat. Use foil helper handles (see page 42) to place the pudding bowl on top of the rack when the water is at a rapid boil. Add more boiling water if necessary; it needs to be high enough to reach halfway up the outside of the bowl. Lock the lid in place. Bring to 15psi over high heat, immediately reduce the heat to the lowest possible setting to stabilize and maintain that pressure, and cook for 25 minutes. Remove from the heat and use the natural release method (see page 31) to depressurize. Carefully open the lid after the pressure drops. Use the helper handles to lift the bowl out of the cooker. To unmold the pudding, run a thin knife around the edge of the bowl and then invert a large plate over the top. Flip it over quickly, and carefully remove the bowl from the pudding. To serve, cut the pudding into wedges and add a dollop of Lemon-Caper Mayonnaise (recipe follows), or regular mayonnaise if desired. ✳ Serves 5 to 6

Lemon-Caper Mayonnaise

1 cup mayonnaise
Juice of 1 lemon
1 teaspoon dried tarragon
1 teaspoon capers
Salt and freshly ground black pepper to taste

Combine all of the ingredients several hours in advance and refrigerate until ready to serve. This goes great with seafood, and makes the best uptown, gourmet-quality sandwiches ever!

Herbed Fresh Tomato Soup

My father, who disliked tomatoes, liked to point out that people once thought the tomato was poisonous, at which mother would remind us children that tomatoes were also called the Apple of Paradise. This heirloom recipe uses fresh, ripe tomatoes to make a well-seasoned, flavorful soup that is de rigueur with grilled cheese sandwiches and a glass of ice-cold milk.

5 tablespoons butter
1 onion, chopped
2 stalks celery, diced
2 tablespoons minced garlic
8 large ripe tomatoes, peeled, cored, and
    coarsely chopped (see page 389)
1 carrot, grated
½ cup finely packed chopped cilantro leaves,
    plus 6 whole leaves for garnish
1 tablespoon dried basil
2 teaspoons dried oregano
2 teaspoons chili powder
½ teaspoon freshly ground black pepper
2 bay leaves
3 (14-ounce) cans chicken broth

Heat 3 tablespoons of the butter in a large pressure cooker over medium heat. Add the onions, celery, and garlic and cook, stirring, for about 3 minutes. Add all of the remaining ingredients, plus 2 cups water. Stir to mix and lock the lid in place. Bring to 15psi over high heat, immediately reduce the heat to the lowest possible setting to stabilize and maintain that pressure, and cook for 15 minutes. Remove from the heat and use the natural release method (see page 31) to depressurize. Carefully open the lid after the pressure drops. Discard the bay leaves. Working in batches, use a blender or food processor to puree the soup. Pass the purée through a fine-mesh wire sieve to remove any bits of peel and seeds. Return the puree to the cooker and simmer, uncovered, over medium-high heat until heated through. Adjust the seasonings to taste. To serve ladle the soup into individual serving bowls and garnish with a single cilantro leaf. ✳ Serves 6

Variation: For a richer-tasting, creamier soup, stir in 1½ cups cream or half-and-half (choose according to your taste buds or waistline) after the pressure cooker is depressurized.

Stewed Fresh Tomatoes

Since they are a fruit and not a vegetable, ripe tomatoes have a touch of sweetness. Stewed tomatoes are flavored with onions, celery, and green bell peppers and they are the perfect side dish to an Italian meal, or add them to stews and soups. When my grandmother served this for lunch, it was ladled over a thick slab of buttery garlic toast topped with melt cheese.

2 tablespoons butter
1 onion, diced
2 stalks celery, thinly sliced
½ cup diced green bell pepper
6 to 8 very ripe Roma tomatoes, peeled
   and cored (see page 389)
3 tablespoons sugar (more or less, to taste)
1 teaspoon salt
½ teaspoon freshly ground black pepper
1 bay leaf

Heat the butter in the pressure cooker over medium heat. Add the onions, celery, and green peppers and cook, stirring, until they are slightly softened, about 3 minutes. Slice the peeled tomatoes about ½ inch thick, saving any juice, and add the tomatoes and juice to the cooker. Add the remaining ingredients and ½ cup water. Stir to mix and lock the lid in place. Bring to 15psi over high heat, immediately reduce the heat to the lowest possible setting to stabilize and maintain that pressure, and cook for 5 minutes. Remove from the heat and use the quick or cold water release method (see page 30) to depressurize. Carefully open the lid after the pressure drops. Adjust the seasonings to taste and serve. ✳ Serves 4

Variations

Add any one or a combination of the following ingredients:

1 pound fresh okra pods, washed, trimmed, and sliced

1 pound green beans, trimmed and sliced diagonally into 1½-inch lengths

1 (10-ounce) can whole kernel corn, drained

Cream of Mushroom Soup

The chicken broth and wine give this soup real body, beyond the usual bland cream and butter taste of most mushroom soups. This soup is great as a meal, but can also be used as a sauce or in recipes in place of the canned version.

Step One: The Mushrooms and Broth
2 ounces dried mushrooms, any variety or
   combination
2 tablespoons butter
½ pound fresh button mushrooms, washed,
   stems chopped, and caps sliced
1 cup finely chopped onions
1 stalk celery, diced
4 tablespoons minced garlic
1 teaspoon salt
½ teaspoon freshly ground white pepper

Miss Vickie's Tips: How to Peel and Core Fresh Tomatoes for Sauces

Cut the stems out of the tomatoes and then make a very shallow × cut on the bottom of each one. One at a time, drop each tomato into boiling water. After 30 seconds, or when the skin begins to peel, quickly remove the tomato with a slotted spoon and place it into a bowl of ice water. Once the tomato has been chilled, remove it from the ice water. The tomato should still be very firm, with the skin wrinkled and hanging off of it slightly. Peel the skin off with your fingers, or use a small sharp paring knife to remove the stubborn pieces, but be careful not to squeeze the tomato. Cut the peeled tomatoes in half over a small bowl, gently squeezing the halves so that the seeds drip into the bowl. Discard the seeds and use the cored tomatoes in your recipes as needed.

¼ teaspoon ground nutmeg

2 bay leaves

½ cup Chablis or any dry white wine

2 (14-ounce) cans chicken broth

1 tablespoon fresh lemon juice

Soak the dried mushrooms in 2 cups hot tap water for 30 minutes. Reserve the mushrooms and soaking water. Heat the butter in the pressure cooker over medium heat. Add the fresh mushrooms, onions, celery, and garlic, and cook, stirring, until they are slightly softened, about 3 minutes. Dice the porcini mushrooms and add the pieces to the pressure cooker. Add the salt, pepper, nutmeg, and bay leaves, and deglaze the cooker with the wine, scraping up all those crusty, brown bits from the bottom. Stir in the broth and lemon juice. Measure the reserved soaking water from the mushrooms and add enough additional water to it to equal 2 cups, adding that to the pressure cooker. Stir to mix and lock the lid in place. Bring to 15psi over high heat, immediately reduce the heat to the lowest possible setting to stabilize and maintain that pressure, and cook for 3 minutes. Remove from the heat and use the natural water release method (see page 31) to depressurize. Carefully open the lid after the pressure drops.

Step Two: Finishing the Soup

4 tablespoons (½ stick) butter

¼ cup all-purpose flour

1 quart half-and-half, at room temperature (warm in the microwave if necessary)

Tabasco sauce to taste

To thicken the soup, make a light roux by melting the butter in a separate saucepan over medium heat. Add the flour and whisk until completely smooth. Continue cooking the roux for a few minutes, stirring constantly to get rid of any flour taste. Gradually pour in the half-and-half, whisking until smooth. Slowly add the white sauce to the mushroom mixture in the pressure cooker, whisking continuously. Bring the soup to simmer over medium-high heat, heating through. Adjust the salt and pepper to taste. At this point, I add a splash of Tabasco, and it really makes the flavors pop! Serve in a heated soup tureen. ✳ Serves 4

Fresh Vegetable Chop Suey

The secret to tender-crisp vegetables in a pressure cooker is using the cold water release method (see page 30), which immediately drops the pressure and stops the cooking process, allowing you to quickly open the lid. When we were growing up, my mom prepared this dish all the time. All of us kids learned how to use chopsticks just to be able show off our expertise by delicately picking out slivers of carrots and slices of water chestnuts—what fun!

1 tablespoon sesame or peanut oil
1 cup sliced fresh mushrooms
2 tablespoons minced garlic
1 tablespoon grated fresh ginger
½ cup chicken broth
1 (6-ounce) can water chestnuts, drained
    and sliced
1 cup bamboo shoots, drained
½ cup chopped cilantro
1 cup sliced red bell pepper
1 cup sliced celery
1 carrot, cut into small matchsticks
2 cups thinly sliced bok choy
2 cups broccoli florets
2 cups chopped green onions, white and
    green parts
1½ cups fresh snow peas
2 cups mung bean sprouts
1 cup pineapple chunks
3 tablespoons oyster sauce
¼ teaspoon Tabasco sauce
⅓ cup soy sauce
2 tablespoons cornstarch
1 tablespoon toasted sesame seeds

Heat the oil in the pressure cooker over medium heat. Add the mushrooms, garlic, and ginger and cook, stirring, until slightly softened, about 3 minutes. Add the chicken broth, then add the next 12 ingredients (through to and including the pineapple) in the order given and do not stir or mix. Lock the lid in place. Bring to 15psi over high heat, immediately reduce the heat to the lowest possible setting to stabilize and maintain that pressure, and cook for exactly 2 minutes. Remove from the heat and use the cold water release method (see page 30) to depressurize. Carefully open the lid immediately after the pressure drops to stop the cooking process. Transfer the vegetables to a serving bowl and set aside while preparing the sauce. Bring the broth in the pressure cooker to a rapid boil, uncovered, and reduce the volume by half. Stir in the oyster sauce and Tabasco sauce, then simmer gently over medium heat. Mix the soy sauce with the cornstarch and add it to the simmering sauce, stirring constantly as the mixture thickens, but do not boil. Return the cooked vegetables to the pressure cooker and toss gently until coated with the sauce and heated through. Transfer to a large serving bowl and garnish with the toasted sesame seeds. ✳ Serves 6

Serving Suggestion: Serve this dish as is, or spoon it over sticky steamed white rice, crisply fried chow mein noodles, cooked ramen-style noodles, or brown rice.

Variation: Add 2 cups cooked and diced chicken, pork, beef, crab, lobster, or shrimp—a great way to utilize small amounts of leftover meats.

Broccoli Florets with Hollandaise Sauce

Few things seem to impress folks more than a good hollandaise sauce, because everyone thinks it's so difficult to make. This quick and easy recipe is anything but hard, but don't tell anyone how simple it is to make this hollandaise sauce. I use it over asparagus or any other fresh vegetables.

Step One: The Broccoli
1 pound fresh broccoli florets

Place the rack in the cooker and add ½ cup water. Place the broccoli in a steamer basket and position it on top of the rack. Lock the lid in place. Bring to 15psi over high heat, immediately reduce the heat to the lowest possible setting to stabilize and maintain that pressure, and cook for exactly 2 minutes. Remove from the heat and use the cold water release method (see page 30) to depressurize. Carefully open the lid immediately after the pressure drops to stop the cooking process. Drain the broccoli and set aside.

Step Two: The Easy Blender Hollandaise Sauce
8 tablespoons (1 stick) butter
4 large egg yolks
3 tablespoons fresh lemon juice
3 drops Tabasco sauce
½ teaspoon paprika

Melt the butter in the pressure cooker over medium heat until bubbling. Remove from the heat. Place the egg yolks, lemon juice, Tabasco sauce, and paprika in a blender. Blend at high speed for 30 seconds, or until creamy and well blended. Reduce the speed on the blender, open the top, and slowly pour in the hot butter in a thin stream. Process the mixture at high speed until it is smoothly blended and thick and creamy. Immediately pour the hollandaise sauce over the broccoli, and serve.

❋ Serves 4 to 5

Fresh Italian-Style Vegetables with Creamy Garlic-Parmesan Cheese Sauce

Here's a deliciously seasoned medley of tender-crisp vegetables with a wonderful melding of Mediterranean-style flavors that come together beautifully in the Creamy Garlic-Parmesan Cheese Sauce.

Step One: The Vegetables

1 onion, cut into wedges
3 stalks celery, chopped
2 carrots, peeled and thinly sliced on the diagonal
1 pound Swiss chard, washed, tough stems removed, and torn into bite-size pieces
1 pound Brussels sprouts, trimmed and halved
1 zucchini, cut into ½-inch slices
1 cauliflower, cut into large florets

Pour ½ cup water into a large pressure cooker and add the rack. Add all of the remaining ingredients in the order given. If necessary, wilt the Swiss chard by steaming it first to reduce its bulky mass. Lock the lid in place. Bring to 15psi over high heat, immediately reduce the heat to the lowest possible setting to stabilize and maintain that pressure, and cook for 3 minutes. Remove from the heat and use the cold water release method (see page 30) to depressurize. Carefully open the lid immediately after the pressure drops to stop the cooking process. Drain the vegetables in a colander, and transfer to a serving bowl.

Step Two: The Creamy Garlic-Parmesan Cheese Sauce

4 tablespoons (½ stick) butter
3 tablespoons minced garlic
½ cup grated Parmesan cheese
½ teaspoon red pepper flakes
½ cup light cream

Melt the butter in the pressure cooker over medium heat. Add the garlic and cook, stirring, for about 3 minutes. Add the Parmesan cheese and red pepper flakes. Slowly add the cream, stirring constantly until smooth and bubbly. Pour the sauce over the vegetables, tossing gently to coat, and serve.

✳ Serves 6

Parsnips and Carrots with Orange Butter Sauce

Parsnips, a sweet, creamy-white root resembling a slender carrot, are becoming more popular on the American table because they're so versatile in soups and stews. Try this vegetable steamed or simply mashed with a little butter. Look for long, slender parsnips, and don't store them near apples, pears, or other fruits, because the ethylene gas produced by these fruits can make parsnips bitter.

Step One: The Vegetables

½ pound parsnips, peeled and sliced
½ pound carrots, peeled and sliced

Place the rack or steamer tray in the bottom of the pressure cooker and add ½ cup water. Add the parsnips and carrots. Lock the lid in place. Bring to 15psi over high heat, immediately reduce the heat to the lowest possible setting to stabilize and maintain that pressure, and cook for 4 minutes. Remove from the heat and use the quick or cold water release method (see page 30) to depressurize. Carefully open the lid after the pressure drops. Drain in a colander and set the vegetables aside while making the Orange Butter Sauce.

Step Two: The Orange Butter Sauce
8 tablespoons (1 stick) butter
2 tablespoons brown sugar
1 tablespoon grated orange zest
¼ teaspoon ground nutmeg
1 tablespoon cornstarch
½ cup orange juice

Melt the butter in the pressure cooker over medium heat. Add the brown sugar, orange zest, and nutmeg. Stir the cornstarch into the orange juice and add it to the butter, whisking as the sauce thickens. Return the carrots and parsnips to the cooker, tossing gently until well coated. Transfer to a serving dish. ✳ **Serves 4 to 5**

Lemon-Buttered Turnip Sticks

Winter roots are very firm, so use a heavy, sharp knife. Place the root on a folded kitchen towel on a cutting board to keep it from slipping around. For the mildest and sweetest tasting turnips choose the smaller, baby turnips that are about 2 inches in size. These matchsticks are so good, even the kids will like them.

> 2 turnips, peeled and cut into long matchsticks
> 3 tablespoons butter
> 1 onion, halved and sliced
> ½ teaspoon sugar
> ½ teaspoon freshly ground black pepper
> ¼ teaspoon ground allspice
> 2 tablespoons fresh lemon juice
> 1 tablespoon chopped fresh parsley, for garnish

Place the rack or steamer tray in the bottom of the pressure cooker and add ½ cup water. Add the turnip pieces. Lock the lid in place. Bring to 15psi over high heat, immediately reduce the heat to the lowest possible setting to stabilize and maintain that pressure, and cook for 2 minutes. Remove from the heat and use the cold water release method (see page 30) to depressurize. Carefully open the lid after the pressure drops. Drain the turnip sticks into a colander and set aside. Heat the butter in the pressure cooker over medium heat. Add the onions and cook, stirring, until soft, about 3 minutes. Stir in the sugar, pepper, allspice, and lemon juice. Return the turnip sticks to the pressure cooker and simmer gently, tossing to coat. Garnish with the chopped parsley and serve hot. ✳ **Serves 4 to 5**

"Potatobagas": Mashed Potatoes and Rutabagas

The rutabaga is often overlooked, and this recipe is a nice introduction to this delicious root vegetable. Rutabagas look very much like a turnip with yellow-orange flesh; in fact, they are often mistakenly called yellow turnips. With its easy preparation and versatility, great nutrition, and excellent flavor, the rutabaga can easily become a family favorite.

 1½ pounds rutabagas, peeled and cut into
  1-inch pieces
 1½ pounds russet potatoes, peeled and cut
  into 2-inch pieces
 6 tablespoons (¾ stick) butter
 ¾ cup buttermilk
 Salt and freshly ground black pepper to taste
 Chopped green onion tops or snipped
  fresh chives

Place the rack or steamer tray in the bottom of the pressure cooker and add ½ cup water. Add the rutabagas and potatoes. Lock the lid in place. Bring to 15psi over high heat, immediately reduce the heat to the lowest possible setting to stabilize and maintain that pressure, and cook for 5 minutes. Remove from the heat and use the natural release method (see page 31) to depressurize. Carefully open the lid after the pressure drops. Drain well. Return the potatoes and rutabagas to the cooker. Add the butter and mash well. Slowly add the buttermilk, using only enough to make the mixture smooth and creamy. Add salt and pepper to taste and stir in the chopped green onions. Transfer the mixture to a serving bowl. ✳ Serves 6

Buttered Red Potatoes with Garlic and Parsley

Although most people think of small red potatoes as "new" potatoes, new potatoes can be any variety of early potato picked before their sugars have converted to starch. Good-quality red potatoes will have a bright red color with few eyes and a smooth, thin, edible skin that only needs to be gently washed. Red potatoes hold their shape after cooking and range from the size of a golf ball to the size of a baseball. For this recipe, I like to choose potatoes that are about the size of a small tangerine.

 8 small red potatoes, washed
 3 tablespoons butter
 2 tablespoons minced garlic
 2 tablespoons chopped fresh parsley leaves
 Salt and freshly ground black pepper to taste

Place the rack in a pressure cooker and add ½ cup water. Add the potatoes to the cooker. Lock the lid in place. Bring to 15psi over high heat, immediately reduce the heat to the lowest possible setting to stabilize and maintain that pressure, and cook for 8 minutes. Remove from the heat and use the natural release method (see page 31) to depressurize. Carefully open the lid after the pressure drops. Transfer the potatoes to a cutting board, and, when they are cool enough to handle, slice them thickly. Empty the cooker, and wipe the inside until dry. Heat the butter in the pressure cooker over medium heat. Add the garlic and cook, stirring, until soft, about 3 minutes. Return the sliced potatoes to the cooker and add the parsley and salt and pepper to taste, tossing gently to coat. When the potatoes are heated through, transfer them to a serving dish. ✳ Serves 4 to 5

Variations

Buttered Red Potatoes with Onion and Dill

8 small red potatoes
3 tablespoons butter
¼ cup finely chopped onion
1 tablespoon chopped fresh dill
Salt and freshly ground black pepper to taste

Cook the potatoes the same as above. Heat the butter in the pressure cooker over medium heat. Add the onion and cook, stirring, until soft, about 3 minutes. Return the sliced potatoes to the cooker and add the fresh dill and salt and pepper to taste, tossing gently to coat. When the potatoes are heated through, transfer them to a serving dish. ✳ Serves 4 to 5

Buttered Dijon Red Potatoes

8 small red potatoes
3 tablespoons butter
1 green bell pepper, seeded and diced
¼ cup finely chopped onion

2 tablespoons Dijon mustard
¼ teaspoon cayenne pepper

Cook the potatoes the same as above. Heat the butter in the pressure cooker over medium heat. Add the bell peppers and onions and cook, stirring, until soft, about 3 minutes. Return the sliced potatoes to the cooker and add the Dijon mustard and cayenne pepper, tossing gently to coat. When the potatoes are heated through, transfer to a serving dish. ✳ Serves 4 to 5

Buttered Herb and Sweet Onion Potatoes

8 small red potatoes
3 tablespoons butter
1 cup sweet Maui or Vidalia onion, halved and thinly sliced
1 tablespoon dried mixed Italian herbs
1 teaspoon ground turmeric
½ teaspoon freshly ground black pepper

Cook the potatoes the same as above. Heat the butter in the pressure cooker over medium heat. Add the onions and cook, stirring, until very soft and golden brown in color, about 3 minutes. Return the sliced potatoes to the cooker and add the Italian seasoning, turmeric, and pepper, tossing gently to coat. When the potatoes are heated through, transfer to a serving dish. ✳ Serves 4 to 5

Mexican-Style Potato Cheese Soup

This soup is very thick and hearty, with just a touch of south-of-the-border spiciness! It's a wonderfully comforting soup for those cold, blustery winter days. Include a loaf of warm, crusty shepherd's bread.

2 mild chiles, such as poblano, pasilla, or
    Anaheim, charred, peeled, seeded, and
    diced (see instructions below)
2 tablespoons butter
1 onion, minced
1 cup chopped celery
2 tablespoons minced garlic
4 white potatoes, peeled and cubed
1 cup chopped carrots
⅓ cup minced cilantro leaves, plus a few
    leaves for garnish (optional)
1 teaspoon ground cumin
1 teaspoon salt
½ teaspoon freshly ground black pepper
2 (14-ounce) cans chicken broth
3 cups milk
1½ cups shredded extra sharp cheddar cheese
1 cup sour cream
⅓ cup instant potato flakes, or more to
    adjust to desired thickness
¼ teaspoon hot sauce, or more to taste

There are two easy ways of roasting peppers for that delicious smoky flavor. Use either a broiler or the flame of a gas stove. When roasting several peppers, it's more convenient to place them under the broiler. Turn the peppers over when the skin begins blacken and char. To roast peppers on top of a gas stove, adjust a burner to high heat. Use long-handled tongs to hold each pepper about 4 inches above the flame, and keep turning the pepper until it is evenly charred on all sides. Place the roasted peppers in a plastic bag so that the steam can loosen the skin. When the peppers are cool enough to handle, just rub the skin off with your fingers. Don't forget to wear rubber gloves when working with hot chiles, and remember not to touch your eyes! After the skin is removed, carefully slit open each chile and remove the seeds. Dice and set aside. Melt the butter in a pressure cooker over medium heat. Add the onions, celery, and garlic and cook, stirring, until softened, about 3 minutes. Add the potatoes, carrots, cilantro, cumin, salt, pepper, and broth. Stir to mix and lock the lid in place. Bring to 15psi over high heat, immediately reduce the heat to the lowest possible setting to stabilize and maintain that pressure, and cook for 4 minutes. Remove from the heat and use the quick or cold water release method (see page 30) to depressurize. Carefully open the lid after the pressure drops. Bring to a simmer, uncovered, and slowly add the milk, stirring gently. Add the cheese, stirring as it melts, and then add the sour cream, heating through. Add the potato flakes a little at a time to thicken the soup to the desired consistency. Adjust the seasonings and add hot sauce to taste. Transfer the soup to a heated serving tureen, and garnish with a few cilantro leaves, if desired. ✳ Serves 4 to 5

Creamy Buttermilk Potato Soup

The original version of this tangy buttermilk soup is probably a hundred years old, a favorite family heirloom recipe dating back to my great grandmother's German roots. Over time it has slowly evolved as it was handed down from one generation to the next. I use white or Yukon gold potatoes for this soup, as they tend to hold their shape better than russets. This is a versatile recipe, and I recommend that you really make it your own with 1-cup additions of fresh or frozen broccoli, cauliflower, baby green peas, corn, or any combination that appeals to your tastes.

2 tablespoons butter
2 cups diced celery
1 onion, diced
2 tablespoons minced garlic
4 white or red potatoes, peeled and cut into ½-inch cubes
1 teaspoon salt
1 teaspoon coarsely ground black pepper
2 (14-ounce) cans chicken broth
1 teaspoon spicy mustard
½ teaspoon Louisiana-style hot sauce
3 cups buttermilk
⅓ cup instant potato flakes, or more to adjust to desired thickness
Dried parsley flakes, for garnish

Heat the butter in the pressure cooker over medium heat. Add the celery, onions, and garlic and cook, stirring, until softened, about 3 minutes. Add the potatoes, salt, pepper, broth, mustard, and hot sauce. Stir to mix and lock the lid in place. Bring to 15psi over high heat, immediately reduce the heat to the lowest possible setting to stabilize and maintain that pressure, and cook for 4 minutes. Remove from the heat and use the natural release method (see page 31) to depressurize. Carefully open the lid after the pressure drops. Whisk in the buttermilk and potato flakes until blended and simmer, uncovered, over low heat until the soup begins to thicken. Adjust the seasonings to taste. Transfer to a soup tureen, and sprinkle parsley flakes on top.

✳ Serves 4

Variation: Add 2 cups cooked or leftover ham or kielbasa at the start of cooking.

"Faked" Potatoes with the Works

When I said, "We're having baked potatoes," someone thought I said "faked potatoes" because they were cooked in a pressure cooker instead of the oven . . . well, it's 30 years later, and I'm still stuck with the play on words describing this recipe. Save your reputation; never let on that your "baked" potatoes are really "faked."

Step One: The Works
1 cup grated sharp cheddar cheese
1 (3-ounce) package cream cheese, softened
½ cup sour cream
4 tablespoons (½ stick) butter, at room
    temperature
1½ teaspoons garlic powder
Salt and freshly ground black pepper to taste
½ teaspoon Louisiana-style hot sauce

Combine all of the ingredients in a bowl and set aside.

Step 2: The Potatoes
6 slices bacon
4 large baking potatoes
½ cup hot milk
½ cup sliced green onion tops

Fry the bacon in the pressure cooker over medium heat until crisp. Drain on paper towels, crumble, and set aside. Pour off all the grease from the cooker. Place the rack in the bottom of the pressure cooker and add 1 cup water, making sure the rack is well above the water line so that the potatoes will steam roast rather than boil. Place the potatoes on the rack and lock the lid in place. Bring to 15psi over high heat, immediately reduce the heat to the lowest possible setting to stabilize and maintain that pressure, and cook for 18 minutes. Remove from the heat and use the natural release method (see page 31) to depressurize. Carefully open the lid after the pressure drops. Test for doneness; a skewer or the tines of a fork should pierce the potato easily and without resistance. If necessary, lock the lid back in place, return to 15psi over high heat, immediately reduce the heat to the lowest possible setting to stabilize and maintain that pressure, and cook for an additional 3 to 5 minutes, or until the potatoes are done. Remove from the heat and use the natural release method (see page 31) to depressurize. Carefully open the lid after the pressure drops. When the potatoes are finished, cut away a 1-inch strip of the skin from the top of each potato. Carefully scoop out the inside of each potato, leaving the shells intact. Mash the potatoes by hand, using a potato masher or ricer for best results. Add the sour cream mixture to the mashed potatoes, stirring until smooth and blended. Add just enough of the hot milk for a smooth and creamy consistency. Spoon the potato mixture back into the empty potato shells, piling high. Top with the crumbled bacon and green onions just before serving. ✳ Serves 4

Cook's Note: To make this with medium-size potatoes, reduce the cooking time to 12 minutes.

Pan-Roasted Potatoes and Red Peppers

This recipe uses the pressure cooker to quickly precook these well-seasoned, pan-roasted potatoes. When you're tired of ordinary potatoes, this is a great side dish that goes well with many other foods. The potatoes are tender on the inside, with a slight roasted crispness on the outside.

Step One: The Potatoes
4 white, red, or gold potatoes

Wash the potatoes. Place the rack in a pressure cooker and add ½ cup water. Lay the potatoes on the rack and lock the lid in place. Bring to 15psi over high heat, immediately reduce the heat to the lowest possible setting to stabilize and maintain that pressure, and cook for 15 minutes. Remove from the heat and use the natural release method (see page 31) to depressurize. Carefully open the lid after the pressure drops. Check for doneness; a skewer or the tines of a fork should pierce the potato easily and without resistance. If necessary, lock the lid back in place, return to 15psi over high heat, immediately reduce the heat to the lowest possible setting to stabilize and maintain that pressure, and cook for a few more minutes. Remove from the heat and use the natural release method (see page 31) to depressurize. Carefully open the lid after the pressure drops. When the potatoes are done, transfer to a cutting board, cut each potato into 8 wedges, and pat dry with paper towels. Empty the cooker and wipe dry.

Step Two: The Pan Roasting
4 tablespoons olive oil
2 red bell peppers, seeded and cut into 1-inch pieces
2 tablespoons minced garlic
2 green onions, white and green parts, chopped
1 tablespoon paprika
1 teaspoon chili powder
½ teaspoon freshly ground black pepper
½ teaspoon salt
½ teaspoon ground cumin

Heat 1 tablespoon of oil in the pressure cooker over high heat; it must be very hot. Add the bell peppers and garlic and cook, stirring, until soft, about 3 minutes. Add the green onions and cook, stirring, until they just begin to wilt, then set the pepper mixture aside in a low oven. Combine the paprika, chili powder, pepper, salt, and cumin in a large sealable plastic bag, shaking until blended. Add the potato wedges a few at a time, shaking gently until they are all coated with the spice mixture. Heat the remaining oil in the pressure cooker over high heat; it must be very hot before adding the potato wedges. Add the wedges to the cooker in batches that will fit without crowding. "Roast" the potato wedges in the cooker, uncovered, over medium-high heat until they are a light golden brown. Turn them once, browning both sides of the wedges until they are crispy. Place each batch in the oven to keep warm until they are all cooked. Combine the potato wedges and pepper mixture in a bowl, tossing gently before serving. ✳ Serves 4

Colcannon

This is the traditional Irish potato and cabbage casserole. A dish of mashed potatoes with just a subtle taste of cabbage and onion makes a wonderful change from ordinary mashed potatoes. This recipe uses the tiered cooking method (see page 38) to keep the potatoes and cabbage separate.

2 potatoes, peeled and diced

4 cups coarsely chopped cabbage

2 leeks, white parts only, washed and thinly sliced

2 tablespoons butter

1 onion, coarsely chopped

½ cup hot milk

½ teaspoon salt

½ teaspoon freshly ground black pepper

Pat of butter, for garnish

Add ½ cup water to a large pressure cooker, place the rack in the cooker, and add the potatoes. Place the cabbage and leeks in a steamer basket and position it on top of the potatoes. Lock the lid in place. Bring to 15psi over high heat, immediately reduce the heat to the lowest possible setting to stabilize and maintain that pressure, and cook for 4 minutes. Remove from the heat and use the quick or cold water release method (see page 30) to depressurize. Carefully open the lid after the pressure drops. Carefully remove the cabbage and leek mixture, drain the potatoes, and set aside. Wipe the cooker dry. Heat the butter in the pressure cooker over medium heat. Add the onions and cook, stirring, until softened, about 3 minutes. Remove from the heat, add the cooked potatoes to the pressure cooker, and add just enough hot milk to mash them by whatever means you prefer, but leave the potatoes somewhat lumpy rather than smooth and creamy. Gently stir in the cooked cabbage and leeks, salt, and pepper, and adjust the seasonings to taste. Return the cooker to low heat and cook until just heated through. Transfer to a serving bowl and top with a pat of butter at the center.

✳ Serves 4 to 5

Cooks Note: Although it's not traditional, you can turn this vegetable side dish into a main course by adding 2 cups cooked chopped ham or sliced kielbasa.

Basic Mashed Potatoes

Mashed potatoes are the quintessential American comfort food. This popular side dish is found on the dinner table in homes everywhere, and, gussied up, it has a starring role on the menus of gourmet restaurants. Everyone has a personal favorite when it comes to mashed potatoes, so alas, there is no one universal method of making mashed potatoes that will suit everyone. Of the two basic varieties of potatoes—boiling or baking—the latter is best suited for mashing because they have a higher starch content. For light, fluffy mashed potatoes, use a potato ricer. For those who like their mashed potatoes with a little more texture, use a potato masher. If you're short on time (and who isn't these days!), an electric mixer used in short bursts on a low setting will turn out mashed potatoes that are somewhere in between. This is the basic recipe for mashed potatoes, with enough variations that you can branch out with something a little fancier whenever you're in the mood.

> 6 medium-size russet potatoes, peeled and quartered
>
> ½ cup whole milk, evaporated milk, half-and-half, whipping cream, buttermilk, or sour cream (your choice)
>
> 4 tablespoons (½ stick) butter or margarine, at room temperature
>
> Salt and freshly ground black pepper to taste

Pour ⅔ cup water into the pressure cooker and add the rack or steamer tray. If necessary, elevate the rack so it is above the water line. Add the potatoes and lock the lid in place. Bring to 15psi over high heat, immediately reduce the heat to the lowest possible setting to stabilize and maintain that pressure, and cook for 6 minutes. Remove from the heat and use the quick or cold water release method (see page 30) to depressurize. Carefully open the lid after the pressure drops. Use a colander to drain the potatoes, and set aside. At this point, you can put them through a potato ricer for a lighter texture, if desired. Reheat the cooker over medium heat, add the milk, and heat just until bubbles begin to form around the edge of the cooker. Add the potatoes, butter, salt, and pepper, and start mashing with a potato masher; or use an electric mixer on a low setting, but do not overdo it or the potatoes will be more like glue. Add more butter if necessary, and continue mashing until the potatoes are smooth and free of lumps. Adjust the seasonings to taste. Transfer the mashed potatoes to a warm bowl, and serve. ✳ Serves 5 to 6

Variations

Garlic and Chives: Add 3 tablespoons minced garlic and ⅓ cup snipped fresh chives or chopped green onion tops while mashing the potatoes.

Bacon and Cheddar: While the potatoes are cooking, fry 6 bacon slices until crisp; drain the bacon and crumble. Mash the potatoes, and then stir in 1 cup shredded sharp cheddar cheese and the bacon.

Horseradish: Add 4 tablespoons prepared horseradish (or adjust to taste) while mashing the potatoes.

Blue Cheese and Rosemary: Add ½ cup crumbled blue cheese and 1 tablespoon finely chopped fresh rosemary while mashing the potatoes.

Chipotle: Add 1 or 2 canned chipotle chiles, drained, seeds removed, and finely chopped, and 1 teaspoon paprika while mashing the potatoes.

Peppered Cream Cheese: Add 1½ teaspoons coarsely ground black pepper and 8 ounces softened cream cheese while mashing the potatoes.

Roasted Garlic: Remove the dry, papery outer leaves from 1 head of garlic. Cut the top off the garlic head to expose the individual cloves. Place the head of garlic in a microwave-safe dish and drizzle with 1 teaspoon olive oil. Cover the dish and microwave on high for 60 seconds. When done, the garlic cloves will be soft and buttery, and they will pop right out with a slight squeeze. Place the garlic cloves and the olive oil in a blender and puree until smooth. Add the roasted garlic paste while mashing the potatoes.

Tropical Treat
Sweet Potatoes

This is an amazing way to serve sweet potatoes, and I have served it both as a side dish and a dessert—I'll let you decide which you prefer.

Step One: The Sweet Potatoes
3 red-skinned sweet potatoes

Wash the potatoes. Place the rack in the pressure cooker and add ½ cup water. Lay the potatoes on the rack and lock the lid in place. Bring to 15psi over high heat, immediately reduce the heat to the lowest possible setting to stabilize and maintain that pressure, and cook for 15 minutes, or until a skewer or the tines of a fork will pierce the potato easily and without resistance. Remove from the heat and use the natural release method (see page 31) to depressurize. Carefully open the lid after the pressure drops. Transfer the potatoes to a cutting board and cut each sweet potato in half lengthwise; then cut the halves into ¼-inch-thick slices. Empty the cooker and wipe it dry.

Step Two: The Toasted Pecans
⅔ cup pecan pieces
½ teaspoon salt

Heat a small heavy skillet over medium-high heat, add the pecans, and cook, stirring frequently to prevent burning, for 3 to 4 minutes, or until the pecans are fragrant and lightly browned. Sprinkle with the salt and set aside.

Step Three: The Tropical Sauce
8 tablespoons (1 stick) butter
½ teaspoon ground cinnamon
¼ teaspoon ground nutmeg

What Is the Difference Between a Sweet Potato and a Yam?

It seems that everyone, including supermarkets, is confused about sweet potatoes and yams. Sweet potatoes are a tropical root from South America. What you see at the grocery store are two varieties of sweet potatoes with different-colored skins. The variety with a yellowish skin is not sweet at all, and it has the texture of a baking potato, making it the best choice for savory dishes like mashed sweet potatoes. The darker, reddish-skinned sweet potato is usually misnamed as a yam, and this type has a sweet, moist flesh that is best used in sweet recipes like candied sweet potatoes. True yams, on the other hand, are from Africa, and they are a large, rough, scaly tuber with a dry and very starchy white meat. The African word *nyami* is the origin of the word "yam," but yams are not commercially grown or marketed in the United States, although they are sometimes found in ethnic or farmer's markets.

¼ teaspoon ground ginger

2 firm bananas, peeled and sliced

¾ cup crushed pineapple, well drained

¾ cup packed dark brown sugar

¼ cup dark rum

Juice of 1 orange

Zest of 1 orange

Heat the butter in the pressure cooker over medium heat. Add the cinnamon, nutmeg, and ginger, frying the spices until they begin to sizzle. Add the bananas, pineapple, and brown sugar and cook, stirring, until the sugar is dissolved. Add the rum, orange juice, zest, and the sweet potato slices, stirring until heated through. To use as a side dish, transfer to a serving bowl and top with the toasted pecans. To serve as a dessert, sweeten to taste, then divide the warm sweet potato mixture among dessert plates, add a dollop of whipped topping or vanilla ice cream, and sprinkle the toasted pecan pieces on top. ✳ Serves 4 to 5

Cream of Sweet Potato Soup

Too often when we think of sweet potatoes, we have a picture of the gooey sweet sort that appear only on Thanksgiving tables and then disappear until the next year. You'll discover a whole new use for sweet potatoes if you think savory and choose the lighter, yellow-skinned variety for this soup, rather than the sweet ones with the reddish skins, because they are more like a regular potato.

2 tablespoons butter

2 leeks, white parts only, washed and sliced

2 stalks celery, chopped

1 onion, chopped

3 tablespoons minced garlic

1 teaspoon ground sage

1 teaspoon curry powder

Salt and freshly ground black pepper to taste

½ cup white wine

2 (14-ounce) cans chicken broth

1 (10-ounce) can condensed cream of celery soup

2 yellow-skinned sweet potatoes, peeled and diced

1 (12-ounce) can evaporated milk

Heat the butter in the pressure cooker over medium heat. Add the leeks, celery, onion, and garlic and cook, stirring, until slightly softened, about 3 minutes. Add the sage, curry powder, salt, and pepper, and deglaze the cooker with the wine, scraping up any brown bits from the bottom. Stir in the broth, canned soup, and sweet potatoes. Lock the lid in place. Bring to 15psi over high heat, immediately reduce the heat to the lowest possible setting to stabilize and maintain that pressure, and cook for 6 minutes. Remove from the heat and use the natural release method (see page 31) to depressurize. Carefully open the lid after the pressure drops. Check for doneness; the potatoes should be tender. Use an immersion blender to puree until smooth. Bring to a simmer, uncovered, over medium heat, and add the evaporated milk, stirring until heated through and well blended. Adjust the seasonings to taste, and serve in a heated soup tureen.

✳ Serves 6

Corn Maque Choux

Onions, bell peppers, and celery are often referred to as the "holy trinity" in Cajun cooking, and I have it on good authority that the food police insist on following this rule. Maque Choux—pronounced "mock shoe," typifies this spicy Southern cuisine.

> 3 tablespoons butter
> ½ cup diced onion
> ½ cup diced green bell pepper
> ½ cup diced celery
> 2 tablespoons minced garlic
> 4 cups whole kernel corn (canned, fresh, or thawed frozen)
> 2 Roma tomatoes, seeded and chopped
> ⅓ cup cilantro leaves, chopped, plus sprigs for garnish
> ⅛ teaspoon cayenne pepper
> ½ cup tomato juice

Heat the butter in the pressure cooker over medium heat. Add the onions, green peppers, celery, and garlic and cook, stirring, until slightly softened, about 3 minutes. Add all of the remaining ingredients and stir to mix. Lock the lid in place. Bring to 15psi over high heat, immediately reduce the heat to the lowest possible setting to stabilize and maintain that pressure, and cook for 3 minutes. Remove from the heat and use the cold water release method (see page 30) to depressurize. Carefully open the lid after the pressure drops. Transfer the corn mixture to a serving bowl with a slotted spoon. Garnish with a couple of sprigs of cilantro, and serve. ✻ Serves 4 to 5

Hearty and Homemade Vegetable Soup

In my mind's eye, I still see my mother rushing to the kitchen sink with a heavy, hissing pressure cooker full of homemade soup in her outstretched hands. Back then, soup was generally a process of elimination: you eliminated whatever you didn't have on hand, and cooked the rest.

> 1 tablespoon dried basil
> 1 tablespoon dried oregano
> 1 teaspoon crushed dried rosemary
> ½ teaspoon red pepper flakes
> ½ teaspoon freshly ground black pepper
> 1 teaspoon salt
> 2 bay leaves
> 1 teaspoon chicken bouillon granules
> 2 (14-ounce) cans chicken broth
> 2 tablespoons minced garlic
> 1 rutabaga, peeled and diced
> 1 turnip, peeled and cubed
> 2 potatoes, peeled and diced
> 2 cups peeled and diced winter squash (acorn, butternut, hubbard, etc.)
> 4 carrots, peeled and diced
> 2 parsnips, peed and sliced
> 1 onion, chopped
> ½ medium-size cabbage, coarsely chopped
> 1 (14-ounce) can whole kernel corn, drained
> 1 (14-ounce) can lima beans, drained
> 1 (28-ounce) can tomato puree
> 1 (28-ounce) can chopped tomatoes, with juice

In a large pressure cooker, add all of the ingredients in the order given; do not stir or mix. Pour in 4 cups water and lock the lid in place. Bring to 15psi over high heat, immediately reduce the heat to the lowest possible setting to stabilize and maintain that pressure, and cook for 5 minutes. Remove from the heat and use the natural release method (see page 31) to depressurize. Carefully open the lid after the pressure drops. Stir to combine the ingredients, and adjust the seasonings to taste before serving. ✳ Serves 6 to 8

Cook's Note: Use any varieties of vegetables that you like. This is a great opportunity to empty the fridge, or just use whatever ingredients are available. There's no right or wrong when it comes to making soup, so be as creative as you can.

Mini Cheese Quiches in Bell Pepper Boats

I once had a garden where the bell pepper bushes tried to take over the world. The only way to stop this threat to civilization was to eat lots of green peppers, and that required many new recipes. As a result, I came up with this interesting way to serve little individual cheese quiches in green pepper boats.

2 large, well-shaped green bell peppers
3 large eggs, separated
1 cup heavy cream
2 tablespoons all-purpose flour
½ teaspoon salt
½ teaspoon cayenne pepper
½ teaspoon ground turmeric
1 cup shredded Gruyère cheese
½ cup bread crumbs
Paprika, for garnish

Cut each of the bell peppers in half lengthwise, remove the seeds and inside ribs. Use an electric mixer to beat the egg whites until they form stiff peaks, and set aside. In a large mixing bowl, combine the cream with the egg yolks, flour, salt, cayenne pepper, and turmeric, whisking until smooth. Stir the cheese and bread crumbs into the milk mixture. Gently fold in the stiffly beaten egg whites. Place the rack in the pressure cooker and add ½ cup water. Place the bell pepper halves in a steamer tray or other shallow metal pan and use foil helper handles (see page 42) to position it on the rack inside the cooker. Carefully spoon the cheese mixture into the bell pepper halves. Lock the lid in place. Bring to 15psi over high heat, immediately reduce the heat to the lowest possible setting to stabilize and maintain that pressure, and cook for 4 minutes. Remove from the heat and use the cold water release method (see page 30) to depressurize. Carefully open the lid after the pressure drops. Carefully lift the pan out of the pressure cooker using the foil helper handles. Transfer the pepper boats to a serving plate and dust a little paprika on the top of each.

✳ Serves 4

Cook's Note: Depending on the size of the bell peppers, you may end up with an extra amount of the quiche mixture. If so, cook the extra in the pressure cooker in buttered ramekins for 4 minutes.

Dutch Vegetable Whip

We never had an actual written recipe for this dish, but I think everyone in my family was born knowing how to make it. "Dutch" in this case is American shorthand for Deutsch, or German, and the original heirloom recipe for this dish was a stovetop version handed down from my great-grandmother, who emigrated from Germany to America in the early part of the last century. It was simple "peasant food," cheaply cobbled together from little bits of whatever vegetables remained in the larder. Slightly sweet with just a hint of apple, it's a nice change from plain mashed potatoes.

½ cup apple juice
3 cups grated potatoes
1 cup grated carrots
1 green apple, peeled, cored, and grated
½ cup chopped onion
½ teaspoon freshly ground black pepper
2 tablespoons butter, plus extra for garnish

Place the rack in a pressure cooker and add the apple juice. Add all of the ingredients except for the butter. Stir to mix and lock the lid in place. Bring to 15psi over high heat, immediately reduce the heat to the lowest possible setting to stabilize and maintain that pressure, and cook for 3 minutes. Remove from the heat and use the natural release method (see page 31) to depressurize. Carefully open the lid after the pressure drops. Drain well, reserving the broth to freeze for future use in stocks. Add the butter to the vegetables, along with a little of the reserved broth if needed, and mash by whatever method you prefer. Adjust the seasonings to taste, transfer to a serving bowl, and garnish with a pat of butter. ✳ Serves 4 to 5

Cooks Note: Save oodles of time by using a food processor for grating the veggies and apple.

Thick 'n' Rich Cream of Potato and Broccoli Soup

This is a good weekday choice for a fast, nutritious dinner when time is short, or you're tired after a busy day. It cooks in 4 minutes, just long enough to set the table and warm up a crusty loaf of bread by the time the cooker depressurizes.

2 tablespoons butter
1 onion, diced
1 cup thinly sliced celery
1 tablespoon minced garlic
½ teaspoon freshly ground black pepper
½ teaspoon dried marjoram
½ teaspoon cayenne pepper
4 potatoes, peeled and diced
3 cups frozen chopped broccoli
2 (14-ounce) cans chicken broth
1 cup hevy cream
1 cup sour cream
1 cup shredded cheddar cheese
⅓ cup instant potato flakes

2 green onions, white and green parts, minced,
for garnish

Heat the butter in the pressure cooker over medium heat. Add the onions, celery, garlic, black pepper, marjoram, and cayenne pepper and cook, stirring, for about 3 minutes. Add the potatoes, broccoli, broth, and 2 cups water. Stir to mix and lock the lid in place. Bring to 15psi over high heat, immediately reduce the heat to the lowest possible setting to stabilize and maintain that pressure, and cook for 4 minutes. Remove from the heat and use the natural release method (see page 31) to depressurize. Carefully open the lid after the pressure drops. Add the cream, bring to a simmer over low heat, and stir in the sour cream and cheese. Add the potato flakes a little at a time until the soup reaches the desired consistency. Serve with the green onions sprinkled on top. ✳ Serves 5 to 6

Cream of Potato Soup with Cheddar Cheese and Pearl Onions

Rich and thick, this soup is great on those chilly days when everyone needs a hot meal in a hurry.

2 tablespoons butter
4 stalks celery, thinly sliced
3 scallions, white and green parts, thinly sliced
1 clove garlic, finely minced

6 potatoes, peeled and cubed
1 (10-ounce) jar pearl onions, drained
1 teaspoon chicken bouillon granules
2 cups chicken stock
1 cup heavy cream
1 cup sour cream
½ cup instant potato flakes
2 cups shredded sharp cheddar cheese
Salt and freshly ground black pepper to taste
Dried parsley flakes, for garnish

Heat the butter in the pressure cooker over high heat. Add the celery, scallions, and garlic and cook, stirring, for about 3 minutes. Add the potatoes, pearl onions, bouillon, stock, and just enough water to barely cover all the ingredients. Stir to mix and lock the lid in place. Bring to 15psi over high heat, immediately reduce the heat to the lowest possible setting to stabilize and maintain that pressure, and cook for 5 minutes. Remove from the heat and use the natural release method (see page 31) to depressurize. Carefully open the lid after the pressure drops. Over low heat, gradually stir in the heavy cream and sour cream. To thicken, stir in small amounts of the potato flakes until the soup reaches the desired consistency. Add the cheese, stirring until it is melted and the soup is hot. Add the salt and pepper, and adjust the seasonings to taste. Sprinkle the parsley on top before serving. ✳ Serves 4 to 5

Italian White Bean Salad with Romaine Lettuce and Feta Cheese

This recipe is a summer favorite of everyone in the family—a well-deserved reputation—and it will be a hit with your family, too!

Step One: The Beans

1 cup dried white beans (navy or great Northern), presoaked for 4 hours

1 tablespoon olive oil

Drain and rinse the beans well. Place in a pressure cooker with enough water to cover by 2 inches, and add the oil. Stir and lock the lid in place. Bring to 15psi over high heat, immediately reduce the heat to the lowest possible setting to stabilize and maintain that pressure, and cook for 10 minutes. Remove from the heat and use the natural release method (see page 31) to depressurize. Carefully open the lid after the pressure drops. Drain the beans and cool in the refrigerator.

Step Two: The Salad

1 red onion, diced

1 green bell pepper, seeded and chopped

1 stalk celery with leaves, finely diced

½ cup grated carrot

½ cup packed cilantro leaves

2 tablespoons garlic, minced

1 tablespoon dried mixed Italian herbs

Salt and freshly ground black pepper to taste

1 (8-ounce) bottle Italian dressing

2 tablespoons fresh lemon juice

6 cups torn romaine lettuce, rinsed and drained

Crumbled feta cheese, tomato wedges, pepperoncini, and chopped green onions, for garnish

After the beans are chilled, place in a large bowl and stir in the red onions, bell peppers, celery, carrots, cilantro, garlic, Italian herbs, and salt and pepper. Add the bottled dressing and lemon juice, and adjust the seasonings to taste. Mix well and refrigerate for several hours or overnight to blend the flavors. To serve, mound a portion of the romaine lettuce on a serving plate and spoon 1 cup of the bean mixture on top. Garnish with the feta cheese, tomato wedges, pepperoncini, and green onions.

✳ Serves 4 to 5

Variation: Add leftover chopped ham, smoked salmon, or sliced pepperoni to turn this salad into a meal.

Vegetable Pie

The basis for this dish comes from one of my grandmother's wartime recipes. Although it's undergone a series of changes over the years, since we no longer have to deal with food shortages, the results are every bit as good as the original. The distinctive ring-shaped mold is the "pie," and it is filled with a complementary sauce, along with vegetables or creamed chicken—always a different combo in my household, where this is a dinnertime favorite.

2 tablespoons butter, plus extra for the mold
   and the bread
½ cup diced zucchini
½ cup diced fresh mushrooms
⅓ cup diced green bell pepper
¼ cup chopped red onion
3 tablespoons minced garlic
1 teaspoon dried thyme leaves
8 slices stale, dense bread, any variety,
   crusts removed
1 (3-ounce) package cream cheese, softened
2 cups evaporated milk
2 cups grated Swiss cheese
2 tablespoons all-purpose flour
1 teaspoon beef bouillon granules
1 teaspoon freshly ground black pepper
4 large eggs, slightly beaten

Generously butter the inside of a 1½-quart metal ring, pudding mold, or tube pan; if your pan has a lid, butter the inside of the lid as well. Heat the 2 tablespoons butter in the pressure cooker over medium-high heat. Add the zucchini, mushrooms, bell peppers, red onions, garlic, and thyme and cook,

stirring, until the vegetables are just crisp-tender, about 15 minutes. Remove from the heat to cool briefly. Meanwhile, butter the bread slices, stack them up and cut into 1-inch cubes, and set aside. In a large bowl, use an electric mixer to beat the softened cream cheese until smooth. Add the milk, Swiss cheese, flour, bouillon, pepper, and eggs, and mix well. Fold in the sautéed vegetables and bread cubes and let the bread soak up the milk. Spoon the mixture into the prepared mold and secure the lid. If your container does not have a lid, butter 1 side of a sheet of aluminum foil and crimp it tightly over the pan. Place the rack in the cooker and add 2 cups water. Using foil helper handles (see page 42), lower the mold into the cooker. Lock the lid in place. Bring to 15psi over high heat, immediately reduce the heat to the lowest possible setting to stabilize and maintain that pressure, and cook for 25 minutes. Remove from the heat and use the natural release method (see page 31) to depressurize. Carefully open the lid after the pressure drops. Carefully open the lid after the pressure drops. To serve, run a knife blade around the inside of the pan and place a serving plate over the top. Quickly invert the pan to unmold the pie.

❋ Serves 4 to 5

Serving Suggestion: This pie can be sliced and served plain with a bit of butter. Or, to dress it up as it was intended, fill the center hole with Roasted Fresh Tomato Sauce (page 410), Chicken à la King (page 197), or Chicken Fricassee (page 199).

Cook's Note: To make fresh bread into "stale" bread, preheat the oven to 200°F and lay the slices on the oven rack. Bake for about 30 minutes or until dry and crisp, and they're good to go.

Roasted Fresh Tomato Sauce

Don't be afraid to try fire-roasting. It takes only a few minutes, deepens the flavor of many vegetables, and adds a smoky touch to this fresh tomato sauce. Serve over steamed vegetables or fresh pasta, or dress up roast beef or pork.

8 ripe plum tomatoes
1 small jalapeño chile, seeded and minced
⅓ cup chopped red onion
¼ cup tightly packed chopped cilantro leaves
2 tablespoons minced garlic
1 teaspoon dried basil
⅔ cup red wine
1 tablespoon fresh lime juice

Fire-roast the tomatoes over a high flame until blistered, charred, and blackened over most of the outside. This can be done on a grill, or use a burner on a gas stove. Cook the tomatoes directly in the flame by spearing them with a fork and turning them as they blacken (like toasting a marshmallow). Once the roasted tomatoes are cool enough to handle, remove and discard the cores. Put the cored tomatoes, along with any pieces of charred skin, in a food processor to puree. Transfer to the pressure cooker and add all of the remaining ingredients, stirring to mix. Lock the lid in place. Bring to 15psi over high heat, immediately reduce the heat to the lowest possible setting to stabilize and maintain that pressure, and cook for 8 minutes. Remove from the heat and use the natural release method (see page 31) to depressurize. Carefully open the lid after the pressure drops. Adjust the seasonings to taste. This sauce will freeze well, so you can use it immediately or freeze it for later use. ✴ **Makes 2 ½ to 3 cups**

Desserts and Sweet Endings

E VEN LONGTIME PRESSURE-COOKER USERS are not aware of the many fabulous desserts that can be prepared under pressure. In many pressure-cooker cookbooks, the dessert choices are often limited to some stewed fruit and a pudding or two. One of the best features of pressure cookery, but also the most often overlooked, is its versatility. Many dessert recipes that are normally baked in the oven can be easily cooked in the modern pressure cooker, with the added bonus that there's no oven heating up the house. Many of these recipes include a master recipe with several variations to expand your menu choices.

Tender fruits are just a beginning; all manner of puddings, custards and flans, and even cheesecakes can be made in the pressure cooker. Fruitcakes are gorgeous, and I don't mean those dried, store-bought monstrosities made with pieces of mysterious, colored—what are those things, anyway? A true, old-fashioned fruitcake is a work of art and deserves a good PR firm to improve its image in this country.

Traditionally, many dessert recipes make use of accessory pans, decorative molds, ramekins, and other insert dishes. In the past, resourceful cooks made do with what was available in their own kitchens, but nowadays there is a wide selection of suitable accessory items available in department stores and gourmet and kitchen shops, as well as from many reputable online outlets.

Molten Mocha Brownie Pudding with Chocolate-Mint Sauce

This decadent mocha brownie will bring even the most jaded chocolate lovers to the table with spoon in hand. Serve with a scoop of vanilla ice cream if desired.

Step One: The Chocolate-Mint Sauce
4 ounces semisweet chocolate pieces
2 ounces unsweetened chocolate, chopped
⅓ cup hot water
¼ cup light corn syrup
¾ teaspoon peppermint extract

Combine both chocolates in a heatproof bowl and microwave on high for 1 to 1½ minutes, or until the chocolate melts. Add the hot water, corn syrup, and peppermint extract, whisking until smooth. This can be made several days in advance and then covered and refrigerated until needed. Before serving, warm the sauce in a microwave using a reduced heat setting.

Step Two: The Brownie Pudding
4 ounces semisweet chocolate pieces
¼ cup unsweetened cocoa powder
¼ teaspoon salt
2 tablespoons butter, plus extra for the pan
2 large eggs, separated
¼ cup sugar, plus extra for the pan
1 teaspoon pure vanilla extract
½ cup chopped pecans

¼ cup plus 2 tablespoons all-purpose flour
2 teaspoons instant coffee granules
2 tablespoons Kahlúa or coffee liqueur

Generously butter the inside of a 1-quart metal pan and dust with sugar, tapping out any excess; set aside while you make the pudding. Place the chocolate pieces, cocoa, salt, and butter into a heatproof bowl and microwave on high for 1 to 1½ minutes, or until the butter and chocolate are melted. Stir to blend, and set aside to cool. In a medium-size bowl, beat the egg whites with an electric mixer on low speed until foamy. Gradually add the sugar, increase the speed to high, and continue beating until they form stiff peaks, then set aside. In a large bowl, beat the egg yolks and vanilla extract with an electric mixer until they are light yellow and stiff enough to look like lightly whipped cream. Slowly add the cooled chocolate and butter mixture to the egg yolks. Gently stir in the pecans, flour, instant coffee, and liqueur, beating just until mixed. With a wire whisk, carefully fold the beaten whites into the chocolate mixture just until incorporated. Do not overmix, or the batter will deflate. Pour into the buttered pan. Only fill the pan ⅔ full, leaving space for the pudding to rise slightly. Generously butter a square of aluminum foil and crimp it over the top of the pudding pan to make a tight lid. Place the rack in the pressure cooker and add 1 cup water. Use foil helper handles (see page 42) to place the pan inside the cooker. Lock the lid in place. Bring to 15psi over high heat, immediately reduce the heat to the lowest possible setting to stabilize and maintain that pressure, and cook for 20 minutes. Remove from the heat and use the cold water release method (see page 30) to depressurize. Carefully open the lid after the pressure drops. Use the foil helper handles to lift the pudding pan out of the cooker and place on a wire rack to cool. Remove the foil covering and let the pudding rest for about 15 minutes. To serve, run a knife blade around the inside of the pan to loosen the sides, and place a serving plate over the top. Quickly invert the pan to unmold the pudding. Top with the Chocolate-Mint Sauce, and serve warm.

❊ Serves 5 to 6

Old-Fashioned Lemon Pudding

I love puddings, but I am usually too busy to fuss with a homemade dessert that requires constant stirring while standing in front of a hot stove. Leave it to the pressure cooker to solve the problem with this tart lemon pudding.

2 large eggs, separated

3 tablespoons butter, plus extra for the bowl

3 tablespoons sugar

⅓ cup all-purpose flour, sifted

1 tablespoon grated lemon zest

¼ cup fresh lemon juice

¼ teaspoon lemon oil, or ½ teaspoon lemon extract

½ cup evaporated milk

Whipped cream, for garnish

Generously butter the inside of a 1-quart, rounded-bottom metal bowl. Meanwhile, bring 1 quart water to a boil in a saucepan or kettle. Using an electric mixer, beat the egg whites in a large bowl until stiff, and set aside. Beat the egg yolks separately until they are light yellow and slightly thickened,

then set aside. In a separate bowl, cream the butter and sugar until light and fluffy, then add the flour, lemon zest, lemon juice, and lemon oil, beating well. Add the milk and egg yolks, beating until combined. Gently fold the mixture into the egg whites. Pour the lemon mixture into the prepared bowl. Do not fill the bowl more than ⅔ full; leave space for the pudding to rise slightly. Cover the bowl tightly with a square of buttered aluminum foil. Place the rack in the pressure cooker, and use foil helper handles (see page 42) to place the pudding bowl on the rack. Pour enough boiling water into the cooker to come ⅓ of the way up the sides of the bowl. Lock the lid in place. Bring to 15psi over high heat, immediately reduce the heat to the lowest possible setting to stabilize and maintain that pressure, and cook for 5 minutes. Remove from the heat and use the natural release method (see page 31) to depressurize. Carefully open the lid after the pressure drops. Use the helper handles to remove the bowl from the cooker. Serve the pudding warm or cold, with a dollop of whipped cream.

❊ Servesv 4 to 5

Master Bread Pudding

The secret of a divine bread pudding is the type of bread chosen. Of course it must be stale, but avoid thinly sliced breads with coarse, porous textures, as they simply cannot hold enough milk for a decent pudding. Choose heavy, dense, fine-textured bread; this is the single most important ingredient for an exceptional bread pudding because it will hold more of the milk and egg mixture. The density is more important than the thickness of the bread, but I find that "Texas toast," or a similar variety of very thickly sliced bread used for French toast, works especially well. According to my grandmother's recipes, the crusts "must" be removed before making bread pudding; to do anything less was just "pure cussed shiftlessness." This is another one of those unwritten laws of the kitchen impressed upon me as a child, and I remain duly wary of the food police, never straying from her exact instructions. It does make a pudding that looks as good as it tastes.

2 cups milk, any variety, or use a combination of milk and cream
4 large eggs, slightly beaten
2 teaspoons pure vanilla extract
½ cup granulated or brown sugar, plus extra for the pan

2 tablespoons all-purpose flour
1 teaspoon ground cinnamon
Dash of salt
8 slices stale, dense bread, any variety, crusts removed
2 tablespoons butter, plus extra for the pan
Whipped cream, for garnish (optional)

Generously butter the inside of a 1½-quart metal ring or pudding mold (or a metal bowl), as well as the inside of the lid. If you don't have this item amongst your pressure-cooker accessories, substitute another metal pan of similar size. In a large bowl, mix the milk, eggs, vanilla extract, sugar, flour, cinnamon, and salt. Spread the bread slices with the butter, stack them up, cut into 1-inch cubes, and arrange them evenly in the mold. Add the milk mixture to the bread a little at a time, letting it soak in before adding more. Continue adding more of the milk mixture as long as the bread will absorb it—this might take as long as a half-hour. When the bread will not absorb any more milk, cover the pudding mold tightly. If your pudding pan does not have a lid, butter one side of a sheet of aluminum foil and crimp it tightly over the pan to make a lid. Place the rack in the pressure cooker and add 2 cups water. Using foil helper handles (see page 42), lower the pudding mold into the cooker. Lock the lid in place. Bring to 15psi over high heat, immediately reduce the heat to the lowest possible setting to stabilize and maintain that pressure, and cook for 25 minutes. Remove from the heat and use the natural release method (see page 31) to depressurize. Carefully open the lid after the pressure drops. Use the foil helper handles to lift the pudding pan out of the cooker, and remove the lid or foil. To serve, run a knife blade around the inside of the pan to loosen the sides, and place a serving plate over the top. Quickly invert the pan to unmold the pudding. Bread pudding is best served warm, and topped with a dollop of whipped cream if desired. ✳ Serves 6

Cook's Note: To make fresh bread into "stale" bread, heat the oven to 200°F and lay the slices on the oven rack. Let them bake for about 30 minutes, or until they are no longer soft, but not dry as toast, and they're good to go.

Variations

Chocolate Chip Bread Pudding: Add ½ cup semisweet chocolate pieces to the bread before cooking; also try it with butterscotch and/or toffee pieces.

Dried Fruit Bread Pudding: Place 1 cup raisins or chopped dried cherries, apricots, peaches, coconut, cranberries, or other chopped dried fruit in a glass bowl with 1 cup water. Heat in a microwave on high for 1½ to 2 minutes, and let stand until the fruit is plumped. Drain and scatter the fruit through the bread cubes before cooking.

Fruited Bread Pudding: Add 1½ cups fresh (or frozen and thawed) chopped or mashed berries, peaches, rhubarb, or bananas to the bread before cooking. Increase the sugar to taste.

Chocolate Bread Pudding: Mix ¼ cup unsweetened cocoa powder into the milk mixture.

Bread Pudding with Nuts: Add ½ cup chopped walnuts, pecans, English walnuts, almonds, or hazelnuts to the bread before cooking.

Eggnog Bread Pudding: Substitute eggnog for the milk, and add ½ teaspoon nutmeg to the milk mixture.

Chocolate Malt Cheesecake

I have to admit that chocolate is one of my favorite vices. This recipe came about quite by accident, when I found I was out of chocolate and grabbed the closest substitute I could find, chocolate malt balls. It still makes me laugh, and since the first "mistake" turned out so well, I've added chocolate malt powder for a more intense malt flavor. Look for malt and chocolate malt powder near the cocoa powder at your supermarket.

Step One: The Crust
2 tablespoons butter, plus extra for the pan
½ cup chocolate graham cracker crumbs
1 tablespoon sugar

Butter the inside of a 7-inch springform pan or any size flat-bottomed pan that will fit inside your pressure cooker. In a small bowl, melt the butter in a microwave and blend in the cracker crumbs and sugar. Use the back of a spoon to pack the crumb mixture into the bottom of the pan and about halfway up the sides.

Step Two: The Filling
11 ounces cream cheese, softened
¾ cup sugar
⅓ cup chocolate malt powder
2 tablespoons all-purpose flour
1 teaspoon pure vanilla extract
2 large eggs, slightly beaten

Use an electric mixer to beat the softened cream cheese until smooth. Add the sugar, malt powder, flour, and vanilla extract, beating with the mixer until well blended. Blend in the beaten eggs, mixing well. Pour the mixture into the center of the crust in the springform pan. Cover the pan tightly with aluminum foil. Place the rack in the pressure cooker and add 2 cups water. Use foil helper handles (see page 42) to lower the pan into the cooker. Lock the lid in place. Bring to 15psi over high heat, immediately reduce the heat to the lowest possible setting to stabilize and maintain that pressure, and cook for 20 minutes. Remove from the heat and use the natural release method (see page 31) to depressurize. Carefully open the lid after the pressure drops. Use the helper handles to lift the pan out of the cooker, remove the aluminum foil, and allow the cheesecake to cool on a wire rack. When cool, run a knife blade around the inside of the pan to loosen the sides. Remove the outer ring of the springform pan and slide the cheesecake onto a serving plate. Refrigerate for several hours or overnight.

Step Three: The Topping
½ cup sour cream
1 teaspoon pure vanilla extract
2 tablespoons sugar
½ cup finely crushed chocolate malt balls
Whole chocolate malt balls, for garnish
(optional)

Stir the sour cream, vanilla extract, and sugar together in a small bowl. Spread over the top of the chilled cheesecake. Sprinkle the crushed chocolate malt balls over the top, and serve. Top each slice with 1 or 2 whole malt balls pressed into the topping, if desired. ✳ Serves 6

Lemon Cheesecake with Fruit Topping

This rich little cheesecake is lemony-tart and goes well with sweet fruit topping.

Step One: The Crust

2 tablespoons butter, plus extra for the pan

½ cup graham cracker crumbs

1 tablespoon sugar

Butter the inside of a 7-inch springform pan, or any size flat-bottomed pan that will fit inside your pressure cooker. In a small bowl, melt the butter in a microwave, then blend in the cracker crumbs and sugar. Use the back of a spoon to pack the crumb mixture into the bottom of the pan and about halfway up the sides.

Step Two: The Filling

11 ounces cream cheese, softened

¾ cup sugar

2 tablespoons all-purpose flour

Zest of 1 lemon

Juice of 1 lemon

1 teaspoon pure vanilla extract

¼ teaspoon lemon oil, or ½ teaspoon lemon
    extract

2 large eggs, slightly beaten

Use an electric mixer to beat the softened cream cheese until smooth. Add the sugar, flour, lemon zest, lemon juice, vanilla extract, and lemon oil, and beat with the mixer until well blended. Blend in the beaten eggs, mixing well. Pour the mixture into the center of the crust in the springform pan, and cover the pan tightly with aluminum foil. Place the rack in the pressure cooker and add 2 cups water. Use foil helper handles (see page 42) to lower the pan into the cooker. Lock the lid in place. Bring to 15psi over high heat, immediately reduce the heat to the lowest possible setting to stabilize and maintain that pressure, and cook for 20 minutes. Remove from the heat and use the natural release method (see page 31) to depressurize. Carefully open the lid after the pressure drops. Use the helper handles to lift the dish out of the cooker, remove the aluminum foil, and allow the cheesecake to cool on a wire rack. When cool, run a knife blade around the inside of the pan to loosen the sides. Remove the outer ring of the springform pan and slide the cheesecake onto a serving plate. Refrigerate for several hours or overnight.

Step Three: The Topping

2 cups fresh or frozen fruit of your choice

¼ cup sugar

Mash the fruit, then add the sugar and sweeten to taste—you'll want the fruit to be more tart than sweet. Or, use chilled canned pie filling in place of the fresh or frozen fruit. Spoon the fruit over the top of the chilled cheesecake just before serving, and then cut the cake into serving portions.

❋ Serves 6

Lemon Pudding Cake

This type of dish is common in England, and it's really like two desserts in one—light lemon sponge cake with its own tangy lemon pudding sauce. This recipe requires a preliminary steaming period before the cooker is fully pressurized, and it cooks at a lower pressure setting to allow the delicate cake part of the pudding to rise.

¾ cup all-purpose flour

1½ teaspoons baking powder

½ teaspoon salt

½ cup (1 stick) butter, softened, plus extra for the bowl

¾ cup sugar

2 large eggs, beaten

Zest of 1 lemon, grated

3 tablespoons fresh lemon juice

¼ teaspoon lemon oil, or ½ teaspoon lemon extract

Powdered sugar, for garnish

Bring 1 quart water to a boil in a saucepan or kettle. Generously butter the inside of a 1-quart, round-bottomed metal bowl. In a separate bowl, combine the flour, baking powder, and salt and set aside. In a large bowl, use an electric mixer to cream the butter and ¼ cup of the sugar until light and fluffy. Gradually add the beaten eggs and mix well. Add the flour mixture in small amounts, beating well after each addition. Spoon the mixture into the prepared pudding bowl. In a small bowl, mix the remaining ½ cup sugar, the lemon zest, the juice, and the lemon oil with 1¼ cups boiling water, stirring until the sugar has dissolved. Carefully pour the lemon mixture into the pudding bowl on top of the cake batter, taking care not to make a crater in the batter. Do not fill the bowl more than ⅔ full; leave space for the pudding to rise slightly. Butter the center of a square of aluminum foil and crimp it tightly over the top of the pudding bowl. Place the rack in the bottom of the pressure cooker and use foil helper handles (see page 42) to lower the pudding bowl into the cooker. Pour enough boiling water into the cooker to come ⅓ of the way up the sides of the bowl. Heat the cooker over medium-high heat and steam the pudding for 15 minutes (see "Miss Vickie Says," below) to allow the cake to rise. At the end of the steaming period, check the water level and add more boiling water if needed to come ⅓ of the way up the sides of the bowl. Lock the lid in place. Bring to 10psi over high heat, immediately reduce the heat to the lowest possible setting to stabilize and maintain that pressure, and cook for 10 minutes. Remove from the heat and use the natural release method (see page 31) to depressurize. Carefully open the lid after the pressure drops. Use the foil helper handles remove the bowl from the cooker, and remove the foil. This dessert is best when served warm. To serve, run a knife blade around the inside of the pan to loosen the sides, and place a serving plate over the top. Quickly invert the pan to unmold the pudding. Dust with powdered sugar before serving. ❋ **Serves 4 to 5**

Miss Vickie Says

There are several methods you can use to steam the bread. For pressure cookers with a spring valve, use a regular lid, or leave the pressure lid ajar and not in the locking position. For a pressure cooker with a removable or weighted regulator, simply remove the regulator from the vent pipe and let the steam escape freely, or leave the pressure lid ajar and not in the locking position.

Caramel Apple Pudding

Like heaven in a bowl, with cake, little morsels of apple, and a ton of rich, buttery caramel sauce for a scoop of vanilla ice cream to melt in. Experiment with other fruits—Caramel Apricot Pudding, peach, pumpkin? Yummy, just think of the possibilities. . . .

Step One: The Pudding
Butter for the pan
All-purpose flour for the pan
2 Granny Smith apples, peeled, cored, and grated
1 cup self-rising flour
¾ cup packed dark brown sugar
½ cup milk
2 tablespoons butter, melted

Generously butter and flour a shallow, 1-quart, flat-bottomed metal pan, like a cake pan, that will fit loosely inside your pressure cooker; tap out any excess flour and set aside. Combine the apples, flour, brown sugar, milk, and butter in a large bowl, mixing by hand until just moistened. Spread the mixture into the prepared pan, leveling the surface.

Step Two: The Sauce
¾ cup packed dark brown sugar
¼ cup (½ stick) cold butter, cut into small pieces
2 tablespoons rum

Bring 1 quart water to a boil in a saucepan or kettle while you make the sauce. Combine the brown sugar, butter, and ¾ cup water in a small saucepan over medium heat. Stir until the sugar is dissolved and the butter melted, then stir in the rum. Slowly pour the sauce on top of the apple pudding in the pan; pour over the back of a spoon to protect the top of the batter. Do not fill the bowl more than ¾ full; leave space for the pudding to rise slightly. If your pan comes with a lid, butter the lid; otherwise, butter a square of aluminum foil and crimp it tightly over the top of the pan. Place the rack in the pressure cooker and place the pan on the rack using foil helper handles (see page 42). Pour enough boiling water into the pressure cooker to cover the lower third of the pan. Heat the cooker over medium-high heat and steam the pudding for 15 minutes to allow the cake to rise (see "Miss Vickie Says," below). At the end of the steaming period, check the water level and add more boiling water if needed to come ⅓ of the way up the sides of the pan. Lock the lid in place. Bring to 15psi over high heat, immediately reduce the heat to the lowest possible setting to stabilize and maintain that pressure, and cook for 25 minutes. Remove from the heat and use the natural release method (see page 31) to depressurize. Carefully open the lid after the pressure drops. Lift the pan out of the cooker immediately; do not let the pudding stand before serving or else the sauce will be absorbed! Spoon the cake and plenty of sauce into individual dessert bowls, and serve. ✳ Serves 4 to 5

Miss Vickie Says

There are several methods you can use to steam the bread. For pressure cookers with a spring valve, use a regular lid, or leave the pressure lid ajar and not in the locking position. For a pressure cooker with a removable or weighted regulator, simply remove the regulator from the vent pipe and let the steam escape freely, or leave the pressure lid ajar and not in the locking position.

Variations: Substitute 1 cup finely chopped dates and ½ cup chopped nuts for the apples.

Banana-Nut Bread with Sticky Toffee Sauce

A simple snack cake can be transformed into a temptingly indulgent dessert with gooey Toffee Sauce.

Step One: The Bread
Butter for the pan
½ cup raisins
2 ripe bananas
2 teaspoons fresh lemon juice
1 cup whole wheat flour
1 cup all-purpose flour, plus extra for the pan
1 teaspoon baking soda
1 teaspoon baking powder
⅛ teaspoon salt
⅔ cup apple juice
¼ cup molasses
2 teaspoons pure vanilla extract
½ cup chopped nuts (walnuts, pecans, English walnuts, or hazelnuts)

To cook through and through, this dense, moist bread needs to cook in a metal tube pan, a ring mold, a traditional pudding mold, or a patterned 7-inch Bundt pan. If you don't have these items in your collection of pressure-cooker accessories, do it the old-fashioned way and substitute tall narrow cans such as 28-ounce food cans or 14-ounce coffee cans—not as pretty a presentation, but it tastes just as good. Bring 1 quart water to a boil in a saucepan or kettle while you make the batter. Generously butter the inside of the mold and dust with flour; tap out any excess flour and set aside. Soak the raisins in very hot water to plump them up.

Mash the bananas in a small bowl and add the lemon juice, mixing thoroughly. In a separate mixing bowl, combine the wheat flour, all-purpose flour, baking soda, baking powder, and salt, and add the apple juice, molasses, and vanilla extract, mixing well. Drain the raisins and add them to the batter, then add the mashed bananas and nuts, stirring until just blended. Pour the mixture into the prepared mold or pan. This bread rises, so do not fill the mold more than ¾ full. If your mold or pan comes with a lid, butter the inside surface. If you're using a container without a lid, butter a square of aluminum foil and crimp it tightly over the top of the mold. Place the rack in the pressure cooker and place the mold on the rack. Pour enough boiling water into the pressure cooker to cover the lower third of the mold. Heat the cooker over medium-high heat and steam the bread for 15 minutes to allow it to rise (see "Miss Vickie Says," below). At the end of the steaming period, check the water level and add more boiling water if needed to come ⅓ the way up the sides of the pan. Lock the lid in place. Bring to 10psi over high heat, immediately reduce the heat to the lowest possible setting to stabilize and maintain that pressure, and cook for 25 minutes. Remove from the heat and use the natural release method (see page 31) to depressurize. Carefully open the lid after the pressure drops. Lift the mold out of the cooker and unmold immediately, letting the bread cool on a wire rack.

Step Two: The Toffee Sauce
¼ cup butter
⅔ cup firmly packed brown sugar
⅓ cup whipping cream
¼ cup molasses
1 teaspoon pure vanilla extract

Melt the butter in heavy 2-quart saucepan over medium heat, then stir in the brown sugar, whipping cream, and molasses. Cook, stirring frequently, until the mixture boils. Boil for 3 minutes, stirring to prevent curdling. Remove from the heat and stir in the vanilla extract. Slice the Banana-Nut Bread and spoon the warm sauce on top.

✳ **Serves 4 to 5**

Miss Vickie Says

There are several methods you can use to steam the bread. For pressure cookers with a spring valve, use a regular lid, or leave the pressure lid ajar and not in the locking position. For a pressure cooker with a removable or weighted regulator, simply remove the regulator from the vent pipe and let the steam escape freely, or leave the pressure lid ajar and not in the locking position.

Rice Pudding

I have childhood memories of rice pudding served in tall parfait glasses, topped with a mound of whipped cream and, just maybe, if we were especially good, a few chocolate sprinkles. I use the PIP cooking method (see page 37) to prepare this recipe, so there's no chance of scorching the pudding.

2 tablespoons butter
1 cup uncooked short- to medium-grain white
    rice, such as Arborio or Calrose rice
1 cup heavy cream
1 cup whole milk
½ cup raisins, soaked in hot water until plump

½ cup firmly packed dark brown sugar
½ teaspoon ground cinnamon
¼ teaspoon ground nutmeg
⅛ teaspoon salt
2 tablespoons molasses
1 teaspoon almond extract

Heat the butter in the pressure cooker over medium-high heat. Add the rice and cook, stirring to coat all the grains with butter, until they look slightly transparent, about 3 minutes. Transfer the rice mixture to a 1-quart, round-bottomed metal bowl. Pour in the milk and all the remaining ingredients and stir to mix. Place the rack in the cooker and add 1 cup water. Use foil helper handles (see page 42) to place the rice bowl inside the cooker. Lock the lid in place. Bring to 15psi over high heat, immediately reduce the heat to the lowest possible setting to stabilize and maintain that pressure, and cook for 8 minutes. Remove from the heat and use the natural release method (see page 31) to depressurize. Carefully open the lid after the pressure drops. The pudding will look thin, but the rice will continue to absorb the milk as it cools. Spoon into dessert glasses and refrigerate until chilled and set.

✳ **Serves 4 to 5**

Variations

Chocolate Rice Pudding: Add 3 tablespoons cocoa powder to the rice mixture before cooking.

Rice Pudding with Dried Fruit: Add 1 cup raisins, chopped dates, apricots or other dried fruits to the rice mixture before cooking.

Master
Tapioca Pudding

Tapioca pudding is comfort food, and almost everyone has a special fondness for this old-fashioned dessert. Look for the original, whole pearl tapioca to make this old-fashioned favorite. The quick-cooking tapioca, which is made by putting the larger pearl tapioca through a grinder, is not suitable for pressure cooking.

2 large eggs
1 cup heavy cream
1½ cups whole milk
⅓ cup small pearl tapioca soaked in
    ¾ cup water overnight
½ teaspoon pure vanilla extract
⅓ cup sugar
⅛ teaspoon salt
1 tablespoon soft butter, do not substitute

Drain the water from the tapioca pearls. Cream the butter and sugar in an electric mixer. Add the eggs and beat until smooth, then add the milk and cream. Stir in the tapioca pearls by hand. Place the rack in the pressure cooker and pour in 1 cup water. Pour the tapioca mixture in a shallow 1 quart stainless steel pan that will fit loosely inside your pressure cooker. Cover tightly with foil and place on a rack using foil helper handlers. Lock the lid in place. Bring to 15psi over high heat, immediately reduce the heat to the lowest possible setting to stabilize and maintain that pressure, and cook for 12 minutes. Remove from the heat and use the quick release method (see page 30) to depressurize. Carefully open the lid after the pressure drops. Lift the pudding out of the pressure cooker and let it cool about 15 minutes. Stir in the vanilla and blend the tapioca pearls that will be at the bottom of the pan. The pudding will look thin, but the starches in the tapioca will thicken and set as it cools. Spoon the pudding into dessert dishes and refrigerate until chilled. Serve with a dollop of whipped cream. ✳ Serves 4

Variations

Chocolate Tapioca Pudding: Add 3 tablespoons cocoa powder plus 1 tablespoon soft butter to the mixture before cooking.

Mocha Tapioca Pudding: Add 3 tablespoons cocoa powder, 2 tablespoons instant coffee, plus 1 tablespoon soft butter to the mixture before cooking.

Chocolate Malted Tapioca Pudding: Add 3 tablespoons cocoa powder, 2 tablespoons malt powder, plus 1 tablespoon soft butter to the mixture before cooking.

Butterscotch Tapioca Pudding: Add ½ cup packed dark brown sugar to the mixture before cooking.

Tropical Tapioca Pudding: Add ⅓ cup chopped dates and ½ cup toasted coconut flakes to the mixture before cooking.

Grandma's Sweet Potato Pie Pudding

A family favorite, this dessert is just as appealing as a sweet potato pie, but without the crust.

Step One: The Sweet Potatoes

2 medium-size sweet potatoes (the sweet, red-skinned variety, not the yellow-skinned)

Place the rack in a pressure cooker and add 1 cup water. Place the sweet potatoes on the rack and lock the lid in place. Bring to 15psi over high heat, immediately reduce the heat to the lowest possible setting to stabilize and maintain that pressure, and cook for 15 minutes. Remove from the heat and use the natural release method (see page 31) to depressurize. Carefully open the lid after the pressure drops. Remove the sweet potatoes from the cooker and let cool. When cool enough to handle, remove the skins and mash with a fork or potato masher to an even consistency. When mashed, the sweet potatoes should total about 1½ cups.

Step Two: The Pudding

2 large eggs, beaten
½ cup heavy cream
2 tablespoons butter, melted, plus extra for the pan
2 tablespoons sorghum molasses
1 teaspoon pure vanilla extract
½ cup packed dark brown sugar
2 tablespoons all-purpose flour
1 teaspoon ground cinnamon
½ teaspoon ground nutmeg
¼ teaspoon salt
½ cup chopped pecans
Whipped cream, for garnish
6 whole pecans, for garnish

Generously butter a shallow, 1-quart, flat-bottomed metal pan that will fit loosely inside your pressure cooker. Bring 1 quart water to a boil in a saucepan or kettle while you make the pudding. In a large bowl, combine the sweet potatoes, eggs, cream, butter, molasses, vanilla extract, brown sugar, flour, cinnamon, nutmeg, and salt, and blend well. Gently stir in the chopped pecans. Pour the sweet potato mixture into the prepared pan. Butter a square of aluminum foil and crimp it tightly over the top of the pan. Place the rack in the pressure cooker and pour in 2 cups boiling water. Use foil helper handles (see page 42) to place the pan on the rack, and lock the lid in place. Bring to 15psi over high heat, immediately reduce the heat to the lowest possible setting to stabilize and maintain that pressure, and cook for 15 minutes. Remove from the heat and use the natural release method (see page 31) to depressurize. Carefully open the lid after the pressure drops. Carefully remove the pudding from the cooker and spoon into parfait glasses or desert dishes. Add a dollop of whipped cream and a whole pecan to each before serving.

✳ Serves 6

Pecan Praline Cheesecake with Hot Fudge Caramel Sauce

A temptingly, rich dessert with a chocolatey crumb crust and a toffee surprise, this cheesecake is topped with toasty pecans and Hot Fudge Caramel Sauce. If you love chocolate and pecans, this cheesecake is for you!

Step One: The Crust
Butter for the pan
2 tablespoons melted butter
½ cup chocolate graham cracker crumbs
1 tablespoon granulated sugar
⅓ cup toffee bits or milk chocolate toffee bits

Butter the inside of a 7-inch springform pan or substitute a flat-bottomed metal pan that will fit inside your cooker. In a small bowl, melt the butter in a microwave, then blend in the cracker crumbs and sugar. Use the back of a spoon to pack the crumb mixture into the bottom of the pan and about halfway up the sides. Sprinkle the toffee bits evenly over the crust.

Step Two: The Toasted Pecans
⅓ cup whole pecans

Preheat the oven to 300°F. Spread the pecans evenly on a baking sheet and bake for 10 to 15 minutes, stirring often, until the pecans are fragrant and lightly browned. Cool, and then finely chop.

Step Three: The Filling
11 ounces cream cheese, softened
½ cup granulated sugar
¼ cup toffee bits or milk chocolate toffee bits, plus extra for garnish
2 tablespoons all-purpose flour
1 teaspoon pure vanilla extract
2 large eggs, slightly beaten

Use an electric mixer to beat the softened cream cheese until smooth. Add the sugar, toffee bits, flour, and vanilla extract, mixing until well blended. Blend in the beaten eggs, mixing well. Pour the mixture into the center of the crust in the springform pan. Cover the pan tightly with aluminum foil. Place the rack in the cooker and add 2 cups water. Use foil helper handles (see page 42) to lower the pan into the cooker. Lock the lid in place. Bring to 15psi over high heat, immediately reduce the heat to the lowest possible setting to stabilize and maintain that pressure, and cook for 20 minutes. Remove from the heat and use the natural release method (see page 31) to depressurize. Carefully open the lid after the pressure drops. Use the helper handles to lift the pan out of the cooker, remove the aluminum foil, and sprinkle toffee bits and the toasted pecan pieces to evenly cover the top of the cheesecake before it cools. Refrigerate and let chill before serving. To unmold, run a sharp knife around the inside of the pan to loosen the sides. Remove the outer ring of the springform pan and slide the cheesecake onto a serving plate.

Step Four: The Hot Fudge Caramel Sauce
¼ cup (½ stick) butter
⅔ cup firmly packed brown sugar
⅓ cup whipping cream
¼ cup light corn syrup
2 ounces semisweet baking chocolate, grated
1 teaspoon pure vanilla extract

This sauce can be made several days in advance and refrigerated until serving time. Melt the butter in a heavy 2-quart saucepan over medium heat, then stir in the brown sugar, whipping cream, and corn syrup, and cook, stirring, until the mixture just comes to a boil. Boil for 3 minutes and remove from the heat. Add the chocolate pieces, stirring until melted and smooth. Stir in the vanilla extract. Cool slightly and transfer to a microwave-safe bowl. Cover and refrigerate until serving time. Just before serving, microwave to warm the sauce if necessary. To serve, cut the cheesecake and place a slice on each dessert plate. Dip a knife in warm water before each cut and wipe clean after each cut. Spoon the Hot Fudge Caramel Sauce over the individual cheesecake slices. ✳ **Serves 4 to 5**

Banana Crème Cups

I think I'm addicted. Not only is this an excellent way to use those overly ripe bananas, but it also tastes decadently rich.

> **Butter for the ramekins**
> **2 ripe bananas**
> **2 tablespoons fresh lemon juice**
> **½ cup soft bread crumbs (see Miss Vickie Says)**
> **½ cup packed dark brown sugar**
> **1 teaspoon ground nutmeg**
> **1 cup heavy cream**
> **2 large eggs, slightly beaten**
> **2 tablespoons dark rum**
> **1 tablespoon pure vanilla extract**
> **Whipped cream, for garnish**
> **12 vanilla wafers, for garnish**

Butter 6 individual 8-ounce ramekins or other heatproof cups of equal size. Use a food processor to puree the bananas and lemon juice together. In a large bowl, combine the bread crumbs, sugar, and nutmeg. Stir in the cream, eggs, rum, vanilla extract, and pureed bananas. Spoon the mixture into the prepared ramekins, then cover each ramekin with a small square of aluminum foil. Place the rack in the pressure cooker and add 1 cup water. Arrange half of the ramekins on the rack. Place a second rack on top of the ramekins and add the second layer of ramekins on top. Lock the lid in place. Bring to 15psi over high heat, immediately reduce the heat to the lowest possible setting to stabilize and maintain that pressure, and cook for 15 minutes. Remove from the heat and use the natural release method (see page 31) to depressurize. Carefully open the lid after the pressure drops. Lift out the ramekins with long-handled tongs and remove the foil. Serve in the cups, warm or chilled as desired. Garnish each cup with a dollop of whipped cream and 2 vanilla wafers just before serving. ✳ **Serves 6**

Miss Vickie Says

There are two types of breadcrumbs: dry—used for crispy coatings and toppings; and soft—used as a filler or softer topping. To make your own breadcrumbs, use stale (day-old) bread, and bake the slices directly on an oven rack in a slow oven (200°F). For soft breadcrumbs the bread is ready when it is slightly dry. For dry breadcrumbs the bread is baked until it is dry throughout. Let the bread slices cool in the oven and then process them in a food processor. Leave plain or season with salt, pepper, herbs, garlic, and onion powder as you wish. Equivalents: 4 slices bread = 1 cup dry breadcrumbs. 3 slices bread = 1 cup fresh, soft breadcrumbs.

Peppery Spiced Poached Apples with Spiced Whipped Cream

Wow! Forget boring, these apples are sweet, spicy, and peppery, and an easy-to-prepare dessert.

½ cup granulated sugar
2 cups dry red wine
2 tablespoons fresh lemon juice
1 whole cinnamon stick
1 teaspoon whole black peppercorns
1 teaspoon whole cloves
3 small Granny Smith apples, peeled, cored, and halved
Spiced Whipped Cream, for garnish (recipe follows)
Coarsely ground black pepper, for garnish

Combine the sugar, wine, and lemon juice in the pressure cooker over medium-high heat and bring to a boil. Tie the cinnamon stick, peppercorns, and cloves together in a cheesecloth bag, add the bag to the cooker, and continue to cook, stirring, until the sugar dissolves. Place the apples in the wine, cut side down, and lock the lid in place. Bring to 15psi over high heat, immediately reduce the heat to the lowest possible setting to stabilize and maintain that pressure, and cook for 4 minutes. Remove from the heat and use the cold water release method (see page 30) to depressurize. Carefully open the lid after the pressure drops. Use a slotted spoon to transfer the apples to a plate, cover with aluminum foil, and keep warm in a low oven. Bring the poaching liquid in the cooker to a boil over medium-high heat, and boil, uncovered, stirring with a wooden spoon to prevent scorching, until reduced and syrupy. Discard the spice bag. Place the apple halves in dessert dishes and lightly sprinkle with the coarsely ground black pepper. Spoon the sauce over each apple half and top with Spiced Whipped Cream. ✳ Serves 6

Spiced Whipped Cream

1 cup whipping (heavy) cream
3 tablespoons powdered sugar
½ teaspoon ground cinnamon
½ teaspoon ground ginger
½ teaspoon coarsely ground black pepper

Beat all of the ingredients together in a chilled bowl with an electric mixer on high speed until soft peaks form.

Variations

Peppery Spiced Poached Pears:
Use 3 pears, peeled, cored, and halved.

Peppery Spiced Poached Peaches:
Use 3 freestone peaches, peeled, pits removed, and halved.

Peppery Spiced Poached Apricots:
Use 12 apricots, pits removed and halved.

Red-Hot Peaches with Balsamic Honey Sauce

During peach season my grandmother canned peaches, blanched and froze peaches, and served an endless variety of peach dishes. These hot and spicy peaches were served with a scoop of vanilla ice cream, and the intense explosion of hot and spicy with a sweet-tart flavor was to die for! I especially remember this dish because it was a special treat just for us kids. Her original recipe started with home canned peaches, and I've modified it for fresh fruit and a smaller amount.

½ cup sugar
2 tablespoons red-hot cinnamon candies
½ cup white vinegar
⅓ cup cranberry juice
1 whole stick cinnamon
1 teaspoon whole cloves
2 tablespoons chopped candied ginger
3 fresh freestone peaches, peeled and pit removed
Balsamic Honey Sauce (recipe follows)

Combine the sugar, candies, vinegars, and cranberry juice in the pressure cooker and bring to a boil over medium-high heat. Tie the cinnamon, cloves, and candied ginger together in a cheesecloth bag, add the bag to the pressure cooker, and continue to cook, stirring, until the sugar and candies dissolve. Place the peaches in the pressure cooker, cut side down, and lock the lid in place.

Bring to 15psi over high heat, immediately reduce the heat to the lowest possible setting to stabilize and maintain that pressure, and cook for 3 minutes. Remove from the heat and use the cold water release method (see page 30) to depressurize. Carefully open the lid after the pressure drops. Use a slotted spoon to transfer the peaches and the spice bag to a glass bowl, and cover with the liquid. Cover the bowl with plastic wrap and refrigerate for 24 hours to allow the flavors to develop. Meanwhile, prepare the Balsamic Honey Sauce. To serve, place the peaches in dessert bowls and pour a spoonful of the prepared sauce over the top of each.

✻ Serves 6

Balsamic Honey Sauce

½ cup honey
¼ cup good-quality balsamic vinegar
1 teaspoon grated lemon zest

Combine the honey, vinegar, and lemon zest in a small bowl and stir to mix well.

Upside-Down Chocolate Fudge Cake

Like two desserts in one, the cake in this recipe separates from the fudge sauce. This recipe requires a preliminary steaming period before the cooker is fully pressurized, and it cooks at a lower pressure setting to allow the delicate cake part of this pudding to rise.

1 cup sifted all-purpose flour
¾ cup granulated sugar
¾ cup packed dark brown sugar
6 tablespoons unsweetened cocoa powder
2 teaspoons baking powder
½ teaspoon salt
½ cup milk
2 tablespoons butter, melted, plus extra
    for the bowl
1 teaspoon pure vanilla extract
Powdered sugar, for garnish (optional)

Bring 1 quart water to a boil in a saucepan or kettle. Generously butter the inside of a 1-quart, round-bottomed metal bowl. In a large mixing bowl, stir together the flour, granulated sugar, brown sugar, cocoa powder, baking powder, and salt and set aside. In a separate bowl, stir together the milk, butter, and vanilla extract. Add the milk mixture to the dry ingredients and stir to mix well. Pour the mixture into the prepared bowl. Do not fill the bowl more than ⅔ full, leave space for the pudding to rise slightly. Butter the center of a square of aluminum foil and crimp it over the top of the pudding bowl, making a tightly sealed covering. Place the bowl in the pressure cooker using foil helper handles (see page 42), and pour enough boiling water into the cooker to cover the lower third of the bowl. Heat the cooker over medium-high heat and steam the pudding for 15 minutes to allow the cake to rise. At the end of the steaming period, check the water level and add more boiling water if needed to cover the lower third of the bowl. Lock the lid in place. Bring to 10psi over high heat, immediately reduce the heat to the lowest possible setting to stabilize and maintain that pressure, and cook for 20 minutes. Remove from the heat and use the cold water release method (see page 30) to depressurize. Carefully open the lid after the pressure drops. Use the helper handles to remove the bowl from the cooker. Serve the pudding warm, spooning portions into individual serving bowls and dusting each with powdered sugar if desired. ✳ Serves 6

Master Spanish Flan

There are many recipes for flan, a smooth, creamy dessert popular in many parts of the world, including Europe, the Caribbean, and the Americas. This recipe has its roots in Spain and is very sweet and rich, and it's traditionally prepared in the pressure cooker.

Butter for the pan
4 large eggs, separated
1 (14-ounce) can sweetened condensed milk
1 cup heavy cream
1 teaspoon pure vanilla extract
¼ cup sugar
½ teaspoon ground nutmeg

½ teaspoon ground cinnamon

½ teaspoon grated lemon zest

⅛ teaspoon salt

Generously butter the inside of 1-quart metal flan pan, or use any shallow, straight-sided, flat-bottomed metal pan that will fit loosely inside your pressure cooker. Beat the egg whites with an electric mixer until foamy, then set aside. Clean the mixer bowl and beaters, and beat the yolks until they are light yellow and stiff enough to look like lightly whipped cream. Slowly add the sweetened condensed milk, heavy cream, vanilla extract, sugar, nutmeg, cinnamon, lemon zest, and salt, and beat until evenly mixed. Carefully fold in the egg whites using a rubber spatula, but do not overmix. Pour the mixture into the prepared pan. Place the rack in the pressure cooker and add 1 cup water. Cover the pan tightly with a sheet of aluminum foil and use foil helper handles (see page 42) to place the pan inside the cooker. Lock the lid in place. Bring to 15psi over high heat, immediately reduce the heat to the lowest possible setting to stabilize and maintain that pressure, and cook for 10 minutes. Remove from the heat and use the natural release method (see page 31) to depressurize. Carefully open the lid after the pressure drops. Use the foil helper handles to lift the pan out of the cooker, and refrigerate the flan in the pan for several hours until completely chilled. Remove the foil covering. Run a knife blade around the inside of the pan and place a serving plate over the top. Quickly invert the pan to unmold the flan.

✳ Serves 5 to 6

Cook's Note: The tart taste of fresh fruits in season, or frozen fruit, goes especially well with this sweet flan. Consider sliced strawberries, peaches, blueberries, raspberries, boysenberries, cherries, or cooked rhubarb.

Variations

Caramel Flan: Before mixing the flan, melt ½ cup sugar in a small heavy skillet over medium heat, stirring until the syrup turns a deep golden caramel color. Immediately pour the caramel into the buttered flan pan, tilting it in all directions to coat the bottom and part way up the sides. Work quickly; the caramel will harden as it cools. The caramel is extremely hot, so use heavy pot holders or oven mitts when handling the pan. Pour the flan mixture into the pan on top of the caramel.

Coconut Flan: Add 1 cup unsweetened coconut flakes to the milk mixture.

Coffee Flan: Add 2 teaspoons instant coffee granules to the milk mixture.

Peppermint Candy Flan: Add ½ cup finely crushed peppermint candies to the milk mixture.

Chocolate Flan: Add ⅓ cup cocoa powder to the milk mixture.

Coconut-Kissed Caramel Flan: Prepare as for Caramel Flan, melting ½ cup brown sugar along with the white sugar. When the sugars have melted, add 1 cup sweetened coconut flakes to the skillet.

Caramel Fruit Flan: Prepare the Caramel Flan as above, coating the flan pan with the caramel. Arrange ½ cup cut or chopped pieces of fresh, canned, or thawed frozen fruit to the center of the pan before pouring in the flan mixture.

Mandarin Orange Flan: Substitute 1 cup orange juice for the evaporated milk. Arrange 1 (11-ounce) can drained Mandarin orange segments in the bottom of the flan pan before pouring in the flan mixture.

Sweet Dumpling Flan with Caramel Sauce

The tiny sweet dumpling squash is true to its name, it's sweet as honey, and only available from September through December. Choose the ones that are heavy for their size; they have a deep yellow to orange meat like pie pumpkins and are delicious in dessert recipes. Cook this flan in a 1-quart metal flan pan, or any shallow, straight-sided, flat-bottomed metal pan that will fit loosely inside your pressure cooker.

Step One: The Squash

2 sweet dumpling squash
1 (14-ounce) can sweetened condensed milk
2 large eggs, slightly beaten
1 teaspoon pure vanilla extract
⅓ cup dark brown sugar
1 teaspoon ground cinnamon
½ teaspoon ground ginger
½ teaspoon salt
¼ teaspoon ground cloves
¼ teaspoon ground nutmeg

Cut each squash in half lengthwise and scoop out the fibrous pith and seeds. Place the rack in the pressure cooker and add ½ cup water. Layer the squash halves on the rack, cut side down, and lock the lid in place. Bring to 15psi over high heat, immediately reduce the heat to the lowest possible setting to stabilize and maintain that pressure, and cook for 8 minutes. Remove from the heat and use the natural release method (see page 31) to depressure. Carefully open the lid after the pressure drops. Remove the squash and scoop out the flesh, cutting it into 1-inch chunks. Put the squash and all of the remaining ingredients in a food processor and blend until it's a smooth puree.

Step Two: The Caramel Sauce

¾ cup granulated sugar

Heat the sugar in a heavy skillet or saucepan over medium-high heat, stirring constantly with a wooden spoon as the sugar melts. Watch closely so that it doesn't burn. When the sugar melts and turns a dark golden caramel color—just like a piece of caramel candy—remove from the heat. Using oven mitts, immediately pour the caramel sauce into a round metal pan of a size that will fit loosely inside your pressure cooker, swirling it around so the caramel evenly coats the bottom. Tilt the pan, letting the caramel coat the sides of the pan as well. Keep tilting the pan to spread the caramel evenly until it hardens.

Step Three: The Flan

Pour the squash mixture into the caramel-coated pan. Place the lid on the pan, or seal the pan with a square of aluminum foil, tightly crimping the edges. Place the rack in the bottom of the pressure cook and add 1 cup water. Use foil helper handles (see page 42) to place the flan pan on top of the rack. Lock the lid in place. Bring to 15psi over high heat, immediately reduce the heat to the lowest possible setting to stabilize and maintain that pressure, and cook for 15 minutes. Remove from the heat and use the natural release method (see page 31) to depressurize. Carefully open the lid after the pressure drops. Use the helper handles to lift the flan out of the cooker, and remove the foil. Unmold the flan into a deep dish such as a decorative pie plate. The melted caramel makes quite a bit of sauce. The flan can be served warm or chilled, according to your preference. ✳ **Serves 4 to 5**

Cook's Note: Delicata, buttercup, butternut, kabocha (Sweet Mama), pie pumpkins, or sugar pumpkins are examples of other sweet squashes that can be substituted for the sweet dumpling.

Master Custard Cups

This classic custard dessert has a delicious appeal for young and old. No matter what your age, babies to grandmothers, the basic egg custard is nourishing and easily digested. Of course, I've included several variations that transform the plain version into a variety of silky smooth desserts sitting in little pools of sweet sauce.

> **Butter for the cups**
> **1 cup heavy cream**
> **1 cup whole milk**
> **2 large eggs, slightly beaten**
> **1 teaspoon pure vanilla extract**
> **¼ cup sugar**
> **¼ teaspoon salt**
> **Ground nutmeg, for garnish**

Generously butter the insides of 6 (4-ounce) custard cups. Using an electric mixer, combine all of the ingredients except for the nutmeg until smooth. Pour the mixture into the prepared cups and dust with the nutmeg. Cover each cup tightly with a square of aluminum foil. Place the rack in the pressure cooker and add 1 cup water. Arrange a layer of cups on the rack. Place a second rack on top of the cups and arrange the rest of the cups on the second rack. Lock the lid in place. Bring to

15psi over high heat, immediately reduce the heat to the lowest possible setting to stabilize and maintain that pressure, and cook for 4 minutes. Remove from the heat and use the natural release method (see page 31) to depressurize. Carefully open the lid after the pressure drops. Lift the cups from the cooker with long-handled tongs and remove the foil covering. Serve in the cups or unmold as desired. To unmold, run a knife blade around the insides of the cups and quickly invert onto individual serving plates. Serve warm or cold. ✳ **Serves 6**

Variations

> **Maple Custard:** Add ⅓ cup maple syrup before cooking.

> **Chocolate Custard:** Add ⅓ cup cocoa powder to the milk mixture.

> **Fruit Custard:** Arrange fresh, canned, or dried fruit in the bottom of each custard cup before adding the milk mixture.

> **Caramel Custard:** In a small heavy skillet over medium heat, melt ½ cup sugar, stirring until the syrup turns a deep golden caramel color. Immediately pour the caramel into each of the cups, tilting them in all directions to coat the bottoms and part way up the sides. Work quickly; the caramel will harden as it cools. The caramel is extremely hot, so use heavy pot holders or oven mitts when handling the cups. Pour the milk mixture on top of the caramel.

> **Butterscotch Custard:** Add 1 tablespoon butterscotch chips and ½ teaspoon butter to the bottom of each custard cup before adding the milk mixture.

> **Taffy-Nut Custard:** Add 1 tablespoon chopped nuts, 2 tablespoons brown sugar, and ½ teaspoon butter to the bottom of each custard cup before adding the milk mixture.

Master Poached
Spiced Fruit

When it's so easy to open up a can, most people forget about the lovely taste of freshly poached fruits. Served warm in the winter and chilled in the summer, seasonal fruit is cooked in spiced sauces, then spooned over cake, ice cream, bread pudding, pancakes, French toast, or breakfast cereal, or just eaten as is.

1 tablespoon minced candied ginger
½ teaspoon whole black peppercorns
½ teaspoon whole cloves
1 cinnamon stick, broken in half
1 (2-inch) strip of lemon peel (no white pith)
1 vanilla bean, split open
1 bay leaf
1 cup sugar
1 cup water or flavoring liquid such as
    fruit juice, fruit-flavored soda, or wine,
    alone or in combination
1 tablespoon fresh lemon juice
Fruit of your choice (see selections below)

Tie the candied ginger, peppercorns, cloves, cinnamon stick, lemon peel, vanilla bean, and bay leaf together in a square of cheesecloth. Add the sugar, water, lemon juice, and spice bag to the pressure cooker and bring to a boil over medium-high heat, stirring until the sugar has dissolved completely. Add your choice of fruit, choosing from the selections below. Place the fruit cut side down in the poaching liquid, and lock the lid in place. Bring to 15 psi over high heat, immediately reduce the heat to the lowest possible setting to stabilize and main-

tain that pressure, and cook for 4 minutes. Remove from the heat and use the cold water release (see page 30) to depressurize. Carefully open the lid after the pressure drops. Transfer the fruit to dessert bowls with a slotted spoon, and serve warm or chilled as desired. Pour a spoonful of the poaching liquid over the fruit, if desired, and serve.

✳ Serves 6

Fruit Selections:

Fresh peaches: 4 peaches, peeled, halved, and pitted. Choose any variety of freestone peaches for easy removal of the peach pit. Peaches are in season from late May through early August.

Fresh pears: 4 pears, peeled, halved, and cored. Firm pears like Bosc, Seckel, and d'Anjou are especially good poached. Different varieties of pears are available year-round.

Fresh apricots: 8 apricots, halved and pitted. Apricots are in season from late May through early August.

Fresh plums: 6 plums (any variety), halved and pitted. Plum season is from June through September.

Fresh cherries: 1 pound sweet cherries, pitted. The season for sweet cherries is May through July.

Fresh nectarines: 4 nectarines, halved and pitted. Nectarines are available from spring through fall.

Fresh bananas: 4 firm, ripe bananas, peeled and halved lengthwise. Bananas are especially good cooked in orange juice. Bananas are available all year long.

Fresh pineapple: 1 small ripe pineapple, peeled, quartered, cored, and cut into ½-inch slices. Increase the cooking time to 5 minutes. Pineapples are available all year long.

Fresh apples: 3 apples, peeled, halved, and cored. I like the flavor and texture of Rome, Pippin, Granny Smith, Gravenstein, or McIntosh, but any firm apple will serve.

Grandma's Bonnet Pudding

This is a very old recipe for a beautiful little steamed, cake-like pudding. The fruit makes a colorful design on the top of the inverted pudding that resembles an old-fashioned lady's hat. Because this pudding needs to rise, a short steaming period is required before the cooker is fully pressured. To keep the pudding from being crushed under high pressure, I also use a lower pressure setting.

1 cup (2 sticks) butter, softened, plus
    extra for the bowl
1 cup sugar
3 large eggs, slightly beaten
1 teaspoon almond extract
1½ cups self-rising flour
Maraschino cherries as desired
1 (16-ounce) can sliced peaches, drained

Bring 1 quart water to a boil in a saucepan or kettle. Generously butter the inside of a 1½-quart round-bottomed metal bowl or pudding mold. Using an electric mixer, cream the butter and sugar together in a large bowl until light and fluffy. Slowly add the eggs, beating continuously. Add the almond extract. Add the flour in small amounts, beating continuously, until well blended. Place 1 maraschino cherry in the bottom of the greased bowl, centering it, and then arrange the peach slices around it in a decorative pattern. Use additional maraschino cherries, halved or quartered, to complete the decorative pattern as you wish. Carefully spoon the batter over the top of the fruit pattern, taking care not to disturb the fruit. Do not fill the bowl more than ⅔ full, leaving space for the pudding to rise slightly. Butter the lid of the pudding mold, or use a buttered square of aluminum foil and crimp around the edge of the bowl, sealing it tightly. Place the rack in the cooker and use foil helper handles (see page 42) to lower the pudding bowl into the pressure cooker. Pour enough boiling water into the pressure cooker to cover the lower third of the bowl. Heat the cooker over medium-high heat and steam the pudding for 15 minutes to allow the cake to rise. At the end of the steaming period, check the water level and add more boiling water if needed to cover the lower third of the bowl. Lock the lid in place. Bring to 10psi over high heat, immediately reduce the heat to the lowest possible setting to stabilize and maintain that pressure, and cook for 20 minutes. Remove from the heat and use the natural release method (see page 31) to depressurize. Carefully open the lid after the pressure drops. Use the foil helper handles to lift the pudding out of the cooker, and remove the lid or foil. To serve, place a serving plate over the top of the pan and quickly invert it to unmold the pudding. Serve warm or cold, as desired. ✳ **Serves 6**

Variations: Use any other varieties of canned fruit to make the pattern on the bottom of the pudding mold. Apricots, pineapple rings or chunks, cherries, and pears are all good choices.

Fabulous Fruitcakes

AMERICANS HAVE A LOVE-HATE relationship with fruitcakes. Misconceptions about fruitcakes inspire many jokes. Even Johnny Carson once said, "There's only one fruitcake in the U.S., and it's passed around year after year from family to family."

What comes to your mind when you think of a fruitcake? Is it a rich, moist cake filled with delicious fruit and nuts, or a dried-out "doorstop"? People tend to dislike fruitcake because so many of them are mass-produced using cheap, inferior ingredients, and those do indeed warrant all the bad press. Commercial fruitcakes sold in supermarkets are often dry, tasteless, and made with mysterious rubbery pieces of colorful, but bitter . . . things. Those yellow-green, candied "things" are pieces of citron, a semitropical citrus fruit that looks like a huge, lumpy lemon, so it's no surprise that a fruitcake is viewed with suspicion and that store-bought versions have given fruitcakes a bad image. Even the so-called gourmet fruitcakes can be full of preservatives and things like melon rinds colored to look like kelly-green cherries.

Real fruitcakes are like a treasure chest of fruits, nuts, and spices, but don't be put off by the long list of ingredients; a fruitcake is supposed to have a lot of good stuff in it. In bygone days, the making of a "great cake" was a leisurely affair stretched out over several days and celebrated with the enjoyable company of good friends and family. A genuine fruitcake is sinfully rich, moist, delicious, and studded with a cornucopia of plump, naturally sweet (not candied!) dried fruits soaked in spirits and mixed with complex spices, and there's not a green candied thing in the lot. Fruitcakes are lavishly decorated with nutmeats, and are soaked with heady liqueurs for several weeks prior to serving.

History of Fruitcakes

Fruitcakes have been around for a long time, and history is full of lore and rumor about their creation. Fruitcake was probably the original high-energy snack food. The oldest reference to fruitcakes dates back to Roman times, when cakes were made with excess fruits and nuts as a means of preserving the harvest. Recipes included native fruits like plums and cherries, pomegranate seeds, pine nuts, and raisins mixed into barley mash.

During the Middle Ages, sweet ingredients such as honey and spices were added. In Europe in the 1700s, a ceremonial type of fruitcake was baked at the end of the nut harvest and consumed the following year to celebrate the beginning of the harvest.

During the Victorian era (1837–1901), fruitcake was very popular, and legend has it that Queen Victoria received a fruitcake for her birthday one year. She put it aside for a year as a sign of restraint, moderation, and her good manners. Fruitcakes were sometimes called the "Queen of Cakes," and were always served to commemorate important occasions. By the end of the 18th century sumptuary laws restricted rich plum cakes—"plum" was a generic word for dried fruit—to Christmas, Easter, weddings, christenings, and funerals because they were considered too decadent. Unmarried girls would put a slice of fruitcake under their pillow at night expecting to dream of the person they would marry.

The English fruitcake tradition came to America with the first colonists. Slices of fruitcake were wrapped up in little packages and tucked into soldier's jackets during the Civil War. In "A Christmas Memory," Truman Capote, who grew up in rural Alabama during the Great Depression, recalls gathering pecans with his cousin one year and baking a fruitcake for Franklin Delano Roosevelt.

In Japan, department stores offer gift boxes of elegant little fruitcakes wrapped in gold foil all year-round. In the South, where fruitcakes are steeped in tradition as well as whiskey, fruitcakes are often placed in heirloom tins that are prominently arranged on the sideboard. Each curing fruitcake is stored with a jigger of whiskey standing in the center hole for the convenience of the person charged with regularly pouring the whiskey over the top of the fruitcake. The jigger was then refilled before the tin was sealed again, leaving it ready for the next "feeding."

Ingredients in Fruitcakes

By tradition, when Labor Day rolled around, everyone in my family knew it was time to start making fruitcakes so that the first one would be ready to cut on Thanksgiving Day. There are dark fruitcakes and light fruitcakes, and some people prefer one more than the other. A light or white fruitcake uses light-colored fruits such as currants, dried apricots and pineapple, and light corn syrup. A dark fruitcake uses darker fruits like raisins, dates, cranberries, and prunes, and dark corn syrup or molasses. The ratio of fruit to batter has always been an issue for serious fruitcake connoisseurs, but the general rule is at least half the weight of the cake should be fruit. A fruitcake with less than a 50:50 ratio is not really a fruitcake, but a plum cake or Dundee cake. A good fruitcake is the result of the best-quality ingredients, and most recipes are fairly tolerant of substitutions, so use the fruits you like best.

The Fruit

If you want a dense, fruit-rich cake, you'll need 2 to 3 pounds of good-quality dried fruits. Select from dried apples, pears, pineapples, dates, peaches, prunes, cranberries, blueberries, cherries, figs, apricots, black and golden raisins, and currants. You can also use dried mango, banana, coconut, and papaya bits, and a little freshly grated lemon or orange peel. For real candied citrus peel and candied pineapple, see the recipes on pages 441–442. To make recipe substitutions and use the fruits that you like, add up the total amount of fruits and nuts called for in the recipe, and then make changes according to your personal preferences. The important thing is that the total amount of fruit and nuts should still be approximately the same as in the original recipe. When you have assembled all the dried fruits, cut them into small pieces with kitchen shears, or chop them with a knife. If the fruits are too sticky, dust them lightly with flour before chopping.

Marinating the Fruit. This step in the preparation should be scheduled at least 48 hours, or better still, 72 hours, prior to the time you want to cook the fruitcake, to allow the fruits time to soak up the marinade and become soft. Without soaking, the dried fruits will continue to dry out and draw moisture from the surrounding cake, leaving you with a dry and crumbling fruitcake suitable only for the trash bin. Don't skimp on the wine; use a good-quality brand that is eminently drinkable. Good choices are Port, sherry, Marsala, Madeira, Malmsey, or Muscat. Choose lighter-colored wines for light-colored fruitcakes, and deeper-colored wines for dark fruitcakes. Even though the heat will destroy most of the alcohol, the rich flavors will remain in the fruits.

Place all the dried fruits in a nonreactive glass or ceramic bowl, and pour in enough wine to cover the pieces completely. Make up a spice bag by tying 2 sticks of cinnamon, 10 whole cloves, 10 whole black peppercorns, and a 3-inch strip of orange peel together in a piece of cheesecloth, and push the bag beneath the surface of the wine. Cover the bowl tightly and refrigerate, allowing at least 2 or 3 days and up to a week for the fruit to absorb the wine. Replenish the wine as needed to keep the fruit pieces covered.

If time is short, you can hasten the "fruits of your labor" by using the pressure cooker to super-marinate them. Place all the fruits, the spice bag, and just enough wine to cover the ingredients in the pressure cooker and lock the lid in place. Bring to 15psi over high heat, immediately reduce the heat to the lowest possible setting to stabilize and maintain that pressure, and cook for 2 minutes. Remove from the heat and use the natural release method (see page 31) to depressurize. Carefully open the lid after the pressure drops. Let stand until cool.

When ready to proceed with the recipe, discard the spice bag and drain the marinated fruit, re-serving the liquid for the recipe. Toss the fruit pieces with a bit of flour just before adding them to the batter; this will keep them from sticking together and sinking through the batter to the bottom of the pan.

The Spices

This is a fruitcake, not a spice cake, so do not go overboard on the spices. Use fresh whole spices whenever possible, and grind them in a coffee mill or spice grinder just before adding them to the recipe. This releases volatile oils and flavors that are long gone in commercial ground spices. Because freshly ground spices are so pungent, you may want to decrease the amounts. If using commercial ground spices, buy them fresh; don't use that can of cinnamon that's been in the back of your cup-board for a decade.

The Nuts

If you like nuts in your fruitcake, use only the freshest, because the oils found in nuts can turn rancid if you plan on keeping your fruitcake in long-term storage. Chop the nutmeats, but don't cut them too small or you won't find them amidst all the pieces of fruit when your cake is finished. The nuts mainly add crunch, but the subtle flavor is lost with so many other ingredients and spices. Pecans, walnuts, English walnuts, and hazelnuts are good choices.

The Suet

Suet adds richness to fruitcake recipes and holiday puddings. Unlike other fat, suet is hard and granular and comes from the solid white fat found around the kidneys and loins of beef and sheep. If you live in England, beef or vegetable suet is easy to find, but in America, the best approach is to ask a butcher to save a pound or two for you and then grind it into small pieces yourself with a grater, food grinder, or food processor. To substitute butter, freeze the required amount, then quickly chop or grate it into small bits and freeze it again. Keep frozen until it's time to add it to the batter.

The Batter

A fruitcake is mostly fruit, with just enough batter to hold the mixture of fruits, nuts, and spices to-gether. The batter will be heavy, so you will need to use a very large bowl, or a large pot if you must, to stir together the batter, fruit, and nuts with a sturdy wooden spoon. See page 442 for a master recipe for fruitcake batter.

The Pans

When cooking a fruitcake in a pressure cooker, you'll need a special pan with a hollow center to ensure that the dense cake is evenly cooked all the way through, and it must be of a size that will fit inside the cooker without touching the sides or lid. An English-style pudding mold with a tight-fitting lid is designed just for this type of cake, but a decorative ring mold, a Bundt pan, or a tube pan will also work, and a square of aluminum foil can serve as a lid. Don't worry if your kitchen isn't stocked with a mold; our grandmothers didn't have them either, and they made do with repurposed coffee or food cans, so you can too. A 1- to 1½-quart mold, or two 28-ounce vegetable cans, will fit inside most 5-quart and larger pressure cookers. A 2- to 2½-quart mold, two 28-ounce vegetable cans, or two 11-ounce coffee cans will fit most 6-quart and larger pressure cookers. See the "Pan Sizes and Volume" chart (page 40) for more information.

Because it is so dense, a fruitcake takes a long time to cook—even in a pressure cooker—and metal pans will conduct heat better and faster than glass or ceramics. Stainless steel, or decorative copper or tinware, molds are the best choice, as they will not react with any ingredient. Aluminum pans may be used, but they may react to certain ingredients. If using a glass, ceramic, or porcelain mold, or a pudding basin (bowl) you will need to increase cooking times by an additional 5 minutes for each 30 minutes of cooking time. See the chart "Quick Guide to Accessories and their Heat-Conduction Properties" (page 41) for more information.

Fruitcakes are very sticky, so getting them out of the pan cleanly can be tricky. Whatever type of pan you're using, it must be lined with greased paper. Even "nonstick" coatings will be overpowered by a fruitcake, so use baking parchment, or do like those resourceful cooks of the past did and substitute brown paper bags, brown mailing paper, butcher's paper, or freezer paper. Don't use waxed paper; it's too thin and will fall apart.

Grease the pans and cut the paper to size, allowing enough to cover the bottom and come up a little above the sides to help unmold the cake. Grease the paper, and, as it softens, smooth it into the shape of the mold without wrinkles, and then flour it. Be sure to grease the lid, too.

Fruitcakes, as a rule, do not use leavening agents other than eggs to rise, so fill the pans up to ⅔ full with batter. It's best to spoon the heavy batter into the pan and then level the batter by tapping the pans on the countertop to remove any trapped air bubbles. Use an elevated rack to accommodate the longer cooking times. Use foil helper handles (see page 42) to lift the heavy fruitcake pan into and out of the pressure cooker.

Fruitcake Glaze

1 cup granulated sugar
⅓ cup corn syrup

Mix together the sugar, ½ cup water, and the corn syrup in a heavy saucepan. Stir over low heat until the sugar is dissolved. Increase the heat to medium-high and boil the mixture, stirring continually, until it reaches the soft-ball stage. On a candy thermometer, the soft-ball stage is between 234°F and 240°F. At this temperature, sugar syrup dropped into cold water will form a soft ball. If you remove the ball from the water, it will flatten like a pancake after a few moments in your hand. It should take 6 to 8 minutes to reach this stage. Brush the hot glaze over the top of the cake, immediately arrange fruit and nuts on top, if desired, and then brush on a final coat of glaze. ✳ **Makes 1⅓ cups**

Hard Sauce

This traditional English pudding topping is known as brandy butter in England, but it really doesn't have the consistency of a sauce because it's refrigerated until firm. A spoonful is placed on your cake or pudding, where it will melt, adding still more decadence for you to enjoy.

1¼ cups sifted powdered sugar
6 tablespoons (1½ sticks) butter, at room
temperature
¼ cup brandy, rum, or whiskey

Using an electric mixer, blend the sugar and butter together until fluffy. Add the brandy and mix until well blended. Scoop the mixture into a bowl, cover tightly, and refrigerate until cold. This is also great served with pumpkin pie, and is extra yummy on raisin toast—if you have any left over, that is.

✳ **Makes about 1 cup**

Decorating a Fruitcake

After cooking, the tops of fruitcakes can be glazed (see recipe above) and decorated with a fanciful pattern of colorful fruits and nuts, if desired. Before the fruitcake is glazed, plan the decorative pattern in advance. Select the fruits—this is a good time to use candied fruits and nuts—and lay out the pattern on a sheet of paper first. The fruitcake must be cooled completely before applying the glaze. Brush the hot glaze over the top of the fruitcake and quickly add the fruits and nuts according to the pattern you designed. When you've completed the decorative pattern on the top of the fruitcake, brush a second layer of the hot glaze over the pieces of fruits and nuts. Allow the glaze to dry before wrapping.

Candied Citrus Peel

It's nothing like the bitter stuff you buy at the supermarket; this is so good that you can eat it like candy.

1½ cups sugar
2 cups rind from oranges, lemons, or other
  citrus fruits, white pith removed

Place the sugar and 3 cups water in a medium-size saucepan and cook over low heat, stirring, until the sugar is melted. Add the citrus rind to the sugar syrup and simmer gently until the peel is translucent. Remove the peels, let them cool, and place in a glass jar with a tight-fitting lid. Let the syrup cool, and then pour it over the peels. Store in the refrigerator for up to 1 week.

✳ **Makes about 1 cup**

Cook's Note: Mix the peels from different kinds of citrus fruits for color and variety.

Serving a Fruitcake

If you are giving a fruitcake as a gift, remove the cloth wrapping and place the cake in a decorative tin container. To serve a fruitcake, it should be at room temperature or slightly warmed. Do not microwave, or you will end up with an inedible brick. Slices of fruitcake can be best reheated by steaming in a pan. Bring the pressure cooker to pressure and then immediately remove from the heat and use the quick release method (see page 30) to depressurize. Carefully open the lid after the pressure drops.

A whole fruitcake can also be warmed by removing all the wrappings and then carefully rewrapping the cake in a double layer of aluminum foil. Place the rack in the cooker and add ½ cup water, and position the fruitcake on the rack. Lock the lid in place. Bring to 15psi over high heat, immediately reduce the heat to the lowest possible setting to stabilize and maintain that pressure, and cook for 3 minutes, followed by the quick release.

When ready to serve, slice the cake in a sawing motion with a sharp, thin knife blade, making each serving about 1 inch thick. Dip the knife in a glass of hot wine before slicing to avoid tearing the fruitcake. A well-aged and cured fruitcake is best served plain to appreciate the complex flavors. Younger fruitcakes can be served with a warm dessert sauce. Rewrap any remaining fruitcake, brush on a little liquor, and store as directed above.

If the fruitcake appears too dry, it can usually be temporarily revived by using the same instructions above for reheating slices. The heat disrupts the starch crystals and releases the trapped moisture back into the cake. After reheating, serve the cake immediately with a hard sauce (see recipe below). This is only a temporary measure, and once the cake cools again, it will return to its dry state.

Candied Pineapple

Another easy recipe that is so much better than the store-bought variety. The only problem is that it doesn't last very long—nobody can resist nibbling.

> 2 (14-ounce) cans pineapple chunks, drained, with juice
> 2 cups sugar
> ⅓ cup light corn syrup

Pour the pineapple juice into a heavy saucepan, and add the sugar and corn syrup. Bring to a boil over medium-high heat and add the pineapple chunks. Simmer until the fruit is transparent, stirring occasionally. Drain, and arrange the pineapple chunks on a baking sheet lined with waxed paper to cool. Store in the refrigerator in a tightly closed container between layers of waxed paper for up to 1 week. ✳ **Makes about 2½ cups**

Master Fruitcake Mix

Read the detailed instructions above before making a fruitcake.

Step One: The Fruit Mixture
> 3½ pounds assorted dried fruits of your choice, chopped
> 4 cups wine, or more as needed
> 2 cinnamon sticks
> 10 whole cloves
> 10 whole black peppercorns
> 1 (3-inch) strip orange peel

Place all of the dried fruits in a nonreactive glass or ceramic bowl, and pour in enough wine to cover the pieces completely. Tie the cinnamon sticks, cloves, peppercorns, and orange peel together in a square of cheesecloth and push the bag beneath the surface of the wine. Cover the bowl tightly and set aside to refrigerate for at least 48 hours, stirring occasionally. Or, see the directions on page 437 to marinate the fruits more quickly in your pressure cooker.

Step Two: The Batter
> 1 cup (2 sticks) unsalted butter, at room temperature, plus extra for the pans
> 1 cup sugar
> 6 large eggs, slightly beaten
> ¼ cup molasses
> ¼ cup wine or sherry
> 2 teaspoons pure vanilla extract
> 2½ cups all-purpose flour
> ¼ teaspoon ground cinnamon
> ¼ teaspoon ground mace

¼ teaspoon ground nutmeg

¼ teaspoon ground cardamom

⅛ teaspoon salt

½ pound chopped nuts of your choice

⅓ cup Candied Citrus Peel (page 441)

Grease 2 (2-quart) traditional pudding molds (or use any of the alternative pans listed on page 439) that will fit loosely inside your pressure cooker, and line them with heavy greased paper. In the bowl of an electric mixer, cream the butter and sugar together until light and fluffy. Add the eggs, molasses, wine, and vanilla extract and mix well, then transfer the ingredients to a large bowl. Sift the flour, cinnamon, mace, nutmeg, cardamom, and salt together and add to the egg mixture 1 cup at a time, mixing well between additions with a wooden spoon. Stir in the marinated fruit, the nuts, and the candied citrus peel in small batches, blending well after each addition. Divide the batter evenly among the prepared molds and cover each pan with a buttered lid or aluminum foil. Place the rack in the pressure cooker and use foil helper handles (see page 42) to place the fruitcake molds in the pressure cooker. Add enough water to cover the lower third of the molds. Lock the lid in place. Bring to 15psi over high heat, immediately reduce the heat to the lowest possible setting to stabilize and maintain that pressure, and cook for 60 minutes. Remove from the heat and use the natural release method (see page 31) to depressurize. Carefully open the lid after the pressure drops. Check for doneness; a wooden pick inserted in the center should come out clean. Remove the fruitcakes from the pressure cooker and take the lid off the pudding molds. Place the molds on a wire rack until completely cool, and then invert and unmold. Carefully remove the greased paper. Depending on what size molds or pans are used, this recipe will yield 2 fruitcakes of about 2 pounds each.

Cook's Note: If you don't have 2 molds, cook the fruitcakes one after the other, washing the mold between uses. Use custard cups to cook the last little bit of batter if it's too small an amount for a regular pan, reducing the cooking time to 10 minutes. After the fruitcakes have cooled, it's time to begin the ripening process and cure them for keeping. Add the first liquor application and wrap as described on page 444.

Pressure Cooking Fruitcakes

Add enough water to reach halfway up the sides of the fruitcake pan, and lock the lid in place. Bring to 15psi over high heat, immediately reduce the heat to the lowest possible setting to stabilize and maintain that pressure, and cook for 45 to 55 minutes, depending upon the pan size. Pans without a hollow center will need 50 to 60 minutes. Remove from the heat and use the natural release method (see page 31) to depressurize. Carefully open the lid after the pressure drops. Fruitcakes made in a pressure cooker are dark, firm, and very moist and may feel sticky to the touch, but the appearance is no indication of doneness. Take care not to overcook the cake. Cool fruitcakes on a rack in the pans in which they were baked. When completely cool, turn them out of the pans and carefully peel off the paper.

The Care and Feeding of a Fruitcake

A fruitcake needs care and feeding for a period of time as it ripens and matures. When people go to the expense and effort to make a really good homemade fruitcake, they often forget that fruitcake is supposed to be aged and cured, just like the best wine. Fruitcakes do taste better with age! Aging is sometimes called "ripening," and it allows the ingredients in the fruitcake to mellow and blend as the tannins in the dried fruits are released. As the fruitcake matures, the skins of the dried fruits, which contain the same tannins that age fine red wines, create similarly complex flavors and aromas. The key, then, to proper aging is to use lots of high-quality dried, well-marinated fruit. The density and high sugar content of homemade fruitcakes prevent bacterial growth and spoilage. Another handy thing about aging is that it allows a busy cook to prepare fruitcakes well in advance of the busy holiday season.

Feeding or curing is the process of adding alcohol to the fruitcake to preserve it for long-term storage and give it that unique flavor associated with the best fruitcakes. Besides adding moistness and flavor, the alcohol also minimizes the sweetness of the ingredients and makes the fruitcake incredibly rich. So how long will a fruitcake keep? When asked that question, the cooks in my family always replied, "'Till it's all eaten." From their earliest history, fruitcakes were made to have a virtually unlimited shelf life, remaining moist and flavorful for years. By custom, fruitcakes were often kept a year in advance of the grand reveal at the holiday table.

After your fruitcake has cooled completely, it is ready to prepare for storage. Fruitcakes intended for short-term storage are handled differently than the ones that are going to keep for several months or longer. To prepare a fruitcake for short-term storage, you'll need a square of cheesecloth large enough to wrap around the fruitcake.

To prepare the fruitcake for longer storage, you'll need a piece of unbleached muslin to wrap around the cake. Muslin is better for long-term storage because it retains more moisture than cheesecloth. In both cases, you will also need a bottle of good-quality brandy, rum, Cognac, bourbon, or whiskey. Pour enough liquor into a small bowl to soak the cheesecloth or muslin until it is completely saturated. The purpose of this liquor-soaked cloth is to protect the surface of the fruitcake and keep it moist as the alcohol is slowly absorbed into the cake.

While the cloth covering for the fruitcake is soaking, slowly pour a jigger of the same liquor over the top of the fruitcake, adding it drop by drop without causing any wet spots. Lay out a sheet of plastic wrap on a large platter to catch any drips, and place the soaked cheesecloth or muslin on the platter. Center the fruitcake in the middle of the cloth. Wrap the well-saturated fabric around the cake, tucking the ends into the hollow center. Wrap the plastic wrap around the wrapped fruitcake, sealing it completely, and then cover tightly with a sheet of aluminum foil. Put the packaged fruitcake in a sealable freezer bag or an airtight plastic container and store it in a cool, dark place, but not the refrigerator.

For best results, a good fruitcake needs to be ripened for at least 4 to 6 weeks prior to serving. During this stage, liquor is regularly added and the cloth wrapping over the surface of the cake is kept moist. Do not apply more alcohol than the fruitcake can absorb; if it begins to pool around the bottom of the fruitcake, invert the cake and wait until the excess soaks in before applying any more. If the cloth wrapping becomes dry, soak it in liquor before rewrapping the cake. The fruitcake will continue to ripen and improve for several months. The ingredients, as well as the temperature and humidity, will affect the condition of the fruitcake. The fruitcake should remain moist at all times; take care that it does not dry out during the curing process.

A well-wrapped and liquor-cured fruitcake that is kept in a tightly closed container will keep for months, or even years. Generally, I use the following rule of thumb for applying liquor:

For short-term storage, put the fruitcake in a sealable freezer bag or an airtight plastic container and use a basting brush to add liquor on the surface of the fruitcake every 2 to 3 days to ripen for 2 weeks. After that time, the cake can be frozen until serving time.

For longer storage of fruitcakes that are made 2 or more months in advance, add 1 jigger of liquor to the fruitcake once a week for the first month, and once a month thereafter, alternating between the top and bottom of the fruitcake for every application. Repeat this process until the fruitcake will not absorb any more liquor.

Bountiful Breakfasts

BREAKFAST IS THE MOST IMPORTANT MEAL of the day, but consumption has declined over the past 25 years, and the determining factor for most adults as to whether or not they will eat breakfast is how much time they have in the morning. There's no need to spend a lot of time on breakfast if you use a pressure cooker to quickly prepare some good old-fashioned favorites or try something a little different.

Master Old-Fashioned Oatmeal

Close your eyes for a moment and flash back to when you were a kid . . . remember breakfast? No dry flakes dumped in a bowl or gluey mush dragged out of the microwave; chances are your mom actually cooked a nice piping hot bowl of stick-to-your-ribs, old-fashioned oatmeal. She may even have used a pressure cooker. Using the PIP method (see page 37) creates a chewier texture, or cook it directly in the cooker for a creamier oatmeal.

1 cup old-fashioned rolled oats
Pinch of salt

Position the rack in the pressure cooker and add ½ cup water. In a small metal bowl that fits inside the cooker, combine the oats, salt, and 2 cups water. Use foil helper handles (see page 42) to place the bowl in the cooker, and lock the lid in place. Bring to 15psi over high heat and immediately reduce the heat to the lowest possible setting to stabilize and maintain that pressure. For chewy oats, cook for 3 minutes, remove from the heat and use the natural release method (see page 31) to depressurize, or, for a smoother, creamier version, cook for 5 minutes, then remove from the heat and use the natural release method (see page 31) to depressurize. Carefully open the lid after the pressure drops. Use the foil helper handles to remove the bowl from the cooker, spoon the oatmeal into individual bowls, and serve. ✳ **Serves 2; recipe can be doubled with no timing adjustments**

Variations

Use alone or in combination

Sweetened Oatmeal: Add ¼ cup, or more to taste, maple syrup, honey, brown sugar, molasses, preserves, or jam after cooking.

Oatmeal with Dried Fruit: Add ½ cup dried raisins, currants, chopped dates, apricots, or other dried fruit before cooking.

Oatmeal with Fruit: Add ½ cup sliced, chopped, or grated fresh, canned, or frozen fruit after cooking.

Oatmeal with Spices: Add ½ teaspoon ground cinnamon, ginger, allspice, or nutmeg before cooking.

Creamier Oatmeal: Replace half the water used with an equal amount of cream before cooking.

Buttered Oatmeal: Add 1 tablespoon butter after cooking.

Flavored Oatmeal: Replace half or all the water with an equal amount of fruit juice before cooking.

Buttered Oatmeal with Walnuts and Raisin-Brandy Sauce

Who said breakfast is boring? Serve up a bowl of gourmet oatmeal that's so good it could be a dessert.

Step One: The Raisin-Brandy Sauce
1 cup raisins
⅓ cup corn syrup
¼ cup brandy
½ teaspoon ground cinnamon

Prepare the sauce the night before to let the raisins plump up in the brandy. Combine all of the ingredients in a small saucepan over medium heat and simmer, stirring to prevent burning, for about 3 minutes. Set aside to cool, then refrigerate overnight.

Step Two: The Oatmeal
3 cups boiling water
¼ teaspoon salt
1½ cups old-fashioned rolled oats
4 tablespoons (½ stick) butter
½ cup chopped walnuts

Add the water and salt to the pressure cooker and bring to a boil over medium heat. Stir in the oats and butter and lock the lid in place. Bring to 15psi over high heat, immediately reduce the heat to the lowest possible setting to stabilize and maintain that pressure, and cook for 5 minutes. Remove from the heat and use the natural release method (see page 31) to depressurize. Carefully open the lid after the pressure drops. Divide the cooked oatmeal between 4 bowls, spoon the Raisin-Brandy Sauce on top, and add the chopped walnut pieces just before serving. ✳ Serves 4

Steel-Cut Oats

I use the PIP—Pan in Pot—cooking method (see page 37) for this recipe, and it's a great way to start the day!

1 cup pre-toasted steel-cut oats
1 tablespoon butter
Pinch of salt

Position the rack in the pressure cooker and add ½ cup water. In a small metal bowl that fits inside the cooker, combine the oats, butter, salt, and 3½ cups water. Use foil helper handles (see page 42) to place the bowl in the cooker, and lock the lid in place. Bring to 15psi over high heat, immediately reduce the heat to the lowest possible setting to stabilize and maintain that pressure, and cook for 5 minutes for chewy oats, or 8 minutes for a smoother, creamier version. Remove from the heat and use the natural release method (see page 31) to depressurize. Carefully open the lid after the pressure drops. Spoon into individual bowls and serve.

✳ Serves 2

Breakfast Hash

Looking for a quick, no-fuss frittata breakfast or brunch? This is one of my favorite morning meals, and it's also a nice change of pace for a light supper. This is a very versatile recipe and the ingredients suit my preferences, but use whatever you like or have on hand.

> 6 slices smoked or Canadian bacon, or
> 1 cup diced ham, sausage, or kielbasa
> 2 cups frozen hash-brown potatoes
> ½ cup bottled salsa
> ¼ cup minced onion
> ¼ cup minced cilantro leaves
> 4 large eggs, slightly beaten
> 1 cup shredded cheddar cheese

Heat the pressure cooker over medium heat, add the meat, and cook until lightly browned on both sides. Cut the meat into bite-size pieces and drain off any excess fat from the cooker. Deglaze the cooker with ⅓ cup water, scraping up any crusty, brown bits from the bottom. Add the potatoes, salsa, onions, and cilantro, stirring gently to mix. Smooth and level out the top of the potato mixture. Pour in the beaten eggs, evenly distributing them over the top of the potatoes. Lock the lid in place. Bring to 15psi over high heat, immediately reduce the heat to the lowest possible setting to stabilize and maintain that pressure, and cook for 4 minutes. Remove from the heat and use the cold water release method (see page 30) to depressurize. Carefully open the lid after the pressure drops. Sprinkle the cheese over the top of the eggs, cover with a regular lid, and let stand for a few minutes or until the cheese is melted. Spoon the hash onto individual serving plates. ✳ Serves 4

Savory Country Grits

A very quick and flavorful alternative to potatoes, this is one of my favorite side dishes. Made from ground hominy, grits are a Southern cousin of Italian polenta, and they are equally good served with breakfast, brunch, or dinner.

> 1 cup coarsely ground yellow corn grits
> (found in some supermarkets and
> health food stores, or order online),
> not quick-cooking varieties
> 2 (14-ounce) cans chicken broth
> 2 tablespoons butter
> 1 teaspoon salt
> ½ to 1 teaspoon Louisiana-style hot sauce,
> to taste
> 1 cup shredded cheddar cheese

Pour 1½ cups water into the pressure cooker and add the rack to the cooker. Place the grits in a 2-quart metal bowl that will fit inside the pressure cooker and pour in the chicken broth, whisking to blend. Add the butter, salt, and hot sauce and stir to mix. Use foil helper handles (see page 42) to place the bowl on the rack inside the cooker, and lock the lid in place. Bring to 15psi over high heat, immediately reduce the heat to the lowest possible setting to stabilize and maintain that pressure, and cook for 20 minutes. Remove from the heat and use the natural release method (see page 31) to depressurize. Carefully open the lid after the pressure drops. Stir in the cheese and serve immediately. ✳ Serves 4 to 5

Sweet Orange Grits

I love yellow grits. In one form or another, grits are popping up on breakfast plates all over, and even gourmet restaurants are coming up with a wide range of new uses for this popular Southern dish.

> 1 cup coarsely ground yellow corn grits (found in some supermarkets and health food stores, or order online), not quick-cooking varieties
> 2½ cups orange juice
> 2 tablespoons butter
> Zest of 1 orange
> 1 teaspoon salt
> ¼ cup packed brown sugar

Pour 1½ cups water into the pressure cooker and position the rack in the cooker. Place the grits in a 2-quart metal bowl that will fit inside your pressure cooker, and pour in the orange juice and 1 cup water, whisking to blend. Add the butter, zest, and salt and stir to mix. Use foil helper handles (see page 42) to place the bowl on the rack. Lock the lid in place. Bring to 15psi over high heat, immediately reduce the heat to the lowest possible setting to stabilize and maintain that pressure, and cook for 20 minutes. Remove from the heat and use the natural release method (see page 31) to depressurize. Carefully open the lid after the pressure drops. Stir in the brown sugar and let stand a couple of minutes until it melts. Serve warm.

✳ Serves 4 to 5

Serving Suggestion: Add milk or cream to taste along with the brown sugar, or try them with maple syrup or a little molasses.

Breakfast Pork Chops with Wedge Potatoes

A good and hearty breakfast or brunch that's quick and easy to get on the table.

> **Step One: The Pork Chops and Potatoes**
> 2 tablespoons butter
> 4 thin-cut pork chops
> Salt and freshly ground black pepper to taste

Heat the butter in the pressure cooker over medium heat. Add the meat, cook until browned on both sides. Pour in ½ cup water. Lay the potato wedges on top of the pork chops and lock the lid in place. Bring to 15psi over high heat, immediately reduce the heat to the lowest possible setting to stabilize and maintain that pressure, and cook for 6 minutes. Remove from the heat and use the natural release method (see page 31) to depressurize. Carefully open the lid after the pressure drops. Transfer the chops and potatoes to a serving platter, sprinkle with salt and pepper to taste, and serve with eggs.

✳ Serves 4

Eggs en Cocotte

This classic dish is called "Oeufs En Cocotte" in French, which means "Eggs in a Casserole," because each egg is cooked in a small ramekin layered between something delectable on the bottom like ham or mushrooms and cheese, and usually a spoonful of cream over the top. Depending on the type of goodies you add, this can be served for breakfast, brunch, a posh luncheon, or an elegantly romantic midnight supper.

>   2 tablespoons softened butter,
>   no substitutions
>   ½ cup grated sharp cheddar cheese
>   ½ finely chopped cooked ham
>   4 large eggs at room temperature
>   4 tablespoons heavy cream (substitute
>   half-and-half, light cream, or
>   sour cream)
>   Freshly ground black pepper
>   4 teaspoons minced chives or green onion tops.

Brush the bottom and sides of 4 small ramekins (about 3 inch diameter) with butter. Divide the ham and cheese between each dish. Break an egg into each dish, add a teaspoon of chives and then 1 tablespoon cream on top to keep the egg from getting too hard. Sprinkle on a few grains of pepper and cover each ramekin with a square of aluminum foil, crimping it around the rim. Place the rack in the pressure cooker and add 1/2 cup water. Position the ramekins on the rack. Depending of the size, you may need to stack two layers. Lock the lid in place. Bring to 15psi over high heat, immediately reduce the heat to the lowest possible setting to stabilize and maintain that pressure, and cook for 4 minutes. Remove from the heat and use the cold water release method (see page 30) to depressurize. Carefully open the lid after the pressure drops. Now glass or ceramic dishes hold the heat so well that the eggs will go on cooking, so we want to quickly remove the ramekins from the cooker with long handled tongs and an oven mitt before the eggs get over-cooked. Discard the foil and place each ramekin on an individual serving plate and serve with toast and butter.

Cook's Note: There are endless variations for the bottom and top layers, but remember the egg is always in the middle. Meats should by precooked so this is a good way to use up those meager little oddments of leftovers that are otherwise too small to use. Softer vegetables like peppers, mushrooms, and onions need only a quick sauté. Harder vegetables, such as potatoes, broccoli, and asparagus, should by precooked because the very quick cooking time for this egg dish won't be long enough to get them soft.

Master Cornmeal Mush or Polenta

This thick porridge made from cornmeal is known as polenta to Italians and gourmet cooks; in Colonial times it was hasty pudding; and it's just cornmeal mush to Southern cooks, who also prepare a meatier version called scrapple. This is a very easy dish to prepare, and it's so versatile that it can be sweet or savory depending on the ingredients. It's eaten as a hot cereal, as a side dish for dinner, or chilled and fried as a crispy bread. Using a pressure cooker makes quick work of this popular dish—no matter what name you prefer.

1 cup yellow cornmeal
½ teaspoon salt
1 tablespoon butter

Mix the cornmeal, salt, and 1 cup cold water in a small bowl and set aside. This will keep the cornmeal from getting lumpy when cooked. Bring 3 cups water to a boil over medium heat in the pressure cooker. Stir the moistened cornmeal into the boiling water and add the butter. Stir constantly over medium-high heat until the mixture begins to bubble. Lock the lid in place. Bring to 15psi over high heat, immediately reduce the heat to the lowest possible setting to stabilize and maintain that pressure, and cook for 10 minutes. Remove from the heat and use the cold water release method (see page 30) to depressurize. Carefully open the lid after the pressure drops. To serve as a hot cereal, spoon into serving bowls, add your choice of sweetener, if desired, and pour in a little milk or cream to taste. ✳ **Serves 6**

Variations

Breakfast Cornmeal Mush: Before cooking the cornmeal, stir in ½ cup chopped fresh or dried fruit, ½ cup toasted nuts, and a dash of ground cinnamon.

Fried Cornmeal Mush: Pour the hot cornmeal mush into a buttered 4 × 8-inch loaf pan, cover with plastic wrap, and chill overnight or until firm. Turn the loaf out of the pan and cut into 1-inch-thick slices. Heat 3 tablespoons butter, bacon drippings, or oil in a small skillet over medium heat, add the slices of cornmeal mush without crowding, and cook each slice until crisp and lightly browned, about 2 minutes on each side. Serve with plenty of butter and a selection of jam, honey, syrup, and molasses, as you would pancakes.

Cheesy Cornmeal Mush: Add 1½ cups grated sharp cheddar cheese, ½ teaspoon ground sage, and ½ teaspoon Louisiana-style hot sauce to the cornmeal mixture after the cooker is depressurized. Stir to mix and cover with a regular lid until the cheese is melted. Serve as a side dish with butter and a sprinkling of chopped green onions.

Blueberry Cornmeal Mush: Add 2 cups fresh or frozen blueberries. If using frozen berries, defrost them between layers of paper towels to absorb excess liquid. Gently stir the blueberries into the cornmeal after the cooker is depressurized. Serve with milk or cream and sugar.

Scrapple: After the boiling water is added to the cornmeal, stir in 1 pound diced or shredded cooked pork (use leftover pork roast, ham, or sausage), ½ cup minced onion, 1 teaspoon ground sage, ½ teaspoon dried thyme leaves, ½ teaspoon freshly ground black pepper, and ½ teaspoon Louisiana-style hot sauce. After the cooker is depressurized, pour the hot cornmeal mush into a buttered loaf pan, cover with plastic wrap, and chill overnight or until firm. Cut into 1-inch-thick slices and follow the frying directions for Fried Cornmeal Mush above.

Farina

If you're old enough not to ask what this is, you may remember that it was often cooked in a pressure cooker, which produces a smooth, creamy texture with no fuss. Farina, Italian for "flour," is a hot cereal marketed in the United States as Cream of Wheat. Protein-rich wheat is milled to a fine granular consistency and then sifted. It is most often served at breakfast and is excellent for very young children.

3 tablespoons farina, such as Cream of Wheat
    (regular, not quick or instant)
Pinch of salt
Milk to taste (optional)
Sugar to taste (optional)

Position the rack in the pressure cooker and add ½ cup water. In a small metal bowl that will fit inside the cooker, add the farina, salt, and 2 cups water. Use foil helper handles (see page 42) to place the bowl in the cooker, and lock the lid in place. Bring to 15psi over high heat, immediately reduce the heat to the lowest possible setting to stabilize and maintain that pressure, and cook for 4 minutes. Remove from the heat and use the natural release method (see page 31) to depressurize. Carefully open the lid after the pressure drops. Spoon into serving bowls and add milk and sugar or your favorite toppings. ✳ Serves 2; recipe can be doubled with no timing adjustments

Hard-Boiled Eggs

Whether you just need one or a dozen, the pressure cooker is a great way to cook hard-boiled eggs. Besides the usual breakfast fare, use this method to quickly cook hard-boiled eggs for egg salad sandwiches, deviled eggs, potato salad, and other dishes.

Place the rack in the cooker. Carefully add any number of fresh eggs as needed. Cover the eggs with water, taking care not to exceed the ⅔-full level, and lock the lid in place. Bring to 15psi over high heat, immediately reduce the heat to the lowest possible setting to stabilize and maintain that pressure, and cook for 5 minutes for hard-boiled eggs. (For medium-soft eggs, cook for 3 minutes; for soft-boiled eggs, cook for 2 minutes.) Remove from the heat and use the cold water release method (see page 30) to depressurize. Carefully open the lid after the pressure drops. Transfer the eggs to an ice-water bath until cool enough to handle. Store in the refrigerator for up to 1 week, or peel and use immediately.

Compote of Spiced Dried Fruits

With the spices, this is a step up from plain stewed fruit and is worthy of being served as dessert as well as breakfast.

Step One: The *Bouquet Garni*
1 whole cinnamon stick
10 whole black peppercorns
10 whole cloves
1 (1 × 3-inch) strip of citrus peel, any variety of citrus fruit

Tie all of the ingredients together in a small square of cheesecloth.

Step Two: The Fruit
1 cup dried prunes or plums
1 cup dried apricots
1 cup pitted dates
½ cup dried figs
½ cup raisins
1 tablespoon sugar
2 tablespoons Port or sherry
2 teaspoons fresh lemon juice
2 tablespoons grated citrus zest, for garnish

Place all of the ingredients, except for the zest, and the *bouquet garni* into a pressure cooker, stir to mix, and add just the minimum amount of water as recommended by the manufacturer to barely cover the fruit. Lock the lid in place. Bring to 15psi over high heat, immediately reduce the heat to the lowest possible setting to stabilize and maintain that pressure, and cook for 5 minutes. Remove from the heat and use the natural release method (see page 31) to depressurize. Carefully open the lid after the pressure drops. Discard the *bouquet garni*. Transfer the fruit compote to serving bowls and add enough juice from the cooker to barely cover. Sprinkle each bowl with some of the grated citrus zest just before serving. Serve warm.

✳ Serves 4 to 5

Cook's Note: Substitute any variety of dried fruits in the proportions that most appeal to your tastes.

Corned Beef Hash

If you need a big breakfast, this is it. No one will leave the table hungry when this, popularly served with fried eggs, is on the menu.

2½ cups diced potatoes
1 (12-ounce) can corned beef, or 2 cups diced leftover cooked corned beef
½ cup minced onion
½ teaspoon Louisiana-style hot sauce

Place the rack in the pressure cooker and add ½ cup water. Mix all of the ingredients together in a large bowl and spread the mixture evenly in a 6-cup flat-bottomed metal pan. Place the pan on the rack in the cooker and lock the lid in place. Bring to 15psi over high heat, immediately reduce the heat to the lowest possible setting to stabilize and maintain that pressure, and cook for 4 minutes. Remove from the heat and use the natural release method (see page 31) to depressurize. Carefully open the lid after the pressure drops. Spoon onto individual plates, and serve. ✳ **Serves 4 to 5**

California Breakfast Hash

An all-in-one egg dish for a fast breakfast. Serve with warmed, buttered flour tortillas and plenty of extra salsa. Try rolling the hash and avocado slices up in a tortilla for a breakfast burrito.

1 tablespoon butter
⅓ cup diced onion
3 cups shredded potatoes
½ cup bottled salsa
1 (4-ounce) can chopped green chiles, with juice
2 cups cooked diced ham, sausage links, or
   browned and crumbled bulk sausage
6 large eggs, slightly beaten
1 cup shredded cheddar cheese
1 cup shredded pepper Jack cheese
2 avocadoes, sliced
¼ cup sliced green onion tops, for garnish

Heat the butter in the pressure cooker over medium heat. Add the onions and cook, stirring, until clear, about 3 minutes. Add the potatoes, salsa, and green chiles with their juice, stirring to mix. Spread the meat on top of the potatoes. Pour the eggs on top and lock the lid in place. Bring to 15psi over high heat, immediately reduce the heat to the lowest possible setting to stabilize and maintain that pressure, and cook for 4 minutes. Remove from the heat and use the quick or cold water release method (see page 30) to depressurize. Carefully open the lid after the pressure drops. Add the cheddar and pepper Jack cheeses and stir to mix. Cover with a regular lid and let stand until the cheese has melted. Using a slotted spoon, transfer the hash to a serving plate, and arrange the avocado slices around the edge. Sprinkle the green onions on top, and serve. ✳ Serves 4 to 5

Eggs à la Goldenrod: Creamed Eggs on Toast

If you're old enough, you may remember this old-fashioned luncheon recipe from high-school home-ec class. It makes a delicious and elegant change of pace from ordinary eggs. The upscale Eggs à la Goldenrod is a very attractive and impressive breakfast dish that can also be served for brunch, as a luncheon entrée, or even as a light supper.

Step One: The Eggs
6 large eggs

Follow the directions on page 454 to cook the hard-boiled eggs in the pressure cooker. Either by hand or in a food processor, finely mince the egg whites. Grate the egg yolks by pushing them through a ricer or forcing them through a wire sieve with the back of a spoon. Set the whites and yolks aside.

Step Two: The White Sauce
2 cups milk
2 tablespoons butter
2 tablespoons all-purpose flour
½ teaspoon salt

¼ teaspoon freshly ground black pepper

⅛ teaspoon cayenne pepper

Heat the milk in the microwave on high power until it is steaming hot but not boiling, about 2 minutes. In a small saucepan, melt the butter over medium heat. When it begins to bubble, add the flour and cook for about 2 minutes, stirring constantly. Add the hot milk and the salt, black pepper, and cayenne pepper, stirring to mix. Simmer over low heat for 3 to 5 minutes, until the sauce reaches the desired thickness. Add the chopped egg whites and stir to mix. The sauce should be thick, but it will thicken even more as it cools, so add a little more milk for a thinner consistency if desired.

Step Three: The Presentation

6 slices white bread, lightly toasted and crusts removed

Paprika, for garnish

Cut 4 pieces of the toast in half diagonally. Cut the 2 extra slices of toast into small geometric shapes—triangles, diamonds, squares, stars, circles, or half-moons. Divide the toast slices between 4 luncheon plates and pour the white sauce over the toast. Sprinkle the grated egg yolks over the top, and stand a few of the geometric shapes upright in the sauce. Dust with paprika before serving.

✳ Serves 4

Cook's Note: Instead of toast, substitute split biscuits, English muffins, hot buttered cornbread, or baked puff pastry shells. To make a heartier version of this dish for dinner, consider the following variations.

Variations

Vegetables: Add ½ cup cooked drained peas, asparagus, diced carrots, or chopped spinach to the White Sauce.

Meat: Add ½ cup chopped cooked ham, crumbled bacon, diced cooked chicken or shrimp, or flaked salmon or tuna, as well as a dash of Tabasco sauce, to the White Sauce.

Cheese: Add 1½ cups shredded sharp cheddar cheese to the White Sauce before adding the egg whites.

Grandma's Spicy Applesauce

Sweet and spicy, this applesauce is the ideal accompaniment to pork and ham. The amount of sugar and spices I've given are the minimum amounts—the finished taste is dependent on the sweetness and flavor of the apples as well as your own personal preferences.

8 cups cored, peeled, and grated apples (about 8 medium-size apples)—use a variety of tart and sweet apples for maximum flavor
½ cup packed dark brown sugar (do not substitute light brown)
1 tablespoon unsalted butter (do not substitute margarine)
2 teaspoons ground cinnamon
½ teaspoon ground cloves
½ teaspoon freshly ground black pepper
½ teaspoon salt
½ cup unsweetened apple juice
1 tablespoon fresh lemon juice

Place all of the ingredients in a large pressure cooker, but do not exceed the ½-full mark for this recipe, because apples tend to foam. Lock the lid in place. Bring to 15psi over high heat, immediately reduce the heat to the lowest possible setting to stabilize and maintain that pressure, and cook for 4 minutes. Remove from the heat and use the natural release method (see page 31) to depressurize. Carefully open the lid after the pressure drops. The apples should be soft enough to mash easily between your thumb and forefinger. If more cooking is needed, cover with a regular lid and simmer over medium heat until the apples are soft enough.

Puree the apple mixture with an immersion blender, or transfer to a food processor, processing in short spurts until the applesauce reaches the desired consistency. Don't overdo it, or the results will be watery. Taste, and adjust the spices and sugar as desired. Ladle into plastic or glass food containers with tight-fitting lids, and refrigerate for up to a week. This recipe is not intended for canning or freezing. ✳ **Makes about 2½ cups; Serves 6**

Variation

Grandma's Special Spicy Apple Butter:
Transfer the finished apple puree to a shallow 9 × 13-inch baking pan and stir in 2 tablespoons bourbon. Bake at 300°F until all the liquid has evaporated and the mixture turns dark brown and is thick and spreadable; this takes between 30 and 50 minutes. To test the consistency, here's how my grandmother did it: chill a small plate in the freezer for a few minutes, and then add a drop of the apple butter to the cold plate. If any liquid seeps out around the edges, the butter isn't ready. Continue cooking until the apple butter tests firm. Time will vary, so check often and stir occasionally until it reaches the desired consistency. Taste and adjust the spices and sugar as desired. Ladle into plastic or glass food containers with tight-fitting lids and refrigerate for up to 2 weeks. Use the apple butter like jam on toast, English muffins, biscuits, pancakes, waffles, or even French toast. Combine with granola and yogurt for a snack, or use in a sandwich with peanut butter.

Index